Value, Capital & Growth

edited by
J.N. Wolfe

Value, Capital & Growth

Routledge
Taylor & Francis Group

LONDON AND NEW YORK

Originally published in 1968 by Edinburgh University Press

Published 2006 by Transaction Publishers

Published 2017 by Routledge
2 Park Square, Milton Park, Abingdon, Oxon OX14 4RN
711 Third Avenue, New York, NY 10017, USA

Routledge is an imprint of the Taylor & Francis Group, an informa business

Library of Congress Catalog Number: 2005046696

Library of Congress Cataloging-in-Publication Data
Value, capital and growth / edited by J. N. Wolfe.
 p. cm.
 Includes bibliographical references.
 ISBN 0-202-30846-4 (alk. paper)
 1. Value. 2. Capital. 3. Economic development. 4. Economics, Mathematical. I. Hicks, John Richard, Sir, 1904- II. Wolfe, J. N. (James Nathaniel).

HB201.V349 2006   2005046696
330—dc22

ISBN 13: 978-0-202-30846-3 (pbk)

Contents

Introduction

This volume is intended to mark the occasion of the retirement of Sir John Hicks from the Drummond Professorship at the University of Oxford. It does not mark Hicks's retirement from academic life, or even from teaching, for he is continuing to teach, and the output of his economic writing appears to be increasing rather than decreasing.

In these circumstances, it would be premature to introduce this book with a summary of the work of the man we honour, or of its place in the history of economic thought. That work is not yet completed. Even were this not so, it would be presumptuous to attempt to pass judgment upon it so soon. Nor is this the appropriate time for a biographical sketch. Much still lies ahead, and we might easily miss the main point of the story. Consider, for instance, where Hicks's recent views on a policy of price deflation, or his participation in the Conservative Party economic seminar may lead!

Such reasons may justify the limitation of my contribution to a few personal recollections of Hicks, Nuffield, and Oxford, mainly in the period (1949–53) when I was most familiar with them. These reminiscences, in themselves merely of passing interest, may help to characterize the man we are honouring in this book.

After graduating from McGill, in 1949, where I had taken my MA by thesis, I landed a scholarship at Glasgow–an exchange scholarship in honour of James McGill. From Glasgow I answered an advertisement by Nuffield College, asking for applications for studentships. I enclosed with my application my MA thesis, which had been on the implications for Hansen's theory of secular stagnation of an accelerator-multiplier model of the Samuelson sort, when the size of the accelerator depended on the level of unemployment (I did not then know of Hicks's forthcoming work on the trade cycle). I was astonished and delighted to be invited to an interview, since it allowed me at least a free trip to the South, and a chance to come face to face with Professor Hicks, whose work I so much admired.

Nuffield College then comprised one small building beside a big parking lot down by the station, plus the 'Wardens' Lodgings' on the Woodstock

vii

Road. I was to stay the night at the latter, and was received by a real butler—a touch of the old system which I have seldom seen repeated, at any rate in academic circles. I remember it as a glorious, sunny day with that touch of frost which is sometimes taken for snow in England. I arrived at the interview in a state of euphoria which was quickly dispelled by the sight of the Board—perhaps fifteen strong—and by the clear hostility of one rather cantankerous member, who appeared to think that any continuation of my studies in economics would be a national disaster. I was in some doubt as to how to fend him off. It occurred to me to extol the virtues of my thesis as my major claim to consideration, and I asked whether Professor Hicks (who had been silent until then) had appreciated its subtlety. This query was no more than a gesture, for I had no reason to think that anyone (let alone the great economist) would have been so misguided as to plough through it. But it emerged that Hicks had indeed read it, and understood it much more thoroughly than I did.

This was my first, and startling, introduction to Hicks's attitude to economics. An infinite patience in selecting students, a thoroughly impersonal pleasure in any advance in the subject, and a confident belief in the ability of those around him, together with the sense of drama thus implied—these constituted the largest part of the explanation of Hicks's almost magical effect upon his students.

At the time of which I write the Nuffield seminar contained, among others, Peter Newman, Gerry Meier, Bob Clower, Alan Walters, Hugh Rose, and George Richardson, and was attended frequently by David Champernowne, Donald Macdougall, and Francis Seton. I venture to say that it was one of the most formidable seminars to be found anywhere at that time. Certainly it was one of the most lively.

I think we all felt that Hicks's comment on any paper would be final, but it was rarely given. More often than not, he would confine himself to maintaining order, perhaps chuckling quietly to himself over some point or other. In spite of this, he always managed to convey the impression that the meeting had been of the highest interest to him, and that he would have commented at length had the discussion not been so vigorous as to make his intervention superfluous.

A notable feature of Hicks's Friday seminars was the attendance, there, of many of the most promising young economists in the world. Hicks always appeared to be able to spot the coming men in economics very early on. I recall, in particular, visits by Kenneth Arrow and Hendrik Houthakker before either of them had become well known. We all noticed the marks of respect shown to them by Hicks. One day, after a very complex talk by Arrow, followed by a long period of silence, Hicks asked me what I had thought of the meeting. I replied that I had been disappointed that there had been so little discussion, and asked him why he thought people had been unwilling to ask questions. Hicks's reply was characteristic: 'Perhaps they were afraid of the answers.'

When visitors came we were often invited up to the Hicks's flat for sherry or coffee. He had an extensive collection of the works of earlier writers, and was always pleased to have the opportunity of showing it. On the whole, though, conversation tended to be careful rather than lively, and this always seemed to me to contrast oddly with his somewhat boisterous seminar. How very lively and amusing a conversationalist he could be, even on the most general subjects, I realized nearly ten years later, when I met him in America. The less restrained atmosphere of America seemed to have a remarkable effect on his personality. At home he was always shy and correct: in America he seemed to me to tend almost to flamboyance. One example may suffice. I recall a dinner at which an earnest American lady, thinking to draw out the visitor, said to him from across the table: 'Oh, Professor Hicks, I do so hope that India solves its population problem, don't you?' To which Hicks, in the best Johnsonian style, replied: 'Ah yes, madam, but it's all hopeless, perfectly hopeless'.

Few theorists possess Hicks's catholicity in economics and his interest in, and appetite for, all branches of applied economics, especially economic history. One of the revelations of my stay at Oxford was his lectures on Italian Renaissance banking, a subject as far from the theory of value as can readily be imagined. Another example concerns his long-standing interest in the affairs of the Oxford University Press, and of a family business of which he is still a director. He has always been a careful and shrewd businessman, but on occasions he seems to me to have allowed his enthusiasm for economics to overcome his habitual caution. It was, I think, in 1955 that he asked me to conduct an economic inquiry into the market for British books in Canada. It was felt at the time that the Canadian market was not contributing sufficiently to British publishing in general, and to the Oxford University Press in particular. Hicks felt that those involved in Canada would welcome such an enquiry, and I was urged into the breach. The result was an exposure to Byzantine labyrinths of intrigue and innuendo whose equal I have not seen again. Something came of it all, but I do not think that any easy improvement was possible.

One of the striking things about Nuffield in those days was how closely knit a community it was. All of us, fellows and students, lunched together in a little room with places, as I recall it, for only sixteen. Perhaps one third to a half at any meal would be students, and one might at any time find oneself lunching between John Plamenetz and Ursula Hicks, or between Philip Andrews and Marjory Perham. It was indeed the most democratic of societies, and certainly there was little expectation and less likelihood that the students would be seen and not heard.

In this society Hicks was in many ways pre-eminent. This was partly due to the numbers of his students, partly to his professional distinction, but mostly to his quiet charm and to the disinterested character of his interventions in college affairs. When I was in my last year he took up the Drummond Professorship and moved to All Souls, and, while Nuffield has prospered greatly since these days, I have had the feeling that it has not developed quite as well as it might have done had he stayed.

To really understand Hicks, however, one must see him as part of his class and time, if a little larger than life. He was educated at Clifton and Balliol, and still seems to me to retain much of the manner and viewpoint of the public school man, with his very stringent code of right behaviour, and the inflexible value of the word as a bond, right down to the predilection for cold baths and the willingness, unusual in academics, to accept physical exertion as a normal part of life. At the time of which I write it was Hicks's normal practice to bicycle to college from his flat up the Woodstock Road – a habit which flabbergasted some of the more bemused North American students.

His interest in gardening has been a long-term passion. At one time he was responsible for laying out parts of the Nuffield gardens. On one occasion he went directly from an important meeting to the gardens to supervise the planting of some new rose bushes. An eminent international trade theorist who happened to be present and who witnessed this operation earned the ire of Ursula Hicks by commenting upon the difficulty of reconciling this activity with the theory of comparative advantage.

Roses have indeed been a continuing interest, and I must regretfully record that a few years ago this nearly proved fatal, a thorn having transmitted tetanus spores through an apparently tough glove. Apart from this ailment, and an earlier serious malady of presumed tropical origin, Sir John has enjoyed the most robust good health. Indeed, a doctor called upon to treat one of his two serious ailments is said to have asked Lady Hicks: 'But doesn't your husband ever catch anything simple, like a cold?'

I have written of the man and his institution. Perhaps it will be felt that I must give *some* account of this volume. It would have been easy, of course, to have produced a very much thicker volume with very many more contributors, and I am sure there will be many who will be grieved at not having been asked. I wished, however, to avoid a difficulty inherent to festschrifts, by confining myself to those authors whose work has been most clearly influenced by the work Hicks has himself done. In the end, homogeneity has had to give way a little to the claims of friendship and close association on the one hand, and to the changing interests of rather obvious contributors on the other.

To the first sort of weakness (if it is a weakness) must be ascribed the inclusion of the fascinating essay in quantitative economic history by Jonathan Hughes. To the second must be ascribed the econometric investigations reported on by Professor Morishima. I do not think, however, that any critic of this volume will cavil at the retention of such impressive and indeed path-breaking papers.

J. N. Wolfe
Edinburgh, January 1968

1

Optimal Capital Policy with Irreversible Investment

Kenneth J. Arrow

Introduction

It is Sir John Hicks's *Value and Capital* which taught us clearly the formulation of capital theory as an optimization problem for the firm. He set a general framework within which all subsequent work has taken place.

If one may generalize a bit roughly, the principal subsequent innovation has been the more explicit recognition of the recursive nature of the production process. As a rough empirical generalization, the links between inputs and outputs at different points of time are built up out of links between successive time points. In discrete-time (period) analysis, this means that outputs at time $t+1$ are determined directly by inputs at time t, independent of earlier inputs; the latter may still have an indirect influence by affecting the availability of the inputs at time t. In continuous-time analysis, which will be employed here, the basic production relation is between the stocks of capital goods and the flows of current inputs and outputs; the earlier past is controlling only in that the stock of capital goods is a cumulation of past flows.

This recursive aspect of the production process simplifies analysis and computation, as was first recognized in the context of inventory theory in the magisterial work of Massé (1946) (unfortunately ignored in the English-language literature) and independently by Arrow, Harris and Marschak (1951). Subsequently, the mathematician Bellman (1957) recognized the basic principle of recursive optimization common to inventory theory, sequential analysis of statistical data, and a host of other control processes in the technological and economic realms and developed the set of computational methods and principles known as *dynamic programming*. Finally, the Russian mathematician Pontryagin and his associates (1962) developed an elegant theory of control of recursive processes related both

1

to Bellman's work and to the classical calculus of variations. The Pontryagin principle, which will be used in this paper, has the great advantage
of yielding economically interesting results very naturally.

This paper follows several others investigating under various hypotheses
the optimal policy of a firm with regard to the holding of fixed capital
(Arrow, Beckmann and Karlin, 1958; Arrow, 1962b; Nerlove and Arrow,
1962; Arrow, 1964). Assume, for simplicity, that there is only one type of
capital good, all other inputs and outputs being flows. Then for any fixed
stock of capital goods, there is at any moment a most profitable current
policy with regard to flow variables; we assume the flow optimization to
have taken place and therefore have defined a function relating operating
profits (excess of sales over costs of flow inputs) as a function of the stock
of capital goods. This function may, however, shift over time, because of
shifts in technological relations and demand and supply conditions (in the
case of a monopoly, there may be shifts in the demand curve; for a
monopsony, shifts in the supply curves of the factors; for a competitive
firm, demand or supply shifts are simply changes in output or input prices).
The cash flow at any moment is the difference between operating profits
and gross investment. We assume throughout a perfect capital market, so
that the aim of the firm is to maximize the integral of discounted cash
flows, where the discounting is done at the market rates of interest (which
may be changing over time).

The problem assumes different forms according to the assumption made
about the cost schedule of capital goods to the firm. To assume that there
is a truly perfect capital goods market to the firm means that, at any moment of time, there is a fixed price of capital goods at which the firm can
buy or sell in any magnitude. In that case, the optimal policy has a special
'myopic' property (see section 1), which is obvious enough once observed,
but which has only recently been given much weight in the literature.

From a realistic point of view, there will be many situations in which
the sale of capital goods cannot be accomplished at the same price as
their purchase. There are installation costs, which are added to the
purchase price but cannot be recovered on sale; indeed, there may on the
contrary be additional costs of detaching and moving machinery. Again
sufficiently specialized machinery and plant may have little value to
others. So resale prices may be substantially below replacement costs.
For simplicity, we will make the extreme assumption that resale of capital

goods is impossible, so that gross investment is constrained to be non-negative. It is clear that this may affect investment policy strongly. Obviously, at a point where a firm would like to sell capital goods at the going price if it could, it will be barred from this disinvestment. More subtly, at a time at which investment is still profitable as far as current calculations are concerned, the firm may refrain from investment if it anticipates that in the relatively near future it would have disinvested if it could. It is this problem which will be studied in the present paper.[1]

In section I, we briefly remind the reader of the myopic optimization rule for the case where investment is costlessly reversible. In section II, we state the model more fully, and note that the case of exponential depreciation can be reduced to that of zero depreciation, which will be considered henceforth. Section III characterizes the solution, in the case of diminishing returns, and section IV indicates how the optimum might be effectively computed. In section V, the case of constant returns to capital is analyzed. Finally, section VI is devoted to some remarks on possible empirical implications.

I. *The Case of Reversible Investment*
A rigorous analysis of this case has been carried out in the earlier publications cited and will follow as a special case of the general reversible case. But the result is obvious once stated: *at each instant, hold that stock of capital for which the marginal profitability of capital equals the cost of capital, by which is meant the sum of the short-term interest rate, depreciation, and the rate of decline in capital goods prices.*

Once stated, the rule will seem banal, for it is one of the standard equations of capital theory. Yet its implications are often ignored. It means that the decision as to the stock of capital to be held at any instant of time is myopic, being independent of future developments in technology, demand or anything else; forecasts for only the most immediate future are needed and then only as to capital goods prices.[2] The argument for this rule is simple; when investment is reversible, then the firm can buy a unit of capital goods, use it and derive its marginal product for an arbitrarily short time span, and then sell the undepreciated portion, possibly at a different price.

This rule defines a demand function for capital very different from Keynes's (1936, Chapter 11) marginal efficiency of capital unless the latter is so interpreted as to make it meaningless. In effect, Keynes's rule is that an investment is justified if and only if the sum of discounted returns at least equals the cost. But the return to a particular investment is not a datum but depends on the total volume of capital in the system. With reversible investment, a natural interpretation is that the given investment is taken to be the marginal investment in every future period, in which case the return in any future period is simply the marginal productivity of capital, net of depreciation and price changes, at that time. *If* the firm follows in the future the myopic rule of equating marginal productivity of capital to the rate of interest, then it is true that the Keynes rule amounts to accepting the same rule today. But the interest of the marginal efficiency concept evaporates, since all the content lies in the myopic rule.

The marginal efficiency rule can easily be misunderstood to mean that, in evaluating future returns, the new investment today is to be regarded as marginal not to a future optimal stock but to the present stock. This is wrong, however. Suppose for example, the marginal productivity schedule is anticipated to be shifting upward over time. Then the sum of discounted profits may exceed the cost because of high returns in the distant future, even though the marginal product may be less than interest in the near future. It is indeed true that it is better to undertake the investment than not to, but these are not the only alternatives. A still better one would be to postpone the investment until it is profitable in the immediate future. It is this possibility of postponement which justifies the myopic rule.[3]

II. *Explicit Formulation of the Model*
The model will be formulated very generally, in some respects at least. We assume one type of capital good, the stock of which is denoted by K. At each moment of time, the operating profit function, $P(K,t)$, denotes the profits obtainable from a given stock of capital, K, by optimal employment of other factors. Thus, the variations of P over time may reflect changes in technology, supply conditions for other factors, or demand conditions. The firm faces a perfect market for liquid capital, but the interest rates may be changing in time, in a known way. Let $\alpha(t)$ be the rate at which receipts at time are discounted back to time 0, the beginning of the optimization period. Then, the (short-term) interest rate at time t is,

$$\rho(t) = -\dot{\alpha}(t)/\alpha(t),$$

where the dot denotes differentiation with respect to time.

We will take the price of capital goods as numeraire. This implies that the interest and discount rates are expressed in terms of capital goods, rather than money, so that the interest rate used here is the money rate of interest less the rate of appreciation of capital goods prices.

Let $I(t)$ be the rate of gross investment. Then the cash flow at time t, in terms of capital goods, is $P(K_t,t) - I(t)$,[4] and therefore the sum of discounted returns is

$$\int_0^\infty \alpha(t)[P(K_t,t) - I(t)]\, dt. \tag{2.1}$$

The aim of the firm is to maximize (2.1) by suitable choice of investment policy, $I(t)$. The evolution of the capital stock, $K(t)$, is determined by its initial value, $K(0)$, and by the investment policy. If we assume depreciation at a fixed exponential rate, δ, then

$$\dot{K} = I - \delta K. \tag{2.2}$$

Finally, the assumption of irreversible investment means that gross investment must be non-negative:

$$I(t) \geqslant 0. \tag{2.3}$$

We also postulate positive but strictly diminishing returns to capital at any moment of time.

$$P_K > 0, \; P_{KK} < 0. \tag{2.4}$$

In the remainder of this section, it will be argued that this problem can be transformed into another, of the same form, but with $\delta = 0$. Then, for the remainder of the paper, we can assume the absence of depreciation with no loss of generality.

Let $\quad x(t) = K(t)\, e^{\delta t}, \; y(t) = I(t)\, e^{\delta t}, \; \beta(t) = \alpha(t)\, e^{-\delta t},$

$\qquad P^*(x,t) = e^{\delta t}\, P(x\, e^{-\delta t},t).$

Then it is easy to calculate that

$$\dot{x} = (\dot{K} + \delta K)\, e^{\delta t} = I(t)\, e^{\delta t} = y$$

and $\qquad \beta(t)[P^*(x,t) - y(t)] = \alpha(t)[P(K,t) - I(t)],$

so that the original problem is transformed into the maximization of

$$\int_0^\infty \beta(t)[P^*(x,t) - y]\, dt,$$

subject to the accumulation condition, $\dot{x} = y$, the initial condition, $x(0) = K(0)$, and the non-negativity condition, $y \geqslant 0$, following from (2.3). The new problem is indeed of the original form, with x and y

replacing K and I, respectively, and $\delta = 0$. Further,

$$P_x^* = P_K, \; P_{xx}^* = e^{-\delta t} P_{KK} \, ,$$

so that conditions (2.4) still remain valid.

III. *The Characterization of the Solution*

We now assume that $\delta = 0$; then we wish to maximize

$$\int_0^\infty \alpha(t)[P(K,t) - I(t)] \, dt, \tag{3.1}$$

subject to $\dot{K} = I$, $\tag{3.2}$

$K(0)$ given, and

$$I \geqslant 0 \, . \tag{3.3}$$

The return to an investment at any moment of time has two parts, the current cash flow and an addition to the sum of discounted future benefits. The latter is equal to the value of a gift of a unit of capital at time t. Let $p(t)$ be this shadow price of capital at time t, discounted back to time 0. Then the (discounted) value of investment at a given time t is

$$H = \alpha(t)[P(K,t) - I] + p(t)I \, . \tag{3.4}$$

H is known in control theory as the Hamiltonian (after the nineteenth-century mathematician who introduced the concept). Then I is chosen so as to maximize H, subject to the condition (3.3).

However, we have to have a principle for determination of the shadow price of capital, p. Pontryagin and associates have shown that $p(t)$ must evolve in time, according to the differential equation

$$\dot{p} = -\partial H / \partial K \, . \tag{3.5}$$

Let us rewrite (3.4) by setting

$$q(t) = p(t) - \alpha(t); \tag{3.6}$$

then $\quad H = \alpha(t)P(K,t) + q(t)I \, . \tag{3.7}$

The maximization of H with respect to I has a rather trivial form. If $q(t) < 0$, then the optimum I, subject to (3.3), must be 0. If $q(t) = 0$, then the optimum I can be any non-negative quantity. This does not mean that I is indeterminate; as will be seen shortly, it is determined by other considerations but not by the requirement that the Hamiltonian be maximized. If $q(t)$ were positive, then there would be no optimum for I; the larger the better. This is, however, incompatible with the existence of an optimal policy, for $q(t)$ would be positive over an interval, and infinite investment over an interval is obviously non-optimal. The point is that a policy of capital accumulation led to such a situation; it would have been better to have invested more earlier, so that the policy followed was non-optimal. We conclude

$$q(t) \leqslant 0; \text{ if } q(t) < 0, \text{ then } I(t) = 0. \tag{3.8}$$

The economic interpretation of (3.8) is straightforward. The comparison of q with 0 is, according to (3.6), a comparison of p with α; since the market price of capital goods is always 1, by the choice of numeraire, $\alpha(t)$ is the market price of capital goods discounted back to time 0, while $p(t)$ is the shadow price (the value of future benefits) similarly discounted. If q is negative, the shadow price is less than the market price, and it does not pay to invest. If $q = 0$, one is just indifferent at the margin between investing and not investing. If q could be positive, it would pay to invest infinitely, but it would also have paid to invest infinitely at an earlier time.

From (3.7), (3.5) becomes

$$\dot{p} = -\alpha(t)P_K, \tag{3.9}$$

which can also be written

$$\alpha(t)P_K + \dot{p} = 0,$$

that is, discounted current returns plus changes in discounted shadow value should be zero, a restatement of the familiar equilibrium relation for the holding of assets, but with shadow prices substituted from market prices.

Since the short-run optimum condition (3.8) has been written in terms of q rather than p, it is convenient to reformulate the differential equation (3.9). From the definition (3.6), and (3.9),

$$\dot{q} = \dot{p} - \dot{\alpha} = \alpha(t)[-P_K - (\dot{\alpha}/\alpha)],$$

or, from the definition of $\rho(t)$,

$$\dot{q} = \alpha(t)[\rho(t) - P_K(K_t, t)]. \tag{3.10}$$

The integral of (10) is straightforward:

$$q(t_1) - q(t_0) = \int_{t_0}^{t_1} \alpha(t)[\rho(t) - P_K(K_t, t)] \, dt. \tag{3.11}$$

Formally, the solution has been completely described. We seek three functions of time, $K(t)$, $q(t)$, and $I(t)$, jointly satisfying the conditions (3.2), (3.3), (3.8), and (3.10), with $K(0)$ given. The initial value $q(0)$ has not been explicitly defined; it has to be such that all these conditions can jointly be satisfied. Primarily, it has to be sufficiently small so that the condition $q(t) \leqslant 1$ holds.

However, a good deal more can be said about the structure of the solution. First, it is necessary to discuss the possibility of discontinuous jumps in the stock of capital. A jump in the stock of capital would require an infinite rate of investment, but from the point of view of the firm there is nothing difficult to comprehend; it is simply the acquisition of a block of capital goods at some instant of time. We will show that it is never optimal to have a jump in the stock of capital except possibly at the very initial point of time.

Since $K(t)$ is monotone increasing, both the left- and right-hand limits exist at every point. Let $K(t)$ have a discontinuity at $t = t_0$, where $t_0 > 0$, and let $K(t_0 - 0)$ and $K(t_0 + 0)$ be the left-hand and right-hand limits, respectively. Since $K(t)$ is increasing, we must have

$$K(t_0 - 0) < K(t_0 + 0).$$

Define

$$r(K,t) = \rho(t) - P_K(K,t). \tag{3.12}$$

Since P_K is strictly decreasing in K,

$$r(K,t) \text{ is strictly increasing in } K \text{ for fixed } t. \tag{3.13}$$

Then we can choose c_1 and c_2, so that

$$r[K(t_0 - 0), t_0] < c_1 < c_2 < r[K(t_0 + 0), t_0].$$

Again, since $K(t)$ is increasing, we must have

$$K(t) \leqslant K(t_0 - 0) \text{ for } t < t_0, \quad K(t) \geqslant K(t_0 + 0) \text{ for } t > t_0,$$

and therefore

$$r(K_t, t) \leqslant r[K(t_0 - 0), t] \text{ for } t < t_0,$$
$$r(K_t, t) \geqslant r[K(t_0 + 0), t] \text{ for } t > t_0.$$

Finally, since $r(K,t)$ is continuous in t for fixed K,

$$r[K(t_0 - 0), t] < c_1 \text{ for } r \text{ sufficiently close to } t_0,$$
$$r[K(t_0 + 0), t] > c_2 \text{ for } t \text{ sufficiently close to } t_0.$$

Combine these statements and recall (3.10):

$$\dot{q}(t)/\alpha(t) < c_1 \text{ for } t_0 - \varepsilon < t < t_0,$$
$$\dot{q}(t)/\alpha(t) > c_2 \text{ for } t_0 < t < t_0 + \varepsilon,$$

for some $\varepsilon > 0$.

But since investment is taking place at time t_0, $q(t_0) = 0$; since $q(t) \leqslant 0$ everywhere, by (3.8), it is impossible that $\dot{q}(t) < 0$ for all t, $t_0 - \varepsilon < t < t_0$, for then we would have $q(t) > q(t_0) = 0$ throughout that interval. Since $\dot{q}(t) \geqslant 0$ for some t, $t_0 - \varepsilon < t < t_0$, we must have $c_1 > 0$; by a similar argument, $c_2 < 0$, which contradicts the assertion $c_1 < c_2$.

An optimal investment policy has no jumps
other than possibly at $t = 0$. $\tag{3.14}$

With this result, we can now investigate more closely the structure of the optimal solution. From (3.8), it is clear that the optimal path consists of time intervals satisfying alternately the conditions $q(t) = 0$ (shadow price and market price of capital goods are equal) and $q(t) < 0$ (shadow price of capital goods less than market price), with zero investment in the latter case. Call the intervals in which $q(t) = 0$ *free* intervals (since the non-negativity condition is not binding on those intervals) and those in which $q(t) < 0$ *blocked* intervals.

In a free interval, $q(t) = 0$ throughout the interval. Hence, $\dot{q} = 0$, or, by (3.10),

$$P_K(K_t, t) = \rho(t) \text{ in a free interval .} \tag{3.15}$$

This is precisely the myopic rule discussed in section 1. In general, let us define the *myopic policy* by the equation

$$P_K(K_t^*, t) = \rho(t); \tag{3.16}$$

under the assumption of diminishing returns, this equation has a unique solution. Then (3.15) is written

$$K(t) = K^*(t) \text{ on a free interval .} \tag{3.17}$$

But $K(t)$ is increasing. Therefore, $K^*(t)$ must be increasing throughout any free interval. If $K^*(t)$ is a well-behaved function, it has alternately rising and falling segments. Refer to any interval which is a rising segment of the graph of $K^*(t)$ as a *riser*.

$$\text{A free interval lies entirely within a single riser.} \tag{3.18}$$

Now consider any blocked interval starting at a time $t_0 > 0$. It was preceded by a free interval and therefore t_0 must lie in a riser. Since neither $K(t)$ nor $q(t)$ have jumps, we must have $K(t_0) = K^*(t_0)$ and $q(t_0) = 0$. Since $I = 0$ on a blocked interval, $K(t)$ is a constant, so that $K(t) = K^*(t_0)$ for all t in the interval.

A blocked interval ending at $t_1 < +\infty$ must be followed by a free interval. By exactly parallel arguments, t_1 must lie on a riser, $K(t) = K^*(t_1)$ for all t in the blocked interval, and $q(t_1) = 0$.

If we recall that by definition $q(t) < 0$ on a blocked interval, then, with the aid of (3.11) and (3.12), we can draw the following conclusions:

On a blocked interval (t_0, t_1) with $t_0 > 0$, $t_1 < +\infty$, (3.19)

(a) $K^*(t_0) = K^*(t_1);$

(b) $\displaystyle\int_{t_0}^{t_1} \alpha(t) r[K^*(t_0), t] \, dt = 0;$

(c) $\displaystyle\int_{t_0}^{t} \alpha(t) r[K^*(t_0), t] \, dt < 0 \text{ for } t_0 < t < t_1;$

(d) $\int_t^{t_1} \alpha(t)r[K^*(t_0), t] \, dt > 0$ for $t_0 < t < t_1$.

Relation (d) is not independent of the others but follows from (b) and (c).

Relations $(b–d)$ have simple interpretations. Suppose it were possible to rent capital goods for some fixed period of time at a price $\rho(t)$ possibly varying in time. Then $P_K - \rho = -r$ is the instantaneous profit. Purchasing a capital good and selling it at the end of the period is exactly equivalent to renting it at rate equal to the market rate of interest; purchasing a capital good and holding it to a point of time where the firm would wish to purchase capital goods anyway is also equivalent to renting. Then (c) assures us that it would be profitable to rent a capital good at t_0 for any term short of the full blocked interval; since in fact the firm has to buy instead of rent and neither can it sell at time t nor does it wish to hold it then, the firm in fact does not purchase. Equation (b) says that at the margin the firm is indifferent between renting and not renting for the entire period. Relation (d) assures that the firm would not wish to rent beginning at any point in the blocked interval and ending at time t_1 (for if it did, it would buy).

There may be a blocked interval beginning at time 0 and ending at a finite time t_1; the stock of capital must be constant at $K^*(t_1)$ and $q(t_1) = 0$. However, there might be an initial jump in capital at time 0 before settling down to the blocked interval; if there is, then $q(0)$ must be zero, since investment is taking place. Then, by the same arguments,

On a blocked interval $(0,t_1)$, with $t_1 < +\infty$,   (3.20)

(a) $K(0) \leqslant K^*(t_1)$;

(b) $\int_0^{t_1} \alpha(t)r[K^*(t_1),t] \, dt \geqslant 0$;

(c) strict inequality cannot hold in both (a) and (b);

(d) $\int_t^{t_1} \alpha(t)r[K^*(t_1),t] \, dt > 0$, $0 < t < t_1$.

To discuss blocked intervals starting at some $t_0 \geqslant 0$, and continuing for all subsequent values of t, it is necessary to note the asymptotic behavior of $q(t)$. Since $p(t)$ was defined as the shadow price of capital, it is necessarily non-negative since $P_K > 0$. Hence, from the definition (3.6) and from (3.8),

$$-\alpha(t) \leqslant q(t) \leqslant 0 .$$

However, we may certainly suppose that $\alpha(t)$ approaches zero as t

approaches infinity; this would certainly be true if the interest rate were bounded away from zero or even approached zero slowly. Then

$$q(+\infty) = \lim_{t \to +\infty} q(t) = 0 . \tag{3.21}$$

Consider now a blocked interval beginning at $t_0 > 0$ and continuing to plus infinity. Then $K(t)$ must be the constant $K^*(t_0)$ and $q(t_0) = 0$, so that, much like (3.19),

On a blocked interval $(t_0, +\infty)$, with $t_0 > 0$, $\qquad$ (3.22)

(a) $\displaystyle\int_{t_0}^{+\infty} \alpha(t)r[K^*(t_0),t]\, dt = 0;$

(b) $\displaystyle\int_{t_0}^{t} \alpha(t)r[K^*(t_0),t]\, dt < 0, \quad t_0 < t.$

Finally, it is possible to have a blocked interval beginning at $t_0 = 0$ and continuing to plus infinity. It may be that the initial stock of capital, $K(0)$, is simply held intact without further investment, or it may be that there is a jump immediately to some value K, which is then never subsequently added to. In the latter case, of course, $q(0)$ must be zero, since some investment has taken place. In any case, by (3.21), $q(+\infty) = 0$.

On a blocked interval $(0, +\infty)$, $K(t)$ is a constant K, with $\qquad$ (3.23)

(a) $K(0) \leqslant K;$

(b) $\displaystyle\int_{0}^{+\infty} \alpha(t)r(K,t)\, dt \geqslant 0;$

(c) the strict inequality cannot hold in both (a) and (b);

(d) $\displaystyle\int_{t}^{+\infty} \alpha(t)r(K,t)\, dt > 0, \quad 0 < t.$

Theorem. The optimal capital policy for a firm with irreversible investment is an alternating sequence of free and blocked intervals, constructed so as to satisfy the relevant conditions among (3.17) – (3.20) and (3.22), (3.23).

IV. *Algorithmic Remarks*

It may not be obvious that the stated conditions really provide a sensible way of computing the optimal policy. In particular, conditions such as (3.19c) and parallel conditions for the other cases refer to the values of a function at every point in the interval and therefore the amount of trial and error needed in successive approximations to the true policy may appear to be prohibitive. But in fact we are seeking only the maxima or minima of certain functions and for these it suffices to search only among local maxima or minima; thus (3.19c) asserts that the maximum value of the indicated function of time be negative and for this it suffices to calculate the integral at local maxima. The local maxima in turns are clearly those zeros of the integrand at which its value changes from positive to negative. If the functions $P(K,t)$ and $\rho(t)$ are well-behaved, there will be only finitely many zeros in any finite period.

Recall from (3.12) and (3.13) that

$$r(K,t) = \rho(t) - P_K(K,t) \tag{4.1}$$

is a strictly increasing function of K for fixed t. By definition of the myopic policy,

$$r(K_t^*,t) = 0 , \tag{4.2}$$

and therefore

$$r(K,t) > 0 \text{ if and only if } K > K^*(t) . \tag{4.3}$$

Label the successive risers 1, 2, ...; for well-behaved functions there are at most denumerably many risers. On any given riser, $K^*(t)$ is a strictly increasing function of t and therefore has an inverse, $t_i(K)$, the time on riser i at which $K^*(t)$ takes on the value K. The function $t_i(K)$ is defined on the range of values which $K^*(t)$ assumes on riser i; let K_i^l be the lower bound of this range and K_i^u the upper bound.

If there is a blocked interval starting on riser i and ending on riser $j > i$, with $K(t) = K$ on that interval, then from (3.19a) the blocked interval starts at $t_i(K)$ and ends at $t_j(K)$. This can, of course, only be possible if,

$$\max(K_i^l,K_j^l) \leqslant K \leqslant \min(K_i^u,K_j^u) , \tag{4.4}$$

for if K were outside these bounds, either $t_i(K)$ or $t_j(K)$ would be undefined. In view of (3.19b), define, for all K satisfying (4.4),

$$q_{ij}(K) = \int_{t_i(K)}^{t_j(K)} \alpha(t) r(K,t) \, dt . \tag{4.5}$$

Then a second condition that must be satisfied is that

$$q_{ij}(K) = 0 . \tag{4.6}$$

We now show that $q_{ij}(K)$ is strictly increasing in K within its range of definition and therefore there is at most one solution to (4.6). First observe that, from (4.2) and the definition of $t_i(K)$,

$$r[K,t_i(K)] = 0 \text{ for all } K \text{ for which } t_i(K) \text{ is defined.} \tag{4.7}$$

Then differentiate (4.5) with respect to K.

$$dq_{ij}(K)/dK = \alpha[t_j(K)]r[K,t_j(K)] \cdot [dt_j(K)/dK] -$$

$$- \alpha[t_i(K)]r[K,t_i(K)] \cdot [dt_i(K)/dK] + \int_{t_i(K)}^{t_j(K)} \alpha(t) r_K(K,t) \, dt .$$

From (4.7), the first two terms vanish; since $r(K,t)$ is strictly increasing in K, $r_K > 0$ everywhere, so that the last integral is positive.

$$q_{ij}(K) \text{ is strictly increasing in } K. \tag{4.8}$$

It is also useful to define,

$$q_i(K,t) = \int_{t_i(K)}^{t} \alpha(t)r(K,t)\,dt; \tag{4.9}$$

(3.19c) requires that $q_i(K,t) < 0$ for $t_i(K) < t < t_j(K)$. As above, we calculate

$$\partial q_i/\partial K = -\alpha[t_i(K)]r[K,t_i(K)] . [dt_i(K)/dK]+$$

$$+ \int_{t_i(K)}^{t} \alpha(t)r_K(K,t)\,dt > 0 . \tag{4.10}$$

$q_i(K,t)$ is strictly increasing in K for fixed t.

Also, $\qquad \partial q_i/\partial t = \alpha(t)r(K,t)$,

so that a local maximum of $q(K,t)$ as a function of time occurs at those values t_0 at which $r(K,t)$ changes sign from positive to negative as t increases. But, from (4.3), it follows that $K^*(t) < K$ to the left of t_0, $K^*(t) > K$ to the right, so that $K^*(t)$ is increasing at t_0 and $K^*(t_0) = K$. Thus, t_0 is on a riser, say k, and $t_0 = t_k(K)$. Hence, at a local maximum, $q_i(K,t) = q_{ik}(K)$ for some k.

In the present notation, the condition (3.19c) is simply that $q_i(K,t) < 0$, $t_i(K) < t < t_j(K)$, for a blocked interval starting on riser i and ending on riser j. It is necessary and sufficient for this that $q_i(K,t) < 0$ at every local maximum in the same interval, and therefore that

$$q_{ik}(K) < 0 \text{ for all risers } k, i < k < j \text{ for which } q_{ik}(K) \text{ is defined.} \tag{4.11}$$

We can also use (4.10) as additional help in screening out conceivable blocked intervals by showing that condition (4.11) is not satisfied. Suppose it has been shown that $q_{ij}(K) \geqslant 0$. By definition, this is equivalent to

$$q_i[K,t_k(K)] \geqslant 0 .$$

From (4.10), $q_i[K',t_k(K)] > 0$ for all $K' > K$. Consider any riser $j > k$ for which K' lies in the range of $K^*(t)$. Since the entire riser j lies beyond the entire riser k, $t_j(K') > t_k(K)$, and it has been shown that

$$q_i(K',t) > 0 \text{ for some } t, t_i(K') < t < t_j(K') ,$$

namely for $t = t_k(K)$. There can be no blocked interval from riser i to riser j with $K(t)$ at the constant level K' for any $K' > K$.

Define now an *eligible* interval as one that satisfies all the necessary conditions for a blocked interval, specifically,

A pair of risers i, j, with $i < j$, form an eligible interval at level K
if $q_{ij}(K) = 0$ and $q_{ik}(K) < 0$ for all risers k, $i < k < j$, for which
$q_{ik}(K)$ is defined.   (4.12)

Note that, from (4.8), there can be at most one K for which $q_{ij}(K) = 0$
and therefore at most one eligible interval between two given risers.

The preceding remarks can be assembled to provide an algorithm for
finding all possible intervals:

Algorithm. Start with any given riser and consider in turn all successive risers. Suppose that we have started with a riser i and reached
riser j. Assume defined a number K_{ij}^d to be defined recursively. Let
$K_{ij}^u = \min(K_{ij}^d, K_j^u)$, $K_{ij}^l = \max(K_i^l, K_j^l)$. If $K_{ij}^u < K_{ij}^l$ then there is no
eligible interval from i to j; proceed to the next riser, with $K_{i,j+1}^d = K_{ij}^d$. If $K_{ij}^u \geqslant K_{ij}^l$ compute $q_{ij}(K_{ij}^u)$. If negative, again there is no
eligible interval from i to j, and so proceed to the next riser, with
$K_{i,j+1}^d = K_{ij}^d$. If $q_{ij}(K_{ij}^u) \geqslant 0$, compute $q_{ij}(K_{ij}^l)$. If positive again there
is no eligible interval from i to j, but now we define $K_{i,j+1}^d = K_{ij}^l$.
Finally, if $q_{ij}(K_{ij}^l) \leqslant 0$, we can find K_{ij} so that $q_{ij}(K_{ij}) = 0$, with
$K_{ij}^l \leqslant K_{ij} \leqslant K_{ij}^u$. Then there is an eligible interval from i to j at level
K_{ij}. To continue the induction, now define $K_{i,j+1}^d = K_{ij}$. To start the
procedure, define $K_{i,i+1}^d = K_i^u$.

Note that K_{ij}^d represents a K-value such that all higher K-values have been
already excluded from consideration by the argument that $q_{ik}(K_{ij}) \geqslant 0$ for
some riser k, $i < k < j$. The computations of $q_{ij}(K_{ij}^u)$ and $q_{ij}(K_{ij}^l)$ are designed to establish the possibility that $q_{ij}(K_{ij}) = 0$ for some K_{ij}. If
$q_{ij}(K_{ij}^u) < 0$, then $q_{ij}(K) < 0$ for all K in the interesting range, K_{ij}^l to K_{ij}^u by
the monotonicity of $q_{ij}(K)$. On the other hand, if $q_{ij}(K_{ij}^l) > 0$, then $q_{ij}(K)$
> 0 in the relevant range; further, we now know that any value of $K > K_{ij}^l$
is ruled out as the level of an eligible interval for risers beyond j.

The Algorithm can easily be extended to find eligible intervals from a
riser i out to infinity. We need only introduce an additional riser at in-
finity, with $t_\infty(K) = +\infty$ for all K, $K_\infty^l = 0$ and $K_\infty^u = +\infty$, and define

$$K_{i\infty}^d = \lim_{j \to +\infty} K_{ij}^d,$$

$$q_{i\infty}(K) = \int_{t_i(K)}^{+\infty} \alpha(t) r(K,t)\, dt.$$

We must finally consider possible blocked intervals beginning at the origin.
First, it will be shown that there cannot be a jump at the origin to a

capital stock greater than $K^*(0)$. For suppose that $K(0+0)>K^*(0)$.
Since $K(t)$ is monotonic increasing, $K(t)\geqslant K(0+0)$ for all $t>0$. On the
other hand, by continuity $K^*(t)<K(0+0)$ for t sufficiently close to 0,
so that $K(t)>K^*(t)$ for $t>0$ and sufficiently small, and, by (4.3), $r(K,t)>$
0, which implies that $q(t)$ is increasing. But this is only possible if $q(0)<0$,
and therefore there was no investment at time 0.

If $K(0)\geqslant K^*(0)$, there is no jump at the origin; if $K(0)<K^*(0)$, the
jump is to a value not exceeding $K^*(0)$. $\hfill(4.13)$

We can now define an eligible interval from time 0 to riser j analogously
to (4.12). First define

$$q_{0j}(K) = \int_0^{t_j(K)} \alpha(t)r(K,t)\,dt.\qquad(4.14)$$

Then, define

the origin, 0, and riser j form an *eligible interval* at level K if the
following conditions are satisfied: (a) $K\geqslant K(0)$; (b) $q_{0j}(K)\geqslant0$;
(c) strict inequality cannot hold in both (a) and (b); $q_{0k}(K)<q_{0j}(K)$
for all k, $1\leqslant k<j$ for which $q_{0k}(K)$ is defined. $\hfill(4.15)$

The algorithm for determining all eligible intervals beginning at the origin
has two branches, according as we are considering $K = K(0)$ or $K>K(0)$.
In the first case, let j_1 be the first riser, if any, for which $q_{0j}[K(0)]\geqslant0$.
Having defined $j_1,\ldots,j_r$, let j_{r+1} be the first riser, if any, for which

$$q_{0j}[K(0)]>q_{0j_1}[K(0)], j>j_r.$$

Then each of the intervals from 0 to some j_r is eligible at level $K(0)$.
In these definitions it is not excluded that one of the j_r's is the riser at
infinity. Also, if the sequence of j_r's is infinite, it follows that the interval
from 0 to infinity at level $K(0)$ is eligible.

For values of $K>K(0)$, the previous Algorithm is fully applicable,
provided we introduce a riser 0, with $t_0(K) = 0$ for all K, $K_0^l = K(0)$, and
$K_0^u = K^*(0)$. Note that, from (4.13), there can be eligible intervals from
the origin at level $K>K(0)$ only if $K_0^l<K_0^u$.

The optimal path, finally, is obtained by choosing eligible intervals in
a mutually consistent manner. Blocked intervals are separated by free
intervals, each of which must lie on a single riser. If there is a jump at the
origin, we understand this to mean that there is a free interval on riser 0.
With this understanding, an optimal policy is described by a finite or
infinite sequence of risers, $i_1, i_2, \ldots$, which satisfy the following conditions:
(a) for each r, there is an eligible interval from i_r to i_{r+1}; (b) the levels,

$K_{i_r i_{r+1}}$, are increasing with r; (c) if the sequence of i_r's is finite, and the last of them is a finite number, then it must be a riser which continues out to infinity (for in this case the optimal policy terminates with a free interval extending to infinity). It is understood that if the sequence of i_r's is finite, the last one may be $+\infty$, in which case it is understood that there is a terminal blocked interval.

To actually find the optimal policy after having listed the eligible intervals is a process of trial and error. Start off with an eligible interval from i_1 to i_2, say, then see if there is an eligible interval at a higher level beginning at i_2, and continue out to infinity unless the continuation becomes impossible. If it does, we go back to some riser at which a choice of eligible intervals was possible and try a different one. There is probably no point in specifying the general algorithm more precisely; in any given concrete situation, one is apt to have considerable qualitative information about the underlying function $P(K,t)$ which can be used to guide the search more precisely.

v. *The Case of Constant Returns*
If we assume constant returns to capital at any given moment of time, much of the previous discussion simplifies considerably. There is of course the possibility of an investment policy which will yield an infinite value for the sum of discounted profits. As usual in treatments of constant returns, we exclude this case. Naturally, as in the usual finite-dimensional case, the policy of investing nothing will then be as good as any other. The only remaining question is that of listing all investment policies which will be no worse than not investing at all.

The assumption of constant returns means that $P(K,t)$ is linear in K and that P_K is a function of t alone, not of K. Then $r(K,t)$ also is independent of K and can be written $r(t)$. When $r(t) > 0$, then $K^*(t) = 0$; when $r(t) < 0$, $K^*(t) = +\infty$; when $r(t) = 0$, then $K^*(t)$ is indeterminate, since all values of K are equally optimal. The time-axis is divided into intervals with $r(t) > 0$ and $r(t) < 0$, respectively, separated by points with $r(t) = 0$. Those zeros of $r(t)$ for which $r(t) > 0$ to the right and $r(t) < 0$ to the left are the analogues of the risers in the diminishing returns case; the same term will be used here. Since the analogue of a free interval becomes an interval on a vertical line, jumps at the risers are not excluded. But no investment can take place except at a riser (including as before a riser at 0).

The solution for this case can be worked out much as before, except that the formulas are much simpler since the magnitudes q_{ij} are now independent of K. The final result can be put simply:

The optimal policies are all those which call for jumps in capital

stock at all risers i (including possibly 0) for which $q_{i_\infty} = 0$. (5.1)

It is useful to note that the condition that infinite profits be impossible is that $q_{i_\infty} \geqslant 0$ for all risers i.

VI. *Econometric Implications*

In econometric application, the function $P(K,t)$ is not itself an observable but rather an expectation, held with subjective certainty, of future profit prospects. It is in the tradition of Professor Hicks's capital model, where actual present and planned future behavior are functions of present and anticipated prices. At any moment, under the model as given, the firm draws up an investment program for the present and future, but the only part of the program that is executed is the immediate investment decision. Hence, we observe at each moment the initial investment of a long-term investment program, with the profit function and the future course of interest rates which are believed in as of that moment. To determine the empirical implications of this model, it would be necessary to add a second relation, showing how the anticipated profit function and interest rates shift with time, possibly in response to new observations on market magnitudes.[5]

This is not the place to go into the possible ways in which anticipations of profit functions and interest rates can be formed, and so we cannot develop here a complete testable version of the theoretical developments of this paper. But there is one striking and definite qualitative implication, that at any given moment either the firm is holding its desired stock of capital (as defined by the profit function of the present moment, and the current rate of interest in terms of capital goods) or there is zero gross investment.[6]

Whether or not this implication is empirically valid can be ascertained only after suitable reinterpretation of the model to apply to the available data. It need only be noted here that loosely speaking the firm may be expected to hold the desired stock of capital until a point of time shortly before an anticipated business cycle peak. At this point, gross investment stops abruptly. The hypothesis therefore resembles that of the flexible accelerator which works on the upswing but not on the downswing, (Hicks, 1950, pp. 44–7) but differs (*a*) by having a less rigid relation between the desired stock of capital and the level of output, and (*b*) by admitting the possibility that the collapse of investment may occur because of anticipation of the end of the boom rather than its actual occurrence.

NOTES AND REFERENCES

[1] Arrow, Beckmann and Karlin (1958) studied in detail a very special case of the present results, in which all prices are fixed, and there is a fixed capital-output ratio, so that revenue is proportional to the smaller of the two quantities, capacity and demand, the latter varying over time. Nerlove and Arrow (1962) dealt with advertising, considered in effect as a capital good. Advertising is clearly irreversible, but it was then not possible to treat the optimal policy in a fully adequate fashion.

[2] Strictly speaking, if depreciation is not exponential, the depreciation term does depend to some extent on the future course of interest rates; for the details, see Arrow (1964).

[3] For other recognitions of the myopic rule for capital policy, see Marglin (1963, pp. 20–7), Kurahashi (1963), and Champernowne (1964, p.185). Fisher's 'rate of return over cost' (1930, pp.155–8) appears to be similar to Keynes's 'marginal efficiency of capital' but in fact Fisher considered returns and costs to be measured relative to the best alternative. If the alternative of postponement is considered, then the myopic rule can be derived, though Fisher does not do so explicitly.

[4] Functions of time, for example, $K(t)$, will also be symbolized by using t as a subscript, e.g. K_t, when typographically convenient, and the time variable may even be suppressed when its presence is clear from the context.

[5] This necessarily brief statement has ignored the possibility of lags between investment decisions and investment realizations, so important in detailed empirical analysis; see Jorgenson (1965). Under conditions of subjective certainty, the calculation of the optimal policy is affected relatively little, since virtually any desired policy for investment realizations can be achieved by a suitably chosen policy for investment decisions, after some initial period. But the investment actually made at any given time will depend upon anticipations of profit functions and interest rates held at some earlier time or times. If these anticipations shift over time, due to new observations on prices and the like or for any other reason, the dependence of actual investment on observed variables will be rather complex.

6 Since any observed moment of time is the initial point of an optimal investment policy computed on the basis of the then currently held anticipations of profit functions and interest rates, there might appear to be a third possibility, that of a jump in capital to a level below that currently desired. But since the anticipations are presumably themselves shifting continuously, we do not expect desired jumps to appear.

2

Trade Liberalization among LDCs, Trade Theory, and Gatt Rules

Jagdish Bhagwati

Political attitudes change rapidly and astonishingly in the field of international commercial policy. To those accustomed to the protectionist policies of the LDCs in the decade and a half since the war, it is remarkable that the LDCs today are actively discussing the issue of trade liberalization among themselves.

Not merely are they discussing it, but several of them have actively engaged in mutual negotiations to get action started. The most striking developments have undoubtedly been those in South America, where the Treaty of Montevideo represented the formal inauguration of LAFTA (The Latin American Free Trade Area),[1] of which Ecuador, Colombia, Peru, Chile, Argentina, Uruguay, Paraguay, Brazil and Mexico are already members, and the Treaty of Managua on *Central American Economic Integration* which has already accelerated significantly the integration process among the member countries Salvador, Guatemala, Costa Rica, Honduras, and Nicaragua (Bell, 1966, chapter 4).

Elsewhere, the current picture is not as much in character, but the outlook points the same way. The *East African Federation*, comprising Tanganyika, Uganda and Kenya, and the UDEAC (Union Douanière et Economique de l'Afrique Centrale), with Congo (Brazzaville), Gabon, the Central African Republic, Chad and the Federal Republic of Cameroon in French Equatorial Africa as its members, are two of the conspicuous examples in the African continent. But they trace their ancestry to colonial periods and their 'integrated markets' have recently been witness to disruption by measures such as *inter-member* QRs, tariffs and surcharges.[2] However, the measures taken by the members to review these developments and *retain* the framework of a generally reduced and low level of trade barriers between member countries, rather than follow post-independence policies of industrialization behind universal trade barriers, themselves signify an *implicit* decision to liberalize trade among themselves.

There have also recently been developments such as the *Regional Cooperation for Development* between Pakistan, Iran and Turkey, which aims explicitly to create 'regional' division of labour with attendant liberalization of mutual trade barriers, and the still-undefined moves towards a *Middle Eastern Common Market*. Asia, however, has witnessed little concrete efforts or ideas in this direction, despite ECAFE's efforts to initiate regional liberalization of trade.[3]

Reasons for Trade Liberalization

The reasons for these efforts at trade liberalization among LDCs are several. First, there is a growing appreciation of the simple fact of inefficiency of specialization which industrialization behind indiscriminate, high trade barriers involves. Many LDCs, especially in the ECAFE region, feel that, starting from the present position of QRS, it is possible to relax restrictions on a mutual basis with other LDCs and reduce 'overlapping' import substitution or industrialization (provided that balance of payments difficulties resulting, if any, are not excessive and payments arrangements are forthcoming to assist in the short-run). The emphasis here is on *economic inefficiency arising from producing things which could well be imported more cheaply from others who are better placed, by natural resources or otherwise, to produce them.*

This argument, however, is eclipsed by the more recent emphasis on *the inefficiency which arises from the inability to exploit economies of scale in industrial activities if one has to industrialize within essentially national markets.* This argument has come up in both African and Latin American contexts and there are three ways in which it can be encountered.

(1) It is often presented, in the African and Central American contexts, in the strongest conceivable terms as a *sine qua non* of industrialization. Individual countries are absolutely *non-viable* because it is impossible to conceive of any industrial activity which can be set up even remotely within sight of its optimum scale in view of the extremely small effective demand. Thus, industrialization cannot be conceived of at all *unless* the markets are widened through trade. Hence the case for international trade liberalization.

(2) The preceding argument overstates the case. The real point is that,

if scale economies cannot be exploited, the real return to investment in industrial activity will fall, raising thereby the resources necessary to achieve the same level of industrialization. The scale of the effective demand in many African countries, for example, is perhaps so small in relation to achievable economies that the increase in costs may be significant; but it is not meaningful to describe the resulting situation as one of 'non-viability'. In the reformulated version, therefore, the argument merely amounts to stating that industrialization, with access to extra-national markets, would be achievable by an LDC at lower cost *via* the resulting exploitation of economies of scale.

(3) Indeed, the 'non-viability' argument comes up, in a different version, in Latin America, among the industrialized countries of Brazil, Argentina and Mexico. They discuss their problems of industrialization in a Fraserian, evolutionary framework and argue that they have 'completed the first stage of industrialization, involving the production of consumer goods', reasonably adequately within national markets. But the 'next stage', involving the establishment of heavy industry, is impossible to contemplate, in view of the scale economies involved, within national frontiers and is conditional upon access to international markets.[4]

Finally, there is the traditional argument that foreign trade can be an instrument for increasing competitiveness and hence the efficiency of industrial activity.[5] The experience of the LDCs has underlined the inefficiencies which arise from domestic monopolies sheltering behind trade barriers. This has been a powerful argument, in Latin America especially, for initiating reductions from very high tariff levels so as to reintroduce some 'measured degree' of competition. Note, however, that this argument presupposes that investment *is* forthcoming; since in most LDCs this itself is frequently a result of fenced-off national markets, the concern with efficiency of investment is something which comes at a *later* stage in the process of industrialization; after all, the LDCs cannot be expected to worry about efficiency unless there is something to be efficient about!

These arguments for trade liberalization are quite sensible, of course, and familiar to economists. Not that they are always used to advantage or with a correct appreciation of their limitations. For example, the fact that economies of scale operate in industrial activities should not make the LDCs, operating a customs union and an industrial allocation policy in

harness (as in East Africa, Equatorial Africa and Central America)
forget that (i) the spatial distribution of demand, (ii) transportation
costs, (iii) the inter-temporal growth of demand at different points of
consumption and (iv) the external economies obtaining *via* the geographical clustering of certain industries are *also* factors to be considered
and that the optimal solutions, even when trade barriers are absent, may
still demand that 'uneconomic scale' plants be constructed in different
member countries in the same activity.[6]

Distinguishing Features of LDC Trade Liberalization

However, the most interesting aspect of the LDC efforts at trade liberalization is that they are characterized by certain patterns which are both
readily discernible and difficult to reconcile with what traditional trade
theory would predict as the behaviour of governments 'rationally' pursuing
economic welfare. The most notable of these features may be listed here
at the outset.

(1) The trade expansion efforts are sought to be on a *preferential* basis,
among a few or all LDCs but *excluding the developed countries*. Where the
preferential groupings fall within the purview of Gatt's Article XXIV
(exempting 100 per cent preferential arrangements from the contractual
commitment to extending MFN treatment to all other Gatt members),
there is no institutional change involved in this demand. But the LDCs
clearly would like to extend the operation of such an exemption to less-
than-100 per cent preferential arrangements among LDCs. They are thus
demanding really the suspension of automatic MFN rights by the developed
Gatt members with respect to the LDC members.

(2) Furthermore, the experience in Latin America in particular shows
that the LDC efforts at tariff cuts and trade liberalization are oriented very
clearly towards *trade diversion*. Looked at from the viewpoint of traditional
trade theory, therefore, the LDC efforts seem to be directed at the wrong
kind of tariff cuts altogether! The acceptance of the increment in intra-
regional trade in LAFTA as an index of its success, without any attempt at
separating out trade diversion from this figure, as also the impatience
exhibited in Latin American circles with the requirement of Gatt's Article
XXIV[7] that the average external tariff must not be greater after a customs
union or free trade area (which would, among other things, make trade
diversion *via* the raising of external tariffs impossible), are pointed

reminders of this divergence between LDC demands and behaviour on the one hand and traditional predictions and prescriptions on the other.

(3) The LDC negotiations and literature are unanimous in insisting upon 'reciprocity' of benefits. This is familiar from the history of tariff negotiations anywhere. The reciprocity takes the form, quite acutely in most LDC cases, of balancing of *incremental* trade flows rather than demands of identical tariffs cuts or any other method. Both the strict insistence on reciprocity and the specific form taken by it are not readily reconciled with what traditional trade theory, as analyzed below, would indicate as the likely pattern of LDC behaviour.

(4) As a corollary to this concern with this form of reciprocity, there is also discernible among many LDCs a preference for negotiations and action on trade liberalization among smaller rather than larger groups. As a consequence, there is already discernible a growing conflict of opinion on whether any *sub*-set of LDCs should be allowed to discriminate against the other LDCs when a less-than-100 per cent programme of tariff cuts, outside the purview of Gatt's Article XXIV, is involved. The dominant trend, however, seems to be in favour of the more 'liberal' version which would permit discriminatory tariff cuts applicable even within a sub-set of LDCS.

There are broadly two sets of issues that arise from these patterns of LDC behaviour and demands. First, is it possible to 'explain' them in terms of the traditional theory of preferential trade liberalization (associated mainly with Viner, Meade and Lipsey[8]) if one makes the additional assumption that the LDC governments act 'rationally' in pursuit of economic welfare? Or do we have to modify the theory itself so that it leads to predictions of behaviour which are consistent with those observed? It is argued, later in this paper, that we indeed require a modified, new theory which fits the observable facts very much better and that such a theory can be obtained by modifying the LDC governments' assumed 'utility function'.

Secondly, in the light of such an 'explanation' of LDC behaviour and demands, the question immediately arises as to what attitude economists *ought* to take concerning the amendments proposed by LDCs in the Gatt rules. The following analysis formulates a conceptual framework which provides a possible case for accepting such amendments, while also examining its limiting assumptions.

Explanation of Distinguishing Features of LDC *Trade Liberalization*

It is possible, of course, to say that the LDCs are 'muddled' and 'irrational'; such views are not as uncommon as one would imagine. They are in fact held especially by those who have not reconciled themselves to the exercise of governmental action and hence cannot admit of its possible rationality.

On the other hand, purely *political* explanations are both possible and undoubtedly relevant. Thus, for example, the desire to liberalize trade *within* the LDC group, to the exclusion of the developed countries, could be explained, partly at least, by reference to a desire to attain 'solidarity' within the LDC group. There are most certainly overtones of such notions as 'solidarity', 'bargaining power', 'political cohesion and strength' and the like in some of the regional LDC groups such as LAFTA and in Central America; they are to be traced to the political dominance of the United States in the area as also the example of the European Common Market which too was enveloped in a political cloak of similar cloth.

There also seems to have been considerable interest shown by some of the developed countries themselves in getting the LDCs to liberalize trade *among* themselves as an 'act of self-help'. This too is to be explained, at least partially, in political terms as an attempt to (i) divert LDC attention away from pressing on with their claims at UNCTAD for concessions from the developed countries, (ii) create predictable dissensions among the LDCs (on issues such as that of discrimination among themselves) and thus break the LDC-block (such as it is) at UNCTAD, and (iii) promote, in particular, *regional* groupings of LDCs which would then be easier to attract into preferential groupings with the developed countries in the region, thus reinforcing the traditional economic and political ties[9] (as with United States and Latin America or EEC and French Africa).[10]

Similarly, the interest in trade-diverting trade expansion may be explained in terms of a *political* inability to lower tariffs on protected, domestic industries. Since producers typically tend to turn into articulate and powerful pressure groups, it is plausible to argue that the politics of democratic systems will reflect producer interests more readily than any others, so that trade-diverting trade expansion is certainly likely to be preferred to trade-creating trade expansion.

While such explanations are certainly relevant, it is also of equal interest to note that practically the entire range of LDC behaviour can be 'explained' by recasting traditional trade theory into a somewhat different mould. This is, in fact, readily done.

Traditional Analysis

The traditional analysis classifies preferential tariff reduction into two ideal categories: (i) trade diverting and (ii) trade creating. Each of these well-known types may be considered, in turn, from the viewpoint of predictions of behaviour that they would generate on the assumption of 'rational' behaviour in the sense discussed earlier.

I. *Trade diverting tariff reduction.* Looked at from the viewpoint of a tariff-cutting country (M), and the partner-country (P) in whose favour the tariff is cut, a trade diverting tariff cut leads to the following situation according to the traditional theory:[11]

(*a*) country M will lose from the trade diversion shifting the source of imports to the higher cost supplier, country P;

(*b*) on the other hand, the cheapening of the commodity, on which the tariff is cut preferentially, may lead to a net consumption gain (Lipsey, 1957);

(*c*) country M can therefore be left as before, or may gain or lose from a trade-diverting tariff cut;

(*d*) as for country P, it will *either* gain from opening trade with country M or by improving its terms of trade with it *or* have its welfare position unchanged if it is a 'large' country (in the Samuelson sense).

The matrix of welfare possibilities from a preferential tariff cut by country M in favour of country P, according to traditional theory, is shown on page 28. Note that, in two cases at least, (1) and (2), there seems to be a clear reason why reciprocity by country P does not represent a *sine qua non* for a tariff cut by country M; whereas, only in three cases (3–5) would it seem that country M could not be induced to cut its tariff on country P without demanding some measure of reciprocity from it. Note also that whereas reciprocity would not be necessary in the cases where trade diversion leads to welfare gains, the insistence on reciprocity would arise most compellingly only in cases where the trade diversion leads to a loss (as will happen in cases 3 and 4) where again all that reciprocity may lead to is a loss to *both* countries instead of one. Thus we *either* fail to provide

rationale for reciprocity at all or provide it in cases where the possibility of
there being preferential tariff cuts at all is dismal.

So far, therefore, the theory fails to explain why the LDCs seem to
prefer trade diverting tariff cuts and simultaneously to insist on reciprocity
(of incremental trade flows). We can, however, go somewhat further than
we have. Within the framework of this analysis itself, there are two ways
in which the reciprocity demands may be justified even in cases where
country M gains from a unilateral, preferential tariff cut causing trade
diversion. On the one hand, we could introduce a game-theoretic formulation into the analysis. For example, in the two cases, (1) and (2), where
country M stands to benefit unambiguously from a preferential tariff cut,
its insistence on a reciprocal tariff cut *could* lead perhaps to a mutual,
simultaneous tariff cut which may make country M even *better off than
under a unilateral, discriminatory tariff cut.*[12]

MATRIX (1). Welfare possibilities under a trade diverting tariff
cut by one country (M) – on traditional theory

	COUNTRY	
possibility	M	P
(1)	gains	gains
(2)	gains	unchanged
(3)	loses	gains
(4)	loses	unchanged
(5)	unchanged	gains
(6)	unchanged	unchanged

At the same time, we could well argue that the alternative to a unilateral
preferential tariff cut by country M is not merely the status quo but could
well be a unilateral *non-discriminatory* tariff cut. Thus it could be argued
that the willingness to cut a tariff preferentially in favour of country P
involves a *potential* loss (or reduction in gain) as compared with a situation
where country M would have cut its tariff non-preferentially, and therefore
the reciprocity demand follows from the consequential (implicit) loss to
country M.[13]

We can somewhat strengthen, therefore, the case for expecting 'rational' governments to press for reciprocity. Note, however, that while reciprocity may be explained along these lines, we cannot so explain the desire for balancing the incremental trade flows – that is, the *specific form* that reciprocity demands take. Moreover, the analysis does not really explain why the sub-set of countries M and P are interested in negotiations for trade liberalization with each other and not with others. To make this implicit but important assumption plausible, we would have to bring in some extraneous, political argument; as argued earlier, a sub-set of countries may well decide to undertake liberalization among only themselves consequent upon a political decision to 'integrate their political and economic systems'. Indeed, some such political assumption would be necessary even to explain why it is that, since *both* countries M and P can lose from such trade diverting trade liberalization despite reciprocity, and such possibilities do not seem to be excluded by any means by recent LDC experience, the LDCs in fact seem to opt nonetheless for such trade liberalization. Unless, therefore, one relies on such political arguments at a crucial stage of the analysis, the traditional theory will not be able to come to grips with even the most obvious features of LDC attempt at trade liberalization.

II. *Trade creating tariff reduction*: When we analyse the case of trade creating tariff cuts, the inability of traditional theory to come to grips with LDC behaviour seems even more evident. Assuming that country M is preferentially cutting its tariff again, if it is a trade creating tariff cut it will lead to the following situation according to traditional theory:

(*a*) country M will lose its inefficient industry, partially or wholly, to country P;

(*b*) country M will consider itself as having improved its allocation or resources and will also derive a consumption gain, leaving it a net gainer; and

(*c*) country P will not or will have gained depending on whether it is or is not 'large'.

The matrix of welfare possibilities under the traditional theory is then as indicated on page 30.

By contrast with the case of trade diverting tariff cuts, we now have one case of harmony of interests and another where the tariff-cutting country gains anyway. In neither case, therefore, would reciprocity appear to be a prime requisite before country M would cut its tariff.[14]

Traditional analysis would then also imply that trade creating tariff cuts will be profitable whereas trade diverting tariff cuts would not be so except where the consumption gain is decisive. Hence we would infer from traditional analysis that trade creating tariff cuts are more likely to occur in practice than trade diverting tariff cuts. This is yet another conclusion which seems to contradict LDC experience.

MATRIX (2). Welfare possibilities under a trade creating tariff cut by one country (M)–on traditional theory

		COUNTRY
possibility	M	P
(1)	gains	unchanged
(2)	gains	gains

Modified 'Utility Function'

Consider, however, the following modification to each LDC's objective or utility function:

(1) let each LDC attach intrinsic significance to the level of import-competing industrial output that trade diversion attracts to each country and trade creation attracts to one country 'at expense of' the other; and

(2) let each country ignore the significance of any possible consumption gain from the cheapening of products in domestic markets subsequent on tariff cuts.[15]

Note further that the addition of these new arguments in the LDC objective function seems quite plausible because, in particular:

(1) the LDCs typically wish to industrialize and hence use tariffs (and/or quantitative restrictions) for this purpose, so that the attraction of import-competing industrial production would be considered a desirable result *in itself*; and

(2) in most cases, the trade pattern of the LDCs involves imports of components, materials and machines, to which the notion of a *consumption* gain is only indirectly applicable.[16]

If these modifications are made, consider what happens in the case of trade diversion examined earlier on traditional lines. The matrix of welfare possibilities will change radically. Country M will now feel that it has 'lost' through having to import the commodities from country P at a higher cost whereas, in its opinion, country P has registered a definite 'gain' because it has now started or expanded production of these commodities. Given therefore this change in the objective function, the matrix reduces to a simple, conflict situation where the tariff cutting country M feels it has lost and the other country P has gained. Reciprocity thus becomes extremely important and no trade diverting tariff cuts or free trade areas / customs unions may therefore be expected to make progress unless reciprocity is built into the arrangements from the beginning.

At the same time, it becomes easy to see that reciprocity would ensure that, by satisfactory distribution of trade-diverted industrialization, both countries could emerge feeling that they have gained from the reciprocal discriminatory tariff cuts.[17] Again, it is easy to see now that the LDCs would prefer to liberalize trade with one another rather than with the advanced countries. Since industrial production has value in itself, the LDCs would consider it disadvantageous to negotiate tariff cuts (on industrial products) with advanced countries (whose competitive strength in manufactures is assumed to be greater) *unless* they are one-way, in their favour, thus ruling out reciprocal tariff cuts (including customs unions and free trade areas) except among the LDCs (who are presumed to be at a more comparable or 'similar' stages of development vis-a-vis one another) and also explaining their well-known insistence on 'non-reciprocity' by LDCs for tariff cuts made by the advanced countries.[18]

For similar reasons, trade creating tariff cuts would, under the modified theory, equally exhibit demands for reciprocity *and* would appear less attractive than under traditional theory, thus corresponding again more closely to observable facts about LDCs. Thus, for example, the matrix of welfare possibilities from such a unilateral tariff cut (Matrix 2) will now be changed. Country M will reduce its estimate of gain (by the amount of the consumption gain, if any) and, more significantly, has a new 'loss' factor because the contraction or elimination of its import-competing manufactures will be considered undesirable *per se*. At the same time, country P will be thought to have *definitely* gained because it has attracted to itself or expanded the manufacturing activity which has declined in country M. The matrix of welfare possibilities thus reduces again to a simple conflict situation where country P is supposed to have gained and country M to have lost. A unilateral tariff cut by country M is thus ruled out and reciprocal tariff cuts by country P become a *sine qua non* of country M's tariff cuts even in trade creating situations. Moreover, since value is attached to industrial production *per se*, the LDCs fail to see any rationale in contracting the output of existing manufactures, so that trade creating tariff cuts seem to them to be 'unnecessary' or 'unfruitful' and hence inferior to trade diverting tariff cuts, which bring more industrial activity to the member LDCs.

If therefore the new theory is accepted, it is possible to explain practically all the puzzling features of LDC negotiations, from reciprocity to preference for trade diverting tariff cuts. The most interesting of these implications may now be brought together and further spelled out:

(1) trade liberalization will *inevitably* be accompanied by considerable interest in 'reciprocity' arrangements, even though traditional theory does not so imply;

(2) trade diverting tariff cuts, provided reciprocity is worked out, are far more likely to be acceptable than traditional theory would imply (the creation or expansion of import-competing, industrial production being a desirable objective in itself);

(3) trade creating tariff cuts will be far less likely to be acceptable, even when reciprocity is worked out, than traditional theory would imply (the decline of import-competing, industrial production being an undesirable objective in itself);

(4) trade diverting tariff cuts, in consequence, are more likely to occur in practice than trade creating tariff cuts, again contrary to what traditional theory would imply;

(5) the 'reciprocity' requirement is further likely to take the form of attention to whether the resulting *incremental trade flows* between the participating countries are balanced: this, in turn, would be an indication of the degree of the production 'advantage' which the new theory stresses as a significant source of gain;[19]

(6) the new theory would also reinforce political explanations in predict-

ing that LDCs would turn to one another for tariff-cutting exercises: trade diversion is more readily practised against the developed countries which still continue overwhelmingly to be the major exporters of industrial manufactures to the LDCs;

(7) the new theory would simultaneously explain the demand to have Gatt's Article XXIV amended so as to allow the *raising* of the average external tariff in a preferential tariff cut (in a 100 per cent programme); if tariffs were to be preferentially cut only from existing levels, and if these tariffs may be expected to be higher on items where trade creation rather than trade diversion is likely,[20] the effort at preferential tariff cuts could be jeopardized by having to concentrate on trade creating rather than trade diverting cuts;

(8) further, in view of the insistence on reciprocity, the preference is likely to be for tariff cuts among smaller groups of LDCs rather than larger groups; reciprocity is easier to work out within smaller groups especially when it takes the specific forms outlined earlier *and* is so important to the participants, whereas smaller groups also make it easier to supplement an 'unpredictable' trade mechanism by a 'more direct' and simultaneous policy of 'industrial allocations' among members;[21] and

(9) the preference for trade diversion is likely to accentuate still further the tendency to prefer smaller groups, for the simple reason that there are more outsiders to divert trade from when the group is smaller.

Indeed, these are all very distinctly the special features of LDC attempts at trade liberalization and of their consequential demands for Gatt revision.

Should Gatt Rules be Changed?
The logical question then is whether it makes economic sense to amend the Gatt rules so as to accommodate the LDC patterns of behaviour and demands. There are three main types of position which can be taken on this general issue.

(1) Either one can be cynical and argue that, after all, countries act exactly as they want to *despite* Gatt membership, so that there is little point in amending these rules. While there is force in the contention that actual practice manages frequently to bypass international obligations – as, for example, with the Gatt rules on export subsidies, which are widely flouted in devious ways – their nuisance value is very evident and they

frequently involve resort to indirect and inefficient ways of achieving legal consistency between international obligations and national action. The very fact that LDCs want Gatt rules changed implies that they must, at least sometimes, be constrictive. So this cynical dismissal of the question must be rejected.

(2) Alternatively, one may argue the opposite case: that, if a sufficient number of countries want a change in the Gatt rules, it will go through and there is no point in arguing the matter any further. Such a cynic may well point to the insertion of Article XXIV, undoubtedly to accommodate an impending European Economic community, which enjoyed equally the support of the United States, while the LDCs were apathetic or reconciled to impotence in influencing events; after all, even traditional theory cannot show that a 100 per cent tariff cut, on a preferential basis, is invariably superior to a partial cut or no cut at all and yet that is exactly what Article XXIV implicitly asserts! If LDCs manage to muster enough bargaining strength, eventually they may well succeed in changing Gatt rules around to suit their demands. But again, unless the developed countries can be persuaded to acquiesce in these amendments, the progress towards them would be inevitably slow and halting. So this form of cynical dismissal of the question must also be rejected.

(3) Indeed, even from an intellectual standpoint, it is necessary to argue through the question whether the LDC demands *ought* to be supported.

In answering this question, one has to be clear about what exactly is the alternative to *not* amending the Gatt rules in accordance with LDC demands. This, in turn, amounts to asking what is really the alternative to LDCs not being allowed to liberalize trade *among* themselves and whether, from an economic point of view, that alternative is superior.

Emphasis is being placed here quite deliberately on defining the most realistic alternative, in comparison with which the possibility of amending Gatt rules in the LDC-suggested direction must be judged. Much too often economic issues are mis-judged because the alternatives considered are really irrelevant. Thus, for example, devaluation was widely considered to be inflationary in its impact because the alternative implicitly considered was that of utilization of reserves to ease the deficit. It was later realized that the correct comparison, from a policy viewpoint, was with alternative adjustment policies, *all* being evaluated subject to non-availability of reserves, and that once this was done it was by no means obvious that devaluation would be inflationary by comparison with, for example, QRS.[22]

The starting point in finding the right alternative to answer our present question seems to be the fact that *industrialization* is among the primary, immediate objectives of the LDCs. One may debate whether this is a desirable, legitimate 'economic' objective or whether it is to be classified as a 'non-economic' objective. Regardless of the precise reasons for considering industrialization as an LDC objective, that the LDCs so consider it is the essential fact to be noted.

If then industrialization is to proceed in an LDC, the immediate consequence of such a decision for most LDCs would be for the imports, of the items in which the import-substitution occurs, to shrink below their level otherwise.[23] *Trade diversion*, in this sense, *is already implicit in the decision to industrialize*. Nothing in current Gatt rules can effectively block an LDC member from undertaking such trade diversion in pursuit of its policy of industrialization.

I. *Case for Gatt Revisions.* From this way of looking at things, the most favourable case for accepting the LDC behaviour and demands emerges as follows.[25]

If the LDCs could be allowed to reduce tariff barriers *among* themselves, this could permit the given trade diversion (implicit in *each* LDC's decision to industrialize) to be carried out at *lower cost* because the trade diversion, while continuing against the non-members, would be eliminated or reduced as among the (member) LDCs. To put it yet differently, and more illuminatingly, the tariff cuts (among the LDCs) would in fact be permitting trade creation among the LDCs in relation to the situation where they would have industrialized behind national tariff walls. The contention then is that, regarded in this light, the apparently trade diverting attempts by LDCs at mutual tariff preferences turn out really to be effectively trade creating.

On this line of argument, several arguments for modifying Gatt rules seem to become persuasive. For example, the automatic extension of MFN treatment by LDCs to the developed members could be removed on the ground that the trade diversion away from the developed countries will take place anyway, thanks to *individual* LDC action, so why hold up the (implicit) trade creation among the LDCs that such an amendment would facilitate?

Similarly, why not modify Article XXIV of Gatt so as to permit the raising of the external average tariff when entering a 100 per cent preferential agreement? If the alternative again is the raising of *national* LDC tariff barriers which Gatt cannot effectively prevent (except when the duties are 'bound'), why not consider the suggested modification of Article XXIV as permitting a less undesirable, alternative procedure which would reduce the LDC-cost of industrialization?

Again, if LDCs will not readily wish to dismantle *existing* lines of industrialization and would rather concentrate instead on ensuring that the *future* doses of industrialization are efficiently made by having wider markets among the LDCs–thus concentrating on the gains from *implicit* trade creation, as defined here–it would appear that the alternative to not letting them discriminate between tariffs on existing and on new industries to come, as Article XXIV would require, is likely to make the LDCs continue the present policies of industrialization in small, domestic markets and thus forgo even the advantages that could accrue from implicit or potential trade creation. By this argument, therefore, there would again be a good case for letting LDCs, even in Article XXIV situations where the LDCs would commit themselves to eventual full integration, discriminate in their progressive tariff cuts between existing and newer industries (much as there is now accepted an asymmetry between manufactures and agriculture).[25]

II. *Arguments against Gatt Revisions*. The above case is, in fact, the most favourable one that can be built up for making some of the Gatt revisions that the LDCs have been demanding. But it rests on two crucial assumptions which need to be spelled out very clearly, for it is around them that economists are likely to divide in their judgment of what changes in Gatt are desirable.

The first crucial assumption (already stated explicitly) is that the LDCs would, in fact, if Gatt rules are not changed, use non-discriminatory tariffs (or quotas) in pursuit of industrialization. While this assumption is plausible, in the light of LDC experience, it *could* be challenged on the dubious argument that the increased cost of the resulting attempt at industrialization behind national tariff walls would itself reduce the degree of trade diversion (and hence economic inefficiency) which LDCs are willing to undertake in pursuit of industrialization.[26]

The second crucial assumption is more serious. The preceding case for

Gatt revisions really presupposes that the LDCs will undertake tariff negotiations in a way which, while discriminatory, does in fact reduce (if not minimize) the mutual cost of any given degree of industrialization among the member countries. There is an important difference between arguing that discriminatory arrangements among LDCs could reduce the mutual cost of member-LDC industrialization and asserting that it would necessarily do so.[27]

Indeed, from the analytical point of view, this way of posing the problem leads to at least three questions of importance and relevance to the present discussion:

(1) If an *arbitrarily-defined* sub-group of LDCs desires to achieve a *given* level of industrialization, within *each* country, what is the *optimal* level and structure of the external tariff which will permit this to be done at *least cost* within the framework of an integrated market? (No such solution need exist, of course, if the level of industrialization within any member cannot be sustained without protection from the other members, thereby violating the presence of an integrated market within the sub-group.)

(2) Within the same, arbitrarily-defined sub-group of LDCs, what is the optimal set of policy instruments for achieving the required level of industrialization within each LDC? Here, the range of policy instruments being considered extends beyond tariff policy.

(3) Given a set of LDCs, each with its own target of industrialization, what is the *optimum sub*-set of LDCs from any *one* LDC's point of view which will permit it to achieve its objective at least cost, assuming for example that the subset will act so as to minimize cost for the group as in (*a*) or (*b*) preceding?[28] It is not clear that LDCs would, in fact, examine their possibilities of preferential arrangements in the careful way that is necessary, so that it is inevitable that economists would be divided on the set of rules that they would like to see at Gatt on the question of preferential tariff arrangements.

The questions concerning Gatt revisions are thus not easily answerable; they involve resort to judgments of a fairly crucial type about what is likely to happen in response to the changes. Even the framework devised in this paper, to strengthen the case for these revisions, cannot make the case for them definitive.

Ultimately, the issue is likely to be judged also in the light of the views which economists have concerning whether the possibility of preferentially reducing trade barriers among LDCs is likely to constitute the only feasible route by which the world will move closer towards freer trade or whether it will only lead to a sustained and more marked fragmentation of the world economy.

ACKNOWLEDGMENTS

This paper has grown out of my having been a member of two United Nations 'Expert Groups', in November 1964 at ECAFE and in February 1966 at UNCTAD, on this general subject. It is really an academic economist's attempt at discovering the rationale, if any, behind the attempts of the developing countries to liberalize trade in certain specific ways which do not 'square with' what economic analysis would predict as 'rational'. Throughout the paper, LDCs mean less developed countries, an identifiable bloc of countries at the UNCTAD now, and Gatt stands for the General Agreement on Tariffs and Trade. I should like to record my general indebtedness to the numerous colleagues on the two United Nations Groups as also to members of a Seminar at I.B.R.D. for their comments. My thanks are also due to Harry Johnson for incisive comments on the penultimate draft of this paper and for drawing my attention to his own work (1965a). The recent work of Linder, Cooper and Massell also relates to some of the questions touched upon in this paper. I am also happy to recall that Sir John Hicks has often shown considerable insight into questions of international trade policy (see *Essays in World Economics*).

NOTES AND REFERENCES

[1] As far as tariff reductions are concerned, Sidney Dell (1966) records that '. . . the LAFTA countries achieved a certain initial measure of success following the entry of the Treaty of Montevideo into force. The first round of negotiations was held in Montevideo from 24 July to 12 August 1961, the second in Mexico City from 27 August to 21 November 1962, the third in Montevideo again from 5 October to 31 December 1963, and the fourth in Bogotá from 20 October to 11 December 1964' (p. 70). For details and evaluation, see chapter 5.

[2] A useful account of the disruptionist trends, immediately after independence of the three East African Territories, is contained in a contribution of Arthur Hazlewood to a forthcoming publication, of the Royal Institute of International Affairs, on Integration in Africa, edited by Hazlewood himself.

[3] The ASA (between Malaya, Thailand and Philippines) and the MAPHILINDO (between Malaya, Philippines and Indonesia) have remained politically utopian in their concept altogether. Several ECAFE conferences have also resulted in Ministerial resolutions on trade liberalization with practically no concrete results. On the other hand, the recent establishment of the Asian Development Bank, with the contribution mainly of Japan and the United States, may lead to the beginning of a more active interest in region-oriented tariff cuts or quota liberalization.

[4] This 'two-stage' method of argument is absolutely 'classical', based on historical observation of industrialization, and has frequently been used to 'establish' the inadvisability of beginning *first* with heavy industry *à la* Soviet Union. It is now well recognized, of course, that no such 'laws' can be derived and the 'Soviet model', which reverses the stages, *can* make considerable sense.

[5] The inefficiency here relates to the lack of incentive, in a sheltered market, for reducing costs to the minimum at *whatever* level of output is chosen by the entrepreneur.

[6] Not merely are these qualifications infrequently appreciated but also there is danger that the industrial allocations among members of a union may, in practice, be the product of 'horse trading'.

[7] 'With respect to a free-trade area, or an interim agreement leading to the formation of a free-trade area, the duties and other regulations of commerce maintained in each of the constituent territories and applicable at the formation of such free-trade area or the adoption of such interim agreement to the trade of contracting parties not included in such area or not parties to such agreement shall not be higher or more restrictive than the corresponding duties and other regulations of commerce existing in the same constituent territories prior to the formation of the free-trade area, or interim agreement, as the case may be.'

[8] The main literature is: J. Viner (1950); J. Meade (1955) and R. Lipsey (1960). There is also the 'monetary' theory of trade discrimination, associated with the names of Frisch, Fleming and Meade, which is not touched upon in this paper, but which would be relevant in understanding payments problems and assessing current IMF rules.

[9] That Raul Prebisch, Secretary General of UNCTAD, has been worried by this aspect of the problem is clear from his address to United Nations Trade and Development Board, stating: 'Unfortunately, there are some symptoms that the spirit of Geneva is not being applied, and that on the contrary there is an aggravation of the tendency towards a system of discriminatory preferences in certain parts of the world. I cannot hide from the Board my great concern at signs in

certain Latin American circles, which are manifesting themselves with increasing force in requests to the United States for a preferential system to be exclusive to Latin American countries' (Dell, 1966, p. 34). Indeed, the fact that LAFTA exists now is likely to make both the demand for, and granting of, such discriminatory preferences by the United States a significant possibility.

[10] Economists are particularly prone to scoffing at such 'fears'. They would be well advised to read, in case they are sceptical, E. M. Carr's (1946) brilliant account of the inevitable interaction of economic philosophy and national political interest.

[11] Note that, in analysis that follows, only the *simpler* analytical models of Viner (1950) and Lipsey (1960), are used. Complications can arise, however, if this is not done. For example, as Lipsey has pointed out, even the consumption effect can be negative if one takes a *three-good* model. Also, as Mundell has shown recently, unless gross substitutability is assumed between the goods of each country in a *three-good*, three-country model, the terms of trade of the partner country (P) with the third country can worsen, thus presumably opening up the possibility of a loss to it.

[12] This aspect of tariff bargaining, which may rationalize certain reciprocity demands even within the *traditional* theoretical framework, has always been ignored by those who voice puzzlement as to the insistence of many countries on reciprocity of one kind or another in tariff negotiations. See, for example, Harry Johnson (1965a) whose elegant analysis neglects altogether this line of argument. Failure to see this line of argument can be traced to many liberal writers, such as Lionel Robbins (1954, pp. 137–8) who recognizes the problem explicitly and tries to account for reciprocity by arguing unconvincingly that the burden of adjustment with unilateral tariff cuts would be less.

[13] This point can be readily seen from Lipsey's well-known diagram. Assume that country M, specialized on producing OR of Y, has an initial, non-discriminatory tariff which leads to trade with country C at price-ratio OC, and consumption at Q with domestic, tariff-inclusive price ratio being P_t and welfare at U_i. If the tariff is eliminated altogether, welfare will increase to U_c. If the tariff is cut only for country P, trade will occur along price-line RP and welfare will be at U_p. Note that $U_p > U_i$ but $U_p < U_c$. See figure opposite.
Therefore, in terms of U_c, there *is* a loss from a preferential tariff removal, even though it is a case where trade diversion increases welfare ($U_p > U_i$).

[14] Again, as with the analysis of trade diversion, we could strengthen somewhat the case for reciprocity by using a game-theoretic formulation or by pointing out the *potential* loss from a discriminatory, as distinct from a possible non-discriminatory, tariff cut.

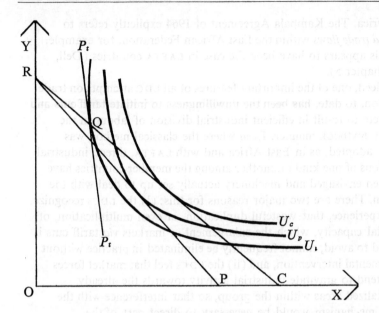

¹⁵ For this reason, though more so by virtue of the difficulty of accepting the notion of 'given preferences' on which the whole theory rests, I have found it useful to develop the welfare theory of trade in my lectures in Delhi in terms of technological efficiency rather than utility rankings. For details on this, see my forthcoming paper (Bhagwati, to appear) on 'Gains from Trade Once Again'.

¹⁶ There is also an associated 'revenue' problem. Where LDCs have levied tariffs for earning revenue, their removal or reduction, on other LDCs, could well result in a loss of revenue in case of trade diversion, if the increment in imports from the resulting cheapening of the item in domestic consumption is not large enough to offset the reduction in the tariff rate. Experience in East Africa and French Equatorial Africa, in particular, suggests that this possible loss of revenue is considered an important 'loss' factor by LDCs in continuing or entering upon integration schemes. This factor is ignored in the text.

¹⁷ It is assumed, in the following analysis, that a decisive weight will usually be attached by LDCs to the question of whether industrial activity expands or contracts in the economy.

¹⁸ This 'principle' of non-reciprocity has been brought up even *within* preferential groupings, as in the special treatment meted out to the less 'developed' members of both EEC and LAFTA, with respect to implementation of tariff cuts.

¹⁹ Evidence of such behaviour by LDC members of common markets and free trade areas is to be found in the experience in LAFTA and in

East Africa. The Kampala Agreement of 1964 explicitly refers to *balanced trade flows* within the East African Federation, for example.

[20] This appears to have been the case in LAFTA countries (Dell, 1966, chapter 5).

[21] Indeed, one of the important features of all LDC attempts on trade expansion, to date, has been the unwillingness to initiate tariff cuts and trust them to result in efficient industrial division of labour in the classical, textbook manner. Even where the classical method was initially adopted, as in East Africa and with LAFTA, direct, industrial allocations of one kind or another among the member countries have now been envisaged and machinery actually set up to deal with the question. There are two major reasons for this: (i) the LDCs recognize, from experience, that wasteful duplication, or even multiplication, of industrial capacity, which the enlargement of markets *via* tariff cuts is intended to avoid, cannot frequently be eliminated in practice without governmental intervention, and (ii) the LDCs feel that market forces would tend to gravitate industrial activity towards the already industrialized areas within the group, so that interference with the market mechanism would be necessary to direct part of the industrialization towards the 'weaker' members. On the other hand, the offsetting disadvantages of such industrial allocations by political agencies, unless managed with reference to economic criteria, could also be significant.

[22] Credit for this insight goes to Egon Sohmen (1958) who, to my knowledge, was the first to reformulate the question of the impact of devaluation upon the price level in this manner.

[23] This argument presupposes, of course, that industrialization will lead to the imposition of tariff (or equivalent QR) protection and that the level of industrialization which free trade will permit falls short of the desired level. Both of these seem to be realistic assumptions, of course, about LDCs.

[24] At the I.B.R.D. seminar, where this paper was presented, Bela Balassa pointed out to me that my way of presenting the strongest case in favour of accepting LDC demands is implicit in the writings of Raul Prebisch, Cooper and Massell and Balassa, although the precise formulation of the argument is different.

[25] This could be done quite readily by permitting a different rate of progressive tariff cuts on these two classes of products and thus effectively lengthening considerably the time over which the existing industries would have to adjust. The fact of growing industrialization and incomes, as also the prospect of an eventually integrated market, would then both induce and permit an orderly decline in the relative and/or absolute level of the industry in the LDC where it is inefficient.

[26] This is, in fact, the type of argument which has long been used by the opponents of foreign aid, such as Milton Friedman, who claim that foreign aid featherbeds many inefficiencies which would become insupportable if the countries receiving aid had to make do with their own resources. This argument, of course, presupposes that the recipient countries agree with these commentators in regarding certain policies as 'inefficient', an assumption which is notoriously invalid – there is a well-known law of intransitivity which operates in these matters: x thinks his economics is better than y's and y thinks the other way around. The effect of withdrawal of aid is more likely to be the reinforcing of the very same policies that these opponents of foreign aid dislike.

[27] The experience in LAFTA, where the tariff cuts seem to have been *undiscriminatingly* trade diverting, can only make one sceptical with respect to the second assumption being discussed here.

[28] Cooper and Massell (1965) raise the somewhat more limited question of whether the LDCs could *reduce* their mutual cost of industrialization through preferential arrangements. They use a constant-cost model, which is somewhat limited for dealing with the questions of importance to LDCs (such as economies of scale); but it is nonetheless a useful device, exploited with great skill by the authors.

3

Income, Wealth, and
the Theory of Consumption

Robert W. Clower and M. Bruce Johnson

A theory is a cluster of conclusions in search of a premiss.
N. R. Hanson *Patterns of Discovery*.

The modern literature on household behavior is a fascinating blend of fact, fancy and computer technology, reflecting the mutual interplay of theory and applications that has long distinguished it from most other fields of economic inquiry. It is an impressive literature, considered either as a collection of *ad hoc* rationalizations of apparent empirical regularities, or as a contribution to positive description of household behavior. Yet when all is said and done, it has added remarkably little to our understanding of underlying causal relations.

The explanation lies, we believe, in the historical isolation of consumption theory from developments in closely related branches of general price theory. Perhaps the most notable shortcoming of the literature is its neglect of dynamic interrelations among income, wealth and consumption implicit in the close connection between saving and asset accumulation (Friedman, 1957a, Houthakker, 1961a, pp. 727–30, 735). This is reflected not only in the predominantly statical orientation of theoretical research, but also in the paucity of empirical studies of balance sheet data in conjunction with related income and expenditure statistics. Recent inquiries, by Spiro (1962), by Ball and Drake (1964), and by Houthakker and Taylor (1966), go some way to remedy these deficiencies; but much remains to be done, particularly at the theoretical level, before they are eliminated.

The purpose of the present paper is to carry this work forward—more specifically, to formulate within the framework of conventional demand analysis a dynamic theory of consumption that is consistent with available empirical evidence. Our discussion is divided into three main sections. In Part I (Theoretical Foundations) we outline a microdynamic theory of household behavior, taking our cue from the elegantly simple model set out in Archibald and Lipsey's famous article (1958, pp. 1–23; Lindbeck, 1963) on value and monetary theory. In Part II (Empirical Superstructure) we impose various restrictions on the behavior relations of our model, drawing for this purpose on survey data from the United States and the United Kingdom. In Part III (Statistical Implications) we develop the aggregative consequences of our theory and collate our findings with results reported in earlier studies, particularly Milton Friedman's influential *Theory of the Consumption Function* (1957b). The nature of our subject compels us to devote substantial space to econometric topics. Our primary aim being to elucidate ideas rather than facts, however, we deal with statistical data explicitly only where its introduction serves to guide or illustrate the theoretical analysis.

I. *Theoretical Foundations*

We begin by examining the planning behavior of a household at an instant of time, temporarily setting to one side all questions involving the execution as distinct from the scheduling of economic plans. The argument is later extended to deal with the intertemporal behavior of measurable income, consumption and saving flows. Following a Samuelsonian maxim (1961), we work throughout with a simple and strong theoretical model to avoid obscuring the intrinsic logic of our analysis in a haze of extraneous details.

Household Planning: Basic Concepts. In keeping with familiar procedure, we consider a household whose decision problem at any given moment of time is to choose among alternative combinations of desired consumption (c) and desired wealth (w), subject to a planning constraint that depends on the actual wealth ($\underline{w}$) of the household at the same moment (Samuelson, 1961; Rolph, 1954; Chase, 1963). We do not inquire into the motives, rational or otherwise, that underlie household attitudes towards spending and saving, nor do we deal explicitly with factors that might influence such attitudes (e.g. expected prices and rates of return, expected income, age, occupation, family composition, previous purchases of durable goods, etc.). On the contrary, we suppose that the household has a short memory and limited foresight, and we ignore all forces affecting choice that conflict with this point of view (Clower, 1963b; Ball and Drake, 1964). Accordingly, we characterize the household's ranking of alternative wealth-consumption combinations by a preference function of the form

$$u = u(w,c), \tag{1.1}$$

in which desired wealth and desired consumption appear as the only explicit variables.

Corresponding to (1.1), we define the set of currently admissible wealth-consumption plans by the budget equation

$$c+v(w-\underline{w}) = 0 , \tag{1.2}$$

where v is a given velocity coefficient. The appearance of the parameter v in (1.2) is dictated by the dimensional difference between the flow variable c and the stock variables w and $\underline{w}$. Since no conceivable experiment will enable us to arrive at independent estimates of v and $\underline{w}$, however, we may gain simplicity without loss of empirical content by setting $v = 1$. On this assumption, the budget equation asserts that the planned (instantaneous) rate of consumption at any given date is numerically equal to the difference between desired and actual wealth at the same date.[1]

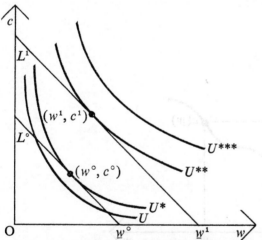

Figure 1.1 Selection of the Optimal Plan

Given the choice alternatives defined by (1.2), we apply the traditional postulate of utility maximization to determine the optimal wealth-consumption combination (w^*,c^*) corresponding to any specified value of actual wealth. This is illustrated in Figure 1.1, where the curves U, U^*, U^{**}, . . ., represent the function $u(w,c)$. If w° is the current wealth of the household, the budget line is $L°$ and the optimal wealth-consumption plan, defined by the tangency of $L°$ with the indifference curve U^*, is $(w°,c°)$. Alternatively, if the current wealth of the household is w^1, the budget line is L^1 and the optimal wealth-consumption plan is (w^1,c^1), and so forth.

Supposing that the decision problem has a unique solution corresponding to any given value of current wealth, we obtain planned consumption at any specified date as a single-valued function of actual wealth at the same date:[2]

$$c^t = c(\underline{w}^t) \,. \tag{1.3}$$

The graph of this function, hereafter referred to as the *consumption locus*, is illustrated in Figure 1.2. Our assumptions impose only one *a priori* restriction on this relation, namely, $c(0) = 0$ (this follows directly from the budget equation (1.2)). Casual empirical considerations suggest that the slope of the consumption locus, that is, the *marginal propensity to consume wealth* (MPCW), is unlikely to be negative; but no such condition is implicit in our model.

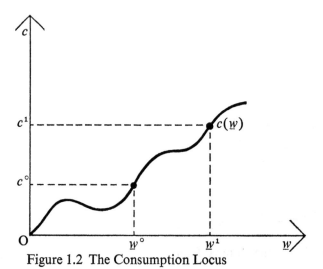

Figure 1.2 The Consumption Locus

The Intertemporal Adjustment Process. The preceding analysis implies that planned consumption at any date t is a function simply of current wealth. This conclusion is in close accord with views advanced on outwardly different theoretical grounds by Milton Friedman (1957b) and by

Modigliani and Brumberg (1954; Farrell, 1959, pp. 687–96). Where these writers regard current wealth as an imperfect proxy for 'permanent' or 'expected' income, however, we regard it as a causal variable in its own right. Correspondingly, where they introduce current income to give operational meaning to the otherwise purely metaphysical concepts of 'permanent' and 'expected' income, we shall introduce it as just one factor (the other being current consumption expenditure) that governs variations over time in objective stocks of household wealth.

Specifically, we assume that *the rate of change of current wealth at any date is equal to the difference between measured income* (y) *and measured consumption* (c) *at the same date.* Symbolically,

$$d\underline{w}^t / dt = y^t - \underline{c}^t . \tag{1.4}$$

This assumption calls for two comments. First, we note that the definition of saving implicit in (1.4) presupposes that assets do not depreciate or appreciate in value, or that exogenous changes in the value of assets are somehow included in measured income and consumption. The second alternative is to be preferred in principle, but the first is easier to manage in practice. For the time being, therefore, we take the easy way out and assume away capital gains and losses. Second, we observe that measured consumption, $\underline{c}^t$, need not bear any simple relation to desired consumption, c^t, at the same date. Again for simplicity, we ignore decision lags and other possible complications and suppose that the value of $\underline{c}^t$ is at all times identically equal to the value of c^t as determined by the wealth-consumption function $c^t = c(\underline{w}^t)$. Given these assumptions, we have only to specify the determinants of measured income before going on to discuss the intertemporal behavior of measured consumption and wealth.

It is customary in discussions of consumer behavior to regard current income as an arbitrary parameter the value of which is determined by social and economic forces over which the individual has no control.[3] We shall adopt the same procedure as concerns one component of total receipts, namely, wage, salary and other *service income*, m^t. Since some portion of household wealth will normally consist of earning assets, we cannot treat rent, interest and other *property income*, n^t, in the same fashion. We shall adopt the simple yet general hypothesis that current property income is a (non-decreasing) function of current wealth: that is,

$$n^t = n(\underline{w}^t) ,$$

where $n'(\underline{w}^t)$ is assumed to be non-negative. Total income at any date is then defined as a function of service income and current wealth by the identity

$$y^t = m^t + n(\underline{w}^t).$$ (1.5)

The graph of (1.5) corresponding to a fixed value of service income, $m^t = m$, is illustrated in Figure 1.3 by the curve $y(w)$, henceforth referred to as the *income locus*. The slope of the income locus represents the increase in property income associated with a marginal increment in wealth, that is, the marginal yield, or marginal rate of return, on wealth. The form of the locus will depend on the structure of the household's asset portfolio. For example, if the household holds: (i) only money, the locus will be horizontal; (ii) only perpetual bonds, linear and rising since the slope will represent the coupon rate of return; (iii) money, bonds, and physical assets in varying proportions, non-linear and variable in slope. The greater the proportion of non-earning assets in the portfolio, the smaller will be the marginal rate of return.

We may now characterize intertemporal adjustment processes. The income locus indicates, for each alternative level of current wealth, the maximum rate of current consumption the household can enjoy without drawing on previously accumulated wealth. The consumption locus (reproduced from Figure 1.2 and superimposed on the income locus in Figure 1.3) indicates what the household's actual rate of consumption will be corresponding to any given value of current wealth. The vertical distance between the income locus and the consumption locus measures realized saving; that is, the current rate of change of actual wealth. Thus the income and consumption functions (1.3) and (1.5), combined with the asset adjustment hypothesis (1.4), define a determinate dynamical system in the single variable $\underline{w}^t$ which, starting from any initial value $\underline{w}^t{}_0$ of wealth at date t_0, generates unique values of measured consumption, income, and wealth for all subsequent dates.

Suppose, for instance, that the value of current wealth at some initial data $t = 0$ is represented by the point $w°$ in Figure 1.3; then current consumption and current wealth will initially tend to increase over time at the rate $y° - c°$.[4] With the passage of time, therefore, the actual values of wealth, income, and consumption all will increase as indicated by the directional arrows originating along the perpendicular $A°$ in Figure 1.3.

Alternatively, if the value of current wealth at initial date $t = 1$ is w^1, then consumption will initially exceed income and wealth will tend to decrease over time. The actual values of wealth, income, and consumption will therefore decline with the passage of time as indicated by the directional arrows originating along the perpendicular A^1 in Figure 1.3.

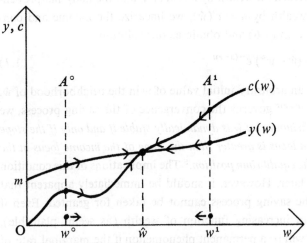

Figure 1.3 The Adjustment Process

In both of these examples, realized saving will converge to zero with the passage of time. That is to say, current wealth will gradually approach a stationary (and stable) equilibrium value ($\hat{w}$ in Figure 1.3) at which current consumption is equal to current income (Spiro, 1962, pp. 339, 342–3). This result holds for all cases in which the consumption locus intersects the income locus from below, provided that only one such intersection occurs for those values of current wealth (e.g. the set $w^1 - w^0$ in Figure 1.3) that are assumed to be admissible. If for some admissible value of wealth the consumption locus intersects the income locus from above, realized saving may or may not converge to zero with the passage of time; for in this case (illustrated in Figure 1.4) one or more of the equilibrium states defined by the consumption and income loci will be dynamically unstable.

Stability Conditions: The Stationary Economy. The exact condition for convergence of the saving process in the neighborhood of any given equilibrium value $\hat{w}$ of wealth is best indicated by approximating the solution of the differential equation

$$dw^t/dt = m + n(w^t) - c(w^t) \tag{1.6}$$

in such a neighborhood—(1.6) being the general form that the asset-adjustment hypothesis (1.4) takes when $m^t = $ constant. Denoting the marginal rate of return on wealth by $r = n'(\hat{w})$, and the marginal propensity to consume wealth by $a = c'(\hat{w})$, we linearize the income and consumption functions in (1.6) and obtain as our solution

$$w^t = \hat{w} - (\hat{w} - w^\circ)\, e^{-(a-r)t}, \tag{1.7}$$

where w° denotes an arbitrary initial value of w in the neighborhood of $\hat{w}$. Since the term $e^{-(a-r)t}$ governs the convergence of the saving process, we see that *the equilibrium value $\hat{w}$ is dynamically stable if and only if the slope of the consumption locus is greater than the slope of the income locus in the neighborhood of the equilibrium position.*[5] The implications of this condition will be discussed later. However, it should be immediately apparent that convergence of the saving process cannot be taken for granted. Even if consumption is an increasing function of wealth (as seems plausible), household saving will be a permanent phenomenon if the marginal rate of return on wealth is sufficiently large or the MPCW sufficiently small (Liviatan, 1965).

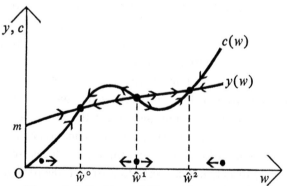

Figure 1.4 Stable and Unstable Equilibria

If the asset-adjustment process is stable, then in the limit as time tends to infinity, consumption will absorb the whole of current income—a proposition which at first sight may seem offensive to common sense.

It would be a serious mistake, however, to discount stability as a practical possibility on this ground. As the illustrative data in Table 1.1 indicate, the convergence of consumption towards income may proceed so slowly in practice as to be observationally unnoticeable–which is to say that observation of the economic system over any *finite* time interval may not provide enough information to enable us to distinguish between stable and unstable asset-adjustment processes.

TABLE 1.1. Time required for 60 per cent completion * of adjustment process, starting at time $t = 0$ $(r = 0.05)$

MPCW	elapsed time
2·00	0·51
1·00	1·05
0·75	1·43
0·50	2·22
0·40	2·86
0·35	3·33
0·25	5·00
0·15	10·00
0·10	20·00

* The exact figure used is 63·2 per cent, corresponding to a value for e^{-x} of 0·368 (i.e., e^{-1}).

Growth, Saving, and the Rate of Return on Wealth. The preceding discussion is applicable only to situations in which the saving process is convergent, and only then on the assumption that the level of service income is fixed. If the saving process diverges for every given value of service income, then *a fortiori* it will also diverge if service income is rising. In neither case can we say anything about the intertemporal behaviour of income, consumption and wealth, except that all will tend to vary with the passage of time.

If the saving process is convergent for every given level of service income, however, definite conclusions can be drawn about the intertemporal behavior of wealth and consumption corresponding to alternative time paths of service income. For instance, if service income varies cyclically (say, as the sine of the time), it can be shown that wealth, total income, and consumption will all vary in a similar fashion – lagging service income by a certain time interval. A more important case for our purposes is that in which service income is assumed to grow over time at a constant exponential rate g; i.e. $m^t = me^{gt}$. If we let $c^t = aw^t$, then the relevant differential equation is $dw^t/dt = me^{gt} + rw^t - aw^t$ which has the solution

$$w^t = \{m/(g+a-r)\}\, e^{gt} + \{w° - m/(g+a-r)\}\, e^{-(a-r)t}. \quad (1.8)$$

The second term in this solution is a transient; hence wealth tends ultimately to grow at the same exponential rate as service income.

Consumption and income must conform ultimately to the pattern set by the growth of wealth. In growth equilibrium, however, there is no tendency for consumption to absorb the whole of income. On the contrary, if we allow sufficient time for transient effects to become negligible, consumption is given by

$$c^t = aw^t = a\{m/(g+a-r)\}\, e^{gt}, \quad (1.9)$$

and gross income by

$$y^t = me^{gt} + rw^t = me^{gt} + r\{m/(g+a-r)\}\, e^{gt}. \quad (1.10)$$

Dividing the first of these equations by the second, we find that

$$c^t/y^t = a/(g+a). \quad (1.11)$$

Thus the *ratio* of measured consumption to measured income approaches a certain constant with the passage of time; but the *absolute* difference between income and consumption increases steadily.

Illustrative values of the consumption/income ratio corresponding to alternative rates of growth and alternative values of a are shown in Table 1.2. The saving-income ratios in the center of the table range from 3 to 12 per cent and probably span most of the cases that are of any practical interest.

It may seem curious that the rate of return on wealth (r) does not play a direct role in the saving process, even in conditions of steady growth. The explanation lies in our earlier decision not to deal with expected rates of return in defining the preference function of the household, for this severs any possible link between growth, realized rates of return, and the marginal propensity to consume wealth. In principle, of course, one should expect prospective yields to have some influence on the MPCW; the question is 'How much influence ?' In general there is no reason to suppose that flows of satisfaction yielded by stocks of money, bonds, factories or old masters are different in degree or kind from those obtained by swallowing tranquillizers or feeding children. Apart from the usual motives of straightening out income streams over time, earning income, and providing a hedge against uncertainty (all of which are probably sensitive to yields) a person may hold assets in order to tyrannize his employees or bank manager, impress his neighbors, provide himself and his heirs with the means requisite to a life of noble contemplation, etc. In all circumstances, one is dealing with alternative forms of immediate gratification, many of which may involve appetites too keen to be blunted by variations in yields—certainly not financial yields.

Whether rightly or wrongly, we assume that prospective yields have no significant effect on the general form of the consumption locus. We do not wish to deny that calculating individuals exist. Our position on this as on most other matters affecting household preferences is much like that of Dostoevsky on history.[6]

TABLE 1.2. Growth and the consumption/income ratio

	GROWTH RATE (g)				
MPCW (a)	·01	·02	·03	·04	·05
·05	·83	·71	·63	·56	·50
·10	·91	·83	·77	·71	·67
·15	·94	·88	·83	·79	·75
·20	·95	·91	·87	·83	·80
·25	·96	·93	·89	·86	·83
·35	·97	·95	·92	·90	·88
·50	·98	·96	·94	·93	·91
·75	·99	·97	·96	·95	·94
1·00	·99	·98	·97	·96	·95
2·00	1·00	·99	·99	·98	·98

II. *Empirical Superstructure*
Although our model of the pure theory of household behavior could be extended in a number of directions, our immediate concern will be

rather to develop and test relevant implications of the version presently at hand.

The Generalized Stability Hypothesis. It is desirable to proceed as far as possible with a minimal set of special assumptions. This must include the hypothesis that household saving at any *given* level of service income converges to zero with the passage of time; otherwise we cannot say anything useful even about the response of individual households to changes in income and wealth. If we confine attention to a group of households for which this hypothesis is valid, however, then we have only to specify the distribution of service income among households to deduce from our model some conclusions about mutual interrelations among group measures of income, wealth, and consumption.

The implications of these restrictions are more extensive than might be suggested by casual reflection. To suppose that asset adjustment processes are universally stable is equivalent to imposing definite 'laws of motion' on individual households. For to any given vector of service incomes there corresponds a unique and dynamically stable set of equilibrium vectors of household consumption, wealth, and gross income. To assume that the form of the service-income distribution is given, is then equivalent to imposing a kind of 'energy conservation' law on the system of households; for what one household loses, another household must gain.

If we suppose further that all changes in household position within any given service-income distribution occur strictly at random, we may invoke the central limit theorem to assert that unique and stable vectors of measured *mean values* of consumption, wealth, and gross income are defined for any stationary level of aggregate service income.[7] Accordingly, we may think of the individual household as a statistical entity the behavior of which is described in terms of the mean values of the variables that it controls. It is then a straightforward matter to introduce non-random factors into the analysis. Changes in aggregate service income, its distribution remaining the same, clearly will lead to changes in the same direction in the mean values of all individual variables. Less obviously, but just as surely, *specified changes in the statistical characteristics of the service-income distribution income can be shown to imply closely related changes in statistical distributions of mean values of individual variables.* We thus arrive at a theory of the 'dynamics of motion' of a system of households that is closely analogous to classical thermodynamics, the most important element of similarity being that we, like the thermodynamicists, are able to pass from models of individual behavior to models of group phenomena by explicit statistical arguments.

Our method of procedure does not represent a break with tradition; on the contrary, it faithfully reflects the spirit if not the letter of Neoclassical equilibrium analysis (Samuelson, 1947, pp. 21–3; Newman and Wolfe, 1961). It does constitute something of a departure, however, from contemporary modes of macroeconomic analysis, where the common practice is either to ignore individuals altogether or to pass from individual to group phenomena by explicit aggregation.

There is a certain irony here: traditional microeconomic analysis is too sophisticated to be statistically manageable, while contemporary macroeconomics is too naïve to be taken seriously. Our aim in this paper is to steer a middle course between the two extremes: to apply methods suggested by Marshall and Walras to models suggested by Keynes. Whether we have chosen the right course remains to be seen. The only way to assess the factual merit of our theory is to apply it to the real world in the way all useful theories–physical, biological, economic, etc.–are always applied, namely, with a considerable amount of intuition and common sense.

Behavior Relations: Empirical Restrictions. As presently formulated, the empirical content of our model is of the second order of smalls. If we are to use the model to interpret published statistics, we must first set some limits to theoretical speculation by imposing empirically plausible restrictions on the basic behavior relations of our system.

(1) *The Income Locus.* The income locus is in the nature of an objective market constraint. The yield to any given household of a marginal increment in wealth will depend on the structure of its asset portfolio as well as the return on particular items in the portfolio; in principle, therefore, marginal yields may vary significantly among households in a single wealth class. As a practical matter, however, we should not expect this to be of any empirical significance. Studies of the portfolio behavior of households in different income and wealth classes indicate that the percentage distribution of broad classes of financial assets (e.g. money, time deposits, government bonds, corporate securities) is related in a systematic way to total wealth (Atkinson, 1956, 1964). As far as durable goods are concerned, it would appear that the majority of households acquire these in fairly well-defined 'priority patterns' (Pyatt, 1964). If these findings are anything to

go by, we may safely regard the marginal rate of return on wealth as a definite number the magnitude of which depends simply on the total asset holdings of the household. Straightforward measures of average yields by wealth class, together with current information about measured income, should provide an adequate picture of the income locus of a typical statistical household.

Although conclusive evidence on the relation between wealth and yields is not available, such evidence as we have suggests that yields are generally higher the larger the income and asset holdings of the household (Atkinson, 1956, pp. 78–9, 128–31) – which is to say that the typical income locus probably displays *positive* curvature. This is attributable to the (apparently quite uniform) tendency of wealthier households to hold larger proportions of equities as compared with direct debt assets and time deposits and related claims (ibid. pp. 63–85). But the yields earned by even the wealthiest households seldom rise as high as 10 per cent on earning assets[8], and the typical portfolio will also include a substantial quantity of non-earning assets. Accordingly, we are probably safe in supposing that the marginal rate of return on total wealth is, on the average, at most 4 to 6 per cent per annum, and that the same rate applies to all households. The substance of the argument that follows would be much the same whether the marginal rate of return were 10 per cent, 6 per cent or zero; and as long as we deal with rates of this magnitude, the curvature of the income locus is of no consequence.

(2) *The Consumption Locus.* The consumption locus, unlike the income locus, is by its nature subjective rather than objective. Indeed, the term 'consumption locus' is little more than a short-hand expression for a vast complex of social, economic, and psychological factors that determine a household's willingness to abstain from consuming its current wealth. To state the same idea in more operational terms: the consumption locus indicates for each possible level of current wealth what level of current income a household must enjoy to be willing to maintain its present wealth intact. This is clearly a meaningful concept. It may also be useful, provided that the forces it summarizes are relatively impervious to sudden change.

Our only *a priori* information about the consumption locus, given the generalized stability hypothesis and the positive slope of the income locus, is that it passes through the origin of the $w-c$ plane and slopes upward from left to right. We may generate additional information only by carrying out conceptual experiments designed to discover what restrictions have to be imposed on individual consumption loci to produce hypothetical data on wealth and consumption that accord with the available statistical evidence.

Let us begin by supposing that all households have linear consumption loci, but that the slopes of different loci vary randomly from one household to another. Then cross-section data on wealth and consumption corresponding to a given distribution of service income will yield a random scatter of wealth-consumption points. Alternatively, suppose that the slopes of individual consumption loci tend to cluster about a common value. Then a cross-section scatter will be heavily concentrated within a certain pie-shaped area of the $w-c$ plane. More generally, we should expect any clustering of consumption loci (whether the loci were linear or not) to be revealed by cross-section data. Conversely, if an actual scatter of wealth-consumption points displays a definite pattern, we should infer from this that individual consumption loci tend to conform to a similar pattern.

Unfortunately, consumption research traditionally has been directed not towards relations between wealth and consumption, but rather towards relations between income and consumption. We cannot settle the issue before us, therefore, by running a regression of consumption on wealth. For this to be possible, we should require detailed information about household consumption expenditures at various levels of wealth. Such data are not available in any collection of published statistics. For both the United Kingdom and the United States, however, we do have information about mean consumption and wealth at various levels of income (Tables 2.1 and 2.2). For the United States alone, moreover, we have some data on the distribution of income and saving within three broad wealth classes (Table 2.3). A combination of these materials should tell us something about the existence and probable character of the 'modal' consumption locus even though the scatter it produces fails to satisfy conventional criteria of statistical relevance.

For purposes of comparison, we have plotted the data in Tables 2.1 and 2.2 as separate scatters in Figure 2.1. The similarity between the data for the US and UK is obvious. In both countries, mean wealth and consumption are, by and large, positively correlated with mean income. Moreover, consumption tends to increase less rapidly than wealth as income increases (with double-logarithmic scales, this is indicated by the negative curvature of the scatters for low income levels, by a slope of less than unity in the linear sections of the scatters). There is an evident difference between the US and UK scatters at the lower end of the income scale, where the UK data indicate a negative correlation between wealth and consumption. But it would be a mistake to pay any attention to this phenomenon; for we know that there are many households in both countries with negative or zero net worth (e.g. about 35 per cent of UK households, 15 per cent of US households (Lydall and Lansing, 1959, p. 60)), and these simply disappear from the wealth distribution when we classify households by income level. That the resulting loss of information is substantial becomes clear when we reflect that the lowest income brackets in both countries will include large numbers of retired people with substantial accumulations of wealth. This alone would explain the truncation of the two scatters and the negatively-sloped section of the UK relation.

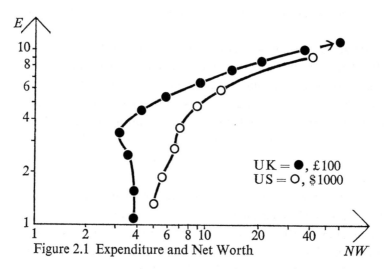

Figure 2.1 Expenditure and Net Worth

The US data on income and saving ratios by wealth classes (Table 2.3) give us a clearer idea of the dispersion of consumption expenditures within different wealth classes. The lowest class in the table (under $1,000) is far enough down the wealth scale to tell us most of what we want to know about the corresponding section of Table 2.1; and the income classifications are sufficiently fine to permit us to gauge the probable distribution of consumption in other sections of the same table.

TABLE 2.1. United Kingdom income units:
mean net worth and expenditure by income classes 1953

income class	gross mean income (£)	mean net worth (£)	mean expenditure (£)
0–99	82	386	101
100–199	146	384	156
200–299	251	356	255
300–399	351	325	347
400–499	466	419	451
500–599	545	563	540
600–699	645	876	646
700–799	742	1372	755
800–899	870	2144	853
1000–1499	1151	3797	1086
1500 and over	2921	16981	2571

Source: Mean gross income and mean net worth are derived from data presented in K. H. Stern, 'Consumers' Net Worth: The 1953 Savings Survey', *Bulletin of the Oxford Univ. Institute of Statistics*, Vol. 18, 1956, p. 12 (table VII). Mean expenditures are calculated from data on income and saving given in L. R. Klein, 'Patterns of Savings', *Bulletin of the Oxford Univ. Institute of Statistics*, Vol. 17, 1955, p. 182 (table IV).

We note first that the maximum entry in each row of Table 2.3 moves from the lowest to the middle to the highest income class as we proceed up the wealth scale. Except in the lowest wealth class, moreover, the saving ratio increases steadily as we move from lower to higher incomes, indicating that consumption expenditure is more concentrated than income at higher levels of wealth. Second, we note that the saving ratio is negative for households with less than $3,000 in current income *and* more than $10,000 in assets, confirming our earlier explanation of the truncation of the distributions shown in Figure 2.1. Finally, we observe that consumption is slightly less than income for households with assets under $1,000 *and* incomes of less than $7,500, which indicates that consumption and income are distributed in much the same way at lower wealth levels. On this ground alone, we should be justified in adding some points to the lower ends of the scatters in Figure 2.1 to indicate that the modal consumption locus extends back towards the origin.

TABLE 2.2. United States spending units: mean net worth and expenditures by income classes

| income class | 1950 | | |
	net mean income ($)	mean net worth ($)	mean expenditure ($)
under $1,000	655	5,073	1,339
$1,000–1,999	1,601	5,487	1,834
2,000–2,999	2,645	6,538	2,809
3,000–3,999	3,633	7,145	3,691
4,000–4,999	4,617	8,990	4,614
5,000–7,499	6,032	12,076	5,809
7,500 and over	11,573	42,932	9,304

Source: Mean net income and mean expenditure are derived from data given in *Study of Consumer Expenditures Incomes and Savings* (The Wharton School and Bureau of Labor Statistics, Univ. of Penn., 1957), Vol. XVIII, Table 1–1, p. 2. The figures on net worth are calculated from aggregate data given in Raymond W. Goldsmith, *A Study of Savings in the United States* (Princeton: Princeton Univ. Press, 1956), Vol. III, Table W–46, p. 122.

(3) *The Negative Curvature Hypothesis.* Taking account of all the considerations mentioned above, we conclude that there is a definite clustering of consumption loci in the w–c plane, with considerable dispersion of individual loci, however, about the modal locus. We infer from this that the modal locus must exhibit less curvature than suggested by the points plotted in Figure 2.1; for a transfer of retired persons from the lower to the middle and upper ranges of the scatter – a direct implication of classifying these units by wealth rather than income – could hardly help but straighten the scatters as presently shown. At higher levels of wealth, the scatters in Figure 2.1 probably conform more or less closely with the modal locus; for at these levels it is clear that current income imposes no direct constraint on current consumption, hence that the observed relation between wealth and consumption is voluntary rather than forced. Finally, we conclude from the information in Table 2.3 that the locus starts somewhere in the neighborhood of the origin and joins the scatters given by our income-classified wealth-consumption data at the point where they tend to become truncated.

The sum and substance of all this may be put more precisely by saying

TABLE 2.3. Distribution of spending units and saving ratios by asset and income classes (non-moving US spending units, 1960–62)

number of units	total assets in 1960	MEAN TWO-YEAR INCOME				
		under *$3,000*	*$3,000* *–4,999*	*$5,000* *–7,199*	*$7,500* *–9,999*	*$10,000* *or more*
	under $1,000					
207	A [1]	37 *	30	25	7	1
	B [2]	9·2	3·7	4·8	†	†
	$1,000– 9,999					
422	A	22	18	29 *	19	12
	B	2·5	9·3	10·7	12·2	15·4
	$10,000 or more					
380	A	14	15	25	14	32 *
	B	−8·7	6·6	13·0	17·5	23·6

[1] Indicates percent of units in wealth class with stated income.
[2] Indicates mean saving ratio of units in stated income class.
* Indicates maximum percentage in row.
† Too few cases to present data.
Source: Charles A. Lininger, 'Estimates of Rates of Saving', Survey Research Center, Economic Behavior Program, University of Michigan, mimeograph, p. 11, Table 2.

that the modal $w-c$ scatter, plotted on double-logarithmic graph paper, is probably linear, and that the corresponding least-squares regression line will most certainly have a slope of less than unity. If this guess is correct, then the implied mathematical relationship between consumption and wealth is given by

$$c = hw^b , \tag{2.1}$$

where h is a positive constant, and b lies between zero and unity.

The graph of the function (2.1) is illustrated in Figure 2.2. In conformity with an old tradition, the relation exhibits negative curvature throughout– suggesting that the marginal urgency of consumption decreases as household wealth increases. In terms of our model, what this means is simply

that the MPCW is a strictly decreasing function of household wealth. As for
the value of b, experiments with alternative graphical regressions using the
wealth-consumption data in Tables 2.1 and 2.2 (supplemented by some
freehand plots of points corresponding to lower levels of wealth than any
shown in Tables 2.1 and 2.2) suggest that it is between 0·35 and 0·40 in
both the United States and the United Kingdom, the value almost certainly
being lower in the UK than in the US. This implies a MPCW ($= bc/w$) of
around 0·10 for the wealthiest households in both countries, which agrees
well with marginal c/w ratios calculated from the data in Tables 2.1 and
2.2. The value of h, assuming that data are expressed in units of £1,000 or
$1,000, as appropriate, appears to be about 2·6 in the US and 0·33 in the
UK. If we convert pounds into dollars at the official exchange rate of 2·4
dollars to the pound, the UK figure would be about 1·08. This suggests that
British households are vastly more thrifty than US households–or, turning
it around, that British households are habituated to a much lower standard
of living than US households.

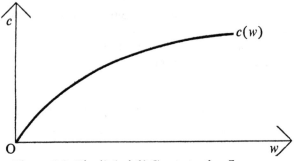

Figure 2.2 The 'Modal' Consumption Locus

From an analytical point of view, the characteristic of the modal consumption locus that merits major emphasis is its negative curvature. If
this restriction is valid, then various implications for observed behavior
follow almost as a matter of course. First, we should expect the wealthiest
households in any society to violate the generalized stability hypothesis;
for at sufficiently high values of w, the MPCW will almost certainly be less
than the marginal rate of return on wealth. The validity of this proposition
is supported by Goldsmith's finding that US households with estates valued
at more than $200,000, unlike households with estates valued at $60,000
or less, tend on the average to go on saving and accumulating assets up to

the very end of their mortal existence (Goldsmith, 1956, vol. 1, pp. 222–4). Second, we should expect wealth in any advanced society to be much more unequally distributed than income. In the US and UK, for example, we should expect the distribution of wealth to be roughly proportional to the *cube* of the distribution of income. The validity of this proposition is supported by Lorenz curves of income and net worth for the US and UK in the middle 1950s (Lydall and Lansing, 1959, p. 61). Third, we should expect the marginal propensity to consume windfall gains to vary inversely with the size of the windfall; and this proposition also appears to be supported by the evidence.[9]

III. *Statistical Implications*

We shall focus attention on cross-section regressions of consumption on income, dealing almost as an afterthought with time-series regressions of income on consumption and consumption on wealth. This procedure happens to reflect our opinion of the relative importance of the two topics and emphasizes the area in which we believe we have something essentially new to say.

The bulk of the present literature on household behavior consists of routine exercises in statistical curve fitting. Any number of variables may be (and have been) entered in this game; the payoff in regression coefficients, standard errors, and t-statistics is always sufficient to make every player look and feel like a winner. Like any mountain of facts, this one has a certain scientific value, but it has yet to produce more than a molehill of usable knowledge. To make sense of statistical regressions, one must start with a clear conception of the mechanism that is supposed to be generating observations; otherwise one cannot determine whether a given set of results is descriptive of household behavior or is just a piece of arithmetic. More specifically, one must develop from microeconomic considerations an explicit set of statistical relations that permits one to assert in advance which results are and which are not consistent with Basman's 'maintained hypotheses' about household behavior (1963).

Cross-Section Relations Between Consumption and Income. Suppose that we have to deal with a group of households for which the generalized stability hypothesis is valid. In these circumstances, our model determines just one time-invariant reduced-form relation between consumption and income corresponding to any given vector $m = (m_1, \ldots, m_i, \ldots, m_N)$ of individual service incomes, namely, the set of equilibrium consumption-income pairs ($\hat{y}_i, \hat{c}_i$) defined by the equations

$$c_i = y_i = m_i + r\hat{w}_i .\tag{3.1}$$

To any given level and distribution of aggregate service income, $\Sigma_i m_i = M$, there then corresponds a scatter of mean values of the variables c_i and y_i that clusters more or less closely about a 45° line through the origin of the $y-c$ plane. In the discussion that follows, we shall be concerned exclusively with these mean values. To avoid notational frills and error terms, however, we shall denote these means by the same letters as have been used heretofore to represent exact values of household variables.

If we adhere strictly to the assumption that variations in household position within the service-income distribution occur strictly at random, every point in the scatter defined by (3.1) will lie on or close to the 45° line; that is, a regression of c_i on y_i will yield a line that coincides with the latter. In a sense, therefore, the 45° line represents the 'true' long-period income-consumption function for a stationary economy, implying that the long-period marginal and average propensities to consume income are identically unity.

The stationary economy is, of course, a theoretical fiction. As a pedagogical device, however, the concept has its uses, for it enables us to isolate and deal effectively with aspects of behavior that a more realistic analysis would simply obscure. For the time being, therefore, we shall maintain the fiction of stationarity and see where it leads.

(1) *The Stationary Economy.* Recalling Schumpeter's classic account of 'The Circular Flow', we remark first that some changes in household position within the service-income distribution (or to use a more convenient phrase, *income permutations*) may be systematic rather than random even in a stationary state. Life-cycle phenomena (emphasized in the Modigliani-Brumberg model of household behavior) and economic survival processes (emphasized in Friedman's permanent income theory) are cases in point. But one can imagine other 'natural forces' – climatic, technological, political, etc. – that would also induce relatively uniform and persistent flows of households from one level to another within a given service-income distribution. In these circumstances, the number of households in any given income class would never change, but the names of the actual households in any class would change over time. Despite the strict stationarity

of the economy, therefore, few households would ever find themselves in a state of equilibrium.

Households that experienced an increase in measured income would, according to our model, temporarily save a significant proportion of the increment; that is, their consumption would tend to rise by less than their income. Points in the $c-y$ scatter associated with such households would thus lie to the right of the 45° line. Similarly, households that experienced a reduction in measured income would temporarily dissave; their consumption would tend to decline by less than income, producing $c-y$ observations to the left of the 45° line. Extending the argument to households as a group, we infer that the scatter of $c-y$ points, instead of clustering closely about the 45° line, would exhibit considerable dispersion–the exact amount depending on the nature of the forces generating income permutations and the speed with which households adapted to changes in income status.

As long as the level and percentage distribution of aggregate service income are given, what one household gains by an income permutation another household must lose. The effect of any given income permutation process is therefore: (i) to produce dispersion in the $c-y$ scatter; (ii) rotate the scatter to the right or left about its mean point; (iii) a combination of (i) and (ii). In no circumstances can the regression line through the scatter lie entirely to the right or left of the 45° line, for this would imply a general movement of households towards higher or lower levels of service income –a contradiction of our stationarity hypothesis. To determine precisely how an income permutation process will affect the $y-c$ scatter, however, we need to obtain an explicit expression for the regression of consumption on income that will be generated by our model during a unit interval of observation.

By hypothesis, income permutation processes operate continuously. The impact of a particular process during a given time interval will therefore be much the same regardless of what specific stretch of calendar time is chosen as the interval of observation. The disequilibrating force of a particular process will depend, however, on the length of the interval of observation, being generally greater the longer the interval.[10] For the purposes of our analysis, it is convenient to think of the interval of observation as that unit of calendar time in which consumption and income flows are expressed. The effect of an income permutation process on a statistically

representative household may then be expressed in terms of the change in
the average value of its service income during a similar (but not necessarily
contemporaneous) time interval.

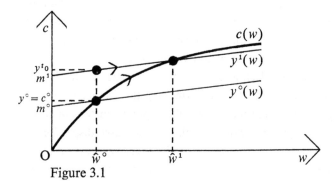

Figure 3.1

This is illustrated in Figure 3.1 where, for the sake of simplicity, we
assume that the household is initially in stationary equilibrium with
$c^\circ = m^\circ + r\hat{w}^\circ$. An increase in service income from m° to m^1 leads to positive
saving, hence to an increase in accumulated wealth and consumption at a
rate per unit time that will depend on the difference between the slopes of
the consumption and income loci. As asserted, the time path of consumption, starting from the initial value c° at, say, date t_0, is defined unambiguously in terms of the change in service income, $m^1 - m^\circ$, and the
properties of the consumption and income loci. Unfortunately, the fact
that consumption at any date $t > t_0$ is related in a definite way to the
change in service income at date t_0 does not mean that the relation can be expressed by a simple formula. Indeed, it cannot be so
expressed; for in general changes in wealth (and consumption) will be
associated with concurrent changes in the MPCW and in gross income.
If our analysis of income-permutation processes is to lead to explicit
regression formulae, therefore, we must first introduce some specialized
assumptions to permit us to establish a simple link between changes in
service income and subsequent variations in consumption expenditure.

We might devise various artful dodges to connect consumption with
service income in an analytically manageable fashion while continuing to
treat gross income and the MPCW as functions of accumulated wealth.

For our purposes, however, it is preferable to adopt a more straightforward and outwardly radical procedure and suppose, first, that $r = 0$, so that gross income is identically equal to service income; second, that the wealth elasticity of consumption is unity, so that the MPCW is a constant. These restrictions do not alter the qualitative characteristics of our model in any significant respect. They do entail potentially significant changes in the quantitative implications of our theory; but whether these are of any practical consequence cannot be decided on *a priori* grounds. Depending on the magnitudes involved, and the applications that we consider, we may discover that even the quantitative implications of our model are in satisfactory accord with the empirical evidence. For the time being, therefore, any misgivings we may have on this score may be held in abeyance. We shall return to the matter after we have developed the statistical implications of our 'special theory' and are in a position to say something definite about its conformity with factual knowledge.

Turning to the task of deriving explicit regression formulae from our model, we begin by assuming that the initial state of the economy at, say, date t_0, is one of stationary equilibrium. Supposing further that $c_i^t = a_i w_i^t$ and $m_i^t = y_i$, we may assert on the basis of the argument in Part I (pp. 46–55) that the consumption of a representative household at the end of a unit time interval starting at date t_0 is given by the equation

$$c_i^{t_0+1} = c_i' = a_i w_i^{t_0+1}$$
$$= a_i \{ m_i'/a_i - (m_i'/a_i) e^{-a_i} \}$$
$$= y_i' - (y_i' - y_i) e^{-a_i}, \tag{3.2}$$

where y_i and y_i' denote, respectively, the (average) service income flows of the household at the beginning and end of the interval (i.e. $y_i' - y_i$ represents the change in the average value of the two flows at the beginning of the unit time interval).

Now the least-squares estimates of the slope and intercept coefficients of the regression of consumption on income at date t_0+1 are defined by the usual formulae as

$$B' = \frac{\Sigma_i (c_i' - \bar{c}')(y_i' - \bar{y}')}{\Sigma_i (y_i' - \bar{y}')^2} \tag{3.3}$$

$$A' = \bar{c}' - B' \bar{y}', \tag{3.4}$$

where barred variables, as is customary, stand for group means. Replacing

c_i' in (3.3) by its equivalent from (3.2), we have

$$B' = \frac{\Sigma_i(y_i'-\bar{y}')^2}{\Sigma_i(y_i'-\bar{y}')^2} - \frac{\Sigma_i(y_i'-\bar{y}')^2 e^{-a_i}}{\Sigma_i(y_i'-\bar{y}')^2} + \frac{\Sigma_i(y_i-\bar{y})(y_i'-\bar{y}')e^{-a_i}}{\Sigma_i(y_i'-\bar{y}')^2}.$$

(3.5)

In general, the weights e^{-a_i} that appear in the last two terms of (3.5) may be expected to vary considerably from one household to another. Referring back to our initial expression for consumption at date t_0+1, we note that the response of a household to a change in income will be quicker the greater its marginal propensity to consume wealth (a_i), which is to say that households with large MPCws will contribute relatively little to the dispersion of the $c-y$ scatter. Neither will such households hold large amounts of wealth. It thus seems plausible to argue that our conclusions about the form of the $c-y$ scatter will not be seriously affected if we replace a_i in (3.5) by a wealth-weighted average of MPCws, namely,

$$a = \Sigma_i(w_i a_i/N).$$

(3.6)

Carrying out the indicated substitution, we rewrite (3.5) as

$$B' = 1 - \left\{1 - \frac{\Sigma_i(y_i-\bar{y})(y_i'-\bar{y}')}{\Sigma_i(y_i'-\bar{y}')^2}\right\}e^{-a}$$
$$= 1 - (1 - s_y r_y)e^{-a},$$

(3.7)

where r_y represents the coefficient of correlation between the income arrays y and y_i, and s_y represents the ratio of the standard deviation of the array y to the standard deviation of the array y'. Under stationary conditions, however, y and y' differ only in the arrangement of their elements, not in the elements themselves; hence $s_y = 1$ and $\bar{c}_i = \bar{c} = \bar{y} = \bar{y}_i$. Given these restrictions, we obtain the following least-squares estimates of the slope and intercept coefficients of the regression of consumption on income at date t_0+1:

$$B' = 1 - (1-r_y)\, e^{-(a)}$$

(3.8)

$$A' = \bar{y}(1-r_y)\, e^{-(a)}.$$

(3.9)

Like any other correlation coefficient, r_y can only assume values between ± 1. If all variations in income flows are strictly random, $r_y = 1$, and the regression line coincides with the 45° line, as indicated earlier. If income permutations are systematic in their effect, r_y will be less than unity; hence B' will be less than unity and its intercept positive. If all households initially have the same service income, $r_y = 0$ and the slope of the regression line will depend simply on the magnitude of the adjustment coefficient $e^{-(a)}$, being smaller the less the value of the exponent (a).[11] Finally, if income permutation processes produce large-scale flows of households from one end of the income scale to the other, r_y may be negative, in which case the slope of the regression line will be negative.[12]

The last case is no doubt rather fanciful, but it is of some theoretical interest for it indicates, what is not at all intuitively obvious, that even if every household responds positively to an increase in service income, a statistical regression of consumption on income may lead to exactly the contrary conclusion. The case may also be of some practical interest, for something approaching it must happen in any society where retirement incomes are substantially below the average for the society as a whole. Since the number of households that move from gainful employment to retirement during any single year is small relative to the total working population, we should not expect the retirement process to produce a negatively sloped $c-y$ scatter for any large sample of households. However, we should expect to observe a significant flattening of the scatter at the lower end of the income scale (because the asset holdings of retired people tend to be well above the average for low-income households as a group), and perhaps some flattening also at the top (because of increased income among persons who replace those who have retired). Such effects have been observed and noted by Friedman (1957b, pp. 48–51), but accounted for on different grounds (namely, 'nonrepresentativeness of the samples or errors in recorded responses . . .').

The simplicity of our regression formulae makes it possible to determine the precise effects of changes in the parameters r_y and a. For if we differentiate B' and A' partially, first with respect to a, next with respect to r_y, we obtain:

$$
\left.
\begin{aligned}
\frac{\partial B'}{\partial a} &= (1-r_y)a\,e^{-(a)} \geqslant 0 \\[6pt]
\frac{\partial B'}{\partial r_y} &= e^{-(a)} > 0 \\[6pt]
\frac{\partial A'}{\partial a} &= -\bar{y}a(1-r_y)e^{-(a)} \leqslant 0 \\[6pt]
\frac{\partial A'}{\partial r_y} &= -\bar{y}e^{-(a)} < 0 .
\end{aligned}
\right\}
\qquad (3.10)
$$

In plain words, our theory implies a higher slope and a lower intercept the greater the marginal propensity to consume wealth, and the higher the correlation between income arrays at the beginning and end of the period of observation. For later discussion, it is relevant to emphasize here that the effects of fluctuating income (lower value of r_y) are statistically indistinguishable from the effects of increased wealth (lower values of a). Thus 'entrepreneurial' households may exhibit relatively low income-propensities to consume either because of uncertain incomes or because their holdings of assets tend to be large relative to their consumption. Similarly, 'proletarian' households may exhibit relatively high income-propensities to consume either because their incomes are stable or because their holdings of wealth are slight relative to consumption. Though the implications of our theory are definite, therefore, they are not unambiguous in empirical import. One must be correspondingly cautious in applying them to practical problems.

We need not suppose that the MPCW as defined by the index (3.6) is the same for all households. Indeed, if we regard our present model as an approximation to a 'true' model for which the negative curvature hypothesis is valid, then we should expect the average MPCW to be higher the lower the average income of the group of households under consideration. Other things being equal, therefore, the slope derivatives in (3.10) may be taken to imply: (i) that cross-section MPCYs will be smaller the higher the average level of household income; (ii) that households with variable incomes will tend to have lower MPCYs than households with steady incomes. A significant portion of Friedman's analysis in the *Theory of the Consumption Function* is directed towards showing that the second of these implications is empirically valid (see particularly his discussion of farm and non-farm families at pp. 58–69, and of occupation characteristics of families at pp. 69–79). His arguments are compelling, considered in the context of his model (which omits explicit mention of adjustment processes); they are merely suggestive in the context of ours. The first proposition accords well with tradition and common sense and has received contemporary support from many writers (Klein and Liviatan, 1957; Friend, 1957; Mayer, 1963; Friend and Taubman, 1966). Resting as it does on non-linearity assumptions, it is disputed by Friedman–though his own charts of farm and non-farm regressions (p. 59) and of income-change groups (pp. 101 and 105) might be considered to lend firm support to the traditional view. From the standpoint of our model, no judgment is warranted, for in none of the studies that we have examined is proper care taken to ensure that 'other things' are in any degree equal.

One implication of our model that we have not so far mentioned must now be emphasized. We refer to the requirement that mean consumption be equal to mean income for households as a group. With minor exceptions, the mean points of actual consumption-income scatters lie off the 45° line. It could hardly be otherwise, for the world from which our observations are drawn is seldom in a state approaching stationarity. This restriction on our model is easily relaxed, provided that we go no further than supposing that the economy with which we have to deal experiences occasional bursts of growth. Sustained expansions of service income, such as characterize all advanced economies, raise some essentially new problems that require separate treatment. (See below, pp. 77–8).

The effects of once-over changes in aggregate service income may be brought out most clearly by temporarily ignoring income permutation processes. On this understanding, the value of r_y may be set at unity since, with the distribution of service income given, changes in aggregate service income must be accompanied by equal proportionate changes in the service income of every household. The effects of such a change in income can then be taken into account in our stationary regression formulae by re-introducing the relative dispersion coefficient $s_y = \sigma_y / \sigma'_y$. A rise in aggregate income implies a value of s_y less than unity. But changes in s_y affect the slope of the regression line in precisely the same manner as changes in r_y. Thus a rise in aggregate service income must reduce, while a fall must increase, the slope of the regression line. Noting further that the intercept of the regression line is affected in precisely the contrary direction by variations in income, we infer that an increase in income will shift the entire regression line to the right, while a decrease in income will shift it to the left.

We conclude that when changes in aggregate service income are combined with income permutation processes, the relevant least-squares coefficients of the regression of consumption on income are given by

$$B' = 1 - (1 - s_y r_y) e^{-(a)} \tag{3.7}$$

(that is, the general formula given earlier (p. 70)) and

$$A' = \bar{y}(1 - s_y r_y) e^{-(a)}. \tag{3.7'}$$

It is evident from the formal similarity between these relations and the formulae (3.8) and (3.9) that changes in the parameters a and r_y will have much the same effect as before, and, as indicated already, that changes in s_y (corresponding to changes in aggregate income) will affect B' and A' in just the same way as changes in r_y. The inclusion in our formulae of the 'shift factor' s_y significantly modifies our earlier conclusions, however, about the range of admissible values of B'. For suppose that all households experience a sudden decrease in service income; that is, suppose that s_y is substantially greater than unity. Then if r_y is sufficiently close to unity, the bracketed expression in (3.7) may be *negative*, in which case the value of B' will be *greater* than unity. In these circumstances, indeed, the value of B' may be greater than $\bar{c}/\bar{y}$, and both may exceed unity. That is to say, *the group marginal propensity to save may be negative.*

At first glance, this possibility seems as fanciful as our earlier case of a negative marginal propensity to consume. On further reflection, however, it is clear that a negative marginal propensity to save is very likely to turn up among household groups that contain large numbers of newly retired persons or large numbers of newly married couples; for both marriage and retirement may reduce effective household income by as much as 50 per cent in a single year.

A striking confirmation of the results suggested by our model is provided by Malcolm Fisher's cross-section analysis of UK households included in the 1953 Savings Survey of the Oxford University Institute of Statistics, from which the data in Table 3.1 are drawn.[13] Notice that negative marginal propensities to save turn up in almost every age group where we should expect to find them, and are notably absent elsewhere.[14]

The significance of Fisher's findings may be brought out more clearly by a graphical illustration. Suppose that we have to deal with a group of households all of which are initially in stationary equilibrium. Then we may suppose that the corresponding $c-y$ scatter is represented initially by a set of points all of which lie on the 45° line as indicated in Figure 3.2 – each point representing households in a particular income class. Now suppose that every household experiences an equal proportionate decline in service income. Supposing that wealthier households are relatively slower to adapt to the change in income status (as suggested by the negative curvature hypothesis), the $c-y$ scatter will shift leftwards from the 45° line as indicated by the arrows in Figure 3.2. The APCY after the shift

TABLE 3.1. UK spending units: 1953 cross-section marginal and average propensities to save * out of net income

occupation		1 (18–24)	2 (25–34)	3 (35–44)	4 (45–54)	5 (55–64)	6 (65 and over)	all ages
Manual	MPSY	·0416	−·0646	·0112 †	−·0013 †	−·1485	−·1542 †	−·0262
	APSY	·0120	−·0075	·0098	−·0019	·0283	−·0990	−·0005
Clerical and Sales	MPSY	−·0422	·0867	·0673	·0821	·0104 †	−·0542	·0391
	APSY	·0076	−·0155	−·0483	·0200	·0109	·0438	−·0086
Managerial	MPSY	−·1165	·1692	·2213	·3063	·1442	−·6166	·2112
	APSY	−·0370	−·0168	·0507	·0574	·0500	−·2731	·0268
Self-employed	MPSY	—|	·7141	·2340	·2362	·6039	·3867	·3594
	APSY	—|	·1979	·2140	·0103	·3010	·1302	·1607
Retired and unoccupied	MPSY	·0932	·1576	−·0438	−·4193	−·3614	−·0293	−·1541
	APSY	−·0150	−·0375	−·0014	−·1706	−·1212	−·0905	−·0958
All	MPSY	·0173 †	·1541	·1476	·1591	·0825	−·0493	·1020
	APSY	·0089	·0004	·0283	·0061	·0215	−·0850	·0034

AGE GROUPS

* Saving excludes purchase of consumer durables.   † Denotes standard error exceeds point estimate.

Source: Assembled from data presented in Malcolm R. Fisher, 'Exploration in Savings Behaviour' *Bulletin of the Oxford University Institute of Statistics*, vol. 18, no. 3 (Aug., 1956), Table 2.1 (p. 232), Table 2.3 (p. 236), Table 2.5 (p. 239), and Appendix A (p. 264).

is indicated by the slope of the ray OA, the MPCY by the slope of the line MM'. As indicated, the 'statistical' MPCY exceeds the 'statistical' APCY, and both exceed unity. But note that *no individual household will ever behave as the statistical results suggest.* To suppose that cross-section regressions of consumption on income accurately reflect individual behaviour responses is to commit a gross fallacy of composition.

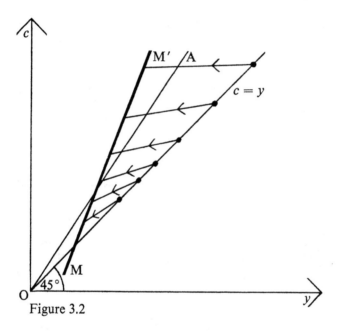

Figure 3.2

(2) *The Nonstationary Economy.* It is evident on *a priori* grounds that estimates of the MPCY based on stationary assumptions will be severely biased unless the state of the economy at the outset of the interval of observation is truly one of stationary equilibrium – biased upward if the economy is growing, downward if the economy is declining. That the amount of the bias may be substantial in practice is indicated by calculating 'typical' MPCYs using direct estimates of r_y suggested by Friedman (0·83 for urban households, 0·69 for farm families), and a value for e^{-a} of 0·82.[15] These calculations yield an MPCY for urban households of 0·86, and an MPCY for farm families of 0·75. A typical value of the MPCY in actual studies of urban families would be about 0·75, and for farm families about 0·60. Thus the bias in our estimates is substantial, and in the anticipated direction.

Whether growth alone can account for the magnitude of the bias is another matter. Recalling our earlier discussion of the effect of growth on the average consumption-income ratio of an individual household, however, it seems plausible to suppose that rates of growth of between 1·5 and 2·5 per cent per annum could produce a reduction of 10–15 per cent in our estimated MPCYS. For if all households in a steadily growing economy had identical MPCWS, the mean point of the cross-section scatter of $c-y$ points would tend at all times to lie on or close to a ray through the origin of slope $a/(g+a)$. Even in the absence of income permutations, therefore, the MPCY would be significantly less than unity for typical values of g and a. A combination of growth and income permutations should thus produce MPCYS that accord closely with actual experience.

Let us check this conjecture by working out the regression implications of a steady-growth model, assuming as before that $y_i^t = m_i^t$ and that $c_i^t = aw_i^t$. Dealing first with a situation in which income permutations are absent, we may describe the equilibrium time path of consumption for a representative household by the relation

$$c_i^t = am_i e^{gt}/(g+a),$$ (3.11)

where g denotes the rate of growth of aggregate income and m_i is a given constant. The relation (3.11) defines what might be described as the 'permanent consumption function' of a steadily growing economy. Since the ratio of consumption to income $(a/(g+a))$ is analogous to Friedman's 'propensity to consume permanent income', we denote it by the same symbol in the discussion that follows: that is, $a/(g+a) = k$ (cf. *TCF*, p. 17).

We next introduce income permutation processes by supposing that the base values of individual service incomes vary over time in a systematic way, the distribution of aggregate service income maintaining the same form at all times. Recalling earlier discussion, the consumption of a representative household will be given in this case not by (3.11) but by

$$c_i^t = k\{y_i' - (y_i' - y)e^{-at}\},$$ (3.12)

where $y_i = m_i e^{gt_0}$ and $y_i' = m_i' e^{gt_0}$ – the household being assumed to be in growth equilibrium, of couse, at date t_0.

Clearly, the only novel effect of growth is to alter the frame of reference from a stationary to an exponential trend. Indeed, since (3.12) has exactly the same analytic form as the corresponding relation in a stationary economy, we may proceed immediately to write out the implied least-squares regression coefficients:

$$B^* = k\{1-(1-s_y r_y)\, e^{-(a)}\} \tag{3.13}$$

$$A^* = \bar{c}(1-s_y r_y)\, e^{-(a)}. \tag{3.14}$$

These formulae gives the stationary coefficients as a special case, for when $g = 0$, $k = s_y = 1$. In general, however, the MPCY implied by (3.13) will differ significantly from that suggested by the stationary case. If g is positive, for example, then k and s_y will both be less than unity; hence the c–y scatter will be substantially flatter than would be true in a stationary state. Conversely, if g is negative, the c–y scatter will be steeper than in comparable stationary conditions.

Let us now recalculate our theoretical MPCYs, assuming that $g = 0.02$ (approximately the rate of growth of real per capita income in the United States during the period 1900–64). Using the same estimates as before of r_y and e^{-a}, we obtain 0·78 as a typical MPCY for urban households, and 0·68 as a typical MPCY for farm households. These values are close enough to actual experience to be considered acceptable. Indeed, with minor adjustments in r_y to levels that are consistent with alternative estimates suggested by Friedman (1957b, p. 187), our theoretical MPCYs can be made to correspond exactly with observed values in any of the studies discussed by Friedman.

We are now in a position to make a tentative assessment of the empirical consequences of assuming that wealth-elasticities of consumption are unity and that the marginal rate of return on wealth is zero. Briefly, the statistical implications of our model do not appear to be significantly affected by either of these restrictions. The explanation may lie in the facts: (i) that our analysis of cross-section regressions is by its very nature confined to impact effects; (ii) that property income is in practice a negligible proportion of gross income for all but a handful of actual households.

By virtue of (i), what appears to be an extremely rough and ready approximation to an adequate model of household behavior may fail to reveal itself as such simply because we do not pursue the implications of the model beyond a single time interval. As we shall discover at a later point in our discussion, the assumption that wealth-elasticities of consumption are unity appears to be consistent also with empirical evidence on the secular relation between consumption and wealth – an apparent contradiction of our earlier conjecture that the modal consumption locus exhibits negative curvature. For reasons that are not clear, therefore, our 'special theory' seems to possess a higher degree of factual validity than could reasonably have been anticipated on *a priori* grounds.

As for (ii), it may be doubted whether our model would perform well in an analysis of the behavior of relatively wealthy households. Even here, however, it is possible to argue that the *direct* impact effects of changes in non-property income are likely to be so large in relation to the *indirect* effects of induced variations in property income as to preclude accurate identification of the latter in empirical data. The moral would seem to be that, in an inexact science like economics, we have less to fear from quantitative than from qualitative errors in the specification of our theoretical models.

(3) *Wealth and Permanent Income*. There is an evident resemblance between our model of a growing economy and Friedman's permanent income theory. Since Friedman's model is known to be in broad accord with the factual evidence, not only for the United States but for a variety of other countries as well, it is desirable for us to show that our theory is capable of reproducing all of Friedman's results. Otherwise we should have to plod through a vast maze of budget-study evidence the central plan of which has already been provided by Friedman.

The relation between Friedman's model and ours may be brought out most effectively by comparing corresponding formulae for the slope coefficient of the $c-y$ regression line. Friedman's (1957b, p. 32) formula, based on the assumption that mean transitory components of income and consumption are uncorrelated with one another and with corresponding permanent components, is simply

$$b = kP_y, \tag{3.15}$$

k being interpreted as the propensity to consume permanent income, P_y as the fraction of any difference in measured income that can on the average be attributed to a difference in permanent income. Our formula (3.13), based on the assumption that variations in measured income produce variations in consumption via their effect on current holdings of wealth, is naturally more complex. Thus, we interpret k as measuring the extent to which differences in steadily rising levels of household income are reflected in current holdings of accumulated wealth. Similarly, we interpret the bracketed portion of our slope formula, that is $(1-(1-s_y r_y)\,e^{-(a)})$ as measuring the extent to which differences in stationary levels of household income are associated with differences in current wealth.

Our k, like Friedman's, represents the propensity to consume permanent income; but in our model, the value of k depends on the rate at which income is growing and the speed with which households adapt to resulting trends in absolute income. Our expression $(1-(1-s_y r_y)\,e^{-(a)})$, by analogy with Friedman's coefficient P_y, may be regarded as the fraction of any difference in measured income that is fully reflected in 'permanent wealth'; but in our model the magnitude of this expression depends not only on the correlation between current and past income but also on the rate at which households adapt to changes in absolute income status.

On this showing, the connection between our theory and Friedman's is at best loose and imprecise. However, the matter is not as hopeless as it appears, for Friedman does not in practice rely on his initial definition of b to interpret observed behavior. On the contrary, in all but a minority of practical applications, he assumes that permanent income is defined in terms of measured income by a differential equation of the form

$$dy_p/dt = \beta(y^t - y_p^t)\,, \tag{3.16}$$

where β denotes a given 'speed of adjustment' coefficient (Friedman, 1957b, p. 143). Starting from any initial value y_p° of permanent income and given any fixed value y° of measured income, this differential equation has the solution

$$y_p^t = y^\circ - (y^\circ - y_p^\circ)e^{-\beta}\,. \tag{3.17}$$

Thus, if we follow Friedman in supposing that permanent consumption at any date t is given by

$$c_p^t = k y_p^t\,, \tag{3.20}$$

we see that permanent consumption will be correlated with the mean transitory component of measured income if this component differs from zero (Eisner, Friedman and Houthakker, 1958, pp. 974–5, 993).

If this interpretation of Friedman's analysis is correct, then the time path of measured consumption for a representative household–assuming the mean transitory component of consumption is identically zero–is given by

$$c^t = c_p^t = k\{y^\circ - (y^\circ - y_p^\circ)e^{-\beta}\}\,. \tag{3.21}$$

If we interpret y_p° and y°, respectively, as measuring the income of the household before and after an income permutation, it is a straightforward exercise to show that the corresponding slope coefficient of the least-squares regression line through the $c-y$ scatter is given not by Friedman's original formula (3.17), but rather by

$$b^* = k\{1-(1-s_y r_y)\,e^{-\beta}\}, \tag{3.22}$$

which is formally identical with our formula for B^* (above, equation (3.13)). Moreover, it includes Friedman's original formula as a special case. For the assumption that mean transitory components of income are zero implies $s_y = 1$, while the assumption that transitory income is uncorrelated with permanent income implies both that $\beta = 0$ and that

$$\frac{\Sigma_i(y_p^\circ-\bar{y}_p)(y^\circ-\bar{y})}{\Sigma_i(y^\circ-\bar{y})^2} = \frac{\Sigma_i(y_p^\circ-\bar{y}_p)^2}{\Sigma_i(y^\circ-\bar{y})^2} = P_y.^{16}$$

If these restrictions are imposed, therefore, $b^* = kP_y = b$ as given by (3.17).

Having restated Friedman's permanent income theory in a form suitable for comparison with our model, we may readily establish points of similarity. Our model, like Friedman's implies an observed regression of measured consumption on measured income for which the ratio of consumption to income declines as measured income increases. Our model, like Friedman's, implies that observed cross-section regressions will shift upward in response to an increase in mean measured income; more generally, that regressions in a growing economy will normally lie farther from the origin of the $y-c$ plane the later the date to which they correspond. Our model, like Friedman's, implies that the mean point of observed regressions will typically lie on or close to a ray of slope $k = a/(g+a)$ through the origin of the $y-c$ plane. Contrary to Friedman's stated belief, his model – like ours – is consistent with Fisher's finding that the marginal propensities to save of certain age and occupational groups are negative. In Friedman's model as in ours, moreover, the slope of the $c-y$ scatter may well be significantly flatter at low than at high levels of measured income, reflecting the influence of life-cycle phenomena. In all of these and in many other *qualitative* respects, there is literally nothing to choose between the two theories of household behavior.

Turning to quantitative comparisons, we begin by observing that our model will yield regression results different from Friedman's only insofar as our estimates of a differ from his estimates of β. This being the case, we confine attention to an issue where the relative magnitudes of a and β are of crucial significance, namely, the close correspondence that Friedman (1957b, pp. 190–5) shows to exist between measured income elasticities of consumption and direct estimates of r_y obtained by correlating income arrays for different years. For purposes of exposition, we shall call the numbers a and β *adjustment exponents* since their values determine the magnitude of the adjustment coefficients e^{-x} in the regression coefficients B^* and b^* defined by (3.13) and (3.20).

If we compute the income-elasticity of consumption at the mean point of the $c-y$ regression, the value so obtained is an estimate of the value of the bracketed expressions in (3.13) and (3.20); that is, $\varepsilon_y = 1 - (1 - s_y r_y) e^{-x}$ (cf. Friedman, 1957b, p. 33). The difference between this estimate of the income-elasticity of consumption and the income-correlation coefficient r_y is thus given by

$$\varepsilon_y - r_y = (1 - r_y) - (1 - s_y r_y) e^{-x}.$$

In normal circumstances, however, we should expect s_y to be close to unity, since its value reflects the rate of growth of aggregate income (roughly speaking, $s_y = 1/(g+1)$). Except in unusual circumstances, therefore, the difference between ε_y and r_y should be approximately equal to $(1 - r_y)(1 - e^{-x})$. Now, this difference clearly will be substantially different from zero unless: (i) income permutations are relatively unimportant (that is, r_y is close to unity); (ii) households adjust very slowly to such income permutations as occur (that is, the adjustment exponent is close to zero). For only in these cases will the slope of the $c-y$ scatter reflect the influence (if any) of income permutations alone–which is what is required if income-elasticities and income-correlation coefficients are to be approximately equal.

As indicated already, the empirical evidence suggests that measured values of elasticities and correlation coefficients are generally very similar. Moreover, both are typically less than unity by a substantial amount. We infer from this that the adjustment exponents β and a must be relatively small (or that our regression formulae are invalid!); for the only alternative is to suppose that s_y is significantly less than unity, and this would require that the rate of growth of aggregate income should typically exceed, say, 10 per cent per annum, which we know to be untrue.

Our estimate of the adjustment exponent a, namely 0·20, is not too large to be consistent with the empirical evidence. Observed differences between elasticities and correlation coefficients are frequently on the order of 0·02–0·04, which is the kind of difference that our model will generate with growth rates of 2 per cent per annum and an adjustment coefficient of $e^{-0.20} = 0.82$. But Friedman's estimate of the probable value of the adjustment exponent β, namely, 0·40–0·70,[17] is much too large to be reconciled with the empirical evidence, for it entails values of the adjustment coefficient $e^{-\beta}$ of only 0·50–0·67. This implies differences between income elasticities and correlation coefficients of 0·04–0·10 for urban households, and differences of 0·15–0·25 for farm households. Our conclusion is that the 'effective horizon'[18] implicit in Friedman's definition of the permanent income concept would have to be considerably longer than the three to five years that he assumes it to be in order to produce anything like the measure of agreement between income-elasticities and income-correlation coefficients that is observed in practice.[19] (The 'effective horizon' implicit in the formula $b = kP_y$, it should be noted, is of infinite length!) Our implicit estimate of the relevant horizon, being based on average rather than marginal consumption-wealth data, may itself be on the small side, and it is nearly 15 years.

The preceding discussion casts doubt on the validity of Friedman's explanation of the temporal relation between consumption and income, for it is largely from his work with time-series regressions of consumption on permanent income that his views about the magnitude of β are drawn. It appears from our analysis that the time-series correlation between permanent income and consumption is spurious: that permanent income is a proxy for a much larger magnitude, namely, household wealth.

This is not the only area where Friedman's theory is open to question; where less idiosyncratic theories – including ours – yield different and rather more plausible results. For example, we should argue that the marginal propensity to save will (other things being equal) tend to decline as we move from lower to higher levels of household income, inferring this result from the negative curvature hypothesis. There is much evidence to support this position, as indicated earlier; but Friedman must oppose it because he assumes that consumption is directly proportional to permanent income.

We should argue that wealth will be distributed much more unequally than income in any advanced society, inferring this from the assumption

that the wealth-elasticity of consumption is less than unity and the generalized stability hypothesis (that is, the tendency of consumption to exhaust
the whole of income). In the absence of shifts over time in the level of the
modal consumption locus, moreover, we should have to argue that the
distribution of wealth will tend to become ever more unequal as aggregate
real income increases. The validity of the first of these implications is not
open to serious argument. As for the second, the evidence suggests no
tendency towards greater inequality in the distribution of income or wealth,
which suggests that (i) the negative curvature hypothesis is invalid, or
(ii) the modal consumption locus is affected in the long run by 'customary'
standards of consumption expenditure. We shall consider these alternatives later; here we merely remark that Friedman's model provides no
definite link between income and wealth – an absurdity of the first order
of magnitude in a theory that purports to say something about saving
behavior.[20]

We should argue that receipts of windfall income will, in general, affect
consumption in the short run [21] in exactly the same way as an increase
in any other kind of income, inferring this from the assumption that
current purchasing power consists simply of current wealth, regardless of
its original source. There is a large literature on this subject, and all of it
seems to support our position (Landsberger, 1966, p. 540; Bodkin, 1966).
Friedman cannot accept the obvious conclusion because he assumes that
changes in measured income affect consumption only insofar as they
produce variations in the household's subjective evaluation of its permanent income – and permanent income is so defined that at most a
minor fraction of windfall receipts will in fact be counted as 'permanent'.

We do not ourselves have serious doubts about where the truth lies
on any of these issues, for we regard the permanent income theory as a
statistically ingenious but economically irrelevant and misleading description of household behavior. A detailed defense of our position is hardly
possible without vastly better information about household asset holdings
than is presently available. Even without such a defense, however, it is
clear from the preceding discussion that our model will perform at least
as well as Friedman's in relation to every cross-section problem that is
considered by him. For where qualitative properties of consumption-
income scatters are concerned, the statistical implications of the two
theories are observationally indistinguishable. Moreover, our model is at

least as simple and plausible as Friedman's in its theoretical foundations, and definitely richer in testable empirical implications. Without further argument, therefore, we may claim that our theory is at least as good as if not marginally superior to, the permanent income theory.

Time Series Regressions. Our model of household behavior appears to be consistent with available budget-study evidence, which is to say that it describes short-run transition processes with reasonable accuracy. Our only remaining task is to compare the secular implications of the model with time-series data on income, consumption and wealth. To avoid indefinite prolongation of an already lengthy paper, we shall focus attention on evidence concerning the empirical validity of the generalized stability and negative curvature hypotheses, both of which have played an important–but so far untested–role in our discussion of cross-section regressions.

(1) *Theoretical Time Profiles.* In time-series analysis, we are concerned with sums of mean values of household variables or, what comes to much the same thing, with the mean points of cross-section scatters of consumption-income and consumption-wealth data. This being the case, we should not expect MPCYs or MPCWs defined by time-series regressions to bear any close relation to corresponding parameters of cross-section regressions. In a stationary economy that experiences income permutations, for example, the cross-section scatter of $c-y$ points will typically define a definite regression line the slope of which will be interpretable as an MPCY. Time-series data for the same economy will produce a 'scatter' that consists of a single point; no MPCY will be defined or definable. If the same economy experiences occasional bursts of growth, time-series observations will produce a scatter of $c-y$ points the form of which will depend on the precise history of the system and on the rate at which households adjust to changes in income; but the cross-section scatter, apart from periods of transition, will maintain its initial form indefinitely even though its mean point shifts ever upward as aggregate income rises. In these examples, we take it for granted that the generalized stability hypothesis is valid. If asset adjustment processes are typically unstable, then we should not expect cross-section or time-series scatters to exhibit any particular pattern, much less to yield estimated MPCYs or MPCWs that are related in any way.

Granted that we can infer little or nothing about time-series regressions from cross-section regressions, and *vice versa*, our procedure at this point must be to develop the time-series implications of our model without regard to income-permutation and other transition processes. To get quickly to the focal issues posed by our stability and negative curvature hypotheses, we shall deal for the most part with a steadily growing economy. This case is by no means as interesting theoretically as an economy that exhibits fluctuations about a rising trend, but that is a subject that merits (and requires) much lengthier treatment than is possible here.

From earlier discussion, we know that in the special case where wealth-elasticities of consumption are unity, the time paths of wealth, income, and consumption of a typical household in a steadily growing economy are given by

$$w_i^t = me^{gt}\{1/(g+a_i-r_i)\}$$
$$y_i^t = me^{gt}+r_iw_i^t$$
$$c_i^t = a_iw_i^t .$$

Even in this special case, however, we should expect the values of the a_is and r_is to vary with the passage of time – the a_is because of changing standards of taste, the r_is because of changing resources and technology. Moreover, there is good reason to doubt the empirical validity of this description of household behavior even if we could suppose that the structure of the model were invariant with respect to time.

These considerations raise what are probably insoluble problems for precise analysis of the secular implications of our theory – or indeed of any model. We have no real alternative but to suppose that our idealized model provides an adequate approximation to 'true' behavior over moderate intervals of time, and to assume that in these circumstances the variables a_i and r_i can be treated as parameters. On this understanding, we can replace the a_is and r_is with corresponding averages (a simple average in case of the latter, a wealth-weighted average in the case of the former) and then sum over the individual decision variables and deal with the resulting aggregates in much the same way as we should deal with their individual components. Needless to say, the inferences that we draw from the resulting mongrelized model are at best plausible; that is, not entirely arbitrary!

If the generalized stability hypothesis holds, the time path of aggregate consumption should be very similar to the time path of aggregate income in a steadily growing economy. Indeed, if wealth-elasticities of consumption are unity, aggregate consumption should be directly proportional to aggregate income, the constant of proportionality being our old friend $k = a/(g+a)$. Common sense and theoretical intuition suggest that a similar relation will hold even if wealth-elasticities of consumption are less than unity, provided that the rate of growth of the economy fluctuates over time between relatively narrow limits, say, $0 < g < 0.05$. For in these circumstances, transient effects will dampen the tendency of the saving ratio to grow larger with the passage of time. The ratio may be expected to vary instead between, say, zero and 0.15, depending on the magnitude of the current growth rate and the size of the average MPCW. We may turn this proposition around and assert with equal or greater confidence that consumption will bear no particular relation to income in a growing or fluctuating economy unless most households in the economy conform to the requirements of the generalized stability hypothesis.

As for the relation between aggregate consumption and aggregate wealth, it should be one of proportionality over relatively long time intervals if wealth-elasticities of consumption are unity and the generalized stability hypothesis is satisfied. If consumption loci typically display negative curvature, however, the consumption-wealth ratio should decline with the passage of time even in an economy that experiences fluctuations around a rising trend. As in the case of the relation between income and consumption, however, we should not expect aggregate wealth to bear any definite relation to aggregate consumption in an economy where few households satisfy the conditions of the generalized stability hypothesis.

The preceding comments would require qualification if the distribution of income were assumed to vary with time; but this does not appear to be an empirically interesting case. Granted that the distribution of income does not alter significantly with the passage of time, we should expect the distribution of wealth to become ever more unequal in a growing economy if the negative curvature hypothesis is valid. Such information as we have suggests that the distribution of wealth has changed relatively little in the US and UK since 1900, but the changes that our theory would suggest might in any case be too slight over periods of one or two generations to be statistically noticeable.

(2) *Observed Time Profiles*. So much by way of speculation. Having indicated in broad outline what time paths we should expect our model to generate, we turn now to historical data for the United States–the only country for which reasonably reliable estimates of household wealth are

available over any considerable period of time. Figure 3.3 shows the time profile of consumption-income points for the period 1900–64, together with the time profile of consumption-wealth points over the period 1945–58 and for selected years prior to 1945 (every year for which household wealth data are available). Since all profiles are plotted on double-log scales, proportionality of variables is implied by a linear relationship of slope +1, and proportionality of variables in different relations by parallel profiles.

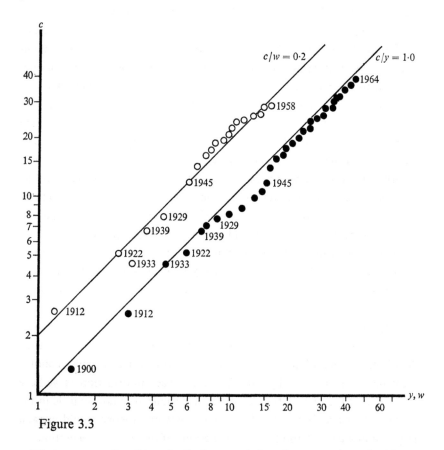

Figure 3.3

That consumption historically has tended to be approximately 90 per cent of income in the United States is well known; the *c–y* profile in Figure 3.3 merely confirms this item of textbook information. It is not perhaps so well known, but is equally true, that consumption historically has tended to be approximately 20 per cent of household wealth (both

TABLE 3.2. Time-series data

	consumption	income	wealth
1900	13·7	15·0	61·5
1912	25·9	30·1	120·7
1922	52·8	59·1	267·4
1929	79·1	83·3	448·1
1933	46·5	45·5	310·6
1939	67·7	70·3	370·8
1940	71·3	75·7	n.a.
1941	81·7	92·7	n.a.
1942	89·3	116·2	n.a.
1943	100·1	133·5	n.a.
1944	109·1	146·3	n.a.
1945	120·7	150·2	622·7
1946	144·8	160·0	678·7
1947	162·5	169·8	752·7
1948	175·8	189·1	799·6
1949	179·2	188·6	821·4
1950	193·9	206·9	920·8
1951	209·3	226·6	993·0
1952	220·1	238·3	1052·2
1953	234·2	252·6	1095·7
1954	241·0	257·4	1198·5
1955	259·5	275·3	1322·1
1956	272·6	293·2	1412·2
1957	287·8	308·5	1450·9
1958	296·5	318·8	1601·8
1959	318·2	337·3	n.a.
1960	333·0	350·0	n.a.
1961	343·2	364·4	n.a.
1962	363·7	385·3	n.a.
1963	383·4	403·8	n.a.
1964	409·4	435·8	n.a.

Source: Consumption, 1900–22: R. W. Goldsmith, *A Study of Saving in the United States* (Princeton, N. J.: Princeton University Press, 1956), Col. 5, Table N–1, Vol. III, minus Col. 2, Table T–1, Vol. I. 1929–64: *Survey of Current Business*, US Dept. of Commerce, Vol. 45, No. 8 (Aug., 1965), Table 5, line 23, pp. 32–3. Income: 1900–22, Goldsmith, op. cit., Col. 5, Table N–1, Vol. III. 1929–64, *S.C.B.*, *op. cit.*, Table 5, line 22, pp. 32–3. Wealth: 1900–58, R. W. Goldsmith, R. E. Lipsey, and M. Mendelson, *Studies in the National Balance Sheet of the United States* (Princeton, N J : Princeton University Press, 1963), Tables III–1d and III–2, line v, pp. 124–7.

measured in current dollars). This finding constitutes an apparent contradiction of the negative curvature hypothesis. Before commenting on that, however, it is interesting to notice that the consumption-income ratio furnished by the data corresponds closely with the figures suggested by our model. The rate of growth of real per capita income (calculated from a series prepared by Simon Kuznets) was 0·017 in the period from 1900–29, 0·00 (that is, nil) in the period 1929–39, 0·024 in the period 1946–4, and 0·017 for the entire period 1900–64. Given a value for *a* of 0·20, these growth figures imply a consumption-income ratio of 0·92 for the periods 1900-64 and 1900–29, ratio of 0·00 for the period 1929–39, and a ratio of 0·89 for the post-war period 1946–64. With due allowance for variations in the consumption-wealth ratio (which has in fact fluctuated over time by as much as 25 per cent of its maximum value), these computations seem to lend strong support to the hypothesis that the observed 'constancy' of the saving ratio reflects nothing more profound than the tendency of consumption to equal income at every point in time. We certainly should not expect consumption to display such a regular pattern of behavior relative to income if the majority of households were unstable accumulators. The empirical evidence thus seems to confirm the validity of the generalized stability hypothesis.[22]

Returning now to the time profile of consumption-wealth points, we begin by noting that the apparent constancy of the consumption-wealth ratio is to some extent an optical illusion. For the one period on which we have continuous data (1945–58), the ratio dropped from just under 0·22 in 1948 to just over 0·18 in 1958 – a reduction of about 15 per cent in 10 years. Considering the relative magnitudes involved in both terms of this ratio, the decline indicated might well be considered precipitous–so much so as to provide strong support for the negative curvature hypothesis. But this position cannot be defended with any force, for the consumption-wealth ratio in 1900 was precisely the same as the ratio in 1948, namely, 0·22.

It is difficult to reconcile these contradictory positions without running into worse problems than are posed by the contradictions themselves. The evidence from budget-study data is so compellingly in favor of the negative curvature hypothesis, however, that one or another reconciliation is almost mandatory. We can think of two rationalizations that seem to us worthy of serious consideration.

The first rationalization is more in the nature of an evasion than an explanation; it involves the supposition that market forces work in such a way that earning assets are valued at a relatively constant proportion of their income yield. The tendency of consumption to exhaust total income at all times would then link consumption with wealth in a similar fashion, producing relative constancy in the proportions between all three magnitudes—income, consumption, and wealth. There is some evidence that a process of this kind is at work. For if one deflates Goldsmith's wealth data with an index of the prices of capital goods, one finds that the ratio of 'real' wealth to 'real' income declines steadily during the period 1900–58. This means that the price level of capital goods historically has increased more rapidly than the price index implicit in the real income (and consumption) series. If we ask, 'Which way did the *true* ratio of consumption to wealth move?', our response must be that we simply do not know. For if we allow for quality changes, the relative rise in market prices of capital goods might be considered to reflect accurately the 'service value' of such goods, leaving us with an approximately constant ratio of real consumption to real wealth; or the relative rise in capital goods prices might be considered to represent an understatement of the service value of wealth held by households, in which case we should argue that the consumption-wealth ratio has after all decreased! One is tempted to conclude from all this that the constancy or non-constancy of the consumption-wealth ratio over periods of more than a decade is not an empirically meaningful problem—and, as we noted earlier, the ratio did decline substantially during the one period for which we have continuous data.

The second rationalization does not require us to question the meaning of the raw statistics on wealth and consumption. It involves the supposition that consumption loci shift over time as per capita wealth rises, marginal consumption-wealth ratios becoming greater as standards of living rise. This conjecture bears an obvious resemblance to Duesenberry's famous 'relative income' hypothesis, and might be defended on similar sociological and psychological grounds. Analytically, the conjecture can be expressed by writing the wealth-consumption function as

$$c = hw^b w^{*(1-b)}$$

where w^* represents a suitable index of 'normal wealth' (e.g. the value of $w^*(t)$ obtained from the solution of a differential equation of the form

$$dw^*(t)/dt = \alpha\{w(t) - w^*(t)\}$$

where α is a positive adjustment coefficient ($0 < \alpha < 1$). A relation of this kind between consumption, wealth, and 'normal wealth' would clearly serve to reconcile the negative curvature hypothesis with the secular constancy of the $c{-}w$ ratio, for it effectively implies that the secular wealth-elasticity of consumption is unity. The same relation would also account for the apparent invariance over time of the distribution of wealth, and for differences among countries (e.g. the US and UK) in consumption spending at given levels of wealth. But these and related themes are much too large to be developed in the present paper.

IV. *Concluding Remarks*

Our analysis of the dynamics of household behavior contains numerous loose ends, and may well raise more questions that it settles. Hopefully it has also contributed to improved understanding of the causal foundations and empirical implications of the theory of consumption.

Our central theme throughout has been that statistical findings, in economics as in any other science, have meaning only insofar as they are associated with explicit conceptual experiments. Facts alone can tell us nothing about the mainsprings of consumer choice; we must assert how households behave and leave it to the facts to determine if our assertions are empirically plausible.

A second theme, closely related to the first, is the need to develop the explicit statistical implications of our theoretical models if we are to recognize and profit from apparent anomalies in observed behavior. Progress in an inexact science like economics is hardly possible unless the consequences of our theories are expressed in terms that are qualitatively comparable with the stochastic relationships that constitute our universe of factual discourse. Neither is progress possible, however, if the only 'theory' we ever use is one that says 'Y can be explained by some set of n variables, $x_1, ..., x_y$, and a collection of associated error terms'—which is just about what contemporary econometrics asserts.

A final theme—implicit in every part of our paper—is that household trading on current account cannot be described satisfactorily, much less explained, without explicit reference to related transactions on capital account. Further progress in consumption theory depends crucially on the future availability of information about all aspects of household balance sheets as well as the usual information about current income and expenditure flows.

NOTES AND REFERENCES

[1] It should be emphasized that the variables c and w represent 'virtual' rather than 'real' magnitudes. Thus we can infer nothing directly from (1.2) about the behavior over time of the 'real' variable $\underline{w}$. Planned current consumption constitutes a virtual drain on real wealth at any given date, but this does not mean that real wealth will actually be depleted over time. The behavior of $\underline{w}$ depends, in fact, on a variety of other circumstances (see below, pp. 49–51).

[2] A similar relation can be defined connecting desired with actual wealth: $w^t = w(\underline{w}^t)$. Since desired wealth is defined in our model in terms of actual wealth and desired consumption, however, all relevant information about desired wealth is already embodied in the wealth-consumption relation (1.3). More precisely, if we combine (1.3) with the budget equation (1.2), we have $w^t = \underline{w}^t - c(\underline{w}^t)$. Accordingly, we shall have no occasion to deal explicitly with desired wealth in the remainder of this paper.

[3] In principle, one should no doubt follow general price theory and include factor services as an explicit decision variable in the preference function of the household. To do so raises a number of awkward complications, however, for one then obtains an 'income function' similar to the consumption and wealth functions defined by our model; hence, it becomes necessary either to develop a specific theory about the form of this function, or to assign specific properties to it. The first alternative is disagreeable; the second is logically equivalent to the procedure that is commonly followed. For further discussion of the matter, see Daniel Suits (1963).

[4] Because all variables to which we shall refer from this point onwards are intended to designate 'real' rather than 'virtual' quantities, we no longer use underlines to distinguish 'measurable' variables. Thus w and y, as used in this sentence, are the same variables as were previously represented by $\underline{w}$ and $\underline{y}$.

[5] If we introduce lagged adjustments of measured consumption to desired consumption, depreciation rates, etc., the effect is to complicate the stability condition, perhaps very considerably, by the addition of adjustment coefficients, side restrictions, etc. Provided that rates of adjustment of actual to desired quantities are sufficiently rapid, however, the simple conditions given here remain valid. As for discrete-time models, the stability condition in the simplest case is that $a - r$ be positive and less than 2, with 'cobweb' phenomena occurring if $a - r$ lies between 1 and 2.

[6] '... one may say anything ... that might enter the most disordered imagination. The only thing one cannot say is that it is rational. The very word sticks in one's throat.'

[7] Cf. Arthur Goldberger (1964, p. 122). We are asserting that the values of relevant variables within each of a large collection of service-income classes will tend to be normally distributed, making it possible for us to view the means for each class as definite values.

[8] The highest yields mentioned by Atkinson are on the order of 7 per cent per annum – approximately the same figure as Stigler arrives at for the average rate of return on manufacturing capital in the United States; see G. J. Stigler (1963, chapter 2).

[9] We refer to information supplied in a recent study by Michael Landsberger (1966) of the response of Israeli households to restitution payments from Germany during the two-year period 1958–9. Landsberger designs a statistical experiment that permits us to view each of five groups of households as being essentially similar except for differences in lump-sum receipts of restitution payments. If our assumption about the form of the consumption locus is valid, the logarithms of the MPCWs calculated by Landsberger (shown in his Table 4, p. 539) should vary inversely with the logarithm of the corresponding windfall receipt; for to say that $c = hw^b$ is to assert that $d \log (dc/dw)/d \log w = \log (bc) - \log w$. If the indicated operations are carried out and the resulting data are plotted as a scatter of log MPCW/log w points, four of the observations turn out to lie almost exactly along a straight line of slope -1. The fifth point (corresponding to an MPCW of $1 \cdot 972$) lies well off the line, but involves an MPCW the point estimate of which is not significantly different from values that would put it on exactly the same line as the other four points. We attach no great significance to a correlation that is based on only five observations – but the extent of the agreement between our prediction and the data is too striking to be altogether ignored.

[10] See Friedman (1957b, pp. 188–9). There are no general rules, of course, for some processes may be cyclic, in which case a proper choice of the unit time interval will eliminate all appearance of change.

[11] Note that if $a = 0$, $B' = r_y$; i.e. income permutation explains the whole of scatter. In general, however, $r_y < B'$.

[12] Friedman's (1957b, p. 32) analysis leads to conclusions much like ours, except that in his model the case $r_y < 0$ does not arise. (The reason for this is indicated below, footnote 16.)

[13] We are indebted to James Richmond for calling this study to our attention.

[14] It is not without interest to mention Milton Friedman's reaction to Fisher's results:

> ... a negative marginal propensity to save contradicts not only the permanent income hypothesis but every hypothesis I know of that has been seriously considered ... Furthermore, it contradicts a host

of other empirical evidence – the propensity to save as computed from cross section budget study data is almost invariably positive. The clear implication is that there is something wrong with [Fisher's] data (Friedman, 1957a, p. 127).

Friedman attempts to account for the apparent anomalies in Fisher's analysis by suggesting that the 'income units' sampled in the UK survey consist in many cases of what would normally be considered mixed households. Subsequent investigations by Fisher (1957) and Klein (1958) failed to support Friedman's suggestion.

[15] The estimates of r_y are from Table 20, line 5, p. 195 of Friedman (1957b); (they are based on a study by John Frechtling, then a member of the staff of the Board of Governors of the Federal Reserve System). The estimate of e^{-a} is based on a value for a of 0·20 – the *average* consumption-wealth ratio in the US over the period 1900–58.

[16] See Friedman (1957b, pp. 31–2). Note that P_y, unlike r_y, must lie between 0 and 1; it cannot assume negative values.

[17] The estimate of 0·40 is based on time-series evidence and is considered by Friedman (1957b, p. 194) to imply an 'average time lag' – namely 2·5 years – that is longer than the lag appropriate for cross-section analysis. The suggested lag for the latter purpose is 1·5 years, which implies an adjustment exponent of 0·67. Hence the limits indicated in the text, i.e. 0·40–0·70.

[18] Defined by Friedman (1957b, pp. 145,150,1934) as twice the value of the reciprocal of the adjustment exponent (i.e. twice the 'average time lag').

[19] This conclusion is given further support by Margaret Reid's analysis of income-elasticities and income-correlations for a sample of farm households whose average income during the period of observation grew at a rate of approximately 40 per cent per annum – implying a value of s_y of about 0·70. The mean income-correlation coefficient in the sample was about 0·50, while the mean income-elasticity was about 0·40. This *negative* difference is directly inconsistent with the naïve version of Friedman's theory. However, it can be accounted for by our interpretation of his model, provided that the adjustment exponent has a value of something less than 0·15. The Reid data cannot be reconciled, however, with an adjustment exponent of 0·40–0·70, for the smallest of these values would just suffice to make the mean income-correlation coefficient equal to the mean income-elasticity (Friedman, 1957b, pp. 192–4).

[20] Friedman (1957b, pp. 16–17) does permit the ratio of human to non-human wealth to influence the value of k, but this link between wealth and saving is about as substantial as the grin of the Cheshire Cat.

[21] It is important to distinguish between short-run and long-run effects. A windfall, in the nature of the case, cannot support a

permanently higher level of consumption unless it is invested in earning assets. If it is not so invested, consumption will be completely unaffected in the long run. In sharp contrast, a salary increase – if it remains in effect – can be used to sustain a permanently higher level of consumption, either directly by being spent as it is received, or indirectly by being invested in earning assets.

   [22] A contrary conclusion is reached by Nissen Liviatan (1965, pp. 225–6) but his analysis rests on the curious assumption that earning assets, unlike money, '. . . are completely illiquid and do not appear . . . as arguments in the utility function' (p. 208). This is equivalent to supposing that the marginal propensity to consume wealth other than money balances is zero. It follows that an increase in holdings of earning assets, however large, will have no *direct* effect on consumption expenditure; such an increase will affect consumption only because it entails an increase in 'permanent' income. Provided that the marginal propensity to consume income from earning assets is less than unity, saving will always be positive as long as households accumulate wealth in the form of earning assets.

   Suppose, for example, that household savings are always invested in perpetual bonds that yield, say, 5 per cent per annum in coupon returns. Suppose further that – other things being equal – households invariably save 100 per cent of any increase in bond income. Then bond holdings obviously will increase without limit as time tends to infinity if the accumulation of wealth has no direct effect on consumption expenditure. However, if an increase of £100 in holdings of bonds produces an increase in consumption of more than £5 per annum (a possibility Liviatan does not admit), saving will converge to zero with the passage of time even though the marginal propensity to consume bond income is zero.

   As we have remarked on several occasions, the MPCWs of certain households may be less than the marginal rate of return on earning assets. Thus Liviatan's model may provide a fairly adequate description of the behavior of a Scrooge, a Rockefeller, or a Getty. But to suppose that the same model is in any way applicable to a Clower, a Johnson, or to most other non-entrepreneurial and non-miserly households, would be almost as silly as to suppose that earning assets are 'completely illiquid'.

4

Taste and Quality Change in the Pure Theory of the True Cost-of-Living Index

Franklin M. Fisher and Karl Shell

1. *Introduction*

The standard theory of the true cost-of-living index gives a rather uncomfortable treatment to taste and quality changes (including the introduction of new goods). The consumer is assumed to have always had an unchanging indifference map, complete with axes for all new goods of whose potential existence he in fact was not aware before their introduction. Similarly, quality change is treated either as an introduction of a new good or as a simple repackaging of an old one equivalent to a price reduction.[1] Yet the justification for the latter procedure has never been satisfactorily set forth, while the former one meets with many of the same difficulties as does the treatment of new goods itself.

If the treatment of new goods and quality change is less than fully satisfactory, however, the treatment of taste change is nonexistent. The assumption of an unchanging indifference map even defined over nonexistent goods is apparently crucial for a theory which is often erroneously thought to answer the question: How much would it cost in today's prices to make the consumer just as well off as he was yesterday? This question cannot be answered without resorting to an arbitrary intertemporal weighting of utilities. Yet taste changes do occur and the cost-of-living index is often carelessly thought to be designed to answer that question (Nat. Bur. Econ. Res., 1961, pp. 51–9; v. Hofsten, 1952).

This paper begins by arguing that the difficulty is due only to a misinterpretation of the theory of the true cost-of-living index. That theory does not in fact seek to answer the question posed above, nor does it make intertemporal comparisons of utility. Indeed, we observe that such a question can never be answered and such comparisons never made because they have no operational content. Incautious application of the theory has avoided facing up to this by the use of an apparently appealing but

97

completely arbitrary and untestable hidden assumption which does no
apparent harm when tastes are constant but which breaks down utterly
when tastes do change.

That assumption, however, is not part of the theory and the question
which the theory does answer retains its meaning whether or not tastes
are constant. The pure theory of the cost-of-living index, rigorously interpreted, accommodates taste changes quite comfortably.

Accordingly, we then go on to consider a case of parametrizable taste
change in full detail. That case can be given the interpretation of consumers
learning more about the properties of a recently introduced good. We
derive the consequences for index number construction of such a circumstance.

Moreover, the rigorous formulation of the theory involved in the treatment of taste change aids also in the treatment of new goods and of quality
change. It does so in two ways. First, the formally acceptable but practically
uncomfortable assumption that the consumer has always known about
unavailable goods and qualities disappears. Second, by focusing attention
on a proper question, the analysis of new goods and quality change becomes relatively straightforward. While it is true in principle that (unlike
the case of taste change) the same analysis could be carried out without
so rigorous a formulation (given the assumption of unchanging tastes for
nonexistent goods), that formulation makes it very clear what is involved.
Asking the right question is a good part of obtaining the answer.

Thus the last two sections of the paper discuss the treatment of new
goods and of quality change respectively and show what kind of information is needed for the handling of these problems in a satisfactory manner.

II. *The Theory of the True Cost-of-Living Index and*
Intertemporal Comparisons of Welfare
As indicated, a frequently encountered view of the true cost-of-living index
is that it is designed to answer the question: 'What income would be
required to make a consumer faced with today's prices just as well off as
he was yesterday when he faced yesterday's income and yesterday's prices?'
The difficulty that is presented by taste changes in answering this question is immediately apparent. What is meant by 'just as well off as he was
yesterday' if the indifference map has shifted?

Yet reflection on this issue shows that the same difficulty appears even if tastes do not change. While it is apparently natural to say that a man whose tastes have remained constant is just as well off today as he was yesterday if he is on the same indifference curve in both periods, the appeal of that proposition is no more than apparent. In both periods, the man's utility function is determined only up to a monotonic transformation; how can we possibly know whether the level of true utility (whatever that may mean) corresponding to a given indifference curve is the same in both periods ? The man's efficiency as a pleasure-machine may have changed without changing his tastes.

Indeed, we have no more justification for saying that a man on the same indifference curve at two different times is equally well off at both than we do for saying that two men who happen to have the same indifference map are equally well off if they have the same possessions. Both statements are attractive for reasons of simplicity and both are completely without any operational content whatsoever. One never steps into the same river twice and the comparison between a man's utility now and his utility yesterday stands on precisely the same lack of footing as the comparison of the utilities of two different men.

Thus, a consideration of the problem of taste change on this inter-pretation of the theory of the true cost-of-living index merely makes explicit a problem that is apparently there all the time. If that theory were really founded upon intertemporal comparisons of utility of the type described, then that theory would be without foundation.[2]

In fact, however, the theory of the true cost-of-living index makes no such comparisons, and rigorous statements of that theory have avoided them. Such statements run as follows: 'Given an indifference map, we compare two *hypothetical* situations, A and B. We ask how much income the consumer in B would require to make him just indifferent between facing B's prices and facing A's prices with a stated income.' Note that the question of whether the consumer has the same utility in A as in B never arises. So long as we remain on this level of abstraction, the point in time and space at which the consumer has the indifference map used in the comparison may be A or it may be B or it may be any other *single* point different from both of these.

In practice, however, the cost-of-living index is meant to compare two real situations rather than two hypothetical ones and A and B become, for example, yesterday and today, respectively. In this case, it is natural to take the indifference map to be used as the one in force at either A or B,[3] and if tastes have not changed so that the two maps are the same, it is easy to slip into the erroneous (but in this case harmless) usage of saying that what is compared are the relative costs of making the consumer at B just as well off as he was at A. If the indifference maps differ, however, such a slip is dangerous and it must never be forgotten that the viewpoint from which the comparison is made is not necessarily identical with either A or B.

Thus, the true cost-of-living index is supposed to represent a comparison between two opportunity or constraint loci not between two utility levels. The first constraint locus is that given by yesterday's income and prices – it is yesterday's budget constraint. The second is a budget constraint defined by today's prices but with income a parameter. The true cost-of-living index does not answer the question: 'How much income would it take today to make me as well off as I was yesterday with yesterday's budget constraint ?' That question is unanswerable. A similar-seeming question which *can* be answered is: 'How much income is required *today* to make me just indifferent between facing yesterday's budget constraint and facing a budget constraint defined by today's prices and the income in question ?' The latter question refers to a choice which can in principle be posed; the former does not.

Note further that the question just posed retains its meaning even if tastes have changed between yesterday and today. It is a question posed entirely in terms of today's tastes and involves a comparison of present and past *constraints*, not a comparison of present and past utilities. As it were, we replace the question: 'Were you happier when young than you are now ?' with the question: 'Would you like to live your youth over again, having the tastes you do now ?' The latter question may seem more fanciful than the former, but it is the one which is operationally meaningful.

It is evident, however, that a second question can also be posed, the answer to which may differ from that to the question just suggested if tastes in fact change. That question is: 'What income would have been required *yesterday* to make you just indifferent between facing yesterday's budget constraint and facing a budget constraint defined by today's prices and the income in question ?' This is the same question as before from the vantage of yesterday's tastes rather than today's. It is equally meaningful, but, we shall argue below, not as interesting.[4]

If tastes do not change, then the answers to the two questions coincide.

In this case also, it is obvious that the required income is precisely that income which would place the consumer today on the same indifference curve as he achieved yesterday. Thus, in the case of no taste change, the cost-of-living index implied by the answers to our questions is precisely that given by the erroneous application of the traditional theory. As indicated in the introduction, however, even in the case of no taste change the advantage of a rigorous formulation is more than aesthetic, since, by focusing attention on a choice between alternative constraints, such a formulation aids in the treatment of problems such as the incorporation of new goods or quality change into the cost-of-living index.

What about the case of taste change, however, in which we have asked two parallel but different questions which (in this case) have two different answers in general? It seems clear that when intertemporal problems are involved, the asymmetry of time makes the question asked assuming today's tastes more relevant than the equally meaningful question asked assuming yesterday's tastes.[5] That this is so may be seen from the following example.

Consider two alternative time paths of prices with the same initial values. In the first, path A, the cost-of-living index considered from the point of view of yesterday's tastes rises, while that considered from the point of view of current tastes stays constant or falls; in the second, path B, the reverse is true. It is clear that the consumer will be better off in every period under path A than under path B, or, equivalently, that in every period, the cost-of-living is higher on path B than on path A. Faced with a choice, rational policy should prefer path A to path B.[6] Indeed, every practical question which one wants the cost-of-living index to answer is answered with reference to current, not base-year tastes. Succinctly, if the prices of goods no longer desired rise and those of goods newly desired fall, a cost-of-living index should fall, not rise. The question of how a man with base-year tastes would view the matter is an operationally meaningful one; it is not a terribly relevant one, however, save insofar as it casts light on the cost of living viewed with current tastes.

This argument has an immediate corollary. The general practice in the construction of consumer price indices is to use Laspeyres indices with base-period quantity weights rather than Paasche indices with current weights. In the case of no taste change, a frequently encountered proposition is that a Laspeyres index overstates price rises and a Paasche index understates them, because of the inadequate treatment afforded substitution effects.[7] If tastes change, however, and if we agree that it is the current-taste cost-of-living in which we are interested, a Laspeyres index loses much of its meaning. That index is a relevant upper bound for a true cost-of-living index with base-year tastes; it need not be such a bound for a true cost-of-living index with current tastes. A Paasche index, on the other hand, retains its property of being a lower bound on the current-tastes index (but may lose it for the base-year-taste index). When tastes change, Laspeyres and Paasche indices cease to become approximations to the same thing and become approximations to different things. As we have just seen, it is the Paasche index which approximates the relevant magnitude; the Laspeyres index becomes less relevant.

Indeed, such relevance as is retained by a Laspeyres index occurs only if taste changes take place in such a way as to make a base-year-taste index differ from a current-taste index in some specific way. If one is willing to specify *how* tastes change and to parametrize that specification, one may obtain results on how a Laspeyres index should be adjusted. This is done for a specific class of cases in the next section. If one is not willing to make such a specification, but believes that important taste changes have taken place, one should put more reliance on a Paasche index and less on a Laspeyres than has traditionally been done.[8]

Before closing this section, it may be well to formalize the question which, we have argued, the true cost-of-living index is designed to answer. Given base period prices of goods $\hat{p}_1, \hat{p}_2, ..., \hat{p}_n$, base period income $\hat{y}$, current prices of goods $p_1, p_2, ..., p_n$, the problem is to find that income y such that the representative consumer is *currently* indifferent between facing current prices with income y and facing base period prices with base period income. The true cost-of-living index is then $(y/\hat{y})$.

Let $u(\cdot)$ be an ordinal utility function derived from the representative consumer's current preference map. The problem reduces to solving for the non-negative values of $x_1, x_2, ..., x_n$, that minimize the expression

$$y = p_1 x_1 + p_2 x_2 + \ldots + p_n x_n, \tag{2.1}$$

where x_i $(i = 1, 2, ..., n)$ is the amount of the ith good that would be purchased at current prices and income y, subject to the requirement that

$$u(x_1, x_2, \ldots, x_n) = u(\hat{x}_1, \hat{x}_2, \ldots, \hat{x}_n). \tag{2.2}$$

$\hat{x}_i$ $(i = 1, 2, \ldots, n)$ is the amount of the ith good that currently would be purchased if the consumer faced base period prices with base period income. That is non-negative $\hat{x}_1, \hat{x}_2, \ldots, \hat{x}_n$ are chosen to maximize utility

$$u(\hat{x}_1, \hat{x}_2, \ldots, \hat{x}_n) \tag{2.3}$$

subject to the budget constraint

$$\hat{y} \geqslant \hat{p}_1 \hat{x}_1 + \hat{p}_2 \hat{x}_2 + \ldots + \hat{p}_n \hat{x}_n. \tag{2.4}$$

It may be noted that a more compact formulation can be given in terms of the indirect utility function (Houthakker, 1951–2, 157–63). Thus, let $\phi(p_1, p_2, \ldots, p_n, y)$ be the indirect utility function, so that $\phi(p_1, p_2, \ldots, p_n, y)$ is the maximal value of $u(x_1, x_2, \ldots, x_n)$ subject to $\sum_1^n p_i x_i = y$. The cost-of-living index is $(y/\hat{y})$, where y is the solution to $\phi(p_1, p_2, \ldots, p_n, y) = \phi(\hat{p}_1, \hat{p}_2, \ldots, \hat{p}_n, \hat{y})$. We have not used this formulation in what follows since taste changes seem to be parametrizable more easily in terms of the direct than in terms of the indirect utility function and because we shall later work with more complicated constraints. However, the properties of the indirect utility function may be useful for future work in this area.

III. *Taste Change*

Consumers' tastes change for a variety of reasons some of which are so mysterious to the ordinary economist that he is unlikely to offer much in the way of a systematic understanding. But certain instances of taste change possess a more systematic structure. For example, it may be known to be the case that a recently introduced electrical appliance, say, increases monotonically in desirability through time during the period in which consumers are learning about the usefulness of the appliance. In such a case, one unit of the appliance in a later year may afford the same service as more than one in an earlier year because of the increase in consumer information but with no physical change in the good itself.

Certain goods seem to suffer similar losses in desirability through time. Dairy products, for which publicity about their possible relationship to certain circulatory diseases has been increasing through time, might be considered to have suffered a systematic decline in desirability to consumers.

These examples raise the important question of just what we mean by a taste change as opposed to a quality change. To take a slightly different idealized case, suppose that consumers suddenly learn to use a certain fuel more efficiently, getting a certain number of BTUs out of a smaller quantity of fuel. If the relevant axis on the indifference map is the amount of fuel *purchased*, then there has been a taste change; if it is the number of BTUs gained from such fuel, there has not been a taste change but a quality change – a change in the opportunities available to consumers. The change can be consistently treated in either way, but the two treatments will differ. When the phenomenon is treated as a quality change, the true cost-of-living index will decline; when it is analysed as a taste change, this will not be the case. The decision turns on whether the cost of living should be said to decrease just because consumers are better at consuming. If we are concerned with the delivery to the consumer of certain 'basic satisfactions', a quality change is involved; this is an extension of the position taken in the construction of hedonic price indices. If, on the other hand, we are concerned with the valuation of opportunities *as available in the market*, then treatment of the change as being one of tastes is more appropriate. Both positions are tenable and both can lead to uncomfortable results if pushed to absurdity. (Suppose on the one hand that the new technique is discovered and popularized by fuel sellers. Suppose, on the other, that there is no change in the technology of fuel use but that people decide they now prefer a lower temperature in their houses.) The present section treats taste changes, the quality change case which is similarly parametrizable being treated in section v.

In this section, the case in which taste change may be parametrized as solely good augmenting is treated in detail. A taste change is said to be good-augmenting if and only if the preference maps can be represented by a utility function whose ith argument is a function of the amount of purchases of the ith good and of the level of some taste change parameter.[9] Following the terminology employed in capital theory, we might call a taste change which is independent of any change in the qualities of the goods a disembodied taste change. In this section, the effect of such taste change upon the value of the true cost-of-living index is studied. We derive results in terms of the parameters of the demand functions which are, in particular, capable of being estimated from market data.

For convenience, assume that only one good, say the first, experiences an own-augmenting disembodied taste change. (Immediate generalization of the results to the case where more than one of the n goods experience own-augmenting disembodied taste changes is discussed at the end of this section.) Let the representative consumer's utility function be given by $u(bx_1, x_2, \ldots, x_n)$, where b is the parameter representing first-good-augmenting taste change and x_i $(i = 1, 2, \ldots, n)$ is the amount of the ith good that is purchased.[10] Also assume that $u(\cdot)$ is an increasing, twice differentiable, strictly quasi-concave function which is defined over the non-negative orthant of an n-dimensional space.[11] For the purposes of this section we also assume that all relevant maxima and minima are given by interior solutions to the first-order conditions. Corner solutions are treated in Section IV.

We now turn to the formal analysis of the problem. If with current tastes the representative consumer faces base period income $\hat{y}$ and base period prices $\hat{p}$ where $\hat{p}$ is an n-dimensional column vector defined by $\hat{p}' = (\hat{p}_1, \hat{p}_2, \ldots, \hat{p}_n)$, his purchases would have been given by the column vector $\hat{x}$ which is defined by $\hat{x}' = (\hat{x}_1, \hat{x}_2, \ldots, \hat{x}_n)$. $\hat{p}_i$ and $\hat{x}_i$ $(i = 1, 2, \ldots, n)$ are respectively the base period price of the ith good and the amount of the ith good that *would have been* purchased if he had faced the base period constraints with current tastes. $\hat{x}$ is found by solving the system of first-order conditions:

$$\begin{pmatrix} \hat{p}'\hat{x} \\ b\hat{u}_1 \\ \hat{u}_2 \\ \cdot \\ \cdot \\ \cdot \\ \hat{u}_n \end{pmatrix} - \begin{pmatrix} \hat{y} \\ \text{---} \\ \hat{\lambda}\hat{p} \end{pmatrix} = 0, \tag{3.1}$$

where $\hat{u}_i (i = 1, 2, \ldots, n)$ denotes the derivative of $u(\cdot)$ with respect to its ith argument evaluated at the point $\hat{x}$. $\hat{\lambda}$ is a non-negative scalar Lagrange multiplier which has the (cardinal) interpretation of the current marginal utility of income when prices are evaluated at $\hat{p}$ and income is $\hat{y}$.

Next we solve for that income y that makes the individual currently indifferent between his current constraints and his base period constraints. y is defined by

$$p'x - y = 0, \tag{3.2}$$

where p is the column vector of current prices, $p' = (p_1, p_2, \ldots, p_n)$, where

p_i $(i = 1,2,\ldots,n)$ is the current price of the ith good. x is the column vector of purchases, $x' = (x_1, x_2, \ldots, x_n)$, that minimizes y subject to $u(bx_1, x_2, \ldots, x_n) = u(b\hat{x}_1, \hat{x}_2, \ldots, \hat{x}_n)$. Constrained minimization of y implies that

$$
\begin{pmatrix} u \\ bu_1 \\ u_2 \\ \cdot \\ \cdot \\ \cdot \\ u_n \end{pmatrix} - \begin{pmatrix} \hat{u} \\ --- \\ \lambda p \end{pmatrix} = 0 , \tag{3.3}
$$

where u_i $(i = 1,2,\ldots,n)$ denotes differentiation of $u(\cdot)$ with respect to its ith argument evaluated at x, $\hat{u}$ denotes $u(b\hat{x}_1, \hat{x}_2, \ldots, \hat{x}_n)$, and λ is a nonnegative Lagrange multiplier.

We are interested in how the true cost-of-living index $(y/\hat{y})$ is affected by taste change. Thus, it is necessary to develop the total derivative of y with respect to b. Base period income $\hat{y}$, base period prices $\hat{p}$, and current prices p are the given data of the problem. We evaluate $(\partial y/\partial b)$ in steps.

Lemma 3.1. $\left(\dfrac{\partial y}{\partial b}\right)_{u=\hat{u} \text{ const.}} = \dfrac{-p_1 x_1}{b}$.

Proof. Total differentiation of (3.3) with respect to b yields:

$$
\begin{bmatrix} 0 & bu_1 & u_2 & \cdots & u_n \\ p_1 & b^2 u_{11} & bu_{12} & \cdots & bu_{1n} \\ p_2 & bu_{21} & u_{22} & \cdots & u_{2n} \\ \cdot & \cdot & \cdot & & \cdot \\ \cdot & \cdot & \cdot & & \cdot \\ \cdot & \cdot & \cdot & & \cdot \\ p_n & bu_{n1} & u_{n2} & & u_{nn} \end{bmatrix} \begin{bmatrix} -\dfrac{\partial \lambda}{\partial b} \\ ------ \\ \dfrac{\partial x}{\partial b} \end{bmatrix} + \begin{bmatrix} x_1 u_1 \\ u_1 + bx_1 u_{11} \\ x_1 u_{12} \\ \cdot \\ \cdot \\ \cdot \\ x_1 u_{1n} \end{bmatrix} = 0 ,
$$

$$\tag{3.4}$$

where u_{ij} $(i,j = 1,2,\ldots,n)$ denotes partial differentiation of u_i with respect to its jth argument and $(\partial x/\partial b)$ denotes the column vector $(\partial x_1/\partial b, \partial x_2/\partial b, \ldots, \partial x_n/\partial b)'$. Denote the nonsingular $(n+1) \times (n+1)$ matrix in

(3.4) by H. Then:

$$\begin{bmatrix} -\dfrac{\partial \lambda}{\partial b} \\ \text{------} \\ \dfrac{\partial x}{\partial b} \end{bmatrix} = -H^{-1} \begin{bmatrix} x_1 u_1 \\ u_1 + b x_1 u_{11} \\ x_1 u_{12} \\ \cdot \\ \cdot \\ \cdot \\ x_1 u_{1n} \end{bmatrix}. \tag{3.5}$$

But from (3.2) and (3.3)

$$\left(\frac{\partial y}{\partial b}\right)_{u=\hat{u} \text{ const.}} = p'\left(\frac{\partial x}{\partial b}\right) = (0 \mid p') \begin{pmatrix} -\dfrac{\partial \lambda}{\partial b} \\ \text{------} \\ \dfrac{\partial x}{\partial b} \end{pmatrix}$$

$$= -(0 \mid p')H^{-1} \begin{pmatrix} x_1 u_1 \\ u_1 + b x_1 u_{11} \\ x_1 u_{12} \\ \cdot \\ \cdot \\ \cdot \\ x_1 u_{1n} \end{pmatrix} \tag{3.6}$$

in view of (3.5). By (3.3), the first row in H is equal to λ times $(0 \mid p')$ so by the definition of the matrix inverse we have that

$$\left(\frac{\partial y}{\partial b}\right)_{u=\hat{u} \text{ const.}} = \frac{-x_1 u_1}{\lambda} = \frac{-p_1 x_1}{b} \tag{3.7}$$

by (3.3), which proves the lemma.

Following the practice in capital theory, a fruitful way to understand Lemma 3.1 is to proceed by measuring the purchases of the various goods in (utility) efficiency units. Let x^*, the vector of purchases *measured in efficiency units*, be defined by

$$x^{*\prime} = (x_1^*, x_2^*, \ldots, x_n^*) = (b x_1, x_2, \ldots, x_n). \tag{3.8}$$

Since the corresponding vector of *prices per efficiency unit* is ($p_1/b, p_2, \ldots,$ p_n), income y can be written as

$$y = (p_1/b, p_2, \ldots, p_n)x^* . \tag{3.9}$$

Holding x^* fixed, differentiating (3.9) with respect to b yields

$$\left(\frac{\partial y}{\partial b}\right)_{x^* \text{ const.}} = \frac{-p_1 x_1}{b} = \left(\frac{\partial y}{\partial b}\right)_{u=\hat{u} \text{ const.}} \tag{3.10}$$

by Lemma 3.1, if x^* and b are such that the system (3.3) is satisfied. Thus the effect on y along a constant utility surface of a first order change in the taste parameter b is the same as the effect on y, holding the amount of purchases measured in efficiency units constant, of a first order change in the taste parameter b.[12]

Now define $(\partial \hat{x}/\partial b)$ to be the column vector with ith entry $(\partial \hat{x}_i/\partial b)$ and let $(\partial \hat{u}/\partial \hat{x})$ be the column vector with ith entry $(\partial u/\partial x_i)$ evaluated at $\hat{x}$.

Lemma 3.2. $\left(\dfrac{\partial \hat{u}}{\partial \hat{x}}\right)'\left(\dfrac{\partial \hat{x}}{\partial b}\right) = 0$.

Proof. Totally differentiating (3.1) with respect to b yields

$$\begin{bmatrix} 0 & \hat{p}_1 & \hat{p}_2 & \cdots & \hat{p}_n \\ \hat{p}_1 & b^2\hat{u}_{11} & b\hat{u}_{12} & \cdots & b\hat{u}_{1n} \\ \hat{p}_2 & b\hat{u}_{21} & \hat{u}_{22} & \cdots & \hat{u}_{2n} \\ \cdot & \cdot & \cdot & & \cdot \\ \cdot & \cdot & \cdot & & \cdot \\ \cdot & \cdot & \cdot & & \cdot \\ \hat{p}_n & b\hat{u}_{n1} & \hat{u}_{n2} & \cdots & \hat{u}_{nn} \end{bmatrix} \begin{bmatrix} -\dfrac{\partial \hat{\lambda}}{\partial b} \\ \text{------} \\ \dfrac{\partial \hat{x}}{\partial b} \end{bmatrix} +$$

$$+ \begin{bmatrix} 0 \\ \hat{u}_1 + b\hat{x}_1\hat{u}_{11} \\ \hat{x}_1\hat{u}_{12} \\ \cdot \\ \cdot \\ \cdot \\ \hat{x}_1\hat{u}_{1n} \end{bmatrix} = 0 . \tag{3.11}$$

The $\hat{u}_{ij}$ $(i,j = 1,2,\ldots,n)$ are the cross partials defined previously but evaluated at $\hat{x}$. Let $\hat{J}$ denote the nonsingular matrix in (3.11). Then from (3.1) and (3.11)

$$\left(\frac{\partial \hat{u}}{\partial \hat{x}}\right)'\left(\frac{\partial \hat{x}}{\partial b}\right) = \hat{\lambda}(0 \mid \hat{p}')\left(\begin{array}{c} -\dfrac{\partial \lambda}{\partial b} \\ \text{------} \\ \dfrac{\partial \hat{x}}{\partial b} \end{array}\right)$$

$$= -\hat{\lambda}(0 \mid \hat{p}')\hat{J}^{-1}\left(\begin{array}{c} 0 \\ \hat{u}_1 + b\hat{x}_1\hat{u}_{11} \\ \hat{x}_1\hat{u}_{12} \\ \vdots \\ \hat{x}_1\hat{u}_{1n} \end{array}\right), \qquad (3.12)$$

which equals zero because $(0 \mid \hat{p}')$ is the first row in $\hat{J}$. Lemma 3.2 is an 'envelope theorem' where the change in $\hat{u}$ due to a first order change in b *ceteris paribus* is exactly equal to the change in $\hat{u}$ due to first order change in b when $\hat{x}$ is allowed to vary optimally (*mutatis mutandis*).

Lemma 3.3. $\left(\dfrac{\partial y}{\partial \hat{u}}\right) = \dfrac{1}{\lambda} > 0$.

Lemma 3.3 taken with Lemma 3.2 has the familiar interpretation that λ is the current marginal utility of income when prices are evaluated at p and income is y.

Proof. Total differentiation of (3.2) with respect to $\hat{u}$ yields

$$H\left(\begin{array}{c} -\dfrac{\partial \lambda}{\partial \hat{u}} \\ \text{------} \\ \dfrac{\partial x}{\partial \hat{u}} \end{array}\right) = \left(\begin{array}{c} 1 \\ 0 \\ \vdots \\ 0 \end{array}\right), \qquad (3.13)$$

where $(\partial x/\partial \hat{u})$ is an n-dimensional column vector with ith entry $(\partial x_i/\partial \hat{u})$. Differentiating (3.2) with respect to $\hat{u}$ and substituting from (3.13) yields

$$\frac{\partial y}{\partial \hat{u}} = p'\left(\frac{\partial x}{\partial \hat{u}}\right) = (0 \mid p')H^{-1}\begin{pmatrix} 1 \\ 0 \\ \cdot \\ \cdot \\ \cdot \\ 0 \end{pmatrix} = \frac{1}{\lambda}, \tag{3.14}$$

because the first row in H is equal to $\lambda(0 \mid p')$.

From (3.1)–(3.3), total differentiation of y with respect to the parameter b gives

$$\frac{\partial y}{\partial b} = \left(\frac{\partial y}{\partial b}\right)_{u=\hat{u}\text{ const.}} + \left(\frac{\partial y}{\partial \hat{u}}\right)\left[\hat{x}_1\hat{u}_1 + \left(\frac{\partial \hat{u}}{\partial \hat{x}}\right)'\left(\frac{\partial \hat{x}}{\partial b}\right)\right]. \tag{3.15}$$

Theorem 3.1. $\dfrac{\partial y}{\partial b} = \dfrac{p_1 x_1}{b}\left(\dfrac{\hat{x}_1\hat{u}_1}{x_1 u_1} - 1\right).$

Proof. Substitute the results of Lemmas 3.1–3.3 into equation (3.15) and then simplify by using equations (3.1) and (3.3) to establish the theorem.

Substituting from (3.1) and (3.3), (3.15) can be rewritten as

$$\frac{\partial y}{\partial b} = \frac{\hat{x}_1\hat{u}_1 - x_1 u_1}{\lambda}. \tag{3.16}$$

Notice that the numerator of the RHS of (3.16) is the *ceteris paribus* increase in current utility when facing base period prices minus the *ceteris paribus* increase in current utility when facing current prices, due to a first order increase in the value of b. By Lemma 3.2, we recognize the numerator of the RHS of (3.16) as the additional compensation in units of utility required to keep the consumer indifferent between base period and current constraints when b changes. Since Lemma 3.3 allows λ the interpretation of the marginal utility of income, the full fraction on the RHS of (3.16) gives the same additional compensation in money units.[13]

Corollary 3.1. If $p = \hat{p}$, then $\left(\dfrac{\partial y}{\partial b}\right) = 0.$

Proof. The corollary is an immediate consequence of Theorem 3.1. The corollary is obvious from consideration of the definition of the true cost-of-living index. After all, if $p = \hat{p}$ then $y = \hat{y}$ for all values of b.

Since we know that $(\partial y/\partial b)$ is zero when current prices equal base period prices, in order to study the effect of taste change on the true cost-of-living index it is natural to investigate the qualitative behavior of $(\partial y/\partial b)$ when prices are displaced from $\hat{p}$. In particular, we want to derive results concerning the sign of $(\partial y/\partial b)$ for values of p different from $\hat{p}$.

To do this, it is convenient to define $z(p) = x_1 u_1$ and to study the effects of price changes upon $z(p)$.

Lemma 3.4. $\dfrac{\partial u_1}{\partial p_1} = \dfrac{u_1}{\lambda} \dfrac{\partial \lambda}{\partial p_1} + \dfrac{u_1}{p_1}$, and

$$\frac{\partial u_1}{\partial p_i} = \frac{u_1}{\lambda} \frac{\partial \lambda}{\partial p_i} \text{ for } i = 2, \ldots, n.$$

Proof. From (3.3) we have that $\dfrac{\partial u_1}{\partial p_i} = \dfrac{1}{b} \dfrac{\partial(\lambda p_1)}{\partial p_i}$ for $i = 1, 2, \ldots, n$. The lemma follows immediately.

Lemma 3.5. $\dfrac{1}{\lambda} \left(\dfrac{\partial \lambda}{\partial p_i} \right) = - \left(\dfrac{\partial x_i}{\partial y} \right)_{p \text{ const.}}$, for $i = 1, 2, \ldots, n$.

Proof. Total differentiation of (3.3) with respect to p_i yields

$$\begin{pmatrix} \dfrac{-\partial \lambda}{\partial p_i} \\ \text{------} \\ \dfrac{\partial x}{\partial p_i} \end{pmatrix} = H^{-1} \begin{pmatrix} 0 \\ \cdot \\ \cdot \\ \cdot \\ 0 \\ \lambda \\ 0 \\ \cdot \\ \cdot \\ 0 \end{pmatrix}, \tag{3.17}$$

where $\left(\dfrac{\partial x}{\partial p_i} \right)$ is a column vector with ith entry $(\partial x_i / \partial p_i)$. The column vector on the RHS of (3.17) has λ for its $(i+1)$st entry with all other entries zero. Therefore

$$\frac{1}{\lambda} \left(\frac{\partial \lambda}{\partial p_i} \right) = -(1\ 0 \ldots 0) H^{-1} \begin{pmatrix} 0 \\ \cdot \\ \cdot \\ \cdot \\ 0 \\ 1 \\ 0 \\ \cdot \\ \cdot \\ 0 \end{pmatrix}, \tag{3.18}$$

where the unit in the column vector in (3.18) appears in the $(i+1)$st entry. The LHS of (3.18) is thus shown to be equal to minus the element in the first row and $(i+1)$st column of H^{-1} which in turn is equal to minus the element in the first row and $(i+1)$st column of the matrix J^{-1} where J is defined by

$$
J = \begin{bmatrix}
0 & p_1 & p_2 & \cdots & p_n \\
p_1 & b^2 u_{11} & b u_{12} & \cdots & b u_{1n} \\
p_2 & b u_{21} & u_{22} & \cdots & u_{2n} \\
\cdot & \cdot & \cdot & & \cdot \\
\cdot & \cdot & \cdot & & \cdot \\
\cdot & \cdot & \cdot & & \cdot \\
p_n & b u_{n1} & u_{n2} & \cdots & u_{nn}
\end{bmatrix}.
$$

This follows because only the first rows of H and J differ and they only differ by a scalar multiple. Consideration of the evaluation of inverses by the adjoint method shows that except for their first entries the first rows of H^{-1} and J^{-1} must be equal. Substituting J^{-1} for H^{-1} in (3.18) and transposing both sides yields

$$
\frac{1}{\lambda}\left(\frac{\partial \lambda}{\partial p_i}\right) = -(0 \ldots 0\ 1\ 0 \ldots 0) J^{-1} \begin{pmatrix} 1 \\ 0 \\ \cdot \\ \cdot \\ \cdot \\ 0 \end{pmatrix} \tag{3.19}
$$

because J^{-1} is a symmetric matrix.

If the first equation in the system (3.3) is replaced by equation (3.2) and the resulting system is totally differentiated with respect to y holding prices constant, then we have

$$
J \begin{pmatrix} \dfrac{-\partial \lambda}{\partial y} \\ \text{------} \\ \dfrac{\partial x}{\partial y} \end{pmatrix}_{p\ \text{const.}} = \begin{pmatrix} 1 \\ 0 \\ \cdot \\ \cdot \\ \cdot \\ 0 \end{pmatrix}, \tag{3.20}
$$

where $(\partial x/\partial y)$ is a column vector with ith entry $(\partial x_i/\partial y)$. It follows immediately from (3.20) that

$$\left(\frac{\partial x_i}{\partial y}\right)_{p \text{ const.}} = (0 \ldots 0 \; 1 \; 0 \ldots 0) J^{-1} \begin{pmatrix} 1 \\ 0 \\ \vdots \\ \vdots \\ 0 \end{pmatrix}, \qquad (3.21)$$

where the unit in the row vector on the RHS of (3.21) appears in the $(i+1)$st entry. The lemma follows after combining (3.19) and (3.21).

Next define the elasticity of demand for the ith good with respect to the first price by

$$\eta_{i1} = \left(\frac{p_1}{x_i}\right)\left(\frac{\partial x_i}{\partial p_1}\right)_{y \text{ const.}}$$

for $i = 1, 2, \ldots, n$.

Lemma 3.6. If $z(p) = x_1 u_1$, then

$$\frac{\partial z}{\partial p_1} = \frac{x_1 u_1}{p_1}\{\eta_{11} + 1\} \quad \text{and}$$

$$\frac{\partial z}{\partial p_i} = \frac{x_i u_1}{p_1}\eta_{i1}, \quad i = 2, \ldots, n.$$

Proof. By Lemmas 3.4 and 3.5

$$\frac{\partial z}{\partial p_1} = u_1\left[\left(\frac{\partial x_1}{\partial p_1}\right)_{u = \hat{u} \text{ const.}} - x_1\left(\frac{\partial x_1}{\partial y}\right)_{p \text{ const.}} + \frac{x_1}{p_1}\right] \text{and}$$

$$\frac{\partial z}{\partial p_i} = u_1\left[\left(\frac{\partial x_1}{\partial p_i}\right)_{u = \hat{u} \text{ const.}} - x_1\left(\frac{\partial x_i}{\partial y}\right)_{p \text{ const.}}\right], \quad i = 2, \ldots, n. \quad (3.22)$$

Because substitution effects are symmetric, in (3.22), $(\partial x_1 / \partial p_1)_{u = \hat{u} \text{ const.}}$ can be replaced by $(\partial x_i / \partial p_1)_{u = \hat{u} \text{ const.}}$. Application of Slutsky's theorem then yields

$$\frac{\partial z}{\partial p_1} = u_1\left[\left(\frac{\partial x_1}{\partial p_1}\right)_{y \text{ const.}} + \frac{x_1}{p_1}\right] \text{and}$$

$$\frac{\partial z}{\partial p_i} = u_1\left(\frac{\partial x_i}{\partial p_1}\right)_{y \text{ const.}}, \quad i = 2, \ldots, n. \quad (3.23)$$

Using the definition of the η_{i1} in (3.23) and rearranging completes the proof of the lemma.

We must now agree on some terminology. We shall call the demand for the first good *price elastic* (*price inelastic*) if $\eta_{11} < (>) -1$. Next, we shall call the ith good a *gross substitute* (*gross complement*) for the first good if $\eta_{i1} > (<) 0$ $(i = 2, \ldots, n)$. Note that this relation is not symmetric; the ith good can be a gross substitute for the first good while the first good is a gross complement for the ith good. This, of course, is due to income effects. The symmetric substitution relationships defined by the substitution terms in the Slutsky equation we shall refer to as those of *net substitutes* or *net complements*.

Theorem 3.2. (A) Suppose $p_i = \hat{p}_i$ for $i = 2, \ldots, n$. If the demand for the first good is price elastic, then $(\partial y / \partial b)$ has the same sign as $(p_1 - \hat{p}_1)$. If that demand is price inelastic, then $(\partial y / \partial b)$ and $(p_1 - \hat{p}_1)$ have opposite signs. If $\eta_{11} = -1$, then $(\partial y / \partial b) = 0$.

(B) Suppose $p_i = \hat{p}_i$ for $i = 1, \ldots, n$ and $i \neq j \neq 1$. If the jth good is a gross complement for the first good, then $(\partial y / \partial b)$ has the same sign as $(p_j - \hat{p}_j)$. If the jth good is a gross substitute for the first good, then $(\partial y / \partial b)$ and $(p_j - \hat{p}_j)$ have opposite signs. If $\eta_{j1} = 0$, then $(\partial y / \partial b) = 0$.

(C) If $p_i = k\hat{p}_i$, $i = 1, 2, \ldots, n$, where k is a positive constant, then $(\partial y / \partial b) = 0$.

Proof. (A) and (B) follow directly from Theorem 3.1, Corollary 3.1, and Lemma 3.6.

(C) Totally differentiating z with respect to k yields

$$k \frac{\partial z}{\partial k} = u_1 x_1 + u_1 \sum_1^n p_i \left(\frac{\partial x_i}{\partial p_1} \right)_{y \text{ const.}} \tag{3.24}$$

by Lemma 3.6 since $k(\partial p_i / \partial k) = p_i$ by hypothesis. But from (3.2), $\sum_1^n p_i \left(\frac{\partial x_i}{\partial p_1} \right)_{y \text{ const.}} = -x_1$. Theorem 3.2 (C) follows from Theorem 3.1 and Corollary 3.1.

Notice that Theorem 3.2 (A) is a *global* result (i.e. it is a result that holds for all values of p_1) when the sign of $(\eta_{11} + 1)$ is independent of the value of p_1. Likewise, Theorem 3.2 (B) is a global result when the sign of η_{j1} is independent of the value of p_j. Theorem 3.2 (C) is an extension of Corollary 3.1. If current prices are all k times base period prices then the income that makes the consumer currently indifferent between current constraints and base period constraints is equal to k times base period income regardless of the value of b.[14]

Theorem 3.2 has important practical implications and may be interpreted as follows. Suppose first that all prices except the jth are the same in the two periods $(1 \leqslant j \leqslant n)$. If tastes did not change $(b = 1)$, the only change in the cost-of-living index would be due to the change in the value of the jth price from $\hat{p}_j$ to p_j and would, of course, be in the same direction. Assuming b to be increasing through time, if $(\partial y / \partial b)$ has the same sign as $(p_j - \hat{p}_j)$, the effect of the taste change is to magnify the effect of the change in p_j. One can express this by saying that the jth good ought to receive increased weight in the index because of the taste change. Similarly, if $(\partial y / \partial b)$ and $(p_j - \hat{p}_j)$ have opposite signs, the effect of the taste change reduces the effect of the change in p_j and the jth good ought to receive a decreased weight. Since we can always analyze a change in more than one price (for our purposes) as a series of individual price changes (because of the definition of the true cost-of-living index), these conclusions are not restricted to cases in which only one price changes between the two periods considered. Thus, Theorem 3.2 suggests that in practice, when computing a cost-of-living index, the recently introduced good should receive more weight (less weight) if demand for it is price elastic (price inelastic) than it would in a price index that does not allow for taste change. Similarly the prices of the goods that are gross complements for the recently introduced good should receive more weight and gross substitutes less weight than they would be given in a traditional price index.

Under certain conditions, we know that the true cost-of-living index $(y/\hat{y})$ is such that

$$\left(\frac{p'x}{\hat{p}'x} \right) < \left(\frac{y}{\hat{y}} \right) < \left(\frac{p'\hat{x}}{\hat{p}'\hat{x}} \right) \tag{3.25}$$

because the price indices on the left and the right do not account for substitution effects. The price index on the left of (3.25) is the (current weight) Paasche index. If tastes have not changed, the price index on the right is equal to the (base-period weight) Laspeyres index, since in that case the vector $\hat{x}$ is equal to the vector $\tilde{x}$, an n-dimensional column vector with ith entry $\tilde{x}_i$ denoting the quantity of the ith good actually purchased during the base period. Since the vector $\hat{x}$ is not observed while the vector $\tilde{x}$ is observed, it is of interest to know the relationship of the Laspeyres index $(p'\tilde{x}/\hat{p}'\tilde{x})$ to the unobserved index $(p'\hat{x}/\hat{p}'\hat{x})$. This is the purpose of the next theorem.

Theorem 3.3. (A) $\dfrac{\partial \hat{x}_1}{\partial b} = \dfrac{-\hat{x}_1}{b}(1+\eta_{11})$

(B) $\dfrac{\partial \hat{x}_i}{\partial b} = \dfrac{-\hat{x}_i}{b}\eta_{i1}, \, i = 2,\ldots, n$.

Proof. Theorem 3.3 can be easily proved by appropriate manipulation of equation (3.11). It is more interesting, however, to analyze the problem when purchases are measured in efficiency units. Let $\hat{x}_1^* = b\hat{x}_1$ be the amount of the first good purchased (measured in efficiency units) when prices are $\hat{p}$. $\hat{p}_1^* = (\hat{p}_1/b)$ is the price per efficiency unit of the first good. The equilibrium amounts of purchases measured in efficiency units depend only upon prices per efficiency unit and income $\hat{y}$. For $\hat{p}_1^*$ fixed, the amounts of equilibrium purchases are independent of the values of b and $\hat{p}_1$. Therefore we conclude that

$$\left(\frac{\partial \hat{x}_1^*}{\partial b}\right)\left(\frac{\partial b}{\partial \hat{p}_1^*}\right)_{\hat{p}_1 \text{ const.}} = \left(\frac{\partial \hat{x}_1^*}{\partial \hat{p}_1}\right)\left(\frac{\partial \hat{p}_1}{\partial \hat{p}_1^*}\right)_{b \text{ const.}} \qquad (3.26)$$

and $\quad \left(\dfrac{\partial \hat{x}_i}{\partial b}\right)\left(\dfrac{\partial b}{\partial \hat{p}_1^*}\right)_{\hat{p}_1 \text{ const.}} = \left(\dfrac{\partial \hat{x}_i}{\partial \hat{p}_1}\right)\left(\dfrac{\partial \hat{p}_1}{\partial \hat{p}_1^*}\right)_{b \text{ const.}}, \, i = 2,\ldots, n$. (3.27)

Using the definitions of $\hat{x}_1^*$, $\hat{p}_1^*$, and η_{11} in (3.26) yields (A). Using the definitions of p_1^* and η_{11} in (3.27) yields (B). The price elasticities of demand $\eta_{i1}, i = 1,2,\ldots,n$, in (A) and (B) are evaluated at $\hat{p}$, $\hat{x}$, and $\hat{y}$.

Again consider the case in which the first good has been recently introduced and thus the value of b has been increasing through time. Theorem 3.3 tells us, e.g. that if the price of the recently introduced good has fallen ($\hat{p}_1 > p_1$) and the demand for the first good is price elastic while the prices of all goods that are gross complements (gross substitutes) for the first good are falling (rising), then $(p'\hat{x}/\hat{p}'\hat{x}) > (p'\hat{x}/\hat{p}'\hat{x})$. In this special case, therefore, the value of the true cost-of-living index lies between the values of the Paasche and Laspeyres price indices (subject, of course, to the qualifications discussed in footnote 7). This result can also be deduced from Theorem 3.2 because in this special case $(\partial y/\partial b) < 0$.

Theorem 3.3 reinforces Theorem 3.2. It tells us that had current tastes been in force during the base period, purchases of gross complements for the recently introduced good would have been greater and purchases of gross substitutes less than was actually the case. Similarly, the demand for the good itself would have been greater (less) if its demand is price elastic.

It follows that in constructing a Laspeyres price index, the price of the recently introduced good should receive more weight (less weight) if demand for it is price elastic (price inelastic). Similarly the prices of goods that are gross complements (gross substitutes) for the recently introduced good should receive more weight (less weight). Theorem 3.2 assures us that similar weight changes should be made in a true cost-of-living index (a Paasche index, of course, needs no such corrections).[15]

We have stated Theorem 3.2 (and interpreted Theorem 3.3) in qualitative terms to give them some practical usefulness. In practice, one might very well be willing to say that a taste change of the sort described (a change in b) has occurred, but it is unlikely that one would be willing to say by how much b has changed. Obviously, if such information were somehow available, our lemmas would yield precise quantitative results.

Theorems 3.1–3.3 can be extended to include cases where more than one good has experienced an own-augmenting taste change. For example, consider the case in which the first two goods have been recently introduced so that the preference maps can be represented by the utility function $u(b_1 x_1, b_2 x_2, x_3, \ldots, x_n)$ where b_1 and b_2 have been increasing through time. In constructing a cost-of-living index, prices of those goods that are gross complements (gross substitutes) for *both* of the recently introduced goods should receive more weight (less weight). If demand for the first good is elastic and demand for the second is inelastic, if the first and second goods are gross substitutes for each other, and if $(b_1/b_2) > 1$ in the current period while $(b_1/b_2) = 1$ during the base period, then the first good should receive more weight and the second good less weight.

Before closing this section, we may briefly ask a second-order question. Do the effects described in Theorem 3.2 get larger with larger price changes or do they decrease as price changes increase? This question is of some interest if attention is to be paid to such effects in practice. Since, as in Theorem 3.2, it suffices to look at one price change at a time, we may answer it by examining $(\partial^2 y/\partial b \, \partial p_j) \ (j = 1, \ldots, n)$.

Define the *net* price elasticity of demand $\eta_{j1}^{[n}$ by

$$\eta_{j1}^{[n} = \left(\frac{p_j}{x_1}\right)\left(\frac{\partial x_1}{\partial p_j}\right)_{u=\hat{u} \text{ const}}, \quad j = 1, \ldots, n. \tag{3.28}$$

Lemma 3.7. $\dfrac{\partial^2 y}{\partial b \partial p_1} = (1/p_1)(\partial y/\partial b)\{\eta_{11}^{[n}+1\} - \left(\dfrac{\hat{x}_1 \hat{u}_1}{b u_1}\right)(\eta_{11}+1)$

and
$$\frac{\partial^2 y}{\partial b \partial p_j} = (1/p_j)(\partial y/\partial b)\eta_{j1}^{[n} - \left(\frac{\hat{x}_1 \hat{u}_1 x_j}{b x_1 u_1}\right)\eta_{j1}(j = 2,\dots,n).$$

Proof. This follows immediately from Theorem 3.1 and Lemma 3.6.

We may now state:

Theorem 3.4. (A) Suppose that $p_i = \hat{p}_i$, $i = 2,\dots,n$. For p_1 sufficiently close to $\hat{p}_1$, $(\partial^2 y/\partial b\, \partial p_1)$ is positive if the demand for the first good is elastic and negative if it is inelastic. Further, if $\eta_{11}^{[n} \geqslant -1$, the same statement holds for all $p_1 > \hat{p}_1$; if $\eta_{11}^{[n} \leqslant -1$, it holds for all $p_1 < \hat{p}_1$.[16]

(B) Suppose that $p_i = \hat{p}_i$ for $i = 1,\dots,n$ and $i \neq j \neq 1$. For p_j sufficiently close to $\hat{p}_j$, $(\partial^2 y/\partial b\, \partial p_j)$ is positive if the jth good is a gross complement for the first good and negative if the jth good is a gross substitute for the first good. Further, if the two goods are *net* substitutes (or if $\eta_{j1}^{[n} = 0$), the same statement holds for all $p_j > \hat{p}_j$; if they are *net* complements (or if $\eta_{j1}^{[n} = 0$), it holds for all $p_j < \hat{p}_j$.

Proof. The statements about sufficiently small price changes follow from Lemma 3.7 and Corollary 3.1. The remaining statements follow from Lemma 3.7 and Theorem 3.2.

Thus, for all cases which can be definitely determined, the second-order effects being examined reinforce the first-order ones already treated. The effects of taste change on proper weights in the cost-of-living index are bigger for bigger price changes. For example, we have already seen in Theorem 3.2 that the weight given a gross complement for the first good should be increased on account of the taste change. We now see that for small changes in the price of that complement this effect gets bigger the bigger the price change, and that this remains true globally if the goods are also net complements and the price of the good in question has fallen. Similarly, if the jth good is a gross substitute for the first good, the weight given the jth good should be decreased as a result of the taste change. The amount of decrease should be greater, the higher is p_j above $\hat{p}_j$, provided that the two goods are net substitutes as well.[17]

IV. *New Goods and Other Corner Solutions*

In the previous section, we restricted our analysis of taste change to cases where the relevant maxima and minima are given by interior solutions to the first-order conditions. This section is devoted to a general analysis of the treatment of corner solutions in the cost-of-living index. The problem of this type that is most frequently encountered in practice is the problem of 'new goods'. For our purposes, a new good is one that is purchased in positive amount during the current period but for which base-period purchases were zero. The opposite case of 'disappearing goods', where purchases of the disappearing goods were positive in the base period but are zero in the current period, is also of practical interest.

Using the vector form of the notation developed in (2.1)–(2.4), the problem is to find that income y that makes the representative consumer currently indifferent between facing current prices p with income y and facing base-period prices $\hat{p}$ and base-period income $\hat{y}$. Formally the problem is to solve for a non-negative vector of purchases x such that:

$$\left(\frac{\partial u}{\partial x}\right) - \lambda p \leqslant 0, \tag{4.1}$$

where $(\partial u / \partial x)$ is a column vector with ith entry $(\partial u / \partial x_i)$, $i = 1, 2, \ldots, n$,

$$x'\left[\left(\frac{\partial u}{\partial x}\right) - \lambda p\right] = 0, \tag{4.2}$$

$$x \geqslant 0 \quad \text{and} \quad \lambda \geqslant 0. \tag{4.3}$$

x is constrained by $u(x) = u(\hat{x})$ or simply

$$u - \hat{u} = 0, \tag{4.4}$$

where $\hat{x}$ solves the system:

$$\left(\frac{\partial \hat{u}}{\partial \hat{x}}\right) - \hat{\lambda}\hat{p} \leqslant 0, \tag{4.5}$$

where $(\partial \hat{u} / \partial \hat{x})$ denotes the vector $(\partial u / \partial x)$ evaluated at $\hat{x}$,

$$\hat{x}'\left[\left(\frac{\partial \hat{u}}{\partial \hat{x}}\right) - \hat{\lambda}\hat{p}\right] = 0, \tag{4.6}$$

$$\hat{\lambda}(\hat{y} - \hat{p}'\hat{x}) = 0, \tag{4.7}$$

$$\hat{x} \geqslant 0 \quad \text{and} \quad \hat{\lambda} \geqslant 0. \tag{4.8}$$

Income y is defined by

$$y - p'x = 0, \tag{4.9}$$

and $(y / \hat{y})$ is the true cost-of-living index.[18]

Inequation (4.1) and equation (4.2) imply that if for any $k = 1, 2, \ldots, n$, $(\partial u / \partial x_k) < \lambda p_k$, then $x_k = 0$. A similar implication is drawn from (4.5) and (4.6). λ and $\hat{\lambda}$ are scalar Lagrange multipliers. In (4.7), if we assume nonsatiation in consumption then the budget constraint holds with equality.

Now assume that the kth good is a new good; that is, $x_k > 0$ with $(\partial u / \partial x_k) = \lambda p_k$ and $\tilde{x}_k = 0$, where $\tilde{x}_k$ is the *actual* amount of the kth good that was purchased during the base period. If tastes have not changed, then $\hat{x}_k = \tilde{x}_k = 0$. The difficulty in this case is that there is no recorded base-period market price for the kth good. In the case of no taste change, the computation of the true cost-of-living index which allows for corner solutions is straightforward. If, for example, the kth good is a new good, the restriction $\hat{x}_k = 0$ is added to the system (4.1)–(4.9) leaving the value of $\hat{p}_k$ as an unknown to be determined in solving the new system. Or equivalently, the system (4.1)–(4.9) is solved for y after assigning to $\hat{p}_k$ any value greater than or equal to the demand reservation price (the lowest price at which demand for the kth good is zero) including the supply reservation price (the highest price at which supply of the kth good is zero) which in some sense is the price that consumers actually faced during the base period.

Note, however, that in the base-period constrained utility maximization problem, the demand reservation price itself is the maximizing value of the shadow multiplier associated with the constraint $\hat{x}_k = 0$, since by definition the demand reservation price is what the representative consumer is willing to pay per unit (locally) for a relaxation of the constraint $\hat{x}_k = 0$.[19]

As stated in section II, it is a well-known proposition in the traditional theory of index numbers (v. Hofsten, 1952, pp. 28–9) (where it is assumed that tastes and qualities are unchanging and that all goods are purchased in positive amounts) that under certain conditions the Laspeyres (base-period weighted) price index $(p'\hat{x} / \hat{p}'\hat{x})$ bounds the true cost-of-living index from above, while the Paasche (current-period weighted) price index $(p'x / \hat{p}'x)$ bounds the true cost-of-living index from below. In the case with new goods, it is obvious that the Laspeyres index bounds the true index from above and is independent of the assignment of base-period price weights to the new goods. If we allow for the complication of new goods, however, the Paasche price index is a lower bound upon the true cost-of-living index only if we assign to the new goods, base-period prices greater than or equal to the demand reservation prices. Note, however, that of all such Paasche indices the largest (and therefore in a sense the greatest lower bound on the true cost-of-living index), is the index in which new goods purchases are weighted by their demand reservation prices. (The analysis for disappearing goods is similar and is left to the reader.)

Thus, if they are known, it is the demand reservation prices themselves which should be used to weight new-goods purchases in the construction of a Paasche index and not simply some arbitrary prices equal to or greater than the demand reservation prices. In particular, *supply* reservation prices are not relevant if the demand reservation prices are known.

This is a natural result if we recall that the demand reservation price measures (locally) the value to the base-period consumer of the relaxation of the constraint stating that the good in question is unavailable. It is the shadow price of that constraint. It is thus the demand reservation price which affects how much income the consumer would be willing to give up to relax that constraint. How much income he would in fact be technologically required to give up to accomplish such relaxation (the supply reservation price) is not directly germane to a theory which runs in terms of indifferent positions. If the demand reservation price is known, the supply reservation price is not relevant.

There remains the difficult practical question as to how one knows the values of demand reservation prices. To ascertain them in general might require a rather detailed demand analysis which might not be available. There are some special circumstances, however, in which demand reservation prices may be less difficult to determine. Suppose that it was known that during a period for which closely-spaced, time-series data are available the supply reservation price of a certain good is falling. With constant tastes and qualities and all other prices constant, the price at which the good was first marketed would then be the demand reservation price. Also, since the supply reservation price is never less than the demand reservation price, supply reservation prices can be used for new goods in the Paasche index and the latter will retain its property as lower bound on the true index (but see footnote 7).

In order to study the effects of new goods on the true cost-of-living index when tastes are changing, the previous analysis can be combined with the analysis of Section III. If, for example, the first good is a new good that has experienced a positive own-augmenting taste change, if the price of the first good has fallen while all other prices have remained constant, and if demand for the first good is elastic, then by Theorems 3.2 and 3.3 the value of the true cost-of-living index is below the value of the Laspeyres index for whatever base-period prices are assigned to the new good. The Paasche index is known to be a lower bound for the true cost-of-living index if and only if the new good is assigned a base-period price greater than or equal to its demand reservation price (subject to the qualification discussed in footnote 8).

v. *Quality Change*

In this section, we take up the problem of quality change.[20] In practice, quality change is handled in the consumer price index (when it is handled at all) by assuming that an improvement in quality in a given good is equivalent to a price reduction in that good. For some cases of quality change, this is obviously the appropriate general treatment. If widgets are sold by the box and twenty widgets now are packed into the same size box as previously held ten, it is clear that this is equivalent to a halving of the price of widgets. Somewhat more generally, if one new widget delivers the same services as two old ones, this may also be considered to be simply a repackaging of widgets and thus equivalent to a price reduction.

Quality change may take other forms than that of simply augmenting the services of just that good whose quality has changed, however, and a simple adjustment of the price of that good may not suffice to account for that quality change in a cost-of-living index. Indeed, we show that such a price adjustment made independently of the amount of all goods purchased is an appropriate one if *and only if* the only effect of quality change is of the good-augmenting type just considered. Then and only then can quality change be considered a simple repackaging of the good in question.

Furthermore, while an adjustment in the price of the quality-changing good can always be made to suffice *locally* (that is, for given purchases of all goods), in general, the price adjustment which must be made will depend on all prices and purchases of all commodities and not simply on the physical characteristics of the quality change. If the new and the old qualities of the good sell in positive amount on the same (perfect) market, then all the information needed to make the appropriate *local* price adjustment for the quality change is of course coded in the difference in the prices of the two varieties. The extension of the same price adjustment to other (perhaps later) situations, however, when other prices change or other related qualities are introduced is appropriate, as stated, only in the pure repackaging case. If the two varieties do not coexist in the same (perfect) market, then even such a local price adjustment must be made to depend explicitly on the quantities of all goods purchased and not simply on physical characteristics, save in the pure repackaging case.[21]

In circumstances other than the simple repackaging case, then, we show that the simplest adjustment of the cost-of-living index may be an adjustment in the price of one or more goods *other than the one whose quality has changed.* While part of the effects of any quality change may well be to augment the services of the quality-changing good, there are likely to be other effects as well and here more than one price change is required.

Thus, for example, suppose that there is a quality change in refrigerators. If this change simply makes one new refrigerator deliver the services of some larger number of old ones, then the simplest price adjustment in the cost-of-living index is indeed an adjustment in the price of refrigerators. On the other hand, if that quality change also increases the enjoyment obtained from a quart of ice cream, then an adjustment in refrigerator price will not suffice; an adjustment in the price of ice cream is also called for. Indeed, if the *only* effect of a refrigerator quality change is to augment the enjoyment obtained from ice cream, then the simplest adjustment is one made *only* in the price of ice cream, even though the quality change takes place in refrigerators. In this case, an adjustment in the price of refrigerators can be made to suffice; the magnitude of that adjustment, however, will depend on the quantities demanded of all goods. An adjustment in the price of ice cream will also suffice; the magnitude of that adjustment, however, will only depend on the quantity of ice cream and the quantity of refrigerators.

Now, of course, this is fairly easy to see in the case of this example. Refrigerators are not directly consumed, rather, they are used as an intermediate good in the production of certain consumption goods, including cold ice cream. Thus, one can argue, since refrigerator services do not enter the utility function directly, the cost of using refrigerator services is but part of the price of the foodstuffs concerned and an improvement in refrigerator quality ought clearly to be accounted for in the prices of just those particular foodstuffs affected. If that quality improvement only changes ice cream enjoyment, then the true quality improvement is in refrigerated ice cream. An adjustment in the price of refrigerated ice cream, however, is most easily done by adjusting the price of ice cream (assuming all ice cream to be refrigerated); an adjustment in the price of refrigerators, on the other hand, affects the cost of consuming other refrigerated foodstuffs as well. Thus, in this simple example, adjustment of the price of ice cream can be made much more simply than adjustment of the price of refrigerators to achieve the same result in the cost-of-living index.

In fact, this is quite a good way to look at the matter and at our results even if refrigerator services do appear in the utility function directly, as is the case in some treatments [22] and as would certainly be the analogous case in treatments of other examples. In this case, refrigerators should *still* be looked on as an intermediate good, affecting the enjoyment of foodstuffs and also the enjoyment of its own services. As before, it is those 'final' goods whose enjoyment is affected by the quality change whose prices should be adjusted to obtain the simplest equivalent change in the cost-of-living index. The fact that one of those 'final' goods happens to have the same name and to be consumed in fixed proportions with the intermediate good does not change this statement. If this is borne in mind throughout, the interpretation of our results will be relatively straight-forward.

We now turn to the formal analysis of the problem. The current (twice differentiable) utility function is given by:

$$u = u(x_1, \ldots, x_n, b) \equiv u(x,b), \tag{5.1}$$

where b is a parameter measuring quality change in the first good, with $b = 1$ being the case of no quality change.[23] As quality change is to take place in the first good, it is natural to assume:

$$u_b(0, x_2, \ldots, x_n, b) \equiv 0, \tag{5.2}$$

where the subscript denotes differentiation with respect to b. However, we shall not make direct use of this property.[24]

As before, in the base period, the consumer has income $\hat{y}$ and faces prices $\hat{p}$. He is also constrained in that period by only being able to purchase a quality of the first commodity for which $b = 1$. The purchases which are made under these conditions are $\hat{x}$, and the corresponding utility level is:

$$\hat{u} = u(\hat{x}, 1). \tag{5.3}$$

The constraints of the present period are defined by some $b \neq 1$ and prices p. The income at which the consumer would be just indifferent between the two sets of constraints is y, and the true cost-of-living index is $y/\hat{y}$. y is thus defined as:

$$y = p'x , \tag{5.4}$$

where x is given as the solution to the problem:

$$\text{Minimize } y \text{ subject to } u(x,b) = \hat{u} . \tag{5.5}$$

x thus satisfies:

$$u(x,b) - \hat{u} = 0 \tag{5.6}$$

$$u_i - \lambda p_i = 0 \quad (i = 1, \ldots, n) ,$$

where λ is a Lagrange multiplier and is the marginal utility of income.[26]

Given $\hat{p}$ and $\hat{y}$, therefore, y is a function of p and b, and we may write:

$$y = y(p,b) . \tag{5.7}$$

Suppose now that we wish to take account of the quality change by a suitable change in the price of the first good. We thus seek a p_1^*, such that:

$$y(p_1^*,p_2,\ldots,p_n,1) = y(p_1,\ldots,p_n,b) . \tag{5.8}$$

For $b = 1$, $p_1^* = p_1$. As b changes from unity, p_1^* will change. Differentiating (5.8) totally with respect to b and rearranging, we have:

$$\frac{\partial p_1^*}{\partial b} = \frac{\partial y/\partial b}{\partial y/\partial p_1^*} . \tag{5.9}$$

We must therefore investigate $\partial y/\partial b$ and $\partial y/\partial p_1^*$.

Lemma 5.1. $\partial y/\partial b = -u_b/\lambda$.

Proof. Differentiate (5.6) totally with respect to b, obtaining

$$\begin{bmatrix} 0 & u_1 & \cdots & u_n \\ p_1 & u_{11} & \cdots & u_{1n} \\ \cdot & & & \\ \cdot & & & \\ \cdot & & & \\ p_n & u_{n1} & \cdots & u_{nn} \end{bmatrix} \begin{bmatrix} -\partial\lambda/\partial b \\ \text{------------} \\ \partial x/\partial b \\ \cdot \\ \cdot \\ \cdot \end{bmatrix} = - \begin{bmatrix} u_b \\ u_{1b} \\ \cdot \\ \cdot \\ \cdot \\ u_{nb} \end{bmatrix} , \tag{5.10}$$

where $\partial x/\partial b$ is an n-component vector whose ith element is $\partial x_i/\partial b$.

Denote the first matrix on the left by D. Then

$$
\begin{bmatrix} -\partial\lambda/\partial b \\ \text{---------} \\ \partial x/\partial b \end{bmatrix} = -D^{-1} \begin{bmatrix} u_b \\ u_{1b} \\ . \\ . \\ . \\ u_{nb} \end{bmatrix}. \tag{5.11}
$$

Now,

$$
\partial y/\partial b = p'(\partial x/\partial b) = (0 \mathrel{\vdots} p') \begin{pmatrix} -\partial\lambda/\partial b \\ \text{----------} \\ \partial x/\partial b \end{pmatrix}
$$

$$
= \frac{1}{\lambda}(0, u_1, \ldots, u_n) \begin{pmatrix} -\partial\lambda/\partial b \\ \text{----------} \\ \partial x/\partial b \end{pmatrix} \tag{5.12}
$$

in view of (5.6).

However, $(0, u_1, \ldots, u_n)$ is the first row of D and the lemma now follows immediately from (5.11) and (5.12).[26]

Lemma 5.2. $\partial y/\partial p_1 = x_1$.

Proof. Differentiate (5.6) totally with respect to p_1, obtaining:

$$
\begin{pmatrix} -\partial\lambda/\partial p_1 \\ \text{-------------} \\ \partial x/\partial p_1 \end{pmatrix} = D^{-1} \begin{bmatrix} 0 \\ \lambda \\ 0 \\ . \\ . \\ 0 \end{bmatrix}, \tag{5.13}
$$

where $\partial x/\partial p_1$ is the n-component vector whose ith element is $\partial x_i/\partial p_1$.

$$
\partial y/\partial p_1 = x_1 + p'(\partial x/\partial p_1) = x_1 + \frac{1}{\lambda}(0, u_1, \ldots, u_n) \begin{pmatrix} -\partial\lambda/\partial b \\ \text{----------} \\ \partial x/\partial b \end{pmatrix}. \tag{5.14}
$$

The lemma now follows as before, since, $(0, u_1, \ldots, u_n)$ is the first row of D.

Thus, $\partial y/\partial p_1 = x_1$. Similarly, if we substitute p_1^* for p_1 and write x_1^* for the corresponding amount of the first commodity purchased, $\partial y/\partial p_1^* = x_1^*$. It is thus clear that as long as $x_1^* \neq 0$, p_1^* is a uniquely defined function of

b (given the other elements of p). Since, at $b = 1$, $p_1^* = p_1$ no matter what the values of the other elements of p and the elements of x are, p_1^* will be independent of any subset of those elements if and only if $\partial p_1^* / \partial b$ is so independent. We therefore concentrate on the latter quantity. To avoid a burdensome notation, we always take that derivative at $b = 1$; only notational changes would be required to perform the analysis at an arbitrary b.

Combining Lemmas 5.1 and 5.2 with (5.9) and evaluating at $b = 1$, we have:

Lemma 5.3. $\quad \dfrac{\partial p_1^*}{\partial b} = \dfrac{-p_1 u_b}{x_1 u_1}.$

Proof. This follows immediately from the two preceding lemmas and (5.6).

Thus we have evaluated the adjustment which must be made in p_1 to give a result equivalent to the quality change involved in a change in b. Clearly, such an adjustment can be made (as long as $x_1 \neq 0$). That adjustment depends in general, however, on all the elements of x. Thus, in the general case, the adjustment cannot be made independent of knowledge of all purchases and the way they affect (u_b / u_1).[27] It is natural to ask under what circumstances the adjustment can be made without such knowledge or, equivalently, under what circumstances an adjustment made from market data in a given situation will retain validity when that situation changes.

Theorem 5.1. (A) A necessary and sufficient condition for $\partial p_1^* / \partial b$ to be independent of $x_2, \ldots, x_n$ is that it be possible to write the utility function in the form:

$$u(x,b) = F(g(x_1,b),x_2,\ldots,x_n) \equiv F(g^*(x_1,b)x_1,x_2,\ldots,x_n)$$

$$(5.15)$$

for some choice of continuously differentiable functions F and g.[28] We write $g(x_1,b) \equiv g^*(x_1,b)x_1$ for ease of interpretation.

(B) A necessary and sufficient condition for $\partial p_1^* / \partial b$ to be independent of *all* the elements of x (including x_1) is that (5.15) hold with g in the form:

$$g(x_1,b) = x_1 h(b) \quad \text{or} \quad g^*(x_1,b) = h(b) \qquad (5.16)$$

for some choice of the function h. (This is the pure repackaging case.)
Proof. (A) By Lemma 5.3, a necessary and sufficient condition for $\partial p_1^* / \partial b$

to be independent of $x_2, \ldots, x_n$, is that u_b/u_1 be so independent. This is equivalent to (5.15) by a well-known theorem of Leontief (1947a, p. 364; 1947b).

(B) In view of Lemma 5.3 and (A), a necessary and sufficient condition for $\partial p_1^*/\partial b$ to be independent of all the elements of x is that (5.15) hold and that, in addition, $\dfrac{u_b}{x_1 u_1}$ be independent of x_1. This means that it is necessary and sufficient that there exist a function $\phi(b)$ such that:

$$\frac{g_b}{g_1} = \frac{u_b}{u_1} = -x_1 \phi(b). \tag{5.17}$$

Now consider a curve in the $x_1 - b$ plane along which g is constant—an indifference curve of g. This is defined by:

$$g(x_1, b) = \bar{g}. \tag{5.18}$$

Differentiating (5.18) totally with respect to b and rearranging:

$$dx_1/db = -\frac{g_b}{g_1} = x_1 \phi(b) \tag{5.19}$$

along that curve. Thus:

$$d \log x_1 = \phi(b)\, db. \tag{5.20}$$

Integrating:

$$\log x_1 = \log \mu(b) + \log c, \tag{5.21}$$

where $\mu(b)$ is an integral of $\phi(b)$, and c is an arbitrary constant. In other words:

$$\frac{x_1}{\mu(b)} = c \tag{5.22}$$

is the equation of the indifference curve defined in (5.18).

Now, we can clearly replace g in (5.15) by any monotonic transformation of $\bar{g}$, adjusting the result by redefining F. Thus we can choose the scale on which g is measured and can do so in such a way as to make $\bar{g} = c$ without changing anything else. If we do this, however, the theorem follows immediately from (5.18) and (5.22), with $h(b) = 1/\mu(b)$.

Some remarks on the theorem are now in order.

First, as observed, part (B) of the theorem is the repackaging case. In this case, it might appear more natural to have b appearing in place of $h(b)$. $h(b)$ appears because the scaling of b is arbitrary. There is no reason not to measure quality change in this case in units of h rather than in units of b, in which case the more natural-appearing result is obtained.

Second, part (B) shows that the repackaging case is the *only* case in which the quality change is equivalent to a *simple* adjustment in the price of the first commodity. Any other case requires knowledge of the elements of x. Another way of putting this is to say that in any other case the adjustment in p_1 will be different at different points in the commodity space.

Third, part (A) shows that, even if we are willing to let the adjustment in p_1 depend on the quantity of the first good purchased, the class of quality changes in the first good which can be so handled is not really much widened. The only generalization is, in effect, to move to a sort of variable repackaging in which the amount of repackaging is allowed to depend on x_1. As soon as a quality change in the first commodity enters in a more general way—for example, by affecting other commodities—an equivalent adjustment in p_1 depends on other elements of x.[29]

Finally, if the conditions of part (A) hold, the dependence of the adjustment on the level of p_1 is of a very simple kind, given x_1. The *percentage* adjustment in p_1 which must be made is dependent only on x_1 in this case, since, given x_1, p_1 enters only multiplicatively in $\partial p_1^* / \partial b$. A similar remark applies to all later results in this section.

Theorem 5.1 can be generalized to give the conditions under which quality change is equivalent to an adjustment in p_1 which depends only on selected elements of x. Thus:

Theorem 5.2. (A) For any $m = 1, \ldots, n-1$, a necessary and sufficient condition for $\partial p_1^* / \partial b$ to be independent of $x_{m+1}, \ldots, x_n$, is that it be possible to write the utility function in the form:

$$u(x,b) = F(g(x_1, \ldots, x_m, b), x_2, \ldots, x_n)$$
$$\equiv F(g^*(x_1, \ldots, x_m, b)x_1, x_2, \ldots, x_n) \tag{5.23}$$

for some choice of continuously differentiable functions F and g.[30]

(B) For any $m = 1, \ldots, n-1$, a necessary and sufficient condition for $\partial p_1^* / \partial b$ to be independent of x_1 and $x_{m+1}, \ldots, x_n$ is that (5.23) hold with g in the form:

$$g(x_1, \ldots, x_m, b) = x_1 h(x_2, \ldots, x_m, b)$$
or $$g^*(x_1, \ldots, x_m, b) = h(x_2, \ldots, x_m, b), \tag{5.24}$$

for some choice of a function h.

Proof. The proof of part (A) follows again from Leontief's theorem. That of part (B) is the same as that given for part (B) of Theorem 5.1, save that the indifference variety of g is taken at fixed values of $x_2, \ldots, x_m$. The values of $x_2, \ldots, x_m$ then become parameters of $\mu(b)$.

Unfortunately, while this generalization allows us to handle a wider variety of quality change than that covered in Theorem 5.1, it still leaves us in the case of repackaging of the first commodity (although the extent of repackaging is now allowed to depend on the quantities of other commodities). It does not touch the case in which a quality change in the first commodity affects other commodities by augmenting their services, for example, the case of refrigerators and ice cream mentioned above being a case in point. This leads us to abandon the notion that simple adjustments in the price of the good whose quality has changed are likely to be generally effective and to ask whether for some quality changes adjustments in *other* prices might not be more appropriate.

Accordingly, we next examine an extreme case in which only an adjustment in the price of the second commodity is called for. There is an asymmetry in the problem. It was reasonable to ask under what conditions an adjustment in p_1 can be made independent of x_2; it is not reasonable to ask under what conditions an adjustment in p_2 can be made independent of x_1. The quality change is embodied in the first commodity and the consumer cannot take advantage of it without purchasing that commodity (see (5.2), for example). It is reasonable to ask under what circumstances an adjustment in p_2 can be made independent of the other elements of x, however, and this we shall do.

We thus replace (5.8) by:

$$y(p_1, p_2^*, p_3, \ldots, p_n, 1) = y(p_1, \ldots, p_n, b) . \tag{5.25}$$

It is clear that the argument leading to Lemma 5.3 shows:

Lemma 5.4. $\dfrac{\partial p_2^*}{\partial b} = \dfrac{-p_2 u_b}{x_2 u_2}$.

We have immediately:

Theorem 5.3. (A) A necessary and sufficient condition for $\partial p_2^* / \partial b$ to be independent of $x_3, \ldots, x_n$ is that it be possible to write the utility function in the form:

$$u(x,b) = F(x_1, g(x_1, x_2, b), x_3, \ldots, x_n)$$
$$\equiv F(x_1, g^*(x_1, x_2, b) x_2, x_3, \ldots, x_n) \tag{5.26}$$

for some choice of continuously differentiable functions F and g.[31]

(B) A necessary and sufficient condition for $\partial p_2^* / \partial b$ to be independent of $x_3, \ldots, x_n$ *and* x_2 is that (5.26) hold, with g in the form:

$$g(x_1,x_2,b) = x_2 h(x_1,b) \quad \text{or} \quad g^*(x_1,x_2,b) = h(x_1,b) \quad (5.27)$$

for some choice of a function h.

Proof. (A) follows from Lemma 5.4 and Leontief's theorem. (B) is proved as before, noting that x_1 is a parameter of the appropriate indifference curve of g in the $x_2 - b$ plane.

This is an interesting case. Whereas what was interesting about Theorem 5.1 was the necessity of the conditions, what is interesting here is sufficiency. Looked at in this way, the theorem tells us that if quality change in good one augments the services of good *two*, then a simple adjustment in the price of the latter good is called for. Once again, an adjustment can be made in this case in the price of good one, but Theorem 5.1 assures us that the adjustment will not be a simple one; it will depend on all commodity purchases. The simple adjustment is one in the price of the second good which is not the good whose quality has changed. If the only effect of a quality change in refrigerators is to make ice cream taste better, the simple adjustment which should be made is in the price of ice cream, not the price of refrigerators. The magnitude of that adjustment will depend on the quantity of refrigerators, and it may also depend on the quantity of ice cream (which is reasonable when one supposes that the effect depends on the ice cream–refrigerator ratio), but, unlike an adjustment in the price of refrigerators, it does not depend on the quantities of other goods.

Such polar cases, however, are too simple. In practice, quality change, even if it takes the relatively simple form of augmenting the services of certain goods, is unlikely merely to augment the services of only one good. A better refrigerator affects goods other than ice cream. Clearly, from Theorem 5.1 and 5.3, a simple adjustment in a single price will not suffice in such circumstances.

Fortunately, however, simple adjustments in more than one price will suffice, and this can be done by using our results simultaneously for more than one good. Thus, suppose that the utility function can be written in the form:

$$u(x,b) = F(g^1(x_1,b),g^2(x_1,x_2,b),\ldots,g^n(x_1,x_n,b)) \quad (5.28)$$

$$\equiv F(g^{*1}(x_1,b)x_1,g^{*2}(x_1,x_2,b)x_2,\ldots,g^{*n}(x_1,x_n,b)x_n)$$

for some choice of continuously differentiable functions, F and $g^1, \ldots, g^n$. This is the case in which every good is augmented, but, if $g^1(x_1, x_i, b) = x_i$ $(g^{*i}(x_1, x_i, b) = 1)$ for all b, then the augmentation of the ith good is zero (and similarly for the first good). This case contains all those turned up in Theorems 5.1 and 5.3; generalization along the lines of Theorem 5.2 is left to the reader.[32]

Since g^1 is to reflect the augmentation of the first commodity itself, it is obviously reasonable to assume that $g^1_1 \neq 0$.[33] Actually, we need only assume that x_1 is uniquely determined given b and g^1, i.e. that there exists a function ϕ, such that:

$$x_1 = \phi(g^1(x_1, b), b). \tag{5.29}$$

With this assumption, our previous results enable us to handle this relatively general case.

Theorem 5.4. If quality change satisfies (5.28) and (5.29), its effect on the true cost-of-living index can be equivalently represented as a set of price adjustments. The percentage adjustment in the first price depends at most on the amount of the first commodity; the percentage adjustment in the ith price $(i = 2, \ldots, n)$ depends at most on the amount of the first and ith commodities.[34]

Proof. In view of (5.29), every $g^i (i = 2, \ldots, n)$ can be written as a function of g^1, x_i, and b. Thus:

$$g^i(x_1, x_i, b) = h^i(g^1, x_i, b) \quad (i = 2, \ldots, n). \tag{5.30}$$

We shall break up the effect of a change in b into its effects on the various commodities, as follows. Let the b appearing as an argument of g^1 be denoted b_1; let the b appearing as an argument of h^i be denoted $b_i (i = 2, \ldots, n)$. We shall begin with all the b_i equal to unity and shall change them to their common post-quality-change value, denoted $\bar{b}$, one at a time.

Thus, set all the $b_i = 1$, save b_1 and consider the effect of changing b_1 from unity to $\bar{b}$. By (5.30), b_1 enters the utility function only through g^1, and hence the condition of (A) of Theorem 5.1 is satisfied. It follows that the effect of b_1 on y can be equivalently represented as an adjustment in p_1. That adjustment (in percentage terms) depends only on x_1 and not on the other elements of x. Further, in view of Lemma 5.3, that adjustment does not depend on the values of the $b_i (i = 2, \ldots, n)$, so there is no need to remake it when we change those values.

Now move b_2 from unity to $\bar{b}$, keeping $b_1 = \bar{b}$ and $b_i = 1$ $(i = 3, \ldots, n)$. With b_1 fixed, g^1 depends only on x_1, so that h^2 depends only on x_1, x_2, and b_2. It is clear that the condition of (A) of Theorem 5.3 is satisfied, so that the effect of the change in b_2 can be equivalently represented as an adjustment in p_2. That adjustment (in percentage terms) depends at most on x_1 and x_2, and, as before, is independent of the values of the b_i $(i = 3, \ldots, n)$.

Next, move b_3 and adjust p_3. This adjustment is independent of the other b_i $(i = 4, \ldots, n)$ and also independent of b_2. Proceeding in this way, we account for all effects of the quality change and the theorem is proved.

Thus any quality change in the first good, every effect of which can be represented as an augmentation of the services of some good[35] can be handled by adjusting in the cost-of-living index the prices of every good whose services are so augmented and *only* the prices of those goods. In the simplest case of this, given in (5.28), those adjustments (taken in percentage terms) depend at most on the quality of the first good purchased, and possibly on the purchased quantity of the good in question. These price adjustments can be made independently. More complicated cases along the lines of Theorem 5.2 can also be handled. Save in the very simplest of all cases, where only the first good itself is augmented, will a change in the price of the good whose quality has changed be sufficient. (Even then, unless the augmentation is constant, the price change will depend on the quantity of the first good that is purchased.) An adequate treatment of quality change in cost-of-living indices must pay attention to cross-good effects.[36]

ACKNOWLEDGMENTS
This research was supported by the Federal Reserve Board Committee on Prices and Price Measurement. We are indebted to Paul Samuelson and Robert Summers for helpful discussions, but we retain responsibility for error.

NOTES AND REFERENCES
[1] An exception is the theory of hedonic price indices where a quality change is regarded as providing a new bundle of old underlying attributes. See Court (1939), Griliches (1961, pp. 173–96), Lancaster (1966), and Stone (1956).

[2] Intertemporal comparisons which do not involve the same set of consumers at both times or geographical comparisons also sharply point up the problem. Following this testament to our ordinalist purity, it is only fair to remark that if the results of our work are to shed light on the construction of a cost-of-living index for a society or even a class within that society the existence of a 'representative consumer' must be assumed. In general, to draw welfare conclusions from aggregate price and quantity data requires interpersonal utility comparisons. For a full discussion of this point, see Samuelson (1947).

[3] Yet this is not inevitable. One can ask how the cost of living in the United Kingdom changed as seen with American tastes or how a man of today would view nineteenth-century price changes.

[4] As already observed, there is a further set of questions in which the tastes are neither those of today nor those of yesterday but are those of a wholly different third situation. For some purposes, these are quite interesting questions to ask, but we shall have nothing to say about them directly in this paper. When the indifference map used in the comparison is one not tied to the situations to be compared, then, of course, we are in the situation envisaged in existing theoretical treatments.

[5] In the case of international or interregional comparisons, both questions have equal interest. The fact that the answers may be quite different is then an inevitable consequence of the fact that people differ. The answer to the question: 'How much income would just make an American with income 100 willing to face British prices?' is not the same as that to the question: 'How much income would make an Englishman indifferent between continuing to face British prices and facing American prices with an income of 100?' Both questions are equally interesting, but they are obviously different. There *is* generally no one answer to both questions and no point in attempting to construct a single index which answers both. One way of looking at the analysis of the next section is as a demonstration of the way in which the answers to the two questions are related if British and American tastes differ in the particular way parametrized in that section.

[6] Note, however, that a policy choice made at the start of the process which did not foresee the taste changes would opt for path B. This is very similar to the myopia problem considered by Strotz (1955–6).

[7] In fact, this proposition is not true if price and income changes are large. This is because of yet another ambiguity in comparing today and yesterday that we have not discussed. The theory of the true cost-of-living index compares the expenditures required yesterday and today to reach a particular indifference curve on a stated indifference

map. But *which* indifference curve is to be used? The natural choices are the indifference curve tangent to yesterday's budget constraint and that tangent to today's. If the indifference map is not homothetic, however, a true cost-of-living index based on the first of these curves (Index A) will not generally coincide with that based on the second (Index B). Yet a moment's consideration reveals that it is Index A which is bounded from above by a Laspeyres index and Index B which is bounded from below by a Paasche index. Unless either the indifference map is homothetic (or obeys other special conditions) or price and income changes are sufficiently small to make Indices A and B close together, there is no reason why the Laspeyres index must lie above Index B or the Paasche index below Index A. Further, both A and B are equally valid and interesting indices.

In this paper, we have, for convenience, concentrated on Index A, that corresponding to the indifference curve tangent to yesterday's budget constraint. Most of our results are equally applicable to Index B, that corresponding to the indifference curve tangent to today's budget constraint. When reading statements about the bounds set by Paasche and Laspeyres indices, however, the discussion of this footnote should be kept in mind. The text implicitly includes the assumption that Index A and Index B do in fact coincide, and we have proceeded on the assumption that in fact the index under discussion is known to be bounded by the Paasche and Laspeyres indices for the case of no taste change. Without that assumption, statements about such bounds apply as statements about the relationship of the bounding index (Laspeyres or Paasche) to the appropriate true cost-of-living index (A or B). We have tried not to overburden the exposition by being explicit about this save in this footnote.

For a discussion of the problems just discussed see v. Hofsten (1952, pp. 28-9) or Malmquist (1953, pp. 221-3).

[8] Note that the implication is not that the true index lies closer to a Paasche index than to a Laspeyres. One does not know this. What one does know is that the Paasche puts a lower bound on changes in the true index, while a Laspeyres fails to have a known relation to it.

The asymmetry between Paasche and Laspeyres indices when tastes change is observed by Malmquist (1953, p. 211).

[9] We treat this case as being the simplest one to analyze. Further, the particular parametrization used not only appears in the theory of technological change but also reappears in the analysis of quality change given below as a result rather than an assumption. Of course, the present section is largely meant as an example of what can be done if an explicit model of taste change is adopted. The necessity for further work is obvious.

[10] Such cases as these may be somewhat more general than the sort of learning effect example given above and continued below. Thus, suppose that the first and second commodities in some sense serve the same needs, so that the utility function can be written as $v(g(bx_1,x_2),$ $x_3, \ldots, x_n)$. Then a change in b might be interpreted as a change in the relative efficiency of the first two commodities in serving those needs, as perceived by the consumer. (Of course, the special form of the utility function in this case has implications for the true cost-of-living index beyond those developed below for the more general case considered in the text.) $u(\cdot)$ serves as a utility function for current *and* base period tastes. If taste change is solely first good augmenting then the units of b can always be chosen such that the first argument can be written as x_1 in the base period. (Also notice for this section $u(\cdot)$ is a function of n arguments. This notation is inconsistent with that of later sections but no confusion should follow.)

[11] If ψ is a scalar-valued function of the vector w, then $\psi(\cdot)$ is said to be (strictly) quasi-concave if for each scalar ξ the set $\{w : \psi(w) \geqslant \xi\}$ is (strictly) convex. See Arrow and Enthoven (1961).

[12] Equation (3.10) is an instance of the class of envelope theorems frequently encountered in the constrained minimization (and maximization) problems of economics. For a discussion of envelope theorems, see Samuelson (1947, pp. 34–5).

[13] Note that there are two effects. An increase in b makes it cheaper today to attain a given utility level, but it also raises the utility level which would have been achieved with yesterday's income and prices. If we were analyzing quality change rather than taste change, only the former effect would be present.

[14] More complicated theorems can be derived from Theorem 3.1, Corollary 3.1, and Lemma 3.6 (or from Theorem 3.2 using the chain property of the true cost-of-living index). For example, we know that if demand for the first good is price elastic and its price has risen ($p_1 > \hat{p}_1$) and if we know that prices have risen for all goods that are gross complements for the first and have fallen for all goods that are gross substitutes for the first good, then we know that $(\partial y/\partial b) > 0$. (Assuming, of course, that for the relevant values of prices, all goods other than the first remain either gross complements or gross substitutes for the first good. The assumption that the sign of $\eta_{j1}, j = 2, \ldots, n$, or of $(\eta_{11}+1)$ does not change when prices change is implicit in much of the discussion that follows.)

[15] It may be thought that these results are obvious. It is natural to expect, for example, that in the situation being analyzed substitutes for the first good will decline in importance and complements will increase. While it is clear that one should indeed expect this as part of the intuitive

meaning of 'substitutes', however, it is not at all clear to us that one would automatically apply such intuition to *gross* substitutes rather than to *net* substitutes or to substitutes defined in yet some different way.

[16] As before, it is implicitly assumed that we remain in ranges of prices in which the elasticity stays on the same side of minus unity and substitute-complement relationships are not reversed.

[17] If the first good is not inferior, certain cases are ruled out. Thus, in this case, the *j*th good must be a net substitute for the first good if it is also a gross substitute. Similarly, if the demand for the first good is inelastic, $\eta_{11}^{[n}$ must be greater than -1.

[18] The systems (4.1)–(4.4), (4.9), and (4.5)–(4.8) are the well-known conditions of Kuhn-Tucker-Lagrange (K T L). The assumption of nonsatiation of consumption guarantees that if (4.1)–(4.9) is solved for y then $(y/\hat{y})$ is the true cost-of-living index. The proof of the optimality of K T L for quasi-concave programming problems with nonsatiation is given in Arrow and Enthoven (1961, pp. 783–8). Nonsatiation also implies that the equilibrium values of λ and $\hat{\lambda}$ are positive.

[19] Arrow (1958, p. 85) discusses the use of demand reservation prices in the construction of a cost-of-living index.

[20] We have already discussed the problem of deciding whether to treat a given change as one in quality or one in tastes. There is a less basic decision as to whether a change in quality should be treated as such or as the appearance of a new good and the disappearance of an old one. This decision (unlike the former one) is largely a matter of convenience. In this section, we assume that it has been made in favor of retaining the same name (or subscript) for a good before and after the change, i.e. in favor of treating the change as one in the quality of a given good.

[21] The use of hedonic price indices (see the references in note 1) is the most sophisticated way now known of using such market information to obtain price adjustments for quality change. It should come as no surprise that the extension of the results of hedonic price index investigations outside the sample period in which the market observations are made is strictly appropriate only in the repackaging case. The theory of hedonic price indices treats a new quality of a given good as a repackaging of a bundle of underlying attributes. Only if the attributes enter the utility function through the 'package' rather than directly, will hedonic price index adjustments be more than locally appropriate. Obviously, to say this is not to disparage the usefulness of hedonic price indices in practice.

[22] For many purposes it is simpler to regard refrigerator services as entering the utility function directly than it is to leave them out. Consumer theory deals with goods traded in the market place, not with later composites of them made up by consumers (such as home-refrigerated ice cream). In any case, to say that refrigerators enter directly rather than

through other goods is a matter of notation at the level of abstraction of most treatments of consumer theory.

[23] There is no reason other than one of convenience why b has to be a scalar. Quality change may take place in more than one attribute of the first good, in which case b would be replaced by $(b_1, \ldots, b_k)$ and the analysis would be essentially unchanged.

[24] It may be noted that the present problem differs from that of taste changes discussed in Section III above in that the change in the utility function is 'embodied' in the first good rather than being 'disembodied'. The parallel to models of embodied and disembodied technical change in production functions is obvious, extending the well-known parallel between the theory of the utility-maximizing consumer and the theory of the cost-minimizing firm. Indeed, some of the results of this section also parallel some of the results in the analysis of such models. We shall return to this in a later footnote.

[25] We assume that $u(\cdot)$ is a strictly quasi-concave function of its first n (non-negative) arguments and restrict our attention to interior minima.

[26] Note that the result is just that which would be obtained ignoring the effects of b on x. Thus a small unit increase in b raises u by u_b which allows a decrease in expenditure by u_b/λ, since $1/\lambda$ is the marginal cost of a unit of utility. As in the analogous case in Section III (and as in the lemma which follows), this is an envelope theorem.

[27] If the new and old varieties of the first good coexist on the same (perfect) market, however, their relative prices will code all the information needed for local adjustment. See the discussion above.

[28] It is natural to take $g(x_1,1) = x_1$, i.e. $g^*(x_1,1) = 1$, but this is not required for our results.

[29] The situation is very similar to that in models of embodied technical change in which a capital aggregate is to be formed or the effect of technical change removed by the use of a quality-corrected capital index, that is, by adjusting the prices of capital goods of different vintages. Under constant returns, technical change must be capital augmenting, analogous to part (B) of the theorem. Under a generalized form of constant returns in which the production functions are homogeneous of degree one in labor and some function of capital, technical change must be capital-altering, a kind of change analogous to the variable repackaging of part (A) of the theorem. See Fisher (1965).

[30] It is natural to take $g(x_1, \ldots, x_m, 1) = x_1$, i.e. $g^*(x_1, \ldots, x_m, 1) = 1$, but this is not required for our results.

[31] It is natural to take $g(x_1,x_2,1) = x_2 = g(0,x_2,b)$, i.e. $g^*(x_1,x_2,1) = 1 = g^*(0,x_2,1)$, but this is not required for our results.

[32] It is natural to take $g^1(x_1,1) = x_1$ and $g^i(x_1,x_i,1) = x_i = g^i(0,x_i,b)$

$(i = 2, \ldots, n)$, i.e. $g^{*1}(x_1,1) = 1$ and $g^{*i}(x_1,x_i,1) = 1 = g^{*i}(0,x_i,b)$ $(i = 2, \ldots, n)$, but this is not required for our results.

[33] If $g_1^1 = 0$ in some open neighborhood in the $x_1 - b$ plane in which $g_b^1 \neq 0$, then b enters the utility function in that neighborhood in some way other than by augmenting the services of the commodities.

[34] If g^1 takes the form of (B) of Theorem 5.3, only dependence on the first commodity is involved; if g^1 takes the form of (B) of Theorem 5.1, the percentage adjustment in p_1 is a constant.

[35] This is quite general in the small, but not in the large.

[36] Is it really much more difficult to say, for example, how the introduction of larger, more powerful cars affects the enjoyment of the services of other prestige items than it is to say how such introduction affects the enjoyment of the services of cars? Both evaluations seem hard to make, but the second one is made in practice. Admittedly, however, the second evaluation can be made implicitly through the use of market data if new and 'old' (but not necessarily used) cars sell on the same perfect market. Even then, as we have seen, that adjustment will generally only suffice while that market situation lasts.

5

Measuring the Quantities
of Fixed Factors

William M. Gorman

1. Introduction

Firms recruit and dismiss workers according to their needs. Similar workers are paid rather similar wages whoever employs them. Despite imperfections, therefore, it seems reasonable to measure labour in efficiency units, weighting each type by its wage rate, assumed to reflect its marginal productivity. Buildings and machinery are less easily shunted around. Once firms have them they are pretty well stuck with them, so they do not buy more just to meet a temporary demand. At any point of time, therefore, there is little reason to expect that the efficiency price of a certain sort of lathe, for instance, will be the same wherever it is used.

In measuring the 'quantity' of capital or any other fixed factor, then, it is dangerous to assume that it is optimally distributed: that is, to use equilibrium conditions.[1]

The central problem of aggregation outside equilibrium was raised by Klein (1946) and solved by Nataf (1948).

Nataf considered T firms, with production equations $f_t(x_t,n_t,z_t) = 0$, $t = 1,2,\ldots,T$ where x_t, n_t z_t are vectors of outputs, and labour and capital inputs respectively. He showed that aggregates $X(x_1,\ldots,x_T)$, $N(n_1,\ldots,n_T)$, $Z(z_1,\ldots,z_T)$ exist which satisfy an aggregate production equation $F(X,N,Z) = 0$, iff[2] subaggregates $X_t(x_t)$, $N_t(n_t)$, $Z_t(z_t)$ exist for each firm, in terms of which its production relation can be written $X_t = N_t+Z_t$. Assuming this to be so, the aggregate production relation can be written $X = N+Z$ where $X = \Sigma a_t X_t$, $N = \Sigma a_t N_t$, $Z = \Sigma a_t Z_t$, the a's being arbitrary positive constants.

That the quantity of capital in an economy, for instance, should be the sum of the quantities in the individual firms, is very acceptable. But what are we to make of the arbitrary weights? Or of the fact that there are many equally acceptable versions of the aggregate relationship? When one thinks of it, this is quite a reasonable phenomenon : after all, the variables in the problem do satisfy T production relations, not one, and, with them, their various combinations. Nevertheless, it makes one rather chary of searching for 'the aggregate production function'.

More disturbing still is the fact that, except for the a's, the definition of these aggregates depends entirely on the existing technology. When the technology changes, so, normally, do the definitions of output, labour and capital.[3] Indeed, if we keep to the canonical form $X = N+Z$, the aggregate production function is completely unaffected by technical change, whose only result is to change the *definition* of the aggregates which enter into it. Griliches (1963) and, more recently, Jorgenson and Griliches (1967) have argued that the fruits of technical change can be imputed largely to changes in the quality of the factors, so that more 'labour' can be extracted from a given work force, for instance, but they would hardly say that the aggregate production function, however construed, has been completely invariant in a period of technical change.

For the same reason, these aggregates will normally have little meaning outside the production sector. The total volume of production, X, for instance, will normally change when Jones produces a hundred more Rhode Island Red eggs and Edwards a hundred fewer, and this even if they use the same techniques and their eggs are indistinguishable. Since the total quantity of individual goods is normally the only link between the demand and supply side in a complete model, this is a serious disadvantage.

These difficulties were discussed by Gorman (1954), where it was shown that, if one allows the a's to depend on the prices as parameters, and if the technology is strictly convex, aggregates can be defined which depend only on the total quantities of the various goods and services produced or used, to the first order in the neighbourhood of equilibrium. To this order of approximation, indeed, they are Paasche indices – measures which are likely to have a meaning in other sectors.[4]

Despite this, Nataf's results are disturbing, not least because they show that aggregation is possible outside equilibrium only in rather special cases.

On the other hand Divisia (1928), Dresch (1938), and Richter have shown that chain base indices frequently work rather well if the productive sector is continuously in a state of instantaneous competitive equilibrium – normally a moving equilibrium of course.

Though this is unlikely for fixed inputs, it is not unreasonable for variable ones. This is the case discussed in the present paper where it is shown that the existence of variable goods and services, which earn, or are paid, their efficiency prices, makes the aggregation of fixed inputs even less likely to be possible, though the interpretation of the aggregates, when they exist, is more acceptable, since they represent the earning power of the corresponding inputs.

II. *Summary* [5]

Consider a collection of *T* productive units: firms in an industry, industries in an economy, sectors in a vintage model. For simplicity call them firms in an economy. They may produce one or more commodities. Some may be intermediate goods, produced by some firms and used by others. The same firm may be a net producer of a good in some situations, a net user in others. They may or may not fall into industries each producing a common group of goods.

Goods are of two sorts: variable and fixed. The *n variable goods* are efficiently distributed, and so have the same *efficiency prices* $p = (p_1, ..., p_n)$ everywhere.[6] The *fixed goods* may or may not be–indeed the same type of fixed input may never be used by more than one firm. While the *variable goods are measured as outputs*, inputs negative, *the fixed goods are all inputs* and will be referred to, and measured as such. They fall into classes which I will call *fixed factors*: I will use 'capital', 'land', 'equipment' and 'buildings' as examples of fixed factors from time to time. I want to find *aggregates* for these fixed factors, which I will call the *quantity of capital, of land*, etc. The *quantity of equipment*, for instance, is required to depend only on the amounts of the various types of equipment used in the individual firms. It is not required to double, for instance, when all these components do so–larger quantities may be proportionately more or less productive–nor to remain constant when a given machine is moved from one firm to another–the new firm may use it more or less efficiently than the old, and, basically what we are looking for is a measure of the productive power of the equipment in the economy, fixed in its present locations.

We distinguish, then, between *fixed inputs*, which may, for example be particular sorts of equipment or buildings, used by particular firms in given quantities, *fixed factors*, such as 'equipment', each a class of fixed inputs, and the *quantity*, e.g. *of equipment*, which may be altered if a particular machine is taken from one firm and given to another.

Let $x_t = (x_{t1}, \ldots, x_{tn})$ be the *production plan* or *net output vector* of the *t*th firm, outputs positive, inputs negative. x_{ti} is its net output of the *i*th variable good. $x = \Sigma_t x_t$ is the *production plan* or *net output vector* for the economy as a whole.

y^r is the *r*th *fixed input vector for the t*th *firm*. If the *r*th fixed factor were equipment, for instance, it would give the amounts of different sorts of equipment owned by the firm. In the case of fixed goods, there is no necessary relationship between corresponding components for different firms, so that the *r*th *fixed inputs vector* $y^r = (y_1^r, \ldots, y_T^r)$ for the economy as a whole is just a list of the corresponding vectors for the individual firms. This is because a capstan lathe, for instance, is as good as its use, and there is nothing to ensure that different firms make equally good use of it. $y_t = (y_t^1, \ldots, y_t^R)$ and $y = (y^1, \ldots, y^R)$, are the *fixed goods vectors* for the *t*th firm and the economy.

We want to find aggregates $Y(y) = (Y^1(y^1), \ldots, Y^R(y^R))$ for the R fixed factors such that the *short run production possibility set* $S(y)$, of production plans which are feasible for the economy as a whole with the fixed inputs y, can be written in the form $\tilde{S}(Y(y))$. The question is: what must the technologies of the individual firms be like for this to be possible? Now the information at the disposal of the individual firms is the prices p of the variable goods, and the quantities y_t of the fixed, available to them. It would seem a good idea, therefore, to specify their technologies in terms of these variables if possible.

Let us assume that the *short run production possibility sets* $S_t(y_t)$, $t = 1, 2, \ldots, T$ for the individual firms, corresponding to $S(y)$ defined above for the economy as a whole, are convex: that is to say that the average of any pair of feasible production plans is also feasible. The short run isoquants, then, are convex, and short run returns decreasing or at least non-increasing. This seems reasonable when we remember that the fixed inputs are fixed in the short run. In Section III it is shown that a knowledge of the *gross profit function* [7]

$$g_t(p, y_t) = \max \sum p_i x_{ti}, [8]$$

given that x_t is a feasible production plan for the *t*th firm when it has the fixed inputs y_t, is equivalent to a knowledge of $S_t(y_t)$ itself in this case.

The conditions which a function has to satisfy in order to be acceptable as a gross profit function are found,[9] and it is shown that $g_t(p,y_t)$ is homogeneous of degree one in y_t iff there is constant returns to scale in the long run, and concave in y_t iff the long run production possibility set is convex.

It is also shown that the optimal production plane is $x_t = g_t'(p,y_t)$ $= (g_{t1}, \ldots, g_{tn})$, when the differential coefficients $g_{ti} = \partial g_t / \partial p_i$ exist, and that the formula continues to hold with a slightly generalized definition of g_t' when they do not.

In Section IV the regularity conditions required for the main analysis are introduced. On the whole these are rather weak: for instance the set over which aggregates are assumed to exist need not be a simple one like the positive orthant, some firms may never use some of the fixed factors, and differentiability is nowhere assumed. However, the aggregates do have to be assumed to be continuous. This is necessary in order to rule out certain trick aggregates which merely transcribe the entire vector y^r in a new code. Nevertheless one would prefer not to assume continuity in a field where lumpiness is so common, if it were avoidable.

The main result in the paper is proved in Section V.

It is easily seen that $S(y) = \tilde{S}(Y(y))$ – so that the short run production possibilities for the economy as a whole depend only on the aggregates $Y(y) = (Y^1(y^1), \ldots, Y^R(y^R))$ – iff the gross profit function for the economy as a whole

$$\Sigma g_t(p,y_t) = G(p,Y(y)), \text{ say.} \tag{1}$$

Let us now define the quantity $Y_t^r(y_t^r)$ of the rth fixed factor in the tth firm by its earning power there at certain base prices q:[10] that is,

$$Y_t^r(y_t^r) = g_t(q,0,\ldots,0,y_t^r,0,\ldots,0) - g_t(q,0).\text{[11]} \tag{2}$$

It is shown that we can take the corresponding aggregate for the economy as a whole in (1) to be

$$Y^r(y^r) = \Sigma_t Y_t^r(y_t^r), \tag{3}$$

the total earning power of the fixed inputs y^r in the economy, and that, in this notation, we can write the gross profit functions in the form

$$g_t(p,y_t) = G_t(p,Y_t(y_t)) = \Sigma c^r(p)Y_t^r(y_t^r) + d_t(p).\text{[12]} \tag{4}$$

for each firm, and

$$\Sigma g_t(p,y_t) = G(p,Y(y)) = \sum c^r(p)Y^r(y^r) + d(p),\ ^{12} \tag{5}$$

where $d = \Sigma d_t$, of course, for the economy as a whole. Since (4) clearly implies (5) which implies (1), it is both necessary and sufficient for it.

I will call the functions $G_t(p, Y_t)$ and $G(p, Y)$ *quasi gross profit functions* because they are defined in terms of the fictional 'quantities' of the fixed factors instead of the actual fixed inputs. They have the same formal properties as ordinary gross profit functions. Similarly I will talk of *quasi production possibility sets* $\tilde{S}_t(Y_t)$, $\tilde{S}(Y)$, and *quasi technologies*, and will say that a firm, or the economy as a whole, produces under *quasi constant returns* if doubling the quantities of the *fixed factors* at its disposal, just permits it to double its net output of each of the variable goods. This does not imply, of course, that it produces under true constant returns, since doubling the fixed inputs need not double the quantities of the fixed factors.[13] According to (4) and (5) the tth firm produces under quasi constant returns iff $d_t(p) = 0$, and the economy as a whole iff $d(p) = 0$.

These results are interpreted in Section VI and VII: the former dealing with the aggregates, the latter with the quasi gross profit functions.

I will summarize the two sections as a unit.

We have already seen that (4) implies that the production possibilities facing the economy as a whole depend only on the total quantities $Y = \Sigma_t Y_t$ of the fixed *factors*. They are therefore the same however these are distributed over the firms: that is the market for the variable goods guarantees that any given distribution of the fixed factors is just as productive as any other – that is, that it is efficient. In fact it is easily shown that $c^r(p)$ is the efficiency price of the rth fixed factor: it is automatically the same in all the firms. It is also the extra profits which an extra unit of the factor will earn any of the firms. Since $c^r(q) = 1$ this confirms that the quantities of the factors are measured in terms of their earning power at these base prices.

Why is this so?

We have already seen that the optimal production plan of a firm is got by differentiating its gross profit function.[14] (4) and (5) therefore yield

$$x_t = \Sigma c^{\prime r}(p)Y_t^r + d_t'(p),\quad x = \Sigma c^{\prime r}(p)Y^r + d'(p), \tag{6}$$

where the primes represent vectors of derivatives. Hence the gift of an extra unit of the rth factor will cause whichever firm gets it to change its production plans in exactly the same way as it would any other [15] and will therefore earn it just the same increase in its profit.

This is serious. Suppose 'equipment' is one of the factors and that a heavy press represents just as much extra equipment to one firm as ten typewriters to another. The gift of the heavy press to it would induce it to change its production of all the variable goods–and use of all the variable inputs–by precisely the same amounts as that of the ten typewriters would the other.

The aggregation of fixed goods, of which capital aggregation is a particular example, is therefore very unlikely to be justified in an economy as a whole, at least with theoretically interesting definitions of the fixed factors. It is perhaps more acceptable for single industries, or, for models of the economy in which the variable goods are themselves highly aggregated, as in vintage capital models, for instance.

Another interpretation of (4)–(6) is as follows: each firm has $(r+1)$ plants, yielding profits $c^1(p)Y_t^1, \ldots, c^R(p)Y_t^R, d_t(p)$, and producing outputs $c'^1(p)Y_t^1, \ldots, c'^R(p)Y_t^R, d_t'(p)$. This interpretation is not always strictly justified, but it is shown in Section VII that it frequently is. The rth plant in each firm, having the same quasi gross profit function, has the same quasi technology, which clearly yields quasi constant returns. The base plants, corresponding to the $d_t(p)$, presumably use fixed factors, specific to the firm itself, and may differ as much as we like among themselves.

These plants are of course only theoretical constructs–normally fictions without physical analogues.

In terms of the quasi technologies, defined in terms of the fixed factors rather than the fixed inputs, these are the only differences between the firms; even these disappear if all the firms [16] produce under quasi constant returns, because each $d_t(p) \equiv 0$, then.

The other way in which firms can differ is, of course, in their aggregation functions

$$Y_t^r(\cdot).\,[17] \tag{7}$$

We have already seen that the quantities of the fixed factors are *measured* in terms of their earning power. They may be *interpreted* either as indices of the quantities of the corresponding fixed inputs or as quantities of fictitious intermediate goods produced from the corresponding fixed inputs in the firms' *fixed factor producing plants* with the production functions (7).

If so we may say that the firms differ only in these plants and in their basic plants, introduced above, their *fixed factor using plants* being identical. I prefer this interpretation in general, because there is no reason why the Y_t^r should double when the corresponding inputs y_t^r do, and there goes my notion of what an acceptable index number should be like.

In one leading case, however, the $Y_t^r(\cdot)$ are homogeneous of the first degree – that in which each of the firms produces under genuine constant returns. In that case, therefore, either interpretation is equally acceptable: in the 'intermediate goods interpretation' we would say that the fixed factors were produced under constant returns. Incidentally the firms also produce under quasi constant returns then, so that they all have the same quasi technology, and so differ only in their factor producing plants.

What about the substitutability relations among the inputs?

Suppose that there are only two variable goods – one an output, the other an input – and let us say that two inputs are complements if increasing the quantity of one increases the marginal product of the other, and substitutes if it decreases it. We see in VII that the fixed factors can be divided into two groups according to whether they are substitutes for, or complements of, the variable input, and that factors in the same group are substitutes, in different groups, complements. The same is true of the corresponding inputs.

III. *Preliminaries: the Gross Profit Function*
Each of the T firms introduced in II is assumed to maximize its gross profit $p \cdot x_t$, given the prices p of the variable goods and quantities y_t of the fixed. More precisely, it choses a *production plan* x_t in its *short run production possibility set* $S_t(y_t)$ to maximize $p \cdot x_t$.

Neglect t and y_t for the moment, since we will be holding them constant in any case, and define the *gross profit function*

$$g(p) = \sup\{p \cdot x : x \in S\}, \quad \text{each } p \in R^n \ ^{18} \tag{8}$$

so that $g(\cdot)$ is
G1 *positively homogeneous of degree one: $g(kp) = kg(p)$, each $k \geq 0$*
G2 *closed convex:* that is
$$U = \{(p,u) : u \geq g(p)\} \text{ is a closed convex set.} \tag{9}$$
Clearly G1–2 are equivalent to
$$U \text{ is a closed convex cone.} \tag{10}$$

Clearly, too,

$$U = \{(p,u): u \geqslant p \cdot x, \quad \text{each } x \in S\}$$
$$= \{(p,u): -zp \cdot x + zu \geqslant 0, \quad \text{each } x \in S, \quad z \geqslant 0\}$$
$$= Z^+, \tag{11}$$

the polar cone [19] of the cone

$$Z = \{(-zx,z): x \in S, \quad z \geqslant 0\}. \tag{12}$$

Whatever the prices, no feasible plan can yield more than $g(p)$. Hence $S \subseteq S^*$, where

$$S^* = \{x: p \cdot x \leqslant g(p), \quad \text{each } p\} = \{x: p \cdot x \leqslant u,$$
$$\text{each } (p,u) \in U\}. \tag{13}$$

In fact

$$S^* \text{ is the convex closure of } S, \tag{14}$$

for

$$\{(-zx,z): x \in S^*, z \geqslant 0\} = U^+ = Z^{++}, \tag{15}$$

which is the convex closure of the cone Z by a well known theorem.[19]

(14) implies that

$$S = S^* \tag{16}$$

iff

S1 S is closed

S2 S is convex.

In the case of *short run* production possibility sets $S_t(y_t)$, S1–2 is a reasonable assumption. The fixed inputs being taken as given, the possibility of increasing returns to scale need not worry us. From now on I will assume S1–2, as well as

S0 S is not empty

for such sets for each individual firm, and hence for the economy as a whole, except where I specify the contrary.

According to (13) and (16), therefore, knowledge of the gross profit function is equivalent to that of the production possibility set, both for the individual firms and the economy as a whole.[20]

Suppose now that we are given a function $g(\cdot)$ which may or may not satisfy G1–2; that is, which may or may not be an *admissible gross profit function*. Define U as in (9), S^* as in (13), $g^*(\cdot)$ from S^* and U^* from $g^*(\cdot)$, as in (8) and (9). Then, easily

$$U^* = U^{++}, \tag{17}$$

the closure of the convex cone spanned by U, so that $U^* = U$, or equivalently

$$g^*(p) = g(p), \quad \text{each } p, \tag{18}$$

iff (10), or, equivalently G1-2. That is (18) holds only for admissible gross profit functions.

S*, as the intersection of a collection of closed half spaces is always closed and convex. Moreover, $U^* = U^{++}$, being a closed convex cone. $g^*(\cdot)$ is always an admissible gross profit function.

Return now to the case where $g(\cdot)$ is an admissible gross profit function. The set

$$R = \{p : g(p) < \infty\} \qquad (19)$$

is a convex cone by G1,2. Because $g(\cdot)$ is closed convex it can be shown that

$g(\cdot)$ is continuous, and has second order partial derivatives almost everywhere, in Int R.[21]   (20)

$g(p) = \lim \inf \{g(q) : q \to p\}$ everywhere.   (21)

We have not so far enquired whether the supremum in (8) is attained. If it is, however, there exists an *optimal production plan* $x \in S$ such that

$$x \cdot p = g(p). \qquad (22)$$

(22) holds at all prices at which x is optimal, while

$$x \cdot q \leqslant g(p), \qquad (23)$$

whether or not x is optimal at q. Hence

$$\phi(q;x) = g(q) - x \cdot q \qquad (24)$$

is minimized with respect to q when $q = p$, and then takes the value zero. Because of (13) and (16), moreover, (22) and (23) imply that $x \in S$. They are therefore both necessary and sufficient for x to be an optimal plan at prices p.

In seeking to characterize these optimal plans explicitly–that is, to find the *supply function*–let us first assume that g is differentiable. Then

$$x = g'(p) = (g_1(p), \ldots, g_n(p)), \qquad (25)$$

where $g_i = \partial g / \partial p_i$. $g'(p)$ is the *gradient* of g at p: that is $(-1, g'(p))$ is the unique normal to $u = g(p)$ there. Since $g(\cdot)$ is convex this local extremum is a global minimum, and since it is positively homogeneous of the first degree, $g = p \cdot q' = \Sigma p_i g_i$ so that (22), and therefore (23), are indeed satisfied; and (25) is indeed both necessary and sufficient for x to be optimal at p.

In general $g(\cdot)$ may not be differentiable. Since $g(q)$ is convex, however, so is $\phi(q,x) = g(q) - x \cdot q$, so that its maximum is attained wherever it has a horizontal tangent plane. That is, where $u = g(q)$ has a tangent plane parallel to $u = x \cdot q$, or, equivalently, where it has a normal parallel to $(-1, x)$. At any such point p

$$g(q) - g(p) \geqslant x \cdot (q - p) \tag{26}$$

because of the convexity of $g(\cdot)$. Setting $q = (k+1)p$, and remembering that $g(\cdot)$ is positively homogeneous of degree one by G1, we see that $kg(p) \geqslant kx \cdot p$, $k \geqslant -1$, which implies (22), and, through (26), (23). If, therefore, we define a *gradient* $\psi'(q)$ at q *of any convex function*, $\psi(q)$, as any vector such that $(-1, \psi'(q))$ is normal to $v = \psi(q)$ at q, we see that (25) remains a necessary and sufficient condition for x to be optimal at p in the non-differentiable case also.

The question of the existence of optimal plans, or equivalently of the attainment of the supremum in (8), is equivalent to that of the existence of a gradient $g'(p)$ of $g(\cdot)$ at p. There are three cases:

(i) $p \notin R$.

$g(p) = \infty$ and there exists an unbounded sequence $\{x^m\}$ in S, such that $p \cdot x^m \to \infty$.

(ii) $p \in \text{Int } R$.

The supremum is attained at a finite point $x \in S$. Otherwise the continuity of $p \cdot x$ in x and the closedness of S would imply the existence of an unbounded sequence $\{x^m\}$ in S such that $p \cdot x^m$ is monotonically increasing. It has a subsequence such that $x_i^m \to +\infty$, $i = 1, \ldots, r$, $x_i^m \to -\infty$, $i = r+1, \ldots, r+s$, $r, s > 0$. Take δ as a vector whose first r components are $+\varepsilon$, next s, $-\varepsilon$, and remainder zero, $\varepsilon > 0$. Then $(p+\delta) \cdot x^m - p \cdot x^m = \delta \cdot x^m \to \infty$. However $p + \delta \in R$ for sufficiently small ε, so that $(p+\delta) \cdot x^m \leqslant g(p+\delta) < \infty$. Hence $p \cdot x^m \to -\infty$, and so is not monotonically increasing.

(iii) $p \in R \cap$ *frontier of R*.

If the supremum in (8) is attainable at a finite x, it can be shown that the optimal facet is unbounded.[22] 'Infinite' plans may not be necessary for maximum profits, therefore, but there is always one which is at least as good as any finite plan.

To summarize. Outside R no finite plan is optimal, inside R there is always an optimal finite plan and all infinite plans are 'infinitely bad', on the frontier of R, there may or may not be optimal finite plans; but, in any case, there are always 'infinite' plans at least as good as any of them.

Once we know R, then, we might as well confine our attention to it. If

S3   *there is free disposal:* $x \in S$ if $x \leqslant x^* \in S$

it would clearly be indefinitely profitable to buy indefinitely large quantities at negative prices. Hence

G3   *R is contained in the positive orthant.*[23]

All these functions and sets should really have t and y_t as arguments, and have direct analogues for the economy as a whole. I wish now to discuss the long run production possibilities and so will introduce the quantities of fixed goods y as an argument in the short run concepts just discussed. I will continue to suppress t.

The *long run production possibility set* is

$$S = \{(x,y) : x \in S(y), \quad y \in \Omega, \text{ say}\}\ [24] \tag{27}$$

so that

$$S(y) = \{x : (x,y) \in S\}, \quad \text{each } y \in \Omega. \tag{28}$$

(8), (13) and (16) immediately imply that there are *constant returns to scale* iff

G4 $g(p,\cdot)$ *is positively homogeneous of degree one* [25]

$g(p,ky) = kg(p,y)$ each $k > 0$, y, $ky \in \Omega$.

The long run production possibility set is itself convex iff

G5 $g(p,\cdot)$ *is concave on* Ω,

given of course that

Ω4 Ω *is convex.*

To see this, observe first that, if $x \in S(y)$ and $x^* \in S(y^*)$, then $\frac{1}{2}(x+x^*) \in S(\frac{1}{2}(y+y^*))$ if S is convex. Hence

$$g(p,\tfrac{1}{2}(y+y^*)) \geqslant \tfrac{1}{2}(g(p,y)+g(p,y^*)). \tag{29}$$

If S is not convex, on the other hand, one can find $x \in S(y)$, $x^* \in S(y^*)$ such that $\frac{1}{2}(x+x^*) \notin S(\frac{1}{2}(y+y^*))$. Since $S(\frac{1}{2}(y+y^*))$ satisfies $S(0-2)$, (13) and (16) imply the existence of a p such that

$$g(p,\tfrac{1}{2}(y+y^*)) < \tfrac{1}{2}(x+x^*) \cdot p \leqslant \tfrac{1}{2}(g(p,y)+g(p,y^*)), \tag{30}$$

which completes the proof.

If

G6 $g(p,\cdot)$ *is strictly concave on* Ω,

where Ω satisfies Ω4, S is strictly convex by (13) and (16) applied to $S(\frac{1}{2}(y+y^*))$, because the weak inequality in (29) becomes strict.

Consider finally the *long run profit function*

$$h(p,q) = \sup \{p \cdot x - q \cdot y : (x,y) \in S\} \qquad (31)$$
$$= \sup \{g(p,y) - q \cdot y : y \in \Omega\},$$

where q is the vector of efficiency prices for the fixed goods. Under decreasing returns $g(p,\cdot)$ is concave. An argument similar to that leading up to (25) shows that

$$q = \dot{g}_2(p,y) = \text{gradient of } g(p,y) \text{ with respect to } y. \qquad (32)$$

If $g(p,\cdot)$ is differentiable but not concave, (32) is the first order condition for maximum profits, but some of the q it yields will correspond to other extrema and will not be true efficiency prices.

Being a profit function, $h(\cdot,\cdot)$ is of course positively homogeneous and closed concave.

IV. *Preliminaries: Formal Statement of the Problem*

We want to be able to write the short sum production possibility set for the economy as a whole in the form

$$S(y) = \tilde{S}(Y(y)), \quad \text{each } y \in \Omega, \qquad (33)$$

say, where

$$\text{Y1} \qquad Y(y) = (Y^1(y^1), \ldots, Y^R(y^R)), \quad \text{each } y \in \Omega,$$

is a vector whose rth component measures the '*quantity of the rth factor*' in the economy as a whole.

I will consider the case where

$$\Omega 1 \qquad \Omega = \Pi_r' \Omega_t^r = \Pi^r \Omega^r = \Pi_t \Omega_t$$

in the obvious notation, [26]

$\Omega 2$ *each Ω^r is nonempty, closed and tube-connected and is bounded below* [27]

$\Omega 3$ *for each factor r, the set*
    $T(r) = \{t : \Omega_t^r \text{ has more than one element}\}$
    contains more than one firm t. [28]

The import of these rather weak restrictions is discussed in the footnotes. In a sense (33) is always true ![29]

To see this: consider any strictly increasing mapping $y^r \to z^r$, where the $N(r)$ components of z^r are nonterminating decimals between zero and one.[30] Define Y^r to be another such decimal, having the first figure of z_1^r in its first place, the first of z_2^r in its second, ..., the first of $z_{N(r)}^r$

in its $N(r)$th, the second of z_1^r in its $N(r)+1$th, ... Clearly we can reconstruct z^r, and therefore y^r, from Y^r, so that we can write the short run production possibility set $S(y)$ in the form $\bar{S}(Y(y))$ whatever the technology. Trick aggregates such as these clearly should be excluded. It is not sufficient to require that admissible aggregates be increasing functions of their arguments, since the trick aggregates are actually strictly increasing. Continuity is the important thing. Accordingly I will require

Y2   *each $Y^r(y^r)$ is continuous in y^r and strongly increasing in each y_t^r*,[31]

so that the range of each $Y^r(\cdot)$ is an interval I^r [32] by $\Omega 1$–2.

Finally I will need

G7   *For some prices q, each $g_t(q,y_t)$ is continuous in y_t and strongly increasing in each y_t^r.*

The import of these requirements, too, is discussed in the footnotes. They are pretty weak.[33]

(8), (13) and (16) immediately imply that (33) holds iff

$$g(p,y) = \Sigma_t g_t(p,y_t) = G(p,Y(y)), \qquad \text{each } y \in \Omega, p. \qquad (34)$$

Clearly G7 implies that

$g(q,y)$ is continuous in y and strongly increasing in each y_t^r,

each $y \in \Omega$.   (35)

With $\Omega 1$–3 and Y1–2, it also implies

$G(q, Y)$ is continuous and strictly increasing in Y,

each $Y \in I = \Pi^r I^r$. [34]   (36)

The proof of (36) is a little technical, and far from our main concerns, so that it is not given here. Those who doubt its validity may prefer to take (36) as a separate requirement – surely an acceptable one.

Our problem now is: given $\Omega 1$–3, Y1–2, G1–2 and G7, under what further conditions does (34) hold?

It will be discussed in the next section.

v. *The Main Theorem*

Theorem: Given $\Omega 1$–3, and Y1–2 and G7, we can write

$$g(p,y) = \Sigma g_t(p,y_t) = G(p,Y(y)), \qquad \text{each } y \in \Omega, p \qquad (37)$$

iff

there exist continuous and strongly increasing subaggregates

$Y_t^r(y_t^r)$, each r, t [35]   (38)

such that

$$g_t(p,y_t) = G_t(p,Y_t(y_t)) = H(p,Y_t(y_t)) + d_t(p) \qquad (39)$$

say all $y_t \in \Omega_t$, p where $Y_t = (Y_t^1, \ldots, Y_t^R)$ and, under an appropriate normalization, which will be used throughout the remainder of this statement of the theorem,

$$Y(y) = \Sigma_t Y_t(y_t) \qquad (40)$$

$$H(p, Y+Z) = H(p, Y) + H(p,Z) \text{ when } Y, Z, Y+Z \in I \quad (41)$$
$$g(p,y) = G(p, Y(y)) = H(p, Y(y)) + d(p), \qquad (42)$$

where

$$d(p) = \Sigma_t d_t(p). \qquad (43)$$

Proof. The sufficiency of (38)–(43) is obvious. I will prove their necessity. Y1–2 and Ω1–2 imply that each $Y^r(y^r)$ attains its minimum value at some point $b^r \in \Omega^r$. Define

$$Y_t^r(y_t^r) = g_t(q, b_t^1, \ldots, y_t^r \ldots, b_t^R) - g_t(q, b_t), \qquad \text{each } t, r \quad (44$$

in the obvious notation, where q is the price vector introduced in G7. Because of G7, these subaggregates, measuring the quantities of the various factors employed in the individual firms, satisfy (38). They have ranges

$$I_t^r = [0, a_t^r], \qquad \text{each } t, r, \text{ say}. \qquad (45)$$

According to (37)

$$G(q, Y^1(b^1), \ldots, Y^r(y^r), \ldots, Y^R(b^R)) -$$
$$- G(q, Y^1(b^1), \ldots, Y^r(b^r), \ldots, Y^R(b^R))$$
$$= \Sigma_t Y_t^r(y_t^r) = Y_r^*(y^r), \qquad \text{say.} \qquad (46)$$

Solve (46) for Y_r in terms of Y_r^* as we can by (36), to get $G(p, Y) = G^*(p, Y^*)$ say, where G^* and Y^* still satisfy Y1,2 and (36). Drop the asterisks to get (37) and (40) in this normalization.

Now vary y_t, if possible, keeping $Y_t(y_t)$ and y_s, $s \neq t$, constant. $g_t = G - \sum_{s \neq t} g_s$ remains unchanged. Hence

$$g_t(p,y_t) = G_t(p, Y_t(y_t)), \qquad (47)$$

say, so that, by (37),

$$G(p, Y(y)) = \Sigma_t G_t(p, Y_t(y_t)) \qquad (48)$$

and, therefore,

$$G_t(p,Y_t) - G_t(p,0) = G(p,Y_t) - G(p,0) = H(p,Y_t) , \qquad (49)$$

say. This immediately yields (39), (42) and (43), where

$$d_t(p) = G_t(p,0) = g_t(p,b_t) , \quad d(p) = G(p,0) = g(p,b) \qquad (50)$$

and, with (48)

$$H(p,\textstyle\sum Y_t) = \sum H(p,Y_t) , \quad \text{each } Y_t \in I_t = \Pi' I_t^r, \quad \text{each } t .$$
$$(51)$$

(51) does not imply (41) immediately since we only proved it when $Y_t^r \in I_t^r = [0, a_t^r\rangle$, each t, r.

Let us first prove (41) for a single firm. That is

$$H(p,Y_t + Z_t) - H(p,Y_t) = H(p,Z_t); \qquad Y_t, Z_t, Y_t + Z_t \in I_t . \qquad (52)$$

Since $H(0) = 0$ by (49), the two sides of (52) are certainly equal when $Y_t = 0$. I will show that they are for any $\tilde{Y}_t \in I_t$ such that $\tilde{Y}_t + Z_t \in I_t$ also. We can increase Y_t to $\tilde{Y}_t$ from 0 by increasing Y_t^1 to $\tilde{Y}_t^1$ first, then Y_t^2 to $\tilde{Y}_t^2, \ldots$ then Y_t^R to $\tilde{Y}_t^R$. I will do so, showing that $H(p, Y_t + Z_t) - H(p, Y_t)$ remains constant, and hence equal to $H(p, Z_t)$, throughout.

First notice that

$$H(p,Y_t + Z_t) - H(p,Y_t) = H(p, Y + Z_t) - H(p, Y) , \qquad (53)$$

where each $Y^r \in I^r = \Sigma^t I_t^r$. Begin with each $Y_t^r = 0$ and each $Y_s^r = d_s^r$, $= \min(\cdot 9 a_s^r, 1)$, $s \neq t$. $\Omega 3$ ensures the existence of at least one $d_s^r > 0$, each r. Increase Y_t^1 from 0 to $\tilde{Y}_t^1$ or $\sum_{s \neq t} d_s^1$, whichever is the smaller, dropping Y_s^1, $s \neq t$, towards zero in such a way as to keep Y constant. The right-hand sides of (52) and (53) are unaffected by these changes: hence, too, their common left-hand side. (52) therefore continues to hold.

If $\tilde{Y}_t^1 \leqslant \sum_{s \neq t} d_s^1$, we now move to the second factor $r = 2$. If not, we next change Y_s^1 back to d_s^1, $s \neq t$, keeping $Y_t^1 = \sum_{s \neq t} d_s^1$. This affects neither side of (52), and we are now in a position to increase Y_t^1 once more, reducing the other Y_s^1 to keep Y constant.

Repeating such moves as often as necessary we finally bring Y_t^1 to $\tilde{Y}_t^1$ without affecting either side of (52), which therefore continues to hold. Doing this for each factor r in turn, we finally get (52) with $Y_t = \tilde{Y}_t$. Since $\tilde{Y}_t, Z_t$ are any pair of vectors satisfying the conditions of (52), this proves that equation in general. This proves (41) for each individual firm. Now I will prove (41) for the economy as a whole. Take any Y, Z

satisfying the conditions of (41). They can be written $Y = \Sigma Y_t$, $Z = \Sigma Z_t$ where the Y_t, Z_t satisfy those of (52). (51) therefore implies

$$H(p,Y+Z)-H(p,Y)-H(p,Z) = \Sigma(H_t(p,Y_t+Z_t) -$$
$$-H(p,Y_t)-H(p,Z_t))$$
$$= 0 \qquad \text{by (52).}$$

(38)–(43) are therefore necessary for (37). Their sufficiency is obvious.

Corollary 1: (41) is a well-known functional equation. Under any of many alternative assumptions, it is equivalent to

$$H(p,Y) = \Sigma^r c^r(p) Y^r. \qquad (54)$$

The one which seems most natural in our case is that,

G8 $\qquad H(p, Y) = G(p, Y) - G(p,0) \geqslant 0 \quad$ each p, $Y \in I$.

Given $\Omega 1$–3, Y1–2, G7–8, then (37) is equivalent to: (38), (40), (43) *and*

$$g_t(p,y_t) = G_t(p,Y_t(y_t)) = \Sigma^r c^r(p) Y_t^r(y_t^r) + d_t(p) \qquad (55)$$

$$g(p,y) = G(p,Y(y)) = \Sigma^r c^r(p) Y^r(y^r) + d(p). \qquad (56)$$

(44), (50) and (55) immediately imply that

$$c^r(q) = 1, \qquad \text{each } r. \qquad (57)$$

VI. *Interpretation of the Aggregates*

Looking first at the formal definition

$$Y_t^r(y_t^r) = g_t(q,b_t^1,\ldots,b_t^{r-1},y_t^r,b_t^{r+1},\ldots,b_t^R) - g_t(q,b_t) \qquad (58)$$

in (44), we see that the quantities of the fixed factors are measured in terms of their earning power at the base prices q. In general, indeed, (55) shows that an extra unit of the rth factor earns the firm lucky enough to get it £$c^r(p)$ at prices p. At the base prices q it earns it £1 by (57).

This 'explains' why the quantities of the fixed factors held by different firms add up, so that

$$Y^r(y^r) = \Sigma^t Y_t^r(y_t^r). \qquad (59)$$

They represent profit earning capacity, and the profits earned by the individual firms add up to the total profits in the economy as a whole.

That the quantity of a fixed factor in the economy should be the sum of the quantities in the individual firms, is highly acceptable, as it is that

$$Y_t^r(\cdot) \text{ is continuous and strongly increasing, each } t,r \qquad (60)$$

as we know from (38).

It would be pleasant, too, if the quantity of a factor were to double, when that of each of the corresponding inputs did so: in general, that is, if

$$Y_t^r(\cdot) \text{ were positively homogeneous of degree one.} \qquad (61)$$

It seems clear that this would happen if there were constant returns to scale, since each added consignment of fixed inputs would be combined with the same variable goods to yield the same increase in profits. We will see later in this section that this is indeed so, so that (61) holds as well as (59) and (60) if each firm works under constant returns to scale.

(59) (60) and (61) comprise between them almost everything which we might wish to require of such measures. The difficulty remains, however, that the aggregates are tied to the particular technology, as in Nataf's case, and that the quantity of the fixed factors in the economy as a whole depends on the distribution of the fixed inputs among the firms, and not just on the total quantity of each of them.[36] The discussion in II makes it clear that this must be so: there are no market forces to ensure that each firm makes equally profitable use of the fixed inputs, because there is no arrangement for mutually profitable exchange of such inputs between the firms. Moreover, the fixed inputs really are *given* in our model, so that there is no question of having to explain them in a wider model of the economy as a whole, in which the demand for them by these firms is faced by a supply from their producers, the only meeting point being the total quantity of each fixed input.

Note, by the way, the absence of Nataf's arbitrary weights in this case. This is due to the fact that the profits of different firms do naturally add up.

There are two natural ways in which we can think of these aggregates: as index numbers of the quantities of the corresponding inputs, or as quantities of the factors, thought of as 'intermediate goods' produced from these with production functions

$$Y_t^r(y_t^r) , \qquad \text{each } t, r \qquad\qquad (62)$$

for individual firms or for the economy as a whole

$$Y^r(y^r) = \Sigma_t Y_t^r(y_t^r) .$$

Either interpretation is perfectly acceptable under constant returns, where (61) holds as well as (59) and (60). However, (61) does not hold in general, and the idea that an index number should double when each of its component series does, seems fundamental to me. In general, therefore, I prefer the 'intermediate good' interpretation, which has the further advantage that the fictitious industries producing these intermediate goods can be introduced into complete models, should one after all wish to determine the *given* Y_t^r.

It will be convenient to write the gross profit functions of the individual firms and the economy as a whole in terms of these fictitious intermediate goods as

$$G_t(p,Y_t) = \Sigma c^r(p) Y_t^r + d_t^{\cdot}(p) \tag{63}$$

$$G(p,Y) = \Sigma c^r(p) Y^r + d(p) \tag{64}$$

as we can by (55) and (56), where, of course

$$Y = \Sigma Y_t, \qquad d = \Sigma d_t. \tag{65}$$

I will call these *quasi gross profit functions*, because they are defined in terms of the fictitious fixed factors instead of the genuine fixed inputs. Similarly, we have the *quasi production possibility sets* $\tilde{S}_t(Y_t)$, $\tilde{S}(Y)$ as against the *production possibility sets* proper $S_t(y_t)$, $S(y)$, *quasi technologies*, and where appropriate, *quasi production functions*.

Because of (64) and (65) the quasi gross profits in the economy as a whole are unchanged if we shift fixed factors about among the firms, keeping the totals constant.[37] Since this quasi gross profit function defines the quasi production possibility set $\tilde{S}(Y)$ for the economy as a whole, this, too, is unaffected. Hence each of the firms must use the fixed *factors* – as contrasted with the fixed *inputs* – equally effectively. This is, the lack of a market for the fixed factory is not felt: in guaranteeing that the variable goods be distributed efficiently over the given fixed factors, the market for the variable goods guarantees that the fixed factors themselves be used as efficiently as possible. Indeed (32) and (55) immediately imply that the efficiency price of the rth factor

$$Q^r = c^r(p), \qquad \text{each } r. \tag{66}$$

Earlier in this section I promised to show formally that we could normalize so that

$$Y_t^r(\cdot) \text{ is positively homogeneous of degree one, each } t,r \tag{61}$$

if each firm produced under constant returns.

According to the argument leading up to G4, in III, constant returns implies

$$g_t(p,ky_t) = kg_t(p,y_t), \qquad y_t, ky_t \in \Omega_t, k \geqslant 0 . \tag{67}$$

Let us assume further that

$\Omega 5$ if $y_t \in \Omega_t$ and $k \geqslant 1$, $ky_t \in \Omega_t$

since it is clearly sufficient for (67) to assume it for all $k \geqslant 1$. (67) then yields

$$\Sigma^r c^r(p)\{Y_t^r(ky_t^r) - kY_t^r(y_t^r)\} + (1-k)d_t(p) = 0 \tag{68}$$

if $y^r \in \Omega^r$ and $k \geqslant 1$. Solving for $Y_t^r(ky_t^r) - kY_t^r(y_t^r)$ we immediately see that

$$Y_t^r(ky_t^r) - kY_t^r(y_t^r) = \alpha_t^r(k), \quad k \geqslant 1, y_t^r \in \Omega_t^r \tag{69}$$

say, since the right hand side of the equation cited is independent of y_t^r. Now

$$\begin{aligned}
\alpha_t^r(ab) &= Y_t^r(aby_t^r) - aY_t^r(bY_t^r) + a\{Y_t^r(bY_t^r) - bY_t^r(y_t^r)\} \\
&= \alpha_t^r(a) - a\alpha_t^r(b), \qquad a, b \geqslant 1 \\
&= \alpha_t^r(b) - b\alpha_t^r(a), \qquad \text{by symmetry}
\end{aligned} \tag{70}$$

so that

$$\frac{\alpha_t^r(a)}{a-1} = \frac{\alpha_t^r(b)}{b-1} = \beta_t^r , \text{ say, } a, b > 1 . \tag{71}$$

Substituting into (69), we get

$$Y_t^{*r}(ky_t^r) = kY_t^{*r}(y_t^r) \qquad \text{if } y_t^r \in \Omega_t^r, k \geqslant 1 \tag{72}$$

as required for (61), where

$$Y_t^{*r}(y_t^r) = Y_t^r(y_t^r) - \beta_t^r, \tag{73}$$

a trivial change of origin.[38] (68) similarly becomes

$$G_t^*(p,Y_t^*) = \Sigma^r c^r(p)Y_t^{*r} \tag{74}$$

so that there are *quasi constant returns to scale*, too, in this normalization: that is, doubling the quantities of the fixed factors available to them just permits each firm to double the net output of each variable good.

This result has an interesting corollary. Consider a vintage model in which there is only one factor, capital, only one capital good – or machine – of each vintage, and constant returns to scale. Let t stand for the vintage, so that the 'firms' are 'plants' of the different vintages. In the appropriate normalization, the gross profit functions are

$$g_t(p,y_t) = c(p)Y_t(y_t), \quad \text{each } t, \tag{75}$$

where the y_t and Y_t are scalars, representing the number of machines used by the tth firm and the amount of capital represented by them. The only positively homogeneous functions of a single variable are

$$Y_t(y_t) = e_t y_t, \quad \text{each } t. \text{[39]} \tag{76}$$

If we normalize so that $e_1 = 1$, this comes to measuring capital in 'equivalent period one machines'. Of course

$$Y = \Sigma Y_t = \Sigma e_t y_t \tag{77}$$

is also measured in this way. Moreover (75) implies that each of the firms, and, by (77), the economy as a whole, has the same quasi gross profit function $c(p)Z$, where Z can be taken to represent either the quantity of capital in an individual firm t, or in the economy as a whole. In terms of equivalent machines, therefore, all the firms, and the entire economy, have the same production possibilities.

VII. *Interpretation of the Gross Profit Functions*
in Terms of Independent Plants
According to (63) and (64) we can write the quasi gross profit functions in the form

$$G_t(p,Y_t) = \Sigma^r c^r(p) Y_t^r + d_t(p); \quad Y_t^r \in I_t^r = [0, a_t^r\rangle \tag{78}$$

$$G(p,Y) = \Sigma^r c^r(p) Y^r + d(p); \quad Y^r \in I^r = [0, a^r\rangle, \tag{79}$$

where, of course,

$$Y = \Sigma Y_t, \quad d = \Sigma d_t, \quad a^r = \Sigma_t a_t^r. \tag{80}$$

(78) and (79) remind one of the relationship $g(p,y) = \Sigma g_t(p,y_t)$ between the gross profit functions of the economy as a whole and of the individual firms which make it up.

Can, then, the components on the right hand sides of (78) and (79) be interpreted as the quasi gross profit functions of individual plants?

We will see below that they often can be, though, of course, the plants in question are mere theoretical constructs, which would normally have no physical existence – mere fictions, in fact. For the moment, assume that we are in such a case, and see what we can learn.

Notice first that the rth plant in both (78) and (79) has a quasi gross profit function

$$c^r(p)Z, \qquad\qquad (81)$$

where Z may be interpreted either as the quantity of the rth factor in the tth firm, or in the entire economy. All of these plants, having the same quasi gross profit function, have the same quasi technology. Moreover it clearly yields quasi constant returns to scale. We may call them the *plants using the rth factor*. Because of the quasi constant returns, doubling the quantity of the rth fixed factor available to the tth firm doubles its net output

$$x_t^r = Y_t^r c''^r(p) \ {}^{40} \qquad\qquad (82)$$

from its plant using this factor.

This helps us to understand why shunting fixed factors back and forth among the firms does not affect what happens in the economy as a whole. Because of the quasi constant returns, the same quantities of the variable goods are associated with each unit of the rth factor, wherever it is located.

In addition to these *fixed factor using* plants, each firm has in general a *basic plant* with gross profit function $d_t(p)$, which produces a net amount

$$x_t^0 = d_t'(p) \qquad\qquad (83)$$

of the variable goods, say, at prices p, however much of the fixed factors are available to it. Because of S1–2 the production possibility sets of these basic plants are necessarily closed and convex. Except for this, they may be of any sort whatever: in particular those in different firms may differ as much as we like. Since the plants using the fixed factors are the same in all the firms, any difference between their quasi technologies appears in the basic plants. We may regard them as using fixed inputs specific to the individual firms, which are not listed in y. In that sense $\Omega 3$ in IV merely tells us that only such fixed inputs as are used in at least two firms are listed, and is not really a genuine restriction at all.

If each firm produces under quasi constant returns, each $d_t(p) \equiv 0$, and so, too, does $d(p)$. There are therefore no specific plants, and all the firms have the same given technology. The only difference between their actual technologies therefore lies in the aggregation functions $Y_t^r(\cdot)$, or, if you like, in the efficiency of their 'fixed factor producing plants', as defined in IV.

We saw in VI, of course, that there are quasi constant returns, in an appropriate normalization if there are proper constant returns. Of course this condition is far from necessary.

For the interpretation in terms of separate plants to be legitimate, each $c^r(\cdot)$ and $d_t(\cdot)$ must satisfy G1 and G2: that is, be positively homogeneous of degree one and closed convex. In finding whether this is so we can use the fact that each $G_t(p, Y_t)$ and $G(p, Y)$, as admissible gross profit functions, do so.

Now

$$d_t(p) = G_t(p,0), \quad d(p) = G(p,0) \qquad \text{by (78) and (79)} \qquad (84)$$

so that they satisfy G1–2 like the G's if $0 \in I_t$ or $0 \in I$ as the case may be. Moreover

$$c^r(p) = \{G_t(p, \tilde{Y}_t^1, \ldots, Y_t^r, \ldots, \tilde{Y}_t^R) - G_t(p, \tilde{Y})\}/(Y_t^r - \tilde{Y}_t^r)$$

$$= \{G(p, \tilde{Y}^1, \ldots, Y^r, \ldots, \tilde{Y}^R) - G(p, \tilde{Y})\}/(Y^r - \tilde{Y}^r) \qquad (85)$$

so that it is certainly positively homogeneous of degree one like the G's and therefore satisfies G1.

The question is: do the $c^r(p)$ also satisfy G2: that is, are they closed convex?

Consider first the case in which $0 \in I_t$, each t, in the chosen normalization, at least one firm t, or the economy as a whole, produces under quasi constant returns, and, for each r, at least one of the entities producing under quasi constant returns permits the use of a strictly positive amount of the rth fixed factor.[41] Then (85) yields

$$c^r(p) = G_t(p, 0, \ldots, Y_t^r, \ldots, 0)/Y_t^r$$

or $\qquad G(p, 0, \ldots, Y^r, \ldots, 0)/Y^r \qquad (86)$

for the entity in question, with Y_t^r or $Y^r > 0$. Hence $c^r(p)$, like the G's, satisfies G2.

In this case, therefore, the interpretation in terms of independent plants is certainly legitimate.

Next let us drop the assumption that any of the firms produces under quasi constant returns. Having done so we are free to use the normalization (44), in which

$$I_t^r = [0, a_t^r\rangle, \quad I^r = [0, a^r\rangle, \quad a^r = \Sigma a_t^r, \qquad (87)$$

and the domains of Y_t^r and Y^r respectively. (84) therefore implies that like the G's

$$\text{each } d_t(p), \text{ and } d(p), \text{ satisfies G1-2.} \tag{88}$$

Let us now assume that

$$\text{each } a_t^r = \infty . \tag{89}$$

This will only be true, of course, if each Ω_t^r is unbounded above, so that there is no upper limit to the potential supply of inputs in any class to any firm, and if having an indefinitely large supply of the inputs in any particular class permits any firm to earn indefinitely large gross profits.

When considering any particular firm t, or the economy, I may certainly require

$$p \in R_t^0 = \{p : d_t(p) < \infty\}$$

i.e. $\quad\quad p \in R^0 = \{p : d(p) < \infty\} = \cap_t R_t^0 \tag{90}$

as the case may be, since the breakdown of an infinite gross profit function into components is of little interest. I will do so.

Taking $\tilde{Y}_t = 0$ and letting $Y_t^r \to \infty$ in (85) we immediately see that each $c^r(p)$ is convex in each R_t^0, and therefore in R^0. Is it closed convex? If not there is a *frontier point q of and in*

$$R^r = \{p : c^r(p) < \infty\} \tag{91}$$

such that

$$\lim \inf \{c^r(p) : p \to q\} = c^r(q) - \gamma; \quad \gamma > 0 . \tag{92}$$

Choose a sequence

$$p^n \to q \text{ such that } c^r(p^n) \to c^r(q) . \tag{93}$$

We have already seen that we may take $q \in R_t^0$ without loss of generality. Assume

$$q \in \text{Int } R_t^0, \quad \text{some } t . \tag{94}$$

Then the sequence $\{d_t(p^n)\}$ is ultimately bounded. Hence it has a limit point

$$d_t(q) + \delta \tag{95}$$

say. Chose a subsequence which converges to this limit and relabel the corresponding $p^n : p^1, p^2, \dots$ (93) continues to hold. Moreover, since $G_t(p, Y_t) = \Sigma c^r Y_t^r + d_t$ is closed convex by G1, $\lim G_t(p^n, Y_t) \geqslant G_t(q, Y_t)$.

Hence
$$-\gamma Y_t^r + \delta \geqslant 0, \quad \gamma \geqslant 0 . \tag{96}$$

Letting $Y^r \to \infty$ in (96), we have a contradiction. If, therefore, $c^r(p)$ is not closed convex, there is a point q in the intersection of R^r with its frontier which is also in the intersection of each R_t^0 with its frontier. If the intersection of all these intersections is empty for each r, the interpretation in terms of independent plants is legitimate, as it is if we consider only prices in a set P which does not contain any such intersections.

Since we know that the efficient output of a set of independent plants is the sum of the efficient outputs of each taken separately.

$$x_t = \Sigma c^{r\prime}(p) Y_t^r + d_t^\prime(p) \tag{97}$$

$$x = \Sigma c^\prime(p) Y^r + d^\prime(p) \tag{98}$$

are the production plans of the individual firms and the economy, where the primes denote gradients, as in the paragraph following (26), when the interpretation in terms of independent plants is legitimate.

Even if it is illegitimate, (97)–(98) are still true whenever all the functions of p are differentiable, as they are almost everywhere in the set where G_t, or G, is finite by (84), (85) and (20).

Since (97)–(98) are the main implications of the representation in terms of independent plants–indeed the only ones in this section–it is not seriously misleading even when illegitimate.

(97) also permits us to examine the substitution and complementarity relationships between the factors and the variable goods. Despite the interpretation of (78) in terms of independent plants for each factor, it turns out that they may be either substitutes or complements for each other, or for the variable inputs.

Admittedly this is in terms of rather jejune, non-Hicksian, definitions of substitution and complementarity.

Because the shadow price of the rth fixed factor

$$Q^r = c^r(p) \tag{99}$$

by (66), we cannot vary it independently. Moreover it is the same however much of the fixed factors the firm has at its disposal, so that the x's and Y's cannot be written as functions of p and Q. Hicks's definitions are therefore difficult to apply and we are thrown back on the idea that two inputs should be *complements* if increasing the supply of one increases the marginal product of the other, and *substitutes*, if it decreases it.[42] Of course this is immediately applicable only if there is a single output and the production function is smooth.[43] Assume this is so and that there is only one variable input. Given its price q in terms of the product as numéraire – that is its marginal product – we can divide the fixed factors into two groups, according to whether they are complementary with it or substitutes for it. I will prove

> *fixed factors in the same group are substitutes, in different groups,*
> *complements.*   (100)

The quantity of the variable input, *measured as an input*, is

$$z = -\Sigma \dot{c}^r(q) Y^r - \dot{d}(q), \tag{101}$$

where the point represents differentiation with respect to q. Now

$$\frac{\partial q}{\partial Y^r} = -\frac{\partial z}{\partial Y^r}\bigg/\frac{\partial z}{\partial q} = \dot{c}^r\frac{\partial q}{\partial z}. \tag{102}$$

Now $\partial q/\partial z \leqslant 0$ because of the declining marginal productivity of the variable input implied by S2. Hence the variable input and the rth fixed factor are

> *substitutes if* $\dot{c}^r \geqslant 0$ [44]
>
> *complements if* $\dot{c}^r \leqslant 0$.   (103)

Moreover, by (99) and (102)

$$\frac{\partial Q^r}{\partial Y^s} = \dot{c}^r\frac{\partial q}{\partial Y^s} = \dot{c}^r\dot{c}^s\frac{\partial q}{\partial z}. \tag{104}$$

which immediately implies (100).

Since the quantity of a factor increases when the corresponding fixed inputs increase, fixed inputs corresponding to factors in the complementary group are complementary with the variable input, to factors in the substitute group are substitutes for it. Moreover fixed inputs corresponding to different factors in the same group are substitutes, while those corresponding to factors in different groups are complements.

As Gorman (1965) has shown,[45] these results hold 'on the average' when there are several variable inputs. However, the average in question is not sufficiently interesting to justify my spelling the result out here.

When discussing the 'independent plants' interpretation of (78), I pointed out that it meant that each firm would make exactly the same use of a unit of a fixed factor as any other. (97) implies that this is true in general, at least 'almost everywhere'.[46]

This is pretty damaging for aggregation. Not everyone will make equally efficient use of a lathe, for instance – indeed some firms may have no use for it at all; but any who use it at all, will produce new variable goods on it in the same proportion as anyone else – *and in the same proportion as someone who gets a new steel press instead.*

Of course firms may vary greatly in the relative efficiency with which they fabricate the different fixed factors from the corresponding inputs, and, if so, will presumably vary greatly in the proportions in which they hold these fixed factors. Or the production from their basic plants may be relatively large. Either phenomenon can lead to different firms producing, or using, the different variable goods in quite different proportions.

Wriggle as I may, however, I cannot persuade myself that this condition for aggregation is remotely likely to be met in practice in an economy as a whole, with theoretically interesting definitions of the fixed factors.

It may be more reasonable for a model of an industry, or in cases where the variable goods are themselves highly aggregated – as in vintage capital models, for instance.

It certainly does not help justify the practice of fitting aggregate production functions.[47]

ACKNOWLEDGMENTS

Earlier versions of this paper were presented at Oxford in 1964 and at the Rome Econometric Conference in 1965. I am grateful to my colleagues at Oxford, the discussants at Rome: André Nataf and Takashi Negishi, and Frank Fisher, Frank Hahn, Leo Hurwicz, David Rowan, Paul Samuelson, John Whittaker and John Wise, for useful comments.

Frank Fisher's paper, which was also presented at Rome (1965), was written before mine. It has since been published. André Nataf's contribution to the Rome discussion is also about to come out. An explanation is in order for publishing a third essay in a limited field. This is it: the three papers differ markedly in method and consequently in structure. They seem to me to be complementary with each other and with John Whitaker's related paper (1966).

NOTES AND REFERENCES

[1] Here, and throughout this paper, equilibria will be perfectly competitive, and the equilibrium conditions: that all goods, or at least all variable goods, have the same efficiency prices everywhere.

[2] 'iff' = 'if and only if' both here and throughout this paper.

[3] Assuming, of course, that the new technology also satisfies Nataf's conditions.

[4] In terms of these aggregates the production relations become $\Pi = PX - WN - RZ$, where P, W and R are Laspeyres indices of prices, wage rates and plant rentals, and Π is the equilibrium profits. The marginal productivity relations $\partial X / \partial N = W/P$, $\partial X / \partial Z = R/P$ therefore hold *everywhere*.

[5] The rest of the paper may be regarded as a mathematical appendix to this rather lengthy summary, to be read only by those technically interested. Sections III–V are the most mathematical.

[6] Of course these need not be uniquely determined: indeed kp will always do as well as p, where $k > 0$, since these are unnormalized accounting prices. What is required is that there be at least one vector of efficiency prices which is the same for all the firms.

[7] This function is a direct analogue to the cost function $K(p,u)$ giving the minimum cost of producing an output u, or reaching a level u of utility, at prices p, whose use has been rather generally known for some time. The first systematic discussion of this class of functions was given in Samuelson (1965).

[8] 'sup' rather than 'max' really, because, in some limiting cases, it may theoretically be profitable to produce infinite quantities of some goods.

[9] They are: that it should be *positively homogeneous of degree one* and *closed convex* in the prices. The former merely means that gross profits increase k fold if each of the prices do, and $k \geqslant 0$. The latter is slightly stronger than ordinary convexity, which would assert that the gross profits at prices $(p+q)/2$ are not greater than the average of those at prices p and q separately. Together, they are equivalent to the statement that the set

$$U_t(y_t) = \{(p,u): u \geqslant g_t(p,y_t)\}$$

is a closed convex cone.

[10] At which it was assumed (G7 in Section IV) that the gross profit functions $g_t(q,y_t)$ were continuous in the y_t, and strongly increasing in each y_t^r: that is, having more of all the fixed inputs in any class actually increases each firm's gross profits *at these prices*. Hence the $Y_t^r(y_t^r)$ are also continuous and strongly increasing.

[11] Here it is implicitly assumed that 0 is admissible as a fixed input vector, while we might, for instance, wish to require aggregability only in a region in the interior of the positive orthant. Actually any

vector b which is admissible as a fixed factor vector will do as a reference vector as well as 0. In Section v, I chose a b which minimizes each $g_t(q,b_t)$, so that the minimum quantity of any fixed factor turns out to be zero.

[12] $Y_t = (Y^1, \ldots, Y_t^R);$ $\qquad Y = (Y^1, \ldots, Y^R) = \Sigma Y_t$ by (3).

[13] I sometimes renormalize the aggregates–measuring them from a new base point to make the a's vanish and get quasi constant returns.

[14] If it is differentiable, which it is 'almost everywhere'. The conclusions below are valid even without differentiability.

[15] If $G_t(p,Y_t)$ is not differentiable, there will in general be many equally profitable production plans both before and after the gift. Any change which is optimal for any one firm is optimal for all.

[16] That is, each firm can just produce twice as high a net output of each variable good if it has twice as much of each factor, or, equivalently, can earn just twice as large gross profits. In general this depends on the origin from which the quantity of equipment is measured. Throughout this section I assume each $Y_t^r(0) = 0$, as in (2).

[17] '$Y^r(\cdot)$' = 'the function Y_t^r'.

[18] n is the number of variable goods. $g(p) = \infty$ if there is free disposal, for instance, and some of the prices are negative. This possibility does not create any real problems.

[19] The polar cone V^+ of a set V is $\{w : v \cdot w \geqslant 0,$ each $v \in V\}$. It is a closed convex cone made up of those vectors which make acute, or right, angles with all the vectors in V. V^{++} is the smallest closed convex cone containing V. $V^{++} = V$, therefore, iff V is itself a closed convex cone. If V is a cone, V^{++} is its convex closure. See, for instance, Karlin (1959) Appendix B.3.

[20] Even if S is neither closed nor convex, the gross profit functions effectively define the competitive market behaviour of firms, or, in general, the efficient behaviour of the economy.

[21] Int R = relative interior of R.

[22] I will sketch the proof for the case where $0 \in S$. It is slightly more complicated if $0 \notin S$.

Let $p \in R \cap$ frontier of R, and take a sequence $\{p+\delta^m\} \notin R, \delta^m \to 0$. Let $\{x^{mk}\}$, each m, be a sequence such that $(p+\delta^m)x^{mk} \to \infty$ each m, as $k \to \infty$. Chose a k for each m such that $(p+\delta^m) \cdot \bar{x}^m \to \infty$ where $\bar{x}^m = x^{mk(m)}$. Write $x^{*m} = \bar{x}^m/(\Sigma \bar{x}_i^m)$ so that $\{x^{*m}\}$ is in the fundamental simplex and therefore has a limit x^*. Chose a subsequence such that $x^{*m} \to x^*$ in the subsequence, and relabel its elements, and the corresponding elements of $\{\delta^m\}$, 1, 2, 3, . . . Set $x^{*m} = x^* + \varepsilon^m, \bar{x}^m = \lambda^m x^{*m} = \lambda^m(x^* + \varepsilon^m)$ when $\varepsilon^m \to 0$. $\lambda^m \to \infty$, of course. Each $\mu x^*, \mu \geqslant 0$ belongs to S, since 0 does and S is closed and convex. Moreover $(p+\delta^m)\bar{x}^m \to \infty$. Hence $\lambda^m(p \cdot x^* + p \cdot \varepsilon^m + \delta^m \cdot x^* + \delta^m \cdot \varepsilon^m) \to \infty$. All but the first element in the bracket certainly tend to zero. Hence $(p+\delta^m) \cdot \bar{x}^m \sim \lambda^m p \cdot x^*$, unless $p \cdot x^* = 0$. This would imply $p \cdot \lambda^m x^* \to \infty$, where $\lambda^m x^* \in S$, so then $g(p) = \infty$, contradicting the fact that $p \in R$. Hence $p \cdot x^* = 0$. Let now $\{\bar{x}^m\}$ be a sequence in S such that $p \cdot \bar{x}^m \to g(p)$. Then $p \cdot [(1-\rho^m)\bar{x}^m + \lambda^m x^*] \to g(p)$ as $\rho^m \to 0$. Yet $\{(1-\rho^m)\bar{a}^m + \lambda^m a^*\}$ is unbounded. This seems the natural interpretation of the phrase 'the facet is unbounded'.

^{23} That is: if $p \in R$, $p \geqslant 0$.
I will use 'strictly positive' to mean $p > 0$, but will not use 'non-negative' at all.

^{24} Ω will be specified below.

^{25} In using this result, I will frequently assume Ω to satisfy $\Omega 5$. If $y \in \Omega$ and $k \geqslant 1$, then $ky \in \Omega$, but this is not necessary for its statement.

^{26} That is: Ω^r is the domain of y_t^r; $\Omega^r = \Pi_t \Omega_t^r$, $\Omega_t = \Pi^r \Omega_t^r$, each r, t.

^{27} *Closure* is for convenience only. Dropping it would make the proof in v slightly more complicated.

Tube connectivity: if y_t^r, z_t^r are distinct points in Ω_t^r, they are joined by a continuous curve whose other points all lie in the interior of Ω_t^r. This is needed in the proof of (36), which is not given in this paper.

Bounded below: there exist $\beta^r > -\infty$ such that $y_t^r \geqslant \beta^r$ if $y^r \in \Omega_t^r$. This seems reasonable. Indeed it would seem reasonable to take $\beta_t^r = 0$. It simplifies the proof in v to have assumed boundedness below, but it is not necessary for the result.

^{28} Required because we have to be able to shunt fixed inputs in each class backward and forward among the firms.

$\Omega 2$ implies that there are y_t^r, $z_t^r \in \Omega_t^r$ such that $y_t^r > z_t^r$ iff $t \in T(r)$.

Y2 therefore implies that Y^r can be changed just by changing y^r_t iff $t \in T(r)$.

^{29} This construction, which replaces a much less elegant one of my own, was suggested to me by Professor L. Hurwicz in the course of a very valuable conversation – very valuable to me at least!

^{30} $1/2 + 1/\pi$ arc tan y is a strictly increasing mapping of $(-\infty, \infty)$ onto $(0,1)$ if we take the principal value of the arc tan.

^{31} *Strongly increasing in y_t^r:* if y_t^r, $z_t^r \in \Omega_t^r$ where $y_t^r > z_t^r$, and if $y_s^r \geqslant z_s^r \in \Omega_s^r$, each $s \neq t$, then $Y^r(y^r) > Y^r(z^r)$. Note that it is not necessary to state that $t \in T(r)$, even though the requirement is empty for $t \notin T(r)$.

The slightly repugnant part of Y2 is the requirement of continuity. One might like fixed equipment to be lumpy. I can only plead
(i) step functions can be indefinitely closely approximated by continuous functions.
(ii) age, etc. of equipment may be thought of as giving some sort

of continuous variability, even if the actual pieces are lumpy.
(iii) One might argue that the flow of services from equipment is
continuously variable, and that it is this flow which determines
production. This would soften the stark contrast between fixed
and variable inputs which underlies my whole analysis.

The real defence is, however, that one cannot hope to get anywhere without continuity because of the trick aggregates mentioned
in the text.

[32] I^r is bounded below and closed below, because Ω^r is. It can therefore be put in the form $[0,a_r\rangle$ by a trivial normalization. Here $[,]$ denote
closed ends, $(,)$ open ends and $\langle,\rangle$ either.

[33] $\Omega 2$ and Y2 can be considerably weakened, but the resulting form
of Y2, in particular, is difficult to understand. Without the order requirements, including (1), it implies the form Y2 given in the text, with its
distasteful demand for continuity.

[34] In Section v, I will need $G(q, \cdot)$ strictly increasing. A brief sketch
of the proof follows:

Take $U, V \in I$ such that $U^r < V^r$, $r \leqslant m$, $U^r = V^r$, $r > m$, and $u, v \in \Omega$
such that $u^r = v^r$, $r > m$ and $Y(u) = U$, $Y(v) = V$.

Assume u^r, $v^r \in \text{Int } \Omega^r$, $r \leqslant m$. They are connected by a curve
$C^r \subseteq \text{Int } \Omega^r$. There exists $\rho^r > 0$ such that $z^r + \rho^r e^r \in \Omega^r$. When $z^r \in C^r$,
$e^r = (1,1,\ldots,1)$.

Define a finite sequence $z^0_r = u^r, \ldots, z^j_r$ on C^r with z^{i+1}_r,
$Y^r(z^{i+1}_r) = Y^r(z^i_r + \rho^r e^r) \geqslant V^r$. Define $z^{j+1}_r = z^j_r + \lambda^r e^r$ such that
$Y^r(z^{j+1}_r) = V_r$. Let the earlier sequences to reach this final point mark
time there until the others catch up. It is easily shown that $\{g(q,z^i_r)\}$ is
a strictly increasing sequence. Hence, $G(q,U) = g(q,u) < g(q,v) = G(q,V)$.

Extend the result to the case when some u^r or $v^r \notin \text{Int } \Omega^r$ by the
continuity of $g(q,y)$.

[35] *Strongly increasing in* y^r_t: if y^r_t, $z^r_t \in \Omega^r_t$, and $y^r_t > z^r_t$, then
$Y^r_t(y^r_t) > Y^r_t(z^r_t)$. (38) is operative iff $t \in T(r)$.

[36] Except in the highly restrictive case in which
$$Y^r_t = \Sigma \, d^r_i (y^r_{ti} - b^r_{ti})$$
in the obvious notation. In this case fixed inputs within each class are
perfect substitutes for each other, the equilibrium price ratio being
d^r_i / d^r_j, whatever the circumstances; so that there is 'really' only one
fixed input in each class. Or, of course, in that in which each fixed input
is used by just one firm, or in the obvious combination of these cases.

[37] This is quite different from keeping the total quantities of the fixed
inputs constant, of course, since different firms will, in general, not use
such inputs equally efficiently.

[38] If $0 \in \Omega$, it comes to taking 0 instead of b in our definition (44)

of Y_t^r–which is surely necessary. In general we can extend the positively homogeneous function $Y_t^{*r}(\cdot)$ over the positive orthant. The extended function vanishes when $y_t^r = 0$.

[39] We can have different coefficients for positive and negative y_t. Formally, therefore, we have to assume $y_t \geqslant 0$ if $y_t \in \Omega_t$. This is quite acceptable.

[40] The prime denotes 'grad' as in the paragraph below (26).

[41] Because of G2, for each r, the same limit of I_t^r must be zero for each firm producing under quasi constant returns. All the same, this is a weak assumption. It will hold, for instance, if $0 \in \Omega_t$, each $t \in \Theta$, say, where Θ is a set of firms producing under genuine constant returns, at least one member of $\Theta \in T(r)$, each r, and, of course, you cannot have negative fixed inputs.

[42] If they are *neutral*, that is if the marginal product is not affected, I will say they are both substitutes and complements. i and j are complements if $\phi_{ij} \geqslant 0$, substitutes if $\phi_{ij} \leqslant 0$ where ϕ is the production function and suffixes denote differentiation, so that the definitions are symmetric, as long as there is sufficient smoothness to yield $\phi_{ij} = \phi_{ji}$, which I assume there is.

[43] We could have several products, and hold their relative prices constant in the definition; in other words the 'single' product might be a Hicksian aggregate. So, for that matter, might the single variable input be. We could talk of declining efficiency prices instead of marginal products if the production functions were not smooth – but then i might be a substitute for j, and j a complement for i.

[44] $c^r > 0$ means, of course, that the input good is an output of the rth plant. What does this matter, since it is only a fictional plant in any case ? If we could have $Y^r \to \infty$, of course, it would be an actual output eventually, but even that is not very disturbing (Gorman, 1965).

[45] There are a pair of idiotic mistakes, which luckily cancel out, in this section of Gorman (1965), and I rule out the possibility of a fixed factor being a substitute for the variable good for the reason given in footnote (43), but the statement in the text is nevertheless true.

[46] 'In general' = 'even if the "independent plant" interpretation is not legitimate'. 'almost everywhere' = 'except on a set of Lebesgue measure zero'.

[47] This criticism holds even when the $c^r(p)$ are not closed convex and not differentiable at the given prices p:

An extra unit of the rth factor changes the production possibilities, and therefore the efficient production plan, for the economy as a whole by the same amount whichever firm t gets it. But the only firm whose individual production plan changes is t. Hence the changes which are profitable are the same whatever firm gets the extra unit.

6

What is a Model?

Roy Harrod

In recent years the word 'model' has come to besprinkle the page of learned articles and books on economics, and, even more so, the examination papers of candidates for degrees in that subject. I have the impression that, for the word 'model', some specific meaning can be formulated, although this meaning is subtle and elusive, and has, to my knowledge, been so far nowhere defined. If the word 'model', which has its aroma of implications, is applied to formulations which are not in fact 'models' in any meaningful sense that may be found for that word, then the implications can lead to false conclusions in relation to those formulations.

In my own case this problem happens to come right home. Many years after I had made certain formulations in the field of growth theory and after Professor Domar had made similar formulations, there began to be references to the 'Harrod-Domar model'. I found myself in the position of Le Bourgeois Gentilhomme who had been speaking prose all his life without knowing it. I had been fabricating 'models' without knowing it. It may be, and I suspect it to be the case, that the word 'model' can, in a meaningful sense, be applied to some of the Harrod-Domar formulations; I also think that to some of those formulations the word 'model' cannot be applied appropriately. I shall return to this theme later in this article.

To make sense of *some* references in the literature to 'model', one has to take the view that it is a substitute for the words 'general proposition'. The number of letters in 'model' is five, whereas that in 'general proposition' is eighteen; thus, if we could take 'model' to be synonymous with ($\equiv$) 'general proposition', that would be economical. But, if there is indeed some subtle and elusive meaning in 'model', as implied by its more sophisticated users, there would be a loss of discrimination, if it came to be accepted that it meant precisely the same as 'general proposition'.

It may serve to focus thought to ask, at the outset, certain questions.

173

(1) Does a 'model' contain one or more propositions that have the character of being 'true or false'? Modern logic undergoes kaleidoscopic changes, and it is a hard task for a layman to keep pace with these. The 'truth table' continues, surely, to be of fundamental importance in logic, and applies, as I understand it, to any group of symbols that contain a connective, whatever that may mean. If there is a connective in the group of symbols, then the 'T or F' attribute applies.

It may be that a 'model' can be constituted by a group of symbols with no connective. Thus one might write 'rate of growth of the G.D.P.', 'capital/output ratio', 'savings ratio'. These symbols might be juxtaposed without any connective.

I have noticed that the word 'useful' is often applied to 'models', in a pragmatic spirit. Thus it might be deemed 'useful' to write the symbols, say G, C and s for the magnitudes mentioned in the last paragraph. There need be no 'connective'. The idea would be that the contemplation of these symbols in juxtaposition might lead on to some worthwhile intellectual process. Perhaps my own 'growth model' might be interpreted in that sense. It grouped together in a small space certain symbols which it would be worthwhile for a thinking agent to dwell on simultaneously. The 'model' would not be 'useful' if the simultaneous contemplation of the symbols bore no intellectual fruit. This minimal interpretation of what is meant by a 'model' is attractive; but I doubt if it is what is actually meant by a 'model' as commonly used in economics; it is less than what is meant in other disciplines; it is also much less than what I meant and, I believe, than what Professor Domar meant, in our formulations.

(2) What is the relation of a model to a hypothesis or to a theory? To get down to brass tacks, but still in the realm of preliminary skirmishing, I would suggest that in this kind of context a 'model' is a formulation that has adjustable parameters.

A digression is necessary here. There is a cloud of ambiguity, I fear, around the word 'parameter'. My own idea is that it can be exemplified as follows:

$$\dot{W} = A + B(x_2)^b + C(x_3)^c + D(x_4)^d + \ldots, N(x_n)^n,$$

where $\dot{W}$ is the rate of increase of wages, $A, B, C, \ldots, N$ and $b, c, \ldots, n$ are constants, x_2 is the rate of increase in the cost of living, x_3 is the rate of increase in trade union membership, x_4 is the level of unemployment, etc.

In my view $A, B, C, D, \ldots, N$ and $a, b, c, d, \ldots, n$ are the adjustable parameters. When one has set up this equation, econometric studies may suggest
specific values for $A, B, C, D, \ldots, N$ and for $b, c, d, \ldots, n$. Once this is
done, these parameters cease to be 'adjustable'.

One might take the line that, when these parameters cease to be 'adjustable', owing to econometric studies, the formulation in question has
become a hypothesis. This, of course, does not mean that the hypothesis
is known to be true. I may insert here that very often in studies that I
have read the number of observables in ratio to the number of 'adjustable
parameters' has been too small to give more than a very low probability
to the specific hypotheses claimed to be established by the observations.

How does one classify the terms? Is a statement in which the parameters
remain adjustable to rank as a 'model' while one with specific numbers
inserted is a hypothesis? Or can one enlarge the scope of the sense of a
hypothesis, to include, as a weaker form of it, a model in which the parameters are still 'adjustable'? In that case some hypotheses would also be
models. And can we also go the other way and include in our category of
'models' hypotheses in which the parameters have already been fixed
(provisionally) by econometric studies?

I would ask a further question here. If the expression 'adjustable parameter' is meaningful, what is an 'unadjustable parameter'? I would suggest
that the meaning of the latter expression relates to a state of intellectual
enquiry, whether due to econometric studies or laboratory experiments, in
which the 'adjustable parameters' have been given specific values in the
hope that these are true, at least in the area of observation to which the
specific formulae are supposed to apply.

But among learned discussants I have found the view that 'the parameters of a system' are constituted by the determining variables. This view
seems to make complete nonsense of the idea of a 'parameter'. There is no
doubt that the coefficients and indices are 'adjustable' parameters. How
can variables possibly be identified with parameters? Surely a variable can
neither be 'adjustable' nor 'unadjustable'.

On the word 'parameter' it seemed expedient to have resort to the *Oxford
English Dictionary*. The definition is:

A quantity which is constant (*as distinct from the ordinary variables*)
in a particular case, but which varies in different cases; esp. a
constant occurring in the equation of a curve or surface, by the

variation of which the equation is made to represent a *family* of such curves or surfaces. (Italics mine.)

This definition seems to be, possibly, applicable to the case of wage determination cited above. The model would hypothetically specify the determining variables for all countries, leaving the parameters (indices and coefficients) to be adjusted from country to country. The model would embody the hope that in a particular country, at least for a certain phase of history, including the near future, the adjustable parameters could be replaced, in consequence of econometric study, by specific numbers. But the influence of any variable such as Trade Union membership, might differ from country to country and its parameters would need adjustment accordingly. Thus the bare model, with its parameters still adjustable would be applicable to all countries, at least for a certain period of history. If a variable that seemed to be one of the determinants in one or more countries, such as the potency of the effective head of state, was deemed to have no influence at all in other countries, for those the coefficient could simply be written as zero. This account seems to make sense; but it is not certain that it expresses what is now meant in all cases, when the word 'parameter' is used.

I would suggest that 'parameter', like 'model', has become something of a show-off word, and that serious economists should be careful in regard to both these words.

It is now expedient to dig deeper, by reference to traditional usage, and to present usages outside economics.

In Bourton-on-the-Water there is a model of that village of considerable size. As the model is inside the village it can, by the Dedekind paradox, never be made complete, however fine the materials available for its construction. The model contains, surely enough, a rough model of itself; but there the matter stops. For completeness there would have to be a model of the model of the model, and so ad infinitum. This model of the village can be said also to be a 'copy' of it, in the sense that the model and the village are, as near as may be, structurally identical. While each is in that sense a copy of the other, it is more natural to apply the word 'copy' to the model, rather than the other way round. The village itself may be regarded as a 'reality' in its own right. In many of the varied uses of the word model, these two features seem to reappear, namely (i) that there are two related objects similar to each other and (ii) that one of the two objects is an independent 'reality', while the other has been fabricated as a copy of it. It may also be a feature common to most users that the model is an approximate, or rough, copy only.

In the case of Bourton-on-the-Water the 'original', to use another word, antedates the model. But in some cases it is the other way round. One may make a model of a projected university building or factory. If it is intended to be helpful, and not something devised for public relations only, one may call it a 'working model'. Again the two features appear, namely, that the model and what it is supposed to be a model of have similar structures, and that the factory is destined to have a 'reality' in some sense that is lacking to the model. We cannot in this case, however, say that the factory is the 'original'.

It may be convenient to make a digression from the main theme here, and refer to a rather different, but still allied, use. One may think of the working model of a factory as something that *ought* to be copied and rendered into a reality. Perhaps the failure to make a correct copy in certain respects might be detrimental to the quality of the factory itself. One sometimes talks of a model husband, or a model farm. Here, what is a model is, so to say, a living reality. But, as with the model of the factory, it is something that *ought* to be copied. As with the model factory, certain objectives will be achieved, only if every husband has a structural similarity in his behaviour to the model husband.

Carrying the analogy still further, Gladstone, in his culminating Free Trade Budget (1860), expressed the hope, quoting Milton, that it

Might serve as model for the mighty world
And be the fair beginning of a time.

The word 'model' has long been used for a person who poses for students in an art school. Here there seems to be an inversion of the relation noted above, which will reappear later; one would say that the live person was the 'reality', while the likenesses painted upon the canvases of the students were copies of the reality. It is not clear, however, whether there is really an inversion here. One might take the painting to be the substantive reality, while the live person is a mere instrument, like the working model of a factory, for the achievement of the grand design, which is the picture itself.

This comes out more clearly when, as in the old days of representative painting, the painter has some large composition, like the Rape of the

Sabine Women, and employs models for the various figures. The models are clearly tools to aid him in his achievement.

The matter becomes more subtle in the case of portraiture. Here at least it would seem that the sitter himself, say a King or Prime Minister, is the substantial reality, and the painting a subordinate object, a mere likeness of the great man. But this fact is perhaps itself expressed by a subtle variation of usage. When the Prime Minister himself comes to the studio to give a sitting, he is not said to be a 'model', but 'the sitter'. Only when some other person comes and puts on the garter robe for the benefit of the painter–the great man having no time for such details–do we use the word model. In relation to the hireling, it is the picture that is the substantial reality and the hireling the model; but in the case of the great man, it is he who is the substantial reality in relation to the picture, although we do not call it a model, but a likeness.

The foregoing sense of model has presumably led on to the use of the word that is now far the commonest in popular speech, namely for a lady who is used to display clothes in a shop. She is like the person who puts on the garter robe for the painter's convenience. There does not seem to be much of the copy idea left in this case. It may be that the model is conceived as such because her figure has a similar structure to that of the grand lady destined to buy the dress. And in this case too the model is the subordinate partner in the copy relation.

I believe that Bohr's model of the atom may have played a crucial part in introducing that word into physics. The idea was, as I understand it, that if one could magnify an atom a billionfold, or by whatever was requisite, one would have a visual object of structural similarity to a model of the solar system correspondingly reduced. It would not be necessary actually to construct such a model, but a visual image might be helpful in advancing thought. The structure of this image would be specified in certain functional equations relating to the mass, etc., of the protons and electrons.

As physics advanced, it became doubtful whether an atom, however much magnified, would really look like a solar system to the naked eye. But the structure of Bohr's equations, as suitably modified in consequence of further experiments, lived on. It was this structure that became the 'model' in our modern more recondite sense.

The old features remained. The structural features displayed in the functional equations were taken to resemble, or anyhow to have a 1 to 1 relation to, the structure of the atom itself. Again, the atom is the 'reality', while the functional equations constitute a tool, enabling one, hopefully, to apprehend the reality.

At this point it may be interesting to note a certain contrariety in usage, as between mathematics and physics. As I understand the matter, a model has the following sense in mathematics.[1] One may write down a number of symbolic expressions, along with rules of interpretation and deduction. These may be said to be in the realm of the highest conceivable abstraction. Then one may come down to earth and contemplate something that is still, of course, abstract, as it must be in mathematics, but is concrete relatively to the formulae previously set out. One might take the row of natural numbers. If concrete is the wrong word, one might at least call this row a 'hard fact'. If the row of natural numbers exemplifies the relations that are set out in the abstract formulations, so that they can be said to be true of it, then the row of natural numbers is a model.

This does seem to be an inversion of usage. In physics the group of functional equations is the model, and it is hoped that real atoms will, by their behaviour as evidenced at second or nth hand in experimental data, exemplify the relations set out in the model. In mathematics the position seems to be inverted. It is that which exemplifies in hard fact the relations set out in a series of formulae that is the model. The relation of the similarity of the model to what it is a model of remains, but in mathematics it seems to be the model that is the substantial reality.

In biological science the meaning appears to shift again. It seems that the word model is applied to a system of functional equations specifying a behaviour pattern, only when this system is taken over from another science, such as physics. A behaviour pattern in physics as expressed in functional equations may give a key for the formulation of laws about bacteriological behaviour. It is this key, taken over from physics, that is the model, while the formulations relating specifically to bacteriological behaviour and expressed in appropriate terms are hypotheses. Thus the equations in physics serve as a model for a similar system of equations that one hopes will prove a correct specification for bacteriological processes.

It is expedient to consider physics a little more closely. It may be that there also a model is distinguished from a set of hypotheses in that there are still adjustable parameters. It is also suggested that a model may not give a full and final account of the reality with which it is concerned, but only pick out certain important features. In this respect the usage of physics may not be far from that of economics.

It may be valuable, for the progress of thinking and investigation, to concentrate on what are hypothetically taken to be the more important determining variables, leaving fringe influences on one side. If one gets approximate verifications for these admittedly incomplete formulations, that may be significant. Modifications in the equations required for fringe influences may be brought in later. It still remains a little difficult to distinguish between a model and a group of hypotheses. Surely an incomplete formulation, viz. omitting fringe influences, would be called an hypothesis. Could one cut through this tangle of terminological inexactitudes (*not* in the Churchillian sense!) by saying that a model is nothing more than a group of hypotheses? That would surely be too simple a solution. It would not accord with the sense in which 'model' is often used in economics. I do not think that this word, as generally employed in economics, *essentially* implies a group of equations, as contradistinguished from a single equation.

There remains one important question to be considered in relation to physics, which makes physics unlike economics. Physics is concerned with entities of which we have (and can have) no direct observation and the question must be asked whether the use of the word model in physics has not some relation to this fact. If this were so, then it would be wrong to think that the use of the word 'model' in economics is analogous to, or authorized by, its use in physics.

We may make a working model of a factory not yet built; we cannot at the outset compare the model with the factory, to see how closely they resemble one another, because the factory does not yet exist. In physics one can *never* compare the model with the reality because one has no direct access to the reality.

Physicists may posit that there is a kind of entity to be named an electron. Certain structural properties are then specified in a series of equations. It is not correct to say that the 'electron' is *defined* by these equations.

Positing an entity, to which the name 'electron' is given, has, in physics, unlike mathematics, the implication that the existence of this entity will somehow show up in and influence the nature of our experience. We just posit that there is a kind of entity to which certain functional equations apply. By a chain of deductions from the equations we build up more complex structures. By carrying on with the deductions to a sufficient extent, we get a structure which ought to have similarity with an empirical structure, as observed in instrument readings or lines on a photographic plate. Having got certain readings, we can argue by a backward deductive process, to show that our readings are consistent with the fundamental structural equations specifying the nature of the posited entity, viz. the 'electron'. Some sort of linkage between the structural equations specified as describing properties of the posited entity and actual observations is an essential part of the definition of that entity. This constitutes the difference between *positing* that there exists an entity to which the functional equations apply and *defining* an entity as being just anything to which the functional relations might apply. Furthermore, if the observations would be consistent, by the deductive chain, not with the functional equations, as originally formulated, but with a modified version of those equations, we are ready to modify them in an appropriate manner. This shows that the original equations should not be taken as a definition, in the proper sense of that word.

It may be objected that I have used the word 'posit' without attempting to define it. I quail before such an attempt, since it would take me into uncharted logical seas. I believe that a perceptive reader will gain an insight into its proposed meaning from the context, even if the ultimate definition is still absent. 'Positing', as used here, is first cousin to 'postulating', or, alternatively, perhaps is a species of 'postulating'. A postulate usually contains two groups of symbols on either side of a connective, both of which are already defined. We 'posit' when we say that 'an entity (or type of entity) exists which is . . .'. On the right hand of 'is' stands a group of symbols, representing properties, which may have to be further specified in a whole series of equations. Some philosophers object to the word 'exist' altogether; in this paper I can explore the matter no further.

I cannot resist the impression that the use of the word 'model' in physics is somehow connected with the fact that it is dealing with a real world of posited entities, none of which can ever be directly observed. And indeed these posited entities may eventually be discarded, like the ether. One cannot exactly say that the ether does not exist because, from the beginning, it was only a posited entity, like the electron or the neutrino. What one can say is that a model which posits ether and then sets up a number of equations specifying its properties is not 'useful'. The legitimacy of using the word 'useful' rather than 'true' in relation to a series of equations is intimately connected with the fact that the entities to which the equations relate are merely posited entities.

Mr Richard Wayne, the physicist, who has been good enough to comment on this paper, has written the following, which provokes thought:

> I wonder whether you are right in stating that the concept of 'ether' did not prove 'useful'. Clerk-Maxwell would not have been able to derive his laws of electro-magnetic radiation at that time without the prop of the ether. Nor would Faraday have been able to make the correlations between his various observations on electric and and magnetic phenomena without his concept of 'lines of force'. Faraday's ideas led in turn to Clerk-Maxwell's formulations, and these are, perhaps, the only important remnant of classical physics to be taken over intact into modern physics. Although the ether was discarded, the equations derived from assuming its existence remain; so I think that the concept was no less 'useful' than the Bohr model of the atom, which served a similar purpose.

Here we have a double idea in regard to posited entities, namely (a) that they may be genuinely 'useful', but only for a time, and (b) that they may also be regarded as having the status of being 'useful' for all time since, during their period of their – what shall we say? – 'active' usefulness, certain advances in thought, valid for all time, were made, that could not have been made at the time in question without their assistance. Whether they could have been made by some more devious route is a matter of historical judgment. One may tremble to wonder whether the Harrod-Domar model, if it has to be downgraded into the category of 'useful' only, will finally be judged to have the better status described under (b) – or, of course, perhaps no status at all.

There still remains the difference between systems that posit certain entities and those that do not. Euclidean geometry may be a case in point. I do not believe that it 'posits' any entities that are *in principle* unobservable. Physicists in the past postulated that the system of relations set out in Euclidean geometry is exemplified in the physical world of what we call space. It is true that in fact a straight line may nowhere exist in the physical world, but it is not, like the electron, a 'posited' entity; its properties may be specified without residue by deduction from its definition;

not so the properties of an electron. Euclidean geometry has obviously been highly 'useful' ((*b*) category of usefulness), and will long continue to be so as an approximative specification of the spatial relations of our world. But we can also affirm that its system of propositions, as deduced from its postulates, has eternal Platonic 'truth', even if they do not apply to our observable world. They could apply to some other world that conformed to the postulates. This can hardly be said of a system containing 'posited' entities, whose properties are not specified by deduction only *without residue.*

Thus it does seem that the boundary line between systems, the maximum claim of which is that they are 'useful', and those that can also claim 'truth', is that which divides systems that comprise posited entities from those that do not.

In economics we are not, I believe, concerned with any entities that are merely posited; all the entities with which economics deals are, in principle at least, directly observable.

My own dynamic equations take a number of forms. The basic one, $G = (s/C)$, is self-evident. G is the increment of income in a period divided by income, s the fraction of income saved and C the capital accumulation during the period divided by the increment of income. I have been content to describe this as a 'tautology'. This need not be regarded as a belittling description. Possible tautologies are infinite in number, and merit may be assigned to the selection of one likely to be fruitful in stimulating thought. Perhaps the electronic computers that we have inside our skulls winnow through millions of tautologies before selecting one for presentation to the conscious mind, just as, so it is said, they go through all permutations of letters when one is trying to remember a name; we give the computer an especially hard task when we wrongly believe that we remember the first letter of the name.

It may be that, when one selects a tautology out of the myriads, one can be held to be presenting a 'model'. But this seems to give that word an inappropriate coverage. In a tautology there can be no adjustable parameters. Nor can there be any question of what is stated being a rough approximation, or one which, while it claims to present the most important determining variables, leaves others out of the formulation as being of minor influence.

I am not, however, happy with the word 'tautology'. It came into favour in my youth in consequence of that movement in logic which discarded the possibility of *a priori* synthetic judgements and divided all statements into tautologies (or deductions therefrom in accordance with arbitrary rules) and those susceptible to empirical test. This movement was due as much to the downfall of Euclidean geometry as to the cogitations of the symbolic logicians. I have been content to use this word during a lifetime of teaching, for example in relation to monetary equations. In the early days it was a smart thing to do; later one became lazy-minded.

I doubt if anyone has a clear idea as to what a tautology is. The conceptual foundations of symbolic logic, as expressed in meta-language, remain very insecure. Progress towards greater refinement and perfection in the techniques of this logic have not, I believe, been accompanied by any improvement in its philosophical position.

I can illustrate one of my difficulties from the Fisherine and Cambridge monetary equations, both, in common parlance, said to be tautological. (Would they have been called 'models', if enunciated at a later date?) The Cambridge equation is *more* tautological than the Fisher equation. Can there be degrees of tautologicality? That does not seem very proper. Both equations are, of course, self-evident.

The value of the four variables in the Fisher equation ($MV = \Sigma pq = PT$) can in principle be independently ascertained for a given period.[2] It may be objected that it is rather difficult to ascertain the value of V (velocity of circulation of money) in practice. It may be replied that the practical difficulty is irrelevant, or, alternatively, that the Fisher equation can be reduced to three terms, by treating MV as a single term, for the value of which it should not be difficult to obtain a rough approximation, e.g. from clearing house returns. We can infer from the equation that, if the observations do not accord with its requirement, then the observations must be wrong. Some fringe definitions may be needed, such as how to deal with loans and gifts. But the main variables in the equation do not have to be defined. Thus the equation may be used to detect errors and omissions, just as the necessary equality of debits and credits in a country's balance of external payments may be so used. If we use index numbers, as with the notation PT (rather than Σpq), then the constituents of the index numbers must be correctly weighted; otherwise we shall get a discordant result.

With the Cambridge equation the whole scene is transformed. We may take the simplest version, $n = pk$, where n is the quantity of money, p is the price of a basketful of goods and k is the number of such basketfuls that the money held by people will purchase. This equation cannot be used to check any statistical data, and it does not matter what index number is used for p. The equation will always be verified by the data, however defective they may be in fact. The reason is that in this equation there are not three values that can be independently ascertained by observation, but two only. k is simply n/p; there is no possible way of evaluating k except by dividing n by p.

This is not to deny that the Cambridge equation has interest. Tautologies often have interest. I hold that it is in some respects more illuminating than the less tautological Fisher equation. Incidentally, it would be quite wrong to say that k is *defined* as n/p. The idea of the amount of value (purchasing power) that people hold in money form is intelligible in its own right.

The fact remains that the Cambridge equation is more utterly tautological than the Fisher equation, although the latter also is self-evident. Until we can have a good definition of degrees of tautologicality, I shall view that word with suspicion.

It might be said that, to give more life to the Cambridge equation, we can substitute for 'the amount of value that people hold in money form' the words 'the amount of value that people *desire* to hold in money form'. But then the equation is no longer self-evident and may be false. If one adds the postulate that people always hold what they desire to hold–a very unsafe proposition–we are back where we were.

My basic equation can be interpreted *either* in the Fisher *or* the Cambridge manner. Cambridgewise we could deduce s from observations of the two values G and C. Or we might have independent statistics for s, as in the combined capital account of national income statistics, and use the formula to check errors in our statistical data.

For the reasons already given (no adjustable parameter and no possibility of empirical verification) it does not seem that this equation should be regarded as a 'model'. The matter may be different when we move on to the variant $G_w = s_d/(C_r)$, where G_w stands for what I called a warranted growth rate, s_d stands for the fraction of income that people desire to save and C_r for the capital required to effectuate the extra output.

We may consider the right-hand side first. The question arises whether what people desire to save is a meaningful concept. We are not discussing the determinants of what people desire to save, which may include the rate of interest, but rather the deeper question of whether they have a desire to save anything in particular. They might just take things as they come. Therefore it would seem that at this point some investigation of a psychological kind is needed. s_d might turn out to be a band within which people were indifferent. One would like to assume provisionally that people do have some definite propensity to save, which would cause an adjustment of behaviour if actual s deviated from s_d, an adjustment by persons in their amount of spending and by companies in their dividend distributions or in their capital outlays.

It would seem that one might be readier to take the meaningfulness of C_r for granted. People do not want to have money locked up in idle capital (except as an adaptation to short-term fluctuations) nor to be short of such capital as is required for efficient production. The value of C_r depends of course on the price of capital disposal and, more importantly, on the relative values of the various kinds of input required to create capital.

C_r is a relation between capital formation and output growth. C_r might be regarded as not meaningful if the output of some capital is nil. Even in the case of public parks and museums, however, one may surely suppose that there is an output of amenity, to which some value could be putatively assigned, even although it is not reckoned as part of the G.N.P. Be it noted that the distinction here referred to, between capital that has no output and capital that has output, is not the same as the distinction between induced and autonomous investment as strongly stressed by Hicks; the latter distinction relates to the sensitivity of current investment plans to current events.

It might be argued, I suppose, that the act of postulating that these two concepts are meaningful is tantamount to setting up a model.

I have long since admitted that there is some difficulty in regard to the status of G_w in this equation.

One way of treating the matter would be to regard the equation as definitional, in which case no question of its truth would arise and it could not be verified (or falsified). G_w would be *defined* as that rate of growth, which, if it took place, would be consistent with people saving what they desired to save and with additional capital being furnished in accordance with requirements. By the basic equation (the so-called tautology) only one rate of growth is consistent with the realization of s_d and C_r.

In the unlikely event of s_d and C_r continuing to have the same value through time G_w would be steady. In practice of course there are likely to be variations, particularly in C_r.

Unfortunately there was another concept involved in my original formulation, namely an implication that G_w was a rate of growth which, if achieved, was self-sustaining because proving satisfactory to entrepreneurs. Thus G_w was taken by me to constitute a dynamic equilibrium, although not a stable equilibrium – but it is not necessary to discuss my 'instability principle' here. The idea was that if everything was turning out well in regard to the size of their stocks and the degree of utilization of their equipment, the entrepreneurs would be content to continue happily in their growth path.

However, at an early date I felt bound to concede to Professor Alexander that this might not be so (Harrod, 1951). If one takes s_d/C_r to be the definition of G_w, then the growth path so specified *may* not represent an entrepreneurial equilibrium. In the article referred to, I felt bound to redefine G_w otherwise than as being simply the quantity that is equal to s_d/C_r. But then we have to leave the happy hunting ground of 'tautologies' and definitions and make empirical investigations into the behavioural parameters (if it is right to use that word) of the representative entrepreneurs. Deeper doubts were expressed in a much later article (Harrod, 1964), to the effect that the behavioural parameters might be such that steady growth could, in a market economy, be sustained only by inflationary doses (or, in other cases, by deflation).

Whether those particular doubts are true or not, we are left with the conclusion that this set-up of equations (model?) calls for empirical investigations into the behavioural parameters of representative entrepreneurs.

I pass to another variant, $s_0 = G_n C_r$. Once again we have to ask whether a concept is meaningful, in this case G_n, the 'natural' rate of growth. We now move right away from the idea of progress being trammelled by what people choose or desire to save. s_0, optimal saving, becomes a desiderand for the economy. The equation assumes that, relatively to it, the natural growth rate is exogenously determined – by population increase and technical progress. (This determination may not be altogether exogenous relatively to *other* variables in the economy.) The difficulty here lies not in the concept of natural growth, but in making a statistical forecast of it.

s_0, optimal saving, is a welfare optimum concept. If it is assumed that, from an economic welfare point of view, output should grow at the greatest feasible rate (making all proper allowances, of course, for an optimal increase of leisure and subject to a correct evaluation of C_r) then, this equation seems to be self-evident. There are no adjustable parameters, and no investigation could verify or falsify it.

But there are some behind-the-scenes troubles. One is the optimal rate of interest, or, better, the optimal minimum acceptable rate of return on capital, which may have some influence on the value of C_r. This optimum depends in turn on the prospective growth rate (thereby simultaneous equations are involved) and on the elasticity of the marginal utility of income schedule. The determination of this elasticity requires econometric study. It has already received some, but not enough; and there may be very great difficulties. If one inserted a tentative guess for this elasticity, say one half, on the basis that likely errors in this could not have much practical effect, then the set-up as a whole would become rather model-like.

There is a further constraint. In certain circumstances the value of s_0, as determined by $G_n C_r$, may reduce consumption to a lower level than is required from an incentive point of view in a growing economy. Here again statistical work, and also field work, are required.

While in very poor economies this constraint may have an important effect on C_r (but this must not be exaggerated, since there are far more important constraints on capital-intensive methods operating there, such as insufficient cadres of qualified personnel and balance of payments troubles) I would suppose that in mature countries it has an insignificant influence. The relative values of inputs and the availabilities of the various kinds of inputs (e.g. inputs of highly specialized technological or managerial man-hours) – we must never forget that the factor market is an imperfect one – are far more important in determining C_r than the acceptable rate of return on capital. Incidentally, it must not be assumed that the ready availability of plenty of technologists and technologically orientated managers always tends to raise C_r; it may sometimes reduce C_r.

Economists, if one may judge, as one now has to, from a small sample of the literature only, too often proceed to this kind of problem by setting up a two-factor model – the word slips out – by choosing capital and labour for their two factors, and by then discussing movements along the production function. No doubt what they say is correct in theory. Some of us have treated this theme in lectures designed to help examination candidates for nearly half a century. Journal articles that seek to advance the subject are a different matter. Even for a class-room it would be much better to choose technologico-manager man-hours and unskilled labour man-hours as the two factors in a two-factor model. This dictum applies even more importantly to international trade theory. This is so, not only because the relative availability of these two factors is probably more important for movements along the production function than the availability of capital and 'labour', but also because capital is a very peculiar kind of factor with special properties, and in a general exposé of production functions one should seek to avoid capital, as being likely to bog one down in problems irrelevant to the central theme.

Associated with this, I detect a continuing tendency to hold that dynamic theory can be regarded as a sort of offshoot of, or an appendix to, static theory. In my opinion, dynamic theory brings into consideration influences that have no place at all in static theory. It must always be remembered that John Stuart Mill failed in precisely this respect; he stated dynamic theory, which had played so potent a part in the work of Adam Smith and Ricardo, in what was, in effect, no more than a series of corollaries to static theory. Thereby in my judgement he killed dynamic theory for a century. This murder, or temporary entombment, was assisted by the new lease of life given to static theory by Jevons, Menger and Walras.

To sum up. I should have preferred that in science, including social science (as distinct from references to model husbands, fair ladies, etc.) the word 'model' should have been confined to formulae relating to posited entities, viz. to entities that we can never directly observe and about the very existence of which we cannot be sure. Such posited entities include not only those of modern physics, but also, by a profounder philosophy, macroscopic entities, like chairs and tables. Locke postulated that these entities of the real world had a structural resemblance to our perceptions of them in respect of primary qualities, like configuration and number. But as regards the secondary qualities of our perceptions, colour, light, etc., all that we can say of the real world is that it has 'powers' that cause these sensations in us, 'powers' with which we can never gain direct acquaintance, but in reference to which we have built up a great structure of equations–the theory of light waves, etc.

There would not, by this restriction, be much scope for models in the social sciences, but some. The unconscious mind is a posited entity, with which we can never direct acquaintance. The laws of its behaviour, as framed by Freud, would constitute a model. Jung provided an alternative model, judged by many to be inferior. Economists are not much concerned with such entities, although perhaps they should be more so. The Freudian model might make them better able to understand (and predict?) the actions of the British economic authorities.

The fact that the subject matter of this kind of model is posited only, gives a meaning to the pragmatic flavour of that word. The fact that we never have acquaintance with these entities means that they can be scrapped if, like the ether, they do not eventually prove 'useful' in explaining the phenomena with which we do have acquaintance. The sense-datum, red, or, indeed, what we call money, cannot be scrapped in that way. Those are things with which we do have direct acquaintance.

If we want to bring 'models' into economics, but to keep them meaningful, we might confine the term to a system of equations, not all of which are tautologies. Some at least might have adjustable parameters. It might be made a condition for the use of the word that some equations explicitly omit to take account of fringe influences. In this sense my system might be called a model, but only if it is taken to include those equations containing adjustable parameters, like the behavioural parameter of the representative entrepreneur or the marginal utility of income schedule.

Whether a single equation, like that cited above about wage increases, should be called a 'model', even if it does include adjustable parameters, is more doubtful. We have the word 'hypothesis'. Perhaps 'model' is appropriate if the equation explicitly excludes fringe influences?

Then we get down to self-evident truths (tautologies), like my basic equation in the form in which it is most often quoted. At this point I have a proprietary feeling. It seems to be downgraded by the appellation 'model', which surely implies either uncertainty or incompleteness or, perhaps, both. If a single tautology can be called a 'model', then that word becomes synonymous with general proposition; such a usage would do violence to our sense that, despite much mishandling, the word still retains a connotation of its own.

Can a respectable economist refer to his model (or models) if he has one? I think that he can, if, unlike Ph.D. candidates, he does so with selectivity and discrimination. *Not* every time he sits down to dinner!

NOTES

[1] I am indebted to Mr John Bell at this point.

[2] In case any non-economists read this book, I should define. M is the quantity of money existing in a given region in a given period, V the average number of times that each unit of money is used in exchange in that period, q is the quantity of each valuable that is exchanged for money, p is the value in money terms of each unit of each of the valuables, P is the general price level and T the quantum of valuables that are exchanged for money.

7

Normal Backwardation

Hendrik S. Houthakker

I. *Statement of the Problem*

There is no book on economic theory from which I have learned more than *Value and Capital*, and this is why (without wishing to slight Sir John Hicks's many more recent contributions) I have chosen a theme from that book for this modest expression of gratitude to its author. It is admittedly a minor theme, but it has its place in the closely-knit fabric of Hicksian economics. I shall not be concerned here with the wider uses to which the theory of normal backwardation is put in *Value and Capital* and elsewhere, and consider it only on its own merits and in its original field of application. In particular I shall deal with the assumptions from which the theory can be derived, and with its empirical validity.

The theory of normal backwardation was first formulated by Keynes (1923) in the ephemeral form of a newspaper article. A somewhat more elaborate, though not necessarily a clearer, statement appeared in the second volume of the *Treatise of Money* (Keynes, 1930), and the version presented there has passed into the literature; the earlier version was apparently never referred to until the later 1950s, when it was rediscovered. Professor Hicks's reference in *Value and Capital* is also to the *Treatise*, and he summarizes the theory in the following words:

> In 'normal' conditions, when demand and supply conditions are expected to remain unchanged, and therefore the spot price is expected to be about the same in a month's time as it is today, the future price for one month's delivery is bound to be below the spot price now ruling. The difference between these two prices (the current spot price and the currently fixed futures price) is called by Mr Keynes 'normal backwardation'. (Hicks, 1939, p. 138)

Actually this statement summarizes Hicks's own argument as well as that

of Keynes, for it is fair to say that *Value and Capital* provided the theory
with a precision that is conspicuously lacking in the *Treatise*. In view also
of the important applications of this theory in *Value and Capital* (especially
in the analysis of interest rates) it should be regarded as the joint product
of Keynes and Hicks.

As is clear from the summary just quoted, the theory of normal backwardation asserts the existence of a bias in futures prices. Contrary to the
traditional view, according to which the futures price 'evenly divides the
bulls and bears' (Hawtrey, 1940), Keynes and Hicks say that the current
futures prices is a downwardly biased prediction of the spot price at delivery
time. It is true that Hicks asserts the existence of bias only for normal
conditions, but Keynes emphasizes that the same holds when there are
excessive inventories; neither of them considers the case when inventories
are below normal, but we shall also discuss that case here.

II. *The Imbalance of Hedging*

Such a bias cannot exist if the futures price is determined only by speculators. In a market consisting only of speculators, the futures price would
necessarily be bid up to the point where the bulls just offset the bears;
we may call this point the 'speculative equilibrium price'. Keynes and Hicks
derive the bias from the existence of another class of participants in futures
trading, namely the hedgers, whose position in the futures market is
balanced by an opposite position in the cash market. In particular for the
futures price to be below the speculative equilibrium the hedgers must be
net short, so that the speculators will be net long and among the latter
the bulls will outweigh the bears. Why then is it that the hedgers are net
short? This is the crux of the theory, and it is precisely here that Hicks
made one of his main contributions. In the *Treatise* Keynes simply took
it for granted that the hedgers will be short in the futures market, though
in his long-forgotten article of 1923 he had shown awareness that this
needs to be proved.

There are in fact two classes of hedgers. The 'short hedgers' are those
who are short in the futures market and long in the cash market (usually
because they hold inventories); the 'long hedgers' are long in the futures
market and short in the cash market [1] (which means they have sold
forward). When people speak about 'hedging' without further qualification
they usually mean short hedging, which according to all available data is

the more common type. The proposition that hedgers as a group are normally net short is therefore empirically well-founded, but the theory also has to explain why this is so.

The explanation put forward by Hicks is essentially along technological lines. Keynes (1923) had already suggested that the producer of a commodity 'needs to look much further ahead' than the consumer [2] and Hicks independently argued that 'technical conditions give the entrepreneur a much freer hand about the acquisition of inputs (which are largely needed to start new processes) than about the completion of outputs (whose processes of production – in the ordinary business sense – may be already begun). Hence the extent to which price risks can be reduced by futures trading would be greater for producers than for consumers, since the latter could always, if the price is too high for them, abandon the activities for which the inputs were intended. He goes on to conclude that the 'desire to hedge planned purchases . . . tends to be less insistent than the desire to hedge planned sales'.

The technological argument, however, is open to two objections, each of which makes the whole unconvincing. In the first place it does not apply to merchants, for whom the commodity is both an input and an output, and for whom technological considerations are clearly irrelevant. It is well known that in most commodity markets these middlemen play a leading part, whereas (at least in the major American markets) the participation of producers is usually negligible. It is not made clear why, if at all, merchants might be more willing to sell futures than to buy futures as a hedge.

But even for producers and consumers the technological argument is unsatisfactory. It is hard to see why producers, after they have been rash enough to start production without arranging for the sale of their products, should suddenly become willing to sell futures at a discount; once having started, they might as well be hung for a sheep as for a lamb. On the other hand consumers cannot always abandon their activities as easily as the technological argument implies, and they may consequently have a strong interest in safeguarding their inputs for later delivery, even at a premium. Thus the manufacturer of a branded product, the demand for which cannot be left unsatisfied without subsequent harm and the price of which cannot be easily changed, lays himself open to great risks if he does not protect himself against rising prices of his inputs.

III. *The Risks of Hedging*

To demonstrate that short hedging normally is larger than long hedging we need a rather different kind of argument. For this purpose let us first consider the risks inherent in these two types of hedging. The idea that there are risks in hedging may seem strange at first sight, for hedging is usually presented as a way of avoiding risk. Most of us have been brought up on the textbook example of the miller who buys wheat at $2.00 per bushel and sells an equal amount of futures as a hedge; then the price of spot wheat drops 10 cents, and lo! the futures price also drops 10 cents, so that the miller gains as much on his futures as he loses on his actuals. Unfortunately such perfect hedges are rare outside the textbooks. In reality the correlation between changes in spot prices and changes in futures prices is usually positive and frequently close, but hardly ever perfect. The risk run by hedgers is that the difference between the spot and the futures price (often known as the 'basis') will change against them.

The 'basis', however, cannot vary without limits, at least not in both directions. In particular the spot price cannot fall below the futures price by more than the cost of carrying inventories from now to the maturity of the futures contract; if it did, a riskless profit could be made by buying spot, selling futures, and making delivery. On the other hand, there is no limit to the amount by which the spot price can exceed the futures price, for the arbitrage operation just mentioned cannot be reversed. A large excess of the spot price over the futures price will encourage consumers to postpone their purchases and suppliers to advance their sales, but this does not provide an absolute limit. Very large excesses of this kind are by no means uncommon. In the month of May, for instance, spot potatoes in New York often sell for about $5.00 per 100 pounds while November potatoes are quoted about $2.50, a discount of 50 per cent for a six-month time period.

As a result of this asymmetry short hedgers have a limited risk, while long hedgers have an unlimited risk, of adverse changes in the basis. Suppose, for example, that the spot price now is one penny per pound above the price of the nearest futures contract, while the carrying charge till maturity is three pence. Then the most that a short hedger can lose is four pence per pound, but his possible gains are theoretically unlimited. The long hedger, on the other hand, cannot gain more than four pence, while his possible losses are unbounded. Of course this does not mean that long hedging is unprofitable on the average, even though a believer in minimax strategies would never engage in it. A potential hedger will evaluate the probabilities of all possible gains and losses, and determine his desired market position accordingly.

It follows from this argument, moreover, that hedging is itself a form of speculation, not on the price itself, but on the 'basis'.[3] Like any form of speculation, hedging involves risk-bearing, and there is no reason *a priori* why speculation on the basis should be less risky than speculation on the price itself. It is, in fact, quite arbitrary to regard hedging as a device for avoiding or reducing risk. It is true that, if the correlation between spot and futures prices is high enough, the risk per unit of inventory (bushel, bale, etc.) is less when the inventory is hedged than if it is not hedged, but this reduced risk per unit will normally be offset by a larger size of the hedged inventory.[4] Traders hedge not to reduce their risk (although this may be an incidental effect), but to increase their profits. From the social point of view hedging is primarily a device not for reducing risk, but for shifting it to those most able or willing to bear it; in this respect hedging is quite similar to insurance.

The above interpretation of hedging is by no means incompatible with the general picture of futures trading given by Keynes and Hicks. It is only at subsidiary points of their reasoning that they appear to have been unduly influenced by the naïve view according to which hedging is merely the result of an afterthought.[5] The emphasis on risk aversion that characterizes their analysis has weakened the force of their argument, but it has not seriously invalidated their conclusions. We shall see later that much the same can be said of another feature of their approach, namely the stress on expectations.

IV. *Determinants of Hedging*

A more important conclusion that can be drawn from Working's analysis of hedging is that the willingness to hedge (whether long or short) depends primarily on two factors:

(*a*) the current level of the basis, which determines the risk per unit, and

(*b*) the correlation between changes in the spot price and changes in the futures price, which determines the effectiveness of hedging.

As to the first of these, we must expect the volume of short hedging to be greatest if the spot price is below the futures price (a situation known in British markets as 'contango'), and to decline as the spot price is higher in relation to the futures price.[6] Conversely long hedging will be larger, *ceteris paribus*, as the spot price is higher relative to the futures price. The effect of the basis, however, is to some extent confounded by the effect of the correlation, for these two factors are not independent of each other. Changes in the spot price are closely correlated with changes in the futures price if futures are a close substitute for actuals. In this context the essential difference between actuals and futures is that the former are specific as regards grade and location, whereas futures contracts can be satisfied with a more or less wide range of grades and locations chosen at seller's option.[7] The futures price will therefore reflect the price of the grade and location in which delivery is likely to be made, but the hedger will in general be interested in some other specification. Hence the correlation between the changes in cash and futures prices can be reduced to the correlation between the changes in cash prices of different grades and locations.

How close this correlation is depends primarily on the size of total inventories. If inventories are large, there will in general be no excessive shortages or surpluses of *particular* grades and locations, so that all prices will tend to move closely together. If inventories are small, however, they are also likely to be unevenly distributed; the market will to some extent disintegrate into submarkets, and the correlation will be less close. The situation will then be similar to that often prevailing in (say) a clothing store at the end of a season; some sizes are so abundant that they have to be marked down drastically, while others are not available at all.[8]

In a seasonal commodity the correlation between changes in the spot price and in the price of a nearby futures contract will therefore rise as the crop reaches commercial hands and fall as it is consumed. This phenomenon is well brought out in Table 1. The entry for cotton 'January', for instance, means that during the 33 years the change in the spot price from each December average to the succeeding January average had a squared correlation coefficient of 0·937 relative to the corresponding change in the monthly average price of the March contract. The bulk of the cotton crop, during this period, reached marketing channels during August and September, while the corn crop is normally harvested in October and November and marketed in the following two or three months. The squared correlation coefficients range from 0·571 to 0·981 and from 0·044 to 0·985 in corn; in both cases the minimum is reached during the principal harvest month and the maximum four months thereafter.

TABLE 1. Squared correlation coefficient between month-to-month changes in the spot price of the contract grade and in a nearby futures price

| | COTTON | | CORN | |
	futures contract	*squared correlation*	*futures contract*	*squared correlation*
January	March	·937	May	·803
February	March	·957	May	·985
March	May	·961	May	·959
April	April	·933	May	·878
May	July	·908	July	·684
June	July	·919	July	·813
July	October	·784	September	·725
August	October	·571	September	·875
September	October	·781	December	·711
October	December	·989	December	·644
November	December	·957	December	·342
December	March	·991	May	·575

Notes: The period of observation extends from August 1931 to July 1954 for cotton (excluding February–July 1951, when price controls were in effect) and covers the calendar years 1930 through 1941 and 1947 through 1954 for corn. The spot price for cotton is the monthly average price for 15/16 inch middling at the 10 'designated' spot markets (7/8 inch before 1937) and for corn the monthly average price of No. 3 Yellow at Chicago. I am indebted to Miss Joy C. Love for research assistance in these and other calculations, which were performed at the Stanford Computation Service.

We see therefore that in a seasonal commodity the correlation pattern favors hedging (both long and short) in the middle of the crop year, but not before and after harvest. In nonseasonal commodities, such as copper, the size of the stock presumably has a similar effect, but it would be somewhat harder to detect it statistically. Actually, as Keynes (1923) emphasized, seasonal commodities are much more important as far as finance is concerned than nonseasonal ones; he even suggested that it 'would be a near thing whether all the ships in the world or the raw cotton available last autumn were worth the more'.

TABLE 2. Mean month-to month change in the spot price on the contract grade and in a nearby futures price

	COTTON			CORN		
	change in spot price	*futures contract*	*change in futures price*	*change in spot price*	*futures contract*	*change in futures price*
January	·32	March	·25	·87	May	−·11
February	·15	March	·14	−4·19	May	−4·20
March	·34	May	·35	2·56	May	1·42
April	·25	May	·31	3·28	May	2·04
May	·08	July	·12	·98	July	·06
June	·30	July	·34	·91	July	1·06
July	·42	October	·79	2·19	September	2·80
August	−·75	October	−·15	·58	September	2·27
September	−·15	October	·11	·21	December	1·40
October	−·15	December	−·16	−10·36	December	−1·86
November	·18	December	·26	−1·54	December	2·94
December	·35	March	·30	4·86	March	2·14

Notes: Prices are in cents per pound for cotton, in cents per bushel for corn. The notes to Table 1 also apply to Table 2.

Let us now return to the other determinant of hedging, namely the basis, and see how it behaves seasonally (Table 2). Since the exact calculation of the basis raises certain technical difficulties, this table shows the average change in the spot price and in a nearby futures price, from which the change in the basis can be inferred. The pattern is again very similar in the two commodities. In the middle of the crop year the algebraic change in the spot price usually exceeds the corresponding change in the futures price, but during the summer and autumn the spot price rises less, or falls more, than the futures price. This seasonal pattern means that short hedging is favored, and long hedging discouraged, during the period when stocks in commercial hands are largest. Conversely, the seasonality of the basis is favorable to long hedging, and unfavorable to short hedging, when commercial stocks are small.[9]

Combining the effects of the two determinants of hedging we find that large stocks favor short hedging both through the basis and through the correlation, and that conversely small stocks discourage short hedging. The case of long hedging, however, is not symmetric, because now the two determinants work in opposite directions. When stocks are large the basis effect is unfavorable to long hedging but the correlation effect is favorable; conversely when stocks are small. What we expect to find, therefore, is that short hedging has a pronounced seasonality, while long hedging does not change much during the crop year. Moreover the volume of short hedging is likely to be much greater than that of long hedging when stocks are large, while the two types should not be very different in size when stocks are small.

TABLE 3. Mean positions of large hedgers at end of each month

| | COTTON | | CORN | |
	long	short	long	short
January	543	1,189	17·8	50·7
February	526	1,055	17·5	47·9
March	502	959	16·1	46·1
April	458	817	14·5	39·1
May	379	726	12·9	32·4
June	403	677	11·9	26·6
July	434	703	13·4	18·9
August	545	711	16·7	18·4
September	570	847	19·4	19·0
October	550	1,115	18·6	30·8
November	534	1,194	19·1	48·0
December	532	1,218	18·2	50·4

Notes: Positions are in thousands of bales for cotton, in millions of bushels for corn. Large hedgers are those whose positions in any one futures contract are at least 200,000 bushels in corn or at least 5,000 bales for cotton. For period of observation see text.

Table 3 illustrates these propositions in the case of cotton and corn. Because of data limitations the periods of observation do not coincide with those in Tables 1, 2 and 4; for Table 3 the period extends from October 1937 to September 1959 for cotton (again excluding February–July 1951) and from October 1937 to September 1965 (excluding October 1940– September 1946) for corn. There is a distinct seasonality in both long and short hedging, but the amplitude is greater in short hedging. Long hedging normally reaches a peak around harvest time, short hedging a few months thereafter, when stocks in commercial hands are largest (in the US farmers rarely hedge). Except for corn in September, average short hedging always exceeds average long hedging, though in some years the relationship is reversed.

The imbalance of hedging thus demonstrated can also be expressed in a different way. In Section II the concept of a 'speculative equilibrium price' was introduced; by analogy we can speak of a 'hedgers' equilibrium price', which would rule in a market where only hedgers hold futures contracts. The seasonality in hedging would depress the hedgers' equilibrium price below the true equilibrium price when stocks are large, because the supply of futures by short hedgers would then exceed the demand for futures by long hedgers. This, as we know, is where the speculators come in.

V. *Speculation, Expectations and the Risk Premium*

We now enter a somewhat more controversial area. While students of hedging may differ in the emphasis they place on various motivating factors, there cannot be much dispute over the preponderance of short hedging over long hedging during the bulk of the crop year.[10] It is also clear that any imbalance among the hedgers must be offset by an equal imbalance among the speculators. But the theory of normal backwardation does not follow merely from the imbalance of hedging and speculation; it rests also on an assumption concerning the speculators, namely that in the long run they will only be net long if by doing so they will earn a profit, usually known as a 'risk premium'. Whether such a premium actually exists is the problem to which we now turn.

By way of a preliminary, something has to be said about the concept of an 'expected price', which has loomed large in discussions of this subject. Both Keynes and Hicks, not to mention a number of other authors, have made this concept central to their analysis (see especially *Value and*

Capital, pp. 124–7). As Hicks has emphasized, the expected price is not the most probable price, but it includes an allowance for risk; it is, in fact a 'certainty equivalent'.

To have thus recognized the importance of uncertainty is of course one of the principal merits of *Value and Capital*. Nevertheless there is reason to question the usefulness of the expected price as a tool of analysis. Among the several objections that can be raised against this concept two are especially damaging.

First, it is essentially a partial equilibrium concept, for it refers to only one market at a time. True, we can conceive of individuals or firms as having expected prices for a variety of commodities, but that does not resolve the difficulty. What is wrong with the concept is the implication that if a trader expects the spot price at some future date to be above the currently quoted futures price, he will buy the futures contract in question. This may be reasonable if there is only one market, but it does not hold if there are several. Thus a trader who confidently expects the price of wheat to rise 10 per cent above the current futures price and the price of cotton to rise 20 per cent will, other circumstances being the same, put his money in cotton and not in wheat. Indeed it is quite possible that a trader will sell a commodity whose price he expects to rise. This may happen, in particular, in hedging. If the trader expects the spot price to rise by 2 cents a pound (after adjustment for carrying charges) and the futures price by 1 cent he may decide (depending on financial constraints) to buy spot and sell futures. This will be profitable if by hedging he can carry an inventory that is more than twice the inventory he could carry without hedging. Knowing his expected price(s) therefore does not tell us much about a trader's market behavior. Among the other factors influencing trader's behavior the income effects (or, more precisely, wealth effects) of past price changes are important, as no reader of *Value and Capital* will be surprised to hear. They are especially relevant to the liquidation, as opposed to the initiation, of market positions, and may explain the occasional instability of speculative markets (see Houthakker, 1961).

The second objection to the expected price context results from diversity in expectations and has been emphasized by Hawtrey (1940). If there are several traders, and their expected prices differ, it is not clear how we should aggregate these prices into the one expected price on which the theory relies. In *Value and Capital* there is an apparent attempt to meet this objection by introducing a 'representative' expected price (p. 126), presumably defined by analogy to Marshall's representative firm, and it is also recognized that differences in expectations may be a minor cause of disequilibrium (p. 133). But these remarks do not come to grips with the real difficulty. This is not so much that differences in expectations will cause speculators to trade with each other, but that the truth of the theory of normal backwardation hinges on the speed with which the body of speculators renews itself, as we shall see in a moment. The latter question could hardly be discussed in terms of a single expected price, no matter how representative.

Actually, the entire concept of an expected price is superfluous, at least in the present context.[11] All we really have to know about traders' behavior is how much they will buy or sell in the aggregate as a function of the prices in the markets considered. For this purpose it does not matter how the expectations of individual traders are described, nor how different individual expectations are summed. These details would matter if the assumption of an expected price led to meaningful theoretical restrictions on observable behaviour, but this does not appear to be the case. The excess demand functions for actuals and futures provide us with complete information on the determinants of prices at any one moment of time. In the simplest case these functions may be written $f(p_0,p_1,k_0)$ and $g(p_0,p_1,k_1)$, where $f(p_0,p_1,k_0)$ describes the excess demand for spot supplies and $g(p_0,p_1,k_1)$ the excess demand for futures, p_0 and p_1 are the spot and futures price respectively, and k_0 and k_1 are shift parameters. Temporary equilibrium (in the Hicksian sense) is then given by the equations

$$f(p_0,p_1,k_0) = s_t$$
$$g(p_0,p_1,k_1) = 0,$$

where s_t is the physical stock at time t; excess demand in the futures market must be zero because the total long position is necessarily equal to the total short position. These equations determine the two prices as a function of the two shift parameters and the size of stocks. The model can be further elaborated by postulating an excess demand equation for changes in the stock, for instance

$$\dot{s}_t = h(p_0,p_1,k_2),$$

where k_2 is another shift parameter.

In a sense the most important thing about the functions just described are the shift parameters, which subsume the effect of a great many variables, including changes in expectations. In a more developed model these parameters would have to be treated as random variables, so that the spot-futures market complex becomes a stochastic process. Unfortunately a model of this kind, if it is to have any claim to realism, must be nonlinear, and this makes its analysis so troublesome that it will not be attempted here.

Pursuing the discussion on less rigorous lines we return now to the balance between hedging and speculation. The volume of net hedging, as we have seen, depends largely on the basis and on the correlation between cash and futures prices, both of which in turn depend largely on seasonal factors manifesting themselves through the size of inventories. As a first approximation we can say that net hedging does not depend on the absolute price of the commodity concerned, though the analysis in the Appendix shows this to be not completely accurate. The volume of net speculation, on the other hand, does depend primarily on the absolute price; the lower the price (*ceteris paribus*) the more speculators are willing to be net long. Thus if short hedging exceeds long hedging, the futures price will be depressed below its speculative equilibrium, but as the two types of hedging come closer to each other, the futures price will also approach its speculative equilibrium. This is roughly what happens during the course of the crop year. Before and during harvest, when commercial stocks are small and short hedging not very different from long hedging, the futures price is near its speculative equilibrium. Then short hedging increases rapidly and the futures price falls below its speculative equilibrium, only to rise again as the short hedges are lifted.

If the speculative equilibrium remained more or less constant during the crop year, those speculators who buy when net hedging is at its maximum (that is, when short hedging has the largest excess over long hedging) and remain long until the beginning of harvest would earn a profit. This profit is the risk premium that rewards them for giving some degree of price insurance to the hedgers. Such is the situation envisaged by Keynes and Hicks, as stated in the passage from *Value and Capital* quoted in the second paragraph of this paper, though of course not in these terms. But in reality the speculative equilibrium price does not stay constant; in the terms of the quotation, conditions are rarely if ever 'normal'. If we want nevertheless to apply the theory of normal backwardation to reality, we have to think of the speculative equilibrium price as a random variable with a constant mean in the long run. Under that interpretation we get very similar statements concerning speculator's profits as in the case of a constant speculative equilibrium, so that the essence of the theory is preserved.[12]

But is this interpretation general enough? Does it apply, for instance, to the age of inflation in which we have lived for nearly three decades? The answer is that long-run trends in the price level do not change the theory appreciably, provided they are more or less unforeseen. If the price of a commodity tends to rise secularly, those who are long will obviously gain more than just a risk premium, provided that such a trend does not undermine the willingness to hedge.[13] In most commodities secular price trends are in any case of little significance compared to the short-run variability of prices. In the rare case of a declining price trend there might be no risk premium at all; since ultimately the risk premium is paid for speculators' contribution to the storage process, such a premium would not be appropriate in a market where supply tends persistently to outrun demand.

A more serious exception to the theory of normal backwardation would arise, however, if the excess demand of speculators for futures contracts were so highly elastic that the size of net hedging would make little or no difference to the prevailing futures price. This is the assumption underlying the pre-Keynesian view of the futures price as an unbiased forecast of the spot price at delivery time; what Keynes and Hicks meant, in effect, was that the excess demand just mentioned is less than perfectly elastic. It is only because of the imperfect elasticity that speculators are able to exact a risk premium from the hedgers.

The question therefore is whether there are enough speculators who will buy futures contracts without the inducement of a risk premium. After all, the casinos of Monte Carlo and Las Vegas do not have to offer a risk premium to find buyers for their contracts – quite the contrary. Although presumably most gamblers lose money, they either keep coming back for more or are replaced by others no less eager to try their luck. Could not the same thing be happening in the futures markets, which also offer considerable excitement at relatively small cost? To determine this, we would need data on the turnover among speculators, but such data are not available. Casual observation suggests that commodity speculators are mostly of a hardy variety, and that the turnover is not very great, though at times of unusual activity the futures markets do attract a number of less durable new-comers. This observation still does not imply that the perennial speculators need a risk premium to stay in the markets; neither does the existence of a body of professional speculators, for the latter could conceivably make their living at the expense of the amateurs rather than of the hedgers.

The existence of a risk premium can therefore not be shown *a priori*. It is an empirical question to which competent students have given different answers. This is not the place for a review of the literature, but by way of a conclusion it may be of interest to consider the data underlying Tables 1 and 2 from this point of view.

TABLE 4. Mean month-to-month price change for each futures contract during its observed life, with and without adjustment for corresponding changes in the spot price

| | COTTON | | | CORN | |
| futures contract | price change | | futures contract | price change | |
	unadjusted	adjusted		unadjusted	adjusted
March	·21	·13	May	·44	·98
May	·22	·12	July	·66	−·31
July	·19	·02	September	1·31	−·44
October	·26	·13	December	1·37	3·36
December	·21	·14			
COMBINED	·22	·11	COMBINED	·87	·60

For this purpose it is necessary to look at the average change in the price of any futures contract during its life from the inception of trading to maturity, or at least during a substantial part of its life.[14] Table 4 gives the average month-to-month price change for the same period as in Tables 1 and 2, and in the same units. These averages need to be adjusted, however, because the overall price level of the two commodities rose during the period of observation. This adjustment has been made by deducting the average month-to-month change in the spot price (from Table 2) during the observed life of each futures contract. Table 4 also contains figures for all contracts combined, obtained by aggregating all monthly price changes irrespective of the contract to which they refer.

Considering first the unadjusted figures we see that they are positive in all nine contracts, and of course also for the combined contracts. In the case of cotton the mean price changes all remain positive after adjustment by the change in the spot price, indicating that on the average futures prices rose more during their life than the spot price. Since we also know from Table 3 that in cotton average short hedging exceeds average long hedging in every month of the year, the observed pattern of price changes is in full agreement with the theory of normal backwardation. The mean adjusted price change is about the same for four of the five cotton contracts, July being the exception. This is merely due to the fact that the June-July price change, which is much larger for futures than for spot, was not included in the observed life of the July contract. The average monthly price changes are in fact much the same for all futures, which is why there was no need to show them separately in Table 1 (a similar remark applies to Table 2).

The pattern of mean adjusted price changes is less regular in corn, where they are actually negative for two of the four contracts. This is also attributable in large part to the exclusion of certain months from the observed life. The mean price change for all four contracts combined, however, remains strongly positive after adjustment, again supporting the theory of normal backwardation. Although no formal statistical test has been undertaken, there can be no doubt that the mean adjusted price changes for all futures combined are significantly different from zero for both cotton and corn.

Of course cotton and corn are only two commodities out of many, and it would be interesting to do the same analysis for others. The two analyzed here were chosen merely because they are (or in the case of cotton, were) important commodities with active futures markets and readily available price data. There is no reason to believe they are unrepresentative.

Finally it is interesting to calculate the numerical magnitude of the risk premium implicit in Table 4. Keynes (1923; 1930) had put it at 10 per cent per annum or more, though he did not bother to cite any evidence worth mentioning. Indeed he did not even make it clear whether the 10 per cent was the risk premium itself or the rate of backwardation (that is, the percentage on an annual basis by which the futures price falls short of the spot price). These two concepts coincide only under very special conditions, but the risk premium is clearly the more interesting of the two. From

Table 4 the average risk premium may be estimated by putting the mean adjusted price change for all contracts combined on an annual basis and dividing it by the mean spot price during the period of observation (which is 20·87 cents per pound for cotton and 106·4 cents per bushel for corn). In this way the risk premium works out at 6·3 per cent for cotton and at 6·8 per cent for corn.

Although these estimates are somewhat less than Keynes's, they are large enough to support his contention that 'the price (of risk bearing) is very high, much higher than is charged for any other form of insurance' (Keynes, 1923, p. 785). Perhaps more important in the context of this paper, they show that the theory of normal backwardation is not only relevant to reality but also of considerable quantitative significance. When Professor Hicks made the concept of a risk premium fundamental to this analysis of dynamics under uncertainty, he put his edifice on solid ground.

APPENDIX

A Portfolio-selection Analysis of Hedging
The model of hedger's behavior developed below is not the only possible one. An alternative model, based on margin requirements, is briefly sketched in Houthakker (1959), and still others are conceivable and perhaps realistic. Here I have chosen a portfolio approach following Markowitz (1959), because it is convenient in bringing out the role of the spot-futures correlation emphasized in the text of this paper. The analysis below, however, does not completely coincide with the less formal one given in the text; in that respect I may perhaps claim to have once more followed the example of *Value and Capital*.

Let p_0 be the cash price and p_1 the futures price, both currently quoted. Let Δp_0 and Δp_1 be the changes in these prices during the next time period, and let x_0 and x_1, be the hedger's positions in the cash and futures markets, which are the unknowns of the problem. The random variables Δp_0 and Δp_1, are supposed to have a (subjective) probability distribution which is normal with means m_0 and m_1, variances σ_0^2 and σ_1^2 and correlation coefficient ρ. The trader's expected profit is then

$$Z(x_0, x_1) = x_0 m_0 + x_1 m_1 \tag{1}$$

and its variance is

$$V(x_0, x_1) = x_0^2 \sigma_0^2 + 2 x_0 x_1 \rho \sigma_0 \sigma_1 + x_1^2 \sigma_1^2. \tag{2}$$

The trader is supposed to maximize

$$Z(x_0, x_1) - \lambda V(x_0, x_1),$$

where $\lambda > 0$ is a measure of risk aversion. There are no financial constraints; in this respect the present model differs from the margin-requirements model mentioned above.

The first-order conditions for a maximum are

$$m_0 = \lambda(2x_0\sigma_0^2 + 2x_1\rho\sigma_0\sigma_1) \tag{3}$$

$$m_1 = \lambda(2x_0\rho\sigma_0\sigma_1 + 2x_1\sigma_1^2), \tag{4}$$

from which we derive, after some manipulation, that

$$x_0 = \frac{m_0 - \rho\sigma_0 m_1/\sigma_1}{z\lambda\sigma_0^2(1-\rho^2)} \tag{5}$$

$$x_1 = \frac{m_1 - \rho\sigma_1 m_0/\sigma_0}{2\lambda\sigma_1^2(1-\rho^2)}. \tag{6}$$

Hence x_0 and x_1 are continuous functions of m_0 and m_1. In reality σ_0 and σ_1 are normally close to each other (though σ_0 is usually slightly larger); if ρ is also close to one (as tends to be true in the middle of the crop year) the coefficients of m_1 in (5) and of m_0 in (6) are both also close to one. Both x_0 and x_1 are then approximately functions of $m_0 - m_1$, which is the expected change in the basis,[15] and x_0 is roughly the negative of x_1. If $m_0 > m_1 > 0$, as will be the case for the period when $\rho \sim 1$, x_0 is positive, so there will be short hedging.

Without making these approximations we can give an intriguing interpretation to the numerators of (5) and (6) in terms of the conditional expectations of the random variables Δp_0 and Δp_1. From the theory of the bivariate normal distribution it is well known that

$$E(\Delta p_1 \mid \Delta p_0) = (\rho\sigma_1/\sigma_0)(\Delta p_0 - m_0) + m_1 \tag{7}$$

$$E(\Delta p_0 \mid \Delta p_1) = (\rho\sigma_0/\sigma_1)(\Delta p_1 - m_1) + m_0. \tag{8}$$

Consequently we find for the numerators

$$m_0 - (\rho\sigma_0/\sigma_1)m_1 = E(\Delta p_0 \mid 0) \tag{9}$$

$$m_1 - (\rho\sigma_1/\sigma_0)m_0 = E(\Delta p_1 \mid 0). \tag{10}$$

It follows that x_0 and x_1 are proportional to the conditional expectations in (9) and (10); in fact it can be proved that they are proportional to the densities at the intersections of the regression lines (7) and (8) with the axes, the proportionality constant being dependent on λ but identical for x_0 and x_1. Two possible patterns are shown graphically in Figures 1 and 2. Here MK corresponds to (7) and ML to the other regression line (8). At K, $\Delta p_1 = 0$, so the distance AK is proportional to x_0; similarly for AL. It will be noted that MK is steeper than ML, which is necessarily true for $0 < \rho < 1$: the slope of MK is $\sigma_1/(\sigma_0\rho)$ and that of ML is $\rho\sigma_1/\sigma_0$, while $\rho < 1 < 1/\rho$. The lines MK and ML are in fact on opposite sides of the line MN, which has a slope of σ_1/σ_0. If Δp_0 and Δp_1 are closely correlated the angle between ML and MK is small, but as ρ decreases the two lines are wider apart, so that AL may become positive instead of negative (see Figure 2, which differs from Figure 1 only in the angle between the regression lines). It may seem that in Figure 2 the value of x_0 must be greater than in Figure 1 because the distance AK is greater, but this is not so. When ρ is changed the constant of proportionality referred to earlier also changes. The correct relationship between x_0 and ρ is given by

$$\frac{\partial x_0}{\partial \rho} = \frac{-(1-\rho^2)\sigma_0 m_1/\sigma_1 + 2\rho(m_0 - \rho\sigma_0 m_1/\sigma_1)}{2\lambda\sigma_0^2(1-\rho^2)^2} \tag{11}$$

$$= \frac{-(1+\rho^2)\sigma_0 m_1/\sigma_1 + 2\rho m_0}{2\lambda\sigma_0^2(1-\rho^2)^2}.$$

Since $1 + \rho^2 < 2$ it then follows from (6) that

$$\frac{\partial x_0}{\partial \rho} > \frac{-2m_1 + 2\rho\sigma_1 m_0/\sigma_0}{2\lambda\sigma_0\sigma_1(1-\rho^2)^2} = \frac{-2\sigma_1 x_1}{\sigma_0(1-\rho^2)}; \tag{12}$$

hence if $x_0 > 0$ and $x_1 < 0$ (corresponding to short hedging) an increase in ρ will lead to an increase in inventories. In that case it can be shown by the same method that an increase in ρ will also lead to an increase in the short position in the futures market ($\partial x_1/\partial \rho < 0$).

From Figure 2 it is clear that unless ρ is high enough there will be no hedging, but the trader will be long in both the cash and the futures market. This is diversification, a more common situation in the investment context discussed by Markowitz. The latter constellation will hold if both

$$x_0 > 0, \quad \text{hence } m_0 > \rho\sigma_0 m_1/\sigma_1 \tag{13}$$

$$x_1 > 0, \quad \text{hence } m_1 > \rho\sigma_1 m_0/\sigma_0. \tag{14}$$

For both these inequalities to hold we must have

$$\rho < \frac{m_0\sigma_1}{m_1\sigma_0} < \frac{1}{\rho}, \tag{15}$$

which, for given positive values of m_0, m_1, σ_0 and σ, can always be satisfied if ρ is small enough.

The two cases depicted in Figures 1 and 2 by no means exhaust the many possibilities that can occur depending on the values of the parameters. The reader will have no difficulty in constructing other cases, of which long hedging is perhaps the most interesting.

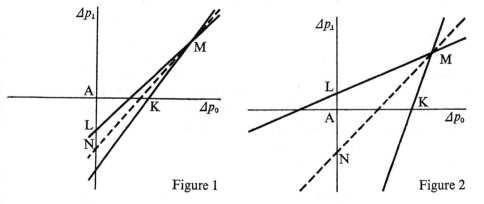

Figure 1   Figure 2

It need hardly be said that the model explored in this appendix is open to serious objections. The assumption of normality, or even the weaker assumption of the existence of second moments, has been questioned by Mandelbrot (1962) on the basis of considerable evidence from commodity markets. It may be possible to construct a theory of hedging on the basis of a stable distribution, as was done for diversification by Samuelson (1965a). The above model also fails to take account of the bounds on the basis implied by the possibility of arbitrage, and in general it ignores transaction costs and the heterogeneity of the cash market; it is also unduly static. Nevertheless it serves to bring out some important properties of hedging which may conceivably be preserved in more realistic models.

NOTES AND REFERENCES

[1] By 'cash market' we mean the market in which transactions in completely specified commodities take place (specified, that is, by grade, location and delivery time). The cash market can be further divided into the 'spot market', concerned only with immediate delivery of physical commodities, and the 'forward market', where delivery is at some later date. The latter is to be sharply distinguished from the 'future market',

in which commodities are not completely specified and which is therefore less suited for the acquisition of physical commodities. This distinction was emphasized by Blau (1944); the earlier failure to make the distinction had resulted in considerable confusion.

² By 'consumer' will always be meant the firm that uses the commodity as an input, not the ultimate consumer.

³ By making this clear Holbrook Working (1953) has put the whole theory of futures trading on a new and more secure foundation. Actually Working classified hedging with arbitrage rather than with speculation, but the effect is the same.

⁴ This matter is discussed in somewhat more detail in Houthakker (1959).

⁵ The naïve view has been most clearly expressed by Kaldor (1939–40, p. 342), who defines hedgers as 'those who have certain commitments, independent of any transactions in the forward market . . . and who enter the forward market in order to *reduce* their risks arising out of these commitments' (his italics). Since hedgers are professionals, the persistent short-sightedness implied by this definition is hard to believe.

⁶ A theory of hedging incorporating these and other elements is set out in the appendix to this paper.

⁷ See Houthakker (1959). It is to be noted that for the point at issue the difference in delivery time between actuals and futures is not essential.

⁸ A closely related phenomenon is the 'convenience yield' of inventories introduced by Kaldor (1939–40). The smaller the total inventories, the larger tends to be their marginal convenience yield.

⁹ This statement is not entirely correct if the hedger's futures position is offset by a forward rather than a spot position (as is necessarily the case in long hedging), since it is physically impossible to be short in the spot market. Unfortunately data on forward prices are not available.

¹⁰ The principal problem here is that the statistics of the US Commodity Exchange Authority, on which all research in this area relies heavily, cover only large hedgers. As Larson (1961) has shown, the inclusion of smaller hedgers is not likely to lead to different conclusions.

¹¹ The concept can only be made useful by postulating some way of inferring expected prices, or changes in expected prices, from observable data. This is sometimes possible, as Nerlove (1958) has shown in the case of agricultural supply functions.

¹² See the important article by Samuelson (1965b).

¹³ Contemporary experience does not suggest any decline in hedging. On the contrary, several old-established markets now show greater volumes of hedging than ever before, corn and cocoa being outstanding examples. It is true that in some important commodities futures trading has declined, notably in cotton, but this is mostly the result of adverse

government policies. On the other hand a number of new futures markets have emerged, one of which (for soybeans) has actually outstripped all others in importance. In the last few years futures trading in livestock and meat has attracted a large amount of speculation and hedging.

[14] For various technical reasons it has not been possible to include in the calculation price changes during the early life of a contract (when in any case trading tends to be very light) or during the month in which it expires (because trading does not cover the full month). In the case of cotton the figures in Table 4 cover monthly averages starting with the eleventh month before maturity and ending with the month before maturity; thus the March future has been taken into account from April through February. For corn the May future is covered from August through April, the July future from November through June, the September future from February through August and the December future from June through November.

[15] In this appendix the words 'expected' and 'expectation' are used as in probability theory, without any Hicksian allowance for risk.

8

Wicksell on the Facts :
Prices and Interest Rates, 1844 to 1914

J. R. T. Hughes

It always has to be remembered that the scope of a law or principle is not
itself written into it, but is something which is learnt by scientists
in coming to understand the theory in which it figures.

Stephen Toulmin *The Philosophy of Science*

Nothing, possibly, is more galling to the mature and careful historian than
the appearance of a one-cause explanation of a long, complex and tortuous
sequence of historical events. What follows is not such a *simpliste* exercise
and I beg to absolve myself of such a crime in advance. However, a reconsideration of the whole history of prices and interest rates during the
reign of the Bank Act of 1844 with the aid *both* of Knut Wicksell's theory
and the results of modern historical research seems worth doing, since
this procedure appears to contribute to solutions to several difficult and
long-standing conundrums.

Our analysis is both novel (by modern standards) and is solidly-based
enough in fact and logic to warrant serious consideration by scholars
interested in the interaction of money and 'real' phenomena.

The analysis is more sweeping than suits the tastes of most scholars,
including, usually, the present author. But by running slightly roughshod
over much of the rich historical detail, I believe I can, in a short space,
contribute both to a better understanding of that detail, and to a clearer
picture of the Bank of England's role in the growth and development of the
British economy in the period in question. I will suggest a mechanism
whereby prices (and perforce much else) were influenced by deviations of
Bank policy from Wicksell-neutrality – an hypothetical world of constant
equalization of the market and the natural rates of interest.[1]

Writing in 1898, Wicksell argued that his new theory explained the paradox,
by then long noted by critics of both the Quantity Theory and the Bank

of England, that, generally, high interest rates were associated with high prices, and low interest rates with low prices. The paradox had been particularly striking in 1891–7 when gold had flooded into Europe and prices failed to rise in the presence of the lowest interest rates in memory. Indeed the Bank of England in 1895–6, while apparently glutted with gold, had faced, for the only time in its history, the astonishing phenomenon of the Banking Department holding in reserve more of the Issue Department's notes than the public was willing to pass in circulation. With Bank Rate sitting at the traditional 2 per cent minimum from 2 February 1894 to 10 September 1896, two and half years, and bankers' rates even lower, prices had not risen.[2]

Wicksell's new theory showed how high market rates could be 'low' if the natural rate were high enough, and low market rates could be 'high' if the natural rate were low enough. Turning to evidence of prices and interest rates for Britain and Germany for 1850–95, Wicksell said that when market rates and prices were high, the natural rate had to be high enough to offset the market rate, and when prices and market rates were low the fall in the natural rate provided a suitable explanatory paradigm.

> In all probability this simple circumstance contains the key to the riddle (Wicksell, 1958, pp. 81–2).

However, Wicksell's examination did not go beyond the two price and interest series he used, and by failing to find an empirical causal mechanism, his paper really only amounted to an assertion that his theoretical construction was not inconsistent with observed facts. It was an appropriate *a priori* explanation. He produced no descriptive mechanism, which explained *why* or *how* the thing he imagined might have come to pass as the data indicated.

The 'riddle' was taken up with great vigour by Keynes in the *Treatise on Money*. At that time he was a modified and enthusiastic Wicksellian, having made Wicksell neutrality a condition for equating (*ex ante*) saving and investment. Keynes investigated several historical episodes he thought his new theoretical construction illuminated, and one was the decade 1886–96. He noted the main features, including the apparent glut of money, the low interest rates and the apparently paradoxical reduction of investment. He thought that, although the causes of the strange phenomena were 'complex and various . . . their general character is fairly obvious to anyone who reads the financial history of the period' (Keynes, 1930, vol. 2, p. 167). He then followed with an account of the historical episodes which, in the confident language of the *Treatise* explained why

> We may conclude, therefore, with considerable confidence that from
> 1891 to 1896 the rate of savings in Great Britain was considerably
> in excess of the rate of investment . . . (Ibid., p. 168).

There had been '. . . no other case where one can trace so clearly the effects of a prolonged withdrawal of entrepreneurs from undertaking the production of new fixed capital on a scale commensurate with current savings' (Ibid., p. 169).

Although he ended this chapter with an assault upon the central bankers for not allowing the market rate to fall fast enough as the natural rate declined (Ibid., pp. 203–6) (an argument repeated again and again in the *Treatise*), he essentially absolved the Bank of England of guilt in 1891–6. They had already tried, he thought. What was needed was the vigorous creation of money demand for goods and services by direct government action to stem the tide of deflation (Ibid., p. 170). Keynes did not attempt to tie the events of the 1890s systematically to any longer historical development.

But when Keynes took up 'Gibson's Paradox' a few pages later (Ibid., pp. 198–203) he went past evidence which might have made him think again. His main table of prices and interest rates might have suggested to him that the decade of 1886–96 was only the dramatic tail-end of a longer movement, impressive throughout. The great swing of inversely-related prices of commodities and consols, the 'Paradox', which brought consol yields to a minimum in 1896 had begun much earlier in the late 1860s.[3] There was no particular reason to suppose that the events of the nineties ended a sequence begun in 1886, nor did Keynes suggest why he 'cut into' the history in 1886, except that there was a slight recovery of prices between 1886 and 1890 (Ibid., p. 164), scarcely an interruption in the long decline from 1873 to 1896.

Keynes also discussed the stickiness of long-term interest rates relative to changes in the natural rate of interest (Ibid., p. 203). At the same time, he minimized the importance of Pigou's suggestion that the psychological impact of 'expectations' might produce an independent influence on prices

(Keynes, 1930, vol. 1, pp. 199–200). But Keynes did not reject this factor altogether, rather, he emphasized the probabilities of wrong guesses, the conflicting nature of the evidence upon which entrepreneurial expectations might be built, and '. . . the facts will soon override anticipations except where they agree' (Ibid., p. 160).

One trouble with both Wicksell and Keynes was the poverty of the historical materials they examined. The whole structure of information, factual and theoretical, was not strong enough to support the conclusions drawn. In both cases the proportions of pure theory to factual information were excessively weighted toward the former, considering that both attempted empirical examinations using their theories. In Economics, as in any science, examination of a 'real world' phenomenon requires thorough knowledge of the identifiable characteristics of the observed phenomenon as well as a theoretical structure of explanatory assumptions.[4] This is not an entirely fair criticism, however, since so much has been done since then on the history of the period. But Keynes was interested in a problem in a period which could hardly be understood without consideration of the relevant temporal antecedents, and Wicksell, although he hedged a good deal about theoretical relationships did not modify *any* of his deductive system to account for problems of reality in the 1898 paper dealing with actual price history.

> If the rate of interest on money deviates *downwards*, be it ever so little, from this normal level prices will, as long as the deviation lasts, rise continuously; if it deviates upwards, they will fall in-definitely in the same way (Wicksell, 1958, pp. 82–3).

Were there no uncertainties, no 'rules of thumb' in business decisions, no 'lessons of experience', no 'traditional behavior'? Wicksell did admit the difficulties of identifying the natural rate statistically, and he did say that his theory would, upon close examination '. . . need modification and completion in some respect or other' (Ibid., p. 89). But, baldly applied to the facts Wicksell examined, with no linking and supporting structure of relevant historical information, Wicksell's empirical 'test' of his theory yielded a much less intellectually satisfying 'explanation' of events than did Keynes's later modification.

We will combine Wicksell's purely theoretical assumptions with some simplifying assumptions about the world which are abstract enough to combine with the theory, but which are 'realistic' enough not to distort reality. Let us first make our simplifying assumptions entirely explicit. Let us begin by making the assumption that the Bank of England's actions were not irrelevant to the fate of the economy's development (the reader who cannot accept this weak assumption as reasonable should stop here). This assumption makes the Bank Act of 1844,[5] in small detail, important. For seven decades that legislation fixed the terms of British central banking. Men were flying airplanes and driving automobiles under the daily influence of legislation which took no note of bank deposits as money [6] or the possibilities of structural balance of payments problems.[7] The Act influenced strategy. The Bank was a private, profit-making institution as well as the nation's major gold depository. The Bank's public strategy was to maintain convertibility at a fixed rate. Its private strategy was to make a profit. Tactics could vary, and did, at times with good results for the level of employment, etc., at times with bad. The Banking Department's reserve of the Issue Department's notes was to be invested enough to yield a suitable return for the proprietors, but was not to be allowed to disappear altogether. Gradually another factor came to the fore, the *duties* of a central bank. The strategy succeeded. Convertibility was maintained for seven decades and the Bank was profitable. The tactical history will not concern us extensively in what follows [8] as we are concerned with a long-period analysis. The tactical results were clearly in accord with strategy, exchanges 'turned', 'speculation' was aborted and so on in each cyclical inflation, and bank reserves were profitably employed in ensuing downswings. Explicit effects upon economic growth, employment, emigration etc., were not part of either strategy or tactics, since they were assumed to be taken care of by the relevant adjustments which followed tactical successes.[9]

We assume that the seven decades contained a normal amount of day-to-day uncertainty in business affairs; that entrepreneurs feared losses, 'insured' against them, and were influenced by experience (balancing hopes for the future against memories of the past). We also assume that the 'natural rate of interest' is a meaningful concept [10] and that its successful identification–a challenge of some magnitude for econometricians–could render conceivable a monetary policy of Wicksell neutrality. Thus, the alternative to the actual history of prices we will study, the contra-factual world, was perfect general price stability (*relative* prices being free to fluctuate).

The next step is to estimate the historical limits of the natural rate, the *range* of possibilities. Here the success of Bank strategy, achieved by varied tactics, provides a set of guidelines. Inflationary episodes, short-term cyclical inflations like 1851–7, were not explosive. After a shakedown, perhaps 10 per cent and a Treasury Letter, prices fell for a time. Since Bank Rate reached its maxima in such episodes, and borrowing from the Bank was not unlimited, the natural rate did not likely exceed the cyclical maxima of Bank Rate, certainly not with any observable effects.[11] That much is fairly simple. But what was the minimum range of the natural rate when prices were falling? This is not so simple. Short market rates did fall below the 'traditional' 2 per cent floor of Bank Rate, in 1894–7, and there is evidence that such was the case for short periods at other times. Here the history of prices gives us a guideline. *So long as prices fell in such circumstances the natural rate was below the market rate.*[12] Cyclical Bank Rate maxima and market rate minima indicate approximate *maximum* ranges for the natural rate over time. We do not know the minima, but we can say something about their locations.

How might the natural rate have moved over time? Actual prices for which we have evidence (Figure 4 below) provide us with guidelines. Leaving out cyclical patterns except for the initial period 1844–7 for the moment ('tactical' problems for the monetary authorities), the price history is as follows: from 1844 to 1847 prices generally rose; from the 1847 crisis to 1849–50 they fell; from 1850 to 1873 they rose (Keynes's 'great mid-nineteenth century investment boom', for reasons only he knew, ran 1855–75) (Keynes, 1930, vol. 2, p. 206); prices fell from 1873 to 1896, and rose from there to 1914.

Now let us set up a simplified model of the world that interests us. For the moment we shall force Wicksell into a somewhat narrower and more regular mould than he really inhabited. But since we shall be guided by the facts as we proceed with the help of this model, the extent to which our conclusions will be unwarranted by hard evidence will be minimized. The modified theory is our intellectual bridge between Wicksell's explicit state-ments and our facts. Figure 1 is not *much* more than Wicksell said. He was interested in price and interest movements. He advanced arguments why price fluctuations were constrained, why neither the natural nor the market

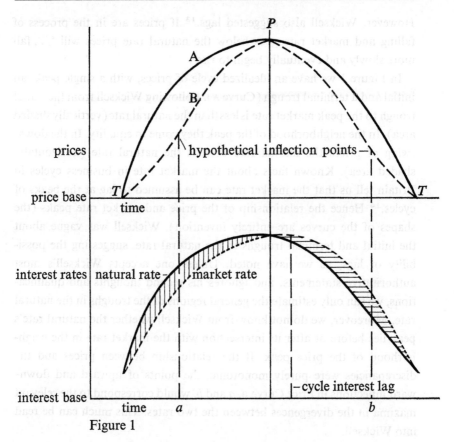

Figure 1

rates would rise or fall indefinitely (Wicksell, 1965, chaps. 8–10). But Wicksell was not wholly unambiguous. He both stated categorically that divergences of market and natural rate had immediate and persistent effects, and said there could be lags. He said the movement of prices was both due to relative and to absolute differences in natural and market rates. For example:

> Our problem is . . . to show that in those periods when upward movements have been observed, the contractual rate of interest – the money rate – was *low* relatively to the natural rate, and that at times of falling prices it was relatively high. . . . If it were possible to ascertain and specify the current value of the natural rate, it would be seen that any deviation of the actual money rate from this natural rate is connected with rising or falling prices according as the deviation is downward or upward (Ibid., p. 107).

However, Wicksell also suggested lags.[13] If prices are in the process of falling and market rate goes below the natural rate prices will '. . . fall more slowly and eventually begin to rise'.

In Figure 1 we have an idealized cycle of prices, with a single peak, an initial and a terminal trough (Curve A). Following Wicksell from the initial trough to the peak market rate is less than the natural rate (vertically shaded area). In the neighborhood of the peak they come to equality. In the downswing of prices the market rate exceeds the natural rate (horizontally shaded area). Known facts about the market rate in business cycles in Britain tell us that the market rate can be assumed to lag at the peaks of cycles.[14] Hence the relationship of the price and market rate peaks (the shapes of the curves are entirely invention). Wicksell was vague about the initial and terminal troughs in the natural rate, suggesting the possibility of lags, as we have noted. Unless one accepts Wicksell's most authoritative statements, and ignores his second thoughts and qualifications, we can only estimate the general regions of the troughs in the natural rate. Moreover, we do not know from Wicksell whether the natural rate's peak lies before or after its intersection with the market rate in the neighborhood of the price peak. If the relationship between prices and the discrepancies were purely monotonic, the points of upward and downward inflections in Price Curve B, *a* and *b*, would correspond to the relevant maxima in the divergences between the two rates. This much can be read into Wicksell.

We shall be using annual data over a seven decade period, so the lags will not present us with problems that are not in accord with the nature of the information conveyed by the data. There is nothing in Wicksell, that I can find, which suggests that he considered that the *adjustment* lags following reversals of the natural and market rate relationships could have been *more than a year*.

We will use the following applications of Wicksell to estimate ranges and movements of the natural rate relative to actual market rates and prices. We must do a bit more very modest theorizing in order to think about entrepreneurial reactions to changes in prices and interest rates.

Let us return to the matter of expectations. Suppose that Figure 1, Price Curve A and the market and natural-rate curves, showed three 'best fit' polynomial regressions derived from actual time series for prices, market and natural rates of interest, over a cycle, either a business cycle or some longer movement. As we know from the saw-toothed charts one ordinarily encounters which depict interest rates and prices, the actual data reveal considerable fluctuations around the regression, which really is only a sophisticated edition of the familiar moving average. In day-to-day transactions entrepreneurs do not experience the smooth curve, but all of the fluctuations, in detail.

Since, as Wicksell noted, there could be considerable short-term reversals of the natural and market-rate relationship, first one and then the other on top, entrepreneurs must adjust to some rule-of-thumb methods, 'wisdom', to deal with this recurrent uncertainty.

We will assume that entrepreneurial memory serves as the 'computer' over time, storing data and continuously calculating a smooth regression.[15] Entrepreneurs are assumed to be aware that, when market rate falls below the natural rate, in the past the opposite has been true at times and might be true again soon enough. Optimism is tempered accordingly. If market rate lies above the natural rate, the depressive influences are similarly mitigated. Short-run experience indicates that no state of affairs will be unchanging. On this logic, incidentally, expectations are about as likely to be a stabilizing influence on economic activity as they are to be totally contributions to 'waves' of optimism and pessimism. I think such considerations may have led Keynes in the *Treatise* to discount expectations.

But we are dealing with history. Men live for several decades of active business life. Memory exists and hence 'wisdom' plays its role; entrepreneurial expectations are tempered by the sum of past experience, sorted and sifted. Hence discounted for present reality, the past plays its rôle and expectations are in this sense cumulative. As is the case today, we will assume that there were 'ratchet effects'.

Consider Figure 2: here we assume that entrepreneurs always know the natural rate and, for simplicity, that the only market rate indicator is the Bank of England Discount Rate and it is a perfect indicator. In case A the natural rate is constant, horizontal to the axis. In case B the natural rate rises at a constant rate. In case C it falls at a constant rate. In case A, whenever the market rate falls below the natural rate, that difference measures the expected probability of profitable borrowing, the vertical maxima being c–d, e–f. If the areas of the triangles formed by deviations of market and natural rates are equal, entrepreneurs make their decisions in the knowledge that there will likely be penalties again for borrowing,

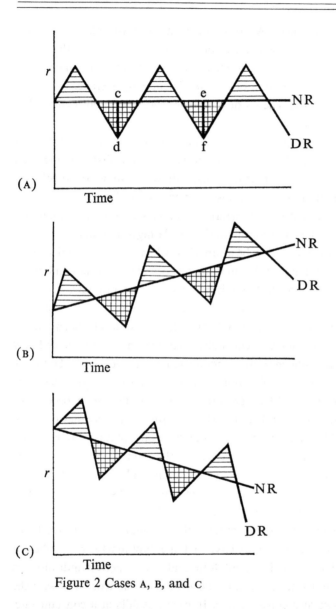

Figure 2 Cases A, B, and C

as in the past, equal to the present inducements. The cumulative effects would depend upon the individual entrepreneur, whether he were a 'bull' or a 'bear' by nature. The point here is that there is nothing either 'bullish' or 'bearish' about these data. If the movements of the market rate above the natural rate are counted positive and those below the natural rate negative, then if the algebraic sums of these movements over time equal zero the *average effects over time, ceteris paribus,* could be the same as if the market and the natural rates had maintained constant equality.

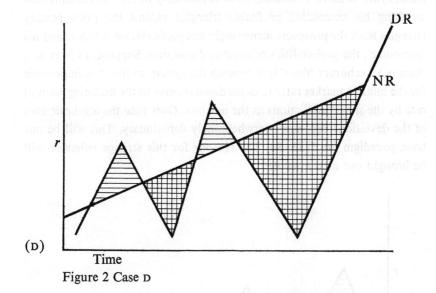

Figure 2 Case D

Cases B and C are just the same, except the diagram has been tilted. In case B, with the natural rate rising, so long as the market rate comes back down appropriately, the rising discount rate has no more cumulatively depressing effect than in its fluctuations of constant ranges as in case A. This follows from Wicksell's theory, but might be surprising to those nursed on the idea that 'rising discount rates are deflationary'. Let us now add a further variation, case D (there are a great number of plausible variations, but we shall confine ourselves to two that are especially useful to us). Here we have a rising natural rate and rising discount-rate maxima; the minima are lower relative to the natural rate. *The sum of movements of discount rate adds up to an inflationary pattern over time even though discount rates go to extraordinary maxima cyclically.* This is going to be our paradigm of period roughly 1850–73. Tactically the Bank Rate is successful, in the sense discussed earlier. Strategically the result is long-period price escalation. The reasons come from history, not theory.

In case C, with the natural rate falling, and the discount rate range going down accordingly there is no necessary net price effect. Falling interest rates are not necessarily 'inflationary'. Moreover, *if the minima should fail to decline by proportions equal to the reductions of the maxima then the decline in the market-rate maxima and minima relative to the natural rate measure a combination of deflationary forces.* An entrepreneur weighing his succeeding profitable triangles against the prior penalty triangles finds the prospects increasingly less profitable on balance, and his 'insurance', the probabilities of success, diminishes. Suppose, as in case E, there is an arbitrary 'floor' laid beneath the system so that it is impossible for the minima market rates to come down relative to the declining natural rate by the same proportions as the maxima. Over time the algebraic sum of the deviations becomes overwhelmingly deflationary. This will be our basic paradigm for 1873–96. The reasons for this strange behavior will be brought out as we proceed.

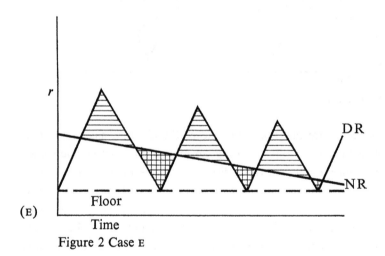

Figure 2 Case E

When the economy 'booms' it takes higher discount rates progressively to the terminal crisis to accomplish the Bank's tactical successes, and conversely in the downswing the Bank's tactical efforts may diminish. But the policy of 'following the market', so long the Bank's stock-in-trade, causes Bank Rate to lag behind price movements. If entrepreneurs know this, then in the upswings of long price movements you could get 'waves' of optimism and in the downswing 'waves' of pessimism.

These innovations in Wicksell's basic arguments are necessary to include enough 'dynamic' elements, changes in time and circumstance, market structure, technical change and the rest, to enable us to be aided by Wicksell.[16]

We again emphasize that it would make no difference to prices in Wicksell's system if the natural rate rose and fell over time, *so long as the market rate rose and fell appropriately*. If the two rates were equal and remained so, they could fluctuate together 'till the cows come home' without disturbing the price level (in Keynes's *Treatise* language, without disturbing the equality of savings and investment – *ex ante*, in the later incarnation).

There is one obvious deficiency in Wicksell's own exposition which I cannot correct here. The theory, as Wicksell left it, cannot be falsified, and thus is not really a theory at all – as it stands.[17] But we shall be using the notion of the natural rate of interest in an ordinal sense only in conjunction with other historical evidence, so that we can hope to produce, overall, a fairly convincing argument.

From 1844 to 1914 the British economy grew, at varying rates, both when prices rose and when prices fell. There were, of course, trade-cycle episodes during the course of this growth. There were also cycles of a less obvious kind, long cycles. At the beginning of the period Britain was the world's major industrial nation, at the end, Britain was *one* of the world's major industrial nations. There had been major changes in the structure of the British economy, in financial institutions, labor force and overseas trade in this period.

The 'long Victorian boom', running from the late 1840s to the early 1870s witnessed a vast and rapid expansion of trade and industrial capacity in Britain. It also witnessed three powerful financial crises, 1847, 1857 and 1866. Because of the first two of these, and because of general interest in the functioning of the Bank Act of 1844, four great Parliamentary enquiries into banking gave posterity a rich mine of information about the monetary side of the developing British economy. (Secret Committee on the Causes of the Recent Commercial Distress etc., 1847–8; Secret Committee of the House of Lords, 1847–8; Select Committee on the Operation of the Bank Act, 1857; Select Committee on the Bank Acts and the Recent Commercial Distress, 1857–8.)

Then came the troubled period of falling prices which ended in 1896. During this period cyclical disturbances were not accompanied by monetary explosions like the earlier ones, and the Bank of England's policies were not subject to further intensive Parliamentary investigation. One result of this is a considerable poverty in our knowledge of monetary and banking development compared to the period up to 1858. Indeed, the role of central-bank policy in 1873–96 has come to be virtually ignored. Concentration at first was placed upon the connection between monetary standards and prices–a source of abundant confusion on both sides of the Atlantic.[18] Recently structural problems have been increasingly stressed, partly because of the implication that many twentieth-century problems, low productivity, backward technology, inability to adjust to changes in taste and all the rest, are rooted in the developments of this earlier period when British industrial supremacy was first challenged. Also, a new overseas empire, the growth of protectionist sentiments together with rising foreign investment stained the period with the sobriquet the 'new imperialism'–another area of modern interest.

Far from producing a consensus, recent investigations into 1873–96 have produced increasing diffuseness. The problems are not easy. Early investigations showed this. Alfred Marshall, before the Gold and Silver Commission, astonished contemporaries with the view that falling prices, falling interest yields and falling profits were consistent with 'prosperity', and he questioned whether complaints about a depression in the 1880s were justifiable at all. So numerous were opinions about the causes of falling prices that an official American commission was forced to order them under 180 separate categories (Layton, 1920).

Modern scholars at first stressed the cyclical characteristics of the late nineteenth century. Then, as interest in growth phenomena came to the fore, the importance of industrial retardation[19] came under intensive study. Increasing Empire and tropical trade meant that Britain was investing and selling in markets which had little growth potential compared to Western Europe and the USA[20] and the period 1873–96 offered abundant examples of decision-making that led to slow growth. The home market was open to foreign products and the question was raised whether this might not have slowed down home demand for domestically manufactured goods as foreign industrial development intensified the competition for markets and raw materials (Hoffman, 1955, pp. 214–15). It was held by some scholars (and contested by others) that Britain's early start in industry produced a burden of obsolete plant and equipment which, for various reasons, including the cheapness of domestic labor, was not replaced in step with technological possibilities. Problems of education, income distribution, capital market imperfections (Saville, 1961)[21] and failure of entrepreneurial recruitment have been held as additional reasons for the slowing down of British industrial growth after 1873 (Habakkuk, 1962, pp. 212–15; Aldcroft, 1964).

Some of the structural arguments are more convincing than others. They all contribute to our comprehension of the sources of general industrial retardation, and to some extent the new structural and quasi-sociological arguments are an embarrassment of riches. Yet the explanations have not been generally convincing and I think this is so because the economy in question was bifurcated, having no analysis of the influence of the *monetary half* of all the circle of transactions. The role of monetary influences has been pushed into the background, and there is no consistent long-run exposition of Bank of England policy which may have contributed to this history. After all, the Bank of England was always there. Profit expectations depended upon present and expected prices and costs. Hence investment decisions could not be independent of monetary influences. We will see that generally a monetary analysis rounds out the set of 'causes' of slower growth after 1873, and is not incompatible with any of them. H. W. Richardson's (1965, p. 131) complaint stands: 'It is as if each authority were trying to outbid the other in the number of "causes" which he can score.' The monetary side does not reduce the number of 'causes'. But it does show that some of the known structural phenomena were not irrational reactions to events. Moreover, addition of the monetary factor seems to me important enough to get at Richardson's cogent objections to the structural arguments:

> . . . the problem to be explained is not why the British economy expanded at a slightly slower rate than the newcomers but why the annual growth rate was half, or less than half, that abroad . . .
> (Richardson, 1965, p. 137).

If it can be shown that central-bank policy framed a long-term environment hostile for investment borrowing in Britain then a deficiency of investment is not surprising. Foreign investment made by British investors shows, after all, that investment funds were available from British sources if the price were right.

The Bank, as we have noted, acted as a private profit-making venture. Currency-school theorists had sought to *free* the Court of Directors from all except profit-making activity by the separation of the Bank into a mechanical gold-to-note and note-to-gold converter, the Issue Department, and a banking business based upon deposits, loans, discounts and investment in the public funds – the Banking department.[22]

There was extant, of course, the rudimentary notion of a central bank, or bank of last resort, for the business community. This developed over time, certainly it was fully acknowledged by Governor Lidderdale's time, if still in question when *Lombard Street* was published. At the beginning of the seven decades, though, the Court of Directors swung into the role of private banker with gusto. In 1845, 1846 and part of 1847 Bank Rate was below market rate as the Bank moved into the private discount business in competition with the rest of the market. After the Panic of 1847 the Bank was sharply criticized for fanning the flames of speculation and inflation by its aggressive policies. The tradition of 'following the market' began then and was not completely abandoned before 1914, although after the 1870s the Bank was willing to make the differential more a matter of its own policy than a reflection of market rates when the occasion arose. Yet it never went back to the aggressive tactics of 1844–7 (King, 1936, chapter 5). In 1852, as the new gold flooded in, Bank Rate dropped to the unprecedented low of 2 per cent. But it never fell below that figure before 1914, no matter what (Ibid., pp. 161–9).[23] Two traditions, following the market, and the 2 per cent floor were thus established with the passing of the first of the seven decades.

Other traditions started then too. The 'Treasury Letter', whereby the Government promised a bill of indemnity should the Bank issue notes in excess of the statutory limit, came first in 1847, again in 1857 with the first 10 per cent, 'panic rate' of Bank Rate, and again in 1866 with the fall of Overend and Gurney. In the Panic of 1873 Bank Rate went to 9 per cent, but not to the traditional maximum, and there was no need for a Treasury Letter. After that it was 1889 and then 1890 and the Baring Crisis before Bank Rate got so much as above 5 per cent. Ten per cent came again only in August, 1914 (Mitchell and Deane, 1962, p. 459).

Within these limits the Bank did a business of discounting bills of exchange, making loans and advances, accepting deposits and buying and selling securities. Profit was the motive, but the limits were imposed by the Bank's experience with the Bank Act of 1844, experience which had been painfully acquired. The Banking Department's reserve of notes was the guide to policy, not the (Issue Department's) gold reserve, as had been the case before 1844, and the two reserves could vary perversely indeed at times (Hughes, 1960, p. 241). It cannot be denied that the Act of 1844 achieved a certain success. The Bank of England note did not become inconvertible, as was threatened in 1836 and in 1825 under the terms of the 1819 Bank Act. The reason was that the Banking Department was bound to run out of its reserve of Issue Department notes completely long before the bullion in the Issue Department was threatened.[24] Hence the 'panic rates' and Treasury Letters in the early days. Although convertibility was secured, there could arise the question of the Banking Department having any reserve of those convertible notes. The Bank had its 'complete dream' of consol sales as security (Bagehot, 1962 ed., p. 33). But in fact, when the old-time panics struck, government action was necessary to relieve the tension.

But those events reflected something else. From the late 1840s to the early 1870s occurred the great Victorian expansion. After 1873 the British economy ceased to 'boom' as it had earlier, and the Bank of England needed no drastic measures further to protect itself from an economy which periodically used more of the medium of exchange than was comfortable under the Act of 1844. Then came the strange depressions of the 1880s and 1890s which seemed to combine great complaint of shortages of money with a glut of gold and low interest rates. What adjustments did the Bank of England make in its policies when the problem changed from primary concern with rapid expansions and reserve shortages to long-periods of slower growth and excess reserves ? Did the 'floor policy' become attuned to the needs of the new era as the 'ceiling' policies had been attuned to capping the old-time booms ? [25]

Our argument will be that here, after the tactical procedures of dealing with booms had contributed to the Bank's strategic success (at whatever short-run cost to traders and financiers) the traditional floor came into play inflexibly and was not altered significantly, and possibly inflicted upon the British economy losses in potential output as great as any that had threatened back in the old boom times. The compression of interest rates from 1873 to 1896, brought about by the unyielding floor, made continued deflation necessary, and gave rise among British investors to an

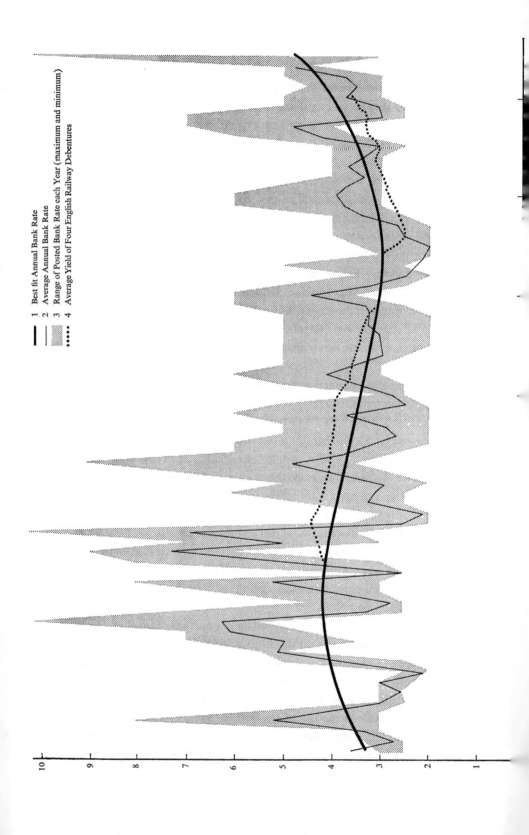

1 Best fit Annual Bank Rate
2 Average Annual Bank Rate
3 Range of Posted Bank Rate each Year (maximum and minimum)
4 Average Yield of Four English Railway Debentures

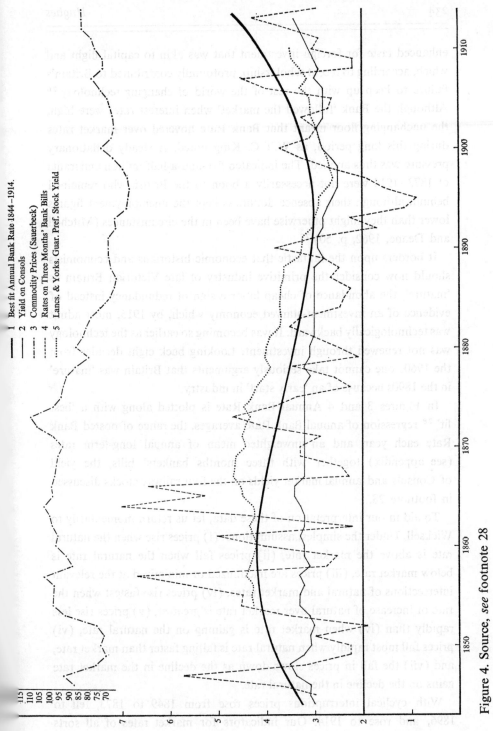

Figure 4. Source, *see* footnote 28

enhanced taste for foreign investment that was akin to capital flight and which, according to recent scholarship, profoundly contributed to Britain's failure to keep up with the rest of the world of changing technology.[26] Although the Bank 'followed the market' when interest rates were high, the unchanging floor meant that Bank Rate hovered over market rates during this long period, as W.T.C. King noted. A steady deflationary pressure was thus applied. The indicated five-and-a-half million emigrants of 1873–1914 were not necessarily a boon to the British who remained behind, although their absence doubtless kept the unemployment figures lower than they might otherwise have been in the circumstances (Mitchell and Deane, 1962, p. 50).[27]

It borders upon the fantastic that economic historians and economists should now consider the primitive industry of late Victorian Britain as 'mature', the abundance of cheap labor a sign of redundancy instead of evidence of an investment-starved economy which, by 1913, most admit was technologically backward. It was becoming so earlier as the technology was not renewed through investment. Looking back eight decades from the 1960s one cannot take seriously arguments that Britain was 'mature' in the 1890s because of an 'early start' in industry.

In Figures 3 and 4 Annual Bank Rate is plotted along with a 'best fit' [28] regression of annual Bank Rate averages, the range of posted Bank Rate each year, and an unweighted mean of annual long-term rates (see appendix) together with three months bankers' bills, the yield of Consols and annual market yields on the four railway stocks discussed in footnote 28.

To aid in our interpretation of these data, let us return momentarily to Wicksell. Under the simplest assumptions: (i) prices rise when the natural rate is above the market rate, (ii) prices fall when the natural rate is below market rate, (iii) prices are maximized or minimized at the relevant intersections of natural and market rates, (iv) prices rise fastest when the rate of increase of natural over market rate is greatest, (v) prices rise less rapidly than (iv) when market rate is gaining on the natural rate, (vi) prices fall most rapidly when natural rate is falling faster than market rate, and (vii) the fall in prices slows down as the decline in the market rate gains on the decline in the natural rate.

With cyclical interruptions prices rose from 1849 to 1873, fell to 1896, and rose to 1914. Our indicators for market rates of all sorts rise to the neighborhood of 1867, fall to the mid-nineties and then rise to 1914.

Following the rules of Wicksell's analysis, the natural rate can be said to have risen irregularly in the first period to 1873 (as prices rose); it fell to 1896, and then rose again to 1914.

Long-term movements in the main interest series used in Figures 3 and 4 are smoothed out by overlapping 9 year averages in Table 1. Generally, they follow the same pattern as does the polynomial fitted curve for annual Bank Rate, with a maximum range roughly from the mid-1850s to the mid-1860s, and the minimum falling in the decade of the 1890s (centering on 1895–6). Why do the interest rates start down in the 1860s and prices rise from 1867 to 1873 ? Several interpretations are possible.

TABLE 1. Nine year moving averages of

	bank rate	3 months bankers bills	yield on consols	average of four English railway debenture yields
1846–54	3·52	3·40	3·20	—
1851–59	4·17	3·91	3·18	4·38@
1856–64	4·72	4·43	3·22	4·29@
1861–69	4·36	4·30	3·27	4·52@
1866–74	3·71	3·71	3·22	4·21
1871–79	3·39	3·22	3·18	3·97
1876–84	3·20	2·84	3·08	3·70
1881–89	3·38	2·79	2·98	3·40
1886–94	3·19	2·47	2·88	3·09
1891–99	2·78	2·05	2·66	2·75
1896–04	3·35	2·82	2·70	2·81
1901–09	3·60	3·09	2·88	3·11
1906–14	3·90	3·33	3·11	3·25@

Sources: *See* footnote 28. 1851–59, 1856–64 and 1861–69 are yields for the Lancashire and Yorkshire Railway only, the 1906–14 number is for the year 1906 only, but like all data in this series from 1863 onwards is the average of four railway yield series.

If the model for the period were taken to be the purely monotonic case (Figure 1, price curve B) then the data in Figure 4 suggest that in the mid-1850s the margin of the natural rate over the market rate was probably at its maximum and the period roughly 1880–7 may have been the maximum of the market rate over the natural rate. These periods correspond, of course, to the strongest part of the expansion of the 1850s (1851 irregularly to 1856, preceding the Panic of 1857) and the well-known 'depression' of the 1880s. It is interesting that Bank Rate was high, relative to its own trend, during this depression (Table 1). No other interest series followed Bank Rate in this regard. W. T. C. King (1936, chap. 5) considered this to be deliberate Bank policy.

If one considers, as Wicksell did, the return to real capital investment as half of the natural rate calculation, but that, in addition, such a yield was not especially volatile in very short periods, then the price rise of 1869–73 may be seen as a 'bubble' on the long-term movement of the natural rate. This rise could have been due to mainly speculative expectations in Britain in association with the inflationary impact of the Franco-Prussian War and its aftermath, together with the strong American boom which ended in the Panic of 1873. Such assumptions would free one of the necessity of supposing that 1869–73 represented a time when there was a fundamental re-evaluation of long-term prospects which led to a strong rise in the expected long-run return to real investment. The slight price recoveries of 1879–80 and the plateau of the late 1880s could be similar cases, although the period at the end of the 1870s did witness a recovery of investment even though unaccompanied by any strong or sustained rise in prices.

The alternative would be simply to take Wicksell at his most dogmatic, place no time limitations upon variations in the natural rate, and argue that rising prices mean that the natural rate exceeds the market rate and falling prices mean the opposite–always. This is the simplest procedure. But from our point of view, with the evidence of sustained long-term movements in both prices and interest rates only barely interrupted by price recoveries at least in 1873–96, there is some merit in considering Wicksell's scheme in a long-term framework and dividing the expectations on investment into two parts, that part related to hoped-for profit from the greater efficiency of new plant and equipment, and that part related to expected increases in profitability due to more transitory speculative hopes, as suggested for 1869–73. The two together equal the expected yield to real investment, but part of it is related to technical efficiency and part to more temporary market phenomena such as war, sudden inflows of bullion, etc.

The data suggest that the strongest long-term upward pressure ended in the years from about 1857–69, with the peak in the 1851–6 period. In the mid-1860s the consol yields and the railway yields both reached their secular peaks and began the long decline to the mid-1890s, centering upon 1896. In the mid-1860s, in association with the Crisis of 1866, Bank Rate hit 10 per cent for the last time prior to 1914 and the three months bill rate hit its last strong peak of the century (Figure 4). The natural rate could already have been declining, as prices were from 1863 to 1869, and then the speculative bubble leading to 1873 brought a tactical Bank Rate resurgence which was not really followed by any other interest rates. Consol yields did not rise, nor did the railway yields in 1869–73 and the rise in the other short-term rate, the three months bankers bill rate, was weak compared to earlier periods of very high Bank Rate (Figures 3 and 4).

The end of the American Civil War in 1865 brought an immediate release from inflationary pressures. As American goods came into the world market, American prices fell and American output rose, the expected yields to British investment (in current prices) could well have justifiably weakened. The 1869–73 rise in prices seen as a bubble on the long-term movement of the natural rate makes sense against this background. Also, of course, the strong gold inflows beginning in 1866 raised the Bank of England's bullion reserve to unprecedented heights (Mitchell and Deane, 1962, pp. 444–5),[29] easing the reserve problem for the banks generally, contributing to lower borrowing costs and making any rise of plateau in the natural rate inflationary. Then why did the Bank of England counter with rising Bank Rate when its reserves were abundant in 1869–73? Again it is a matter of tactics. As Hawtrey (1938, pp. 90–2) points out, the apparently abundant reserve of notes of the Banking Department was only maintained by a constant battle against exports as German gold purchases began in 1871 to go on the Gold Standard and interior demand for notes rose with prices up to 1873.

After 1873 there is no problem about significant increases in the natural rate until 1896. The long-run fall in the natural rate was rapid enough that even lower market rates did not offset the deflationary effects. Lower costs with falling prices, periodic failure to invest at home and the attraction of investment abroad certainly helped form the basis of the falling natural rate.[30] With the slow-down in export demand existing plant and equipment could do the output job without straining capacity. The Bank of England did not see its reserve rise significantly in the 1880s (Mitchell and Deane, 1962, pp. 444–5),[31] and here perhaps lies the explanation of the rise and plateau in Bank Rate in the 1880s when the trend of other interest rates was downward. It is here, in about 1880–6 that the deflationary pressure may have been greatest, the excess of market over the natural rate greatest.

The natural rate's maxima after 1873 cannot have seriously been above the various Bank Rate maxima cyclically, as the latter sufficed in every case to do the usual things credited to it, including adding a full stop to any previous tendency for prices to rise. The minimum natural rate clearly occurred around 1894–6 when prices reached their trough, Bank Rate was at its 2 per cent floor, three months bills yielded less, and other indicated market rates were at their minima. The natural rate rose after 1896, indicated by the rise in prices *together with market rates*. Bank Rate left the 2 per cent floor for good – 'it was no more heard of' (Clapham, 1944, vol. 2, p. 370) – indicating an end of the compression which had lasted since 1873.

Wicksell's analysis suggests that 2 per cent in 1894–6 was *too high*; had Bank Rate been less, market rates generally would have fallen eventually below the natural rate, and a recovery would have been sparked. Is this reasonable? Keynes (1930, vol. 2, p. 170), writing of this episode in the twenties, weakened at this point, and called for the government.

As we have noted, the Bank had developed a clear set of procedures to handle booms in the panics of 1847, 1857 and 1866. In between Bank Rate had been dropped sharply, as can be seen in Figure 3, but not so sharply as to repeat the 'errors' of 1845–7 when the Bank was charged with fostering speculation with too low a minimum. It was low enough, though, to employ the reserve at a suitable level. Two per cent was the floor. But so long as the natural rate was rising, these reductions of Bank Rate and associated declines in market rate gave traders renewed 'insurance', relatively large margins of possible yields over borrowing costs. Also, widening the spread of the interest rate structure provided more 'space' in which financial intermediaries of all kinds could operate. Thus the very high maxima of the 1849–73 expansion did not kill secular growth, even if, in each cycle, activity was damped by successful Bank of England tactics. And this brought strategic success, as it was both profitable, turned the exchanges and all the rest.

But when the natural rate was falling from 1873 to the mid-nineties, while the same tactics as before were followed on the ceilings, with easier successes (no more 10 per cent and no more Treasury Letters), *the floor remained fixed*. As the natural rate declined faster than market rates (indicated by falling prices together with falling market rates) the structure was compressed. Periodic drops in Bank Rate were of smaller amplitude, shortening the insurance margin, and leaving larger and larger unused reserves. Finally, at the trough of the long compression, the Bank was glutted, and, as noted, in 1895 found itself in the fantastic position of holding in idle reserve more of the Issue Department's notes than the public held.

How low would Bank Rate have needed to go to 'force' the notes out? Recall that Bank Rate was not 'market rate'. Our market rate indicators are in the range of 2·5 to 3 per cent in the compression trough, apart from three months bankers bills which, at annual rates, hit just under 1 per cent. But the three months bankers bill rate was then rock-bottom; *it was a rate not available for ordinary businessmen*. By then, the compression of the interest structure must have sharply reduced the area of profitable operations for financial intermediaries of all sorts, making the profitable area for borrowing and lending extremely narrow. The living area of Professor Hicks's 'hierarchy of specializations' among financial intermediaries was being crushed. The consequences were bound to be debilitating for the economy at large. Indeed, W.T.C. King indicated that the Bank of England had, by staying at 2 per cent, just enabled the discount houses to maintain profitable operations (Hicks, 1965, pp. 285–7; King, 1936, p. 311). Natural rate could have been in the range of the spread of the market rates, low enough, but not unreasonably low; that is, it is hard to imagine the natural rate as low as either Bank Rate or the banker bill rates even if such a thing is conceptually possible.

Hence Bank Rate of 1·5 or 1 per cent might have dropped the market rate, if the Bank had attracted enough business to itself to force the other financial institutions to compete. But the rule of the 1844–7 episode was to keep the Bank from competing aggressively for discounts and the tradition was a floor of 2 per cent.

Application of Wicksell to this history raises what is perhaps a more fundamental question. There was nothing *necessary*, historically inevitable, about the depressions of the late nineteenth century, and the extreme conditions of the eighties and nineties during the compression. Suppose a flexible 'floor policy' had existed earlier, in the 1880s or the 1870s. Ranges of early Bank Rate variations, as high as 5 to 7 per cent following earlier periods of tight money (Figure 3), applied in 1873–96 would have dropped Bank Rate below 2 per cent, even below 1 per cent when Bank Rate bumped along its 2 per cent minimum floor. As the compression developed foreign investment became popular; in Cairncross's phrase, foreign investment became a 'sink' for unemployable British funds.

This view supplies answers to four questions. (i) Brinley Thomas's analysis was based upon investment funds which seemed to be income-invariant, so that as British income fell, or grew slowly relative to foreign, British funds flowed out. We see that they were in fact squeezed out, as many have noted, at the expense of domestic investment, except in the early 1890s, and even there, when domestic investment stagnated, foreign investment remained far above the levels of the late 1870s (Cairncross, 1953, tables 38 and 40). (ii) Richardson had no explanation of the doldrums in innovation which came with such frequency in 1873–96, he just assumed that a 'lull' came about following the great developments of midcentury. Why should there have been such a lull? A healthy economy innovates, obsolete plant is torn out and replaced. New industries grow up. Retardation in individual industries need not necessarily permeate the whole economy. Replacement of old industries by new in the Kuznets-Burns analysis *is part of growth itself* (Kuznets, 1954, p. 253–7; Burns, 1934, pp. 270–81). Why not in Britain in this period?

Modern scholarship has suggested a number of answers. Clearly there could be no one answer to such a question. We add a monetary reason for the stagnation of investment in 1873–96. Bank tactical policies plus the inflexible interest floor kept market rates too high as the natural rate fell. Foreign investment was not an unfortunate accident, but was a rational market reaction to the long compression in Britain. (iii) What happened to British entrepreneurs? In his criticism of Habakkuk and Erickson,

Richardson (1965, p. 139) emphasizes the failure of British entrepreneurship cannot by itself explain the stagnation.

> If such a case is to be justified, it is necessary to explain why the economy which produced the most dynamic entrepreneurs in the first half of the nineteenth century produced the most inefficient in the second half.

Part of the answer must lie in the growth of the Victorian caste system treated by Habakkuk and Erickson. But also the compression was a poor environment indeed for any sort of entrepreneurial revolution. As Richardson emphasizes, had there been industry-creating innovations generally, as was the bicycle industry in the 1890s, and as there were in other countries in machinery, electricity and chemicals, etc., the loss of investment funds abroad would not have been so severe, and would not have continued so powerfully in the early twentieth century at the expense of domestic development. This flight of funds was to some extent cumulative. (iv) The long depressions and short expansions of 1873–96 were, again, partly a product of the compression. It is not the case that '. . . obviously the causes of a declining rate of growth are not the same as the causes of a secular price fall' (Richardson, 1965, pp. 145–6). Obviously, such things are not unconnected. Investment is a function of profits and profit expectations–total revenue minus total cost. Total revenue equals price times quantity, total cost equals average cost times the number of inputs, including labor. With falling prices and sticky wages a problem arises regarding profits. The profit level may be maintained by productivity-increasing investment, but not so easily as profits can be raised if prices are rising, and wages lag behind price increases. If, as was the case in 1873–96, investment fails to raise productivity sufficiently to offset declining prices and sticky wages, then growth will be slow. In such circumstances the sources of the fall in prices are also sources of a declining rate of growth. The compression of 1873–96 is such a source.

Insofar as foreign investment robbed the British economy of needed home investment, so much was Britain's ability to compete in rapidly growing industrial countries weakened, and so much was the drift into Empire trade encouraged. An earlier drop in the floor might have lifted the economy, and the interest-rate crush of 1892–6 might never have come. While this analysis neither supports nor weakens Musson's argument that a slowing down of industrial growth after 1873 or so was 'inevitable', one can say that our analysis makes such a slow-down 'not surprising'.

The losses of men and capital were no boon to Britain, unless one assumes that their contribution to world output and demand was necessarily higher abroad than at home, an assumption about secular diminishing returns and the viability of the British economy which would require really bold arguments.[32] What is usually argued is that the British did extremely well out of a bad situation (Richardson, 1965, pp. 145–6). However, as recent scholars have noted, a habit was formed, and when more favorable conditions returned with the rise in the natural rate after 1896 the outflow of capital continued and British industry did not refresh its technology. Growth was even slower than before. As Thomas (1954, pp. 228–30) put it, 'the accomplished old rentier' continued to provide others with capital when his own estates were crying for sustenance.

Thus, with some interpretation and the addition of relevant factual information Wicksell's theory is more than just the empirical rule he laid down in his 1898 paper and in *Interest and Prices*. Given an historical and statistical mechanism based on modern research Wicksell does seem to provide a key. Without such historical foundations Wicksell's theory long remained an *a priori* explanation – one of many. What Keynes missed, that modern scholarship has provided, is a set of explanations for secular shifts in the natural rate. We can now see how the very odd monetary phenomena of the seven decades can be squared with the results of hard historical scholarship about growth, trade, foreign investment, the structure of industry and the record of emigration. What has been missing in the general picture has been a systematic way to explain the complex events in the City, which, in spite of cyclical upheavals, yielded an illusion of secular stability where there was investment and technological stagnation, and excessive liquidity when that liquidity was 'spilled on the ground', as Keynes put it. Economic theorists scarcely had time to consider Wicksell in his Keynesian clothes, before the clothes themselves were transmogrified into those of the *General Theory* and the analysis of natural and market rates was long ignored, apart from polite textbook references, in the Keynesian Revolution and its aftermath.

What held the market rate behind rises in the natural rate to 1873, what slowed the market rate's decline to 1896, and what held it back afterwards ? Keynes (1930, vol. 2, p. 206) noted its stickiness. As he put it:

> Between 1820 and 1900 . . . the rate of interest did not fall fast
> enough to keep investment level with savings, except during the
> great mid-nineteenth-century investment boom, 1855–1875.

During the compression of 1873–96, the shortest market rate (three months bankers bills) does not fall below the traditional Bank Rate minimum of 2 per cent until 1894. Was it kept up long before 1894 by the Bank's unwillingness to go below 2 per cent, unwillingness to repeat the 'errors' of 1844–7 and actively compete for discounts ? Why did the Bank refuse to go lower ? What, apart from 'tradition' really was the magic of 2 per cent ? For a Wicksellian analysis the 2 per cent minimum becomes as interesting an historical phenomenon as the old 10 per cent peaks have been. Scholars have mainly been interested in the 'tactical' mechanisms at the peaks of interest movements. But tactics at the floors are equally deserving of study if the details of the compression are to be completely understood. For example, when King indicated that somehow business was available for discount houses at a profit during the period when the rates on three months bankers bills were below the 2 per cent floor, was he suggesting collusion between the Bank and the discount market ? An agreement to hold the line on discount rates would have been effective if the major houses and the Bank agreed. Such an agreement would not have been unwelcome to the commercial banks who lent the discount market funds at call. At least a minimal trend of profitability was maintained to keep financial intermediaries alive by keeping the structure artificially high, if compressed. But a 1 per cent Bank Rate might have done a better job. Since the compression was due to the failure of market rate to fall appropriately with the natural rate, one might easily conclude that Keynes let the Bank off too easily.[33]

There is a final, entirely speculative point. We have referred earlier to ratchet effects on business decisions. What about in the Court of Directors ? Thomson Hankey was a member in 1838 during the first skirmishes between Palmer, Torrens and Overstone. According to Clapham (1944, vol. 2, p. 357), in 1890, forty-two years later, Hankey moved, as a member of the Court, that the Bank cease publishing its minimum rate and go back to an active discount business at rates below 2 per cent. Hankey was then eighty-five years old. The Bank of England was ruled by a self-perpetuating oligarchy. Perhaps they remembered the past too well when the compression started and the men of 10 per cent were still about in the Parlour. Their robust willingness to staunch an outflow of bullion with a whacking Bank Rate increase developed in an era when the British economy knew powerful 'booms' (when the natural rate was rising) and fast recoveries from ensuing crises. Until retirements and death changed the Bank's management, such ratchet experience in the Court of Directors was additionally deflationary, as vigorous tactical increases in discount rates during a secular decline in the market rate, together with a fixed floor, could not help but dampen the ardour of traders who were influenced by interest costs. The compression was over by 1897, but that was more than three decades after the fall of Overend and Gurney, 10 per cent and the last Treasury Letter. There had been no great boom for a generation. Younger men in the Court had not known booms and powerfully rising prices. As the natural rate and prices rose perhaps the old deflationary influences were weakened at the Bank with the passing of the men of 10 per cent; perhaps there was an inflationary ratchet at work in the Bank. Prices did indeed rise (Figure 2). Had Bank Rate been dropped lower after 1896 a new boom in investment might have been engendered. But when the natural rate rose after 1896 the Bank's floor rose too. Although this did not stop prices from rising it could have helped to keep market rate close enough to investment yields to discourage domestic investment. As it was the foreign investment habit kept new domestic capital outlays at lower levels than might otherwise have been the case, and no new boom came before 1914.

All this may be summarized in a few sentences. Generally, from the mid-1840s to the late 1860s and early 1870s, by Wicksell's scheme and related historical evidence, movements of the natural and market rates of interest were favorable to domestic investment because of the Bank of England's willingness to drop Bank Rate down sharply after cyclical periods of high interest rates. The economy was one of strong expansion, and the high Bank Rate maxima, although tactically successful in capping booms, did not produce secular dampening effects. From the mid-1870s to the mid-1890s, although maximum tactical Bank Rates came down, the *range* of the spread of Bank Rate (Figure 3), and of interest rates generally, was sharply reduced by the maintenance of an arbitrary floor. As a matter of policy, Bank Rate was kept above other market rates whenever possible. Prices were falling with market rates, and hence the natural rate was falling too. The compression produced a profoundly deflationary situation, which encouraged emigration and foreign investment. Industrial growth slowed down. After the late 1890s when prices recovered and market rates rose, so did the natural rate. But emigration rose and foreign investment boomed – 'Britain's lost opportunity', as Brinley Thomas put it. The Bank of England's arbitrary floor was not touched again before 1914.

Our formal model is no touchstone and by itself explains little. But there is now a well-developed body of solid historical information which is consistent with this policy analysis and which, indeed, as Wicksell claimed, this analysis helps to illuminate. One general growth factor which has been largely ignored by modern scholarship concerning Britain in this period has been central-bank policy. Possibly the presumed 'automacy' of the gold-standard adjustments, and possibly the existence of monetary analyses in nearly all short term cyclical studies have contributed to the lack of a longer-term monetary-policy framework. It is such a framework that we have tried to produce here.

Such is one interpretation of the seven decades when Peel's Bank Act ruled the Gold Standard. Our interpretation, relying mainly upon recent scholarship, but also illuminated by some of the Keynes's insights is, like Wicksell's 1898 paper, not inconsistent with the facts. We have now added an historical and statistical mechanism which purports to explain *why Wicksell's empirical rule works*. It is intellectually satisfying?

ACKNOWLEDGMENTS

The author is indebted to the J. S. Guggenheim Memorial Foundation, the Purdue Research Foundation and the Krannert Graduate School which defrayed computer expenses; also to Mark Ridgway, Kenneth Young and Professor George Horwich.

NOTES AND REFERENCES

[1] *Capital and Growth* (Hicks, 1965) took up Wicksell again for long-run growth considerations. The pristine theory may be examined in 'The Influence of the Rate of Interest on Commodity Prices' (Wicksell, 1958); also *Interest Rates and Prices* (Wicksell, 1965). J. M. Keynes

notes the main Continental adapters, up to 1930, and amended the
theory (Keynes, 1930). (All references here are to the 1953 edition.)
Volume I, pp. 154–5, 186, 196–220, contain the main development
and discussion of the theory. Its use occurs extensively in the historical
narratives given in Volume II. George Horwich (1966) has recently fired
a Wicksellian salvo.

[2] Mitchell and Deane (1962). See 'Banking and Insurance', Table 2
for reserve figures and Table 9 for Bank Rate. The modern economist
may not comprehend these figures. Let me explain. The Banking Department reserve of the Issue Department's notes in these figures stood at
£27·3 millions in 1895, the Issue Department's 'Circulation' of its own
notes was £25·8 millions. The latter were in the hands of the public.
In 1896 the numbers were £32·3 millions and £26·5 millions. In any
year the sum of the two was supposed, under the terms of the Bank
Act of 1844, to equal the Issue Department's gold reserve plus the
fiduciary issue, notes issued against Issue Department securities ear-
marked for that purpose pursuant to Article V. The fiduciary issue in
1895, for example, was £16·8 millions, leaving an indicated gold reserve
of £36·3 millions; the figure in Mitchell and Deane is £36·4 millions.
The error presumably is accounted for by rounding, discrepancies in
accounting dates, etc. Similarly, in 1896 the gold reserve of the Issue
Department indicated by the note figures was £42·0 millions; the figure
given by Mitchell and Deane is the same. The fiduciary issue as of 1895
can be found in Palgrave (1903), p. 223.

[3] See Figure 3. Source, Mitchell and Deane (1962), Table 8.
Consol yields on an annual basis rose from 3·0 in 1852 to 3·4 in 1865–6
and declined irregularly to 2·5 in 1896–8.

[4] For *empirical* work the proper mixture is a vexing problem. See
Basmann (1965), Hughes (1966).

[5] There now exists an extensive literature on the Bank Act of 1844.
It has never been clear just who were the main persons who influenced
Sir Robert Peel, who, as Prime Minister, pushed the Act through parlia-
ment. The basic idea came from Ricardo (1824). In chapter 10 of
Hughes (1960), is given a brief summary of the history of the Act with
references to the main modern works treating the subject, as of 1960.
Since then Professor F. W. Fetter (1965) has covered the ground again.
Fetter leans toward Colonel Torrens as the major intellectual influence;
traditionally it was Samuel Jones Lloyd (Lord Overstone) who was
supposed to have been the *éminence grise* of this legislation. The narrow
truth of the matter is not known, even though Fetter made an exhaustive
effort to push back this particularly arcane frontier of knowledge.

[6] Moreover, Torrens (1857, pp. 8–11), at least at one stage of his
long and erratic career, explicitly denied the moneyness of bank money

– cheques. He did think that bills of exchange were almost money, pp. 11–18. There was much grousing about this, ranging from gold-coin purity to J. S. Mill's catholicity. See Hughes (1960, pp. 232–3).

[7] Lord Overstone in particular was the pillar of orthodoxy on the immediate and universal effects of the supposed price-specie-flow mechanism. See his long answer to Q. 3645, of the Commons Committee on the Bank Acts (1857).

[8] This is a matter of brevity. If I may be permitted a slight pre-sumption, I shall assume that the critical reader will be able to see in my own published work on the complexities of short-run Bank of England tactics, and of cycles more generally, that I am well aware of the importance of what I am omitting. E.g., Hughes (1956); chapter 10 and appendix 5 of Hughes (1960); Hughes and Rosenberg (1963).

[9] Hawtrey (1938), Clapham (1944), Morgan (1943), Feavearyear (1963), King (1936), are perhaps the standard running accounts of the Bank's developing tactics during the period concerning us. Einzig (1962, chapters 15–18) has some interesting detail on these issues. Recently A. G. Ford (1962; 1965; 1964) has added significantly to our know-lege of the cyclical impact of the Bank's actions in the late nineteenth and early twentieth centuries. The latter paper is particularly explicit about the tactical success of Bank Rate – success from the Bank's point of view. 'But it must be emphasized that, while a sustained rise in Bank Rate, if it cut overseas lending by making new issues more difficult brought immediate relief without burden to the British economy, never-theless the last rise in Bank Rate to its cyclical peak had the less happy result in the next year or so of provoking a fall in exports. Thus the balance of payments would then have tended to worsen again but for the depressive effects of falling exports on incomes and on imports – the automatic mechanism', p. 30. The Bank's tactics protected its reserve at the cyclical peak, and made its contribution to the long-term strategy of convertibility. Moreover, a check of earnings figures in appendices C and D of Clapham (1944), ii, pp. 433–5 and the charts pp. 440–2 will establish that such tactics also made profound contributions to the Bank's other strategic goal, profitability. *The crisis were the years of greatest earnings.* The *Cunliffe Report* stated 'The provisions of the Act of 1844 so applied to that system have operated both to correct un-favorable exchanges and to undue expansions of credit' (Ford, 1962, p. 4). Such testimonials could be multiplied. *The Bank's tactics worked so far as the Bank's strategy was concerned.* Or as Lord Overstone put it before the Lord's Committee of 1847 when asked about the necessity of applying the Bank's 'screw' during a crisis at the peak of a boom when the Bank Act allowed of no *ad libitum* issues of bank notes: 'In fact, the patient, however painful the operation may be, must submit

to it if it becomes necessary ? – yes.' See Hughes (1960, p. 322). The
Bank's tactics could be sharp medicine indeed, but all evidence shows
them to have been successful from the Bank's strategic point of view.
One can be appalled by this history, but, given the terms of the 1844
Bank Act, it is difficult to see what the Bank's alternatives could have
been so long as the Act was in force.

[10] By 'meaningful' I mean a concept like 'equilibrium price', a useful
reference point. It is helpful when considering Wicksell to bear in mind
that all transactions take place *at the market rate* except when it happens
to equal the natural rate. Apart from that, 'natural rate' is a reference
point, that level of interest-payment flows which would stabilize the
general price level, something easily imaginable, and something central
bankers are in fact talking about with phrases like 'full employment
without inflation', etc. Thus an argument that central bankers ought
to make the market rate equal the natural rate is an argument that the
effects of central bank policy on prices ought to be to stabilize them
and prevent general movements.

[11] Wicksell was vague about turning points in price and interest
movements in his theory in a way that rivals the Marshallian style.
We will turn to this problem shortly.

[12] In the full exposition of this theory given in *Interest Rates and
Prices*, Wicksell (1965, p. 120) gives the problem of turning points a
cavalier treatment: e.g. 'If, for any reason whatever, the average rate
of interest is set and maintained *below* this normal level, no matter how
small the gap, prices will rise and go on rising; or if they were already
in the process of falling, they will fall more slowly and eventually begin
to rise.' The first part of this statement is solid, but the second part
nullifies the authority of the first part, and suggests both lags and
monotonic relationships, etc. Such things are not rare in Wicksell.

[13] Footnote 12.

[14] A.D. Gayer, W.W. Rostow, A.J. Schwartz (1953). Price series
measured against the NBER nine stage cycle generally show a III–V
conformity up to 1850: vol. II, Table 61, p. 537; Tables pp. 802–15,
discussion in chapter IX, for the expansion '. . . the most appropriate
pattern is I–V', p. 819. In the market rates included in the financial
series thus measured, tables, vol. II, pp. 858–79, discussion pp. 915–22
generally show a lag beyond the stage V peak to stage VII. See p. 883.
Market rates thus lagged prices by two NBER cycle stages up to 1850.
Although less precisely measured afterward, the lag is a well-known
phenomenon up to 1914, especially in connection with the Bank of
England's policy of following the market. Keynes (1930, vol. 2, pp. 203–
6) advanced a series of arguments about the institutional origins of the
market-rate lag relative to price movements and the natural rate.

15 This sentence is for those who refuse to consider that memory and experience influence economic decisions. I appeal to their respect for machinery, hoping that the human brain can be considered at least a poor second to modern computer 'hardware'.

16 Why was Keynes ambivalent about expectations in the *Treatise* (1930) ? After all, the *General Theory* is full of off-the-cuff psychological effects. I think that in spite of his historical excursions he was not thinking like an historian. Hence his belief that ultimately the facts would rule over expectations. True doubtlessly, except that in a *flow* of events over time, 'ultimately' doesn't happen in any final sense. The new day dawns, with new hopes, dangers, demands, all determinants of expectations, all to be used again as new decisions must be made. Keynes's change on this score in the *General Theory* is especially strong in the marginal efficiency of capital and the motives for liquidity preference.

17 If there is no way to try the theory out against data under varying assumptions to determine the conditions under which the predictions will not be in accord with observations, we cannot know whether we understand the phenomena under investigation or whether we simply are making true statements which may be entirely trivial as far as causal forces are concerned. See John R. Platt (1964, pp. 145–7).

18 A brief survey of the main conclusions of early investigations into 1873–96 is found by W. T. Layton (1920), chapter VII.

19 Income growth apparently slowed down after 1890 while growth of industrial output slowed down soon after 1870. The modern emphasis on the 'Great Depression' as a growth problem, rather than a cyclical one, received its major impetus with E. H. Phelps-Brown and S. J. Handfield-Jones (1952) 'Study in the Expanding Economy', *Oxford Economic Papers*, New Series, 1952. D. J. Coppock (1956) countered, moving the climacteric back to the 1870s (which was more comfortable for most economic historians). From there the scope of enquiry broadened and deepened. A. E. Musson (1959) re-examined the issue; then came John Saville (1961); Coppock (1963) countered then Musson (1963) was back a year later after which both Coppock (1964) and Musson (1964) appeared in tandem. H. W. Richardson (1965) produced a summary and critique of these papers and others, and books, which, although not focused primarily upon 1873–96, dealt with it in passing. William Ashworth (1966) also joined in the discussion. Since the evidence upon which all arguments about growth rests is primarily quantitative, and the discussion has now been extensively developed, the later papers deal perforce primarily with critical analyses of the data and their interpretation. The 'Great Depression' of 1873–96 still exists as an historical phenomenon in the sense that all agree that industrial

growth slowed down then and no one has yet called it either the Great
Constant or the Great Expansion. But the roots of the phenomena of
1873–96 are now seen to be complex indeed and the extent to which
1896 marks the end of any 'depression' except in the movement of
prices and interest rates is now in question, since the evidence shows no
decisive pickup in industrial growth after prices rose in 1897. In none
of these analyses was the monetary system given a crucial role. This
perhaps reflects the growing sophistication of economics itself as well
as the modern distaste for over-simplified explanations of things, which
the old-time monetary analyses certainly did produce. One does not
object to such progress, but there *was*, after all, a central bank and a
monetary system in 1873–96. As an aside, let it not be thought that
the fate of agriculture has been lost sight of; T. W. Fletcher (1961)
found that the depressing effects upon agriculture of downward moving
prices in 1873–96 was mainly limited to corn and has been generally
exaggerated.

[20] British exports to Asia rarely exceeded those to USA before the
1850s. Then, in 1858, after the Crisis of 1857, in conjunction with the
consolidation of British rule in India and a decisive shift in British
overseas lending toward Asia, the Asian share surged ahead of exports
to USA, except for the solitary period 1871–2, for the rest of the century.
By 1910 exports to Asia were 20·5 per cent of the total, compared to
only 12·7 per cent to all of North America. Exports to Africa and Latin
America also had more or less overtaken those to North America,
although not in every year. British exports to Europe had declined as a
proportion of the total, but less dramatically than the proportional
decline in exports to USA (Schlote, 1952, pp. 157–60; Jenks, 1938,
p. 214). The conjunction of this shift in British overseas trade distribution has been widely held to be a shift toward easy, but relatively
stagnant markets (Meyer, 1965; Berill, 1960). Saul (1960, chapters 8–9)
notes the many advantages to Britain of the Empire trade (especially
in multilateral clearings) but deplores both the maintenance of textiles
and railway materials manufacturing in Britain which this trade encouraged and also the temptation fostered in the hearts of British traders
to avoid, or withdraw from the rapidly growing but more competitive
markets in Europe and America. Charles Kindleberger (1961), argues
that in the late nineteenth century Britain's main exporting manu-
facturers had become overspecialized and thus remained inflexibly tied
to traditional products and hence to areas that wanted them. He shows
the shift in the direction of cotton exports away from Europe and
America to Asia and Africa as a particularly dramatic example, pp.
295–300. To him, p. 295, British export growth was 'bound to decline'
in any event.

[21] The argument about the early start began with an exchange in 1955–6, Marvin Frankel (1955) and Donald Gordon (1956) argued against the early start thesis, i.e. that an early start need necessarily impose a constraint upon subsequent growth and Frankel (1956) answered him. The attack upon the early start thesis was renewed by Edward Ames and Nathan Rosenberg (1963). Richardson's (1965, pp. 139–40) argument against Ames and Rosenberg is that both USA and Germany did not start out as mainly agricultural countries but that each was, instead, a 'highly industrialized late-comer'. I cannot imagine the evidence upon which this assertion is based.

[22] R. G. Hawtrey (1938) is oddly ambiguous about this. Again and again his accounts of increases or decreases in the gold supply and the reserve of notes are written as if the two were merely automatic reflections of one another. Apart from the Bank's deposits, there was no automatic way for the two reserves to change simultaneously or even in uniform directions. Sales and purchases of securities, loans and discounts raised or reduced, constituted the only connection, apart from deposits, between the Issue Department's gold and the Banking Department's reserve of notes. See, for example, the descriptions of changes in gold and note reserves in chapter III. By not dealing with these matters explicitly Hawtrey leaves the impression that somehow a change in the Issue Department's gold hoard should be reflected by an appropriate change in the Banking Department's note reserve. The connection, when there was one, apart from deposits, had to be made by active Bank transactions in the money market and Bank policy was thus more 'authority' than it was 'rules'.

[23] Keynes (1930, vol. 1, p. 196) objected to the historical consequences of following the market as merely 'a belated and inadequate effort to follow a movement of the natural-rate'. T. M. Weguelin (Governor in 1857), in his evidence before the Select Committee on the Operation of the Bank Act (1857), clearly accepted the new technique as a convenient way to avoid any return of the troubles of 1847. See also R. S. Sayers's (1957, pp. 10–13) arguments that following the market was the only practical policy after 1873 when growth and change in the City of London greatly weakened the Bank's quantitative control. In fact, during much of the period 1873–96 the Bank stayed deliberately above the market. As King (1936, chapter 9) emphasized, the tendency after the early 1870s for the Bank to cut loose from the market existed whenever the Bank felt the need. Mostly this need was for Bank Rate to rise relative to market rate. The Bank realized that its quantitative control had been weakened since the 1840s and 1850s and that its Bank Rate policy had to be adapted accordingly. This usually meant that the differential was for Bank Rate to be well

above market rate. Since the experience of pre-1847 was not to be
repeated, the Bank would not compete aggressively when interest rates
were low. Bank Rate, which had been for so long above market rate,
came back into closer contact after 1898 when market rates were rising.
I do not know why the floor was held at 2 per cent after the 1850s even
when, in the 1880s and 1890s, the margin of Bank Rate over market
rate was exceptionally large. The problem is not that Bank Rate should
stay above market rate to protect the reserve, but that 2 per cent should
be the floor no matter what. 'John Bull cannot stand 2 per cent' was a
saying in the press in the period before 1873. Yet John Bull had to stand
a lot of it from the mid-1870s to the mid-1890s. Hawtrey (1938, p. 250)
is perfectly laconic about this extraordinary phenomenon: 'Two per cent
is the customary minimum below which Bank Rate has never been reduced,
but the market rate of discount has frequently been below 1 per cent.'

[24] This *need not* have been the case, but was in practice. As noted in
footnote 2 above, the Bank could not have paid all of its notes in gold
because of the fiduciary issue. How either the Banking or the Issue
Department or both were 'drained' was a matter to be discovered in
practice; it was not a theoretical problem. After 1844 in times of pressure
the public wanted notes as well as gold. When gold flowed out of the
Issue Department, either into circulation or out of the country, notes
were also withdrawn from the Banking Department (there was a tendency for balance of payments crises and internal financial pressure to
coincide). In the big 1847, 1857 and 1866 crises it was the reserve of
notes and not the gold which gave out or threatened to. This outcome
was a surprise to those who supported the 1844 Bank Act. As Sir
Francis Baring said in a speech in the House following the 1847 Crisis:
'It certainly never entered into the contemplation of anyone considering
the subject prior to the passing of the Act that £7,000,000 of gold
should run off and yet the notes in the hands of the public should
rather increase than diminish' (Hughes, 1960, p. 236). The Bank was
placed in reduced circumstances by the Act of 1844 so far as its dis-
cretionary reserve was concerned and by fighting tactically in times of
pressure to preserve its own liquidity it acted strategically to preserve the
convertibility of the pound, that is, it maintained the Issue Department's
gold reserve.

[25] Musson (1959) provides a good bibliography on the period 1873–
96 viewed as a cyclical problem.

[26] Footnote 23 above.

[27] Ashworth (1966, p. 18), ignoring the emigration of the late nineteenth century, says that the unemployment data show no '. . . declining
efficiency of deployment'. Such a solution to any nation's unemployment
problems might yield such results among the remaining labour force.

[28] Bank Rate $= 3 \cdot 218 + 0 \cdot 136t - 0 \cdot 006t^2 + 0 \cdot 00006t^3$, $t = 1, 2, \ldots 71$, covering the years 1844 to 1914. The equation chosen is a matter of judgment. I am using it for purposes of illustration only, against which movements of other actual data may be compared visually in Figures 3 and 4. The annual Bank Rate data come from the Board of Trade and are annual means of their monthly averages. They were published monthly and by year in the annual *Statistical Abstracts*, and can be found compiled in several places, most recently in Sidney Homer (1963), pp. 208–9 and 418. These data are partly weighted by time because the annual average is a straight arithmetic mean of monthly averages of days at each rate. We tried computing annual Bank Rate with each rate weighted by the number of days actually at each rate and found the results in no way significantly different from the Board of Trade averages. Range of Bank Rate may be found in Mitchell and Deane (1962), pp. 456–9; railway debenture series in both Figures 3 and 4 come from sources cited below; yield on consols, Mitchell and Deane (1962), p. 455; commodity prices, ibid. pp. 474–5; rates for three months bank bills, ibid. p. 460. Additional data for nineteenth-century interest-rate movements are always useful to scholars. The data included for yields on railway debentures in Table 1 and Figures 3 and 4 were computed in connection with the work in this paper, but should be of more general interest. They originate from price data collected by Robert A. Macdonald (1912). Space does not permit publication of these numbers here; I will make them available to any interested scholars.

[29] Only in 1852 had the gold reserve been above £20 millions on an annual basis. The reserve figure went from £14 millions in 1866 to £20·2 millions in 1867, declined to £17·8 millions in 1869, and was £22·9 millions again in 1871.

[30] The phases of variations in domestic and foreign investment in this period are well known. In addition to the sources cited in footnote 19 above, see Alexander Cairncross (1953), chapter VII, Tables 38 and 40; Brinley Thomas (1954), esp. chapter VI,; Saul (1960), chapter V. With cyclical variations total net investment was shaped like a flat U from 1871 to 1913. The main cyclical recoveries in domestic investment were 1870–4, 1876–8, 1880–2, 1895–6, 1898–1902. Cairncross's (1953, Table 38) 1874 figure of £68·8 millions for new construction was not reached again until 1897, although in 1877–8 it was nearly reached. Foreign investment went from £28·1 millions in 1870 to £63·4 millions in 1873; slumped sharply to the early 1880s (including years of apparent net imports), then rose irregularly from £9·3 millions in 1880 to £85·6 millions in 1890. Foreign investment was high through most of the depression of the 1880s. The early 1890s produced a famous paradox; the slump in domestic investment was not matched by any 'compensating'

rise in the outflow of British investment funds (although foreign
investment did not fall back to the low levels of the 1870s). Doubtless
this was due to the world-wide fall in prices and interest yields in the
early 1890s so that for once foreign temptations were slight when
British yields were low. But also, as can be seen in Figure 3, as the
Bank Rate maxima rose after 1896 the floor rose too and even though
the compression was lifted as the natural rate rose, it would have been
more potentially encouraging for investment had Bank Rate fallen
lower after high rates, as had been the case up to 1873. The great
upsurge after the 1880s did not begin until 1905. Foreign investment was
thus not always an attraction. But the compression of 1873–96 provided
a background of pressure which made foreign investment more attractive than it would otherwise have been. The matter of the substitutability of domestic and foreign investment has not been solved to
everyone's satisfaction, although many now agree with Cairncross's
remark that after 1875 foreign investment became a 'sink' for unemployed British investment funds, and was generally undertaken at the
expense of domestic investment to the detriment of British economic
growth – a conclusion most agreeable to my present thesis (Richardson,
1965, pp. 143–4). After 1900 other factors come into play which we
will treat presently.

[31] The Bank's bullion hit £31·3 millions (annual data) in 1879, fell
and was less than £27 millions from 1880 to 1894, including two years,
1886 and 1888 below £20 millions.

[32] An argument that Keynes (1930, vol. 2, p. 188) was not loath
to make.

[33] A quantity-theory approach to this whole history is, of course, an
alternative. If one pursues that path an interesting observation occurs.
Although the results of that approach are beyond the scope of this
paper, I might mention some interesting results. The Bank's reserves
were low relative to demand obligations only tactically, and even though
for some periods growth of the bullion reserve and note reserves were
slow, they were generally more than adequate, especially in the 1880s
and 1890s. See both Hawtrey (1938) and King (1936), for the discussions of reserves in the relevant periods. If the sum of all central-bank
demand claims against the Issue Department's gold reserve (that is,
notes outside the Bank – the Banking Department's own hoard of Issue
Department notes – deposits in the Banking Department) are divided by
Feinstein's income estimates, then a ratio results which can be thought
of as the potential demand in aggregate for the gold in use. This
number dips to long-term low values from 1881 onwards to 1913 in
every year save 1884–5 and 1894–8. The increase in transactions in
$P = (MV/T)$ was lowering prices. A charitable view would be that the

Bank's directors, in spite of the apparently bulging reserves, were somehow aware that the gold standard, for all its apparent reserve stability,
would inexorably reproduce the wild financial panics of old if the
economy should boom again, since even at slower rates of growth the
bullion reserve was not growing rapidly enough to maintain central-
bank liquidity ratios of the 1870s. This deserves to be pursued further,
but is really another paper. The point is that while by conventional
ratios of reserves to liabilities the Bank was generally in liquid condition,
potentially they were not.

9

A Partial Theoretical Solution of the Problems of the Incidence of Import Duties

Murray C. Kemp

The problem of the incidence of import duties is extremely complex. It is indeed too large and difficult to be handled shortly.

Alfred Marshall *Memorandum on the Fiscal Policy of International Trade*

The central problems of tariff theory concern the relations between import and export duties on the one hand, and product and factor prices, at home and abroad, on the other. Professional discussion of these problems has a long history, extending back to Robert Torrens and John Stuart Mill, and, at least for the world of two commodities most commonly studied, has culminated in a substantial measure of agreement. It is now common ground that a tariff normally will turn the terms of trade in favour of the tariff-imposing country and normally will shift the internal or domestic price ratio to the advantage of the imported commodity.

But to each proposition there is an admitted exception. These exceptions constitute the grand paradoxes of tariff theory. The first paradox we owe to Marshall, who, in his *Memorandum on the Fiscal Policy of International Trade*, suggested the possibility that in the face of 'Giffen effects' of sufficient severity, the terms of trade may move against the tariff-imposing country:

> ... a general tax on the importation of wheat into England ... might increase rather than diminish England's total demand for wheat: and, unless it lead to a greater increase of supplies from England herself, it might raise and not lower the net price which foreigners obtained for their wheat (Marshall, 1926, p. 382).

Actually, Marshall's statement of the conditions for this perverse outcome is defective; but it is not difficult to patch it up, and there can be no doubt about the *possibility* of perversity (Kemp, 1966a). The second paradox derives from the possibility that the world terms of trade may move so far in favour of the tariff-imposing country that, even with the tariff added, the domestic price ratio will move in the same direction. The possibility that a 'protective' tariff may fail to protect was first noted by Marshall (1926, p. 373), but it was not until the publication of Abba Lerner's 'Symmetry' article (1936, pp. 306–13) that precise conditions for the outcome were available. Later again, Lloyd Metzler (1949a; 1949b) discussed the possibility with great thoroughness.[1]

Most treatments of tariff theory, including the fundamental contributions of Marshall (1923; 1926) and Lerner (1936) have rested on highly restrictive assumptions concerning the international mobility of factors. Specifically it has been assumed that all factors of production are perfectly immobile between countries. Moreover, it has been customary to ignore the possibility of international indebtedness.[2] These assumptions need no defence as a device for clarifying ideas and getting the main forces at work in focus. Nor I hope is it necessary to argue the desirability of exploring more general models.

In the present essay I shall examine the familiar questions within the confines of a model which differs from those employed by Marshall and Lerner in that capital will be assumed to be perfectly mobile, free to move from country to country in response to profit incentives. I shall be especially interested in the degree to which the two paradoxes are preserved after this change of assumptions.

It will be further assumed that there are just two trading countries, the 'home' and the 'foreign' country, two consumer goods, and two factors of production, labour and capital (thought of in physical terms). Labour will be assumed to be quite immobile between countries. Markets will be considered to be perfectly competitive, all participants being well informed about trading and investing opportunities. In particular, both factor markets will be assumed to be competitive so that, whatever commercial policy is pursued, full employment is assured. Both factors will be considered to be in fixed supply; that is, the population of each country will be assumed to be stationary, and in each country net saving will be assumed to be zero. Production functions will be taken to be homogeneous of first degree, but may differ from country to country. It will be assumed that, initially, free trade prevails and that the proceeds of any tariff subsequently imposed are turned over to the public of the tariff-imposing country. No account will be taken of the possibility that one country may retaliate against the tariffs imposed by the other. Finally, it will be assumed that each country is an exporter; that is, we rule out the extreme possibility that the creditor country exports nothing.

Marshall's views concerning the intricacy of tariff theory, cited at the head of this essay, are as valid today as sixty years ago. Even with the simplifying assumptions set out above, the analysis will be sufficiently complicated. It will therefore be developed in gentle stages, beginning with the most special cases and moving steadily towards greater generality. In the present section each country is assumed to specialize in the production of its export good, the foreign country producing the first commodity, the home country the second. First we consider the familiar case in which, both before and after the imposition of a tariff, net international indebtedness is zero. Then we pass to an intermediate case in which net indebtedness is non-zero but constant, independent of the tariff. The theoretical value of this case lies in the fact that it enables us to isolate the implications of the mere existence of international indebtedness, uncomplicated by variations of the level of indebtedness in response to changes in the rate of duty. Finally, the possibility of such variations is allowed for.

Only the simplest cases can be discussed readily without resort to algebra. It seems best therefore to adopt a mathematical form of exposition at the outset. This requires some notation. Thus we denote by D_i the home demand for the ith commodity, by X_i the home output of the ith commodity, and by $E_i (\equiv D_i - X_i)$ the home excess demand for the ith commodity. (In the case considered in this section, that of complete international specialization, $X_1 \equiv 0$ and $E_1 \equiv D_1$). The home price of the second commodity in terms of the first is denoted by p and the *ad valorem* rate of import duty by τ. I_i stands for the net income of the home country, in terms of the ith commodity. The amount of equipment lent abroad is denoted by K. (If the home country is a net debtor, K is negative.) Asterisks relate the variables to the foreign country. Thus p^* stands for the world terms of trade, E_i^* for the foreign excess demand for the ith commodity, etc.

The excess demand functions must be specified with care. Failure to pay attention to this detail has been responsible for much confusion in the literature, chiefly concerning the relative scopes of *ceteris paribus* and *mutatis mutandis* implicit in definitions of price elasticity of demand. Evidently the demand for a commodity can be written as a function of the price ratio and of net income; thus $D_1 = D_1(1/p, I_2)$ and $D_2 = D_2(p, I_1)$. The output of a commodity, on the other hand, depends on the price ratio and on the amount of capital lent to or borrowed from the foreign country; thus $X_1 = X_1(1/p, K)$ and $X_2 = X_2(p, K)$. It follows that $E_1 \equiv D_1 - X_1 = E_1(1/p, I_2, K)$ and $E_2 \equiv D_2 - X_2 = E_2(p, I_1, K)$. The price elasticity of home import demand is now defined as

$$\eta_1 \equiv \frac{1}{pE_1} \cdot \frac{\partial E_1}{\partial(1/p)}.$$

The price elasticity of foreign import demand is defined similarly as

$$\eta_2^* \equiv \frac{p^*}{E_2^*} \cdot \frac{\partial E_2^*}{\partial p^*}.$$

Finally, the home marginal propensity to import is defined as

$$m_1 \equiv \frac{1}{p} \cdot \frac{\partial E_1}{\partial I_2} = \frac{1}{p} \cdot \frac{\partial D_1}{\partial I_2}$$

and the foreign marginal propensity to import as

$$m_2^* \equiv p^* \frac{\partial E_2^*}{\partial I_1^*} = p^* \frac{\partial D_2^*}{\partial I_1^*}.$$

[The two marginal propensities to buy exports are $m_2 \equiv p(\partial E_2/\partial I_1) = p(\partial D_2/\partial I_1)$ and $m_1^* \equiv (1/p^*)(\partial E_1^*/\partial I_2^*) = (1/p^*)(\partial D_1^*/\partial I_2^*)$].

Net home income, in terms of the second commodity, is composed of three parts: total output, foreign earnings (possibly negative), and the tariff proceeds. Thus if the home country is on balance a creditor, its net income is

$$I_2 \equiv X_2 + \frac{Kr_1^*}{p^*} + T_2,$$

where r_1^* is the marginal product of capital abroad, in terms of the first commodity, and $T_2 \equiv \tau E_1/p^*$ is the tariff revenue. The net income of the foreign country consists of two parts, total output and its (negative) foreign income:

$$I_1^* \equiv X_1^* - Kr_1^*.$$

If, on the other hand, the home country is a net debtor, its income is

$$I_2 \equiv X_2 + Kr_2 + T_2 ,$$

where r_2 is the marginal product of capital at home, in terms of the second commodity. (Recall that in this case $K < 0$.) The net income of the foreign country is then

$$I_1^* \equiv X_1^* - p^* Kr_2 .$$

Further notation will be introduced as required.

Case 1: Zero Net International Indebtedness. In this familiar case, both outputs, X_1^* and X_2, are constants, independent of the tariff. r_1^* and r_2 also are constant. Our basic equation expresses the requirement that international payments be in balance:

$$D_1(1/p, I_2) - p^* D_2^*(p^*, I_1^*) = 0 . \tag{1}$$

To (1) are added an equilibrium equation relating the domestic and world price ratios:

$$p(1+\tau) = p^* \tag{2}$$

and three definitional equations:

$$I_2 \equiv X_2 + T_2 \tag{3}$$

$$I_1^* \equiv X_1^* \tag{4}$$

$$T_2 \equiv \frac{\tau}{1+\tau} \cdot \frac{1}{p} \cdot D_1(1/p, I_2) . \tag{5}$$

Differentiating through (1)–(5) with respect to τ, solving for $dp^*/d\tau$, and recalling that $\tau = 0$, we obtain

$$dp^*/d\tau = p\left(\frac{\eta_1 + m_1}{1 + \eta_1 + \eta_2^*}\right). \tag{6}$$

Introducing the Slutzky decomposition, $\eta_1 = \bar{\eta}_1 - m_1$, where $\bar{\eta}_1$ is the pure substitution elasticity of import demand, and writing $\Delta = 1 + \eta_1 + \eta_2^*$, (6) reduces to

$$dp^*/d\tau = p\bar{\eta}_1/\Delta . \tag{6'}$$

Since $\bar{\eta}_1$ is necessarily negative, the sign of $dp^*/d\tau$ depends on that of Δ, the familiar 'one plus the sum of the elasticities of import demand'. The coefficient $1/\Delta$ translates the tariff-inspired change in import demand into a change in the world terms of trade.

The commonsense of (6) and (6′) is not difficult to unearth. The tariff has two direct or immediate effects: it raises the price of imports, and it creates revenue which is distributed to the public and spent in accordance with the latter's preferences. The effect of the higher price normally is to curtail the demand for imports and is, in any event, proportional to m_1, the marginal propensity to import. We therefore have two effects weighing on opposite sides of the balance. The net effect is proportional to $(\eta_1 + m_1)$ which, as we have just seen, is necessarily negative. Thus the direct effect of the tariff is to curtail import demand. The ultimate effect on the world terms of trade is then determined by the value of Δ. In the stable case in which $\Delta < 0$ the tariff turns the terms of trade in favour of the home country.

Having discovered the effect of the tariff on the world terms of trade, it is a simple matter to calculate its effect on the internal price ratio p. From (2) we learn that

$$dp/d\tau = dp^*/d\tau - p .$$

Applying (6), we find that

$$dp/d\tau = -p\left(\frac{\eta_2^* + m_2}{\Delta}\right), \tag{7}$$

or, resorting to Slutzky's decomposition of η_2^*,

$$dp/d\tau = -p\left[\frac{\bar{\eta}_2^* + (m_2 - m_2^*)}{\Delta}\right]. \tag{7'}$$

Equations (7) and (7′) confirm Marshall's and Lerner's conclusion that, even under stable circumstances (with $\Delta < 0$), the internal price ratio may move in either direction. In particular, the tariff fails to protect the imported commodity if $\eta_2^* + m_2 > 0$, that is, if the home country's marginal propensity to import exceeds (minus) the foreign country's price elasticity of import demand.

Case 2: Non-Zero but Constant International Indebtedness. In this case also, both outputs are constant. Again we are free of complicating production effects and can treat r_1^* and r_2 as constants. However, the basic equation of international balance is now more intricate, its precise form depending on the international balance of indebtedness.

(a) If the home country is a net creditor ($K > 0$), our basic equation takes the revised form

$$D_1(1/p, I_2) - p^* D_2^*(p^*, I_1^*) = Kr_1^* . \tag{8}$$

This differs from (1) in containing on the right-hand side a term for interest payments to the home country. The new definitions of income are

$$I_2 \equiv X_2 + T_2 + Kr_1^*/p^* \tag{9}$$

and

$$I_1^* \equiv X_1^* - Kr_1^* . \tag{10}$$

Equations (2) and (5) carry over. Thus our new system comprises (2), (5) and (8)–(10). Differentiating with respect to τ, solving for $dp^*/d\tau$, and defining $\xi \equiv Kr_1^*/D_1$, the proportion of the home country's imports financed by its foreign earnings, we obtain a generalization of (6):

$$dp^*/d\tau = p \left[\frac{\eta_1 + m_1}{\Delta - \xi(\eta_2^* + m_2)} \right], \tag{11}$$

or, resorting to the Slutzky decomposition of η_1,

$$dp^*/d\tau = \frac{p\bar{\eta}_1}{\Delta - \xi(\eta_2^* + m_2)} . \tag{11'}$$

Evidently little is changed by the recognition of international indebtedness. Under stable conditions the tariff must turn the terms of trade in favour of the home country. Only the conditions of stability have changed. It is now a necessary and sufficient condition of stability that $\Delta - \xi(\eta_2^* + m_2)$ be negative. Negative Δ is no longer either necessary or sufficient.

Armed with (11) it is a simple matter to calculate the effect of the tariff on the internal price ratio:

$$dp/d\tau = dp^*/d\tau - p$$

$$= -p(1-\xi) \left[\frac{\eta_2^* + m_2}{\Delta - \xi(\eta_2^* + m_2)} \right] . \tag{12}$$

Equation (12) is a generalization of (7), which emerges as a special case when $\xi = 0$. As with zero indebtedness (case 1), it is possible, even under stable conditions, for the domestic price ratio in the tariff-imposing country to move against the 'protected' commodity. Bearing in mind that ξ, and therefore $(1-\xi)$, is a positive fraction, the condition for this curious outcome is seen to remain unchanged: $\eta_2^* + m_2 > 0$.

(b) If, on the other hand, the home country is a net debtor ($K < 0$), the fundamental equation of international balance becomes

$$D_1(1/p, I_2) - p^* D_2^* (p^*, I_1^*) = p^* Kr_2 . \tag{13}$$

The revised right-hand term represents (minus) the interest payable to the foreign country. The new definitions of income are

$$I_2 \equiv X_2 + T_2 + Kr_2 \tag{14}$$

$$I_1^* \equiv X_1^* - p^* Kr_2 . \tag{15}$$

Thus our new system comprises (2), (5) and (13)–(15). Differentiating with respect to τ, solving for $dp^*/d\tau$, and defining $\zeta^* \equiv -Kr_2/D_2^*$, the proportion of the foreign country's imports paid for by its earnings abroad, we obtain an alternative generalization of (6):

$$dp^*/d\tau = p(1-\zeta^*)\left[\frac{\eta_1 + m_1}{\Delta - \zeta^*(\eta_1 + m_1^*)}\right] \tag{16}$$

$$= \frac{p(1-\zeta^*)\bar{\eta}_1}{\Delta - \zeta^*(\eta_1 + m_1^*)} . \tag{16,}$$

ζ^*, and therefore $(1-\zeta^*)$, is a positive fraction. It follows that the numerator of (16') is unambiguously negative and that, under stable conditions $[\Delta - \zeta^*(\eta_1 + m_1^*) < 0]$, the terms of trade must move in favour of the tariff-imposing country, as in Cases 1 and 2(a).

From (16) we may calculate the effect of the tariff on the internal price ratio:

$$dp/d\tau = dp^*/d\tau - p$$

$$= -p\left[\frac{\eta_2^* + m_2 + \zeta^*(m_2^* - m_2)}{\Delta - \zeta^*(\eta_1 + m_1^*)}\right] \tag{17}$$

$$= -p\left[\frac{\bar{\eta}_2^* + (m_2 - m_2^*)(1-\zeta^*)}{\Delta - \zeta^*(\eta_1 + m_1^*)}\right] . \tag{17'}$$

Equation (17) is an alternative generalization of (7). As with zero international indebtedness (Case 1), it is possible even under stable circumstances, for the domestic price ratio to turn against the 'protected' commodity. Whether the critical value of m_2 is larger or smaller in the present case depends on the relative values of m_2 and m_2^*.

Case 3: Variable International Indebtedness. After the above finger exercises, we must now allow for the major complication that K is itself related to the rate of duty and that therefore all outputs and marginal products must be treated as variables. Again it is necessary to distinguish two subcases, according to the balance of international indebtedness.

(*a*) If the home country is a net creditor we revert to (2), (5) and (8)–(10), with X_1^*, X_2 and r_1^* understood to be functions of K. To help pin down the additional variable K we add the equilibrium condition that the rate of return on capital be everywhere the same:

$$r_1^*(K) - p^* r_2(K) = 0. \tag{18}$$

We also require two additional definitions:

$$\delta^* \equiv \frac{K}{r_1^*} \cdot \frac{dr_1^*}{dK} = \frac{K}{dX_1^*/dK} \cdot \frac{d^2 X_1^*}{dK^2}$$

is the elasticity of foreign returns with respect to imported capital, and

$$\delta \equiv \frac{K}{r_2} \cdot \frac{dr_2}{dK} = \frac{\cdot K}{dX_2/dK} \cdot \frac{d^2 X_2}{dK^2}$$

is the elasticity of home returns with respect to exported capital. With diminishing returns to proportions, we have $\delta^* < 0 < \delta$ and $(\delta^* - \delta) < 0$.

Differentiating through (2), (5), (8)–(10) and (18), and solving for $dp^*/d\tau$, we obtain

$$dp^*/d\tau = \frac{p\bar{\eta}_1}{\Delta - \xi \left[\eta_2^* + m_2 + \dfrac{1 - \delta^*(m_2^* - m_2)}{\delta^* - \delta} \right]}. \tag{19}$$

Equation (19) is a further generalization of (6). Our earlier conclusion that under stable conditions the terms of trade must turn in favour of the tariff-imposing country, remains unshaken. Only the stability conditions have changed to allow for the tariff-inspired capital movements. The reader should at this point compare (6'), (11') and (19).

From (19) one deduces the effect of the tariff on the internal price ratio:

$$dp/d\tau = dp^*/d\tau - p$$

$$= -p(1-\xi) \left(\frac{\eta_2^* + m_2 + \dfrac{\xi}{1-\xi} \cdot \dfrac{1 - \delta^*(m_2^* - m_2)}{\delta^* - \delta}}{\Delta - \xi \left[\eta_2^* + m_2 + \dfrac{1 - \delta^*(m_2^* - m_2)}{\delta^* - \delta} \right]} \right). \tag{20}$$

Equation (20) is a generalization of (7) and (12). It is clear that the price ratio may move in either direction, even under stable conditions. The curious possibility that the tariff may fail to protect the imported commodity materializes when

$$\eta_2^* + m_2 > -\frac{\xi}{1-\xi} \cdot \frac{1-\delta^*(m_2^*-m_2)}{\delta^*-\delta} .$$

The familiar Lerner-Metzler condition emerges as a special case when $\xi = 0$.

(b) It remains to consider the case in which the home country is a net debtor. The relevant system of equations comprises (2), (5), (13)–(15) and (18), with the understanding that all outputs and marginal productivities are functions of K. Since $K < 0$, we have $\delta^* > 0 > \delta$ and $(\delta^* - \delta) > 0$. Differentiating with respect to τ and solving for $dp^*/d\tau$, we obtain the desired generalization of (6) and (16):

$$dp^*/d\tau = \frac{p(1-\xi^*)\bar{\eta}_1}{\Delta - \xi^*(\eta_1+m_1^*) + \frac{\xi^*}{\delta^*-\delta}[(m_2^*-m_2)\delta-1]} . \qquad (21)$$

Again we find that, under stable conditions, the terms of trade must move in favour of the tariff-imposing country.

Finally, from (21) we may calculate the outcome for the domestic price ratio:

$$dp/d\tau = dp^*/d\tau - p$$

$$= -p\left(\frac{\eta_2^* + m_2 + \frac{\xi}{\delta^*-\delta}[(m_2^*-m_2)\delta^*-1]}{\Delta - \xi^*(\eta_1+m_1^*) + \frac{\xi^*}{\delta^*-\delta}[(m_2^*-m_2)\delta^*-1]} \right) . \qquad (22)$$

Equation (22) is, of course, a generalization of (7) and (17). Again it has turned out that even in stable circumstances the domestic price ratio may move in either direction.

It has been implicit in our discussion of Case 3 that K is not prevented by the poverty of capital endowments from varying in response to profit incentives. In those boundary cases in which K would otherwise increase in response to a tariff, but is prevented from doing so by virtue of the fact that K has already reached one or other of the two limits determined by the capital endowments of the two countries, we are back to Case 2.

We emerge from this partial survey of cases with the tentative impression that the recognition of international indebtedness and capital mobility does not call for any major modifications of accepted theory. It remains true that the terms of trade must move in favour of the tariff-imposing country, and it remains true that the domestic price ratio may move in either direction. Whether these conservative conclusions survive the abandonment of the simplifying assumption that both countries specialize completely remains to be seen.

So far we have not encountered Marshall's paradox, that the terms of trade may move against the tariff-imposing country. Perhaps this possibility emerges only in a world of incomplete specialization. A final verdict must await the analysis of the following section. At this stage we may note that in the opinion of Marshall himself (1926, p. 382) a domestic source of supply of the imported commodity renders his case less rather than more likely.

We turn briefly to the alternative possibility, that at least one country produces something of each commodity, and immediately plunge into a consideration of the most complicated case, that in which capital is internationally mobile.

Case 1: Foreign Country Incompletely Specialized. Suppose first that the foreign country is incompletely specialized. The rate of return to capital abroad, r_1^*, is then independent of the overall factor ratio abroad and, in particular, of K. It does depend, however, on the foreign price ratio p^*. We must therefore re-write the condition of capital market equilibrium as

$$r_1^*(p^*) - p^* r_2(K) = 0 . \tag{23}$$

(*a*) If the home country is a net creditor, the balance of payments condition must be written as

$$D_1(1/p, I_2) - p^* E_2^*(p^*, I_1^*, K) = K r_1^*(p^*) , \tag{24}$$

with I_2 defined by (9) and

$$I_1^* = X_1^* + p^* X_2^* - K r_1^*(p^*) . \tag{25}$$

Thus our new system is composed of (2), (5), (9) and (23)–(25). Differentiating this system and solving for $dp^*/d\tau$, we obtain [3]

$$dp^*/d\tau =$$

$$\frac{p \bar{\eta}_1}{(1-\xi)\left\{\Delta + \dfrac{\xi}{1-\xi}[\bar{\eta}_1 + \omega_1^*(m_2 - m_2^*) - (\omega_1^* - 1)^2/\delta] + m_2^* X_2^*/E_2^*\right\}} \tag{26}$$

where $\omega_1^* \equiv (p^*/r_1^*)/(dr_1^*/dp^*)$ may be of either sign but must be greater than one in magnitude.[4] If the foreign export industry is relatively capital-intensive, $\omega_1^* < -1$; if it is relatively labour-intensive, $\omega_1^* > 1$. We conclude that under stable conditions the terms of trade must turn in favour of the tariff-imposing country. (Of course, the stability conditions have changed again, this time to allow for the incomplete specialization of the foreign country.) And, as the reader may easily check, the Marshall-Lerner-Metzler outcome remains possible.

(b) If the home country is a net debtor, the balance of payments condition becomes

$$D_1(1/p,I_2)-p^*E_2^*(p^*,I_1^*,K) = p^*Kr_2(K) . \tag{27}$$

The appropriate definitions of income are

$$I_2 = X_2+T_2+Kr_2(K) \tag{28}$$

and

$$I_1^* = X_1^*+p^*X_2^*-p^*Kr_2(K) . \tag{29}$$

These three equations replace (9), (24) and (25) in our system. Differentiating the new system (2), (5) and (27)–(29) with respect to τ, and solving for $dp^*/d\tau$, as usual, we obtain

$$dp^*/d\tau =$$

$$\frac{p(1-\xi^*)\bar{\eta}_1}{\Delta-\xi^*\left\{\eta_1+m_1^*-\dfrac{(\omega_1^*-1)}{\delta}[\omega_1^*-1-\delta(m_2-m_2^*)]\right\}+m_2X_2^*/E_2^*} . \tag{30}$$

We conclude again that, under stable conditions, the terms of trade must move in favour of the tariff-imposing country and the home price ratio may move in either direction.

Case 2: Home Country Incompletely Specialized. Suppose, next, that the home country is incompletely specialized. One might expect perhaps that our conclusions for this case would differ only in detail from those just reached for the case of complete home specialization. This, however, is not so; it turns out that in this case, the terms of trade may turn against the tariff-imposing country. Given the new pattern of specialization, r_1^* depends on K only, and r_2 depends on p, or (more conveniently) on $1/p$, only. The condition of capital market equilibrium is therefore

$$r_1^*(K)-p^*r_2(1/p) = 0 . \tag{31}$$

(*a*) If the home country is a net creditor, the balance of payments condition must be written

$$E_1(1/p,I_2,K) - p^*D_2^*(p^*,I_1^*) = Kr_1^*(K) \tag{32}$$

with I_1^* defined by (10) and

$$I_2 = X_1 + pX_2 + Kr_1^*(K)/p^* + T_2, \tag{33}$$

where the proceeds of the duty are now

$$T_2 = \frac{\tau}{1+\tau} \cdot \frac{1}{p} \cdot E_1(1/p,I_2,K). \tag{34}$$

Thus our new system consists of (2), (10) and (31)–(34). It yields $dp^*/d\tau =$

$$\frac{(1-\xi)^{-1}p\left\{\bar{\eta}_1 - \frac{\xi\omega_2}{\delta^*}[(1-\omega_2)+\delta^*(m_2-m_2^*)]+m_1X_1/E_1\right\}}{\Delta + \frac{\xi}{1-\xi}\left\{\bar{\eta}_1 + \frac{1-\omega_2}{\delta^*}[(1-\omega_2)+\delta^*(m_2-m_2^*)]+m_1X_1/\xi E_1\right\}}, \tag{35}$$

where $\omega_2 \equiv (1/pr_2)/[dr_2/d(1/p)]$, like ω_1^*, may be of either sign but must be greater than one in magnitude. From (35), it is clear that, under stable conditions (negative denominator), the terms of trade may decline. The plausibility of this new possibility may be established by noting two implications of incomplete home specialization. Suppose, tentatively, that the world terms of trade are unchanged, so that the tariff forces up the home price of the first commodity. Since something is produced of the first commodity, the price change results in an increase in home income (in terms of the second commodity), and therefore in an increase in the demand for imports. The price change also raises the return to the factor used relatively intensively in the first industry. If that factor is capital, there will result a return flow of capital from abroad. This return flow will force up r_1^*, the reward of capital invested abroad. It will result therefore in an international redistribution of income in favour of the home country and in a net increase in the home country's demand for imports. It is possible that this double boost to home import demand may outweigh the remaining effects of the increase in price (including the possible stimulation to home production of the imported commodity afforded by the price-induced return flow of capital). If this should be the case, we should have to abandon our tentative assumption that the world terms of trade are unchanged in favour of the conclusion that they move against the home country.

It is not difficult to see that under the present assumptions the Marshall-Lerner-Metzler outcome is still possible.

(b) If the home country is a net debtor the balance of payments condition becomes

$$E_1(1/p,I_2,K)-p^*D_2^*(p^*,I_1^*)-Kp^*r_2(1/p) = 0 . \tag{36}$$

The appropriate definitions of income are

$$I_2 = X_1/p+X_2+K\bar{r}_2(1/p) \tag{37}$$

and

$$I_1^* = X_1^*-Kp^*r_2(1/p) . \tag{38}$$

From (2), (31), (34) and (36)–(38) we calculate that

$$dp^*/d\tau =$$

$$\frac{p(1-\xi^*)\left\{\bar{\eta}_1-\dfrac{\xi^*}{1-\xi^*}\cdot\dfrac{\omega_2}{\delta^*}[(1-\omega_2)-\delta^*(m_2-m_2^*)]+m_1X_1/E_1\right\}}{\Delta-\xi^*[\bar{\eta}_1+(1-\omega_2)(m_2-m_2^*)+(1-\omega_2)^2/\delta^*]+m_1X_1/pD_2^*} . \tag{39}$$

Thus, as in case 2(a), both the terms of trade and the home price ratio may move in either direction.

We have at last found a case in which Marshall's paradoxical outcome is possible. However, this case bears little relation to the circumstances Marshall had in mind. Inferiority of the imported commodity at home is neither necessary nor sufficient for his outcome. Indeed one cannot even be sure that negative m_2 makes Marshall's outcome more likely; whether it does so depends on ω_2. Moreover, his conjecture that a domestic source of supply of the imported commodity renders his case less likely is revealed to be the opposite of the truth (Marshall, 1926, p. 382). In fairness to Marshall, however, it must be recalled that he had in mind a world in which factors of production are internationally immobile.

Case 3: *Both Countries Incompletely Specialized.* Suppose finally that both countries produce something of each commodity. The possible effects of a tariff are in this case more varied than in any other cases studied. The analysis of these effects is, however, quite uncomplicated, for it can proceed without reference to demand conditions and without paying attention to the balance of international indebtedness.

Since the foreign country is incompletely specialized, the rate of return to capital, r_1^*, is independent of the overall factor ratio abroad and, in particular, of K. It depends only on the foreign price ratio p^*. Similarly, since the home country is incompletely specialized, r_2 depends only on the domestic price ratio p. Therefore since capital is internationally mobile we may write the following condition of equilibrium in the world capital market:

$$r_1^*(p^*) = p^* r_2(1/p), \tag{40}$$

or, recalling that when the commodity markets are in equilibrium, so that $p^* = p(1+\tau)$:

$$r_1^*(p^*) = p^* r_2 [(1+\tau)/p^*]. \tag{41}$$

Differentiating with respect to τ, and solving for $dp^*/d\tau$, we obtain

$$dp^*/d\tau = \frac{dr_2/d(1/p)}{(dr_1^*/dp^*) - r_2 + (1/p)[dr_2/d(1/p)]},$$

or, translating into elasticities,

$$dp^*/d\tau = \frac{p\omega_2}{\omega_1^* + \omega_2 - 1}. \tag{42}$$

It follows that

$$dp/d\tau = (dp^*/d\tau) - p = \frac{p(1-\omega_1^*)}{\omega_1^* + \omega_2 - 1}. \tag{43}$$

Thus the home country's terms of trade must improve if ω_1^* and ω_2 are of the same sign, that is, if each country's export commodity is relatively capital-intensive or if each country's import commodity is relatively capital-intensive. However, the terms of trade cannot improve so markedly that the home country's internal price ratio moves in favour of the exported commodity – the tariff cannot fail to protect the imported commodity. In other cases, where ω_1^* and ω_2 are of opposite sign, both the external and the internal terms of trade may move in either direction, the outcome depending on the relative magnitudes of ω_1^* and ω_2. For these other cases, however, we have the following sweeping generalization: *the two price ratios must move in the same direction; in particular, any improvement in the external terms of trade must be so great that it carries the internal terms of trade with it, so that the tariff fails to protect the imported commodity.*

An interesting, though totally unrealistic special case is that in which production functions are the same at home and abroad. For then $\omega_2 = \omega_2^*$ (defined as $(1/p^*r_2^*)[dr_2^*/d(1/p^*)]$) and, since $\omega_1^*+\omega_2^* = 1$,[5] we find ourselves dividing by zero in (42) and (43). Evidently our method of analysis breaks down in this case. The reason is not far to find. If production functions are the same everywhere, and if neither country is completely specialized, any tariff, however small, results in a capital movement of such magnitude that all trade ceases (other than the one-way 'trade' necessitated by interest payments) and the terms of trade are undefined.

The discussion has been supported by a substantial number of simplifying assumptions and it has seemed expedient to carry it through with a minimum of turning to right and left. The main task completed, however, we may note several avenues along which generalization may be sought, as well as a few of the alternative directions the discussion could have taken.

In a more extended treatment it would have been desirable to generalize by allowing for the possibility that the initial state is not one of free trade, for the possibility that foreign earnings are taxed, for the possibility that foreign investment is attended by special risks which call for compensating premia of foreign returns, or for the possibility that the tariff proceeds are spent partly by the public and partly by the government of the tariff-imposing country.[6]

If attention is confined to the case of incomplete international specialization, the first and last of the four extensions can be accommodated by (40) as it stands; the other two extensions call for only minor changes. Consider first the possibility that the home country imposes a tax on capital earnings at the rate $100t$ *per cent* and that the foreign country imposes a tax at the rate $100t^*$ *per cent*. Then, in the absence of an international tax agreement, (40) must be re-written as

$$(1-t-t^*)r_1^* = (1-t)p^*r_2 \qquad \text{if the home country is a net creditor}$$

$$(1-t^*)r_*^1 = (1-t-t^*)p^*r_2 \quad \text{if the home country is a net debtor.}$$

If, on the other hand, a tax agreement reciprocally exempts foreign earnings from home taxation, (40) becomes

$$[1-\max(t,t^*)]r_1^* = (r-t)p^*r_2 \quad \text{if the home country is a net creditor}$$

$$(1-t^*)r_1^* = [1-\max(t,t^*)]p^*r_2 \quad \text{if the home country is a net debtor.}$$

Consider next the possibility that home investors demand an earnings premium of 100π *per cent* on investment abroad and that foreign investors require a premium of $100\pi^*$ *per cent* on investment in the home country. Then the revised form of (40) is

$$r_1^* = (1+\pi)p^*r_2 \quad \text{if the home country is a net creditor}$$
$$(1+\pi^*)r_1^* = p^*r_2 \quad \text{if the home country is a net debtor.}$$

The problems of tariff incidence have been tackled in a more general setting than is customary. From the point of view of general trade theory, however, the discussion has been illustrative only. The implications of technical improvements, of population growth, indeed the whole of comparative statical trade theory, can be reworked along similar lines.

NOTES AND REFERENCES

[1] See also Koo (1953), Baldwin (1960), and Bhagwati and Johnson (1961).

[2] Marshall (1923, pp. 188–9, 349–50), however, is a partial exception. Marshall allowed for the possibility that the tariff-imposing country may be a net debtor. But his treatment, at this particular point, is inadequate. For he assumed that the offer curve of the debtor country could be obtained by horizontally displacing the zero-indebtedness curve by an amount proportional to the interest payments (expressed in terms of the debtor's export commodity). This simple device is however valid only in very special circumstances.

[3] In this and other calculations of this section use is made of the duality relations $\partial r_1^*/\partial p^* = \partial X_2^*/\partial K$ and $\partial r_2/\partial(1/p) = -\partial X_1/\partial K$, where the derivatives on the right-hand side are defined *mutatis mutandis*. For proofs, see Samuelson (1953–4) and Kemp (1966b).

[4] See Kemp (1964, p. 12), where it is shown that the reciprocal of ω_1^* must lie between plus and minus one: $-1 < 1/\omega_1^* < 1$.

[5] Thus
$$\omega_1^* + \omega_2^* = \frac{1}{r_1^*}\left[p^*\frac{dr_1^*}{dp^*} + \frac{dr_2^*}{d(1/p^*)} \right]$$
$$= \frac{1}{r_1^*}\left(p^*\frac{\partial X_2^*}{\partial K} + \frac{\partial X_1^*}{\partial K} \right) \quad \text{(from footnote 3)}$$
$$= \frac{r_1^*}{r_1^*} = 1 \,.$$

[6] Both Marshall and Lerner discussed the extreme possibility that the government itself spends the entire tariff revenue.

10

Time, Interest, and
the Production Function

Charles Kennedy

In *Capital and Growth*, Sir John Hicks spends some time in examining a puzzle that arises during the course of his discussion of Harrod-type macrodynamics. When certain particular assumptions are made about entrepreneurs' expectations, a difference equation for income is obtained such that

$$Y_t = \frac{v}{v-s}Y_{t-1},\tag{1}$$

where v is the investment coefficient and s the savings ratio (Hicks, 1965, p. 118). This equation only makes sense so long as $v > s$, and since v is a stock-flow relation and will depend on the length of the period, there is no complete assurance that this condition will hold.

Now I believe that this particular puzzle, which has also been noticed by R.C.O. Matthews (1959, pp. 14, 50) and R.G.D. Allen (1959, p. 79),[1] is of a great deal wider significance than might appear from the rather special context in which it has arisen. The Harrodian approach to growth theory is essentially a demand-determined model, and it is for this reason that the precise way in which expectations are formed is so important. But it is recognized that a theory of growth that is formally very similar can be obtained in a supply-determined model. In such Domar-type macrodynamics, as we may call it, the same puzzle can arise, and whether it does so or not will in this case turn on whether the production function is unlagged or lagged.

Modern critics of the use of a production function in capital theory, for example Mrs Robinson (1954), have tended to lay emphasis on the inappropriateness of using 'capital' as a factor of production, in view of the heterogeneity of capital goods in real life. I have never myself attached very much importance to this objection. This is partly because I

275

think that for many purposes the assumption of a single type of capital good – a 'machine' – is a powerful and useful simplification. More important, however, is the fact that the recent application of matrix algebra has enabled capital theorists to handle a heterogeneous collection of capital goods without very much difficulty.

In my own view, a more legitimate object of criticism is the imprecision with which time has been treated in models using a production function, whenever period analysis has been employed. This is not, of course, for want of recognition of the problem – there is scarcely a subject that has received more attention in the literature. Nevertheless, it is still rare to find a consistent treatment: very often writers who do not explicitly introduce a lag into the production function assume one implicitly; and writers who do explicitly introduce a lag do not always follow through with the full implications of the assumption.[2]

The purpose of this paper is to attempt to clear up some of these matters by looking at a number of models on the assumption first that all production functions are unlagged and secondly that there is a uniform one-period lag in all production functions. I am well aware that the use of the latter assumption is not the only, or indeed the most realistic, way of taking recognition of the fact that the production process takes time. It is, however, the simplest way; and a number of matters can be elucidated with its help. In what follows, the term 'production function' will be used in an entirely general sense, to include cases where there are fixed input-output coefficients as well as cases where factor proportions are variable.

The notion of a production function with a one-period lag is intelligible enough. But the notion of an unlagged production function raises certain conceptual problems that had better be discussed beforehand. In the case of the production of consumption goods, what it implies is that the consumption goods produced during a period can be consumed at the same time as they are being produced. Rightly or wrongly, economists have found little difficulty in accepting this. But the analogous implication for the production of capital goods is another matter. It is that the capital goods produced during a period can themselves be used in the production of the output of the period. Such an idea has no meaning in terms of economic reality. The production process does in fact take time, and for this reason there is a strong *prima facie* case for preferring a lagged production function to an unlagged one. Nevertheless, the conceptual implausibility of the unlagged case in no way precludes a formal treatment of it, and it is this formal treatment that will be undertaken in what follows.

After these preliminaries, we can begin the analysis. It will be convenient to start with Domar-type macrodynamics because of its close formal similarity to the Harrod-type macrodynamics referred to at the outset. In the unlagged case, the investment undertaken in period t will make possible a rise in output during the same period. With a given capital-output ratio (c) and a given proportion (s) of output saved, we obtain:

$$Y_t - Y_{t-1} = \frac{1}{c}I_t = \frac{s}{c}Y_t . \tag{2}$$

In the lagged case, the investment undertaken in period t will make possible a rise in output in the succeeding period. With the same capital-output ratio and savings ratio, we obtain:

$$Y_{t+1} - Y_t = \frac{1}{c}I_t = \frac{s}{c}Y_t . \tag{3}$$

Difference equations for the unlagged case and for the lagged case can then be written:

$$Y_t = \frac{c}{c-s}Y_{t-1} \tag{4}$$

$$Y_{t+1} = \frac{c+s}{c}Y_t . \tag{5}$$

These difference equations are formally identical with those discussed by Hicks (1965) in his chapter on Harrod macrodynamics. If c is large compared to s, the two equations are very close; and if the period is shrunk to the limit so that continuous time is used, they become identical.

It is when c becomes small that the two equations begin to differ in their properties. While the lagged equation (5) continues to behave properly whatever the value of c, the unlagged equation definitely misbehaves when c is reduced to the value of s.

As will become clearer in the next section, $c = 1$ is really the critical value at which the unlagged model starts to misbehave. For, if the output of the current period can be used as a capital good in the same period, and if further the capital-output ratio is less than one, then it follows that the output possibilities of the period will be unlimited. The fact that not all of output is used in this way, that is, that some of it is consumed, means that the economy is prevented from taking advantage of these possibilities. For this reason it appears that the critical value of c is when $c = s$, but this is because, in Domar-type macrodynamics, only the quantitative aspects of growth are considered. We shall soon find that a value of c of less than one has some disturbing consequences for the price system. It is indeed already time to abandon what Hicks calls the 'fixprice' method and to turn to a model in which prices as well as quantities are in question. For it is evident that the price system will not be unaffected by the choice between an unlagged and a lagged production function.

Much of the rest of this paper will take as its standard of reference the outline model presented in chapter XII of *Capital and Growth*. I fear we shall have to tamper with it in some respects later on, but for the moment we can set it out almost exactly as Hicks did.[3] It is a two-sector two-factor model: labour and tractors are used to produce corn, and labour and tractors are used to make tractors. The one respect in which I shall depart from Hicks's own treatment is in assuming that tractors last for ever. Hicks was able to justify a neglect of depreciation without having recourse to that assumption, but for our purposes it will be simpler to make it. The assumption will be relaxed in a later section and depreciation formally introduced into the model. It will be remembered that a feature of the notation is that Greek letters are used to mark a reference to the consumption sector and the corresponding Roman letters to refer to the capital-goods sector.

Let

π be the price of the consumption good (corn),

p be the price of the capital good (tractor),

w be the wage of labour,

q be the earnings (quasi-rent) of the capital good,

r be the rate of profit,

α (capital)
β (labour) } be production coefficients in consumption good production,

a (capital)
b (labour) } be production coefficients in capital good production.

In equilibrium, we then have the *price equations*

$$p = aq + bw \tag{6}$$
$$\pi = \alpha q + \beta w \tag{7}$$

and, by definition

$$q = rp. \tag{8}$$

By substitution, three *relative-price equations* are obtained

$$\frac{p}{w} = \frac{b}{1-ra} \tag{9}$$

$$\frac{q}{w} = \frac{rb}{1-ra} \tag{10}$$

$$\frac{\pi}{w} = \beta + \frac{rab}{1-ra}.^{4} \tag{11}$$

On the quantity side, let

ξ be the output of the consumption good (corn),

x be the output of the capital good (tractors),

L be the labour employed,

K be the stock of capital (number of tractors),

g be the rate of growth.

In equilibrium, we then have the *quantity equations*

$$K = ax + \alpha\xi \tag{12}$$
$$L = bx + \beta\xi \tag{13}$$

and by definition

$$x = gK. \tag{14}$$

By substitution, the following *relative-quantity equations* are obtained

$$\frac{K}{\xi} = \frac{\alpha}{1-ga} \tag{15}$$

$$\frac{x}{\xi} = \frac{g\alpha}{1-ga} \tag{16}$$

$$\frac{L}{\xi} = \beta + \frac{g\alpha b}{1-ga}. \tag{17}$$

Such, in barest outline, is the model to be considered. The main features to be noted at the moment are first, the *duality* of the quantity system and the price system, equations (15–17) being exactly similar in form to equations (9–11); secondly, the fact that both r and g have the same maximum value–if wages are not to be negative we must have $r < 1/a$, and if consumption is not to be negative we must have $g < 1/a$.

When we look at the above system from our own particular point of view, we find we cannot accept it just as it stands. For, if we look at the system of price equations (6–11), we see that they assume implicitly an *unlagged* production function. The price of a good is simply equal to the cost of hiring the factors to produce it. There is no cost of 'waiting' included, as there would have to be if the production function were lagged.

On the other hand, the system of quantity equations (12–17) implicitly assumes a *lagged* production function. It is clear from equation (14) that K must be interpreted as the capital stock at the beginning of the period. But, if this is so, then equation (12) makes it clear that the output x of capital goods is not available for use until the next period. Hence the production function must be lagged.

Thus, the whole system, as it stands, is a hybrid system.[5] In order to make it consistent, we must either adapt the quantity-equations to an unlagged production function, or adapt the price equations to a lagged production function. Let us tackle the former task first.

All we have to do is to replace equation (12) by an equation which allows for the fact that the output of capital goods is available for use in the current period, that is

$$K+x = ax+\alpha\xi .\tag{18}$$

Equations (13) and (14) are unaffected, so that by substitution we obtain as relative-quantity equations in the place of (15–17) the following

$$\frac{K}{\xi} = \frac{\alpha}{1-g(a-1)}\tag{19}$$

$$\frac{x}{\xi} = \frac{g\alpha}{1-g(a-1)}\tag{20}$$

$$\frac{L}{\xi} = \beta+\frac{g\alpha b}{1-g(a-1)} .\tag{21}$$

So long as a is large, this amendment makes little difference to the earlier model, since the difference between a and $(a-1)$ will not be of great importance. If we shrink the period to the limit and work with continuous time, the difference disappears altogether. But it will be no surprise to find that equations (19–21) start to misbehave as soon as a becomes less than one. For in this case there will be no reason for a limit to the possible rate of growth of output. It will be interesting to see whether this possibility of unlimited growth is frustrated, as in the case of Domar-type macrodynamics, by a savings ratio of less than one, but before this point is examined, it will be useful to have a look at what happens to the price system when a becomes less than one.

At first sight it looks as if the relative-price equations (9–11) are still well-behaved when a is less than one, but closer inspection reveals that this is not the case. It is still true that there is an upper limit to the rate of profit (r) but this upper limit ($1/a$) is now greater than one. And a rate of profit greater than one is not possible. In market-place terms, it would imply that it was cheaper to buy a tractor than to hire one, and this is obvious nonsense.

In fact, the delinquency of the price system when $a < 1$ is more serious than that of the quantity system. For whereas the latter can be kept straight by a sufficiently low savings ratio, the same is not true of the former. To elucidate this point, it will be necessary to establish a relationship between the rate of growth, the rate of profit and the savings ratio. In order to do so, we shall assume a classical savings function, i.e. that there is no saving out of wages, but that a certain proportion (s_1) of profits is saved. With this assumption, Hicks establishes a relationship as follows:

$$px \text{ (investment)} = pgK = s_1(rpK) \text{ (saving)} \tag{22}$$

so that $g = s_1 r$. (23)

However, this equation assumes that owners of capital goods receive quasi-rents only on the capital they hold at the beginning of the period, and this assumption presupposes a lagged production function. With an unlagged production function, we would have

$$px = pgK = s_1 rp(K+x) \tag{24}$$

so that $g = \dfrac{s_1 r}{1 - s_1 r}$. (25)

It is evident from this equation that g will be limited so long as $s_1 r < 1$. Since, from the relative-price equations, r cannot be greater than $1/a$, it follows that g will be limited so long as $a > s_1$.

This result may be compared with the one found for Domar-type macrodynamics. The point of importance in the present context, however, is that a savings ratio out of profits of less than a will not ensure that r is less than one. This means that although it may prevent indefinite growth during the period, it does not prevent the price-system from possibly going awry.

This completes the discussion of the basic model for the unlagged case. We have seen that the unlagged model is usable if a is large, but that it develops grave weaknesses when *a* is less than one. We shall return to the model again briefly after depreciation has been introduced into the analysis. It is now time to examine the lagged model, which fortunately behaves rather better.

In the lagged case, we can retain the original system of quantity equations (12–17), and it is the price equations (6–11) that require alteration. The cost of 'waiting' has to be included in the cost of the products, and for this purpose it is necessary to introduce a rate of interest (i). The two price equations (6) and (7) can then be replaced by

$$p = (aq+bw)(1+i) \tag{26}$$
$$\pi = (\alpha q+\beta w)(1+i) . \tag{27}$$

The rate of interest (i) is distinct from r, which is the rate of profit on capital goods already in existence, but there is a simple relationship between them. Since the capital goods last for ever, the present owner of a tractor will earn a rent of q in all future periods as well as the current one. Discounting future values, we obtain

$$p = q+\frac{q}{1+i}+\frac{q}{(1+i)^2}+\frac{q}{(1+i)^3}+ \cdots \tag{28}$$

By substituting rp for q (equation (8) still holds) and summing the series, we obtain

$$i = \frac{r}{1-r} \tag{29}$$

and $$r = \frac{i}{1+i} . \tag{30}$$

Equations (26) and (27) can then be written in the form

$$p(1-r) = aq+bw \tag{31}$$
$$\pi(1-r) = \alpha q+\beta w . \tag{32}$$

By substituting equation (8) into these equations (31) and (32), we obtain in the place of equations (9–11) the following relative-price equations

$$\frac{p}{w} = \frac{b}{1-r(a+1)} \tag{33}$$

$$\frac{q}{w} = \frac{rb}{1-r(a+1)} \tag{34}$$

$$\frac{\pi}{w} = \frac{1}{1-r}\left[\beta+\frac{r\alpha b}{1-r(a+1)}\right] . \tag{35}$$

If r is relatively small and a relatively large, there is little difference between this set of equations and the unlagged set (9–11). The difference begins to matter as a becomes smaller. Moreover, the lagged set now behave properly when $a < 1$, since the new upper limit to r of $1/(a+1)$ cannot be greater than one. Hence the possibility of r being greater than one is ruled out.

One result of the consistent treatment of the price and quantity systems undertaken in earlier sections may be found a little disappointing. No matter whether one takes the lagged or the unlagged case, the strict duality of the price and quantity equations has been lost. *Time, so to speak, has interfered with the duality of the system!*

The duality can be partially, but not completely, restored for the lagged system, if the relative-price equations (33–35) are rewritten in terms of the rate of interest instead of the rate of profit. Substituting equation (30) in equations (33–35) we obtain:

$$\frac{p}{w} = \frac{b(1+i)}{1-ia} \tag{36}$$

$$\frac{q}{w} = \frac{ib}{1-ia} \tag{37}$$

$$\frac{\pi}{w} = (1+i)\left[\beta + \frac{i\alpha b}{1-ia}\right]. \tag{38}$$

This is almost certainly the most illuminating form in which to set out the relative-price equations. The correspondence between the rate of growth and the rate of interest is closer than that between the rate of growth and the rate of profit.[6]

Moreover, the effect of the savings ratio on the system is more easily seen if we use the rate of interest rather than the rate of profit. With a lagged model the value of investment in any period will be equal to the discounted value of the capital goods being produced. Hence, in the place of equation (22), we have

$$p(1-r)x = p(1-r)gK = s_1 rpK \tag{39}$$

assuming a 'classical' savings function as before; from which it follows that

$$g = s_1 \frac{r}{1-r} \tag{40}$$

or $g = s_1 i$. $\tag{41}$

If all profits are saved, we obtain the familiar result that

$$g = i. \tag{42}$$

Notice, however, that in this case the rate of growth is equal to the rate of interest and not to the rate of profit.

Returning to the relative-price equations, we see that the 'waiting' term $(1+i)$ appears in equations (36) and (38). This is just where we should expect to find it. The cost of 'waiting' affects the relation of product prices to the wage, but does not affect the factor-price ratio q/w. Thus, no 'waiting' term appears in equation (37).[7]

It is this 'waiting' term that still mars the complete duality of the price and quantity equations. The hankerer after complete duality could, I suppose, just save the situation by replacing the product prices by discounted product prices. However, my own view is that this would be carrying the worship of the new God Duality to too great lengths.[8] It is better in my opinion to regard complete duality as being a feature only of the continuous-time vanishing-lag model, and to recognize that a lag in the production function spoils this to some extent, though it should still leave us enough duality to satisfy our spiritual needs.

The assumption that capital goods last for ever must now be relaxed. For this purpose, we can adopt (*mutatis mutandis*) the treatment used by Hicks in his chapter xiv. A certain proportion of the capital goods used in each sector has to be made good in any period, and we may as well call this proportion the rate of depreciation in that sector.[9] Consistently with Hicks's notational scheme, let

d be the rate of depreciation in the capital-goods sector,

δ be the rate of depreciation in the consumption-good sector.

Let us start as before with an unlagged production function. However, I do not think we need spend very much time over the unlagged case, because the superiority of the lagged model over the unlagged one will already have become apparent to the reader. There is just one point that the examination of the unlagged case brings out, and for this purpose we can, I think, confine ourselves to the quantity side, and it will not be necessary to establish more than one relative-quantity equation.

We have as before

$$K+x = ax+\alpha\xi. \tag{43}$$

We shall not need the labour-requirement equation, but we have now a new *accumulation* equation

$$gK = x - dax - \delta \alpha \xi .$$ (44)

By substitution we can obtain

$$\frac{x}{\xi} = \frac{\alpha(g+\delta)}{1-da-g(a-1)} .$$ (45)

The point that seems worth bringing out is as follows. For the model to be feasible we must have a value of *da* less than one. There would be no point in making tractors if we used up more tractors in making them than we produced. Let us now examine the case of purely circulating capital. In this case, *d* will be equal to one. Hence *a* must be less than one. But when *a* is less than one the equation misbehaves, since there is no limit to the possible rate of growth. In other words, we cannot use an unlagged production function in the analysis of the case of purely circulating capital – a conclusion that seems worth recording, though it should hardly surprise us.

For completeness, the lagged model with depreciation had better be set out in full. The algebraic manipulations required are no different in kind from those already used in earlier sections, and I will spare the reader the algebra and present merely the bare results.

On the price side, we have

$$p(1-r) = qa + pda(1-r) + wb$$ (46)

$$\pi(1-r) = q\alpha + p\delta\alpha(1-r) + w\beta$$ (47)

$$q = pr .$$ (48)

Two points are worth mentioning. Since production takes time, it is only fair to assume that depreciation takes time as well. Hence, the depreciation terms in equations (46) and (47) have a discounting factor $(1-r)$. Secondly, *q* must now be interpreted as the *net* earnings of a tractor. If you hire a tractor for a period you must pay the owner *q* and hand back the tractor intact at the beginning of the next period.

From these three equations, the relative-price equations can be obtained. As before, they are simpler if expressed in terms of the rate of interest rather than the rate of profit. We have

$$\frac{p}{w} = \frac{b(1+i)}{1-(i+d)a}$$ (49)

$$\frac{q}{w} = \frac{ib}{1-(i+d)a} \qquad \qquad (50)$$

$$\frac{\pi}{w} = (1+i)\left[\beta + \frac{(i+\delta)\alpha b}{1-(i+d)a}\right]. \qquad (51)$$

On the quantity side, we have

$$K = ax + \alpha\xi \qquad (52)$$
$$L = bx + \beta\xi \qquad (53)$$

and $\qquad gK = x - dax - \delta\alpha\xi$. $\qquad\qquad (54)$

From these three equations, we can obtain the relative-quantity equations

$$\frac{K}{\xi} = \frac{\alpha[1+a(\delta-d)]}{1-(g+d)a} \qquad (55)$$

$$\frac{x}{\xi} = \frac{(g+\delta)\alpha}{1-(g+d)a} \qquad (56)$$

$$\frac{L}{\xi} = \beta + \frac{(g+\delta)\alpha b}{1-(g+d)a}. \qquad (57)$$

The relative-price equations (49–51) and the relative-quantity equations (55–7) are so similar in form to their opposite numbers in the everlasting tractor case (36–8 and 15–17) that little new comment is required. In suitable places, we find $(i+d)$ or $(i+\delta)$ instead of i, and $(g+d)$ or $(g+\delta)$ instead of g. The only other new feature is the complication that occurs in the numerator of equation (55). This is the result of differential rates of depreciation. With a uniform rate of depreciation in both sectors, the complication would vanish.

I shall make no formal attempt to generalize from the two-sector model to the case, discussed by Hicks (1965) in chapter XIV, where there are many capital goods. I shall, however, hazard a few intuitive remarks. In the place of our single capital-capital coefficient a, which played so important a role in the two-sector model, we now have a matrix of such a-coefficients. I should guess that provided some at least of these a-coefficients were large enough, unlagged production functions would be usable; but that smaller values of these a-coefficients could lead the unlagged model into delinquency, by allowing unlimited growth on the one hand and a rate of profit greater than one on the other. With lagged production functions, I should expect the system to be free of these difficulties, but I should also expect to see a 'waiting' term appear in the price equations. I should guess, further, that it is the rate of interest rather than the rate of profit that can be more appropriately cast in the role of *dual* to the rate of growth. In short, I believe that the more important results derived from the examination of the two-sector case are also applicable to the matrix case, but I must of course warn the reader that the basis for this belief is not at all sure.

The time has come for an assessment, and I must ask myself some awkward questions: Is the rather pedestrian analysis of the preceding sections of any importance whatsoever? Or the even more pressing one: Is it anything like good enough to offer in a volume of essays written in honour of Sir John Hicks, especially since I have had to take liberties with some of his own work? The answer to both of these questions must be 'No and Yes'. No, because the main points we have been concerned with are in truth very small ones. So long as we receive our salary payments frequently enough, it really does not matter very much whether we are paid in advance or in arrear. For a similar reason, it does not matter very much if economists tend to identify the rate of profit on existing capital (r) with the rate of interest $[r/(1-r)]$. If we go to the limit and use a model with continuous time, the two become identical in any case. Like the problem of arc *versus* point elasticity this is just another example of a type of problem that economists as a profession habitually make very heavy weather of–the difference that it makes when a variable varies discontinuously rather than continuously.

But there is a point of some subtlety here that our assumption of uniform one-period lags is in danger of obscuring. For consider what is happening when we make the period shorter. Two things are really happening at the same time, which are in principle distinct, but which appear inseparable because of the assumption of one-period production lags. On the one hand, the period itself is getting shorter. On the other hand, the production lag is getting shorter. The distinction is important, because the two things have different effects. The shrinkage of the period itself brings the rate of interest closer to the rate of profit. The shrinkage of the production lag reduces the importance of the discounting factor in the price equations. Now there is no reason why we should make these two things happen simultaneously. We could for example halve the length of the period while keeping the production lag the same by making it a two-period lag. We could go further and work with continuous time while still maintaining a finite production lag. In this case the rate of interest would become identical with the rate of profit but we would still need a discounting factor in our price equations.[10]

It is on points like these that some of the most long-standing controversies in economics have turned: the question of whether interest should be regarded as the yield on a stock or rather as the premium attaching to present goods over future goods, the whole dispute over productivity theories of interest and *agio* theories. I hope that the spelling out undertaken in the foregoing sections may have cast some light on them, or at least have put them in proper perspective.

The upshot would appear to be something like this. So long as we work with continuous time and vanishing lags, these different theories of interest are all equally acceptable, since they come to the same thing. But as soon as we introduce finite production lags, we have to take the first step down the Austrian path by introducing a discounting factor into our price equations.[11] And as soon as we work with discrete periods, we have to draw a distinction between the rate of interest and the rate of profit.

My own knowledge of these famous controversies owes practically everything to Schumpeter's (1954) superb account of them in *History of Economic Analysis*. At the end of it all, however, one cannot help feeling that he may have exaggerated their scientific importance. If it were not too depressing a note on which to conclude, I should be inclined to say that the two propositions.

'this paper has been concerned with some very small points', and
'this paper has been concerned with some of the grand themes of economic controversy'
are not necessarily inconsistent with one another!

NOTES AND REFERENCES

[1] Allen 'notices' the puzzle by setting it as an exercise for the student. Rather a fast ball for him to have to face so early in his innings!

[2] I certainly intend these strictures to apply to some of my own writings.

[3] In setting out the model, I shall not scruple to use Hicks's own words without further acknowledgment. To attempt a complete paraphrase would be merely tiresome. I have, however, made minor changes in the arrangement of some of the equations. Needless to say, our own account

of the model will restrict itself to what is necessary for the particular purpose in hand. It should certainly not be regarded as a substitute for Hicks's own analysis, for which the reader must of course refer to the text itself.

⁴ Hicks has aptly called equation (11) the *wage equation*.

⁵ Hicks is, of course, not alone in using a hybrid model of this kind. Dorfman, Samuelson and Solow (1958, pp. 317–18), implicitly use an unlagged model in their discussion of own-rates of interest, even though this discussion is set in the general context of a lagged model. The whole of chapters 11 and 12 of this work is of course relevant to the subject-matter discussed in the present paper.

⁶ It is not a weakness of the system that i can be greater than one when a is less than one. It is clear from equation (30) that, whatever the value of i, r will be less than one, and this is what matters.

⁷ I am sure Hicks (1965, p. 140) is right to insist that it is this equation that should be called the 'factor-price equation'.

⁸ If this way out were adopted, I think there would be a risk of confusion between it and the more legitimate case of duality between quantities in future periods and discounted prices, that arises in the von Neumann growth model. Cf. Allen (1959, p. 603 *et seq.*) The discounting factor that enters into our equations (36) and (38) above is necessary not because the prices refer to future periods) they refer to the current period) but because of the lag in the production functions.

⁹ We need the 'death rate' of tractors for the quantity equations, and for the price equations we need the 'rate of depreciation'. The identification of the rate of depreciation with the death rate is justified only if we make the special assumption about the nature of depreciation that Meade has called 'depreciation by evaporation', i.e. that the death rate of tractors is independent of their age distribution. Reluctant as we may be to make this unrealistic assumption, it seems to be the only way of maintaining any simplicity in our equations. The complications that arise if we adopt a more plausible assumption, e.g. depreciation by sudden death after a given number of years, may be regarded as another example of the way in which time-lags can spoil the duality of the price and quantity equations. Cf. Meade (1961) especially chapters 1 and 8, appendices II and III, and the other references he cites in the footnote to chapter 8.

¹⁰ Our examination of the unlagged case in the text was an attempt to do the opposite, that is, to retain a finite period while making the production lag zero. As we saw, it led us into difficulties.

¹¹ But we need not go the whole Austrian way with Mrs Robinson and do away with physical capital altogether.

11

The Principle of Two-stage
Maximization in Price Theory

Nissan Liviatan

I. *Introduction*

One of the most important methodological contributions made by Sir John R. Hicks's classic work on *Value and Capital* (1946 ed, p. 312–13) is the 'Composite-Good Theorem', which states that a group of commodities with fixed relative prices can be treated analytically as an ordinary individual commodity. It is on the basis of this theorem that Hicks was able to reduce the general multicommodity model to a two-dimensional indifference curves diagram where all but one of the commodities are lumped into a single composite good. To prove this theorem Hicks applies (in an appendix) advanced-calculus techniques which became the usual tools for analyses of this kind. The purpose of this paper is to show how the composite good theorem and some of its important applications in the theory of the firm can be derived alternatively by a principle which can be called 'Two-Stage Maximization' (in short TSM).[1] The advantage of this approach is both in its mathematical simplicity and in its intuitive appeal.

II. *Illustrations of the Principle of TSM*

We may illustrate the principle of TSM by a well known example from the theory of the firm. Consider a competitive firm with a production function $y = f(x_1, \ldots, x_n)$ where y denotes output and x_i denotes inputs and where the corresponding prices are denoted by p_y and p_i. It is assumed that for any set of prices there exists a unique maximum for the profit function

$$r = p_y f(x_1, \ldots, x_n) - \sum_{i=1}^{n} p_i x_i.$$ Suppose we determine the optimal set of

inputs by solving [2] the set of first order conditions (which equate, for each factor, the value of marginal product with factor price). Denoting this set by $\bar{x}_1, \ldots, \bar{x}_n$ we may compute optimal value of output by $\bar{y} = f(\bar{x}_1, \ldots, \bar{x}_n)$.

Similarly we may compute the optimal value of total cost (c) by $\bar{c} = \sum_{i=1}^{n} p_i \bar{x}_i$
and of profits by $\bar{r} = p_y \bar{y} - \bar{c}$.

In textbooks on price theory the optimal value of y is usually determined by an alternative, two-stage, procedure. In the first stage one determines the minimum value of cost which is required to produce any specified level of output. This leads to a (total) cost function $c = c(y)$ and to a corresponding profit function, say $g = p_y y - c(y)$. In the second stage one maximizes g as a function of y to determine the optimal value of output. Note that in the first stage we get rid of all n inputs, which are represented in the second stage by $c(y)$. Consequently the second stage profit function involves only one variable, namely y.

Two fundamental properties of the foregoing TSM, which are intuitively clear, should be noted. First we know that g as a function of y must possess a maximum if this is true of completely specified profit function. Secondly, TSM is consistent in the following sense. Denote the value of y which maximizes g by y' and similarly let $c' = c(y')$ and $g' = p_y y' - c(y')$. Then we must have $y' = \bar{y}$, $c' = \bar{c}$ and $g' = \bar{r}$ (where $\bar{y}$, $\bar{c}$ and $\bar{r}$ are the optimal values of these variables which result from maximizing the completely specified profit function $r = p_y f(x_1, \ldots, x_n) - \sum_{i=1}^{n} p_i x_i$).

The foregoing TSM can be easily converted into one where *both* stages involve maximum problems, which is the type of TSM with which we shall be concerned. In the first stage we determine the maximum value of output, say y_m, for any specified level of total cost. This leads to a functional relationship (of the nature of a production function) $y_m = y(c)$, which is of course the inverse function of $c(y)$. In the second stage we maximize the corresponding profit function, say $w = p_y y(c) - c$, with respect to c. Again it is intuitively clear that w, as a function of c, does have a maximum. It is also quite clear that this TSM is consistent in the foregoing sense. In particular, denote the value of c which maximizes w by c^*, and similarly let $y^* = y(c^*)$ and $w^* = p_y y^* - c^*$. Then we have $y^* = \bar{y}$, $c^* = \bar{c}$ and $w^* = \bar{r}$.

III. *A Basic Composite Good Theorem*

We shall now apply the principle of TSM to derive a useful composite good theorem which will be applied later to establish some of the basic propositions in the theory of the firm. Let us first define an aggregative production function of a certain type which plays a fundamental role in the following theorem. Suppose that the firm is faced with a particular set of constant prices which will be referred to as 'base-point' prices and denoted by $p_y^\circ, p_1^\circ, \ldots, p_n^\circ$. Let the firm operate under a cost constraint concerning the outlay on the inputs $x_{k+1}, \ldots, x_n$ ($0 \leqslant k < n$), so that in any situation the firm must spend a predetermined sum on these inputs, say

$$v = \sum_{t=k+1}^{n} p_t^\circ x_t.$$ The value of maximum profits at base point prices, to be

denoted by max r_b,[3] will then depend on the value of the cost constraint v. Under these conditions we may define a functional relationship between max r_b and v, say max $r_b = R(v)$.

From $R(v)$ we may derive the function which will appear in our theorem.

Define $z = p_y^\circ y - \sum_1^k p_j^\circ x_j$, so that z is 'gross profits' at base point prices

before deducting v, i.e. $z = r_b + v$. Then for each value of v there exists a maximum value of z given by max $z = $ max $r_b + v$. This leads to a functional relationship $z = R(v) + v \equiv F(v)$ which specifies the maximum

value of z for any given value of $v \left(= \sum_{t=k+1}^{n} p_t^\circ x_t \right)$. The variables z and v

constitute the composite goods of the following analysis whose purpose is essentially to specify the conditions under which $F(v)$ can be considered as an ordinary production function.

Let us divide all the commodities entering the production function into two groups where the first group includes $y, x_1, \ldots, x_k$ and the second includes $x_{k+1}, \ldots, x_n$, where $0 \leqslant k < n$. Suppose that the relative prices within each of the two groups remain constant throughout the analysis. This is of course equivalent to saying that the prices within each of the two groups vary in the same proportion, that is

$$\frac{p_y}{p_y^\circ} = \frac{p_j}{p_j^\circ} = p_z \, (j = 1, \ldots, k); \quad \frac{p_t}{p_t^\circ} = p_v \, (t = k+1, \ldots, n), \qquad (1)$$

where p° denotes the foregoing 'base-point' (or 'initial') prices which are treated throughout as constants. It is important to note that under assumption (1) there is a one-to-one correspondence between any set of current prices $p_y, p_1, \ldots, p_n$ and the pair p_z, p_v, so that any one of these sets determines uniquely the other. We shall also make use of the important fact that p_z and p_v, which are the price indices of the two groups, can be considered as the prices of the composite goods z and v in the sense that $p_z z$ and $p_v v$ satisfy the following 'value identities'

$$p_z z = p_z p_y^\circ y - \sum_{j=1}^{k} p_z p_j^\circ x_j = p_y y - \sum_{j=1}^{k} p_j x_j \qquad (2)$$

$$p_v v = \sum_{t=k+1}^{n} p_v p_t^\circ x_t = \sum_{t=k+1}^{n} p_t x_t \,. \qquad (3)$$

Thus the outlay on the composite input v equals the total outlay on its components.

We may now state the fundamental theorem. Under assumption (1) the foregoing function $z = F(v)$ has the following property: if we use it to form the (profit) function

$$q = q(v; p_z, p_v) = p_z F(v) - p_v v \qquad (4)$$

with p_z and p_v [defined by (1)] as parameters, then *for any set of p_z and p_v* (i) q as a function of v will possess a maximum, and (ii) the optimal values which correspond to max q, denoted by stars, satisfy $q^* = \bar{r}$,

$z^* = F(v^*) = p_y^\circ \bar{y} - \sum_{j=1}^{k} p_j^\circ \bar{x}_j = \bar{z}$ and $v^* = \sum_{t=k+1}^{n} p_t^\circ \bar{x}_t = \bar{v}$ [where the barred

variables denote as usual the optimal values resulting from the maximization of $r = p_y f(x_1, \ldots, x_n) - \sum_1^n p_i x_i$].

Thus the theorem states that under assumption (1) we may carry out, for any set of current prices, the usual profit maximization procedure treating $z = F(v)$ as an ordinary production function and $q = p_z F(v) - p_v v$ as an ordinary profit function, and obtain the correct answers concerning the optimal values of q, z, and v.

The proof is a direct application of the principle of TSM. We shall first show that if we carry out a first stage maximization of profits for given values of $v\left(= \sum_{j=1}^{k} p_j^\circ x_j\right)$, then under assumption (1) this will lead to the function $q(v; p_z, p_v)$ for any set of current prices. We shall then show that $q(v; p_z, p_v)$ being a second stage profit function, can be consistently maximized with respect to v.

Under assumption (1) we may write the completely specified profit function for any set of current prices as [see (2) and (3)]

$$r = p_z\left(p_y^\circ y - \sum_{j=1}^k p_j^\circ x_j\right) - p_v\left(\sum_{t=k+1}^n p_t^\circ x_t\right) = p_z z - p_v v. \tag{5}$$

Consider a TSM of (5) for any *arbitrary* set of p_z and p_v. In the first stage we maximize r for given values of v. However, holding v constant means holding $p_v v$ constant. Consequently maximizing r under these conditions implies maximizing $p_z z$ and hence z for given values of v. We have seen however that these conditional maxima of z are given by the function $z = F(v)$, which is independent of current prices. Substituting $F(v)$ for z in (5) we may express the first stage maximum profits by $p_z F(v) - p_v v$ which is the function $q(v; p_z, p_v)$ of our theorem. We have thus established the fact that under (1) the first stage of maximization will result in (4) for any set of current prices.

Since $q(v; p_z, p_v)$ results from a maximization of the original profit function *under a constraint* of the form $v = \sum_{t=k+1}^n p_t^\circ x_t = $ constant, it follows immediately that the values specified by $q(v; p_z, p_v)$ can never exceed the *unconstrained* maximum of profits which we denoted by $\bar{r}$. Denoting the value of $\bar{r}$ at any set of p_z and p_v (which correspond of course to a certain set $p_y, p_1, \ldots, p_n$) by the function $\bar{r}(p_z, p_v)$, we may express the foregoing conclusion as

$$q(v; p_z, p_v) \leqslant \bar{r}(p_z, p_v) \tag{6}$$

for any values v, p_z and p_v.

Consider now the maximum profit position for any arbitrary set of p_z and p_v where we have

$$\bar{r} = p_z\left(p_y^\circ \bar{y} - \sum_{j=1}^k p_j^\circ \bar{x}_j\right) - p_v\left(\sum_{t=k+1}^n p_t^\circ \bar{x}_t\right) = p_z \bar{z} - p_v \bar{v}. \tag{7}$$

If we take $\bar{v}$ as a given parameter then it is easily seen that $\bar{z}$ is the *maximum* value of z which can be attained with any set $x_{k+1}, \ldots, x_n$ which satisfies the constraint $\sum_{t=k+1}^n p_t^\circ x_t = \bar{v}$. For if this were not the case then it would have been possible to increase $p_z z$, and hence profits, without increasing $p_v v$. This contradicts, however, the assumption that we started from a maximum profit position. Hence $\bar{z}$ *is* the maximum value of z attainable with $\bar{v}$. We may therefore write $\bar{z} = F(\bar{v})$. Substituting in (7) we obtain $\bar{r} = p_z F(\bar{v}) - p_v \bar{v} = \bar{q}$, which specifies a point on the second stage profit function $q(v; p_z, p_v)$. Since this is true for any set (p_z, p_v) we may write

$$q(\bar{v}; p_z, p_v) = \bar{r}(p_z, p_v). \tag{8}$$

Now (8) together with (6) implies that for any set (p_z, p_v), q, as a function of v, has a maximum which equals $\bar{r}$ and that this maximum is attained at $\bar{v}$, i.e. $v^* = \bar{v}$.[4] It also follows that $\bar{z} = F(\bar{v}) = F(v^*) = z^*$. This completes the proof.

It should be noted again how the fundamental assumption (1) entered the proof. Using this assumption in (5) enabled us to express each of the value sums $p_y y - \sum_{j=1}^{k} p_j x_j$ and $\sum_{t=k+1}^{n} p_t x_t$ as a product of two functions: one depending on current quantities only $\left(z = p_y^\circ y - \sum_{j=1}^{k} p_j^\circ x_j \text{ and } v = \sum_{t=k+1}^{n} p_t^\circ x_t \right)$ and the other on current prices only $\left(p_z = \dfrac{p_y}{p_y^\circ} = \dfrac{p_j}{p_j^\circ} \text{ and } p_v = \dfrac{p_t}{p_t^\circ} \right)$. It is this separability of price and quantity elements that makes it possible to arrive at our results. This point will be discussed in greater detail in the concluding section.

IV. _Applications of the Composite Good Theorem_

Let us first restate some well-known results of the single input case where $y = f(x_1)$. The problem of profit maximization can be formulated as follows: Maximize $r = p_y y - p_1 x_1$ under the production constraint $y - f(x_1) = 0$. This is represented diagrammatically in Figure 1 by the tangency at the point E_1 of the total product curve $y = f(x_1)$ with the highest isoprofit line of the family $r = p_y y - p_1 x_1 = $ constant. The important thing to note in Figure 1 is that in the neighborhood of the maximum profit position the production function is concave, that is, the marginal product is decreasing. This is a restriction on the production function imposed by the existence of a regular maximum of profits. As a result of this restriction we know that when p_1/p_y (the slope of the isoprofit line) decreases the tangency point must shift to the right of E_1, say to E_2, so that both y and x_1 must necessarily increase.

Let us return to the more general case of n inputs and to the composite production function $z = F(v)$. Since the composite profit function $q = p_z F(v) - p_v v$ has a maximum, we know that $z = F(v)$ must be tangent to an upward sloping line $z = \dfrac{q}{p_z} + \dfrac{p_v}{p_z} v$ and that it must be subject to the same concavity restriction as the production function in Figure 1. Consequently as p_v/p_z decreases both z and v must increase. We are now ready to derive some fundamental propositions.

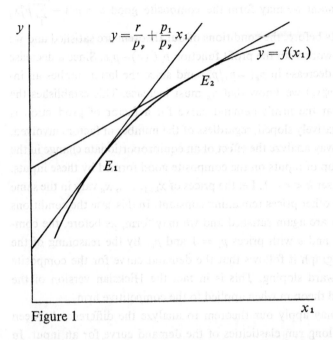

Figure 1

Consider first the effect of an increase in p_y on the supply of y. In this case it is convenient to set $k = 0$ (it should be recalled that k is the number of inputs in the group on which z is based). We then have $z = p_y^\circ y$ and $p_z = p_y/p_y^\circ$, so that z is trivially a composite good ('all' prices in this 'group' change in the same proportion). Since we consider a change in p_y only, all other prices $p_{k+1}, \ldots, p_n$ (where $p_{k+1} = p_1$) remain constant, which means of course that *relative* prices in this group remain constant too. We may therefore form a composite good $v = \sum_{t=1}^{n} p_t^\circ x_t$ with price $p_v = 1$. Since the conditions of our theorem are satisfied we may work with the profit function $p_z F(v) - p_v v$. Now an increase in p_y means an increase in p_z which in turn implies an increase in $z = (p_y^\circ y)$ and hence also in y. This establishes the fact that the supply function is upward sloping. (Note that the foregoing effect on output will also result from an equiproportional decrease in all input prices, that is, in p_v.)

Let us now analyze the effect of a reduction in the price of an input (p_n)

on its quantity. Here it is convenient to set $k = n-1$ so that $p_v = p_n/p_n^o$ and $v = p_n^o x_n$. In this case v is trivially a composite good. Since all other prices are constant we may form the composite good $z = p_y^o y - \sum_{1}^{n-1} p_j^o x_j$ with $p_z = 1$. As before, the conditions of our theorem are satisfied and we may therefore work with the profit function $p_z F(v) - p_v v$. Since a decrease in p_n means a decrease in $p_v (=p_n/p_n^o)$ and since the latter implies an increase in $v (=p_n^o x_n)$ we know that x_n must increase. This establishes the proposition that the firm's demand curve for a factor of production is necessarily negatively sloped, regardless of the number of factors involved.

In a similar way analyze the effect of an equiproportionate change in the prices of a group of inputs on the composite good formed by these inputs. In this case we set $k < n - 1$. Let the prices of $x_{k+1}, \ldots, x_n$ vary in the same proportion, all other prices remaining constant. In this case the conditions of the theorem are again satisfied and we may form, as before, the composite goods z and v with prices $p_z = 1$ and p_v. By the reasoning of the foregoing paragraph it follows that the demand curve for the composite input is downward sloping. This is in fact the Hicksian version of the composite good theorem when applied to the competitive firm.

Finally we may apply our theorem to analyze the difference between short run and long run elasticities of the demand curve for an input. In particular we shall establish the well-known proposition that the foregoing demand curve is more elastic in the long run, regardless of the number of factors involved. Consider the long run effect of a change in p_n on x_n, starting from a long run equilibrium position and assuming that $x_1, \ldots, x_n$ are all freely variable. We have seen that this case can be analyzed in terms of the composite production function $z = F(v)$, which specifies the maximum values of $z \left(= p_y^o y - \sum_{j=1}^{n-1} p_j^o x_j \right)$ attainable with given values of v. Since in this case $v (= p_n^o x_n)$ is proportional to x_n it will be more convenient to define a composite production function $G(x_n)$ so that $z = F(p_n^o x_n) \equiv G(x_n)$. The profit function will then be $q = p_z G(x_n) - p_n x_n$.

Suppose now that some of the inputs $x_1, \ldots, x_{n-1}$ are fixed in the short run at their initial long run optimum values, while x_n is freely variable. Denote the maximum values of z, which can be attained in the *short run* for given values of x_n by the function $G^s(x_n)$. It is then clear that $G^s(x_n) \leqslant G(x_n)$ for all values of x_n, since in the long run one can always produce as much gross profits as under various short run constraints. It is also clear that if the firm does not deviate in the short run from the long run optimal value of x_n then we must have $G^s(x_n) = G(x_n)$.[5] However, if the firm does vary x_n in the short run, then because of the rigidities in some of the x_j's it will not be possible to attain in the short run that level of z which is attainable in the long run when all inputs are optimally adjusted. (This argument is familiar from the theory of cost functions.) In the latter case we therefore have $G^s(x_n) < G(x_n)$.[6]

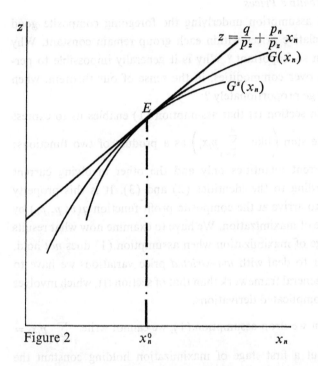

Figure 2

This situation is illustrated in Figure 2 where at the long run equilibrium point E we have $G^s(x_n^o) = G(x_n^o)$ while for $x_n \neq x_n^o$ we have $G^s(x_n) < G(x_n)$. If prices remain unchanged then E is also a short run equilibrium so that the relevant isoprofit line ($q = p_z z - p_n x_n = $ constant) is tangent to *both* curves at E. Now it is clear from the diagram that the curvature of $G^s(x_n)$ at E must be greater than that of $G(x_n)$, i.e. the 'value of marginal product' curve corresponding to $G^s(x_n)$ is steeper. Consequently a decline in p_n will cause a greater response in the demand for x_n in the long run.

In the foregoing analyses we have not considered the effect of a change in the price of an individual commodity on the quantity of another individual commodity. For example, we have seen that when p_n declines $z = p_y^o y - \sum_1^{n-1} p_j^o x_j$ must increase, but we do not know under what conditions (say) y will increase or decrease. It can be shown that our analytic technique can be applied to these problems as well, but this lies outside the scope of the present paper.[7]

v. *Constancy of Relative Prices*

The fundamental assumption underlying the foregoing composite good theorem is that relative prices within each group remain constant. Why is this assumption so important? Why is it generally impossible to perform aggregation over commodities, in the sense of our theorem, when prices do *not* change proportionately?

We have seen in section III that assumption (1) enables us to express each current value sum $\left(\text{like } \sum_{t=k+1}^{n} p_t x_t\right)$ as a product of two functions: one involving current quantities only and the other involving current prices only, according to the identities (2) and (3). It is this property which enables us to arrive at the composite profit function $q(v; p_z, p_v)$ by way of a first stage of maximization. We have to examine now what results from the first stage of maximization when assumption (1) does *not* hold. However, in order to deal with *unrestricted* price variations we have to start with a more general framework than that of section III, which involves somewhat more complicated derivations.

Since now, when we drop assumption (1), we cannot write $\sum_{t=k+1}^{n} p_t x_t = pv$, let us carry out a first stage of maximization holding constant the *current* value sum $\sum_{t=k+1}^{n} p_t x_t$, to be denoted by E. Proceeding in the standard manner let us maximize the completely specified profit function under the constraint $\sum_{t=k+1}^{n} p_t x_t = E$, where E is treated as a parameter.

Form the function

$$L = p_y f(x_1, \ldots, x_n) - \sum_{i=1}^{n} p_i x_i - \lambda \left(\sum_{t=k+1}^{n} p_t x_t - E \right) \tag{9}$$

with λ as a Lagrange multiplier. The first order conditions are obtained by equating to zero the partial derivatives of L with respect to $x_1, \ldots, x_n$. Together with the cost constraint this yields the following system:

$$L_j - p_y f_j(x_1, \ldots, x_n) - p_j = 0 \quad (j = 1, \ldots, k) \tag{10}$$

$$L_t = p_y f_t(x_1, \ldots, x_n) - (1 + \lambda) p_t = 0 \quad (t = k+1, \ldots, n) \tag{11}$$

$$\sum_{t=k+1}^{n} p_t x_t - E = 0 , \tag{12}$$

where the subscripts of L and f denote partial derivatives with respect to the appropriate input. Let us divide (10) by p_y, (12) by p_n and let us eliminate $(1 + \lambda)$ from (11) by substituting $1 + \lambda = p_y f_n / p_n$ from the nth equation. Then our system becomes

$$f_j(x_1, \ldots, x_n) = \frac{p_j}{p_y} \quad (j = 1, \ldots, k) \tag{13}$$

$$\frac{f_t(x_1, \ldots, x_n)}{f_n(x_1, \ldots, x_n)} = \frac{p_t}{p_n} \quad (t = k+1, \ldots, n-1) \tag{14}$$

$$\sum_{t=k+1}^{n} \frac{p_t}{p_n} x_t = \frac{E}{p_n} . \tag{15}$$

By solving the foregoing system we may express the optimal value of x_i as a function of the parameters on the right hand side, which yields

$$x_i = D^i \left(\frac{E}{p_n}, \frac{p_1}{p_y}, \ldots, \frac{p_k}{p_y}, \frac{p_{k+1}}{p_n}, \ldots, \frac{p_{n-1}}{p_n} \right) \quad (i = 1, \ldots, n) . \tag{16}$$

Let us now return to the profit function which can be written identically as

$$r = p_y \frac{Q}{p_y} - p_n \frac{E}{p_n} \tag{17}$$

where

$$Q = p_y f(x_1, \ldots, x_n) - \sum_{j=1}^{k} p_j x_j \tag{18}$$

denotes 'gross profits' at *current* prices. Substituting (16) in (18) and dividing by p_y we obtain Q/p_y as a function of the same arguments as in (16):

$$\frac{Q}{p_y} = M \left(\frac{E}{p_n}, \frac{p_1}{p_y}, \ldots, \frac{p_k}{p_y}, \frac{p_{k+1}}{p_n}, \ldots, \frac{p_{n-1}}{p_n} \right) . \tag{19}$$

Finally substituting (19) in (17) we may express the constrained maximum value of profits (say r_m) as a function of the parameters of the first stage of maximization. This yields the second stage profit function

$$r_m = p_y M\left(\frac{E}{p_n}; \frac{p_1}{p_y}, \ldots, \frac{p_k}{p_y}, \frac{p_{k+1}}{p_n}, \ldots, \frac{p_{n-1}}{p_n}\right) - p_n \frac{E}{p_n}. \qquad (20)$$

Note that $M(\cdot)$ must be a function which specifies *maximum* values of 'deflated gross profits' Q/p_y for given values of 'deflated outlay' E/p_n at any set of relative prices. This is due to the fact that maximizing r for a given E/p_n implies the maximization of Q/p_y for that value of E/p_n.

Now, for any given set of relative price parameters [written to be right of the semicolon in $M(\cdot)$ above] we may maximize (20) with respect to E/p_n, treating it as an ordinary input, to obtain the optimal values of profits, Q/p_y and E/p_n. By the argument of section III it can also be established that the maximization is consistent. However, we have not succeeded in arriving at a production function with the ordinary analytic properties. In particular, the form of the relationship between Q/p_y and E/p_n will vary with every change in the relative price parameters in $M(\cdot)$. It is this dependence of the production relationship on market prices which destroys the analogy between (20) and the ordinary production function in the theory of the firm.

Let us introduce again assumption (1). In this case the relative price parameters become ratios of *base point* prices, that is, constants, and can therefore be ignored. Using (1), (2) and (3) we may express (20) as

$$r_m = p_z \left[p_y^\circ M\left(\frac{v}{p_n^\circ}, \frac{p_1^\circ}{p_y^\circ}, \ldots, \frac{p_k^\circ}{p_y^\circ}, \frac{p_{k+1}^\circ}{p_n^\circ}, \ldots, \frac{p_{n-1}^\circ}{p_n^\circ}\right) \right] - p_v v. \qquad (21)$$

Note that under (1) $\dfrac{Q}{p_y} = \dfrac{p_z z}{p_z p_y^\circ} = z\dfrac{1}{p_y^\circ}$. It follows therefore from the properties of $M(\cdot)$ that the expression in the square brackets in (18) is a function which specifies maximum values of z for given values of v. It can therefore be identified with $F(v)$ and consequently (21) can be identified with the function $p_z F(v) - p_v v$ of our theorem. In this case the analogy with an ordinary profit function is preserved since $F(v)$ like $f(x_1, \ldots, x_n)$ is independent of current prices.

ACKNOWLEDGMENT

I wish to thank D. Patinkin for suggesting many improvements to
an earlier draft.

NOTES AND REFERENCES

[1] A sketch of this principle has been presented (Liviatan, 1966, p. 52).

[2] We refer of course to that solution which corresponds to the *maximum* of profits.

[3] The subscript b indicates that profits are measured at *base point* prices, i.e. $r_b = p_y^\circ y - \sum_1^n p_i^\circ x_i$.

[4] It is easy to prove that this maximum is unique if the maximum of the completely specified profit function is unique.

[5] Since then the firm can remain in the short run with the set $x_1, \ldots, x_n$ which is optimal in the long run.

[6] This excludes the special case where the marginal products of $x_1, \ldots, x_{n-1}$ are independent of x_n in the whole range. In this case, starting from a long run optimum, we shall have $G^s(x_n) = G(x_n)$ for all values of x_n.

[7] These analyses are considered in detail in my forthcoming book *Topics in Price and Capital Theory*.

12

Two Classical Monetary Models

Cliff L. Lloyd

There are, under current discussion in the journals, at least two notions of the consumers demand for money which, within the traditions of monetary theory, appear to be clearly 'acceptable'.[1] One of these has received impetus from the work of Patinkin (1956) and others. It supposes, in essence, that people hold money because they want to. They gain utility from so doing. The utility accrues directly to real balances rather than to money as such, but it is money that is held. The other approach, recently discussed by Clower (1963b) and others, supposes that money is held, not because people want to hold it, but because they must. They are constrained so to do by the workings of the economic system. It will be the purpose of this paper to discuss the empirical implications of this latter model. Clower has shown that a particular case of this model is consistent with Say's Law, Walras's Law, homogeneity of degree zero of excess demand functions in money prices alone, the determination of absolute prices by the quantity theory and the classical 'invalid' dichotomy. Since this list includes almost everything that has ever been claimed for a theory of money the model in which people hold money because they are constrained so to do must be a good one indeed. Elsewhere (Lloyd, 1964), we have shown that the Patinkin model is lacking in known empirical implications. We shall show here that the constraint model is not so lacking. It is rich in empirical content. Perhaps it is too rich.

Suppose that the consumer chooses those quantities $x_1, \ldots, x_n$ of commodities $1, \ldots, n$ that maximize his utility function

$$U = U(x_1, \ldots, x_n) \tag{1}$$

subject to a budget constraint

$$\sum_{i=1}^{n} x_i p_i + M = L + Y \tag{2}$$

305

and to an additional constraint

$$M = k \sum_{i=1}^{n} x_i p_i,$$ (3)

where p_i is the price of commodity i, Y is money income, L is initial money holdings, M is final money holdings and k is a positive constant. The consumer holds money because he is constrained so to do by equation (3). The model has been characterized (Valavanis, 1955) as one in which each man faces his own little quantity equation. Note that by observing the size of the consumer's money holding and the value of his total consumption, we may derive the value of his k empirically.

Consider first the comparative-static properties of this model. Since money does not enter the consumer's utility function, and since we are concerned only with quantities $x_1, \ldots, x_n$ which satisfy both constraints, we may substitute equation (3) into equation (2) to obtain a single constraint on the consumer's decision variables $x_1, \ldots, x_n$

$$(1+k) \sum_{i=1}^{n} x_i p_i = L + Y.$$ (4)

We seek those values of $x_1, \ldots, x_n$ such that (1) is a maximum subject to (4).[2] The first order conditions for this maximum are

$$U_i = \lambda(1+k)p_i \qquad i = 1, \ldots, n$$

$$(1+k) \sum_{i=1}^{n} x_i p_i = L + Y.$$ (5)

The second order sufficient conditions are that

$$\begin{vmatrix} 0 & (1+k)p_1 & \cdots & (1+k)p_J \\ (1+k)p_1 & U_{11} & \cdots & U_{1J} \\ \cdots & \cdots & \cdots & \cdots \\ \cdots & \cdots & \cdots & \cdots \\ (1+k)p_J & U_{J1} & \cdots & U_{JJ} \end{vmatrix} (-1)^J > 0, J = 2, \ldots n,$$ (6)

where all border-preserving principal minors of like order are of like sign. When $J = n$ call the determinant in (6) K. Since K is symmetric, we may, without ambiguity, write the cofactor of $(1+k)p_i$, K_i. Similarly, let K_{ij} denote the cofactor of U_{ij} in K. We suppose that $K \neq 0$.

It is a straightforward matter to differentiate conditions (5) partially and solve the resultant simultaneous equation systems to get the following comparative static results:[3]

$$\frac{\partial x_s}{\partial y} = \frac{K_s}{K} = \frac{\partial x_s}{\partial L} \tag{7}$$

$$\frac{\partial x_a}{\partial p_r} + (1+k)x_r\frac{\partial x_a}{\partial y} = (1+k)\lambda\frac{K_{rs}}{K}. \tag{8}$$

Combining (2) and (3) so as to eliminate $\sum_{i=1}^{n} x_i p_i$ and arranging terms, we get

$$M = \frac{k}{(1+k)}(L+y). \tag{9}$$

Thus $\qquad \dfrac{\partial M}{\partial y} = \dfrac{k}{(1+k)} \tag{10}$

and $\qquad \dfrac{\partial M}{\partial p_r} = 0.[4] \tag{11}$

We shall see below that there exists a level of money holdings, $M = ky$, such that if the consumer attains it, he will hold it. He will neither hoard nor dishoard money. At other levels, he will either hoard (if $M < ky$) or dishoard (if $M > ky$). Thus, the consumer's demand function being

$$x_i = x_i(p_1, \ldots, p_n, L, y), \tag{12}$$

week-to-week variations in money holdings, prices and income constant, will lead to week-to-week variations in the consumption of commodity i,

$$dx_i = \frac{\partial x_i}{\partial L}dL.$$

Should a single price p_r vary by dp_r from one week to the next, during which period other prices and income are held constant and L varies through hoarding by ΔL, then the resultant variation in x_i would, by equation (12) be approximated by

$$dx_i = \frac{\partial x_i}{\partial p_r}dp_r + \frac{\partial x_s}{\partial L}\Delta L. \tag{13}$$

Thus $\qquad \dfrac{\partial x_i}{\partial p_r} = \dfrac{dx_i}{dp_r} - \dfrac{\partial x_s}{\partial L}\dfrac{\Delta L}{dp_r}. \tag{14}$

The terms on the right hand side of (14) being observable, so is $\partial x_i/\partial p_r$.

All the variables on the left hand side of (8), the modified Slutsky equation, are observable. Conditions (6) imply all the usual things about the substitution term on the right hand side of (8). Moreover, equations (10) and (11) offer *additional* empirical ramifications of the theory.

Unlike the Patinkin model, the constraint model that we are examining possesses all the usual empirical results of consumer demand theory and more too.

Nor have we exhausted the empirical ramifications of the model. Money does not depreciate and it cannot be traded except during some 'week'. Accordingly, the amount of money with which the individual begins week t is the same as the amount with which he ends week $t-1$. Equation (9) may be rewritten

$$M_t = \frac{k}{1+k}M_{t-1} + \frac{k}{1+k}y .$$ (15)

This is a linear first-order difference equation and since

$$0 < \frac{k}{1+k} < 1 ,$$

the equation has the unique solution

$$M_t = \left(\frac{k}{1+k}\right)^t (M_0 - ky) + ky ,$$ (16)

which converges monotonically to

$$M = ky .$$ (17)

Since k can be observed, result (17) offers an additional empirical test of the theory. But why stop there ? On the basis of (15), having observed the value of k, we can always predict exactly how much additional cash the consumer will hoard *in each subsequent period* so long as his income does not change unpredictably. Moreover, we may aggregate this information and predict the future demand for money to hoard for the entire economy.

By equation (16) M_t converges monotonically for all $k > 0$. For any consumer then, the time path of money hoarding will converge monotonically to some level, ky. The nature of this path will have certain characteristics which will not vary with the individual. To illustrate these, consider a young man starting out in life. Suppose, for convenience, that for him $k = 1$. Let him have no money hoarded as yet and an income of $100.00 per week. According to equation (17) his equilibrium money hoard will be $100.00. Let us examine the path whereby he ultimately saves up this $100.00. Putting the appropriate values for the variables into equation (15) our theory predicts that during period 1 he will hoard $50.00. The following week he will hoard an additional $25.00, etc. In general, for any value of $k > 0$ and any fixed value of $y > 0$, if $M_0 < ky$ the consumer will, in the first period in which he earns money, *hoard the largest absolute amount of any period in his entire career.* His rate of hoarding will thereafter fall off for so long as his income remains fixed. This is true regardless of variations in prices which may occur. According to this model, a consumer, on fixed income, will add most to his money hoardings when he is youngest and will slack off as he matures. Frugality, the model implies, is a characteristic of youth.

II. *A Minimal Classical Model*

The classical model that we have been examining, while it admittedly abstracts from a vast array of possibly important complications has a good deal to recommend it. It is rich in implications regarding consumer behavior. In addition to this it is, as Clower has shown, in keeping with traditional notions regarding monetary theory. Must one who wishes to employ such a classical model saddle himself with such odd implications regarding consumer hoarding? Must we, in general, associate such implications with classical monetary theory? It is the purpose of this section to show that we need not.

Consider the properties which economists have traditionally sought in a monetary theory. Consumers, it is thought, do not desire money as such; rather it is sought for the goods that it will buy. Thus, Patinkin assumed that consumers gained utility from holding real balances, while in the model just discussed consumers are *constrained* to hold a certain part of the value of what they spend on consumption in the form of money. These are simply alternative ways of supposing that the consumer will demand sufficient funds to purchase a typical bundle of commodities, that is, that money is not desired for itself but for what it will buy. Let that be the case. What then can we say about the demand for money? Should all prices double then, clearly, the price of the 'typical bundle of commodities', whatever the bundle might include, would double. If, at the same time, the individual's initial money holding and money income should double then he would be able to consume as before and to hold twice as much money. Moreover, twice as much money would just buy the 'typical bundle of commodities', the price of which has doubled. If the consumer demands money for its command over a typical bundle of commodities only, then he will want twice as much after the above changes as before them. His demand for money will be homogeneous of degree one in prices, income and initial money holdings. Thus, the consumer's demand function for money may be written

$$M = f(p_1, \ldots, p_n, y, L), \tag{18}$$

where $f(\lambda p_1, \ldots, \lambda p_n, \lambda y, \lambda L) = \lambda f(p_1, \ldots, p_n, y, L). \tag{19}$

The notion that money is not demanded for itself but for what it will buy implies that the consumer's demand for money is homogeneous as shown in equations (18) and (19). It is this characteristic of the demand function for money which is the hallmark of an acceptable monetary theory. Accordingly, it is this characteristic that we will use. We will continue to consider a model in which people hold money not because they want to, but because they must.

Let the consumer choose those values of $x_1, \ldots, x_n$ that maximize

$$U = U(x_1, \ldots, x_n) \tag{20}$$

subject to

$$M + \sum_{i=1}^{n} x_i p_i = y + L \tag{21}$$

and to $M = f(p_1, \ldots, p_n, y, L),$

where the function f is as shown in (19). We may combine (18) and (21) to get

$$f(p_1, \ldots, p_n, y, L) + \sum_{i=1}^{n} x_i p_i = y + L, \tag{22}$$

and simply maximize (20) subject to (22). The first order conditions for this maximization are given by

$$U_i - \lambda p_i = 0 \qquad i = 1, \ldots, n$$

$$f(p_1, \ldots, p_n, y, L) + \sum_{i=1}^{n} x_i p_i = y + L.$$

Differentiating these conditions partially with respect to the various parameters, we generate the comparative-statics implications of the model for the individual consumer. These are

$$\frac{\partial x_r}{\partial y} = \left(1 - \frac{\partial M}{\partial y}\right)\frac{A_r}{A} = \frac{\partial x_r}{\partial L} \tag{23}$$

and $$\frac{\partial x_r}{\partial p_s} = -\left(x_s + \frac{\partial M}{\partial p_s}\right)\frac{A_r}{A} + \lambda\frac{A_{rs}}{A} \tag{24}$$

$$
\text{where} \quad A = \begin{vmatrix} 0 & p_1 & \cdots & p_n \\ p_1 & U_{11} & \cdots & U_{1n} \\ \cdots & \cdots & \cdots & \cdots \\ p_n & U_{n1} & \cdots & U_{nn} \end{vmatrix}
$$

and A_r is the cofactor of P_r in A while A_{rs} is the cofactor of U_{rs}.

Combining equations (23) and (24) we get

$$
\frac{\partial x_r}{\partial p_s} + \frac{\left(x_s + \dfrac{\partial M}{\partial p_s}\right)}{\left(1 - \dfrac{\partial M}{\partial y}\right)} \frac{\partial x_r}{\partial y} = \lambda \frac{A_{rs}}{A} . \tag{25}
$$

Every term on the left hand side of (25) is observable. Moreover, estimation of these terms would require observation of the same number of parameter changes as would estimation of the usual Slutsky equation terms. The interpretations of the terms of (25) are the usual ones. The first is the price effect, the second is an income effect and they sum to a substitution effect having all the usual properties.

To better understand the term multiplying $\partial x_r / \partial y$ in (25) consider the variation in income which would be required to so compensate the individual for a rise dp_s in p_s, that he *could* exactly purchase the bundle of commodities after the price and income rise that he *did* purchase before them. To begin with, the consumer buys x_s units of commodity s. Each of these units has risen in price by dp_s. Accordingly, the consumer would need $x_s \, dp_s$ in additional income to just maintain his purchase of x_s. In addition to this, should p_s rise the individual will be constrained by (18) to change his money holdings. For this purpose he would need additional income in the amount $(\partial M / \partial p_s) \, dp_s$. Should the consumer experience an income change of $[x_s + (\partial M / \partial p_s)] \, dp_s$ he would be able to maintain his consumption of all commodities intact, were he to spend this new income on commodities. Notice, however, that he may not. Any income increase must in general, be partly hoarded.[5] If we wish exactly to compensate him for a change in price of dp_s we must change his income so that the marginal propensity to consume out of the new income equals

$$
(x_s + \partial M / \partial p_s) \, dp_s .
$$

In this model the consumer's marginal propensity to consume is given by $1 - \partial M / \partial y$.

Accordingly, we seek dy such that

$$\left(1-\frac{\partial M}{\partial y}\right)dy = \left(x_s+\frac{\partial M}{\partial p_s}\right)dp_s .$$

Thus $\quad dy = \dfrac{\left(x_s+\dfrac{\partial M}{\partial p_s}\right)}{\left(1-\dfrac{\partial M}{\partial y}\right)}dp_s .$ \hfill (26)

The reader may easily verify from (25) that a consumer confronted with a simultaneous change of dp_s in p_s and the dy shown in equation (26) will adjust his consumption of x_r according to a substitution effect alone. Thus the coefficient of $\partial x_r/\partial y$ in (25).

Since the substitution effect of (25) has the usual properties this model has the usual number of empirical ramifications. These, of course, are altered to account for the consumer's hoarding behavior.

The time path of consumer hoarding may be ascertained as before by recognizing that

$$L_t = M_{t-1} .$$

Substituting this into (18) and writing the latter as a difference equation, we get

$$M_t = f(p_1,\ldots,p_n,y,M_{t-1}) , \hfill (27)$$

where variables without t subscripts are supposed constant over time. We know nothing of this equation save that it is homogeneous of degree one in all its variables. There is no implication of the sort of time path exhibited by the previous model. We will suppose that if there exists an economically meaningful solution to (27), then it is unique. That is to say, for any set of prices and income if there is any real, positive level of money holding such that, once it is attained, the consumer will be able to maintain it indefinitely, then that level of money holdings is unique.

It is our claim that the model under discussion is a minimal classical model, that it possesses the basic characteristics of the classical model without complicating extras. We have shown above that, in contrast to the Patinkin model, this model has clear empirical implications. We have shown in the previous paragraph that, in contrast to the Clower model, this model does not predict peculiar hoarding behavior on the part of consumers. We will now show that, as with the Clower model, a special case of the current model preserves the various classical monetary properties which Clower has shown a special case of the previous model to possess.

In particular, we shall now show that, if we follow Clower in confining our attention to situations in which all consumers have adjusted their holdings of money to the desired full-equilibrium level, then:

(1) Walras's Law is an identity;

(2) Say's Law is an identity so long as consumers are in equilibrium;

(3) Commodity excess demand functions are homogeneous of degree zero in money prices;

(4) Money prices are determined by a form of the quantity theory;

(5) The classical 'invalid dichotomy' is valid.

Following Clower, we replace y by

$$\sum_{i=1}^{n} \bar{x}_i p_i \,,$$

where $\bar{x}_i$ is the consumer's initial endowment of commodity i.

The consumer varies his money hoarding from period to period according to equation (27). Should a situation be reached in which

$$M_t = f(p_1, \ldots, p_n, y, M_t) \,,$$

that is, in which

$$M_t = M_{t-1} = L \,,$$

then the consumer may be said to be in full equilibrium. He will have so adjusted his holdings of money that he is satisfied to maintain them as long as prices and his income remain constant.

Supposing that the consumer's initial endowment of commodities is constant we will write his money holding constraint

$$M = F(p_1, \ldots, p_n, L) \,. \tag{28}$$

Since the function f above satisfies equation (19) and since the consumer's initial endowment of commodities is supposed fixed, it must be the case that

$$F(\lambda p_1, \ldots, \lambda p_n, \lambda L) = \lambda F(p_1, \ldots, p_n, L) \,. \tag{29}$$

The demand for money is homogeneous of degree one in prices and initial money holdings.

For full equilibrium the consumer must be maximizing his utility subject to his budget restraint, equation (20), and to his money hoarding restraint, (28). In addition, he must be satisfied to keep his money holdings intact.

For each individual the following relations must hold,

$$M + \sum_{i=1}^{n} x_i p_i = \sum_{i=1}^{n} \bar{x}_i p_i + L;$$

$$M = F(p_1, \ldots, p_n, L);$$

and $\quad M = F(p_1, \ldots, p_n, L) = L.$ $\qquad$ (30)

We may now establish our five propositions:

(1) Walras's Law is an identity. By this we mean that, for any set of prices, Walras's Law must be true. Since the consumer takes prices as given, for *any set* of prices he must adjust his demand for commodities to satisfy (21). Hence (21) is an identity for all permissible values of consumer demand. Aggregation of equations (21) over all consumers leads to Walras's Law. Hence Walras's Law is an identity, true for any set of prices.

(2) Say's Law is an identity so long as consumers are in equilibrium. By this we mean that, for any set of prices, Say's Law will be true so long as consumers are in equilibrium. Should consumers be in equilibrium, then equations (21), (28) and (30) are all true whatever the prices. In particular, equations (21) and (30) are true. Combining these yields

$$\sum_{i=1}^{n} x_i p_i = \sum_{i=1}^{n} \bar{x}_i p_i, \qquad (31)$$

for any set of prices. Aggregating equation (31), an identity so long as consumers are in equilibrium, yields Say's Law as such an identity.

(3) Commodity excess demand functions are homogeneous of degree zero in money prices. So long as the consumers are in equilibrium equation (31) must be true. So long as equation (31) is true if all prices are doubled the consumers, given initial endowments of commodities, will continue to buy the same final bundles of commodities. The budget restraints are not changed by the doubling of all prices. Accordingly, whatever bundle of commodities maximized the consumer's utility function before prices were doubled will continue to do so when they are doubled. Hence statement (3).

(4) Money prices are determined by a form of the quantity theory. Consider the quantity equation in the form

$$MV = PT.$$

This is either a definition of velocity, in which case it is without behavioral significance or it is (coupled with the notion that V is a constant) a relationship between the quantity of money and the level of money prices. The latter case is the interesting one. It would assert that, should the quantity of money (say) double, then so will money prices double. It would also assert that, should all money prices double, so would the demand for money. We will first show that in the absence of distribution effects the quantity theory as a relationship between the quantity of money and the level of money prices is true in our model. We will then show that the quantity theory determines money prices. In doing this we will also establish the truth of statement (5).

Since (28) is a function, for any vector $p_1^\circ, \ldots, p_1^\circ, L_n^\circ$ there is one and only one M° such that

$$M^\circ = F(p_1^\circ, \ldots, p_n^\circ, L^\circ).$$

In full consumer equilibrium

$$M^\circ = L^\circ = F(p_1^\circ, \ldots, p_n^\circ, L^\circ)$$

by equation (30). Suppose that all prices are multiplied by λ. What is the appropriate full equilibrium money holding, that is, what is $M' = L'$ such that

$$M' = L' = F(\lambda p_1^\circ, \ldots, \lambda p_n^\circ, L')?$$

By assumption, if there exists a solution to difference equation (27) then it is unique. Accordingly, for any set of prices there can be only one M_t such that $M_t = f(p_1, \ldots, p_n, M_t)$. By equation (29)

$$M' = \lambda L^\circ = f(\lambda p_1^\circ, \ldots, \lambda p_n^\circ, \lambda L^\circ)$$

is such a solution. Accordingly, it is the only such solution. Should all prices (say) double then each individual's demand for money will double. So, therefore, will the aggregate market demand double.

Now consider a doubling of the quantity of money. Since we wish to abstract from distribution effects suppose that each person's quantity of money is doubled. Should all prices be doubled, then by (29) each consumer would just hold all his new money. By equation (21) he will be able to just continue to consume his previous consumption bundle. Each consumer would have the same wealth and the same tastes after the doubling as before it. Clearly the new prices would be an equilibrium set. Under the usual assumption that the equilibrium is unique the new prices would be *the* equilibrium set. Should the quantity of money be increased by a factor λ, then, in the absence of distribution effects, all prices will be increased by the same proportion.

If we take any price, p_i, and let M^* be the aggregate demand for money, then, so long as all markets are cleared and consumers are in full equilibrium, there exists a constant of proportionality α_i such that

$$M^* = \alpha_i p_i, \qquad i = 1, \ldots, n .   \tag{32}$$

Moreover, should M^* or $p_1, \ldots, p_n$ vary as discussed above this constant of proportionality remains fixed. Equation (32) says simply that prices are proportional to the quantity of money. It is thus a form of the quantity theory.

Consider the real sector of the economy, excluding money. We wish to attempt to determine relative prices in the real sector alone. Let

$$r_i = \frac{p_i}{p_n}$$

be the relative price of commodity i. Then $r_n = 1$ and commodity n is the numeraire. We thus have $n-1$ variables $r_1, \ldots, r_{n-1}$ to be determined in the real sector. We have one excess demand function for each of the n commodities. By Say's Law, the aggregation of equations (31), these excess demand functions are dependent so that one may be dropped. Under the usual equation counting convention, we may thus determine the $n-1$ relative prices in the real sector alone. We thereby establish $r_1, \ldots, r_{n-1}$.

(5) Following the method of the 'invalid dichotomy' we then turn to the quantity theory, equation (32). Letting $i = n$ we have

$$p_n = \frac{M^*}{\alpha_n}$$

whence we may determine money prices from our knowledge of $r_1, \ldots, r_{n-1}$ determined in the real sector as follows:

$$p_i = r_i p_n , \qquad i = 1, \ldots, n-1 .$$

Thus, statements (4) and (5) are true.

ACKNOWLEDGMENTS

I am grateful for helpful comments from Syed Ahmed, Charles Plott, E. J. R. Booth, and, particularly, James Quirk. I am also grateful to the Purdue Research Foundation, who sponsored part of this work. Of course, responsibility for the paper is entirely my own.

NOTES AND REFERENCES

[1] See section II below.

   [2] When the maximization is written in this form, it is clear that consumers demand functions must be homogeneous of degree zero in prices, income and initial money holdings. Should all of these variables be (say)

doubled, then neither equation (1) nor equation (4) would be changed in any way. Accordingly, neither would the values of $x_1, \ldots, x_n$ for which (1) is a maximum subject to (4).

[3] The second equality of (7), that is, $\dfrac{\partial x_s}{\partial y} = \dfrac{\partial x_s}{\partial L}$, is an obvious artifact of any weekly model that includes money holding.

[4] If as we will suppose below, the consumer receives a weekly endowment of commodities, $\bar{x}_1, \ldots, \bar{x}_n$, rather than an amount of money income, y, then y in (9) should be replaced by $\sum_{i=1}^{n} \bar{x}_i p_i$, and (11) becomes

$$\frac{\partial M}{\partial p_r} = \frac{k}{1-k}\bar{x}_r .$$

[5] Note: This is a variation in hoarding because of an *income* change. $\partial M / \partial y$ as opposed to $\partial M / \partial p_r$, which we have already accounted for.

13

Information and Period Analysis
in Economic Decisions

H. B. Malmgren

Period analysis has been used with much success in the analysis of macro-economic processes. Sir John Hicks's own work is perhaps the most outstanding example. However, most of the theoretical discussion has not really been made to relate to microeconomic problems, in spite of the power of this framework for analyzing dynamic processes.

Sir John Hicks's most recent book *Capital and Growth*, develops further his earlier discussions of individual intertemporal period equilibrium, and in so doing touches upon a number of conceptual problems in analyzing microeconomic decisions. His interesting discussion stimulates much thought even though his main attention is focused elsewhere on capital growth. Some aspects of microeconomic decisions, however, still seem to have been given insufficient recognition. Questions come to mind such as: How long should a distinct decision period be? What should be decided in one period rather than in another? What factors are considered in making decisions in any given period, and how do these relate to when a decision is made? What links decisions in one period with those in another?

Any decision-maker must not only make decisions, he must decide when to review those decisions in the light of new information and the actual evolution of the process he has decided upon. The information used in the initial decision may have been incomplete, or incorrect. Having decided upon one course of action, at some point he must check results to determine whether to continue on the same course or change to another. Just as the correctness of a decision may depend upon the accuracy of information, so the length of the period of time before a decision is reviewed will depend upon expectations about when new information will become available. That period may be infinitely short, in which case continuous re-evaluation is going on, at some high cost of information-processing. Or it may be very long, in which case re-evaluation may be undertaken long after circumstances will have changed. Thus, one gathers information, decides, and then allows events to unfold for some period, when new observations are taken and the cycle begins again.

In order to determine what is the correct observation interval it may be useful to first look at the evaluation and decision process itself. Information relevant to a decision has a value, and acquiring it often entails a cost. The value of information can be said to be the value of the gain derived from using it. Thus in a simplistic theory one might calculate the cost of an increment of information and the return from employing it, subtracting the former from the latter to see what the net gain, or profit is. This formulation, adopted by a number of economists in recent work on theories of organizational decision-making, is not, however, fully satisfactory. How can an entrepreneur know in advance what a particular increment of information is worth in advance, that is, before collecting and assimilating it? In fact, he often cannot know, and thus he must rely on the expected value as an indicator. On the cost side, what the information might cost will depend upon such things as how complicated it is, how much must be known before a useful summary fact can be derived, and how similar the information may be to facts already known.

In addition, if we are dealing with dynamics, as we are in period analysis, the time element during a decision provides further complications. The introduction of time brings forward a problem of decision strategy for an entrepreneur. Collecting information and deciding takes time (indeed, the costs of a decision and the collection of the requisite information might be reckoned in terms of costs per unit of time taken to evaluate and decide). If the entrepreneur is a perfectionist, and is unwilling to decide without comprehensive data, he may find his data out of date by the time it is all put together. He will thus have to work out some kind of strategy with respect to his decisions. This strategy will be partly informational (what he should consider and what he should disregard) and partly expectational (what he should do in relation to what he thinks others, both producers and consumers, will do).

In the first instance, the entrepreneur must rely to a large extent on prior information, on past history and experience, so as to leave himself free to consider events which have turned out differently from his previous period's expectations and new events which do not fit very well into old pigeon-holes. Now some decisions will be based on events which will not be substantially altered if the entrepreneur waits until some later period and makes no current decision. If there were no advantage or disadvantage to waiting in this case, the entrepreneur would be indifferent between deciding now and deciding later.[1] There may, on the other hand, be an advantage in waiting if one expects new information to appear in later periods which would be helpful in making a decision, so long as the set of events will not be altered significantly during the interim. Such new information might, for example, arise from repeated observations between now and the latest possible decision date sufficient to establish some regularity, and therefore a higher degree of certainty, in one's information.

Some sets of events will at times be stable, and at other times unstable; that is, at some moments a large number of variables may be fluctuating considerably, perhaps due to random disturbances or to absence of any expectational equilibrium among the entrepreneurs in the economy. During such periods of instability it would not pay to collect information unless enough information could be collected over the period of fluctuations to allow prediction of some kind of trend or other pattern. This might sometimes require an excessively rapid rate of assimilation of data. Unless information from past assessments during stable periods were sufficient to make a forecast for future periods, it might be better for the entrepreneur to wait until that part of the environment which concerned him settled down again, and information could be collected more cheaply which would not be out of date so quickly (Shackle, 1952, pp. 11–12).[2] If it were possible to evaluate, decide, and achieve results of a decision faster than the rate of fluctuation in the variables of the system, it would of course be possible that such rapid decisions would be worthwhile, provided that the cost of rapid decision did not offset the gain from the activities chosen. In addition, the gestation period of an investment or current productive activity will partly determine the relative efficacies of rapid and slow decisions. The time allowed for observation must in this case, be shorter than the length of time to attain fruition of the chosen activity (Marschak, 1949, pp. 184–9).[3]

There are other cases of decisions where certain possible events may still be open to choice in subsequent periods regardless of the decision made currently. This type of case attracted the attention of Professors Modigliani and Cohen (1961). They argued that the value of a future constraint or parameter is irrelevant to a current decision if the optimal value of the first period decision can be determined without knowledge of the specific form of the constraint or the value of the parameter. They suggested that a parameter would be 'totally irrelevant' if it were irrelevant no matter what its value might turn out to be, and 'conditionally irrelevant' if its value falls within some pre-determined range. Thus if a parameter were conditionally irrelevant only an amount of effort sufficient to ascertain whether it was in or out of a specified range would be necessary. Modigliani and Cohen did not, however, explain how one knows which variables are irrelevant before all are evaluated. They propose that the entrepreneur compute the 'expected pay-off' with and without the information, assuming that the entrepreneur has in mind a suitable probability distribution. The parameter is then supposedly worth estimating according to whether the pay-off with the information is greater than without. This seems to be circular reasoning, since in each case computing the expected pay-off necessitates estimating the parameter value at least roughly.

Some estimate must also be made of totally irrelevant parameters, if the entrepreneur is to know they are in fact totally irrelevant. Any decision to commit oneself to a course of action which extends over more than one planning period does constrain choice in subsequent periods during the life of that course of action. If one erects a factory building without installing machinery in the first period, the possible choices in subsequent periods are constrained, though wide. The production function, insofar as it is thought to be a 'catalogue of alternative techniques' for planning purposes, changes its shape once a particular technique of production is chosen. Clearly the only totally irrelevant events are those which will occur beyond the decision horizon: that is, after the effects of the decision now will have fully matured. But in this case events are irrelevant because they are not part of the particular production plan at any future date within the duration of that plan. This is not very revealing.[4]

Let us take, then, another tack. The length of a decision period must be related to the speed of adjustment of expectations. Sir John Hicks (1965, p. 63) suggests that the length of a period should equal the expectational lag. This seems reasonable. On the other hand, different kinds of changes within the bounds of the overall economic plan of a business firm take place at different speeds. The pace of technological change in the development of alternative machines may not match the pace of changing market conditions for the firm's products, or its changing wage structure.

One means of breaking up this temporal difficulty is to think of periods of varying lengths, overlapping one another, with the duration of each dependent upon the particular group of variables relevant to a particular decision. This is realistic. Capital expenditure decisions in practice involve entirely different data and entirely different time horizons to production and inventory scheduling decisions. The decision period for a factory manager (e.g. a weekly production report) may be longer than for a shop foreman (e.g. a daily labor productivity appraisal). The sales manager may be planning within periods of time which represent entire seasons. Moreover, the variable which might be adjusted may vary in each case: the sales manager may adjust prices at the end of a selling season, the shop manager may adjust machine speeds at the end of a day, and the board of directors may adjust long-term capital spending decisions every six months or year.

What this means is that a Marshallian short-run equilibrium could exist within a given production planning period, and that expectations and realizations could be consistent during that period, and yet at the end of that period a decision could be called for to adjust production or price, as a result of the transpiration of events during the course of an independent capital planning decision period. Moreover, the information relevant to each type of decision period being different, a temporary change in market prices, for example, may affect some kinds of decisions within a firm, where the period is short, and not affect others, where the period is much longer. The effect of this is that the traditional concept of the economic production function of the firm needs to be adjusted. Instead of a single function, we must think of a number of different functions, or economic activity plans, coexisting, relating to each other in some ways but not others.

Thus, it will often be useful to divide up information collection and decision activities so that variables which relate closely to each other, and which vary with some regularity or can be observed with some regularity, be partitioned off. If the variables are sufficiently regular in their relations with one another, the observation of only one of them may be a 'sufficient indicator' of what is transpiring. In order to limit the amount of information collection in each period, the indicator, or a few indicators, may be measured, and a general re-evaluation of all the variables made only when the indicator, or indicators, break through some reasonable limits of variation.

In other words, the economic decision-maker will partition his decision environment into classes or types of decision problems. This partitioning into such decision modules will have a time dimension and a grouping-of-variables dimension. (From a practical point of view, we see this process in operation in all business firms. Different types of decisions are made at different points in organizations, using different types of data assessed at entirely different points in time.)

For each decision about a subset of events, there will be two types of decision links which will also have to be considered. The first is the relation of one period's decision to that of another, regarding the same economic activity. When considering whether to invest in a particular activity or production process, the firm may lay out a multi-period production plan based upon expectations and upon engineering data to determine whether or not to make the investment. If the investment is then made, future decisions regarding this activity are constrained to variations in the variable cost elements of the activity. The general process may not be reviewed unless something turns out to be quite wrong with the original expectations. If general expectations go badly unrealized, the entire activity may be reorganized. Otherwise, only minor decisions will be required (such as ensuring that the number of defectives in daily production is minimized). This general activity may thus be considered as fixed for certain period of time, say three years, although decisions relating to day-to-day labor utilization of the machine or process in question may be made daily or weekly.

The second link is that between the outcome of one decision subset and that of another. Within firms, we may suppose that the interactions are considerable. Otherwise, why would the firm control several activities and make a variety of types of decisions? Among firms, this link will involve different kinds of variables, but it will still exist as a relevant factor in evaluating alternative courses of action. These two types of links, the intertemporal relationship of decisions and the interdependence of outcomes of decisions, must be taken into account when partitioning the information and decision structure into decision modules.

This information-processing and decision-making structure cannot itself be completely varied each period. To do so would require high expenditures for modest gains, and would probably result in missing deadlines for decisions. The routinization of what to observe, information collection, and decision in some stable bureaucratic pattern is, in other words, an economically rational method of handling decisions.

A theory of the optimal choice of (i) length of decision period and (ii) information structure partitions would thus be extremely complex. In addition, as noted earlier, it would have to take into account the effects of other decisions upon the outcomes of any particular decision under analysis: What should the entrepreneur do in relation to what he thinks others will do ?

Now it is clear that a rigid conceptual framework and information-flow process would be relatively useless in a rapidly changing environment. There is an economic incentive, then, to use such a decision apparatus for activities that are sufficiently controllable, or sufficiently predictable, that the apparatus provides efficient decisions. The more regular and predictable the environment, the more efficient will the decisions be. New ideas, new technologies or new methods of dealing with problems, may be introduced, but new developments must not totally disrupt the value of the existing information structure. If they do, such new developments could not be really exploited, because there would be insufficient time and too high a cost attached to assimilating their nature and likely effects. There is an economic incentive, then, to maintain the *status quo* and to vary it only slowly.[5]

Can we theorize about equilibrium using this conceptual framework ? At a point in time, looking forward into the future, a decision could be thought to be in equilibrium when the proposed allocation of activities among future periods, or substitution over time, to use Sir John Hicks's term, is optimal, given the information and expectations available. That, however, is equilibrium in a planning sense only. The period may finish, outcomes may be found to differ from expectations, and stock disequilibrium may result. Among several firms, an *ex ante* market equilibrium would require that everyone base his decisions on the same set of information as everyone else, or that the various plans would have to be independent in terms of their consequences. For many types of decisions, such a perfect market equilibrium will not be likely. There will always be some incentives to adjust at the end of each decision period, as the consequences of past decisions, based on incomplete information, unfold. Thus to postulate that the market as a whole is in planning equilibrium, or moving towards it, is to postulate a great deal.

One way of saving the concept of equilibrium in relation to this microeconomic conceptual framework is to focus more thought on the stability of the system. If there is a high degree of stability or regularity of movement among a large portion of the variables which affect the whole market, unexpected outcomes in some areas will not destabilize the whole system. On the contrary, decision-makers would be free to concentrate their efforts on events which turn out significantly different from expectations, because most activities are unfolding according to past expectations. Within firms, stabilization of events through controls of various kinds, and routinization or regularization of information flow and decisions, provides one type of market stability. To the extent that expectations and decisions of firms are consistent with one another, the basis for market stability is laid. Where decision outcomes are highly interdependent, as in oligopoly, stability may only exist where each acts in a manner which is highly predictable by others. This will usually require avoiding aggressive, or 'surprise', tactics, or employing them only in selected areas. Sir John Hicks's well-known reference to the desire for the quiet life comes to mind – the pursuit of the quiet life is at least a partial condition for economically efficient decisions by many firms.

Thus general market equilibrium, following this line of reasoning, would have to be construed as a rather loose kind of equilibrium. It will usually be characterized by pockets of stock disequilibrium, and thus there will be continual incentives to change courses of action in light of realizations. The equilibrium may be sub-optimal in the sense of not fully using all available resources. But that is fully consistent with the whole stream of macroeconomic thought in recent decades. The equilibrium could be thought of as an area of convergent expectations, where realizations and expectations will be sufficiently consistent so that overall changes from period to period will not trigger an unstable upward or downward movement.

This framework has been laid out more to throw light on conceptual problems than to develop a finished theory of optimal decision-making. The conceptual framework, nonetheless, seems to me to help in dealing with many of the very same issues which Sir John Hicks raised in his own attempt in *Capital and Growth* to wrestle with long-term capital stock equilibrium and growth equilibrium problems. What is needed next is some more precise theories about optimal decision-making involving learning and search processes, in the context of a changing environment.

NOTES AND REFERENCES

[1] However, he may not be indifferent if he wishes to decide about other sets of events at the same time, for if the other decisions must be taken now, he will have more time to consider them if the time-indifferent decision is postponed.

[2] Professor Shackle has called this a position of subjective stability; a position where the individual feels 'that the number of unanswered questions is at a minimum, and is likely rather to increase on balance, through the obsolescence of some of the data now in his possession, than to decrease through the acquisition of fresh knowledge'.

[3] It is in this sense that Professor Marschak suggested that a decision might profitably be postponed if the 'liquidity' of the investment considered were low and the likelihood of a shift in the state of the environment high.

[4] While I have given little general value to the Modigliani-Cohen conceptual framework, it should be noted that their scheme could be made useful for day-to-day operating decisions concerning certain subsets of events within the constraints of an overall economic plan of the firm. In fact, they mainly based their ideas on inventory and production scheduling problems, which might readily be dealt with by this conceptual approach. But the overall economic plan of a firm, of which inventory scheduling is merely a subset, is a multiperiod plan dealing with future, as well as today's, investment, sales, price, and production alternatives. (Their conceptual approach also embodies another class of parameters called 'practically irrelevant' parameters; but this class provides no insights, in my view, that are not better examined in other ways.)

[5] This stabilization of events and the development of a controlled information structure provide a rationale for the existence of firms themselves (Malmgren, 1961).

14

On Hicksian Stability

Daniel McFadden

I. Introduction

J. R. Hicks first raised the question of the stability of a general equilibrium system in *Value and Capital*, and suggested as an answer his now-classic stability conditions:

> What do we mean by stability in multiple exchange ? Clearly . . .
> that a fall in the price of X in terms of the [numéraire] commodity
> will make the demand for X greater than the supply. But are we to
> suppose that it must have this effect (a) when the prices of other
> commodities are given, or (b) when other prices are adjusted so as
> to preserve equilibrium in the other markets ? . . . Strictly, we should
> distinguish a series of conditions: that a rise in the price of X will
> make supply greater than demand, (a) all other prices given, (b)
> allowing for the price of Y being adjusted to maintain equilibrium
> in the Y-market, (c) allowing for the prices of Y and Z being
> adjusted, and so on, until all prices have been adjusted. . . . I propose
> to call a system in which all conditions of stability are satisfied
> *perfectly stable* (Hicks, 1946, p. 66).

However, formulating the price adjustment mechanism in the multiple exchange model as a system of ordinary differential equations, P. A. Samuelson (1941, 1942, 1944) showed that in general perfect stability was neither a necessary nor sufficient condition for dynamic stability. Samuelson went on to argue: 'Why any system should be expected to possess *perfect* stability, or why an economist should be interested in this property is by no means clear.'

Commenting on Samuelson's results in a note to the second edition of *Value and Capital*, Hicks writes:

> My discussion of static equilibrium in this book was intended as no
> more than a preliminary to what I called economic dynamics; thus

the discussion of static stability was deliberately and explicitly timeless. And when I passed on to my dynamics, the discussion of
stability remained timeless, at least in this sense: that I assumed
the process of adjustment to a temporary equilibrium to be completed within a short period (a 'week'), while I neglected the movement of prices within the week, so that my economic system could
be thought of as taking up a series of temporary equilibria. In
adopting this device, I was following in the tradition of Marshall,
though I was of course aware that the assumption of an 'easy passage to temporary equilibrium' required more justification when it
was applied to my problem of many markets than it did when
applied to Marshall's case of a single market. . . .

Professor Samuelson has turned some much heavier mathematical
artillery than mine onto this precise issue, and has undoubtedly
made important progress with it. He drops the assumption of a
quick and easy passage to temporary equilibrium, assuming instead
that rates of price-change are functions of differences between
demands and supplies. His whole theory thus becomes dynamic
in a different sense than mine, but one which is perhaps more acceptable to mathematicians. . . .

In terms of this new technique, my static theory can be 'dynam-
ized'; it is possible to inquire into the stability of the static system
in the sense of investigating whether the movements set up when
a system is initially out of equilibrium will converge upon an
equilibrium position. Since Professor Samuelson's system has a
new degree of freedom, it is not surprising that his stability conditions are different from mine and more elaborate than mine; his
system may fail of stability, not only for my reasons, but because
of a lack of adjustment between rates of adaption in different
markets, or rates of response by persons trading. All this opens
a most promising line of investigation, which is clearly by no means
exhausted by the work hitherto done on it.

Professor Samuelson's work thus represents an important advance
in our knowledge of the mechanics of related markets; his 'dynamiz-
ing' of static theory is a notable achievement. But I still feel that
something is wanted which is parallel to *my* dynamic theory, and
I miss this in Professor Samuelson's work. By my hypothesis of

essentially instantaneous adjustment, I reduced the purely mechanical parts of my dynamic theory to the simplest terms – it is now quite evident that I oversimplified it. But in so doing I did leave myself free to make some progress with the less mechanical parts – expectations and so on. I still feel that this procedure has its uses, and I should be sorry to abandon it altogether in favor of a pure concentration on mechanism (Hicks, 1946, p. 336).

In the quotation above, Sir John Hicks alludes to the intimate connection between his conditions of perfect stability and the basic assumptions of Marshallian partial equilibrium analysis, and suggests that the sequential adjustments to temporary equilibria associated with partial equilibrium analysis capture the spirit of his 'dynamics'. He then asks whether this view of stability has a parallel within the framework of Samuelson's 'dynamic stability'. An affirmative answer is given in this paper. The assumptions of partial equilibrium analysis are first formalized and shown to be essentially equivalent to Hicks's perfect stability conditions. Then, for any economy satisfying these assumptions, a class of dynamic processes is shown to be dynamically stable in the sense of Samuelson. These dynamic processes are found to be 'close' to the sequential adjustments to temporary equilibria which Hicks envisioned. Thus, a synthesis of Hicksian and dynamic stability conditions can be achieved, providing a justification, within the framework of dynamic stability theory, for the application of Hicksian stability conditions in economic problems.

The assumptions of partial equilibrium analysis are formalized in Section II of the paper. Section III relates the partial equilibrium assumptions to the properties of Hicksian matrices. Sections IV and V give, respectively, local and global stability theorems.

II. Hicksian Stability and Partial Equilibrium Analysis

Although the issue of Hicksian versus dynamic stability can be raised in any dynamic system, we shall for concreteness consider the multiple exchange model. Consider an economy with n commodities, labeled $1, 2, \ldots, n$. The price of commodity i, assumed to be non-negative, is denoted by p_i.[1] The aggregate excess demand for commodity i is denoted by x_i, and is given by an excess demand function $x_i = h_i(p_1, \ldots, p_n)$. In vector notation, $\underline{p} = (p_1, \ldots, p_n)$, $\underline{x} = (x_1, \ldots, x_n)$, and

$$\underline{x} = \underline{h}(\underline{p}) = (h_1(\underline{p}), \ldots, h_n(\underline{p})). \tag{1}$$

The *i*th market is in *equilibrium* if it has zero excess demand or if commodity *i* is a free good in excess supply.

The dynamic price adjustment mechanism formulated by Samuelson states that the rate of change in the price of the *i*th commodity is positive when that commodity is in excess demand, and negative when it is non-free and in excess supply. This dynamic process can then be described by a series of difference equations of the form [2]

$$\Delta p_i(t) = p_i(t+1) - p_i(t) = c_i H_i(p(t)) \qquad (i = 1, \ldots, n), \quad (2)$$

where $p(t) = (p_1(t), \ldots, p_m(t))$ denotes the price vector prevailing at the point of time t; c_i is a positive *rate of accommodation* in market i; and $H_i(p(t))$ satisfies the conditions:

(a) $x_i = h_i(p(t)) > 0$ implies $H_i(p(t)) > 0$;

(b) $x_i = h_i(p(t)) < 0$ and $p_i(t) > 0$ imply $0 > H_i(p(t))$ [and $p_i(t+1)$ $= c_i H_i(p(t)) - p_i(t) \geqslant 0$]; and

(c) if market i is in equilibrium, then $H_i(p(t)) = 0$.

We shall term $H_i(p)$ the *market demand index* for commodity i. An often-analyzed case is one in which the market demand index for a commodity equals its excess demand or is a sign-preserving function of its excess demand. In vector notation, the system (2) will be written

$$\Delta p(t) = H(p(t))C, \qquad (3)$$

where C is a diagonal matrix of the rates of accommodation c_i, and H is a row vector of the functions H_i. In the case that the market demand indices are continuously differentiable, an analysis of the stability of this system in a neighborhood of the general equilibrium is conveniently carried out using a Taylor's expansion of (3),

$$\Delta p(t) = (p(t) - \bar{p}) A(\bar{p}) C + \text{remainder}, \qquad (4)$$

where $\bar{p}$ denotes a general equilibrium price vector satisfying $H(\bar{p}) = 0$, and $A(p)$ denotes the Jacobian matrix of $H(p)$ evaluated at p:

$$a_{ij}(p) = \partial H_i(p)/\partial p_j \qquad (i,j = 1, \ldots, n). \qquad (5)$$

A *partial equilibrium price vector* for a given subset of markets is one which achieves equilibrium in the subset markets, given fixed prices in the remaining markets. Consider a single primary market i, and suppose that the remaining markets can be divided into two subsets such that prices are fixed for the markets in one subset, and are adjusted to maintain partial equilibrium in the other subset for each primary market price. The resulting excess demand in the primary market depends only on its own price and the fixed prices, and is termed the *compensated excess demand* for the primary market i, conditioned on the subset of markets which adjust to partial equilibrium.

Marshallian partial equilibrium analysis studies price behavior in a single primary market, postulating that price behavior in remaining markets can be ignored. Two types of external market behavior are consistent with this postulate:

(1) The structure of the primary market varies smoothly with the external market price, and this external price does not change significantly over the period of analysis.

(2) The external price effectively adjusts to maintain partial equilibrium in its market, so that the *compensated* primary market can be analyzed.

Even more basic to the Marshallian analysis are the assumptions that a unique partial equilibrium price exists in the compensated primary market, and that excess demand in this market is positive when its price falls below its partial equilibrium level. The conditions for perfect stability by Hicks correspond precisely to these assumptions.

A dynamic price adjustment mechanism which is consistent with the partial equilbrium assumptions above for a given primary market i must have, relative to the rate of price adjustment in this market, a very rapid rate of adjustment in markets where 'partial equilibrium is maintained', and a very slow rate of adjustment in markets where prices are 'fixed'. Hence, if we require that partial equilibrium analysis be applicable to *each* market $i = 1, \ldots, n$, then we should be able to rank these markets in order of decreasing 'rates of accommodation'. Then, the dynamic adjustment process would be essentially 'sequential': the first market would be brought into approximate equilibrium, maintained there while the second market was adjusted, and so forth.

The geometry of the Marshallian assumptions in the case of two commodities is illustrated in Figure 1. The contours of zero excess demand in each of the markets 1 and 2 are plotted, and the sign of excess demand on each side of each of these curves is indicated. For each value of p_2,

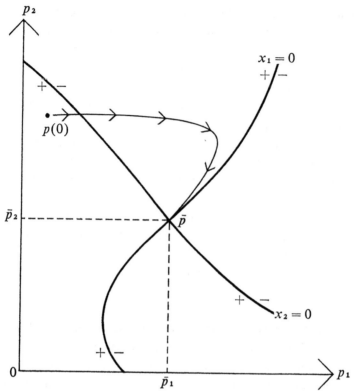

Figure 1 Structure of Partial Equilibrium Analysis

the locus $x_1 = 0$ determines a unique partial equilibrium price in market 1. The compensated excess demand for market 2, conditioned on partial equilibrium in market 1, is given by values of x_2 for prices in the locus $x_1 = 0$, and has the property that this excess demand is negative when p_2 is above the market 2 equilibrium price $\bar{p}_2$. One can see clearly in this diagram that the dynamic price adjustment mechanism suggested above should be stable under the Marshallian assumptions: Starting from an initial price vector $p(0)$, the price in market 1 will adjust rapidly toward the locus $x_1 = 0$. After p_1 is close to this locus, prices will move, much more slowly, along the locus to equilibrium. In the remainder of this paper, we shall verify formally this intuitive result.

A formalization of the assumptions of partial equilibrium analysis which will be shown to admit stable dynamic processes of the type just described is summarized in the following postulate:

Assumption 1 (*Hicks's Perfect Stability*) *The markets of the economy can be ranked (and this ranking can be taken, without loss of generality, to be their labeling* 1, 2, . . ., *n*) *such that for each market* i ($i = 1$, . . ., *n*), *the following conditions hold:*

(1) *given any fixed prices in markets* $i+1$, . . ., *n, there exists a unique partial equilibrium price vector for markets* 1, . . ., *i. Further, these partial equilibrium prices for the first* i *markets can be written as continuously differentiable functions of the remaining prices.*

(2) *the compensated excess demand function for commodity* i, *conditioned on the subset of markets* 1, . . ., $i-1$ *adjusting to partial equilibrium, is negative when its price is above its partial equilibrium level and is positive when its price is below its partial equilibrium level.*

Several features of our form of the Hicks conditions should be emphasized. First, the assumption is on the *static* structure of the economy and involves no dynamics, even though it was motivated by dynamic considerations. Second, the assumption imposes conditions on the *sign* of excess demands and the regularity of the equilibrium, but imposes no conditions of continuity or differentiability on the excess demand functions or demand indices away from partial equilibria. Third, the conditions are assumed to hold only for a single ranking of the markets, rather than for all possible rankings of markets, as in Hicks's original formulation.

III. *Perfect Stability and Hicksian Matrices*

Consider a square matrix $\underline{A}$ of order *n*, and let A_i denote the upper left-hand principal minor of $\underline{A}$ with order *i*:

$$A_i = \begin{vmatrix} a_{11} & \cdots & a_{1i} \\ \cdot & & \cdot \\ \cdot & \cdot & \cdot \\ \cdot & & \cdot \\ a_{i1} & \cdots & a_{ii} \end{vmatrix} \qquad (i = 1, \ldots, n).$$

The matrix $\underline{A}$ is called *Hicksian* if A_1 is negative and the principal minors alternate in sign; i.e. $(-1)^i A_i$ is positive for $i = 1, \ldots, n$.

In the case that the market demand indices are continuously differentiable in a neighborhood of the general equilibrium price vector $\bar{p}$, Assumption 1 will be shown to imply that the Jacobian matrix $\underline{A}(p)$ of $\underline{H}$ is Hicksian at some price vector p^0 which is as close as one pleases to $\bar{p}$. The upper left-hand principal minor of $\underline{A}(p)$ of order *i* will be denoted by $A_i(p)$. Throughout the remainder of the paper, the notation '[i' will be used as a subscript on a vector to denote the subvector with components from i through n; e.g., $p_{[i} = (p_i, \ldots, p_n)$. Similarly, the subscripts 'i]', 'i[', and '] i' will be used to denote subvectors with components i] $= (1, \ldots, i)$, $i[= (i+1, \ldots, n)$, and] $i = (1, \ldots, i-1)$, respectively. Under Assumption 1, there exist unique partial equilibrium prices in the first i markets which can be written as continuously differentiable functions of the prices in the remaining markets. Denote these functions by

$$p_j = f_{i,j}(p_{i+1}, \ldots, p_n) \qquad j = 1, \ldots, i, \tag{6}$$

or more compactly, $p_{i]} = f_i(p_{i[})$. By assumption, the system (6) is a unique solution for $(p_1, \ldots, p_i)$ in the system of equations

$$0 = H_j(p) \qquad j = 1, \ldots, i. \tag{7}$$

Suppose $\underline{H}(p)$ is continuously differentiable in a neighborhood $\underline{N}$ of $\bar{p}$. Then, for any solution $(f_i(p_{i[}), p_{i[})$ of (7) which is contained in $\underline{N}$, a converse of the implicit function theorem due to Bernstein and Toupin (1962) can be applied to establish that $A_i(p)$, the Jacobian of (7) with respect to $p_{i[}$, assumes non-singular values for some price vector $(p'_{i]}, p_{i[})$ with $p'_{i[}$ as close as one pleases to $f_i(p_{i[})$. Starting with $i = n$, a recursive argument then establishes the existence of points p^0 arbitrarily close to $\bar{p}$ where $A(p^0)$ has all principal minors $A_i(p^0)$ non-zero. With little loss of economic generality, Assumption 1 can then be strengthened to

Assumption 1* The conditions of Assumption 1 hold, the market demand index functions $\underline{H}$ are continuously differentiable in a neighborhood of the general equilibrium price vector $\bar{p}$, and all the principal minors $A_i(p)$ of the Jacobian of $\underline{H}$ are non-zero at $\bar{p}$.

Under this assumption, the own price derivative of the compensated market demand index function for commodity i, conditioned on achievement of partial equilibrium in markets $1, \ldots, i-1$, is negative. Further, when the price vector $p_{i[}$ attains its general equilibrium level $\bar{p}_{i[}$, this derivative, evaluated at $\bar{p}_i$, equals $A_{i-1}(\bar{p})/A_i(\bar{p})$, with $A_0(p) = 1$ by convention. Hence, $\underline{A}(\bar{p})$ is Hicksian under Assumption 1*.

iv. *A Local Stability Theorem*

A remarkable theorem by Fisher and Fuller (1958) on the stabilization of matrices allows us to establish immediately the local stability of the dynamic process (2), provided the rates of accommodation c_i are small and are ranked in size in the manner suggested in our discussion of

Marshallian analysis. The relevance of the Fisher-Fuller theorem for stability analysis was first noted by P. Newman (1959). The local stability theorem given below was communicated to me in essentially its present form by J. Quirk.

Theorem 1. Suppose Assumption 1* holds. Then, there exists a positive scalar ε_0 such that if (a) *the positive rates of accommodation c_i satisfy $c_1 < \varepsilon_0$ and $c_i / c_{i-1} < \varepsilon_0$ for $i = 2, \ldots, n$, and* (b) *the initial price vector satisfies $| \underline{p}(0) - \bar{p} | < \varepsilon_0$,[3] then the dynamic process (2) is stable, and all the characteristic roots of the matrix $\underline{A}(\bar{p})\underline{C}$ in the Taylor's expansion (4) of the dynamic process (2) are real, negative, distinct, and less than one in modulus.*

Proof. Since $\underline{A}(\bar{p})$ is Hicksian and $\underline{A}(p)$ is continuous in a neighborhood of $\bar{p}$, there exists $\varepsilon_1 > 0$ such that $\underline{A}(p)$ is Hicksian for $| p - \bar{p} | \leqslant \varepsilon_1$. The corollary to the Fisher-Fuller theorem given in Appendix A then establishes the existence of a scalar $\varepsilon_2 > 0$ such that for $\underline{C}$ satisfying $c_i / c_{i-1} < \varepsilon_2$, $\underline{A}(p)\underline{C}$ has real, distinct characteristic roots which are bounded negative. Choosing $c_1 < 1/n\| \underline{A}(\underline{p}) \|$ for all $\underline{p}$ in the ε_1-neighborhood ensures that the roots will have modulus less than one. Take $\varepsilon = \min(\varepsilon_1, \varepsilon_2)$.

For $| \underline{p}(t) - \bar{p} | \leqslant \varepsilon$, the dynamic process (2) can be written in the form
$$\Delta \underline{p}(t) = \underline{H}(\underline{p}(t))\underline{C} = (\underline{p}(t) - \bar{p})\underline{A}(\underline{p}^{\triangle}(t))\underline{C},$$
where $\underline{p}^{\triangle}(t) = \theta \bar{p} + (1-\theta)\underline{p}(t)$ for some scalar θ satisfying $0 < \theta < 1$. The norm $| \underline{p}(t) - \bar{p} |$ then satisfies

$$| \underline{p}(t+1) - \bar{p} |^2 - | \underline{p}(t) - \bar{p} |^2 = (\underline{p}(t) - \bar{p})[2\underline{A}(\underline{p}^{\triangle}(t))\underline{C} + \underline{A}(\underline{p}^{\triangle})\underline{C}\underline{C}'\underline{A}(\underline{p}^{\triangle})'](\underline{p}(t) - \bar{p})' < 0$$

for $\underline{p}(t) \neq \bar{p}$, since the matrix in square brackets is negative definite. Hence, the solution is contained in the neighborhood $| p - \bar{p} | \leqslant \varepsilon$ and converges to $\bar{p}$. Q.E.D.

When the system of market demand index functions $\underline{H}(\underline{p})$ is linear, Theorem 1 establishes stability globally (i.e., for arbitrary $\underline{p}(0)$).

v. *A Global Stability Theorem*

A global stability result analogous to the local stability theorem proved above can be established using the geometry of the partial equilibrium system. The class of dynamic processes which are proved stable again are of the type illustrated in Figure 1, with the markets adjusting to partial equilibrium essentially in a sequential fashion.

Theorem 2. Suppose Assumption 1* holds, and assume that the market demand index functions $\underline{H}(p)$ are continuous for all non-negative p. Given a positive bound M, there exists a positive scalar ε (which depends in general on M) such that if (a) the positive rates of accommodation c_i satisfy $c_1 < \varepsilon$ and $c_i/c_{i-1} < \varepsilon$ for $i = 2, \ldots, n$, and (b) the initial price vector satisfies $|\underline{p}(0) - \bar{p}| \leqslant M$, then the dynamic process (2) is stable.

Discussion of the Proof. The formal proof of this theorem will follow closely the geometric argument for stability given in Figure 1. The first market price in the solution is shown to monotonically approach its corresponding partial equilibrium value until the solution is trapped in a neighborhood of the locus of partial equilibria for market 1. Then, the second market price vector approaches its compensated partial equilibrium value, and so forth, until the price vector is trapped in a neighborhood of general equilibrium.

The theorem will be proved in five steps: *Step* 1 constructs a rectangle which is later shown to contain the solution when hypothesis (a) of the theorem is satisfied. *Step* 2 introduces a system of notation which is used in the proof, and *Step* 3 establishes several geometric implications of the partial equilibrium assumptions. *Step* 4 establishes the value of ε required in the hypothesis of the theorem. *Step* 5 establishes a basic induction step which guarantees that after some time t_n, the solution will be trapped in a small neighborhood of the general equilibrium. Theorem 1 is then applied to complete the proof that the system is stable.

Proof. Step 1. First, a rectangle $\underline{R}^*$ is constructed in such a way that it contains the partial equilibrium values of any component which might result when succeeding components are in $\underline{R}^*$. In particular, all non-negative prices satisfying $|\underline{p} - \bar{p}| \leqslant M$ will be contained in $\underline{R}^*$. Define the functions

$$b_i(\theta) = \text{Max}\{|f_{i,i}(p_{i[}) - \bar{p}_i|\,|\,|p_{i[} - \bar{p}_{i[}| \leqslant \theta\}$$

for $\theta \geqslant 0$ and $i = 1, \ldots, n-1$. Define a scalar $\theta_{n+1} = nM + \sum_{i=1}^{n-1} b_i(M) + 1$. Then define scalars $\theta_n, \theta_{n-1}, \ldots, \theta_1$ by the recursion formula $\theta_i = \theta_{i+1} + 4\theta_{n+1} + 3b_i(\theta_{i+1})$. Define a box $\underline{R}^* = \{p \geqslant 0|\,|p_i - \bar{p}_i| \leqslant \theta_i, i = 1, \ldots, n\}$ and let $\underline{R} = \{p \geqslant 0|\,|p_i - \bar{p}_i| \leqslant 2\theta_i, i = 1, \ldots, n\}$ be a larger box containing $\underline{R}^*$.

Step 2. We now introduce a system of notation for neighborhoods of partial equilibrium price vectors. The structure of these neighborhoods is illustrated in Figures 2 and 3. Let α denote a positive scalar. The sets

$$\underline{S}_i(\alpha) = \{p \text{ in } \underline{R} \mid H_i(p) \leqslant -\alpha\},$$
$$\underline{D}_i(\alpha) = \{p \text{ in } \underline{R} \mid H_i(\geqslant p)\alpha\},$$
$$\underline{E}_i(\alpha) = \{p \text{ in } \underline{R} \mid |H_i(p)| \leqslant \alpha\}$$

denote, respectively, points in $\underline{R}$ where excess demand in market i is bounded negative, bounded positive, and near zero. The set

$$\underline{T}_i(\alpha) = \{p \text{ in } \underline{R} \mid |p_{i]} - f_i(p_{i\bar{i}})| \leqslant \alpha\}$$

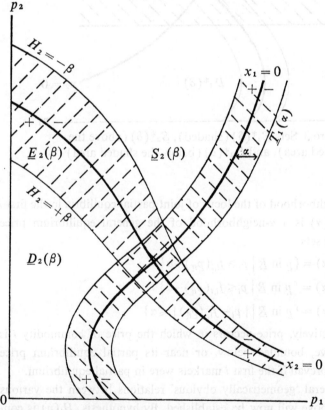

Figure 2 Sets $\underline{E}_2(\beta)$ (shaded northeast–southwest), $\underline{T}_1(\alpha)$ (shaded northwest–southeast), $\underline{S}_2(\beta)$ (northeast of the $H_2 = -\beta$ contour), and $\underline{D}_2(\beta)$ (southwest of the $H_2 = +\beta$ contour)

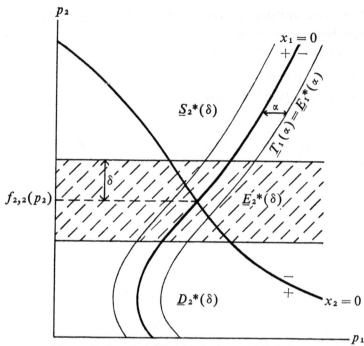

Figure 3 Sets $\underline{E}_2{}^*(\delta)$ (shaded), $\underline{S}_2{}^*(\delta)$ (above the shaded area), and $\underline{D}_2{}^*(\delta)$ (below the shaded area)

denotes a neighborhood of the locus of joint partial equilibria in the first i markets. ($\underline{T}_n(\alpha)$ is a α-neighborhood of the general equilibrium price vector $\bar{p}$.) The sets

$$S_i^*(\alpha) = \{p \text{ in } \underline{R} \mid p_i \geqslant f_{i,i}(p_{i\underline{l}}) + \alpha\},$$

$$\underline{D}_i^*(\alpha) = \{p \text{ in } \underline{R} \mid p_i \leqslant f_{i,i}(p_{i\underline{l}}) - \alpha\},$$

$$\underline{E}_i^*(\alpha) = \{p \text{ in } \underline{R} \mid \mid p_i - f_{i,i}(p_{i\underline{l}}) \mid \leqslant \alpha\}$$

denote, respectively, price vectors in which the price of commodity i is bounded above, bounded below, or near its partial equilibrium price which would prevail if the first i markets were in partial equilibrium.

Step 3. Several 'geometrically obvious' relations between the various sets defined above will now be established. By hypothesis, $\underline{H}_i(p)$ is continuous, and if the first $i-1$ markets are in partial equilibrium and p_i is bounded above its partial equilibrium level, then $\underline{H}_i(p)$ is negative (by Assumption 1). Then, $\underline{H}_i(p)$ is uniformly continuous on the compact set $\underline{R}$, and is bounded negative on the set $\underline{S}_i^*(\varepsilon) \cap \underline{T}_{i-1}(\delta)$ for sufficiently small δ. Hence, we can conclude

Given $\varepsilon > 0$, there exist δ, $\gamma > 0 (\delta \leqslant \varepsilon)$ such that $\underline{S}_i^*(\varepsilon) \cap \underline{T}_{i-1}(\delta)$ is contained in $\underline{S}_i(\gamma)$. The result holds when $\underline{S}$ is replaced by $\underline{D}$. (8)

By Assumption 1, the partial equilibrium prices $f_i(p_{i\underline{\mathfrak{t}}})$ are continuously differentiable on the compact set $\underline{R}$. Hence, there exists a scalar $\mu(\mu > 1)$ such that [Note: $f_{i-1}(f_{ii}(p_{i\underline{\mathfrak{t}}}), p_{i\underline{\mathfrak{t}}}) \equiv f_{i\underline{\mathfrak{1}},i}(p_{i\underline{\mathfrak{t}}})$]

$$| f_{i-1}(p_i, p_{i\underline{\mathfrak{t}}}) - f_{i,\underline{\mathfrak{1}}i}(p_{i\underline{\mathfrak{t}}}) | \leqslant \mu | p_i - f_{i,i}(p_{i\underline{\mathfrak{t}}}) |$$

for p in $\underline{R}$. If p is in $\underline{T}_{i-1}(\varepsilon) \cap \underline{E}_i^*(v)$, then

$$| p_{\underline{\mathfrak{1}}i} - f_{i,\underline{\mathfrak{1}}i}(p_{i\underline{\mathfrak{t}}}) | \leqslant | p_{\underline{\mathfrak{1}}i} - f_{i-1}(p_i, p_{i\underline{\mathfrak{t}}}) | + | f_{i-1}(p_i, p_{i\underline{\mathfrak{t}}}) - f_{i,\underline{\mathfrak{1}}i}(p_{i\underline{\mathfrak{t}}}) |$$

$$\leqslant \varepsilon + \mu | p_i - f_{i,i}(p_{i\underline{\mathfrak{t}}}) | \leqslant \varepsilon + \mu v,$$

and we conclude

$$\underline{T}_{i-1}(\varepsilon) \cap \underline{E}_i^*(v) \text{ is contained in } \underline{T}_i(\varepsilon + \mu v). \tag{9}$$

Step 4. A series of bounds will now be established, among them the value of ε required in the hypothesis of Theorem 2. Choose a positive scalar $\varepsilon_n(\varepsilon_n < 1$ and $\varepsilon_n \leqslant \theta_{n+1}/4)$ which satisfies Theorem 1. Then, define a series of scalars $v_n, \varepsilon_{n-1}, v_{n-1}, \ldots, v_2, \varepsilon_1$ recursively as follows:

Given $\varepsilon_i > 0$, choose $v_i(\varepsilon_i/2\mu \leqslant v_i < \varepsilon_i/\mu)$ such that $\underline{S}_i^*(v_i/2) \cap \underline{T}_{i-1}(\varepsilon_i - \mu v_i)$ is contained in $\underline{S}_i(\delta)$ and $\underline{D}_i^*(v_i/2) \cap \underline{T}_{i-1}(\varepsilon_i - \mu v_i)$ is contained in $\underline{D}_i(\delta_i)$ for some $\delta_i > 0$ and then choose $\varepsilon_{i-1} = \varepsilon_i - \mu v_i$. (The scalar μ is given in (9). That this recursive definition is possible follows from (8) and the observation that $\varepsilon_i - \mu v_i$ can be made as close to zero as we please.) Finally, define $v_1 = \varepsilon_1/2\mu$, and choose δ_1 such that $\underline{S}_1^*(v_1)$ and $\underline{D}_1^*(v_1)$ are contained in $\underline{S}_1(\delta_1)$ and $\underline{D}_1(\delta_1)$, respectively. Define $\delta = \min \{\delta_1, \ldots, \delta_n\}$, where the δ_i are given by the recursive procedure above.

Let $G \geqslant 1$ be a upper bound on $| \underline{H}_i(p) |$ for p in $\underline{R}$ and $i = 1, \ldots, n$. Now, choose ε to be the *smallest* of the numbers $v_1/8nG\mu$, $\delta/2nG\mu$, $\theta_{n+1}/\delta G$, and $v_1\delta/6nG\theta_1$. The matrix $\underline{C}$ will now be assumed to satisfy the hypotheses of the theorem for this ε.

Using (9) and the condition $\varepsilon_i = \varepsilon_{i-1} + \mu v_i$ given by the recursion above, one obtains the useful condition

$$\underline{T}_{i-1}(\varepsilon_{i-1}) \cap \underline{E}_i^*(v_i) \text{ is contained in } \underline{T}_i(\varepsilon_i). \tag{10}$$

Step 5. Suppose a given matrix $\underline{C}$ satisfies the hypotheses of Theorem 2 for the ε given in the previous step. Define a sequence of times t_i, $i = 1$, $\ldots n$, by the following recursive procedure (define $t_0 = 0$ and $t_{n+1} = +\infty$): Given t_{i-1}, define t_i as the largest integer which is less than $t_{i-1} + 3\theta_1/\delta c_i$.

We shall now give an induction argument which shows that (a) up until time t_{i-1}, market i exhibits 'insignificant' price changes, so that the solution remains in the rectangle $\underline{R}^*$, (b) after time t_{i-1}, the price in market i approaches its partial equilibrium value monotonically until, by time t_i or before, it is trapped in a neighborhood $\underline{E}_i^*(v_i)$ of this equilibrium value, and (c) after time t_i, the price vector is trapped in a neighborhood $\underline{T}_i(\varepsilon_i)$ of the locus of partial equilibrium price vectors for the first i markets.

We shall require the following bound: for $k > i$

$$t_i c_k \leqslant c_k \sum_{j=1}^{i} \frac{3\theta_1}{\delta c_j} \leqslant \frac{3\theta_1 i}{\delta} \frac{v_1 \delta}{6nG\theta_1} \leqslant \frac{v_1}{G}. \tag{11}$$

Define a norm $V_i(\underline{p}) = |p_i - f_{i,i}(p_{it})|$ for $i = 1, \ldots, n$, and note that $\underline{E}_i^*(v_i) = \{\underline{p} \text{ in } \underline{R} \mid V_i(\underline{p}) \leqslant v_i\}$. The basic induction step can now be stated:

Lemma. If the Induction Hypothesis below holds for time t', then it remains valid when t' is replaced by $t'+1$.

Induction Hypothesis. At the time t (with i defined so that $t_{i-1} \leqslant t < t_i$), the following conditions hold:

(a) $\underline{p}(\tau)$ *is in $\underline{R}^*$ for $\tau \leqslant t$;*

(b) $\underline{p}(\tau)$ *is in $\bigcap\limits_{k=1}^{j} \underline{E}_k^*(v_k) \subseteq \underline{T}_j(\varepsilon_j)$ for $t_j \leqslant \tau \leqslant t_{j+1}$*

for $j = 1 \ldots, i-2$ and is in $\bigcap\limits_{k=1}^{i-1} \underline{E}_k^*(v_k) \subseteq \underline{T}_{i-1}(\varepsilon_{i-1})$ for $t_{i-1} \leqslant \tau \leqslant t$;

(c) $V_i(\underline{p}(t_{i-1})) \leqslant \theta_i - 2\theta_{n+1} - b_i(\theta_{i+1})$;

(d) $V_j(\underline{p}(t)) \leqslant \text{Max}\left\{ v_j, V_j(\underline{p}(t_{j-1})) - \dfrac{c_j \delta}{2}(t - t_{j-1}) \right\}$

for $j = 1, \ldots, i$.

Proof of the lemma. Suppose the induction hypothesis holds for t. Then $|p_i(t+1) - p_i(t)| \leqslant Gc_i \leqslant \theta_{n+1}/2 < \theta_i$ for each i, and $\underline{p}(t+1)$ is in $\underline{R}$.

The proof will now be carried out in three phases. In Phase 1, (b), (c), (d) will be shown to hold for $t+1 \leqslant t_i$ with the index i held fixed. Phase 2 will verify condition (a). Finally, Phase 3 will verify that (b), (c), (d) continue to hold when $t+1 = t_i$ and the index i is advanced in (b), (c), (d). This will prove the lemma.

Phase 1. Consider the case where $t+1 \leqslant t_i$, and (b), (c), (d) are considered without advancing the subscript i for $t+1 = t_i$. Condition (c) continues to hold without induction. The next chain of arguments will establish that condition (d) holds in this case.

Suppose first that for some $j \leqslant i$, we have $p(t)$ in $\underline{S}_j^*(v_j/2) \cap \underline{T}_{j-1}(\varepsilon_{j-1})$. From Step 4, $p(t)$ is then in $\underline{S}_j(\delta_j)$, implying $H_j(p(t)) \leqslant -\delta_j$. Further, $p_j(t+1)-f_{j,j}(p_{jt}(t+1)) \geqslant v_j/2-|\,p_j(t+1)-p_j(t)\,|-\mu|\,p_{jt}(t+1)-p_{jt}(t)\,| \geqslant v_j/2-Gc_j-\mu Gnc_{j+1} \geqslant v_j/4 > 0$. Hence,

$$V_j(p(t+1))-V_j(p(t)) = p_j(t+1)-p_j(t)-$$
$$-[f_{j,j}(p_{jt}(t+1))-f_{j,j}(p_{jt}(t))] \quad (12)$$
$$\leqslant -\delta_j c_j+\mu\,|\,p_{jt}(t+1)-p_{jt}(t)\,|$$
$$\leqslant -\delta_j c_j+\mu Gnc_{j+1} \leqslant -\frac{\delta}{2}c_j,$$

using the inequalities satisfied by ε. If $p(t)$ is in $\underline{D}_j^*(v_j/2) \cap \underline{T}_{j-1}(\varepsilon_{j-1})$, a similar argument again establishes that $V_j(p(t+1))-V_j(p(t)) \leqslant -\delta c_j/2$.

Next suppose that for some $j \leqslant i$, we have $p(t)$ in $\underline{E}_j^*(v_j/2) \cap \underline{T}_{j-1}(\varepsilon_{j-1})$. Then,

$$V_j(p(t+1)) \leqslant V_j(p(t))+|\,p_j(t+1)-p_j(t)\,|+$$
$$+|\,f_{j,j}(p_{jt}(t+1))-f_{j,j}(p_{jt}(t))\,|$$
$$\leqslant v_j/2+v_1/4+\mu\,|\,p_{jt}(t+1)-p_{jt}(t)\,| \leqslant v_j,$$

where the bounds on ε have again been utilized.

But under the induction hypothesis, $p(t)$ is in one of the cases we have just considered. Hence, for each $j \leqslant i$, either $V_j(p(t+1)) \leqslant v_j$ or $V_j(p(t+1))-V_j(p(t)) \leqslant -\delta_j c_j/2$. Therefore, condition (d) of the induction hypothesis holds.

From condition (d), one then has $p(t+1)$ in the intersection of $\underline{E}_j^*(v_j)$ for $j = 1, \ldots, i-1$, which implies by an application of (10) that $p(t+1)$ is in $\underline{T}_{i-1}(\varepsilon_{i-1})$. Hence, condition (b) holds.

Phase 2. Condition (a) will now be verified. Consider first a market k for $k > i$. Then, by (11),

$$| p_k(t+1) - \bar{p}_k | \leqslant | p_k(t+1) - p_k(0) | + | p_k(0) - \bar{p}_k |$$
$$\leqslant Gc_h t_i + \theta_{n+1} \leqslant v_1 + \theta_{n+1} \leqslant 2\theta_{n+1} \leqslant \theta_k , \qquad (14)$$

and the components $i+1, \ldots, n$ of $p(t+1)$ are in $\underline{R}^*$.

To establish (a) for the remaining markets, we shall employ the inequality

$$| p_j - \bar{p}_j | \leqslant | p_j - f_{j,j}(p_{jt}) | + | f_{j,j}(p_{jt}) - \bar{p}_j |$$
$$\leqslant V_j(p) + b_j(| p_{jt} - \bar{p}_{jt} |) \qquad (15)$$

From condition (d) established for $t+1$ in Phase 1 above, $V_i(p(t+1)) \leqslant$ Max $\{ v_i, \; V_i(p(t_{i-1})) \} \leqslant \theta_i - b_i(\theta_{i+1}) - 2\theta_{n+1}$. Then, (15) establishes $| p_i(t+1) - \bar{p}_i | \leqslant \theta_i$. An induction argument completes the demonstration: Suppose $| p_j(t+1) - \bar{p}_j | \leqslant \theta_j$ has been established for markets $k+1$ to n ($k < i$). Then, condition (b) implies $V_k(p(t+1)) \leqslant v_k$, and $| p_k(t+1) - \bar{p}_k | \leqslant v_k + b_k(\theta_{k+1}) \leqslant \theta_k$. Hence, (a) holds.

Phase 3. Consider the case where $t+1 = t_i$. Phase 1 established conditions (c) and (d) at t_i when the subscript $i-1$ is maintained. The second term in the bound on the right-hand side of (d) then satisfies

$$V_i(p(t_{i-1})) - \frac{c_i \delta}{2}(t_i - t_{i-1}) \leqslant \theta_i - \frac{c_i \delta}{2}\left(\frac{3\theta_1}{\delta c_i} - 1 \right)$$

$$\leqslant \theta_i - \tfrac{3}{2}\theta_1 + \frac{c_i \delta}{2} < 0$$

by the construction of the t_i and the bounds on ε. Hence $V_i(p(t_i)) \leqslant v_i$, and (b) holds with i replaced by $i+1$.

To show (c) in this case, we make the expansion

$$V_{i+1}(p(t_i)) \leqslant V_{i+1}(p(0)) + | f_{i+1,i+1}(p_{i+1,t}(0)) - \bar{p}_{i+1} | +$$
$$+ | p_{i+1}(t_i) - p_{i+1}(0) | + | f_{i+1,i+1}(p_{i+1,t}(t_i)) - \bar{p}_{i+1} | . \qquad (16)$$

From Step 1 of the theorem proof, the first two terms on the right-hand-side of (16) are bounded by θ_{n+1}. By (11), the term $| p_{i+1}(t_i) - p_{i+1}(0) |$ is bounded by v_1. By (a), established for t_i in Phase 2 above, the last term is bounded by $b_{i+1}(\theta_{i+2})$. Hence,

$$V_{i+1}(p(t_i)) \leqslant \theta_{n+1} + v_1 + b_{i+1}(\theta_{i+2})$$
$$\leqslant \theta_{i+1} - 2\theta_{n+1} - b_{i+1}(\theta_{i+2}),$$

since $\theta_{i+1} - 2\theta_{n+1} - b_{i+1}(\theta_{i+2}) = 2\theta_{n+1} + 2b_{i+1}(\theta_{i+2})$ and $v_i \leqslant \theta_{n+1}$. Hence, (c) holds when i is advanced to $i+1$, $t+1 = t_i$.

Finally, note that (d) holds at $t+1 = t_i$ and i not advanced by the results of Phase 1. Then, it holds by definition when i is advanced to $i+1$. Q.E.D. Lemma.

From condition (b) of the induction hypothesis, the solution will be contained in $\underline{T}_n(\varepsilon_n)$ after time t_n. Hence, Theorem 1 can be applied to establish that the solution converges to the general equilibrium price vector $\bar{p}$. Q.E.D. Theorem 2.

Theorem 2 may be generalized in several directions:

(1) If there are sub-groups of markets which are stable for more general dynamic processes than the essentially sequential processes we have considered, then Theorem 2 can be generalized to establish the stability of a process which is essentially sequential between subgroups.

(2) In more general dynamic systems than the multiple market model, transformations of the dynamic system, $\Delta p(t) = \underline{H}(p(t))\underline{B}\underline{C}$, where $\underline{B}$ is an $n \times n$ matrix, may be possible and may result in a system which is Hicksian. Theorem 2 can then be applied to establish the stability of this modified system. For example, in the case that $\underline{H}(p(t)) = (p(t) - \bar{p})\underline{A}(\bar{p})$ is linear and $\underline{A}(\bar{p})$ is non-singular, there always exists a sequence of column permutations and sign changes which reduces $\underline{A}(\bar{p})$ to a Hicksian matrix. Then Theorem 1 would establish the stability of the transformed system.

(3) If the bounds (8) and (9) on the structure of the neighborhoods of partial equilibria and the upper bound G on the market demand index functions hold uniformly in M, then Theorem 2 holds for a value of ε independent of M.

(4) If no continuity assumptions are imposed on the market demand index functions H_i other than the condition that they be bounded away from zero when their own prices are bounded away from their partial equilibrium values, the proof of Theorem 2 still establishes that, given any small neighborhood of the general equilibrium, there exists $\varepsilon > 0$ such that for $\underline{C}$ satisfying the hypotheses of Theorem 2, the dynamic process (2) will converge to the given neighborhood. This result could be applied, for example, to the case where the levels of excess demand for some commodities are discrete, leading always to finite jumps in some prices.

(5) Theorem 2 continues to hold if the market demand index functions and rates of accommodation are no longer autonomous, but depend on

time, provided the bounds used on these functions hold uniformly in time. In particular, if the rates of accommodation converge to zero, but converge at a slow enough rate so that their partial sums diverge, then the dynamic system (2) can be made stable even under the relaxed assumptions on the H_t suggested in the previous paragraph.

The assumption of the existence of partial equilibria employed in obtaining the stability results of this paper is intuitively reasonable in many economic models. Further, it is an implication of some of the conditions commonly imposed in the analysis of multi-market stability. In particular, if a condition of strong gross substitutability holds globally or if the Jacobian matrix of $\underline{H}$ has a negative dominant diagonal,[4] then the partial equilibrium conditions will be satisfied. We now demonstrate these propositions rigorously:

Theorem 3. Suppose an economy satisfies the following conditions (for commodities $i = 1, \ldots, n$):

(a) the excess demand functions are homogeneous of degree zero and continuously differentiable,

(b) the differential form of the gross substitutability condition holds,[5] and

(c) Walras's law holds and the supplies of commodities are bounded.

Then, Assumption 1 holds.

Proof. Assume $p_n > 0$. The theorem is proved by induction. Suppose we have established that partial equilibria exist in markets $1, \ldots, i-1$, and satisfy Assumption 1. Let $p_{ji} = f_{i-1}(p_{[i})$ denote these equilibrium prices, as before, and let

$$z_j = h_j(f_{i-1}(p_{[i}),p_{[i}) \equiv \xi_{i-1,j}(p_{[i}), \quad j = i, \ldots, n$$

denote the compensated excess demand functions in the remaining markets. Suppose further that the compensated demand functions $\xi_{i-1,j}(p_{[i})$ satisfy the differential gross substitutability assumption, are homogeneous of degree zero in prices, and satisfy the 'modified' Walras's law,

$$\sum_{j=i}^{n} p_j \xi_{i-1,j}(p_{[i}) \equiv 0.$$

We now demonstrate that these conditions hold for markets $1, \ldots, i$. Applying a lemma established by Arrow and Hurwicz (1959, Lemma 1, p. 89), one has $\xi_{i-1,i}(0,p_{i[}) = +\infty$. The homogeneity and gross substitutability properties imply that $\partial \xi_{i-1,i}(p_i, p_{i\mathsf{C}})/\partial p_i < 0$. By the modified Walras's law,

$$\xi_{i-1,i}(1, p_{i\mathsf{C}}/p_i) = - \sum_{j=i+1}^{n} (p_j/p_i)\xi_{i-1,j}(1, p_{i\mathsf{C}}/p_i).$$

But the Arrow-Hurwicz lemma implies $\xi_{i-1,j}(1, p_{i\mathsf{C}}/p_i) > 0$ for $p_{i\mathsf{C}}/p_i$ sufficiently small, $j = i+1, \ldots, n$. Hence, $\xi_{i-1,i}(+\infty, p_{i\mathsf{C}}) < 0$. By continuity, there then exists $p_i = f_{i,i}(p_{i\mathsf{C}})$ such that $\xi_{i-1,i}(f_{i,i}(p_{i\mathsf{C}}), p_{i\mathsf{C}}) = 0$. Applying an implicit function theorem, we establish that $f_{i,i}(p_{i\mathsf{C}})$ is continuously differentiable, and

$$\partial f_{i,i}/\partial p_j = - \frac{\partial \xi_{i-1,i}}{\partial p_j} \bigg/ \frac{\partial \xi_{i-1,i}}{\partial p_i} > 0 \text{ for } j = i+1, \ldots, n,$$

where $f_{i,i}$ is evaluated at $p_{i\mathsf{C}}$ and $\xi_{i-1,i}$ is evaluated at $(f_{i,i}, p_{i\mathsf{C}})$. Now consider the compensated excess demand functions

$$z_j = \xi_{i-1,j}(f_{i,i}(p_{i\mathsf{C}}), p_{i\mathsf{C}}) = \xi_{i,j}(p_{i\mathsf{C}}), \quad j = i+1, \ldots, n.$$

The modified Walras's law and homogeneity of degree zero are easily verified for these functions. Further, for $j, k = i+1, \ldots, n$ and $j \neq k$,

$$\frac{\partial \xi_{i,j}}{\partial p_k} = \frac{\partial \xi_{i-1,j}}{\partial p_i} \frac{\partial f_{i,i}}{\partial p_k} + \frac{\partial \xi_{i-1,j}}{\partial p_k} > 0,$$

where ξ_{ij} is evaluated at $p_{i\mathsf{C}}$ and $\xi_{i-1,j}$ is evaluated at $(f_{i,i}(p_{i\mathsf{C}}), p_{i\mathsf{C}})$, establishing the gross substitutability property for market i, and proving the induction step. Q.E.D. Theorem 3.

Theorem 4. Suppose an economy has market demand index functions $\underline{H}(p)$ which are continuously differentiable and suppose that a general equilibrium price vector $\bar{p}$ exists. Suppose further that the Jacobian matrix $\underline{A}(p)$ of $\underline{H}(p)$ has a negative dominant diagonal for all nonnegative prices.[6] Then, the system satisfies Assumption 1.

Proof. Under the hypotheses, every principal sub-matrix of $\underline{A}(p)$ also has a negative dominant diagonal. Two theorems of McKenzie (1960, Theorems 1 and 2, p. 49) establish that these principal submatrices are non-singular and negative definite. Hence, the matrix $\underline{A}(p)$ is Hicksian for all p. A strong implicit function theorem (the global univalence theorem of Gale and Nikaido (1965)) then establishes the existence of a unique solution for a partial equilibrium price vector in any subset of markets. Q.E.D. Theorem 4.

VI. *Conclusions*

Theorems 1 and 2 above verify formally the suggestion made by Sir John Hicks that his perfect stability conditions should be sufficient for the dynamic stability of a price adjustment process which is 'close' to the Marshallian concept of movement through a series of temporary equilibria. The class of essentially sequential price adjustment mechanisms we have studied cannot be put forth seriously as a model of empirical price behavior (except possibly in certain systems where one market is known to adjust much more rapidly than another: as, for example, in the case of a rapidly adjusting bond market and a slowly adjusting durables market, or in the case of a rapidly adjusting domestic market and slowly adjusting international market). On the other hand, the results have theoretical value in that they provide a dynamic framework in which partial equilibrium analysis can be rigorously justified. Further, they allow the model builder to verify satisfaction of stability conditions (and meet the requirements of Samuelson's correspondence principle) with minimum effort, freeing him to pursue more complex representations of the static structure. While the cost in terms of realism is high in restricting one's analysis to models satisfying the partial equilibrium assumptions, the literature of economics attests to the value of added descriptive detail for particular markets. Finally, the possibility of stabilization of a variety of dynamic systems is suggested by Theorems 1 and 2 in the case that the matrix $\underline{C}$ is an instrument of the economic planner or programmer.

APPENDIX : STABILIZATION OF MATRICES

A fundamental theorem due to Fisher and Fuller (1958) forms the basis for our analysis of local stability. A slightly strengthened version of this result is the

> *Fisher-Fuller Theorem (Strong Form)*–*Suppose $\underline{A}$ is a real $n \times n$ matrix with the property that the upper left-hand principal minor A_i of each order $i = 1, \ldots, n$ is non-zero. Then, there exists a positive scalar ε such that if the real diagonal matrix $\underline{C} = diag.\ (c_i)$ satisfies $c_i A_i / A_{i-1} < 0$ (where $A_0 = 1$) for $i = 1, \ldots, n$ and $|c_i|/|c_{i-1}| < \varepsilon$ for $i = 2, \ldots, n$, then the characteristic roots of $\underline{AC}$ are real, negative, and distinct.*

This result is stronger than the original Fisher-Fuller theorem in that lower bounds on the c_i of the form $\alpha \varepsilon < |c_i|/|c_{i-1}|$, where α is a positive scalar, $\alpha < 1$, are no longer required in the proof. The method of proof used by Fisher and Fuller is to show that $\underline{A}\underline{C}$ has real characteristic roots which lie close to the values $r_i = c_i A_i / A_{i-1}$, provided ε is sufficiently small.

First, choose ε small enough so that $|r_i| > 4|r_{i+1}|$, and choose c_n so that $r_n = -1$ (the matrix $\underline{C}$ can be rescaled to any desired level of r_n). Employing a lemma on the approximation of roots of polynomials, Fisher and Fuller establish that a sufficient condition for $\underline{A}\underline{C}$ to have real characteristic roots λ_k satisfying $|\lambda_k - r_k| < \frac{1}{2}$ is that the following inequality be satisfied for each k.[8]

$$1 > \frac{\sum\limits_{s=1}^{n-1} |r_k|^{n-s} \cdot |r_1||r_2|\ldots|r_{s-1}||r_{s+1}|m_s}{\frac{1}{2}|r_k| \cdot \prod\limits_{i=1}^{k-1}|r_i - \frac{3}{2}r_k| \cdot \prod\limits_{i=k+1}^{n}|\frac{1}{2}r_k - r_i|} = (*),$$

where the m_s are positive constants determined by the matrix A. This expression can be rewritten in the form

$$(*) = \frac{2^{1+k-n}\left[\sum\limits_{s=1}^{k-1}\left|\frac{r_k}{r_s}\right| \cdot \prod\limits_{i=s+2}^{k}\left|\frac{r_k}{r_i}\right| m_s + \sum\limits_{s=k}^{n-1}\left|\frac{r_{s+1}}{r_k}\right| \cdot \prod\limits_{i=k}^{s-1}\left|\frac{r_i}{r_k}\right| m_s\right]}{\prod\limits_{i=1}^{k-1}\left|1 - \frac{3}{2}\frac{r_k}{r_i}\right| \cdot \prod\limits_{i=k+1}^{n}\left|1 - 2\frac{r_i}{r_k}\right|}$$

(products $\prod$ over empty index sets are taken to equal one). Using the condition $|r_i| > 4|r_{i+1}|$, one can establish the inequality

$$(*) < 2\left(\frac{8}{5}\right)^{k-1}\left[\left|\frac{r_k}{r_{k-1}}\right|\sum\limits_{s=1}^{k-1}m_s + \left|\frac{r_{k+1}}{r_k}\right|\sum\limits_{s=k}^{n-1}m_s\right].$$

For $|c_{i+1}/c_i| < \varepsilon = 2^{-n-1}\left(1 + \sum\limits_{s=1}^{n-1}m_s\right)^{-1} \cdot \min\limits_{k=1,\ldots,n-1}|A_k^2/A_{k+1}A_{k-1}|$,

the right-hand side of this expression will be less than one, and the sufficient condition for the validity of the theorem holds.

The following corollary establishes that the Fisher-Fuller theorem above holds uniformly when $\underline{A}$ varies continuously over a compact set.

Corollary. Suppose the matrix $\underline{A}(p)$ is a continuous function over p contained in a compact set $\underline{N}$, and has $A_i(p)$ non-zero on $\underline{N}$. Then there exists $\varepsilon > 0$ such that if $\underline{C}$ satisfies the conditions of the Fisher-Fuller theorem, then the characteristic roots of $\underline{A}(p)\underline{C}$ are real, distinct, finite, and bounded negative uniformly for $\underline{p}$ in $\underline{N}$.

The bound established for $|c_{i+1}/c_i|$ in the proof outline of the theorem above is found to depend on the terms m_s and A_k, which are continuous functions of determinants of various sub-matrices of $\underline{A}(\underline{p})$. Further, the $A_k(\underline{p})$ are bounded away from zero on $\underline{N}$. Hence, the bound for $|c_{i+1}/c_i|$ is continuous in $\underline{p}$, and achieves a positive minimum on $\underline{N}$.

ACKNOWLEDGMENTS

I am particularly indebted to Professor Josef Hadar, who contributed many ideas to the first version of this paper read at the Boston Meeting of the Econometric Society, 1963. The local stability results which have been added to this revised paper were communicated to me in essentially their present form by Professor Jim Quirk. This research was supported by the University of Pittsburgh and the Mellon Foundation, with additional support from the University of California and the University of Chicago.

NOTES AND REFERENCES

[1] The prices p_i may be thought of as 'normalized' prices, and a numéraire commodity $n+1$ with price one may also be present in the economy. In our analysis, it is *unnecessary* to assume that such a 'non-normalized' system is behind our model and related to it by homogeneity and Walras's law. However, it is a special property of the class of dynamic processes we consider that, when this relationship does hold, the solutions of the 'normalized' ($p_{n+1} = 1$) and 'non-normalized' (p_{n+1} modified by the dynamic process) systems are almost identical. The only additional restriction required is that the rate of accommodation in market $n+1$ be low enough so that p_{n+1} remains positive.

[2] The results of this paper are unchanged if the difference equations (2) are replaced by differential equations $dp_i(t)/dt = c_i H_i(\underline{p}(t))$.

[3] The notation $|\underline{p}| = \left(\sum_{i=1}^{n} |p_i|^2\right)^{\frac{1}{2}}$ and $\|\underline{A}\| = \left(\sum_{i,j=1}^{n} |a_{ij}|^2\right)^{\frac{1}{2}}$ is used for the Euclidean norms of a vector $\underline{p}$ and a matrix $\underline{A}$.

[4] A matrix $\underline{A} = (a_{ij})$ is said to have a negative dominant diagonal if there exists a positive diagonal matrix $\underline{C}$ such that $-a_{ii}c_i > \sum_{j \neq i} |a_{ij}| c_j$ for all i. For a full discussion, see McKenzie (1960).

[5] Differential gross substitutability requires that $\partial h_i(\underline{p})/\partial p_j$ be positive for $i \neq j$, while Walras's law requires that $\sum_{i=1}^{n} p_i h_i(\underline{p})$ be identically zero.

[6] The normalized price system, where commodity $n+1$ has price $p_{n+1} = 1$, will tacitly be assumed in this theorem.

[7] The expression (*) is a bound on the ratio $|g((1\pm\delta)r_k)/|f((1\pm\delta)r_k)|$ used by Fisher and Fuller (1958, equations (14)–(20), p. 442), taken with $\delta = \frac{1}{2}$.

15

Accumulation Programs of Maximum Utility and the von Neumann Facet

Lionel W. McKenzie

The study of optimal programs of economic growth which maximize a sum of utility was begun by Frank Ramsey (1928). He considered the case of a stationary population with no technical progress, except that which is explained by capital accumulation, no uncertainty about the future, and a single aggregate output that serves both as capital good and consumption good. His primary objective was to determine the rate of saving at any time prescribed by an optimal program of capital accumulation of unlimited duration.

Ramsey chose to consider a utility sum with no time discounting. Such a sum over an infinite future will be infinite for many programs between which it will not distinguish. To get round this difficulty Ramsey introduced a level of utility saturation and replaced the utility sum by a sum of differences between the utility enjoyed at saturation and the actual level of utility. If the saturation level can be reached by some program of accumulation, this differential sum will be finite for that program, and this program may be regarded as better than any program for which the differential sum is larger. Therefore, the criterion of maximizing the utility sum can reasonably be replaced by that of minimizing the differential sum, the shortfall from saturation, and the new problem will ordinarily have a solution.

The saturation level for utility can arise, according to Ramsey, either from an upper bound on the utility function itself or from an upper bound on the level of output that can be achieved through increasing the quantity of capital. Even if one does not wish to accept the notion of a bounded utility function, the bound on output from given population and given natural resources is entirely in accord with common sense. Indeed, if one allows for the need to replace capital as it wears out, and for the fact that this also uses labor, a bound on total capital accumulation is strongly

23   353

recommended, even if output with unlimited capital supplies is not limited. However, a bound on capital accumulation would also suffice to define a saturation level of utility.

Ramsey did not bring out the point explicitly, but the appeal of his substitute criterion probably comes from the fact that a program which achieves a lower shortfall from saturation than another program will thereby also have the property that its utility sum over a finite period will exceed this sum for the same period for the other program provided the period is long enough. The criterion was explicitly phrased this way in recent work of Hiroshi Atsumi (1965) and Christian von Weizsacker (1965).

In recent years Ramsey's work has been extended in various ways. Uncertainty about the future of tastes and technology has been introduced by Mirrlees (1965). Atsumi (1965) and Koopmans (1965) have dealt with the case of an increasing population without scarce natural resources. Atsumi (1966) and Gale (1966) extended the model to consider more complicated technologies where the number of goods produced may exceed one. And simple forms of technical progress have been introduced by Weizsacker and Mirrlees. Also a straightforward extension of the Ramsey case to many goods was made by Samuelson and Solow (1956).

In this recent work two main themes have been present, the proof that infinite optimal programs converge to a saturation level and the proof that infinite optimal programs exist. Koopmans (1965) used methods very close to those of Ramsey to give these proofs for his model. The new feature of Koopman's model is a population which increases at a constant exogenous rate. Ramsey had not faced the question of summing utility over populations of different sizes, but the logic of his summation over years would seem to imply that people living in different years should be treated equally. However, Koopmans shows that the Ramsey type of argument will not work unless future utility is discounted at a rate at least equal to the rate of population growth. This is the course adopted by Koopmans and described as maximizing a sum of per capita utility over time.

Atsumi (1965) independently of Koopmans adopted the same expedient of summing per capita utilities and applying the Ramsey criterion, which he explicitly interpreted in terms of finite sums which eventually exceed the finite sums of any competing path. Atsumi did not concern himself with the existence question for infinite paths but proved the convergence of optimal paths to saturation paths in the sense of paths with maximum sustainable per capita utility. These saturation paths had already been characterized by Phelps, Joan Robinson, and others. However, Atsumi was the first to combine an expanding population with more than one produced good. Also, unlike Samuelson and Solow, he was able to avoid assuming strict convexity of the production set, apart from homogeneity, by using methods akin to those applied by Radner (1961) and myself (1963) to the von Neumann model. He proved the asymptotic convergence of optimal paths to saturation paths in a generalized Leontief model (1966). He also derived a generalization of the expression for the optimal saving ratio in a neo-classical model.

Finally, David Gale (1966) has treated both the asymptotic convergence of optimal paths defined by the Atsumi-Weizsacker criterion and the existence of such optimal paths in linear production models with a finite set of activities. However, he has avoided some of the problems incident to introducing many goods by using a strictly concave utility function, defined on activity levels rather than on goods.

My purpose in this paper is to deal with the problems of asymptotic behavior of optimal paths using the Atsumi-Weizsacker criterion in a fully general production model. This allows an extension of Gale's result on the existence of infinite optimal paths. I follow Atsumi and Koopmans in assuming a steadily expanding population without scarce natural resources. The special limitations of the production set involved in strict convexity or in the absence of joint production are avoided. Two main results are derived. First, in a quite general model with a (weakly) convex transformation set, the finite optimal paths are shown to lie close, for all but a fixed number of periods, to a certain facet of the transformation set. This facet is characterized by the presence of the input-output combinations that provide the maximum sustainable utility. Indeed, a subset of the facet is described to which the optimal paths approach for all but a fixed number of periods. Second, it is shown that when this subset of the facet is a single point (where maximum sustainable utility will be realized) infinite paths exist which have a slightly weakened form of Atsumi-Weizsacker optimality.

I. *The Model*

We shall deal with an economy in which there are n kinds of durable and non-durable goods which can be accumulated as capital stocks. The quantities of these goods per capita at time t are the components of a vector $k(t) \geqslant 0$ in E_n, an n-dimensional Euclidean space. We assume that the development of the population over time is specified and also the rate at which natural resources are exhausted. Then it is reasonable to suppose that the per capita utility that can be achieved through consumption of goods and services during the period from t to $t+1$ depends only on the initial and terminal capital stocks per capita $k(t)$ and $k(t+1)$. This gives rise for each t to a transformation set $Y(t)$ in E_{2n+1} composed of points $(u(t),k(t),-k(t-1))$ where $u(t)$ is a per capita utility level achievable in the tth period with initial capital stocks $k(t-1)$ and terminal capital stocks $k(t)$.

In the present discussion the model will be specialized further by supposing that $Y(t)$ is a constant set Y for all t. The rationale for this specialization may be taken to be a constant rate of expansion for population, whose composition is fixed, and the absence of scarce natural resources. However, the depletion of resources, a varying rate of population growth, and technical progress could be so offsetting as to achieve the same result. The first formal assumption is

(1) Y is a closed convex subset of E_{2n+1}. Also $(u,k',-k) \in Y$ implies $(u(1),k'(1),-k(1)) \in Y$ when $u(1) \leqslant u$, $0 \leqslant k'(1) \leqslant k'$, and $k(1) \geqslant k$.

The second part of Assumption 1 is an assumption of free disposal. The assumption of convexity may be defended on the same grounds here as in the theory of production with linear activities. In the theory of production convexity results if the level of a productive activity may be continuously varied with all inputs and outputs changing in the same ratio, and if the productive activities are independent, so that the possibility of realizing one activity is not dependent on the levels of other activities. In the present model utility may be treated as an output resulting from combining capital goods and certain types of people.

Indeed, transformation set Y may be derived from a more basic activities cone. Suppose there are r types of people and the initial population is represented by a vector L in E_r. Let the initial capital stocks vector be K and the terminal vector K'. Let U be the utility generated over the period. Then there is a cone Y^Δ in $E_{2n+2r+1}$ whose elements have the form $z = (U,K',L',-K,-L)$. We are considering the section of this cone given by all elements of the form $z' = (U,K',\rho \bar{L},-K,-\bar{L})$. $\bar{L}$ has the composition of the actual population and $|\bar{L}| = 1$.[1] ρ is the population expansion factor. Corresponding to z' there is an element $y = (u,k',-k) \in Y$ with $u = \rho^{-1}U$, $k' = \rho^{-1}K'$, and $k = K$.

There is no reason to expect the section of Y^Δ at $|\bar{L}|$ to be strictly convex since V is generated by independent activities involving people of differing tastes doing different jobs in various independent industries and consuming different bundles of services. On the other hand, the convexity of Y^Δ does not depend on convexity of the individual utility functions. The fact that the quantities of a finite number of types of people are made to vary continuously is an approximation of the same order of realism with the same assumption made for goods. The continuous variation of all quantities is used to provide the convexity that we need.

Let us say that k is expansible with respect to Y, or simply expansible, if there is $(u,k',-k) \in Y$ and $k' > k$. A further assumption is

(II) There is a capital stock vector k^Δ which is expansible with respect to Y.

In other words, there is a level of capital stocks from which it is possible to accumulate larger per capita stocks of all types. Finally, we assume

(III) (*a*) For any number ξ there is a number η, depending on ξ, such that $|k| \leqslant \xi$ and $(u,k',-k) \in Y$ implies $u < \eta$ and $|k'| < \eta$.

(*b*) There is a number ζ, and a number $\gamma < 1$, such that $(u,k',-k) \in Y$ and $|k| \geqslant \zeta$ implies $|k'| < \gamma |k|$.

Thus if initial stocks are bounded, terminal stocks are bounded and utility is bounded above. Also there is a limit above which accumulation per capita cannot be sustained. This is reasonable since capital goods are subject to some wear from time alone and labor services are needed to restore them.

II. *The Turnpike Theorem*

Consider the set $V = \{u,k'-k\}$ of vectors in E_{n+1}, where $(u,k',-k) \in Y$. V is convex and closed since Y is convex and closed. Consider the subset V^+ of V defined by $v \in V^+$ if $k' \leqslant k$, where $v = (u,k',-k)$. By Assumption III(*b*), $|k| < \zeta$ must hold for $v \in V^+$. Then, by Assumption III(*a*), v is bounded for $v \in V^+$. Since Y is closed, it is easily seen that V^+ is compact. Also by Assumption II, V^+ is not empty. Thus there is a point $v^* \in V^+$ where $v^* = (u^*,k^{*\prime}-k^*)$ and u^* is maximal for $v \in V^+$.

Let us say that k is not saturated, with respect to Y, if there is k' such that $(u,k',-k') \in Y$ and $k' > k$. It is useful to assume with regard to k^*

(IV) k^* is expansible, and not saturated, with respect to Y.

This says that further accumulation can occur from k^* and, moreover, there exist stocks of goods per capita, larger than those which allow maximum utility per capita to be realized, that can be sustained in a process belonging to Y. We may show

Lemma 1. There is a vector $p^* \in E_n$ such that $p^* \geqslant 0$ and, for $(u,k'-k) \in V$,

$$u+p^* \cdot (k'-k) \leqslant \mu$$
$$u^*+p^* \cdot (k^{*\prime}-k^*) = \mu . \tag{1}$$

Moreover, we may choose $\mu = u^*$ and $k^{*\prime} = k^*$.

Proof. v^* is a boundary point of V, since $v^* \in$ int V contradicts the maximality of u^* for v in V^+. Since V is convex, there is a vector $(\pi,p) \in E_{n+1}$ such that $(\pi,p) \neq 0$ and, for $(u,k'-k) \in V$

$$\pi u+p \cdot (k'-k) \leqslant \mu$$
$$\pi u^*+p \cdot (k^{*\prime}-k^*) = \mu , \tag{2}$$

for some number μ. By free disposal, $(\pi,p) \geqslant 0$ holds and $k^{*\prime}$ may be assumed equal to k^*. Then it follows from (2) that $\pi u^* = \mu$. Suppose $\pi = 0$. Since k^* is expansible by Assumption IV, there is $v \in V$ where $v = (u,k'-k^*)$ and $k' > k^*$. For this v, $\pi u+p \cdot (k'-k^*) > \mu$, in violation of (2). Therefore, $\pi > 0$. We may choose $\pi = 1$. Also it is sometimes useful to choose p^* relative interior to the set of p which satisfy (2) with $\pi = 1$.

Let F be the set of $y = (u,k',-k)$ such that $y \in Y$ and

$$u+p^* \cdot k'-p^* \cdot k = u^* . \tag{3}$$

Since the left side of (3) is $<u^*$ for any element y of Y where $y \notin F$, we see that $(1,p^*,p^*)$ is a normal to the convex set Y in the points of F, which include $y^* = (u^*,k^*,-k^*)$. I shall refer to F as the von Neumann facet of Y and y^* as a von Neumann point. y^* may not be unique but the set N of all points $y \in F$ for which $y = (u,k',-k)$ with $k' \geqslant k$ is convex and need not exhaust F. N is the set of all von Neumann points.

I wish to consider paths of capital accumulation departing from an initial stock per capita $k(0)$. We adopt the Atsumi-Koopmans objective of maximizing the sum of per capita utility over the planning period, which in this section is finite, and reach an assigned terminal (final) stock per capita $k^\triangle$. This may be arbitrarily chosen within limits of feasibility.

Equivalently, we will maximize $\sum_{t=1}^{T} \rho^{-t}U(t)$. That is to say, maximizing per capita utility is equivalent to discounting the sum of individual utility at the rate of population increase.

The choice of this objective can be defended in several ways. One way is to assume that each period the existing population is interested only in its own future welfare, but that each type of population grows at the rate ρ and the distribution of income over the types of people remains the same over time. Then if mortality is ignored, discounting at the rate $\rho - 1$ is justified at each moment of decision. The mortality rate would justify a higher discount rate except to the extent that it is compensated by an interest in the welfare of the unborn. That this interest should exactly offset the effects of mortality, however, regardless of the level of ρ, is clearly *ad hoc*.

There is another source of interest in a discount factor equal to the growth factor. This comes from the general theory of maximization in linear production models where the objective is to maximize terminal stocks in pre-assigned proportions. In the case where the desired goods are overproduced in the initial von Neumann equilibrium, and the surplus stocks can grow at the von Neumann growth rate also, the present theory may be applied in the derivation of asymptotic results (see McKenzie, 1967, and Winter, 1965). This is easily interpreted in the present case. The von Neumann growth factor here is ρ, the maximum rate of population growth. Population is produced in the model from population and a subsistence supply of consumption goods. Utility is produced by consumption, but it is not an input to the process of population growth. The population growth rate ρ' is a policy variable to be chosen each period. Then if utility is treated an an input to an activity whose output is ρ times the input of utility, the maximization of the terminal stock of utility,[2] when $\rho' = \rho$, is equivalent to the Atsumi-Koopmans objective, since $\sum_{t=1}^{T} \rho^{T-t+1} U(t) = \rho^{T+1} \sum_{t=1}^{T} \rho^{-t} U(t) = \rho^{T+1} \sum_{t=1}^{T} u(t)$. Moreover, it is known from earlier work that for large T, ρ' will be close to ρ most of the time in a maximal program where U is the only desired terminal stock (McKenzie, 1967). But when ρ' approaches ρ the problem of the present paper arises, and if the assumptions are met, the asymptotic results derived here will apply.

Although this problem can arise in any closed linear model with a terminal objective, it may seem very special that the maximal growth rate ρ_1 for over-produced goods should be exactly equal to ρ in the technology which only uses over-produced goods. However, this is the unique *distinguished* case which does arise. The other possibility is $\rho_1 < \rho$, and then complications do not appear.

Let us define a path of accumulation as a sequence $\{k(t)\}$, such that there is a sequence $\{u(t)\}$, and $(u(t),k(t),-k(t-1)) \in Y$ for each t. I wish to consider paths of accumulation lasting T periods, departing from a given initial stock per capita $k(0)$ and reaching a given terminal stock per capita $k(T)$. Moreover, we will confine our attention to stocks $k(0)$ from which there exists a finite path $\{k(t)\}$, $t = 0, \ldots, \tau$, and $k(\tau)$ is expansible. The existence of a stock $k(\tau)$ is guaranteed by Assumption II. Then there is $(u,k'-k(\tau)) \in V^+$.

In order to conduct our argument we want to show that from any point in Y which allows stocks to expand we can pass by a finite path of accumulation to a von Neumann point of Y. It is convenient to prove

Lemma 2. (Gale.) Suppose $k(0)$ is expansible, and k is sustainable. Then there is an infinite accumulation path $\{k(t)\}$, $t = 0, 1, 2, \ldots$, in which $k(t) \to k$ as $t \to \infty$.

Proof. Since $k(0)$ is expansible there is $y' = (u',k',-k(0)) \in Y$ and $k' > k(0)$. Since k is sustainable there is $y = (u,k,-k) \in Y$. Since Y is a convex set, $\lambda^t y' + (1-\lambda^t)y = y(t) \in Y$ for $0 < \lambda < 1$. Write $y(t) = (u(t), k'(t), -k(t-1))$. Then $k'(t) = \lambda^t k' + (1-\lambda^t)k$ and $k(t) = \lambda^{t+1}k(0) + (1-\lambda^{t+1})k$. We must select λ so that $k(t')-k(t) > 0$. This is equivalent to $k'-k-\lambda(k(0)-k) > 0$, which holds for λ sufficiently near 1. Then it is implied by free disposal that $\{k(t)\}$ is an accumulation path. Since $\lambda(t) \to 0$ in the limit as $t \to \infty$, $k(t) \to k$. We shall need the

Corollary. Suppose $k(0)$ is expansible and k is not saturated. Then, for τ sufficiently large, there is an accumulation path $\{k(t)\}$, $t = 0, \ldots, \tau$, such that $k(\tau) = k$.

Proof. Since k is not saturated, there is $k' > k$ where k' is sustainable. By the Lemma there is a path $\{k(t)\}$, $t = 0, 1, 2, \ldots$, such that $k(t) \to k'$. Then for some τ, $t \geq \tau$ implies $k(\tau) > k$. By free disposal $k(\tau)$ may be set equal to k.

The Corollary to Lemma 2 says that any per capita stock can be reached provided that an even larger stock is sustainable and that the initial stock allows accumulation to begin. Given that these conditions are met by the initial and terminal stocks, we will first prove that when T is sufficiently large, the normalized input-output vector $(u(t),k(t),-k(t-1))$ must stay near F most of the time if the sum of per capita utility is maximized over the path. The Radner theory for closed models of growth can be applied here, as Atsumi has shown, and, indeed, the argument is simpler in the open model. Let $d(F,y) = \min |z-y|$ for $z \in F$.

Lemma 3. (Atsumi) Let $y = (u,k',-k) \in Y$. For any $\epsilon > 0$, there is $\delta > 0$ such that $d(F,y) > \epsilon$ implies $u + p^* \cdot (k'-k) < u^* - \delta$, given $|k| \leq \zeta$.

Proof. If the assertion were false, there would be a sequence $y(s)$ for $s = 1, 2, \ldots$ with $d(F,y(s)) > \epsilon$ for all s and $u(s) + p \cdot (k'(s)-k(s)) \to u^*$. However, $|k(s)| \leq \zeta$ and Assumption III(b) imply that $|k'(s)|$ is bounded. Then, by III(a), $y(s)$ lies in a bounded region for all s. Thus there is a point of accumulation $\bar{y} = (\bar{u},\bar{k}',-\bar{k})$, and $\bar{u} + p^* \cdot (\bar{k}'-\bar{k}) = u^*$, although $d(F,\bar{y}) > \epsilon$. This contradicts (1) and establishes the lemma.

We may now prove an asymptotic result. Let $\{k(t)\}$ be a path of capital accumulation, lasting for T periods, with initial stocks $k(0)$ and terminal stocks (per capita) $k(T)$. We will say that $\{u(t)\}$ is a utility path associated with $\{k(t)\}$ if $(u(t),k(t),-k(t-1)) \in Y$ for all t. We will say that $\{k(t)\}$ is an optimal path from $k(0)$ to $k(T)$ if the per capita utility sum $\sum_{t=1}^{T} u(t) \geq \sum_{t=1}^{T} u'(t)$, where $\{u'(t)\}$ is any utility path associated with any T-period accumulation path $\{k'(t)\}$ leading from $k(0)$ to $k(T)$. Also if $\{k(t)\}$ is an accumulation path and $\{u(t)\}$ is an associated utility path, we will call $\{y(t)\}$ a production path associated with $\{k(t)\}$ if $y(t) = (u(t),k(t),-k(t-1)) \in Y$ for all t.

We may now prove the turnpike theorem.

Theorem 1. Suppose $k(0)$ is expansible and $\bar{k}$ is not saturated. Then, for large T, there is an optimal path $\{\bar{k}(t)\}$, $t = 0, \ldots, T$, leading from $k(0)$ to $k(T) = \bar{k}$. Let $\{\bar{y}(t)\}$ be the associated production path. Then given any $\epsilon > 0$, there is N such that $d(F,\bar{y}(t)) > \epsilon$ holds for not more than N periods.

Proof. By the corollary to Lemma 2 for T large enough a path $\{k(t)\}$ exists from $k(0)$ to $k(T) = \bar{k}$. By Assumption III(b), the set of all T-period paths from $k(0)$ to $\bar{k}$ is bounded. Then from the fact that Y is closed, a T-period path $\{\bar{k}(t)\}$ exists for which the utility sum $\sum_{t=1}^{T} \bar{u}(t)$ is a maximum for all T-period paths from $k(0)$ to $\bar{k}$.

Since, by Assumption IV, k^* is not saturated, there is also an accumulation path lasting N_0 periods, for some $N_0 \geqslant 0$, leading from $k(0)$ to k^*. Moreover, since, by Assumption IV, k^* is expansible, there is an accumulation path lasting N_1 periods, for some $N_1 \geqslant 0$, leading from k^* to $\bar{k}$. Let $T > N_0 + N_1$. Finally, since $(u^*, k^*, -k^*) \in Y$ by the definition of a von Neumann point, from $t = N_0$ to $t = T - N_1$, there is an accumulation path $\{k(t)\}$ where $k(t) = k^*$. Let $\{k(t)\}$, $t = 0, \ldots, T$, where $k(T) = \bar{k}$, represent the combination of those three paths in sequence, and let $\{u(t)\}$ be an associated utility path with $u(t) = u^*$ for $t = N_0$ to $t = T - N_1$.

Let $u' = \sum\limits_{t=1}^{N_0} u(t)$ and $u'' = \sum\limits_{t=T-N_1+1}^{T} u(t)$. Then the utility sum along this 'comparison path' is at least $(T - N_0 - N_1)u^* + u' + u''$. This sum must not exceed $\sum\limits_{t=1}^{T} \bar{u}(t)$ for the optimal path.

On the other hand, it follows directly from (1) that

$$\bar{u}(t) \leqslant u^* - p^* \cdot (\bar{k}(t) - \bar{k}(t-1)).$$

By Lemma 3, when $d(F, \bar{y}(t)) > \varepsilon$ and $|k(t)| < \zeta$, there is $\delta > 0$ such that $\bar{u}(t) \leqslant u^* - p^* \cdot (\bar{k}(t) - \bar{k}(t-1)) - \delta$. This provides a 'valuation ceiling' for the utility sum. However, it is a consequence of Assumption III(b) that $|\bar{k}(t)| < \zeta$ for $t > N_2$ for some $N_2 \geqslant 0$. Thus putting the utility sum between the 'floor' established by the comparison path and the 'valuation ceiling', we obtain

$$(T - N_0 - N_1)u^* + u' + u'' \leqslant \sum_{t=1}^{T} \bar{u}(t) \leqslant Tu^* - \qquad (4)$$
$$- p^* \cdot (\bar{k} - k(0)) - \tau\delta,$$

where $N_2 + \tau$ is the number of periods when $d(F, \bar{y}(t)) > \varepsilon$. This inequality requires

$$\tau \leqslant \delta^{-1}((N_0 + N_1)u^* + p^* \cdot (k(0) - \bar{k}) - u' - u''). \qquad (5)$$

Thus N may be chosen equal to $N_0 + N_1 + N_2 + N_3$ where N_3 is any number larger than the right side of (5).

Corollary. The conclusion of Theorem 1 continues to hold if $k(0)$ and k^* are not necessarily expansible, but finite paths exist leading from $k(0)$ to $k^\triangle$ where $k^\triangle$ is expansible, and from k^* to $k^{\triangle\triangle}$ where $k^{\triangle\triangle}$ is expansible.

III. *Convergence on the von Neumann Facet* [4]

If a stronger result is to be reached than approximation to the von Neumann facet the structure of the facet must be studied. The number of processes $y = (u, k', -k)$ that lie in F and are positively linearly independent can be infinite. However, the maximum number of processes that lie in F and are independent is equal to the dimension of F plus 1. Let the dimension of F be $r-1$, and choose r linearly independent vectors $y(j)$ which lie in F. Define

$$A = [k(1) \ldots k(r)], \qquad B = \begin{bmatrix} u(1) & \ldots & u(r) \\ k'(1) & \ldots & k'(r) \end{bmatrix}.$$

Then for any $y \in F$, we may write

$$y = \begin{bmatrix} B \\ -A \end{bmatrix} x, \; x \in E_r, \; \sum_{j=1}^{r} x_j = 1 . \tag{6}$$

The x_j are allowed to be any real numbers.

We shall say that a production path $\{y(t)\}$, $t = 1, \ldots, T$, lies on F if $y(t) \in F$ for these t. Let

$$\bar{A} = \begin{bmatrix} k(1) & \ldots & k(r) \\ 1 & \ldots & 1 \end{bmatrix}, \qquad \bar{B} = \begin{bmatrix} k'(1) & \ldots & k'(r) \\ 1 & \ldots & 1 \end{bmatrix}.$$

Then the necessary condition (6) for $y \in F$, implies that the sequence $\{x(t)\}$, $t = 1, \ldots, T$, corresponding to $\{y(t)\}$ on F, satisfies

$$\bar{A}x(t+1) = \bar{B}x(t) . \tag{6'}$$

From the definition of F we know there is at least one solution of (6'), $x(t) = x^* \geqslant 0$, for all t. Moreover, there is such a solution where $y^* = \begin{bmatrix} B \\ -A \end{bmatrix} x^*$ lies in the relative interior of F. Otherwise, F would not be minimal.[5] However, the fact that F is minimal follows from the choice of p^* to lie in the relative interior of the set of p such that $(1, p)$ satisfies (2).

Let $X = \left\{ x \mid y = \begin{bmatrix} B \\ -A \end{bmatrix} x, \sum_{j=1}^{r} x_j = 1, \text{ and } y \in F \right\}$. Then $x^* \in \text{int } X$, the interior of X. Necessary and sufficient conditions for a production path $\{y(t)\}$, corresponding to an accumulation path $\{k(t)\}$, to lie on F are (6') and $x(t) \in X$ in each period. X is a convex set by the convexity of F.

Since $x^* \in \text{int } X$, if x is another constant solution of (6'), for small α, $x' = x^* + \alpha x$ will also lie in X and define a path $\{y(t)\}$ on F, which is constant. Indeed, if $\{x(t)\}$ is any cyclic solution of (6'), not necessarily constant, it may be combined with x^* to give another solution of (6') which lies in X and generates a path on F. These paths lie on F for arbitrarily large t, if α is chosen small enough.

In order to characterize all paths on F, it is necessary to examine the general solution of (6'). This can be done by examining the canonical form of the (possibly singular) pencil of matrices $\bar{B} - \lambda\bar{A}$. (This theory may be found in Gantmacher (1959).) The canonical form is reached by pre-multiplying and post-multiplying $\bar{A}$ and $\bar{B}$ by nonsingular real matrices P and Q of orders $n+1$ and r respectively. This amounts to defining new composite goods and new activities in a way to simplify as far as possible the relation of $\bar{A}$ and $\bar{B}$ as linear transformations. The composite goods and activities use negative as well as positive weights. However, they often may be interpreted as variations of the quantities of goods and activities from positive levels.

We will say that a matrix L is a diagonal block of a matrix C if L is a submatrix of C and all elements of C that lie outside L and in a row or a column that contributes to L are zero. The canonical matrix for $\bar{B} - \lambda\bar{A}$ may have diagonal blocks:

$$L_1, \ldots, L_p; \quad L'_1, \ldots, L'_q; \quad N_1, \ldots, N_s; \quad J - \lambda I .$$

Also, if needed, 0 columns and rows must be added, to bring the order of the block diagonal matrix up to that of $\bar{B} - \lambda\bar{A}$, which is $(n+1, r)$. Each submatrix L_i has the form

$$L_i = \begin{bmatrix} 1 & -\lambda & & & 0 \\ & 1 & -\lambda & & \\ & & \ddots & \ddots & \\ & & & \ddots & \ddots \\ 0 & & & 1 & -\lambda \end{bmatrix} .$$

Its order is $(\varepsilon_i, \varepsilon_i + 1)$. Each submatrix L'_i has the form

$$L'_i = \begin{bmatrix} -\lambda & & & 0 \\ 1 & -\lambda & & \\ & 1 & \ddots & \\ & & \ddots & -\lambda \\ 0 & & & 1 \end{bmatrix} .$$

Its order is $(\eta_i + 1, \eta_i)$. Each submatrix N_i has the form

$$N_i = \begin{bmatrix} 1 & -\lambda & & & 0 \\ & 1 & -\lambda & & \\ & & \cdot & \cdot & \\ & & & \cdot & \cdot \\ & & & & \cdot & -\lambda \\ 0 & & & & & 1 \end{bmatrix}.$$

Its order is (u_i, u_i). Finally, $J - \lambda I$ is a rational canonical form minus λ times the identity matrix of the same order.

Write $\bar{B}_1 - \lambda \bar{A}_1 = C_1$ for the canonical form of $\bar{B} - \lambda \bar{A}$. $\bar{A}$ and $\bar{B}$ multiplying elements of E_r on the right define linear transformations from E_r to E_{n+1}. The zero columns of C_1 correspond to the common right null spaces of $\bar{A}$ and $\bar{B}$. However, since the columns of $\begin{bmatrix} \bar{B} \\ -\bar{A} \end{bmatrix}$ are linearly independent, the right null space of $\begin{bmatrix} \bar{B} \\ -\bar{A} \end{bmatrix}$ cannot have dimension exceeding 1, and this is the same subspace as the common right null space of $\bar{A}$ and $\bar{B}$. In this subspace of E_r the solution of (6′) is completely arbitrary, but no difference is made to the corresponding capital stock vectors k and k'. Then we see from (3) that the utility produced is not affected either.

The L_i arise from disjoint null spaces of $\bar{A}$ and $\bar{B}$ in E_r. There is a one dimensional subspace of each of these null spaces associated with a submatrix L_i. The 1 in the upper left corner of L_i represents a variation of output which needs no variation of input. Then the following columns represent the use of the preceding output variation as an input variation to produce a new output variation until finally the $-\lambda$ in the lower right hand corner represents the absorption of the last input variation without producing a further output variation. Thus ε_i is the number of transformations before the initial effect is entirely cancelled. Each submatrix L_i may give rise to a transient modification of a solution of (6′), which affects x and k and may affect u as well. By starting such transients in each period at appropriate levels a solution may be constructed that grows at an arbitrary rate, in particular at the rate 1 of the solution x^*. However, (1) implies that the utility accruing along the new constant path is again u^*.

Multiplying elements of E_{n+1} on the left, $\bar{A}$ and $\bar{B}$ also define linear transformations from E_{n+1} to E_r. The submatrices L_i' arise from disjoint left null spaces (in E_{n+1}) in the same way that the L_i arise from disjoint right null spaces (in E_r). However, the submatrices L'_i generate transient solutions of $(6')$ that depend on an initial input variation and cannot be continued beyond η_i periods, since the final output variation is not usable. Similarly, the submatrices N_i arise from null spaces of $\bar{A}$ to which no null spaces of $\bar{B}$ correspond. In this case, as for the L_i, an output variation occurs with no input variation. But, as for the L'_i, the final output variation cannot be absorbed, so the solution cannot be continued beyond the first u_i periods.

Finally, the submatrix $J - \lambda I$ corresponds to a subspace in which $\bar{A}$ is non-singular. In this subspace the solutions of $(6')$ may be expressed in terms of the characteristic roots of J and associated characteristic vectors by classical formulas. In the case of real roots the characteristic roots are diagonal elements of J, and among the real roots is the root 1 for which $Q^{-1}x^*$ may serve as a characteristic vector.

The solutions of $(6')$ may be expressed in terms of the columns of Q and P^{-1}. First, note that $\bar{A}x(t+1) = \bar{B}x(t)$ is equivalent to

$$P^{-1}\bar{A}_1 Q^{-1} x(t+1) = P^{-1}\bar{B}_1 Q^{-1} x(t).$$

Since Q is non-singular and its order is (r,r), its columns span E_r. Thus any sequence in $x(t)$ can be expressed by means of a sequence of linear combinations of the columns $q(j)$ of Q. But $Q^{-1}q(j)$ is a vector with its jth component equal to 1 and all other components 0. Thus $\bar{A}_1 Q^{-1}q(j)$ is equal to the jth column of $\bar{A}_1$ and $\bar{B}_1 Q^{-1}q(j)$ is equal to the jth column of $\bar{B}_1$. These columns have only one non-zero component if they intersect the blocks L_i, L'_i or N_i and no more than two non-zero entries in other cases. However, a sequence $\{x(t)\}$ is already a solution if it satisfies $\bar{A}_1 Q^{-1} x(t+1) = \bar{B}_1 Q^{-1} x(t)$. The multiplication of this equation by P^{-1} will give the variation in capital stocks generated by the solution. In the simplest cases this variation is a column of P^{-1}. In the general case it is a linear combination of columns of P^{-1}, which can express any arbitrary variation of stocks, since the order of P^{-1} is $(n+1, n+1)$ and its columns span E_{n+1}.

For illustration consider a simple L block,

$$L = \begin{bmatrix} 1 & -\lambda & 0 \\ 0 & 1 & -\lambda \end{bmatrix}.$$

Let $q(1)$, $q(2)$, $q(3)$ be the columns of Q with the same indices as the columns of C_1 that intersect L. Then $x(t) = 0$, $t < \tau$, $x(\tau) = q(1)$,

$x(\tau+1) = q(2)$, $x(\tau+2) = q(3)$, $x(t) = 0$, $t > \tau+2$, is a solution of (6'). In the subspace of E_r on which this L block operates

$$Q^{-1}q(1) = \begin{pmatrix} 1 \\ 0 \\ 0 \end{pmatrix}, Q^{-1}q(2) = \begin{pmatrix} 0 \\ 1 \\ 0 \end{pmatrix}, \text{ and } Q^{-1}q(3) = \begin{pmatrix} 0 \\ 0 \\ 1 \end{pmatrix}.$$

Then

$$\begin{pmatrix} 0 \\ 0 \end{pmatrix} = \bar{A}_1 Q^{-1}q(1) = \bar{B}_1 Q^{-1}\begin{pmatrix} 0 \\ 0 \end{pmatrix}$$

$$\begin{pmatrix} 1 \\ 0 \end{pmatrix} = \bar{A}_1 Q^{-1}q(2) = \bar{B}_1 Q^{-1}q(1)$$

$$\begin{pmatrix} 0 \\ 1 \end{pmatrix} = \bar{A}_1 Q^{-1}q(3) = \bar{B}_1 Q^{-1}q(2)$$

$$\begin{pmatrix} 0 \\ 0 \end{pmatrix} = \bar{A}_1 Q^{-1}\begin{pmatrix} 0 \\ 0 \end{pmatrix} = \bar{B}_1 Q^{-1}q(3).$$

The corresponding variations in capital stocks are $P^{-1}\begin{pmatrix} 1 \\ 0 \end{pmatrix} = p(1)$, $P^{-1}\begin{pmatrix} 0 \\ 1 \end{pmatrix} = p(2)$. Here $\begin{pmatrix} 1 \\ 0 \end{pmatrix}$ and $\begin{pmatrix} 0 \\ 1 \end{pmatrix}$ represent vectors in E_{n+1} whose

other components are all equal to 0. The explicit components correspond to the rows of C_1 which intersect L. Suppose a solution of this type that lasts three periods is started up in every period. Then after the first three periods a constant solution $x(t) = q(1)+q(2)+q(3)$ is obtained for all subsequent time. The corresponding variation of capital stock is

$$\begin{pmatrix} k(t) \\ 0 \end{pmatrix} = p(1)+p(2).$$

Since (6') implies that $\sum_{i=1}^{r} x_i(t)$ is constant, it follows that $\sum_{i=1}^{r} q_i(j) = 0$

for $j = 0, 1, 2$, and $p_{n+1}(j) = 0, j = 1, 2$.
   A simple example for an L' block is

$$L' = \begin{bmatrix} -\lambda & 0 \\ 1 & -\lambda \\ 0 & 1 \end{bmatrix}.$$

Using a notation like that in the preceding example, there is a solution in the form $x(\tau) = q(1)$, $x(\tau+1) = q(2)$, but it cannot be continued beyond $x(\tau+1)$, and it requires an initial investment of stocks to begin. In detail,

$$Q^{-1}q(1) = \begin{pmatrix} 1 \\ 0 \end{pmatrix} \text{ and } Q^{-1}q(2) = \begin{pmatrix} 0 \\ 1 \end{pmatrix}, \text{ and}$$

$$\begin{pmatrix} 1 \\ 0 \\ 0 \end{pmatrix} = \bar{A}_1 Q^{-1}q(1)$$

$$\begin{pmatrix} 0 \\ 1 \\ 0 \end{pmatrix} = \bar{A}_1 Q^{-1}q(2) = \bar{B}_1 Q^{-1}q(1)$$

$$\begin{pmatrix} 0 \\ 0 \\ 1 \end{pmatrix} = \bar{B}_1 Q^{-1}q(2).$$

The initial input is $P^{-1}\begin{pmatrix} 1 \\ 0 \\ 0 \end{pmatrix} = p(1)$. Then $P^{-1}\begin{pmatrix} 0 \\ 1 \\ 0 \end{pmatrix} = p(2)$ is produced

and used, but $P^{-1}\begin{pmatrix} 0 \\ 0 \\ 1 \end{pmatrix} = p(3)$ and $p(3)$ cannot be used on F.

An example for an N block is

$$N = \begin{bmatrix} 1 & -\lambda \\ 0 & 1 \end{bmatrix}.$$

There is a solution in the form $x(t) = 0$, $t < \tau$, $x(\tau) = q(1)$, $x(\tau+1) = q(2)$, but it cannot be continued beyond $x(\tau+1)$. In detail,

$$Q^{-1}q(1) = \begin{pmatrix} 1 \\ 0 \end{pmatrix}, \quad Q^{-1}q(2) = \begin{pmatrix} 0 \\ 1 \end{pmatrix}, \text{ and}$$

$$\begin{pmatrix} 0 \\ 0 \end{pmatrix} = \bar{A}_1 Q^{-1}q(1) = \bar{B}_1 Q^{-1}\begin{pmatrix} 0 \\ 0 \end{pmatrix}$$

$$\begin{pmatrix} 1 \\ 0 \end{pmatrix} = \bar{A}_1 Q^{-1}q(2) = \bar{B}_1 Q^{-1}q(1)$$

$$\begin{pmatrix} 0 \\ 1 \end{pmatrix} = \bar{B}_1 Q^{-1}q(2).$$

The initial output is $P^{-1}\begin{pmatrix} 1 \\ 0 \end{pmatrix} = p(1)$. This is used to produce $P^{-1}\begin{pmatrix} 0 \\ 1 \end{pmatrix} =$

$p(2)$ which is not usable on F.

The block $J - \lambda I$ presents no special problem unless there is a zero characteristic root. This gives rise to a block that, in a simple case, takes the form

$$D = \begin{bmatrix} -\lambda & 0 \\ 1 & -\lambda \end{bmatrix}.$$

This is like an L' block with the last row missing; that is, no final output is produced. As in the case of an L' block an initial input is needed. A solution has the form $x(\tau) = q(1)$, $x(\tau+1) = q(2)$, $x(t) = 0$, for $t > \tau + 1$. In detail

$$\begin{pmatrix} 1 \\ 0 \end{pmatrix} = \bar{A}_1 Q^{-1} q(1)$$

$$\begin{pmatrix} 0 \\ 1 \end{pmatrix} = \bar{A}_1 Q^{-1} q(2) = \bar{B}_1 Q^{-1} q(1)$$

$$\begin{pmatrix} 0 \\ 0 \end{pmatrix} = \bar{A}_1 Q^{-1} \begin{pmatrix} 0 \\ 0 \end{pmatrix} = \bar{B}_1 Q^{-1} q(2).$$

The initial input variation is $P^{-1} \begin{pmatrix} 1 \\ 0 \end{pmatrix} = p(1)$. This is used to produce a variation $P^{-1} \begin{pmatrix} 0 \\ 1 \end{pmatrix} = p(2)$ that is absorbed with no variation in output.

We find then that the only parts of the solution of (6') which can influence the asymptotic results are those which arise from a zero column of C_1 or from the quasidiagonal blocks L_t and $J - \lambda I$. If a zero column is present, let it be the first column of C_1. Let $q(1)$ be the first column of Q, where $P(\bar{B} - \lambda \bar{A})Q = \bar{B}_1 - \lambda \bar{A}_1$. Then $x(0,t) = \alpha_t q(1)$ is a solution of (6') for any sequence of real numbers α_t. Let $q(i,0), \ldots, q(i,\varepsilon_i)$ be the columns of Q corresponding to L_t. Then $\alpha_{it} q(i,0) + \ldots + \alpha_{it-\varepsilon_i} q(i,\varepsilon_i) = x(i,t)$ is a solution where the α_{it} are arbitrary real numbers for all t. Whereas $\bar{A}q(1) = \bar{B}q(1) = 0$, $\bar{A}q(i,1) = \bar{B}q(i,0) = p(i,1)$ where $p(i,1)$ is an appropriate column of P^{-1}. Thus the solution $x(i,t)$ has an effect on the capital stock vector k. Moreover, if $\alpha_{it} = 1$ for all $t \geqslant 0$, the resulting solution $x^\triangle(i,t)$ is constant for $t > \varepsilon_i$ and $x^* + \alpha x^\triangle(i,t)$ is a constant solution of (6') for these t and lies in X for all sufficiently small α. Since (1) implies that all constant paths of F have $u(t) = u^*$, $u^\triangle(i,t) = 0$.

The final block $J - \lambda I$ gives rise to the type of solutions recognized in the theory of systems of ordinary difference equations of the first order.

24

J is further decomposed into blocks J_{ij}, which take two forms. If λ_j is real, the associated blocks are

$$J_{ij} = \begin{bmatrix} \lambda_j & & & 0 \\ 1 & \cdot & & \\ & \cdot & \cdot & \\ & & \cdot & \cdot \\ 0 & & 1 & \lambda_j \end{bmatrix}.$$

If λ_j is complex, its complex conjugate $\bar{\lambda}_j$ is also a root, and associated with the pair $\lambda_j, \bar{\lambda}_j$ there are blocks

$$J_{ij} = \begin{bmatrix} 0 & 1 & 0 & & & \\ -|\lambda_j|^2\,2R(\lambda_j) & 1 & & 0 & & \\ 0 & 0 & 1 & & & \\ & & -|\lambda_j|^2\,2R(\lambda_j) & 0 & 1 & 0 \\ & & & \cdot & & \cdot \\ & 0 & & & \cdot & \cdot \\ & & & & \cdot & \cdot \\ & & & & & -|\lambda_j|^2\,2R(\lambda_j) \end{bmatrix}$$

J has zero elements outside these blocks. The order of J_{ij} is $(\delta_{ij}, \delta_{ij})$. $R(\lambda_j)$ is the real part of λ_j and $|\lambda_j|$ is the absolute value. If $\bar{A}_J$ and $\bar{B}_J$ are matrices which represent the linear transformations $\bar{A}$ and $\bar{B}$ on the subspace corresponding to $J - \lambda I$, the λ_j, and their complex conjugates, are the characteristic roots of $|\bar{A}_J^{-1}\bar{B}_J|$.

For each block J_{ij}, where $\lambda_j \neq 0$, there is a solution of $(6')$ of the form

$$x(i,j,t) = \sum_{s=1}^{\delta_{ij}} q(i,j,s)(J_{ij}^t a)_s,$$

where a is a vector of dimension δ_{ij} of arbitrary constants a_s and the $q(i,j,s)$ are the columns of Q corresponding to the columns of the J_{ij} block. To derive this result, note that if $x(t)$ is a solution, then $x(t) = Qz(t)$ where $\bar{A}_1 z(t) = \bar{B}_1 z(t-1)$. But, for the subspace of E, on which J_{ij} operates, this last equation is equivalent to $z_{ij}(t) = J_{ij} z_{ij}(t-1)$, where $z_{ij}(t)$ is the part of $z(t)$ that corresponds to the columns of the J_{ij} block. Then $z_{ij}(t) = J_{ij}^t z_{ij}(0)$. Put $a = z_{ij}(0)$ to obtain the formula.

If $a \neq 0$, the expression in parentheses goes to 0 with increasing t if $|\lambda_j| < 1$, and is unbounded with increasing t if $|\lambda_j| > 1$. Since Q is nonsingular, the same behavior holds true for the corresponding solutions $x(i,j,t)$. The associated vector of capital stocks is also unbounded, since the final component of the solution vector is constant by $(6')$. However.

by Assumption III(b), $|k(t)| \geqslant \zeta$ implies $|k(t+1)| < \gamma |k(t)|$, $\gamma < 1$. Thus ζ is eventually a bound on $|k(t)|$, and this implies that the weight of any component $x(i,j,t)$ for $|\lambda_j| > 1$ must be small in a solution of (6') which describes a path of accumulation lying on F for a large number of periods.

The only remaining solutions arising from $J + \lambda I$ are those solutions $x(i,j,t)$ for which $|\lambda_j| = 1$ or $\lambda_j = 0$. In the case $\lambda_j = 0$ no output is produced after δ_{ij} periods. Thus components arising from these blocks have no effect on solutions for $t > \delta_{ij}$. The solutions for $|\lambda_j| = 1$ are cyclic, and not constant except for those associated with $\lambda_j = 1$, among which is x^*. Let $x(j,t)$ be a real solution belonging to λ_j and $\bar{\lambda}_j$ for $|\lambda_j| = 1$. Then it follows from $x^* \in$ int X that for sufficiently small α, $x^* + \alpha x(j,t)$, will also lie in X for all t with $1 \leqslant t \leqslant T$, however large T may be. Since (6') implies $\sum_i x_i(j,t) = \sum_i x_i(j,t+1)$, it follows that $\lambda_j \neq 1$ implies

$$\sum_i x_i(j,t) = 0$$

for all t. Let E^* be the subspace of the space E_r which is spanned by those columns of Q which are associated with a zero column of C_1, the quasi-diagonal blocks L_i, and the diagonal blocks J_{ij} for $|\lambda_j| = 1$. Let $X^* = X \cap E^*$. Finally, let $W = \left\{ y \,\middle|\, \begin{bmatrix} B \\ -A \end{bmatrix} x = y \text{ for } x \in X^* \right\}$. We may prove

Lemma 4. Let $\{x(t)\}$, $t = 1, \ldots, T$, be a sequence of vectors in E_r that satisfy equation (6') and the condition $\sum_{i=1}^{r} x_i(t) = 1$. Assume for the corresponding sequence $\{k(t)\}$ that $|k(t)| \leqslant \zeta$ and

$$y(t) = (u(t),k(t),-k(t-1)) = \begin{bmatrix} B \\ -A \end{bmatrix} x(t).$$

Then for any $\varepsilon > 0$, there is $N > 0$ such that $d(y(t),W) < \varepsilon$ for all t with $N < t < T - N$. N is independent of T.

Proof. Let S_1 be the subspace of E_r which is spanned by the columns of Q that are associated with those J_{ij} whose λ_j have $|\lambda_j| > 1$. Let Q_1 be the submatrix of Q formed of these columns. Define S_2 in the analogous way for $|\lambda_j| < 1$. It is implied by the preceding analysis of (6') that after r periods $x(t)$ will be in the vector sum of S_1, S_2, and E^*. Let J_1 and I_1 be matrices representing the transformations $\bar{B}$ and $\bar{A}$ on S_1, and J_2 and I_2

similarly for S_2. Then with respect to the projection $x_1(t)$ of $x(t)$ on S_1, (6′) may be written

$$x_1(t) = Q_1 z(t)$$
$$z(t+1) = J_1 z(t),$$

where all the characteristic roots of J_1 have absolute value less than 1. Then $J_1^t \to 0$ as $t \to \infty$. This implies that N_1 exists such that $|x_1(0)| < \zeta$ and $t > N_1$ implies $|x_1(t)| < \frac{1}{2}\varepsilon$. In the same way $|x_2(T)| < \zeta$ implies there is N_2 such that $|x_2(t)| < \frac{1}{2}\varepsilon$ for $t < T-N_2$. Therefore, N may be chosen to be the maximum of r, N_1, and N_2.

Since the equality in (1) is realized for any path $\{y(t)\}$ which lies on F, and $\mu = u^*$, we have, for $y(t) = (u(t), k(t), -k(t-1))$,

$$\sum_{t=1}^{s} u(t) + p \cdot k(s) - p \cdot k(0) = su^*. \tag{7}$$

Suppose $\{y(t)\}$ is generated according to (6) by a sequence of activity vectors $\{x(t)\}$ in the interior of X. Consider a modified sequence defined by $x'(t) = x(t) + \alpha q(i,t)$ for $t = 0, \ldots, \varepsilon_i$, $x'(t) = x(t)$, otherwise, where $q(i,0), \ldots, q(i,\varepsilon_i)$ are the columns of Q corresponding to the quasi-diagonal block L_i. As we have seen, for small α, $x'(t) \in$ int X and generates a path on F, since $\bar{A}q(i,0) = 0$, $\bar{B}q(i,0) = \bar{A}q(i,1), \ldots, \bar{B}q(i,\varepsilon_i-1) = \bar{A}q(i,\varepsilon_i)$, and $\bar{B}q(i,\varepsilon_i) = 0$. Then $k'(0) = k(0)$ and $k'(\varepsilon_i+1') = k(\varepsilon_i+1)$. Moreover, by (7) $\sum_{t=1}^{\varepsilon_i} u(t') + p \cdot k(\varepsilon_i+1) - p \cdot k(0) = \varepsilon_i u^*$, so

$$\sum_{t=1}^{\varepsilon_i} u(t') = \sum_{t=1}^{\varepsilon_i} u(t).$$

The introduction of solutions associated with the L_i makes no difference to the utility sum after the transient fluctuation in capital stocks has passed. Thus maximizing utility in choosing a path on F will not eliminate the arbitrary element due to an L_i block. By the same type of argument it has already been shown that modification of $\{x(t)\}$ by $q(1)$ has no effect on utility, where $q(1)$ spans a common null space of $\bar{A}$ and $\bar{B}$ on E_r. The same considerations indicate that the effects of cyclic modifications of $x(t)$ will cancel out over a full cycle. Thus in the absence of specific initial conditions the result of Lemma 4 is as definite an asymptotic result as we can reach for paths on F.

In order to prove an asymptotic result for arbitrary optimal paths by means of Theorem 1 and Lemma 4, we must show that a path $\{y(t)\}$

which lies near the von Neumann facet F must also lie near a path $\{y'(t)\}$ satisfying the conditions of Lemma 4. We prove

Lemma 5. Let $\{y(t)\}$, $t = 1, \ldots, T$, be a production path in Y.

Let $\{y'(t)\}$ be defined by $y'(t) = \begin{bmatrix} B \\ -A \end{bmatrix} x'(t)$, where $\{x'(t)\}$

satisfies (6') for $t = 1, \ldots, T$. For any $T \geqslant 1$, $\delta > 0$, there is an $\varepsilon > 0$ such that if $d(y(t),F) < \varepsilon$ for all t, then there is a sequence $\{y(t')\}$ where $|y(t) - y(t')| < \delta$ for $t = 1, \ldots, T$.

In the general case, a difficulty arises in proving this lemma that does not occur when $\bar{A}$ and $\bar{B}$ both possess inverses. Thus it would not be possible simply to appeal to the analogous lemma proved for the generalized Leontief model in my former paper (1963). The difficulty is that $\bar{B}x = \bar{A}w$ may have no solution in w for some choices of x. The corresponding formula for the normalized matrices is $\bar{B}_1 Q^{-1} x = \bar{A}_1 Q^{-1} w$. The obstacle to a solution arises when there is a row of $\bar{B}_1$ which contains a non-zero element while the same row of $\bar{A}_1$ is zero throughout. This may happen in two cases. First, it holds for the last row of any L'_i block. Thus if a solution is to exist for w, it is necessary that $(Q^{-1}x)_s = 0$ if the sth column is a last column of an L'_i block. The second case arises for the last row of an N_i block. It is also necessary that $(Q^{-1}x)_s = 0$ if the sth column is the last column of an N_i block.

Proof of Lemma 5. By the fact that $d(y(t),F) < \varepsilon$, $y'(1)$ which satisfies $|y(1) - y'(1)| < \delta$ can be found by putting $\varepsilon = \delta$. Suppose a sequence $\{y'_{\tau-1}(t)\}$ can be found for any δ_1 for $t = 1, \ldots, \tau - 1$, where $\tau - 1 < T$, and $|y(t) - y'_{\tau-1}(t)| < \delta_1$ for each t. To prove the lemma we must show that this implies that a sequence $\{y'_\tau(t)\}$ also exists with $|y(t) - y'_\tau(t)| < \delta$ for $t = 1, \ldots, \tau$. Let $\{y'(t)\}$ be defined for $t = 1, \ldots, \tau - 1$, and choose ε so that $|y(t) - y'(t)| < \delta_1$ for $t < \tau$. Let $y'(\tau - 1) = (u'(\tau + 1), k'(\tau - 1), -k'(\tau - 2))$. Then

$$\begin{pmatrix} k'(\tau - 1) \\ 1 \end{pmatrix} = \bar{B}x'(\tau - 1).$$

Assume $(Q^{-1}x'(\tau - 1))_s = 0$ for all s such that the sth column of $\bar{A}_1 + \lambda\bar{B}_1$ intersects the last $T - \tau + 1$ columns of submatrices L_i or N_i when these columns are present. We will say that such an $x'(\tau - 1)$ is feasible. Then

$P\begin{pmatrix} k'(\tau - 1) \\ 1 \end{pmatrix}$ lies in the subspace spanned by the columns of $\bar{A}_1$. Therefore, there exists $x'(\tau)$ such that $\begin{pmatrix} k'(\tau-1) \\ 1 \end{pmatrix} = P^{-1}\bar{A}_1 Q^{-1} x'(\tau) = \bar{A} x'(\tau)$. We

define $y'(\tau) = \begin{bmatrix} B \\ -A \end{bmatrix} x'(\tau)$.

Assume $d(y(\tau),F) < \varepsilon$. Then there is $y \in F$ for which $|y - y(\tau)| < \varepsilon$ and
$y = \begin{bmatrix} B \\ -A \end{bmatrix} x$. Let $y = (u,k',-k)$ and $y(\tau) = (u(\tau), k(\tau), -k(\tau-1))$.
Then $|k(\tau-1)-k| < \varepsilon$, so $|k'(\tau-1)-k| < \varepsilon + \delta_1$. By the continuity of
the linear transformation defined by A, for $k'(\tau-1)$ near k, we may choose
$x'(\tau)$ near x. In turn this implies $y'(\tau)$ near y, using the definition of $y'(\tau)$.
This shows that ε and δ_1 may be chosen, which is to say, ε may be chosen,
so that $|y'(\tau)-y(\tau)| < \delta$. Notice also that the definition of $x'(\tau)$ implies
that $(Q^{-1}x'(\tau))_s = 0$ for all s such that sth column intersects the last
$T-\tau$ columns of submatrices L_t or N_t, when these columns are present.
Thus if a sequence $\{y'_{t-1}(t)\}$ can be found for any $\delta_1 > 0$ and if $x'(\tau-1)$
is feasible, a sequence $\{y'_t(t)\}$ can be found and $x'(\tau)$ can be chosen to
be feasible. It only remains to show that $x'(1)$ can be chosen to be feasible
for any $T > 0$.

Let $y(t) = (u(t),k(t),-k(t-1))$, $t = 1, \ldots, T$. In the way described
earlier, the proximity of $y(1)$ to F allows the choice of $y = (u,k^\Delta,-k) \in F$
such that k is near $k(0)$ and k^Δ is near $k(1)$, where $\begin{pmatrix} k \\ 1 \end{pmatrix} = \bar{A}x, \begin{pmatrix} k^\Delta \\ 1 \end{pmatrix} = \bar{B}x$.
Then the proximity of $y(2)$ to F allows the choice of $y' = (u',k'^\Delta,-k')$ so
that k' is near $k(1)$, and k'^Δ is near $k(2)$, where $\begin{pmatrix} k' \\ 1 \end{pmatrix} = \bar{A}x'$, and $\begin{pmatrix} k'^\Delta \\ 1 \end{pmatrix} =$
$\bar{B}x'$, and so forth. Although $\begin{pmatrix} k^\Delta \\ 1 \end{pmatrix}$ may not be expressible by $\bar{A}z$ for any z,
$\begin{pmatrix} k' \\ 1 \end{pmatrix}$ is so expressed with $z = x'$. Moreover, k^Δ is near k', since both are
near $k(1)$. Let us refer to an L_t block or an N_t block as an infeasible block.
The components of $w^\Delta = P \begin{pmatrix} k^\Delta \\ 1 \end{pmatrix}$ which correspond to the last rows of infeasible blocks can be made as small as we like through making $(k^\Delta - k(1))$
small. Suppose a component w_i^Δ is large relative to the approximation of
w^Δ to $w(1) = P \begin{pmatrix} k(1) \\ 1 \end{pmatrix}$, where $(\bar{A}_1 z)_i = \delta$ implies $(\bar{B}_1 z)_j = \delta$ and the
jth row of $\bar{A}_1$ is zero. That is, the ith component of w^Δ corresponds to

the next to last row of an infeasible block. Since k^Δ is near k', w^Δ is near w' and $w_j^{\prime\Delta}$ is large relative to the approximation of w'^Δ to $w(2) = P\begin{pmatrix} k(2) \\ 1 \end{pmatrix}$.

But this contradicts $k(2)$ near k'' where $\begin{pmatrix} k'' \\ 1 \end{pmatrix}$ is expressible as $\bar{A}x''$, for some x''. Continuing this argument until $t = T$, if necessary, it must be that by the choice of ε the absolute value of a component of $w = P\begin{pmatrix} k^\Delta \\ 1 \end{pmatrix}$ which corresponds to any of the last $T+1$ rows of an infeasible block can be made as small as desired. These are the only components of w that can lead to a capital stock $k'(T)$ that is not expressible as $Ax'(T)$. We may term them the infeasible components. Not all components of w can be infeasible since w near $w(0)$, w^Δ and w' near $w(1)$, and so forth, would then imply $\left| \begin{pmatrix} k(T) \\ 1 \end{pmatrix} \right|$ could be reduced below 1 by choosing ε small enough. We now choose $\begin{pmatrix} k'(0) \\ 1 \end{pmatrix} = P^{-1}w'(0)$, where $w_i'(0) = w_i$ when the ith component is feasible and $w_i'(0) = 0$, otherwise. Then $x'(1)$ is chosen so that $(Q^{-1}x'(1))_j = 0$ if the jth column intersects one of the last T columns of an infeasible block, and $(Q^{-1}x'(1))_j = (Q^{-1}x)_j$, otherwise. Thus $\begin{pmatrix} k'(0) \\ 1 \end{pmatrix} = P^{-1}A_1Q^{-1}x'(1)$ will hold. Since $x'(1)$ is feasible and $|x(1)-x'(1)|$, and therefore $|y(1)-y'(1)|$, can be made arbitrarily small, the induction is successfully begun. This completes the proof of Lemma 5.

We now have it that optimal paths of accumulation where the technology is given by Y will lie near the von Neumann facet F for all save a certain number N_1 of the total number of periods, given the initial and terminal capital stock vectors, regardless of the length of the path $T \geqslant N_1$. Also a path $\{y(t)\}$ which remains near enough to F for a number of periods T_1 will stay near a sequence $\{y'(t)\}$ of vectors whose associated $x'(t)$ satisfy (6') during these periods. Finally, $\{y'(t)\}$ will stay near the subset W of F for all periods save initial and terminal sequences of length N_2 independent of T_1. This suggests that the production vector associated with an optimal path with assigned initial and terminal stocks can stay outside a given neighbourhood of W for no more than a fixed number of

periods, however long the accumulation path may be. This is the substance
of the second theorem.

   Theorem 2. Let $\bar{y}(t) = (\bar{u}(t),\bar{k}(t),\bar{k}(t-1))$. Suppose that $k(0)$ is
   expansible and $k(T)$ is not saturated. Then for any $\varepsilon > 0$, there is
   N such that if $\{\bar{y}(t)\}$, $t = 1, \ldots, T$, is associated with an optimal path
   $\{\bar{k}(t)\}$ with initial and terminal stocks equal to $k(0)$ and $k(T)$,
   then $d(W,\bar{y}(t)) > \varepsilon$ for not more than N periods. N depends upon ε.

Proof. The proof requires assembling the results of Theorem 1, Lemma 4,
and Lemma 5. We may fix N_1 according to Theorem 1 so that $d(F,\bar{y}(t)) \geqslant \delta$
for no more than N_1 periods, where δ is a positive number which may be
chosen arbitrarily small and N_1 depends on δ. From the proof of Theorem
1 we see that N_1 may be chosen so that during the remaining $T-N_1$
periods, $|\bar{k}(t)| \leqslant \zeta$ also holds.

   By Lemma 5 for any $N_2 \geqslant 0$ and $\varepsilon > 0$ there is a $\delta > 0$ such that
$d(F,\bar{y}(t)) < \delta$ for N_2 (or fewer) consecutive periods ensures that there is

a sequence $\{y'(t)\}$ for these periods where $y'(t) = \begin{bmatrix} B \\ -A \end{bmatrix} x'(t)$ and

$(x'(t),x'(t+1))$ satisfies (6′) for all pairs of immediate successors, and
$|\bar{y}(t)-y'(t)| < \tfrac{1}{2}\varepsilon$ for each t.

   By Lemma 4 for any $\varepsilon > 0$ there is N_3 such that during any consecutive
sequence of periods $d(W,y'(t)) < \tfrac{1}{2}\varepsilon$ for all t except N_3 periods at the
beginning and end of the sequence. Select $N_2 > 2N_3$. Suppose $d(F,y(t)) < \delta$
holds from period t_1 to period t_2. Then $d(W,y'(t)) < \tfrac{1}{2}\varepsilon$ provided that
there is $\tau_1 \geqslant t_1$ and $\tau_2 \leqslant t_2$ and $\tau_1+N_3 < t < \tau_2-N_3$. Thus for such t,
$d(W,y(t)) < \varepsilon$. But appropriate τ_1, τ_2 exist for all t which satisfy $t_1 +N_3 <
t < t_2-N_3$. Consequently $d(W,y(t)) < \varepsilon$ must hold for all periods in a
sequence of periods between times when $d(F,y(t)) \geqslant \delta$ exceptf or $2N_3$
periods in the sequence. But the number of such sequences cannot exceed
N_1+1. Thus an upper bound on the number of periods when $d(W,y(t)) > \varepsilon$
can hold is $2N_3(N_1+1)$. We may take N to be this number. Note that for
any ε an N_3 may be chosen, and for any N_3 an N_2 may be chosen. Then
for N_2 and ε, there is an appropriate δ from which N_1 may be determined.
Thus there is N for any arbitrary $\varepsilon > 0$, and the theorem is proved.

IV. *Efficiency Prices*

In order to prove the existence of infinite optimal paths we must derive
the efficiency prices which are associated with an optimal program

according to the theory of activity analysis. The goal of the program is the maximization of $\sum_{t=1}^{T} u(t)$ given $k(0)$ and $k(T)$, where $y(t) = (u(t),k(t),$ $-k(t-1)) \in Y$.

Let $E(t)$ be an $n+1$ dimensional Euclidean space with a basis whose first component represents a quantity of utility and whose remaining n components represent stocks of goods. For example, $(u,k') \in E(t)$, and $(0,-k) \in E(t)$. Let $E = \prod_{t=0}^{T} E(t)$. E is the Cartesian product of the $E(t)$.

Thus $z = \prod_{t=0}^{T} z(t) \in E$ where $z(t) \in E(t)$ for $t = 0, \ldots, T$. Write

$$z((\tau)) = \prod_{t=0}^{T} z(t)$$

where $z(t) = 0$ for $t \neq \tau$. We may write $z(t) = (z_u(t),z_k(t))$. We will say $y = (u,k',-k) \in Y$ corresponds to $(z(t),z(t-1))$ when $z(t) = (u,k')$ and $z(t-1) = (0,-k)$. Define the intertemporal production set $Y((t)) = \{z((t))+z((t-1)) \,|\, y \in Y \text{ and } y \text{ corresponds to } (z(t),z(t-1))\}$. Let $Y_T = \sum_{t=0}^{T} Y((t))$. Define the feasible set $Z = \{z \in Y_T | z(0) = (0,z_k(0)),$ $z_k(0) \geq -k(0), z_k(t) \geq 0, t = 1, \ldots, T-1, z_k(T) \geq k(T)\}$. Suppose $Z \neq \emptyset$.

We wish to consider a point $\bar{z} \in Z$ such that $\sum_{t=1}^{T} \bar{z}_u(t)$ is maximal over Z.

The existence of such a point is guaranteed if Z is bounded above in $z_u(t)$. However, this is easily seen by use of Assumption III. We also define a preferred set

$$B = \left\{ z \in E \,\Big|\, \sum_{t=1}^{T} z_u(t) > \sum_{t=1}^{T} \bar{z}_u(t), z_k(0) \geq -k(0), z_k(t) \geq 0 \right.$$

$$\left. \text{for } t = 1, \ldots, T-1, z_k(T) \geq k(T) \right\}.$$

Suppose $z' \in Y_T \cap B$. Then by the definitions of B and Z, $z' \in Z$. Moreover $\sum_{t=1}^{T} z'_u(t) > \sum_{t=1}^{T} z_u(t)$, which contradicts the maximality of $\bar{z}$ in Z. Therefore, no such point z' can exist.

Both Y_T and B are convex sets. By the Minkowski separation theorem there is a vector $\bar{q} \in E$ and a real number μ such that $\bar{q} \cdot z > \mu$ for $z \in B$

and $\bar{q} \cdot z \leqslant \mu$ for $z \in Y_T$. Write $\bar{q}(t) = (\bar{q}_u(t), \bar{q}_k(t))$. Since $z_k(t)$ is unbounded above for $z \in B$, it must be that $\bar{q}(t) \geqslant 0$. Let $\bar{B}$ be the closure of B. Since $\bar{z} \in \bar{B} \cap Y_T$, $\bar{q} \cdot \bar{z} = \mu$. Also $\bar{q}_u(t) = \alpha$, a given number, for all t. Otherwise, there would be points $z \in B$ near $\bar{z}$ with $\bar{q} \cdot z < \mu$. We choose $\bar{q}$ and μ so that $\alpha = 1$.

Any $z \in Y_T$ may be expressed $\sum_{t=0}^{T} (z((t)) + z((t-1)))$, where $z((t)) + z((t-1)) \in Y((t))$. Let $\mu(t) = \bar{q}((t)) \cdot \bar{z}((t)) + \bar{q}((t-1)) \cdot \bar{z}((t-1))$. Then $\mu = \sum_{t=0}^{T} \mu(t)$. Also $\bar{q}((t)) \cdot z((t)) + \bar{q}((t-1)) \cdot z((t-1)) \leqslant \mu(t)$ for all $z((t)) + z((t-1)) \in Y((t))$. But $z((t)) + z((t-1)) \in Y((t))$ is equivalent to $y \in Y$ where $y = (u, k', -k)$ and $z(t) = (u, k')$, $z(t-1) = (0, -k)$. Therefore, replacing $\bar{q}_k$ by $\bar{p}$, we have

$$u + \bar{p}(t) \cdot k' - \bar{p}(t-1) \cdot k \leqslant \mu(t)$$

$$\bar{u}(t) + \bar{p}(t) \cdot \bar{k}(t) - \bar{p}(t-1) \cdot \bar{k}(t-1) = \mu(t), \quad t = 1, \ldots, T, \qquad (8)$$

for any $(u, k', -k) \in Y$. In (8) we have taken $\bar{z}(t)_k = 0$, $t = 1, \ldots, T-1$. This is permissible by the assumption of free disposal. Thus we have proved

> **Lemma 6.** Let $\{\bar{y}(t)\}$ be an optimal path of T periods where
> $\bar{y}(t) = (\bar{u}(t), \bar{k}(t), -\bar{k}(t-1))$, $\bar{k}(0) \leqslant k(0)$, and $\bar{k}(T) \geqslant k(T)$. Then
> there exists a sequence of prices of goods $\bar{p}(t)$ and real numbers
> $\mu(t)$ such that (8) is satisfied for all $y = (u, k', -k) \in Y$.

We will refer to $\{\bar{p}(t)\}$ as a sequence of efficiency prices for the optimal sequence $\{\bar{y}(t)\}$.

It is convenient (though not essential) for the subsequent argument to have infinite price sequences for infinite production paths. Consider an infinite production path $\{y(t)\}$, $y(t) = (u(t), k(t), -k(t-1))$, $t = 1, 2, \ldots$, every initial segment of which is an optimal finite path given the terminal stock vector of the segment. By Lemma 6 there is for each initial segment a sequence of efficiency prices which satisfy (8). An infinite path with optimal initial segments will be said to have finite optimality. We may prove

> **Lemma 7.** (Malinvaud, 1953; 1962) Suppose $\{y(t)\}$, $t = 1, 2, \ldots$,
> is a production path that has finite optimality. If the associated
> efficiency prices are bounded over all initial segments, there is a
> price sequence $\{p(t)\}$, $t = 0, 1, \ldots$, whose initial segments are
> efficiency prices for the initial segments of $\{y(t)\}$.

Proof. Let $\{y_T(t)\}$ and $\{p_T(t)\}$ be an initial segment of $\{y(t)\}$ terminating at $y(T)$ and an associated sequence of efficiency prices. There is a sequence $\{\mu_T(t)\}$ associated with $\{p_T(t)\}$ satisfying (8). Moreover, $\mu_T(t)$ is bounded over t and T, since $p_T(t)$ is bounded, and also $y(t)$ is bounded by Assumption III. Consider the sequence $\{p_T(0)\}$, $T = 1, 2, \ldots$. Since $p_T(0)$ is bounded, there is a convergent subsequence $p(0)_{T_i} \to p(0)$, where $i = 1, 2, \ldots$, and $T_{i_1} > T_{i_2}$ for $i_1 > i_2$. Then there is a further subsequence of $\{p_{T_i}(0)\}$ that we may write $\{p_{T_j}(0)\}, j = i_1,$ $i_2, \ldots$, with $p_{T_j}(0) \to p(0), p_{T_j}(1) \to p(1)$, and $\mu_{T_j} \to \mu(1)$. Continuing this procedure we derive infinite sequences $\{p(t)\}, t = 0, 1, \ldots$, and $\{\mu(t)\}$, $t = 1, 2, \ldots$. By continuity these sequences satisfy (8) with $y(t) = (u(t), k(t), -k(t-1))$. Thus the initial segments of $\{p(t)\}$ give efficiency prices for the initial segments of $\{y(t)\}$.

v. *Existence of Optimal Paths*

In a model with a transformation set Y that is not strictly convex it is necessary to weaken the Atsumi-Weizsacker definition of optimality. Let $\{y(t)\}, t = 1, 2, \ldots, y(t) = (u(t), k(t), -k(t-1))$, be an infinite production sequence. We will say that $\{y(t)\}$ is optimal if the following is true: Let $\{y'(t)\}, t = 1, 2, \ldots, y'(t) = (u'(t), k'(t), -k'(t-1))$, be any other production path where $k'(0) = k(0)$. Then for any $\varepsilon > 0$ there is T such that $t > T$ implies $\sum_{t=1}^{T} (u'(t) - u(t)) < \varepsilon$. This weakening does not seem to be significant unless the utility function is merely ordinal. However, the fact that we sum utilities over time implies that the utility function is defined except for an affine transformation, and thus it is not merely ordinal.

Even with the weaker criterion of optimality infinite optimal paths will not always exist in our model. A deep reason for this failure seems to be the fact that some points of W may have 'larger' terminal stocks than others, so that it is worthwhile to go from the point with 'larger' stocks to another. But this may not be possible on F. Then the closer the transition hugs F the better it may be, and the longer it will take. Thus there will be an infinite sequence of paths each better than the last, while the limit path never leaves the initial point and is the worst path of all. Gale has given examples that fit this description. To avoid the difficulty we will assume

(v) The set $W = \{y^*\}$.

In other words, the set W is a unique von Neumann point on F. This means that in the block diagonal canonical form of $\bar{B}-\lambda\bar{A}$ there are no L blocks and no blocks $J_{ij}+\lambda I$ where $|\lambda_j| = 1$ and $\lambda_j \neq 1$. Moreover, 1 is a simple root of $\bar{A}_J^{-1}\bar{B}_J$. Then $\bar{A}_J^{-1}\bar{B}_J$ is a Frobenius matrix by the definition of Uzawa (1961).

In order to use Lemma 7, it will be necessary to bound the efficiency prices associated with any infinite production sequence whose initial segments are optimal. This will require a slightly stronger version of Assumption IV. Let us say that k is a subsistence stock if there is $(u,k', -k) \in Y$ and there is no $(u',k'', -\alpha k) \in Y$ for $\alpha < 1$. The revised assumption is

(IV') With respect to the transformation set Y, k^* is expansible, not saturated, and not a subsistence stock.

In addition to IV' we will need a direct corollary of Theorem 2,

Lemma 8. Any infinite path which is finitely optimal converges to W. *Proof.* Suppose $\{y(t)\}$, $t = 1, 2, \ldots$, is finitely optimal and does not converge to W. Then there is $\varepsilon > 0$ and $d(y(t),W) > \varepsilon$ for $t = t_1, t_2, \ldots$, where the t_i are all distinct. But by Theorem 2, there is N such that $d(y(t),W) > \varepsilon$ for no more than N periods for a finite optimal path $\{y(t)\}, t = 1, 2, \ldots, T$. If $T > t_N$, there is a contradiction, so $d(y(t),W) \to 0$ as the lemma asserts.

As a consequence of Lemma 8, it is sufficient to bound the efficiency prices in some neighborhood of W, that is, in view of Assumption V, in some neighborhood of y^*. This is proved in

Lemma 9. There are $\eta > 0$ and $\bar{p} \geqslant 0$ such that $d(y^*,\bar{y}) < \eta$, $\bar{y} \varepsilon Y$, $\bar{y} = (\bar{u},\bar{k}', -\bar{k})$, and

$$u' + p' \cdot k' - p \cdot k \leqslant \mu$$
$$\bar{u} + p' \cdot \bar{k}' - p \cdot \bar{k} = \mu, \text{ for all } (u',k',-k) \varepsilon Y, \qquad (8')$$

imply $p' < \bar{p}$.

Proof. Suppose the lemma is false. Then there is a sequence

$$(p'(s),p(s),\mu(s)), \quad s = 1, 2, \ldots,$$

that satisfies (8') with $\bar{y}$ replaced by $y(s) = (u(s),k'(s),-k(s))$ where $y(s) \to y^*$ and $|p'(s)| \to \infty$. But by Assumption IV' there is a point $y^\Delta \varepsilon Y$ where $y^\Delta = (u^\Delta,k^\Delta,-k^*)$ and $k^\Delta > k^*$. Then $u^\Delta + p'(s)\cdot k^\Delta - p(s)\cdot k^* \leqslant \mu(s)$ must hold. Let $q(s) = (1,p'(s),p(s),\mu(s))$ and

$$q^\Delta(s) = q(s)/|q(s)|.$$

There is a subsequence $\{q^\Delta(r)\}$, $r = s_1, s_2, \ldots$, of $\{q^\Delta(s)\}$, such that

$q^\triangle(r) \to q^\triangle = (q_u^\triangle, q_k'^\triangle, q_k^\triangle, \mu^\triangle)$. But $q^\triangle$ satisfies (8′) when $\bar{y}$ is replaced by the limit y^* of the sequence $\{y(s)\}$, or

$$q_u^\triangle u^\triangle + q_k'^\triangle \cdot k^\triangle - q_k^\triangle \cdot k^* \leqslant \mu^\triangle$$

$$q_u^\triangle u^* + q_k'^\triangle \cdot k^* - q_k^\triangle \cdot k^* = \mu^\triangle .$$

Subtracting the second of these relations from the first, we obtain $q_u^\triangle(u^\triangle - u^*) + q_k'^\triangle \cdot (k^\triangle - k^*) \leqslant 0$. If $|q^\triangle(s)|$ is unbounded, $q_u^\triangle = 0$, $q_k'^\triangle \cdot (k^\triangle - k^*) \leqslant 0$. Since $q_k'^\triangle \geqslant 0$ and $(k^\triangle - k^*) > 0$, this implies that $q_k'^\triangle = 0$, and $q_k^\triangle \cdot k^* + \mu^\triangle = 0$. Then $q_k^\triangle \cdot k \geqslant q_k^\triangle \cdot k^* > 0$ must hold for all $k \geqslant 0$, where $(u, k', k) \in Y$. However, by Assumption IV′ there is $(u, k, \alpha k^*) \in Y$ where $\alpha < 1$. This is a contradiction, since $q_k^\triangle \cdot \alpha k^* < q_k^\triangle \cdot k^*$. Thus $q(s)$ is bounded, which implies that $p'(s)$ is bounded and the lemma follows.

The final preparation needed for the proof that an infinite optimal path exists is to show that an infinite path exists that is finitely optimal.

Lemma 10. Assume that $k(0)$ is expansible. There is a path $\{y(t)\}$, $t = 1, 2, \ldots$, where $y(t) = (u(t), k(t), -k(t-1))$ and every initial segment of $\{y(t)\}$ is optimal.

Proof. Let $\{k(T)\}$, $T = 0, 1, \ldots$, be a sequence of stock vectors where $k(T) \to k^*$. According to Lemma 2, $\{k(T)\}$ may be chosen so that there exists a production path $\{y_T(t)\}$, $t = 1, \ldots, T$, for every $T \geqslant 1$ and $y_T(1) = (u(1), k(1), -k(0))$, $y_T(T) = (u(T), k(T), -k(T-1))$. Then by closure of Y, there is an optimal path of T periods between $k(0)$ and $k(T)$ for every $T \geqslant 1$. Since $\{y_T(0)\}$, $T = 1, 2, \ldots$, is bounded by Assumption III, there is a convergent subsequence $\{y_{T_s}(0)\}$, $s = 1, 2, \ldots$, say $y_{T_s}(0) \to \bar{y}(0)$. Then a subsequence of this sequence $\{y_{T_r}(0)\}$ may be chosen such that $y_{T_r}(1) \to \bar{y}(1)$. Continuing this selection, we may derive a sequence $\{\bar{y}(t)\}$, $t = 1, 2, \ldots$, where $\bar{y}(t) = (\bar{u}(t), \bar{k}(t), -\bar{k}(t-1))$ and $\bar{y}(t) \in Y$ for all t by closure of Y. Moreover, $\{\bar{y}(t)\}$, $t = 1, \ldots, T$ is the limit of a sequence of optimal T periods paths. Thus by closure of Y it is an optimal T period path, given the terminal stock $\bar{y}(T)$. The sequence $\{\bar{y}(t)\}$, $t = 1, 2, \ldots$, satisfies the conditions of the lemma.

We are now ready to prove the existence of an optimal path by the method of Gale.

Theorem 3. Under Assumptions I, II, III, IV′, and V, if $k(0)$ is expansible, there is an infinite optimal path $\{\bar{y}(t)\}$,

$$\bar{y}(t) = (\bar{u}(t), \bar{k}(t), -\bar{k}(t-1)) \in Y, \quad \bar{k}(0) \leqslant k(0) .$$

Proof. We will show that a path $\{\bar{y}(t)\}$ that satisfies Lemma 10 is optimal. Let $\{y(t)\}$, $t = 1, 2, \ldots$, where $y(t) = (u(t), k(t), -k(t-1))$, be any other path in Y. By the proof of Theorem 2, if $d(y(t), y^*) > \varepsilon > 0$ for an infinite number of periods, $\sum_{t=1}^{T}(u(t)-u^*) \to -\infty$, as $T \to \infty$. On the other hand, Theorem 2 implies $\bar{y}(t) \to y^*$. Also, (4) implies that

$$\sum_{t=1}^{T}(\bar{u}(t) - u^*) \geqslant u' + u'' - (N_0 + N_1)u^*.$$

In this formula u' and N_0 are fixed independently of T. Let u be derived from $y' = (u, k', -k^*) \in Y$ where $k' > k^*. y'$ exists by Assumption IV. Then for sufficiently large T, the convergence of $\bar{y}(t)$ to y^* will give $k' > \bar{k}(T)$. Thus N_1 may be chosen equal to 1, and $u'' = u$. This justifies

$$\sum_{t=1}^{T}(\bar{u}(t) - u^*) \geqslant u' + u - (N_0 + 1)u^* \quad \text{for all } T > T_1, \text{ where } T_1 \text{ is a fixed}$$

number. Thus infinite paths for which $\sum_{t=1}^{T}(u(t)-u^*) \to -\infty$ as $T \to \infty$ need not be considered, that is, it is sufficient to consider paths $\{y(t)\}$ where $y(t) \to y^*$.

By Lemma 9, we may apply Lemma 7 to obtain a sequence of goods prices $\{\bar{p}(t)\}$, $t = 0, 1, \ldots$, whose initial segments are efficiency prices for the initial segments of $\bar{y}(t)$. Then $\bar{p}(t)$ and $\bar{y}(t)$ satisfy relations (8) with some sequence of real numbers $\{\bar{\mu}(t)\}$. Summing the second relation, we obtain $\sum_{t=1}^{T}\bar{u}(t) = \bar{p}(0).\bar{k}(0) - \bar{p}(T).k(T) + \sum_{t=1}^{T}\bar{\mu}(t)$. Summing the first relation, we obtain $\sum_{t=1}^{T}u(t) \leqslant \bar{p}(0).k(0) - \bar{p}(T).k(T) + \sum_{t=1}^{T}\bar{\mu}(t)$. Therefore, subtracting the first sum from the second, we obtain $\sum_{t=1}^{T}(u(t) - \bar{u}(t)) \leqslant \bar{p}(T).(k(T) - \bar{k}(T))$. This inequality holds for every $T = 1, 2, \ldots$, and $|k(T) - \bar{k}(T)| \to 0$, as $T \to \infty$ by the fact that both sequences of stock vectors converge to k^*. Then for any $\varepsilon > 0$ there is N such that $\sum_{t=1}^{T}(u(t) - \bar{u}(t)) < \varepsilon$ for $T > N$, and $\{\bar{y}(t)\}$ is an optimal path by the definition we have adopted. Note from the proof of Theorem 3 that the set of infinite optimal paths is precisely the set of infinite paths that are finitely optimal.

ACKNOWLEDGMENTS

The research on this paper was begun at the Rochester Conference on Mathematical Models of Economic Growth, sponsored by the Social Science Research Council in the summer of 1964. It was continued at the Stanford Conference on Optimal Growth, sponsored by the Mathematical Social Science Board of the Center for Advanced Research in the Behavioral Sciences in the summer of 1965. In the course of my research I have benefited greatly from the advice of David Gale and Johannes Kemperman. During both the Conferences and in other periods my work was supported by the National Science Foundation.

NOTES AND REFERENCES

[1] If x is a vector in n dimensional Euclidean space, $|x| = \sum_{i=1}^{n} |x_i|$, where $|x_i|$ is the absolute value of x_i.

[2] The idea of accumulating utility as a stock was suggested to me by a remark made by Roy Radner at the Cambridge Conference on Activity Analysis in the Theory of Growth and Planning sponsored by the International Economic Association in the summer of 1963.

[3] The analysis of paths on the von Neumann facet found in this section was stimulated by a paper (1964) delivered to the Faculty Seminar of the Department of Economics of the University of Rochester by Michio Morishima. He in turn gives much credit for the stimulation of his ideas to Sir John Hicks.

[4] F is minimal in the sense that it is the smallest facet of Y that contains all the von Neumann points of Y.

16

Free Trade and Development Economics

Gerald M. Meier

The first part of this essay's title may appear old-fashioned; the second, too fashionable! There is, however, merit in striving to maintain the continuity of economic thought while reformulating traditional principles to illuminate better contemporary problems, always a characteristic of Sir John Hicks's (1950–1) writings. Some fifteen years after Sir John's paper on 'Free Trade and Modern Economics', it may again be appropriate to attempt to throw some new light on the old story of free trade versus protection, and to cast Sir John's paper into even more modern terms. The strongest arguments for protection now stem not so much from the economics of full employment, as was the case when Sir John wrote, but from the economics of underdevelopment. And as Sir John observes, if there is any branch of economic theory which is especially relevant to underdevelopment economics, it is the theory of international trade (Hicks, 1965).

In the first section, we shall appraise the contemporary arguments for protection to accelerate development. We shall then proceed to examine the effects of protectionist policies as actually practised by developing countries. The last section relates the current demand for trade preferences to the issue of protection.

Notwithstanding the changes in economic thinking brought about by Keynesian economics, the new welfare economics, and programming analysis, the free trade doctrine is fundamentally unassailable from the standpoint of static efficiency conditions. Economists have generally remained reluctant to admit other exceptions to the free trade case beyond the time-honored (but increasingly restricted) infant industry and re-formulated optimum tariff arguments.

The challenge of development, however, has moved the free trade-

385

protection issue into a new context. Dynamic and structural problems of poor countries now appear to transcend the criterion of maximizing world production efficiency under static conditions. Once we allow for market imperfections, externalities, and the criteria of intertemporal optimality – all of which are prominent in underdevelopment economics – we may indeed wonder if the conditions justifying trade restrictions are not widespread in developing countries.

There is no doubt that the assumptions of the received theory of international trade appear unrealistic for a developing country – and it is this which gives rise to protectionist arguments that are *prima facie* attractive. At the same time, the economics of development can easily become confused with the 'economics of discontent' within a newly-independent nation, so that protection is also advocated as a means of attaining the 'superior way of life of an industrial society', or increasing 'national power through self-sufficiency', or 'avoiding dependence on foreigners'. These are, however, non-economic objectives, and though they may be valued for their own sake, they do not constitute an economic argument for protection as a means of increasing real income.

We shall leave these non-economic considerations on one side and restrict our discussion to the more serious economic arguments only: in particular, those arguments that contend that a protectionist policy will strengthen a development program by enabling the developing country to enjoy a larger share of the gains from trade, increase its rate of capital formation, and promote the growth of its 'infant manufacturing sector' (Meier, 1963).

The first argument – that a poor country can alter the distribution of the gains from trade in its favor, and thereby directly raise its real income – is based on the terms-of-trade argument for protection. An expected deterioration in their terms-of-trade is a pervasive concern among poor countries. This pessimism rests partly on an extrapolation of the alleged secular deterioration in their commodity terms-of-trade, and partly on an expectation that future improvements in primary production, together with a low income elasticity of demand for primary products, will lower the prices of their exports, relative to imports. It is, therefore, argued that restrictions on exports or imports may result in a rise in export prices or a fall in import prices, so as to forestall the anticipated deterioration or bring about an improvement in the terms-of-trade.

The use of the terms-of-trade as an index of welfare clearly dies hard. And for developing countries, it is only too easy to overemphasize and misuse this argument for protection. On the one hand, the argument focuses on the commodity terms-of-trade and tends to neglect movements in the single factoral terms-of-trade or income terms-of-trade which are more significant for analyzing the effects on real income and the capacity to import. Attention should not be diverted from efforts to raise productivity in exportables and improve the single factoral terms-of-trade, and from the need to expand the volume of exports and improve the income terms-of-trade. Nor should the argument be overextended to claim that if a primary producing country expects a future deterioration in its terms-of-trade, or fluctuations in its export prices, it should impose industrial protection. Even if the country's comparative advantage in primary production is expected to decline in the future, it does not follow that the country should forgo the present gains from trade that can still be realized as long as there is a current comparative advantage in such production. Only if the future competitive adjustment to secularly changing comparative advantage cannot be relied upon, and some advance planning is required for the transfer of resources out of exports, is there a need for protection. Even then, this may be an inferior solution compared with alternative domestic policy measures to stimulate such a transfer. Similarly, even though primary exports may be subject to greater variability of earnings than industrial exports, it does not follow that average earnings in primary production are necessarily lower than they would be in industrial production, and that real income over the cycle would be enhanced by protection. Although fluctuations in export receipts have adverse effects on the continuity of a country's development program, these effects are more appropriately avoided by stability measures than by protective trade policies.

Properly interpreted, the terms-of-trade argument reduces to the optimum tariff argument. When the marginal terms-of-trade diverge from the average terms-of-trade, and a distortion in international markets arises under free trade between the foreign rate of transformation in production and the marginal rate of substitution in consumption, there is then a case for an optimum tariff to offset this distortion and bring about the marginal equivalencies of a Pareto national optimum.

This argument is analytically valid, and if a developing country could exploit national monopoly or monopsony power, it could trade on better terms by appropriately taxing its exports or imposing a tariff on its imports. But few, if any, of the developing nations can exercise sufficient monopoly or monopsony power to effect an international transfer of real income through an improvement in their terms-of-trade. The practical relevance of this argument is only slight in view of alternative sources of supply for foodstuffs on the part of importing countries, the capacity of industrial importers to develop synthetics as substitutes for natural raw materials, and the relatively small size of any one poor country's domestic market for a specific import.

A second category of protection arguments concentrates on the need to raise the savings ratio and increase investment. The favorable effects of trade on capital accumulation could readily be included in Mill's 'indirect effects, which must be counted as benefits of a high order'. For trade provides an opportunity to exchange goods with less growth potential for goods with more growth potential, thereby quickening the progress that results from a given effort on the savings side (Hicks, 1959). Moreover, the capacity to save increases as real income rises, through the more efficient resource allocation associated with international trade. And the stimulus to investment is strengthened by the realization of increasing returns in the wider markets that overseas trade provides. By allowing economies of large-scale production, the access to foreign markets also makes it profitable to adopt advanced techniques of production which require more capital; the opportunities for the productive investment of capital are then greater than they would be if the market were limited to only the small size of the home market (Hicks, 1959). Thus, within the neoclassical framework, it could be concluded that above and beyond the static gains from trade that result from the more efficient resource allocation with given production functions, international trade also transforms existing production functions and induces outward shifts in the production possibility frontier.

But could not protection do even better and contribute to a more rapid rate of capital formation? One possibility is to increase the savings ratio through controls on imports of consumer goods. The objective of greater investment will not be realized, however, if consumption expenditure merely shifts from imports to domestic production of importables. A reduction in consumption expenditure, and not a mere change in its composition, is, of course, what is needed for an increase in the volume of savings. Even if the imports of consumer goods are reduced in order to be replaced directly by imports of capital goods (goods with a higher growth potential), the new capital imports will not constitute a net contribution to capital formation unless there is also a corresponding act of domestic saving. The efficiency of protection as a means of increasing investment is, thus, contingent upon a complementary domestic policy of mobilizing additional saving.

Following the Galenson-Leibenstein criterion of the allocation of investment resources (Galenson and Leibenstein, 1955) we might also think that it is justified to protect capital-intensive projects which yield high profits that will be ploughed back into an expansion of the industry. But even if we do not contradict the Galenson-Leibenstein criterion (as we should do) and assume that the capital-intensive project will promote savings, a protectionist policy to accomplish this would still involve inefficient production and a consumption loss. Instead of fostering such inefficient production, it would be better to use domestic taxation policies to raise the level of savings – assuming that the country has the capacity to do so, and that the taxes do not, in turn, introduce other distortions entailing a real cost.

Protection may also be advocated as a means of capital formation through its inducement of foreign direct investment to escape the import controls. A differentiated tariff structure may be particularly effective in encouraging the final stages of manufacture and assembly of parts within the tariff-imposing country when there is an import duty on finished products, while intermediate goods and materials remain untaxed or taxed at a lower rate. Provided that there is a sufficiently high domestic demand for the product of the foreign manufacturer, and other conditions are favorable for foreign investment, protection can attract such 'tariff factories'. The crucial question, though, is whether foreign investment should be so encouraged in the import-competing sector, rather than in some other sector of the economy. An analysis of the benefits and costs of foreign investment, according to alternative patterns of resource allocation, might indicate no net benefit from foreign investment in importables or a lower net benefit than from allocation to another sector.

While the foregoing has been concerned only with an increase in the level of savings, the formulation of a development plan also raises questions of what should be the optimal rate of saving over time and the terminal capital stock at the end of a multi-period production plan. This introduces the complex problems of dynamic optimum theory that Hicks has analyzed in *Capital and Growth*. The optimum position reached under free trade does not necessarily comprise optimality of the saving decision and multiperiod optimality of capital accumulation. It is certainly possible to argue that the time path of saving is less than optimal from the stand-point of some social objective when saving decisions are individually made under imperfect foresight. And, when it is recognized that the outputs of the current period become the inputs of the next period, there is no reason to believe that the free trade output is necessarily equivalent to the optimal plan of production.

Nonetheless, although the statement of the optimal saving problem calls into question the assumptions on which welfare propositions of static trade theory rest, it is merely an unsupported assertion that protection would better satisfy the criterion of optimal saving or efficient capital accumulation. The models that have been used in growth theory to explore these questions have all been restricted to a closed economy. The negative criticism of free trade simply suggests that development planning rather than reliance on the market mechanism might better approach the optimal rate of saving. But this refers only to development programming–not protection. The positive case for protection as a means of attaining the optimal rate of saving has yet to be presented.

What does happen in the practice of development programming, how-ever, is that planners do not worry about the optimality of the saving decision, but simply treat it as a 'political' decision. They also plan in terms of a definite time horizon and assume knowledge of the future techniques and trade possibilities and consumption patterns–all of which amounts, in effect, to assuming perfect foresight. In this framework, the traditional welfare propositions of trade theory remain valid (Bhagwati, 1963).

Of all the protectionist arguments, most appealing to developing coun-tries are those advocating trade restrictions to promote the growth of the 'infant manufacturing sector' or an 'infant economy'. These arguments invoke the existence of market imperfections and externalities to contradict the free trade prescription. In this vein, it has been maintained that there are 'four special reasons for industrial protection in underdeveloped countries–the difficulties of finding demand to match new supply, the existence of surplus labor, the large rewards of individual investments in creating external economies, and the lopsided internal price structure disfavoring industry' (Myrdal, 1956, p. 279). These reasons are interrelated and may be interpreted as an extension of the infant industry argument to the 'growing up' of the economy as a whole.

The infant industry argument is a logically valid part of this argument. But again, on closer analysis, its applicability may be quite narrow. At best, protection can only make the production of importables more profitable, but cannot create the necessary capital or skills required by the industry at the outset. As Professors Nurkse and Hirschman have observed, before an industry can be protected, it must first be created. Assuming, however, that this prior problem has been solved, the protected industry must still meet not only the 'Mill test' of acquiring sufficient skill and experience to overcome an historical handicap, but also the 'Bastable test' of realizing a sufficient saving in costs to compensate for the high costs of the learning period (Kemp, 1960, pp. 65–7). We should also recognize that, even though there may be losses on early operations during the learning period, if the future scale of output is sufficient to enable the current rate of interest to be earned on the initial amount invested in learning the job, the investment will be profitable for private enterprise; there is then no case for a protective tariff if there are only internal economies of scale – not external economies. Should the learning process, however, be external to the firm in the sense that all the knowledge and experience gained through 'learning by doing' is not appropriable, the social benefit would exceed the private benefit of investment in learning industrial production techniques, and there would then be a case for State support.

While the infant industry argument maintains that the industry's present costs are too high, it might also be claimed that the demand for its product is too low, and that protection is needed to create demand to match new supply. This argument is, however, restricted simply to promoting the demand for import substitutes; but there is no indication why this particular pattern of development is preferable to any alternative pattern. The fundamental question of whether development ought to be through import substitution is simply assumed away. Even if the argument is extended to the 'balanced growth' thesis, the special emphasis on import substitutes is still unwarranted. For the 'balanced growth' doctrine calls only for a balanced pattern of investment in a number of different industries, including agriculture; it does not emphasize import-competing industries, and there is nothing in the doctrine itself to favor general protection for industry over other policies designed to promote extensive investment. Further, as Professor Nurkse was careful to note in formulating the 'balanced growth' doctrine, the case for output expansion for the home market depends on the requirement that the amount of resources is increasing at a sufficient rate so that domestic output can expand without neglecting export production and giving up the benefits achieved through international specialization (Nurkse, 1959, pp. 41–8).

A more persuasive argument for industrial protection is that externalities in production cause the market evaluation of comparative advantage to diverge from the investment criterion of social profitability, so that governmental support of the industry that yields external economies is needed to correct the market mechanism.

Recognizing this problem, the linear programming approach to development planning attempts to include a number of non-market phenomena by using accounting prices in evaluating the allocation of resources. By this method, the optimal pattern of trade is determined simultaneously with the optimal allocation of investment resources. Again, however, the programming approach is distinct from the protection issue. The objective of efficiency in trade is not superseded by the principles of development programming. On the contrary, the programming approach to resource allocation may just as readily show that the country's development policies are actually over-emphasizing import substitution and neglecting the potential gains from trade (Chenery, 1961).

It is by no means self-evident that the most significant net external economies are to be realized in the domestic production of importables rather than in alternative investment opportunities in the export sector, or domestic industries, or public overhead capital. Further, it is necessary to distinguish whether the net external economies are reversible or irreversible. For if the gains to other enterprises do not continue after protection is withdrawn, the protection must then be permanent to keep the reversible external economies utilized. The case of irreversible external economies merges with the infant industry situation that requires only temporary intervention, but this does not apply to reversible external economies.

Finally, it is contended that industrial protection can increase the developing country's real income by facilitating a redistribution of labor from agriculture to industry when wages in industry exceed the opportunity cost of labor to the economy (Hagen, 1958). A structural disequilibrium in the labor market causes the allocation of labor between agriculture and industry to be inefficient: in effect, production occurs on an inferior transformation curve within the maximum possible production frontier based on a uniform wage, and a suboptimal position is selected on the inferior transformation curve because private costs of production exceed social costs. The commodity price ratio, then, diverges from the domestic rate of transformation, so that the optimum conditions characterized by the equalities of the foreign rate of transformation, domestic rate of trans-formation, and domestic rate of substitution in consumption are violated under free trade. Given that the marginal product of labor is higher in the importable manufacturing sector than the agricultural sector, but that industrial wages exceed agricultural wages for labor of equal quality, it is argued that industry should be protected to overcome the excessive wage differential and bring private costs in line with social costs. If the distortion in factor allocation is removed by protecting the importable manufacturing industry, it is believed that real income can then be raised relatively to the free trade situation.

There is merit in this argument, subject to some qualifications (as we have now come to expect of most protectionist arguments). If the con-sumption loss is not to exceed the production gain, the increase in the aggregate cost to buyers of the protected product must be less than the increase in income to factors which shift to the protected industry. It is also necessary that the wage differential be due to non-economic causes that make the industrial wage rate exceed the agricultural wage rate by a margin larger than can be accounted for by the disutility or higher economic costs incurred by labor in the industrial sector.[1]

Another variant of the factor disequilibrium argument relies on the alleged existence of disguised unemployment in the agricultural sector. Even if the actual wages are equal in the industrial and agricultural sectors, the market wage diverges from the true social cost of labor when the marginal productivity of labor in agriculture is zero, or at least below the average product (which sets the minimum transfer wage for industrial employment), while the cost to industrialists of hiring the surplus labor is considerably higher than its marginal product. Equalization of wages in the two sectors would then still leave labor's marginal product in industry above its marginal product in agriculture. In this situation, it is again claimed that protection can bring about a better utilization of domestic resources if secondary industries are protected in order to offset the divergence between private money costs and true social marginal costs.

Rarely, however, is conclusive evidence offered that there actually is in agriculture a substantial amount of labor that could be released with no effect on production if there is not, at the same time, an increase in the supply of cooperant factors, a reorganization of agricultural production, or an extension of the 'normal' working day for those remaining on the land. If the remaining workers have to be provided with economic incentives to make up the total of labor time, the transfer of the 'disguised unemployed' is not socially costless (Myint, 1964). There is a cost represented by the extra resources necessary to produce those incentive consumers' goods that have to be provided for the remaining workers to induce them to market their food surplus. An additional social cost is incurred when increased investments in housing and equipment are required for workers transferred to the industrial sector. Greater employment in this sector will also lead to extra consumption of food, which is a significant social cost in a country with a limited supply of food. These collateral costs should not be underestimated, even if total output might be maintained in the agricultural sector after underemployed workers are transferred to the sheltered industrial sector.

Moreover, even assuming the existence of disguised unemployment, it still does not follow that industrialization through protection is the best utilization of the underemployed. The major consequence of surplus labor in agriculture is low productivity, but the basic remedy for this is capital formation, not industrialization as such. The disguised unemployed constitute an 'investible surplus' which can be applied to other capital-formation projects—not the least of which could be the construction of rural overhead capital and other capital projects which can help to transform the traditional structure of agricultural production.

It may also be questioned whether protection is an effective measure for stimulating the necessary labor mobility, in so far as disguised unemployment cannot be attributed to any deficiency of demand. It is, instead, due to real causes, such as land shortage, capital deficiency, and the lack of skills and organization needed to utilize the underemployed labor in other activities (Hicks, 1959). Labor mobility might, therefore, be better encouraged by public investment in overhead capital, education and training, land tenure reforms, and other extra-economic measures that remove the social and institutional barriers to mobility.

Finally, when disequilibrium in the capital market is considered along with disequilibrium in the labor market, it may be that even if the private cost is, in agriculture, too low because wages are depressed, and in industry too high compared with what it would be if the disguised unemployed competed freely in the labor market, the exact opposite may exist in the capital market (Myint, 1964). It is generally true that rates of interest are considerably higher and capital is more overvalued in the agricultural sectors of poor countries than in the industrial sectors, so that the private return on capital invested in agriculture is less than the social return. The critical question, therefore, is whether manufacturing costs as a whole are overstated relatively to agricultural costs. This depends on the relative capital-labor ratios in the two sectors and the relative sizes of the wage and interest rate differentials between the two sectors. It is possible that the counterbalancing effects of the higher interest rate in agriculture and the higher capital-labor ratio in industry may more than offset the overvaluation of labor in industry.

While we have presented specific criticisms to each of the foregoing arguments, a more general criticism can be submitted. Neo-classicists would have maintained that, under conditions of market imperfections and externalities, the deviations from ideal output would be better corrected by alternative domestic policies instead of protection. Nowadays, we may make essentially the same point (but more rigorously) by utilizing the theory of the second-best. Thus, only the optimum tariff argument meets the criterion of the 'first-best'; when world market prices diverge from relative opportunity costs in international trade, an optimum tariff can offset this international distortion and equate the domestic price ratios facing producers and consumers with the marginal rates of transformation between commodities in international trade. But it is important to recognize that if these divergencies are in domestic production or factor use, instead of in foreign trade, so that domestic prices do not reflect domestic opportunity costs, the appropriate remedy is a tax or subsidy on domestic production or factor use, rather than a tax or subsidy on international trade.[2] When it is a divergence between domestic price ratios and domestic rates of transformation that is to be corrected, a tariff will itself introduce a new divergence between either the marginal rate of substitution in domestic consumption or the marginal rate of transformation in foreign trade; the tariff might then possibly result in a net economic loss compared with the free trade situation.[3] An optimum subsidy is then superior to restricted trade.

Thus, aside from the optimum tariff and capital formation arguments, the foregoing arguments come down to arguments for subsidies as superior to a tariff policy. For the case of an infant industry in which the social rate of return exceeds the private, or the social rate of discount is less than the private interest cost, the appropriate policy is subsidization of the investment in the learning process of the infant industry. For the case of external economies in manufacturing, the appropriate policy is again a subsidy on the activity giving rise to the externalities so as to remove the divergence between the higher monetary private cost and the lower real social cost of production in industry. And, similarly, the case of a distortionary wage differential between the agricultural and industrial sectors calls for a subsidy per unit of labor used in industry equal to the difference in unit labor cost prevailing in industry and the true marginal opportunity cost, rather than a tariff protecting the output of the industry.[4]

If we now leave the theoretical arguments behind, and consider the developing countries' experience with commercial policy, what effects can we single out as having been most significant in practice ?

It is immediately apparent that the theoretical arguments have truly been left behind–not these arguments but balance of payments considerations have induced the extensive use of trade controls. The underlying inflationary strains exerted by the demands of a development program, fluctuations in export earnings, and an overvalued currency have exerted continuing pressure on the balance of payments. And this has been met in an *ad hoc* fashion by imposing quantitative restrictions over a wide range of imports. When there are random price rises in the non-protected sectors, and the continuing inflationary pressure is met by simply another *ad hoc* round of import controls, it is impossible to sustain an effective and selective protectionist policy (Myint, 1964, pp. 189–90). At the same time, as long as inflationary monetary and fiscal policies are pursued in combination with an unwillingness to devalue, the wide range of import restrictions becomes self-justifying because of the increased incentives to import and the greater difficulties of exporting. Thus, while there are theoretical arguments for protection, it has been exceedingly difficult to practice a rational protectionist policy within the actual setting of inflation, chronic balance of payments pressure, and fixed exchange rates. As has been said of Latin American countries (Macario, 1964), *ad hoc* balance of payments measures, temporary to begin with, have become permanent in most cases and more general in their scope, giving rise to a form of protectionism which has been characterized by extemporaneousness, lack of autonomy (since it is primarily motivated by external causes), extremely high levels and indiscriminate application, with the basic objective being import substitution at any cost, regardless of which industries it is most expedient to develop and how far the process should be carried.

To the extent that 'permanent' tariffs have been embedded among the quantitative restrictions, they have had a strong influence in favoring domestic substitution of consumer goods. This is in part attributable to the easy appeal of restricting most severely 'luxury' and 'semi-luxury' imports for balance of payments reasons. Even more significantly, the tariff rates have been differentiated by stages of production, with the rates of duty rising from the raw material to the semi-fabricated to the fabricated stages. Higher rates have also been set on consumer goods than on capital goods, and on 'non-essential' than 'essential' consumer goods. Because of this cascading of tariff rates by production stages, the effective or implicit rates of protection of value added in producing the higher-tariff goods at successive stages of the production process have been greater than the nominal or explicit commodity tariff rates on these goods.[5] By maintaining low tariff rates on inputs, the developing countries have been able to increase generally the degree of effective protection afforded by the tariff on finished products.

Moreover, application of the differentiated tariff structure has not been accompanied by sufficiently strong domestic measures to raise the level of domestic saving. The result has been rising demand for the domestic output of consumer goods and the unplanned growth of consumer-goods industries providing substitutes for the products that can no longer be imported. Instead of adopting domestic measures to discourage such production, the developing countries have actually encouraged home production of import-substitutes by subsidizing the manufacturing sector through a variety of domestic policies. The general practice has been to offer various incentives to manufacturing by the remission of taxes, availability of cheaper credit, provision of industrial estates, and subsidized transport and power facilities. Although it is difficult to measure the subsidies given to the manufacturing sector when the internal price structure is distorted and market prices differ from more realistic accounting prices, the indirect evidence would indicate a substantial degree of subsidization. This subsidization by internal measures reinforces the relatively easy access to imports of intermediate goods and capital goods, thereby encouraging all the more the domestic production of finished goods that are being subsidized by the pattern of differential tariffs.

As a result of the complex of policies followed, it can well be argued that in many of the developing countries import substitution has passed beyond the stage where it is economic and has had deleterious repercussions for resource allocation in the economy as a whole. In view of the narrow home markets which prevent exploitation of economies of scale, the technological inefficiencies, and the monopolistic market structures that are sheltered behind high protection, it is readily understandable why the domestic prices of importables have been much higher than foreign prices. In view of the differentiated tariff structure, the protection of value added makes the excess cost of the domestic fabrication process substantially higher than appears from simply the nominal tariff rates on commodities or from the excess of the domestic price over the foreign price. The excess cost per unit of protected activity (value added) becomes even larger if we calculate not only the excess cost of domestic value added, but also the consumption cost of protection.

These high subsidies on the final manufacturing stages are much larger than can be justified by presumed external economies, distorted wage rates, inelasticity of the demand for traditional exports, or *de facto* overvaluation of the currency (Johnson, 1964). If, for example, the effective rate of protection on the domestic process of fabrication makes the domestic cost three times as much as the foreign, the protection would only be economically advantageous if the alternative opportunity cost of the domestic factors used were less than one-third of their money earnings. Or, it would only be economical to invest in importables rather than exportables if the reallocation of domestic factors to the export industries would increase foreign exchange earnings by less than one-third of their value. If we included the costs of the domestic policies that are subsidizing the manufacturing sector (tax concessions, etc.), the cost of import-substitution would be even greater. Although more empirical studies are needed, the few country studies that do exist clearly indicate the excess cost of production of import-substitutes (Power, 1963; Macario, 1964).

The strategy of 'development *via* import substitution' has also failed to be net saving of foreign exchange. The import content of investment has been very high as imports of intermediate materials and capital equipment have increased (Maizels, 1963); the policy of 'industrialization from the top downwards', with emphasis on the assembling of imported components and the final stages of manufacture, has meant that the value added domestically has often been only a small percentage of the value of the finished product. The high import-intensity of the process of import substitution has even led in many of the developing countries to imports rising at a faster rate than the growth of national product, and in some cases the value of the inputs imported for the new industries has been greater than that of the goods replaced by domestic production.

Nor has the import substitution policy been successful in absorbing much of the underemployed labor. A relatively capital-intensive technology has been used in the import-competing sector–in part, because the price of imported capital goods has been kept relatively low by means of the differential tariffs and preferential exchange rates, and in part, because the high protection on finished goods has induced the establishment of 'tariff factories' which have simply duplicated the capital-intensive techniques of advanced foreign production. Further, when domestic factor prices have risen at the same time as low tariffs have been maintained on imported intermediate inputs, it is not surprising that the participation of domestic factors in the protected industries should have been relatively low.[6]

Further, in contrast to the historical experience of some countries that are now advanced (Chenery, 1960, pp. 624–51) the import-substitute industries in less developed countries have not been able to proceed on to such an efficient point as to enter export markets. The historical evidence shows that the rise of industry through import-replacement in the presently-advanced countries, and the subsequent decline in cost of tradables relative to non-tradables as income rose, was in large part due to systematic changes in supply conditions, not simply to a change in the composition of demand with rising income (Chenery, 1960). The changes in factor supply, especially the growth in capital stock per worker and the increase in education and skills of all kinds, were instrumental in causing a systematic shift in comparative advantage as per capita income rose. But the favorable supply conditions that emerged in other countries have not been duplicated in underdeveloped countries that have simply undertaken a policy of industrial protection. In addition, the indiscriminately broad-scale type of protection has led to an extensive range of consumer goods industries, producing small quantities of a large variety of goods for the home market, instead of the intensive specialization that is required for entry into the export market. The overdiversification effected through indiscriminate protection has actually inhibited the concentration of effort and specialization needed for the development of an export industry (Johnson, 1964; Macario, 1964).

Finally, a policy that is designed simply to replace imports does nothing to guarantee cumulative growth. Import-replacement is a once-for-all occurrence in any one industry, but there still remains the problem of sustaining the industrialization momentum beyond the point of import replacement. Even on an industry by industry basis, the future scope for continuing import-substitution has become extremely limited. Having already replaced the technologically-simple consumer manufactures, many of the developing countries would now have to turn to the replacement of manufactured intermediate inputs and capital goods. But the remaining import industries are characterized by more complex technology, increasing capital-intensity, and a progressively smaller domestic market in relation to the minimum efficient units of production. Further substitution in this direction is therefore more difficult, and the excessive cost of protection becomes progressively higher.

If we now view the development process in more general terms and consider the effects of import substitution on aggregate growth, the case against continuing import replacement becomes even stronger. For if on the one side there has been a subsidization of importables there has been on the other side a levy on the rest of the economy. In particular, import-substitution policies have conflicted seriously with the strategic roles that agriculture and exports must have in the development process.

From the experience of development planning, it has become abundantly clear that the agricultural bottleneck is a major obstacle to accelerated development. The rate at which nonagricultural sectors can grow depends on the rate of increase in agricultural supplies, and a country's rate of development must be restrained when the agricultural base is neglected. Higher agricultural productivity is necessary to supply foodstuffs for the industrial workers and growing population, to supply raw materials for expanding domestic industry, to raise the demand for nonagricultural commodities, to provide additional foreign exchange earnings, and to contribute to capital formation. And all this cannot be simply a once-for-all accomplishment, but must be cumulative, with a *growing* food surplus, etc., as the industrial sector expands (Myint, 1964). In practice, however, the average annual rates of growth in the supplies of agricultural materials and foodstuffs have been declining over the past decade, and the foreign exchange scarcity has been intensified, with a consequent limitation on the pace of the development program.

It is not merely coincidental that agricultural output has lagged at the same time as import-substitution policies have been pursued. Urban exploitation of agriculture has only too commonly materialized, and agriculture has been heavily taxed by attempts to develop *via* import-replacement. Even more inhibiting than the direct taxation of agriculture have been the indirect levies imposed through rising prices of industrial inputs for agriculture, price controls on agricultural products, the neglect of investment in agriculture, and the diversion of resources into the home production of importables.

Not only has agriculture producing for the home market been impeded, but so too has agriculture producing staple primary products for export. Such exports have been taxed under the guise of terms-of-trade considerations, and a great part of the proceeds from exports obtained through export duties, discriminatory exchange rates, and the activities of the government marketing boards have been diverted to industrial development. The rise in home consumption of foodstuffs, especially in the industrial urban sector, has also limited the export surpluses of foodstuffs. And those countries that export non-food staples and import foodstuffs have attempted to become more self-sufficient in food by diverting agricultural resources from their traditional exports.

More generally, import restrictions have discriminated heavily against the developing countries' exports. The protection given to importables has been equivalent to a tax on exports in so far as it has raised the production costs of exports by increasing the prices of factors that are used in both the export and import-competing sectors, and has increased the cost of inputs for exports. While the policy of industrialization through import-substitution has subsidized the imports of intermediate inputs, it has had the effect of taxing exports. The implications of the theoretical discussion of the symmetry between import and export taxes have indeed had considerable relevance to reality.[7] And while the home cost of producing exports has risen, the unwillingness to adjust the overvalued exchange rate has also held back export flows that might otherwise have been achieved. In addition, the profitable sheltered home market for importables has attracted scarce capital and entrepreneurship away from the export sector. Under these conditions, it has been difficult to maintain a competitive position even for export commodities for which world demand has grown, and several of the developing countries have suffered a decline in the proportionate share of the world market for their key export commodities.

Instead of realizing, however, that the policies associated with import-substitution have reacted on their exports and agriculture, most of the developing countries have simply interpreted the slow growth in export proceeds and lag in agricultural output as evidence of the need to intensify their import-substitution policies, thereby impeding all the more an improvement in the performance of exports and agriculture. It is this self-justifying character of import-substitution policies that has made it so difficult to shift the emphasis of development planning away from import-replacement to the improvement of agriculture and exports. With progressive import-substitution, however, the implicit taxation of agriculture and exports has increased, and the waste of resources through the real excess costs of import substitution has increased over time, thereby cancelling out part or all of the gains in productivity that should have by this time accrued through development programmes.

It is notable that there is now increasing awareness of the limitations to a strategy of development *via* import-substitution. Indeed, the most significant aspect of the first United Nations Conference on Trade and Development was to recognize the defects of an inward-looking policy of industrial development, and to place greater emphasis on the alternative of export promotion.[8] The poor countries remain, however, pessimistic regarding their prospects for primary product exports, and are instead emphasizing the potential for the development of industrial exports. But here again, in order to promote manufactured exports, the developing countries are arguing for a departure from free trade principles. Instead of being willing to adjust the exchange rate to an equilibrium level and reduce restrictions on imported inputs, so as to in effect subsidize their exports, the poor countries shift the onus for their inability to export manufactures on to the advanced industrial nations and insist that these countries should now grant preferences on their imports of manufactures.

Spokesmen for the less developed countries argue in particular for two types of preferential arrangements: (1) developed countries should grant general 'across-the-board' preferences to all less developed countries on manufactures and semi-manufactures without requiring preferences from the less developed countries in return (an exception to Article I of Gatt)[9] and (2) less developed countries should be allowed to discriminate in favor of one another without having to enter into a full-fledged customs union or free trade area comprising substantially all the commerce of the member nations (an exception to Article XXIV of Gatt).

We may now examine the issues raised by these proposals.

As between general preferential arrangements and regional preferential arrangements, a stronger economic case can be made for the latter, even though the less developed countries place greater stress on the former.

On theoretical grounds, a partial customs union or preferential tariff association among less developed countries can now be supported by appeal to the theory of second-best. If tariffs exist outside a customs union, and the customs union maintains an external tariff, it is then no longer necessarily true that reducing tariffs among members of the union will raise welfare; all that we can really conclude is that the second-best optimum for the tariffs among the members will be something greater than zero and less than the tariffs on outside imports. Contrary to Gatt's insistence on zero tariffs within the union, it follows that the second-best optimum is some kind of preferential area rather than a complete customs union or free trade area: 'when only some tariffs are to be changed, welfare is more likely to be raised if these tariffs are merely *reduced* than if they are completely *removed*' (Lipsey, 1960, p. 506). There is no economic justification in maintaining, as Gatt does, that 100 per cent discrimination is permissible but less than 100 per cent is not.

Moreover, once we realistically take as our starting point the fact that the less developed countries are using trade restrictions to promote import-replacement industries, the relevant choice is obviously not between free trade or import substitution in a preferential tariff association, but rather between the present practice of import substitution within national frontiers or within the proposed preferential tariff association. There is then considerable force to the argument that import substitution on a regional basis may enable the member countries to protect a given amount of industry at a lower real cost in terms of income forgone than do the present policies of national import substitution and compartmentalized industrialization in every developing country (Cooper and Massell, 1965).

Through a preferential tariff association, trade in manufactures among the less developed countries might be considerably expanded, in view of the restrictions that these countries have imposed against one another's manufactures as well as those from the more developed countries. And by their quality, specifications, and design, the manufactures produced in a less developed country are also more appropriate for marketing in another less developed country than in advanced industrial countries. But the very advantage that a preferential trading arrangement might have in bringing about a more rational location of industry, with industry concentrated in the lowest-cost producing country, is also its main drawback to prospective members. For this implies, of course, that other member countries will have to suffer a contraction in their industrial sectors. The members are certainly unlikely to benefit equally with respect to the growth of their industries, and some will be only too prone to believe that other members are gaining at their expense. Unless a regional preferential arrangement fosters competition among the local industries of the member countries and allows industrial production among the members according to their comparative advantages, there is little to commend it; but if it does so, some members will undoubtedly prefer to resort to their own national policies of industrialization.

For this reason, together with the belief that the scope for expanding exports of manufactures to one another is limited, and the fact that such an expansion does not raise the supply of foreign exchange from the more developed countries, the less developed countries have given regional preferences only minor emphasis relative to their demand for the granting of general preferences by the advanced countries.

In large part, the case for general preferences rests on the less developed countries' grievances against the trade policies of the developed nations and the mechanism of bargaining for tariff reductions under Gatt. Although the average *ad valorem* tariff rate on the developed countries' imports of manufactures does not appear excessively high, it is argued that this does not truly reflect the high incidence of the developed countries' tariff barriers. Some of the highest tariff rates are on imports of labor-intensive and technologically-simple consumer goods that are of special interest to the developing countries. It is also contended that the European Economic Community and the European Free Trade Area have created additional protection against exports from the infant industries of less developed countries, and the Associated Overseas Territories enjoy preferences in the EEC to the detriment of the exports of other less developed countries. Of most significance is the complaint that the escalation of tariff rates in the industrial countries according to the degree of processing is especially discouraging to the export of processed goods from the developing countries. There is considerable justification to this grievance: empirical studies do show that effective rates of protection on value added in the developed countries are much higher than the nominal tariff rates on commodities (Balassa, 1965).

Non-tariff restrictions (witness the use of quantitative restrictions, internal taxes and revenue duties, practices of customs administration, and agreements to avoid 'market disruption' such as in the case of cotton textiles) also inhibit the developing countries' exports of manufactures. Finally, it is observed that if a developing country were to resort to export subsidies instead of seeking the alternative of preferences, the advanced country would then impose countervailing duties nullifying the export subsidy.

If the tariff structures and non-tariff restrictions of the advanced countries thwart export promotion, so too, it is argued, have the negotiations under Gatt failed to liberalize trade to the benefit of the developing countries. Against the background of the types of commercial policy problems encountered before the war, the historical origins of Gatt were not such as to recognize the special problems of trade for an under-developed country. Instead of giving positive assistance for exports, Gatt only assists the developing countries by way of concessions for special protectionist policies. And instead of recognizing that a developed country and an underdeveloped country are not equal, the premise of Gatt is egalitarian. It is claimed, however, that equal tariff treatment under the principle of non-discrimination has really meant preferred tariff treatment for the advanced industrial nations. This is because the negotiations for tariff reductions have depended upon the willingness of the principal-supplier nations to enter into such negotiations; the commodities for which there has been trade liberalization have been those predominantly supplied by the industrial countries; and while trade has expanded among the developed countries, the most-favored-nation extension of these trade concessions has meant little to the less developed countries. By their choice of the items for reciprocal tariff reduction, the advanced countries have therefore actually been able to practice indirect discrimination against the less developed countries, notwithstanding the most-favored-nation principle.[10] A departure from the most-favored-nation principle is therefore urged to allow preferred treatment and deliberate assistance for the exports of developing countries.

In more positive terms, the case for general preferences is based on a realization that development cannot come merely through aid, or through import-substitution, but must now come through trade. The volume of net aid has been too small, has actually declined, and cannot be expected to rise significantly. The deficiencies of industrialization through import-replacement have already been noted. And yet, the less developed countries cannot expect trade negotiations on a multilateral non-discriminatory basis to result in any substantial increase of their exports. If the alternative strategy of 'development through trade' is to be followed, preferences are claimed to be necessary for an expansion of manufactured exports. Only then will the industries in developing countries enjoy sufficiently large markets to reduce their costs of production, and their infant industries will be enabled to mature.

Indeed, a major argument for preferences is that infant industry protection (which is now allowed by Gatt and widely practiced by the developing countries) should be extended to world markets instead of being restricted to only the domestic market. In essence, the argument for preferences is for the 'internationalizing' of protection – a logical extension of the infant industry argument. Other protectionist arguments, such as the 'attraction of private foreign investment' or the 'overcoming of wage differentials', can also be logically extended into an argument for preferences, the internationally protected industry now being an export industry instead of an import-competing industry as under national protection.

The extension of the infant industry argument may have a certain tactical appeal, but we should be clear on its implications. Although the case for infant industry protection depends essentially on external economies, it is difficult to comprehend the relevance of this when the externalities arise in the preference-receiving country but the governmental assistance is to be provided by the preference-granting country. Moreover, whereas national protection of an infant industry entails the subsidization of domestic producers by domestic consumers, the preference-giving country would subsidize industrial imports from the less developed countries by transferring income from the consumers of the preference-giving country to producers in the preference-receiving country, and that is quite a different matter. Complex procedural and administrative problems are also involved if preferences are to be granted only to the products of industries that are selected as having the greatest infant-industry potentialities. A system of common preference rates, on the other hand, would apply to even those industries that do not need the large size of world markets to realize economies of scale and a competitive position. And if we were to take the present level of protection in the less developed countries as indicative of how much protection through preferences would be needed for exporting industries, it would in most cases amount to much more than preferences could realistically provide. It is also question-begging to assert that preferences need be only temporary: if the external economies are reversible or the exporting industries do not become truly competitive, the preferences would have to be permanent. But even more to the point, the wrong question is being begged: as previously discussed, the infant industry situation is a case of domestic distortions that should be removed by domestic subsidies, not by commercial policy. A preferential arrangement is only second-best, or even third-best if it leads to trade diversion in the preference-granting country, as it is most likely to do when preferences are given to the high cost infant industries instead of to only those lower cost industries that have already demonstrated a capacity to export competitively.

Perhaps the strongest argument in favor of preferences is that it may allow foreign aid to be increased in the disguised form of trade policy. If trade preferences would enable the exporters of the developing countries to charge the domestic prices of the importing country instead of the world market price, the effect would be to transfer resources from the richer to the poorer countries just as under aid. Given that foreign aid programmes will not otherwise be increased, and that trade preferences might be politically easier for a developed country to accept than a direct increase in aid, then an increase in aid through trade policy would be a desirable second-best (Johnson, 1966). Moreover, by operating through exports, 'aid' in this form might yield the important dynamic benefit of exposing the developing country to the stimulating effects provided by the opportunities and pressures of international competition, instead of supporting, as aid has done in the past, the highly costly inward-looking policies of import-substitution.

Increased trade will not be equivalent to aid, however, if the preference-receiving country is enabled to export more but only at the same prices as prevailed before. In this situation, the less developed country would realize only the 'normal' gains from trade – that is, the ability to import goods that are worth more than the goods that could have been produced at home with the resources used to produce the additional exports. In so far as import-replacement policies are excessively costly, this gain could be considerable; but it still could never be so great as to equal the value of the additional export proceeds if these were received as a free grant. Further, the argument that preferences substitute for aid may just as readily cut the other way and provide the preference-granting country with an excuse for reducing its aid programme. The net result of aid through trade policy might then be to leave the poor country with less of a transfer of real resources from the aid-giving country than would otherwise have occurred.

Beyond the doubts that we have expressed about the infant industry and aid arguments for preferences, our final judgment on trade preferences must turn on two essential questions: Would preferences be effective in substantially increasing export earnings ? And would the benefits of such a policy exceed its costs ?

Any conclusion on the potential efficacy of trade preferences must depend on detailed empirical studies of the application of a specific preferential arrangement to particular countries. Although we are so far without such studies, we may at least note the division of opinion that has been expressed on the basis of general and preliminary evidence. On the one hand, Professor Patterson (1965; 1966) has concluded that only a very limited number of industrial exports would be promoted by preferences.

This conclusion rests on the calculation that, given the existing level of tariff rates on manufactured items in the major developed countries and a reasonable expectation of the outcome of the Kennedy Round of tariff negotiations, preferences applied at a 50 per cent rate to the assumed post-Kennedy-Round tariff would yield an average preference that is in the neighborhood of only 5 per cent. A price advantage of only 5 per cent, or even 10 per cent if duties were zero, would not be a decisive factor in making it possible for less developed countries to take markets in developed countries away from both domestic producers in those countries and from producers of comparable manufactured goods in other industrial countries.

Objecting to this conclusion, Professor Johnson has rightly observed that the protective effects of existing tariff schedules cannot be evaluated by reference to the duty rate on commodities, as done by Professor Patterson, but must be measured by the substantially higher effective rates of protection of value added in the production processes that turn out the goods. Utilizing Professor Balassa's (1965) data which demonstrate that the effective protection rates on manufactures that are of export interest to the less developed countries are in the neighborhood of 25 to 50 per cent, and in particular cases even higher, Professor Johnson reaches a more optimistic conclusion regarding the potential expansion of exports from the preference-receiving countries. Moreover, the preference-receiving producers might be allowed to compete even more effectively with domestic producers in the preference-granting countries than is suggested by the calculated effective protection rates, because the preferences might reduce the subsidies to domestic production given by the tariffs on finished goods, without reducing the taxation of domestic production implicit in the tariffs levied on other goods used as inputs in the production processes of the preference-giving country. Owing to the higher materials cost imposed on them by the duty on their material inputs, for which they would receive no compensation via the tariff on the final product, the domestic producers in the preference-granting country might even be subjected to negative protection against producers in the preference-receiving country. Analysis on effective protection lines therefore leads Professor Johnson to submit that within existing tariff structures, trade preferences for developing countries, even if not at the 100 per cent level, might provide powerful incentives for the expansion of the industrial exports of the less developed countries.[11]

Even if we accept the most favorable assessment of the assistance that can be provided by preferences, the question remains whether the benefits would exceed the costs. It must first be recognized that preferences will be more effective, the higher are the non-preferential tariffs on imports from other developed countries. In the process of making preferences effective for less developed countries, the preference-granting countries might thereby be led to keep trade restrictions on imports from other developed countries higher than they otherwise would be. Having once granted preferences, the developed countries might also find it politically impossible to engage in any trade liberalization in other directions. Further, preferences are likely to be subject to quotas by product or country and to other barriers against market disruption in the preference-granting countries. Thus, preferences may cause deviations from the free trade principle that extend beyond the granting of preferences.

Further, if trade diversion results in the preference-granting country, as it is most likely to do when preferences are based on infant industry considerations, there is a misallocation in international resource allocation. If industry is attracted from a preference-granting country to a preference-receiving country, the misallocation is intensified. And if, as already noted, preferences act to shelter the export industries from international competition and to replace or reduce aid, then there are additional costs.

More fundamentally, the overriding objection to preferences is simply that it *is* a departure from the principle of non-discrimination. After the discriminatory practices of the 1930s, recognition of the most-favored-nation clause was a hard-won achievement that has the great merit of ensuring that third parties will not be discriminated against by bilaterally negotiated tariffs. In contrast, to be fully effective, the application of preferences really calls for a gradation of preferences that would provide highly selective discrimination, giving greater preferences to some products than others, to some countries than others, and for different periods of time. If it is to fulfil its objectives, a preferential trading system must discriminate according to the immediate results desired. This contrasts with the principle of non-discrimination which places ultimate value on the generality and neutrality of commercial policy. In other words, the principle of non-discrimination can be justified by reference to a standard that transcends the immediate result that is achieved and is capable of uniform application, whereas discrimination cannot be decided with reference to any standard that can be stated in terms more general than its own result. If discrimination is to be effective, it must be a device of expediency or a matter of what is most convenient or agreeable at a particular moment to some countries; but this is its major deficiency as a principle of commercial policy. For its application then depends upon a political, arbitrary, or variable judgment. This would unfortunately reinforce divisive elements in the international economy, as between the less developed countries and the developed countries and among the countries of each group, just at a time when more international cooperation is needed to support foreign aid and international monetary reform. It was an accomplishment of Gatt to take the longer view and attempt to establish commercial principles of enduring value. This should not now be lightly dismissed.

Instead of supporting preferences which amount to an inversion of protection in favor of the less developed countries, we thus come back to an emphasis on free trade as the direction in which the developed and less developed countries alike should move. While the argument for preferences is right in stressing the objective of expanding export earnings, the means advocated are misplaced. More desirable would be freer trade in manufactures, instead of a proliferation of preferences and further restrictions on efficient resource allocation. To expand exports from the developing countries, it is especially important now to emphasize the removal of trade restrictions imposed by the developed countries as well as the developing countries. The grievances of the developing countries regarding the commercial policies of the advanced countries are legitimate and should be met by a removal of tariff differentials and trade liberalization. If the advanced countries were willing to follow the dictates of the free trade doctrine, they would even reduce their tariffs unilaterally without awaiting the willingness of other countries to reduce their tariffs. Together with a removal of tariff differentials, a unilateral reduction of tariffs by the developed countries on products of particular importance to the less developed countries without full reciprocity could be of considerable significance in stimulating exports from the less developed countries, without incurring the costs of preferences.[12]

To allow their export industries to become more competitive and be in a position to take advantage of tariff reductions by the developed countries, the developing countries must also eliminate their costly policies of import substitution and reduce their trade barriers. The cost disadvantages of these policies may indeed be greater than any competitive advantage that preferences could bestow. It must be re-emphasized that devaluation and a reduction in import restrictions could be equivalent to a subsidy on exports; these measures constitute the most effective action that the less developed countries can immediately take to increase their exports. In addition, the developing countries could promote their exports through disinflationary policies, the special encouragement of private foreign investment into the country's export sector, and a variety of governmental measures of assistance at the micro level to overcome the special costs and disincentives of engaging in the export trade.

Finally (and perhaps too elliptically), we may conclude by noting that in an international economy that is not only tariff-ridden but also subject to recurrent balance of payments crises which act against a removal of trade restrictions, the promotion of development through trade may ultimately have to depend on reform of the international monetary system. Just as Sir John in his 'Free Trade and Modern Economics' was most concerned over the case for import restriction as a means of facilitating full employment without weakening the balance of payments (Hicks, 1950–1), so too, in the pursuit of development, we must still be attentive to the constraint that the balance of payments imposes on trade liberalization. Lagging exports and the discipline of the balance of payments now exercise under the gold-exchange standard a drag on international development and lead to protectionist policies to promote development, just as lagging investment and the discipline of a balanced budget once exercised a fiscal drag on domestic expansion and led to protectionist policies to promote employment. The less developed countries now limit the size of their development plans and impose import restrictions out of balance of payments considerations, and foreign aid programmes also encounter balance of payments restraints in the reserve-currency countries. A genuine movement towards free trade may therefore have to await the provision of more elasticity in the international monetary system and an increase in international liquidity. The very survival of Gatt, with its principle of non-discrimination, may indeed depend on modification of the International Monetary Fund in order to provide a monetary framework that is more conducive to a liberal trade system. But all this is another story that deserves its separate telling.

NOTES AND REFERENCES

¹ Bhagwati and Ramaswami (1963) offer eight reasons for the existence of a wage differential between the industrial and agricultural sectors, only four of which involve genuine distortions that make the gap between industrial and agricultural wages greater than can be accounted for by 'net advantages' as between agricultural and industrial work.

² Bhagwati and Ramaswami (1963, pp. 44–50), and H. G. Johnson (1964, pp. 8–11; 1965, pp. 9–30).

A free trade purist might consider a subsidy to be a type of protection because it encourages directly some domestic industries at the expense of others; but, unlike the tariff, it does not create a disparity between the home market and foreign prices of the affected commodities.

³ Given unusually restrictive conditions with respect to elasticities of home demand and supply, a tariff may allow the increase in producers' surplus (or government revenue) to be greater than the loss in consumers' surplus that results from the tariff. Even under these conditions, however, as long as a tariff entails some consumption cost, the tariff is inferior to a subsidy when it is a matter of offsetting a domestic distortion. This is proved by Bhagwati and Ramaswami (1963, pp. 44–7).

⁴ A tariff could make the foreign and domestic rates of transformation equal, but it would destroy the equality between the domestic rate of substitution and foreign rate of transformation.

A policy of subsidization of industrial production, or of taxation of agricultural production, could equate the domestic and foreign rates of transformation and the domestic rate of substitution; but, since it would not eliminate the inefficiency of labor-use induced by the excessive wage differential, it would achieve this equality only along the inferior trans-formation curve within the maximum attainable production possibility frontier.

In contrast, and in a superior fashion, a policy of subsidizing the use of labor removes directly the wage differential against the industrial sector; and both the inefficiency in labor allocation and the divergence of commodity prices from opportunity costs are simultaneously eliminated. The marginal equivalencies of the domestic and foreign rates of trans-formation and domestic rate of substitution are then achieved along the maximum attainable production possibility frontier.

⁵ For a fuller discussion of the theoretical implications of 'escalation' in tariff rates, see H. G. Johnson (1964).

The effective rate of duty indicates the excess of domestic value added obtainable through the imposition of tariffs, as a percentage of value added in a free trade situation. Professor Johnson provides a rigorous proof, in terms of an input-output system, that the effective rate of protection will be higher than the nominal tariff rate if the weighted-average tariff rate on imported inputs is lower than the tariff rate on the output. See also W. M. Corden (1963, pp. 197f.).

For illustrations of the effects of differential tariffs in practice, see Macario (1964, pp. 74–83), G. M. Radhu (1965, pp. 527–51).

[6] Under reasonable assumptions which take general equilibrium repercussions into account, Professor McKinnon (1966) has shown that the participation of domestic factors per unit of gross output in the protected industry is even likely to decline significantly relative to the use of imported intermediate inputs, as the tariff rate is raised on imported finished goods.

[7] See A. P. Lerner (1936, pp. 306–13). Professor McKinnon has generalized Lerner's discussion to show that levying an *ad valorem* tariff *t* on the *foreign* price of one class of imports is equivalent to taxing exports as a per cent of their *domestic* price, together with subsidizing previously untaxed imports as a percent of their *domestic* price at the same *ad valorem* rate *t*.

[8] The defects of industrialization based on import-substitution are concisely summarized in the Report of the Secretary-General of UNCTAD (1964, pp. 21–2).

[9] A large number of alternative preferential arrangements have been suggested by different countries, but the varying details of these proposals do not affect the logic of the ensuing discussion.

[10] The 'linear' approach of the Kennedy Round reduces the relevance of this criticism, although the exceptions list and the 'tariff disparities' procedure might still allow some indirect discrimination.

[11] Johnson (1966, pp. 15–18). Professor Johnson is, however, careful to note that the developing countries must be able to respond effectively to such export opportunities; that their price and cost levels are now often well above world market levels, and frequently the excess is substantially greater than the tariff-created excess of domestic over world market prices in the developed countries; and that preferences would be of no avail unless they were accompanied by drastic reform of the currency-overvaluation and protectionist import-substitution policies that make the less developed countries unable to compete in world markets (p. 18).

[12] Instead of passing the burden of adjustment on to other developed countries, as under preferences, the policy of unilateral reduction of tariffs might require a liberalized domestic assistance program for the domestic industries that would confront greater competition from exports of the less developed countries. This is especially so because these industries are most likely to be the low-wage and already depressed industries of the advanced country.

17

An Economic Test of Sir John Hicks's
Theory of Biased Induced Inventions

Michio Morishima and Mitsho Saito

I. *Introduction*

Some of the factors that determine the growth of output through time act from within the economic sphere, while others act from the outside of it. Technology has often been regarded as an autonomous factor developing at an externally given rate; many mathematical and econometric models of economic growth have been worked out on the assumption that technology progresses independently of economic events. Against this line of approach, theoretical economists have occasionally emphasized the importance of economic influences on the development of technology.

The idea of induced invention has a long history certainly dating back as far as Marx who argued that increases in the productivity of labour accompanied by the accumulation of capital brought about a continuing rise in the organic composition of capital (that is, the ratio of machines to labour) which would, in turn, induce changes in productive methods in the direction of saving labour; otherwise the death of the capitalist production system could not be avoided sooner or later. Schumpeter's theory of innovation has long been one of the most celebrated and comprehensive among those theories stressing mutual conditioning of economic fluctuations and technical change. Among the British 'innovators' in the 1930s such as Harrod, Hicks, Joan Robinson and others, who paved the way for the contemporary theory of invention, Sir John Hicks (1932) has classified inventions into induced and autonomous inventions and has paid particular attention to biased technological progress induced by a change in relative factor prices. Mrs Robinson (1956) has then argued how innovations are diffused throughout the economy, while Simon (1951) and Morishima (1958) have discussed trigger effects of an invention in one industry on the techniques adopted by other industries.[1] In the vintage models of economic growth recently discussed by Johansen (1959),

Solow (1960), Kaldor and Mirrlees (1960), and others, technical progress is regarded as being embodied in new machines, so that when there is no new capital accumulation, it is impossible to reveal technical progress, though technology may (as they assume) develop, as a science of industrial arts, at an externally given rate. Arrow (1962a) has been concerned with a model in which all advance in technical knowledge is treated as the result of capital accumulation. Finally, the 'invention possibility frontier' now discussed by Kennedy (1964), Samuelson (1965a) and other writers will lead to a new theory of induced invention.

Among these alternatives, we are concerned in this paper with Sir John's approach; his hypothesis that a change in the relative factor prices stimulates the invention of new methods of production biased in the direction of using the now cheaper factor to save the expensive one is successfully tested on time series data for the United States over the period 1902–55. To the knowledge of the present authors, there are no such econometric investigations in spite of the recent rapid accumulation of literature in this field. Our work may, however, be compared in many respects with investigations by M. Brown and J. Popkin (1962) and by P. A. David and Th. van de Klundert (1965); so the rest of the introduction is devoted to giving comments on their papers with the purpose of establishing the *raison d'être* of this paper.

In order to account for the increase in output of the United States non-farm domestic sector, 1890–1958, Murray Brown and Joel Popkin have fitted a production function of the Cobb-Douglas type to various sub-periods and have found that there was no non-neutral technological change within each of the 'technological epochs', 1890–1918, 1919–37, and 1938–58. They take account of neutral and biased inventions, but they all are considered as autonomous. Let X_{t_r}, K_{t_r} and N_{t_r} be total output, employed capital and labour in year t_r of the epoch r, respectively; let A_r, z_r, b_r and c_r be Cobb-Douglas parameters. We have

$$X_{t_r} = A_r K_{t_r}^{a_r} N_{t_r}^{b_r} t_r^{c_r},$$

the total differential of which may be analyzed into four parts:

$$\frac{dX_{t_r}}{X_{t_r}} = \left[\frac{dA_r}{A_r} + c_r \frac{dt_r}{t_r} + \log t_r \, dc_r\right] + \left[\log K_{t_r} \, da_r + \log N_{t_r} \, db_r\right] +$$

$$+ \left[a^r \frac{dK_{t_r}}{K_{t_r}} + b^r \frac{dN_{t_r}}{N_{t_r}}\right] + \left[(a_r - a^r)\frac{dK_{t_r}}{K_{t_r}} + (b_r - b^r)\frac{dN_{t_r}}{N_{t_r}}\right],$$

where $a^r = a_r/(a_r+b_r)$ and $b^r = b_r/(a_r+b_r)$. According to Brown and Popkin, the part in the first brackets on the right-hand side gives output change attributable to neutral technological change, while the part in the second brackets to non-neutral change; the third bracketed part measures contributions of changes in inputs to output change that would be obtained if constant returns to scale prevailed; and the final part takes account of the exploitation of economies of scale.[2] By interpreting all differentials as discrete changes and putting $\Delta a_r = a_{r+1} - a_r$, $\Delta A_r = A_{r+1} - A_r$, etc., Brown and Popkin have estimated these four effects experienced between 'epochs', that is, between 1890–1918 and 1919–37, and between 1919–37 and 1938–58. They have observed, among other things, that 'neutral technological change appears to be lowest in the first epoch and becomes increasingly more important in the second and third'.

We do not wish to belittle their interesting new idea of a 'technological epoch' and their procedure for estimating it statistically, but we must not overlook the fact that K_{t_r} and N_{t_r} are measured in arbitrary units. Let N'_{t_r} be the employed labour measured in a new unit which is q times the old unit, denoted as N_{t_r}. We have

$$X_{t_r} = A_r K_{t_r}^{a_r}(N'_{t_r}q)^{b_r}t_r^{c_r} = A'_r K_{t_r}^{a_r}N_{t_r}^{\prime b_r}t_r^{c_r},$$

so that $A'_r = A_r q^{b_r}$. Hence,

$$\frac{dA'_r}{A'_r} = \frac{dA_r}{A_r} + \log q \, db_r \, .$$

It is, therefore, seen that the change in output that is attributed to neutral technological change in the new unit system includes not only the corresponding term in the old unit system but also some part of the output change which, in the old unit, is considered part of the term due to non-neutral change. This shows that there is an arbitrary element in the Brown-Popkin estimates of the effects of neutral and non-neutral inventions. (A similar arbitrariness is found in Brown's other work with J. S. de Cani.[3])

On the other hand, David and van de Klundert have fitted a production function with constant elasticity of substitution,

$$V_t = [(E_L L_t)^{-\rho} + (E_K K_t)^{-\rho}]^{-1/\rho},$$

to observations on the US private domestic economy for the period 1899–1960. In this expression V_t, K_t and L_t stand, respectively, for total output, employed capital and labour in year t; the coefficients E_K and E_L represent the levels of efficiency of the conventional inputs of capital and labour; and ρ is the substitution coefficient that gives the elasticity of substitution σ as $\sigma = 1/(1+\rho)$.

David and van de Klundert designate the capital-labour ratio as k and the ratio of wages to rentals as π. They put the familiar relationship that follows from the marginal productivity conditions in competitive situations in the form

$$k_t = \pi_t^{\sigma/(1-\sigma)}(E_L/E_K).$$

They have made the following four hypotheses:

(1) The above equation holds for the desired capital-intensity k^* and the normal (or long-run) ratio of factor shares π^*.

(2) The actual ratio of factor shares π is higher than π^* when the rate of unemployment U is abnormally high, so that [4]

$$\pi_t^* = \pi_t a(1-U_t)^\alpha \qquad a>0,\ \alpha\geqslant 0.$$

(3) The actual or true degree of capital-intensity k is distinguished from the observed degree of capital-intensity $\hat{k}$. The ratio of k to $\hat{k}$ gives the rate of utilization of the existing capital stock. Percentage changes in it are assumed to be a constant fraction of the concurrent percentage changes in the rate of employment of labour; thus

$$k_t = \hat{k}_t b(1-U_t)^\beta \qquad b>0,\ \beta>0.$$

(4) An increase in the ratio of the desired capital-intensity in period t to the observed capital-intensity in period $t-1$ induces an increase in the ratio of the actual capital-intensity in period t to the observed capital-intensity in period $t-1$; it is, therefore, postulated that

$$k_t/\hat{k}_{t-1} = (k_t^*/\hat{k}_{t-1})^\gamma \qquad 0<\gamma<1.$$

Substitution of the last three equations into that which precedes them yields

$$\log \hat{k}_t = v_0 + v_1 \log \pi_t + v_2 \log \hat{k}_{t-1} + v_3 \log(1-U_t) + \log(E_L/E_K).$$

According to David and van de Klundert, a technological change is said to be biased into the direction of labour-augmentation (or capital-augmentation) when it causes an increase (or a decrease) in the relative efficiency of labour E_L/E_K. When the elasticity of substitution σ is less than unity, this classification of biased inventions amounts to being equivalent to Sir John's, that is to say, a labour-augmenting (or capital-augmenting) bias in technical change amounts to the same thing as a labour-saving (or capital-saving) invention in the sense of Hicks if and only if $\sigma < 1$. An additional hypothesis introduced by David and van de Klundert specifies the behaviour of the relative efficiency of labour through time. They assume that E_L/E_K follows, with stochastic disturbances, a path with an exponential trend that is expected to be decisively biased in the direction of labour-augmentation:

$$(E_L/E_K)_t = c\, e^{v_4 t} \varepsilon_t \qquad c>0,\, v_4 >0,$$

where ε_t stands for the stochastic term. This, together with the last equation for k, yields

$$\log \hat{k}_t = v_0' + v_1 \log \pi_t + v_2 \log \hat{k}_{t-1} + v_3 \log (1-U_t) + v_4 t + \log \varepsilon_t ,$$

an equation fitted to the observations on k_t, π_t and U_t.

It should be noticed that although David and van de Klundert correctly point out the close relationship of their classifications of innovations to Hicks's, their approach summarized in the above is very different from his theory developed in a famous chapter of *The Theory of Wages*. One of Sir John's problems in that chapter is to ask the real reason for the predominance of labour-saving inventions which has been observed throughout modern history. He divides E_L/E_K (or more exactly $(1-b)/b$ below) into two parts, exact and stochastic, and explains the former by means of economic variables relating to the scarcity of labour and capital. Accordingly, in his view many biased technical changes should not be regarded as exogenous phenomena as David and van de Klundert do, but should endogenously be explained as results of economic calculation.

In this paper we follow David and van de Klundert in assuming production functions of the CES type but differ from them in making a (Hicks-like) hypothesis of induced inventions. Our model is built in Section II and is, in Section IV, fitted to data for the US economy in the period 1902–55. In estimating the regression coefficients we use a method of selective estimation, whose description is given in Section III. On the basis of these estimates, the final section is devoted to an examination of the effects of technical change on the capital-labour ratio and the relative sharing of aggregate income between labour and capital.

From the results obtained we conclude, like Brown and Popkin, that innovations have been strongly labour-saving in the first half of the period (that is, before the Great Depression) but mildly capital-saving in the second half, and, like David and van de Klundert, that technical progress has been labour-saving in the whole period. It is also observed that the dominant factor that has led to the rise in the capital-labour ratio is, in the first half of the period, the spurt of labour-saving inventions in the twenties and, in the second half, substitution of capital for labour induced by the rapid increase in wages. Finally, from the comparison of our index of biasedness of technological progress with David's and van de Klundert's yearly estimates of relative labour efficiency E_L/E_K (including not only the estimated trend values but also the residuals of the regression) we observe that the development of technology treated by them as wholly exogenous could, to a significant extent, be explained, like our series, by a number of variables certainly belonging in the economist's province.[5]

II. *The Model to be Estimated*

We owe to Sir John Hicks the well-known dual classifications of technical invention into 'labour-saving', 'neutral', and 'capital-saving' inventions and into 'autonomous' and 'induced' inventions. He has suggested a hypothesis that autonomous inventions are evenly distributed in a random way with no bias in one direction or another. Another hypothesis of his is that if relative prices of the factors of production change in favour of using a factor, say capital, entrepreneurs are stimulated to adopt inventions of the labour-saving type, that is, such methods of production that increase the marginal product of capital more than they increase the marginal product of labour.[6]

This theoretical set-up by Sir John is examined by splitting the whole economy into two sectors, agricultural and non-agricultural, and by fitting an aggregate production function to time series data for the United States over the period 1902–55.[7] Let X_1 and X_2 be agricultural and non-agricultural products, respectively. Let H_1 and N_1 be capital and labour inputs that agriculture uses to produce output X_1; similarly, let H_2 and N_2 denote capital and labour inputs that the non-agricultural sector transforms into X_2, respectively. We postulate that the production of each sector is subject to a transformation function of the CES type; we have

$$X_1 = a_1 [b_1 H_1^{-c_1} + (1-b_1) N_1^{-c_1}]^{-d_1/c_1}, \tag{1}$$

$$X_2 = a_2 [b_2 H_2^{-c_2} + (1-b_2) N_2^{-c_2}]^{-d_2/c_2}, \tag{2}$$

where a_1 and a_2 are the efficiency coefficients, b_1 and b_2 the distribution coefficients, c_1 and c_2 the substitution coefficients, and d_1 and d_2 the returns-to-scale parameters.[8] When perfect competition prevails, each sector's marginal rate of substitution between labour and capital should equal their relative prices; hence we get

$$\frac{wN_1}{qH_1} = \left(\frac{1-b_1}{b_1}\right)\left(\frac{H_1}{N_1}\right)^{c_1}, \tag{3}$$

$$\frac{wN_2}{qH_2} = \left(\frac{1-b_2}{b_2}\right)\left(\frac{H_2}{N_2}\right)^{c_2}, \tag{4}$$

where w is the money wage rate and q the earnings (quasi-rent) of the capital goods. It follows from these equations that an increase in the wage rate relative to the quasi-rent induces *ceteris paribus* a rise in the capital-labour ratio in each industry, while an increase in b_i (that is, a technical change in industry i into the direction of saving labour) has *ceteris paribus* a similar effect to the capital-labour ratio of that industry.

Sir John has offered a view that a change in the relative prices of the factors of production will lead to an invention that economizes the use of a factor which has become relatively expensive. A change in the relative prices, if it is so powerful that it affects choice of techniques, should be a reflection of a more or less lasting scarcity of the factors. We assume that as labour (or capital) becomes more scarce, the production functions will be shifted in the labour-saving (or capital-saving) direction. On the other hand, Sir John's classification of induced inventions implies that, according as an invention is labour-saving, neutral, or capital-saving, it gives rise to an increase, no change, or a decrease in the parameters b_1 and b_2, respectively. Therefore, when labour (or capital) becomes scarce, b_1 and b_2 are increased (or decreased). We measure, throughout this research, the scarcity of labour by the employment ratio multiplied by the ratio of the gross investment to the existing stock of capital and the scarcity of capital by the index of capacity utilization similarly weighted. The investment-capital ratio should appear as weights, because a high employment of labour and a high utilization of capital should be discounted when entrepreneurs are pessimistic about the future, so that their current investment activities are low. We assume that there is a time lag of one year between a change in the scarcity of a factor and its effects on b's. Since capital, unlike labour, is not freely transferable from sector to sector, it is quite possible that one sector fully utilizes the stock of capital it has, while another does not. We assume, however, for the sake of simplicity that there have been no significant differences in the degree of capital utilization between the agricultural and the non-agricultural sectors; and we use the index of capacity utilization for the non-agricultural sector to measure the scarcity of capital not only in that sector but also in the other, that is, in agriculture. We may now formulate the Hicksian postulate of induced inventions as follows:

$$\left(\frac{1-b_1}{b_1}\right)_t = \beta_{10}\left(h\frac{I}{K}\right)_{t-1}^{\beta_{11}}\left(n\frac{I}{K}\right)_{t-1}^{\beta_{12}} m^{c_1}, \tag{5}$$

$$\left(\frac{1-b_2}{b_2}\right)_t = \beta_{20}\left(h\frac{I}{K}\right)_{t-1}^{\beta_{21}}\left(n\frac{I}{K}\right)_{t-1}^{\beta_{22}} m^{c_2}, \tag{6}$$

where h is the index of capacity utilization (for the non-agricultural sector), n the employment ratio of labour (for the whole national economy), I the gross investment (national), K the existing stock of capital (national), and m a constant depending on the units of measuring capital and labour inputs H and N. β's are constants to be estimated; we expect β_{11} and β_{21} to be positive and β_{12} and β_{22} negative.

Let us next assume that both sectors similarly respond to scarcity of the factors, so that $\beta_{11} = \beta_{21}$ and $\beta_{12} = \beta_{22}$. Let the total capital input be denoted by H and the total labour input by N. Evidently,

$$\frac{wH}{qH} = \frac{wN_1}{qH_1}\frac{qH_1}{qH} + \frac{wN_2}{qH_2}\frac{qH_2}{qH}.$$

In view of (3), (4), (5) and (6) this may be put in the form

$$\left(\frac{wN}{qH}\right)_t = \left(h\frac{I}{K}\right)_{t-1}^{\beta_1}\left(n\frac{I}{K}\right)_{t-1}^{\beta_2}\left[\beta_{10}m^{c_1}\left(\frac{H_1/X_1}{H/X}\right)_t\left(\frac{H_1}{N_1}\right)_t^{c_1} g_t + \right.$$

$$\left. +\beta_{20}m^{c_2}\left(\frac{H_2/X_2}{H/X}\right)_t\left(\frac{H_2}{N_2}\right)_t^{c_2}(1-g_t)\right]u_t, \tag{7}$$

where X is total output, that is, the sum of X_1 and X_2, both being measured in 1929 dollars; g is the share of the agricultural output in total output, X_1/X; β_1 and β_2 are the elasticities of $((1-b_1)/b_1)_t$ with respect to $(hI/K)_{t-1}$ and $(nI/K)_{t-1}$ respectively, which the two sectors have, by assumption, in common with each other, that is $\beta_1 = \beta_{11} = \beta_{21}$ and

$\beta_2 = \beta_{12} = \beta_{22}$; u denotes the disturbance term and is regarded as being affected autonomous inventions.

We now make the following three assumptions for the sake of simplicity in the estimation of the parameters. (Those assumptions, as will be seen soon, are rather restrictive but are needed for the aggregate relationship derived from individual CES production functions also to be of the CES form.) First, the part in the brackets of the above expression gives the weighted average of

$$\beta_{10} m^{c_1} \left(\frac{H_1 / X_1}{H / X} \right)_t \left(\frac{H_1}{N_1} \right)_t^{c_1} \quad \text{and} \quad \beta_{20} \, m^{c_2} \left(\frac{H_2 / X_2}{H / X} \right)_t \left(\frac{H_2}{N_2} \right)_t^{c_2} .$$

We assume that the weights g_t and $(1 - g_t)$ remain in a range in which the arithmetic average is approximately proportional to the corresponding geometric average,

$$\beta_{10}^{g_t} \beta_{20}^{1-g_t} m^{c_1 g_t + c_2 (1-g_t)} \left(\frac{H_1 / X_1}{H / X} \right)_t^{g_t} \left(\frac{H_2 / X_2}{H / X} \right)_t^{1-g_t} \left(\frac{H_1}{N_1} \right)_t^{c_1 g_t} \left(\frac{H_2}{N_2} \right)_t^{c_2 (1 - g_t)} .$$

Second, assume that g_t is in a range where the geometric average of H_1 / X_1 and H_2 / X_2 with weights g_t and $1 - g_t$ may safely be regarded as a constant proportion of the arithmetic average H / X. Finally, capital-intensities, H_1 / N_1 and H_2 / N_2, of the two sectors are assumed to vary proportionally, so that they may be replaced by $\alpha_1 H / N$ and $\alpha_2 H / N$ with certain constants α_1 and α_2, respectively. Hence the formula of the distribution of income among workers and capitalists can now be written

$$\left(\frac{wN}{qH} \right)_t = \beta_0 \left(h \frac{I}{K} \right)_{t-1}^{\beta_1} \left(n \frac{I}{K} \right)_{t-1}^{\beta_2} (\log^{-1} \beta_3)^{g_t} \left(\frac{H}{N} \right)_t^{c_1 g_t + c_2 (1 - g_t)} u_t \quad (8)$$

with constants β_0 and β_3.

In estimating this equation we make use of the technique of pooling cross-section and time series data. It is evident that equation (8) may be put in the following form:

$$\log \left(\frac{wN}{qH} \right)_t - (c_1 g_t + c_2 (1 - g_t)) \log \left(\frac{H}{N} \right)_t$$

$$= \log \beta_0 + \beta_1 \log \left(h \frac{I}{K} \right)_{t-1} + \beta_2 \log \left(n \frac{I}{K} \right)_{t-1} + \beta_3 g_t + \log u_t. \quad (9)$$

We substitute for c_1 and c_2 the estimates from the cross section sample, $c_1 = -0 \cdot 175$ and $c_2 = 0 \cdot 120$, the former being taken from Griliches

(1964), and the latter being the average of the ACMS estimates with the weights of industrial gross value added.[9] To obtain estimates of β_i's, the new variable on the left-hand side of (9) is regressed on $\log (hI/K)_{t-1}$, $\log (nI/K)_{t-1}$ and g_t by applying the method of selective estimation discussed in the next section.

III. *A Method of Selective Estimation*

In statistical estimation of parameters of a model on the basis of a set of sample observations on the variables concerned, we must, among other things, assume that they have all been generated from the same structure by the same stochastic mechanism. This implies that the samples should have already been selected so as to fulfil, at least approximately, the *ceteris paribus* assumption that there had been no exogenous shift in the parameters defining the probability distributions of stochastic variables and no shifts in the economic-technical structural parameters. But no statistically rigorous and practically applicable principle of selection has yet been found; in the present state of econometrics we can only select observations on the basis of more or less arbitrary outside information as many practising econometricians usually do.[10]

In spite of the unavailability of a satisfactory principle for finding black sheep, they must be withdrawn from the flock. Homogenization is important, especially when we are concerned with estimating effects of technological changes. In equations (5) and (6) the stochastic terms reflect a class of (non-neutral) autonomous inventions, while the systematic parts reflect induced inventions. It would be restrictive and unrealistic to assume that autonomous inventions occur in a random way according to the classical least-squares hypotheses about the disturbance term. Technical progress is often a volatile, irregular phenomenon; it is quite conceivable that autonomous inventions with a significant bias in one direction are more likely to be produced in some particular years than in others. If we were non-selective in data and blindly accepted the hypothesis that autonomous inventions should be unbiasedly distributed over a long period, we might obtain seriously distorted estimates for the parameters.

In order to escape arbitrariness in subjective individual judgments that appear to be inevitable when we select observations on the basis of outside information, an objective or mechanical selection procedure, though not fully satisfactory, should be used as a test. In the present investigation the relevant time series data are homogenized in the following way. To estimate parameters of a linear relationship

$$Y_t = \beta_0 + \beta_1 X_{1t} + \beta_2 X_{2t} + \ldots + \beta_k X_{kt} + e_t, \quad t = 1, 2, \ldots, n, \quad (10)$$

between the regressand Y and k explanatory variables $X_1, X_2, \ldots, X_k$, where e stands for the disturbance term, we first group n given observations on $Y_t, X_{1t}, \ldots, X_{kt}$, in an arbitrary way, into two distinct classes A_0 and B_0, each including $n/2$ observations. We then obtain, on the basis of the sample observations classified in A_0, a set of least-squares estimators of β's and apply Wallis's (1951) tolerance-interval test to each observation belonging to B_0.[11] Eliminating from B_0 those observations that are shown to be outside their respective tolerance intervals, we form a sub-group B_1 of B_0. The second step of our procedure is to estimate equation (10) on the observations in the 'selected' set B_1 and to compute tolerance intervals for the observations in A_0; if some of them fall outside the intervals thus obtained, we eliminate them from A_0 to get a subset A_1.[12]

Next we fit equation (10) to the observations in A_1 and test whether those in B_0 belong to the same linear structure. Those observations which have been seen to pass the test form a new group B_2, on the basis of which (10) is re-estimated. From these last estimates, we again make tolerance-interval tests whether the observations in A_0 come from the same relation as those in B_2, in order to get a new 'selected' group A_2. Proceeding in the same way until we finally get two sets of observations A_r and B_r such that $A_r = A_{r-1}$ and $B_r = B_{r-1}$, we are provided with a set of homogenized observations, that is the join of A_r and B_r, because all the observations belonging to B_r are inside the tolerance intervals computed from that relation which is estimated on the observations in A_r and *vice versa*.

It should be noted that the above homogenization will depend on the initial division of the available data into groups A_0 and B_0; it is possible and will usually happen that one grouping turns out to exclude some observations, while another to exclude different ones. When the total number of different pairs of groups that can be selected out of a set of n observations is not large, we can make a test for each of them and see how often a particular observation would be discarded. But in a practical case where that number is very large, we can only draw a random sample of an appropriate size, say fifty, from the enormous range of possibilities and apply our homogenization test to the groups thus drawn. Those observations which these selected trials frequently discard may safely be regarded as being heterogeneous to all others with respect to the linear structure being estimated.

The final paragraph of this section is devoted to a few remarks on conceivable obstacles to the proposed procedure for finding a set of homogeneous observations. First, we may imagine a case in which the test results in discovery that those observations rejected as 'heterogeneous' are widely and more or less evenly distributed throughout the whole set of the available data. If this happens, it is doubtful whether there are homogeneous observations. Second, for some initial grouping of the whole set of observations into A_0 and B_0, it may happen that our stepwise homogenization procedure does not succeed in finding, after a finite number of iterations, a unique subset (A_r, B_r) such that every member of A_r lies in the tolerance interval associated with the corresponding forecast that is made on the basis of the structural equation derived from the observations in B_r, and *vice versa*. For example, it is conceivable that our iteration procedure yields sets A_2 and B_2 such that $A_2 \neq A_1$ and $B_2 \neq B_1$, but $A_2 = A_0$ and $B_2 = B_0$; then we have a cycle starting from A_0 and returning to it through B_1, A_1, and B_0 in order. The procedure will be repeated endlessly and give no consistent solution. Finally, it may be noted that a process starting from A_0 and a process starting from the complement B_0 of A_0 may result in different homogenizations. In spite of the logical possibilities of these perverse cases, it seems that they would rarely happen in practice; in fact, we have met none of them in one hundred trials (that is fifty independent trials plus their complements).

IV. *Application of the Proposed Method*

We divided the sample period 1902–55 into three subperiods: 1902–41, 1942–6, and 1947–55. The war period was eliminated on an *a priori* basis; and the method described in the preceding section was first applied to the data of the prewar period, and the structural equation obtained was then found to fit, with a dummy variable subjoined, close to the observations of the postwar period. Forty observations in the prewar period can be divided into two groups of the same size in $\frac{1}{2} \times \binom{40}{20}$ different ways—a number approximately equal to $6 \cdot 89 \times 10^{10}$. By random sampling, fifty different groupings were drawn, and the test was applied to each of them.

We begin by making some general remarks on common features of the results. First, with no exception the groupings we drew were found to converge, after several iterations of our stepwise homogenization procedure, to a set of 'homogeneous' observations. Second, the number of iterations was small, 2 to 7. Third, with each grouping specified, we can start two processes of iterations, primary and complementary, from either of the initial groups; but, as far as our 50 sample groupings were concerned, it was seen that both these processes selected exactly the same set of observations as homogeneous. The final remark is of the most general character; the ordinary least-squares regression method, applied to a single equation model such as ours, has a chance of leading to biased and inconsistent results. Our conclusions drawn below are, however, subject to the assumption that single equation biases are not serious.

TABLE 1. Frequencies with which the time series observations turned out singular in the fifty tolerance-interval tests

$$p = 90\% : \gamma = 95\%$$

Year	13	19	21	22	31	32	33	35	41
Frequency	7	19	50	15	4	22	19	2	49

$$p = 95\% : \gamma = 95\%$$

Year	19	21	22	32	33	41
Frequency	1	49	1	9	7	29

The tolerance interval defines a range within which at least p per cent of non-sample observations belonging to the given population are expected to lie with probability of γ per cent; tolerance interval tests were made at two different levels of probability; at $p = 0.90$ and $\gamma = 0.95$, and at $p = 0.95$ and $\gamma = 0.95$. Table 1 summarizes the results of our fifty independent trials. Those years which were dismissed by the test at least once are all listed in the first row. The second row shows the frequency with which a particular year failed to pass the test; for example, with $p = 0.90$ and $\gamma = 0.95$, the set of observations for 1913 lay outside of the tolerance interval in seven cases out of the 50 tests, while that for 1921 was discarded as singular (or heterogeneous) in all 50 tests. The test with $p = 0.90$ and $\gamma = 0.95$ has led to the following findings. The years which were rejected as being not homogeneous with high frequencies were 1921

(100 per cent) and 1941 (98 per cent). These were followed by 1932 (44 per cent), 1933 (38 per cent), 1919 (38 per cent) and 1922 (30 per cent). The other years were dismissed with percentages less than 14 per cent; and thirty-one out of the forty years never failed in the tests. With $p = 0.95$ and $\gamma = 0.95$, on the other hand, the years 1921 and 1941 were dismissed with such high frequencies as 98 and 58 per cent, respectively, while 1932 and 1933 were discarded with 18 and 14 per cent, all other years having never or only once failed in the fifty tests. These results would suggest that a mild homogenization follows from regarding 1921, 1932, 1933, and 1941 as singular years when there were extremely unusual random shocks or structural changes; while, at a more rigorous level of homogenization, two years 1919 and 1922, in addition to the above four years, have to be counted as singular.

From the viewpoint of qualitative history also, it seems that these years may reasonably be discriminated from others. 1919 is the year immediately after World War I, which forms, together with the following three years, 1920, 1921, and 1922, a period of transition from war to peacetime production. In those years businessmen felt uncertain about future prospects; the economy experienced a strong postwar boom and a sudden, sharp downswing. 1932 and 1933 are the years in the midst of the Great Depression. At the end of 1941 the United States joined in World War II, although prior to that time she had been gradually preparing for action. Increasing amounts of military spending were powerfully stimulating the American economy. Although it is very difficult to discover specific inventions, autonomous or induced, which made those years odd members in the sample, there is no doubt that they are the years when we had abnormal exogenous shocks.

The result of fitting equation (9) to the data for the years, 1902–41, are presented in Table 2.[13] The number appearing in parentheses below the regression coefficients are the values of t-statistics which are used for testing the null hypotheses that the corresponding coefficients are not significantly different from zero. The measure of goodness of fit $\bar{R}^2$ is adjusted for degree of freedom; d is the Durbin-Watson statistic.

The estimation method assumes that the random disturbances are drawn from a set of mutually independent normally distributed variables with common expectation (zero) and common variance. Table 2 shows that the value of the d-statistic was computed at 0.89 when no years were

TABLE 2. Selective and non-selective estimations of equation (9) on 1902–41 observations

	COEFFICIENTS OF				$\bar{R}^2$	computed d	2.5% level of significance d_L	d_U	calculated Smirnov test statistic
	$\log\left(h\frac{I}{K}\right)_{-1}$	$\log\left(n\frac{I}{K}\right)_{-1}$	g	1					
i. No years excluded	0·796 (1·458)	−0·807 (1·366)	7·530 (10·482)	−0·214 (0·847)	0·77	0·89	1·25	1·57	0·092
ii. 1921,32,33, & 41 excluded	1·063 (2·986)	−1·175 (3·027)	8·315 (16·795)	−0·615 (3·285)	0·90	1·46	1·20	1·56	0·040
iii. 1919, 21, 22, 32, 33 & 41 excluded	1·296 (4·235)	−1·439 (4·307)	8·469 (20·208)	−0·732 (4·560)	0·93	1·64	1·17	1·55	0·029

excluded (regression (i)), at 1·46 when four years, 1921, 1932, 1933, and 1941, were excluded (regression (ii)), and at 1·64 when two more years, 1919 and 1922 were excluded (regression (iii)). It is worth observing that the value of d of regression (iii) is greater than the upper bound for acceptance of the hypothesis of no serial correlation at a probability level of 2·5 per cent, whereas the corresponding value of regression (i) is less than the lower bound, and that of regression (ii) lies between the lower and upper bounds. Thus the residuals of regression (iii) may be regarded as fulfilling the hypothesis of random disturbances, though it is rejected in favour of the hypothesis of positive autocorrelation in the case of regression (i), and the test is inconclusive in the case of regression (ii).

By applying the Smirnov test procedure (Kendall and Stuart, 1961, pp. 450–2), regressions (i), (ii) and (iii) are favourably tested for the hypothesis of normally distributed disturbances. The calculated values of the Smirnov test statistic are listed in Table 2; they are seen significantly less than the respective critical values of the asymptotic distribution of that statistic for a probability level of 10 per cent.

It is obvious that the selection by the tolerance-interval method should be consistent; that is to say, those observations which a number of iterative tolerance-interval tests have revealed to be 'singular' should themselves be outside of the tolerance intervals which are computed from the equation estimated on the basis of the suggested exclusions of observations. In our case, the four years listed in the row (ii) of Table 2 should be outside the tolerance intervals computed from regression (ii). They turned out to be so; in fact, they were found to be outside a range within which at least 95 per cent of non-sample observations are expected to be with probability of 95 per cent. In a similar way, it was seen that the selection of the six years listed in the row (iii) was consistent with respect to the test with $p = 0·90$ and $\gamma = 0·95$.

From Table 2 it is also seen that the signs of the regression coefficients are in accord with those which are expected on the basis of theoretical considerations. The t-statistics associated with the capacity utilization and the labour employment variable are poor in regression (i) with no observations being excluded. When the four or six abnormal years are excluded, however, all the coefficients obtained become significantly different from zero with 99 per cent level of confidence. Furthermore, in both regressions the coefficient of the labour employment variable is seen to be significantly greater in modulus than the coefficient of the capital utilization variable. And this last finding would lead to a view that, other things being equal, inventions have a decided bias in the labour-saving direction.[14]

We have so far neglected the observations in the postwar period which are now combined with the prewar observations so as to estimate the parameters of the overall structure. For this purpose we first computed tolerance intervals for the postwar 9 observations (1947–55) by the use of the sample (ii) or (iii) estimated on the basis of the prewar selected observations, and found that all the postwar observations did not lie within the corresponding tolerance limits. These findings would naturally lead to a hypothesis that there were some structural changes in the transition from the prewar to the postwar period.

We attempted to account for possible structural change by introducing an additive 'dummy variable' *D*, which assumed *zero* values for prewar years and *unit* values for postwar years. We found that the coefficients of the dummy variable were significantly positive; so that it is seen that the method of production was more capital-saving in the postwar period, 1947–55, than it was in the prewar period.

The pooling of the observations in both periods was made on the assumption that the parameters of the equation other than the constant term had remained unchanged throughout the whole period except the four or six abnormal years and the war period. Comparing the prewar sample (ii) (or (iii)) in Table 2 with the prewar and postwar sample (ii′) (or (iii′)) in Table 3, we find that the estimated values of the corresponding coefficients are very close to each other. To test the equality between them, we may follow the procedure developed by Gregory C. Chow (1960). The calculated *F* ratio of Chow's test for equality of coefficients was 1·72 in the case of comparing (ii) and (ii′) and 2·05 in comparing (iii) and (iii′). These are less than the respective critical values, 2·85 and 2·87, at the five per cent level of significance; the assumption of the equality between the coefficients (except the dummy variable term) is thus strongly corroborated in both cases.

Finally, comparing Tables 2 and 3 with each other, it is seen that the values of *t*-statistics for all regression coefficients and *d*-statistics remain unchanged between regressions (ii) and (ii′) and between (iii) and (iii′). It is also seen that the calculated values of the Smirnov test statistic for regressions (i′), (ii′) and (iii′) are all in favour of the normality assumption.

TABLE 3. Selective and non-selective estimations of equation (9) on 1902–41 and 1947–55 observations

	COEFFICIENTS OF					computed $\bar{R}^2$ d	2·5% level of significance d_L d_U	calculated Smirnov test statistic
	$\log\left(h\dfrac{I}{K}\right)_{-1}$	$\log\left(n\dfrac{I}{K}\right)_{-1}$	g	D	1			
i′. No years excluded	0·786 (1·578)	−0·789 (1·464)	7·482 (11·362)	0·382 (5·028)	−0·184 (0·800)	0·77 1·10	1·29 1·64	0·092
ii′. 1921,32,33 and 41 excluded	1·041 (3·072)	−1·137 (3·072)	8·210 (17·393)	0·458 (8·358)	−0·552 (3·119)	0·90 1·49	1·25 1·63	0·041
iii′. 1919,21,22,32,33 and 41 excluded	1·266 (4·191)	−1·391 (4·227)	8·355 (20·272)	0·480 (9·975)	−0·663 (4·186)	0·92 1·63	1·22 1·63	0·033

We may now strongly confirm that apart from some sporadic, anomalous changes, systematic biased technical changes have been induced during the first half of this century.

v. *Distribution and Biased Invention*

On the basis of the *point* estimates of the parameters listed in the bottom row of Table 3, we attempt, in this final section, to decompose changes in the relative shares of factors in output into four parts attributed to induced and autonomous (biased) technical changes, changes in the industrial composition and changes in the prices of the factors of production. We also attempt, on the same basis, to decompose changes in the capital-labour ratio into four similar components. All conclusions drawn below should be qualified, however, by remarks that the parameter estimates used are subject to sampling errors.

Let us write

$$s_t = \frac{1}{r_1 g_t + r_2(1 - g_t)}. \tag{11}$$

As r_1 and r_2 are the reciprocals of the elasticities of substitution of the agricultural and non-agricultural production functions, it is seen that s_t is the harmonic average of the sectoral elasticities of substitution. Taking account of the relationships $r_i = 1 + c_i, i = 1, 2$, we have from (8) and (11)

$$\left(\frac{wN}{qH}\right)_t = \left[\beta_0\left(h\frac{I}{K}\right)_{t-1}^{\beta_1}\left(n\frac{I}{K}\right)_{t-1}^{\beta_2}(\log^{-1}\beta_3)^{g_t}u_t\right]^{s_t}\left(\frac{w}{q}\right)_t^{1-s_t}, \tag{12}$$

or

$$\left(\frac{H}{N}\right)_t = \left[\frac{\left(\frac{w}{q}\right)_t}{\beta_0\left(h\frac{I}{K}\right)_{t-1}^{\beta_1}\left(n\frac{I}{K}\right)_{t-1}^{\beta_2}(\log^{-1}\beta_3)^{g_t}u_t}\right]^{s_t}. \tag{13}$$

To find an approximate change in the ratio of workers' income to capitalists' income, we carry out logarithmic differentiation of (12) and interpret differentials as discrete change to obtain

$$\Delta \log\left(\frac{wN}{qH}\right)_t = s_t\beta_1\Delta\log\left(h\frac{I}{K}\right)_{t-1} + s_t\beta_2\Delta\log\left(n\frac{I}{K}\right)_{t-1} + s_t\Delta\log u_t +$$

$$+ s_t\beta_3\Delta g_t + \log\left(\frac{N}{H}\right)_t\Delta\log s_t + (1-s_t)\Delta\log\left(\frac{w}{q}\right)_t. \tag{14}$$

As $\Delta \log \left(\dfrac{wN}{qH}\right)_t = \Delta \left(\dfrac{wN}{qH}\right)_t \Big/ \left(\dfrac{wN}{qH}\right)_t$, (14) gives the percentage change in $\left(\dfrac{wN}{qH}\right)_t$ split into six terms: The first term on the right-hand side of (14) stands for the effect on the distribution of income of a technical invention that is induced by an increase in the degree of utilization of capital and is biased into the direction of saving capital, the second term for the effect of an invention induced by an increase in the rate of employment of labour and biased into the direction of saving labour, the third term for the effect of an autonomous invention, the fourth and fifth terms together for the two effects, direct and indirect (*via* s_t), of a change in the share of the agricultural product in the total output, and the last term for the effect of a change in the price ratio between labour and capital service. They are called the induced invention effect (that is, the sum of the first two terms), the autonomous invention effect, the industrial composition effect (that is, the sum of the fourth and fifth terms), and the price effect, respectively.[15]

Let us now define the operator $G(\ \ )$ as

$$G(\ \ ) = \log^{-1}(\ \ ) - 1 .$$

Putting $\Delta \log [h(I/K)]_{t-1} = \log [h(I/K)]_t - \log [h(I/K)]_{t-1}$ etc. in (14) and denoting the mean of the ith term on the right-hand side of (14) over a certain subperiod (t_0, t_1) by A_i, we have calculated, for various subperiods,

$$G(A^*), \quad G(A_1+A_2), \quad G(A_3), \quad G(A_4+A_5), \quad G(A_6),$$

where A^* represents the sum of all A_i's. $G(A^*)$ gives the average annual percentage change in the relative share of income $(wN/qH)_t$, which is attributed to the induced invention effect $[G(A_1+A_2)]$, the autonomous investment effect $[G(A_3)]$, the industrial composition effect $[G(A_4+A_5)]$ and the price effect $[G(A_6)]$. It is clear that the equality

$$G(A^*) = G(A_1+A_2)+G(A_3)+G(A_4+A_5)+G(A_6)$$

is not exactly correct but may be regarded as a reasonable approximation.

In a broader classification, the industrial composition effect may be placed in the same category as the induced and autonomous invention effects. The aggregate of these three effects yields the total technology effect $G(A^{**})$, where A^{**} is the sum of the first five A_i's. It is seen that the average total technology effect is nearly (but not exactly) equal to the sum of the component effects, $G(A_1+A_2)$, $G(A_3)$, $G(A_4+A_5)$; and it is further added to the average price effect to approximate the average total effect.

It is not surprising that we have obtained very small price effects for all subperiods, because the (harmonic) average of the sectoral elasticities of substitution, s_t, is close to unity (ranging from 0·945 to 0·909). As is seen from Table 4, they are all less than 0·3 per cent per year. On the other hand it follows from $s_t < 1$ that an invention of labour-saving technology tends to decrease the relative share of labour, and *vice versa*. The figures listed in the column 'total technology effect' of Table 4 show that there were powerful technological changes in the direction of saving labour in the first half of our sample period, while, in the second half, inventions strongly biased in the opposite direction experienced during the Great Depression were followed by a number of inventions which were practically neutral.

TABLE 4. Decomposition of the average annual percentage changes in the relative income share into components

| | | TECHNOLOGY EFFECT | | | | |
	TOTAL EFFECT $G(A^*)$	total $G(A^{**})$	induced inventions $G(A_1+A_2)$	autonomous inventions $G(A_3)$	industrial composition $G(A_4+A_5)$	PRICE EFFECT $G(A_6)$
1902–29 [a]	−2·2	−2·2	−0·1	0·5	−2·5	−0·1
1929–55 [b]	1·0	0·9	0·6	0·6	−0·3	0·2
1929–38 [c]	2·7	2·4	3·3	−3·0	2·3	0·3
1938–55 [d]	0·0	−0·1	−1·0	2·8	−1·8	0·1
1902–55 [e]	−0·9	−0·9	0·2	0·5	−1·6	0·0

[a] Excluding 1919, 21, and 22.
[b] Excluding 1932, 33, and 1941–6.
[c] Excluding 1932 and 33.
[d] Excluding 1941–6.
[e] Excluding 1919, 21, 22, 32, 33, and 41–6.

From Table 4 we also see that the allocation of the average annual percentage change in wN/qH among the induced invention effect, the autonomous invention effect and the industrial composition effect is different from subperiod to subperiod. In 1902–29, the induced invention effect was practically neutral, while the autonomous invention effect was slightly capital saving. But the industrial composition effect was so powerful that it lowered the relative share at the average rate of 2·5 per cent per year. The rapid industrialization was responsible, especially in the twenties, for shifting the aggregate production function into the direction of saving labour. On the other hand, in 1929–38 the induced invention effect was capital saving at 3·3 per cent per year. It is natural that in the depression period, during which the amount of capital decreased but the labour force increased at a steady rate, business firms were interested in labour-using techniques of production.[16] In 1938–55, however, the induced invention effect emerged with labour saving bias as a result of the persistence of high level employment and a rapid increase in wages. It is noted that in the second half of the period the induced invention effect took a big share in the total technology effect, whereas it played a negligible role in the first half.

In terms of the index of the technological effect defined below, our results may be compared with the previous results by David and van de Klundert. Let us fix the average elasticity of substitution s_t at the value s_0 in 1902, and compute

$$\log M_t = \log\left(\frac{wH}{qH}\right)_t - (1 - s_0)\log\left(\frac{w}{q}\right)_t \tag{15}$$

for each t. As the variance of s_t is very small, it is seen from (12) and (14) that M_t may be regarded as a proxy for that part of wN/qH which is attributed to induced and autonomous inventions and changes in the industrial composition. On the other hand, we have from the David-van de Klundert production function

$$\left(\frac{wN}{qH}\right)_t = \left(\frac{E_K}{E_L}\right)_t^{1-\sigma}\left(\frac{w}{q}\right)_t^{1-\sigma}, \tag{16}$$

a relationship, which David's and van de Klundert's index of relative labour efficiency E_L/E_K is required to fulfil in the long run. As their estimate of σ is less than one, it is seen from (15) and (16) that M_t is comparable with the reciprocal of $(E_L/E_K)_t$, that is, with $(E_K/E_L)_t$, the time paths of both indices being plotted in Figure 1 on a semilogarithmic scale.[17] The similarity of the two paths suggests that David and van de Klundert could have explained at least some part of E_K/E_L by economic variables such as the rate of utilization of capital, the rate of employment of labour and so on. The path of M_t reveals that technical changes in the direction of saving labour have been dominant in the first half of the sample period, while those in the other direction have successively appeared in the thirties. By fitting a linear semilogarithmic trend to the series of M_t, we find that there is a highly significant upward tendency of the index in the thirties as well as a downward tendency in 1902–29. The period of saving capital is shorter than the period of saving labour, so that we observe a general tendency of saving labour over the whole sample period.

Our findings may be compared with conclusions of other studies. David and van de Klundert (1965, pp. 382–4) have arrived at the following four conclusions: (i) Over the period 1899–1960 technical change was not neutral but was biased in the direction of saving labour. (ii) In 1900–18 labour saving technical change took place more rapidly than the long-term trend rate. (iii) In 1919–45 there was no significant tendency to save one factor relative to the other. (iv) In the postwar period, 1946–60, technical changes of the labour saving type appeared at a rate even faster than that experienced prior to 1919. We find from Figure 1 that the time path of our index M_t also displays the alleged tendencies (i), (ii) and (iii), but its behaviour in the postwar period contradicts what David and van de Klundert have found. It is interesting to see that they have observed peaks of labour saving inventions in the years, 1921 and 1932, which we have picked out as singular by the procedure of selective estimation.

Brown and Popkin (1962, pp. 406–8) have found that the sample period, 1890–1958, may be divided into three technological epochs, 1890–1918, 1919–37 and 1938–58, within which observations have been seen to be homogeneous with respect to non-neutral technology; by comparing the epochal estimates of the Cobb-Douglas parameters with each other they have noticed a labour-saving technological change between the first and the second epoch and a capital-saving one between the second and the third. Roughly speaking, these findings are in line with ours except that the neutrality of technical inventions within 1902–18 clearly contradicts the movements of our index and the David-van de Klundert index.

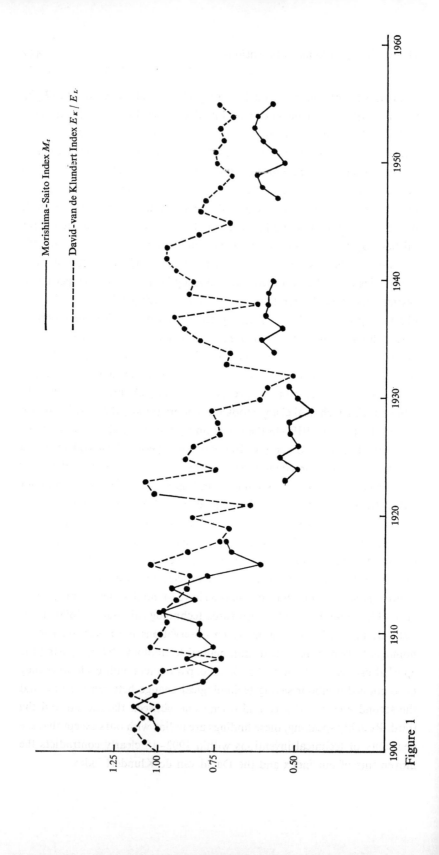

———— Morishima-Saito Index M_t

– – – – David-van de Klundert Index E_K / E_L

Figure 1

The Brown-Popkin trichotomy has recently been revised by Brown (1966, pp. 148–59); he has proposed, in his book, a new division of the period 1890–1960 into four technological epochs: 1890–1906, 1907–20, 1921–39 and 1940–60. The reader might be interested in observing that our singular years, except 1932 and 1933, form boundaries of his (or Brown's and Popkin's) technological epochs.

TABLE 5. Decomposition of the average annual percentage changes in the capital-labour ratio into components

| | TOTAL EFFECT | TECHNOLOGY EFFECT | | | | PRICE EFFECT |
		total	*induced inven-tions*	*auto-nomous inventions*	*industrial com-position*	
1902–29 [a]	1·1	2·2	0·1	−0·5	2·6	−1·1
1929–55 [b]	1·1	−0·8	−0·6	−0·6	0·3	2·0
1929–38 [c]	1·0	−2·4	−3·2	3·1	−2·2	3·5
1939–55 [d]	1·2	0·1	1·0	−2·7	1·9	1·1
1902–55 [e]	1·1	0·9	−0·2	−0·5	1·6	0·2

[a] Excluding 1919, 21, and 22.
[b] Excluding 1932, 33, and 41–6.
[c] Excluding 1932 and 33.
[d] Excluding 1941–6.
[e] Excluding 1919, 21, 22, 32, 33, and 41–6.

The final part of the paper is devoted to a similar decomposition of the average annual percentage change in the capital-labour ratio into the induced and autonomous invention effects, the industrial composition effect and the price effect. The logarithmic differentiation of equation (13) yields

$$\Delta \log\left(\frac{H}{N}\right)_t = -s_t\beta_1\Delta \log\left(h\frac{I}{K}\right)_{t-1} - s_t\beta_2\Delta \log\left(n\frac{I}{K}\right)_{t-1} -$$

$$- s_t\Delta \log u_t - s_t\beta_3\Delta g_t - \log\left(\frac{N}{H}\right)_t\Delta \log s_t + s_t\Delta \log\left(\frac{w}{q}\right)_t. \quad (17)$$

The sum of the first two terms gives the induced invention effect, the third term the autonomous invention effect, the sum of the fourth and fifth terms the industrial composition effect and the last term the price effect. The three effects other than the price effect constitute the total technology effect. It follows from (14) and (17) that the total technology effect and its components on the capital-labour ratio are identical with those on the relative income share, except that they are opposite in sign.

Let us concentrate our attention on the price effect. In the first half of the period, 1902–29, the wage rate increased so mildly that the price effect tended to diminish the capital-labour ratio at an average rate of 1·1 per cent per year; and this negative price effect was exceeded by a strong technology effect with labour saving bias. As for the second half, 1929–55, however, we got a big positive price effect (at the rate of 2·0 per cent per year), reflecting rapid increase in the wage rate during that period. It is seen that there remains a positive net effect after subtracting from this price effect the corresponding technology effect that emerged in the opposite direction at the rate of 0·8 per cent per year. We conclude this paper by saying that the commanding factor in the movement of the capital-labour ratio is different between the first and the second half of the period; it was the technology effect in the first half, but the price effect in the second half.[18]

ACKNOWLEDGMENTS

We are indebted to Professors L. R. Klein, University of Pennsylvania, H. Oniki, Tohoku University, and M. Sawamura, Kobe University of Commerce, for valuable comments and to Mr K. Nakagawa for computational assistance. Thanks are also due to Professors M. Brown and J. W. Kendrick, both of George Washington University, for permitting us to use their time series data.

NOTES AND REFERENCES

[1] Mansfield (1961) has made an econometric investigation of the diffusion and imitation of technology.

[2] The same decomposition is maintained in Brown's new book (1966), pp. 159–64.

[3] See footnote 16 below.

[4] They have made this assumption because labour's share displays a tendency to move inversely to the rate of employment over the course of the trade cycle.

[5] Note that David and van de Klundert have identified the elasticity of substitution and other parameters on the basis of the assumption that the index E_L/E_K has an exponential trend.

[6] See Hicks (1963), pp. 121–7.

[7] For the sources and the units of measurement of the data, see Appendix below.

[8] The production functions (1) and (2) are homogeneous of degrees d_1 and d_2, respectively; increasing, constant, or decreasing returns to scale prevail when d_t exceeds, equals, or falls short of unity. Although considerable evidence can be collected for the constant returns to scale (cf. Walters (1963, pp. 26–7 and 31–6)), Brown and Popkin (1962) have observed that the US nonfarm domestic sector enjoyed increasing returns to scale in 1890–1918, and Dhrymes (1965) has recently observed that the US two-digit manufacturing industries are subject to slight increasing returns to scale. Griliches (1964) has also shown that substantial economies of scale have prevailed in the US agriculture.

[9] The elasticities of substitution corresponding to these c_is are 1·212 and 0·893 in the agricultural and the non-agricultural sectors, respectively. The gross values added are taken from Leontief's 1929 Input-Output Table (1951). Also see Arrow, Chenery, Minhas and Solow (1961), p. 227. $c_2 = 0·120$ has to be interpreted as a mere rough proxy since the ACMS estimates are available only for principal manufacturing industries, while the non-agricultural sector includes both manufacturing and tertiary industries. Dhrymes's estimates allowing for variable returns to scale give $c_2 = 0·383$ with the weights of the 1929 gross values added. This value of c_2 implies that the elasticity of substitution of the non-agricultural sector is 0·723.

[10] Cf., for example, F. M. Fisher (1962, pp. 1–18).

[11] The Wallis test has been used by Brown and Popkin (1962) to find technological epochs.

[12] This second step of the selection is necessary, because the group A_0 whose elements are all assumed homogeneous in the first step may itself include heterogeneous observations.

[13] We have tried to reproduce equation (9), using the Dhrymes estimate, $c_2 = 0·383$, instead of the ACMS estimate, $c_2 = 0·120$, and have obtained

$$\log\left(\frac{wN}{qH}\right)_t = \underset{(3·8)}{1·19} \log\left(h\frac{I}{K}\right)_{t-1} - \underset{(3·8)}{1·32} \log\left(n\frac{I}{K}\right)_{t-1} + \underset{(21·9)}{9·47}\, g_t +$$

$$+ (-0·175\, g_t + 0·383(1-g_t)) \log\left(\frac{H}{N}\right)_t - \underset{(6·0)}{1·00},$$

with $\bar{R}^2 = 0.94$ and $d = 1.69$ for the period 1902–41, excluding the six abnormal years, 1919, 1921, 1922, 1932, 1933, and 1941.

[14] One might argue that, as soon as a selective procedure is undertaken, the meaning of the t-statistics disappears, for different results are supplied, depending on the researcher's subjectiveness in selecting observations. But we think that t-statistics will still be meaningful if observations are selected in the way we have done. We have first asked whether given observations may all be considered as coming from the same population. This question has been answered with 'No', but it has also been seen that a homogeneous group of observations may be formed by discarding a number of observations. A least-squares hyperplane has been fitted to the homogeneous observations thus selected, just as it is fitted, in natural sciences, to observations obtained by well-controlled experiments; so that our t-statistics are meaningful.

[15] Brown and de Cani (1963) have regarded the movement of the relative share as a resultant of the following three factors: non-neutral invention, change in the elasticity of substitution, and change in the relative factor price. But, as they have recognized, their measure of non-neutral technical invention, i.e. γ_2 in their notation, cannot be invariant with the units of measurement of labour and capital inputs. Moreover, we can show that since the elasiticity of substitution and other parameters may change from one technological epoch to another as Brown-de Cani estimates of them really do, the time shape of γ_2 (as well as its magnitude) depends on the units of measurement; in fact, γ_2 may decrease between one technological epoch and another if capital and labour are measured, say, in the conventional units of measurement but may increase during the same period of time if other units are chosen. This is an absurdity, of course; the direction of bias of an invention from the neutral one should be independent of the units of measurement.

[16] Though the rate of growth in labour force was low in the thirties, it was larger than the rate of capital accumulation in that period.

[17] We adjust the index M_t such that $M_{1902} = 1$, whereas David and van de Klundert have set the value of E_K/E_L in 1900 at unity.

[18] On the basis of the Dhrymes estimate $c_2 = 0.383$, the regression

$$\log\left(\frac{wN}{qH}\right)_t = 1.17 \log\left(h\frac{I}{K}\right)_{t-1} - 1.28 \log\left(n\frac{I}{K}\right)_{t-1} + 9.36\, g_t +$$
$$\phantom{\log\left(\frac{wN}{qH}\right)_t =}\;(3.8)\phantom{\log\left(h\frac{I}{K}\right)_{t-1}}(3.8)\phantom{\log\left(n\frac{I}{K}\right)_{t-1}}(22.2)$$

$$+(-0.175\, g_t + 0.383\,(1 - g_t))\log\left(\frac{H}{N}\right)_t + 0.46\, D_t - 0.93$$
$$\phantom{+(-0.175\, g_t + 0.383\,(1 - g_t))\log\left(\frac{H}{N}\right)_t}(9.4)(5.8)$$

(with $\bar{R}^2 = 0.94$ and $d = 1.69$) is obtained for the period 1902–55 excluding the abnormal years, 1919, 1921, 1922, 1932, 1933, and 1941–6.

This leads to essentially the same conclusions about changes in the relative income share and the capital-labour ratio. The only change deserving attention is that the price effect on the relative income share is now estimated to be bigger than before, since the Dhrymes elasticity of substitution is lower than the ACMS.

Appendix

The sources and the units of measurement of the time series data are listed below.

(1) Gross national product X (billions of 1929 dollars): Kuznets (1961) Column (1) (B. Variant III) of Table R–22, pp. 555–6, and Column (9), (Variant III) of Table R–2, p. 487.

(2) Gross investment I (billions of 1929 dollars): For 1902–18, *net investment* (annual increment of *capital stock* series by Klein-Kosobud (1961), Table II, pp. 179–80) plus *capital consumption allowances* (Kuznets (1961), Column (4) minus Column (5) of Table R–22, pp. 555–6). For 1919–55, Kuznets (1961), the sum of Columns (1) to (3) of Table R–5, p. 492.

(3) Capital input H (billions of 1929 dollars): h multiplied by K.

(4) Existing stock of capital K (billions of 1929 dollars): (*beginning of year capital stock* plus *end of year capital stock*) divided by 2. *End of year capital stock:* Klein–Kosobud (1961), *capital stock* of Table II, pp. 179–80, and the series (1945–55) extrapolated by the net investment of Kuznets (1961), the sum of Columns (3) and (6) of Table R–5, p. 492.

(5) Labour input N (billions of manhours per year): Kendrick (1961), *total, including military* of Table A–X, pp. 311–13, and Kendrick's unpublished estimates for 1954–5.

(6) Index of capacity utilization h (full capacity = 1): Brown (1966), *first approximation* series of Table D2, p. 206.

(7) Employment ratio n (full employment = 1): 1 minus *unemployment ratio. Unemployment ratio:* Lebergott (1957), *per cent of civilian labor force* of Table 1, pp. 215–16, and the corresponding figure by the Bureau of the Census for 1955.

(8) Earned income wN (billions of current dollars): Klein-Kosobud (1961), *Earned income*, of Table III, pp. 183–4, and the series (1954–5) extrapolated by the Department of Commerce series on employee compensation and income from self-employment. For the years after 1941 we

have made the same adjustment as Klein and Kosobud (1961, p. 182, footnote 2) did to the earned income series.

(9) Capital income qH (billions of current dollars): *National income* minus wN. *National income:* Kuznets (1961), Column (1) (B. Variant III) of Table R–23, pp. 557–8, and Column (6) (Variant III) of Table R–1, p. 486.

(10) Ratio of agricultural product to total product g: *Agricultural product* divided by X. *Agricultural product:* Kendrick (1961), Column (8) of Table A–III, pp. 298–301, and the series (1954–5) extended by the Department of Commerce series.

18

Hicksian Stability, Currency Markets, and the Theory of Economic Policy

Robert A. Mundell

The stability analysis introduced by Hicks has been one of the most successful failures in economic theory. Originally developed to integrate statical and dynamical general equilibrium theory, it was used as a bridge between dynamics and comparative statics:

The laws of change of the price system, like the laws of change of individual demand, have to be derived from stability conditions. We first examine what conditions are necessary in order that a given equilibrium system should be stable; then we make an assumption of regularity; that positions in the neighborhood of the equilibrium position will be stable also; and thence we deduce rules about the way in which the price-system will react to changes in tastes and resource (Hicks, 1939, p. 62).

But the stability conditions were not founded on an explicitly-formulated dynamic system. Hicks had defined stability along conventional lines: '... In order that equilibrium should be stable, it is necessary that a slight movement away from the equilibrium position should set up forces tending to restore equilibrium ...' but concluded that stability requires that 'a rise in price makes supply greater than demand, a fall in price demand greater than supply'. This is indeed the stability condition corresponding to a dynamic system in which excess demand causes a rise in price, but, as Samuelson pointed out, the proposition is not explicitly derived as the condition of convergence of such a dynamical system. The problem may be considered trivial in the case of a single market,[1] but it raises difficulties in analysis and interpretation in the case of multiple exchange (exchange of more than two commodities), as Hicks foresaw:

What do we mean by stability in multiple exchange? Clearly, as before, that a fall in the price of X in terms of the standard commodity will make the demand for X greater than the supply. But

are we to suppose that it must have this effect (a) when the prices
of other commodities are given, or (b) when other prices are adjusted
so as to preserve equilibrium in the other markets ?' (Hicks, 1939,
p. 66).

To resolve the difficulty Hicks introduced his concepts of 'perfect' and
'imperfect' stability. He noted first that it was necessary to distinguish a
series of conditions, namely, that a rise in the price of X will make supply
greater than demand, (a) all other prices being given, (b) allowing for the
price of Y being adjusted to maintain equilibrium in the Y-market, (c)
allowing for the prices of Y and Z being adjusted, and so on, until all
prices have been adjusted. He then defined as *imperfectly stable* a system
in which a rise in price of a commodity causes excess supply for the commodity after all repercussions are allowed for, and as *perfectly stable* a
system in which a rise in price causes excess supply regardless of how many
other prices are adjusted to attain equilibrium values in their respective
markets.[2]

Samuelson (1941) criticized Hicks's concept of stability on the grounds,
as stated above, that 'stability conditions are not deduced from a dynamic
model, except implicitly'. Hicksian stability is not equivalent to 'true'
dynamic stability and the Hicks conditions are neither necessary nor
sufficient for the convergence of the dynamical system implicit in Hicks's
dynamics, that is, the dynamic system Samuelson postulated as the 'natural
extension' of the Walrasian system. True dynamic stability requires that
the roots of the characteristic equation of the dynamic system have
negative real parts, and this requirement is not equivalent to the Hicks
conditions.[3]

Samuelson's criticism undermined the logic of Hicks's method. But the
conditions of stability produced by that method retained an important
place in the literature. Samuelson had already observed that the Hicks
conditions were equivalent to the conditions of 'true' dynamic stability
in the symmetrical case. Metzler (1945) showed that they were equivalent
in the case of gross substitutes, and also necessary (but not sufficient) for
stability to be independent of the speeds of adjustment.[4] Morishima proved
that they were equivalent. They are also sufficient conditions for convergence of any *non-oscillating* system, since Hicksian (perfect) stability
implies the absence of positive real roots. They are, moreover, conditions
which, if not satisfied, yield anomalous comparative statics results, and

thus seem, at least for a price system, to be necessary conditions for useful applications of the Correspondence Principle, at least in the context of analysis of the Walrasian system. Thus, even though Hicks's *method* seems to lack theoretical justification,[5] the Hicks *stability conditions* produced by that method have proved exceedingly useful.

How can a wrong method yield useful results? Leaving aside coincidence, the answer may lie in the two-way character of the Correspondence Principle. Samuelson had observed that

not only can the investigation of the dynamic stability of a system yield fruitful theorems in statical analysis, but also known properties of a (comparative) statical system can be utilized to derive information concerning the dynamic properties of a system.

(Samuelson, 1942.)

When Hicks is specifying the signs of changes in excess demands when a given price is put above or below its equilibrium value, various subsets of other prices remaining constant, he is at the same time implying specific comparative statics results. Provided these results correspond to *known* properties of a statical system the conditions implied should be related to stability conditions if the *reciprocal* character of the Correspondence Principle is valid.

Another reason why the Hicks *method* may appear more reasonable than Samuelson's original criticism of it suggests is that our knowledge of the precise laws governing dynamical systems is scanty. The empirical 'output' according to the methodology of the Correspondence Principle is a set of comparative statics results, while the empirical 'input' is (a) the nature of the dynamic processes, and (b) the assumption of stability. Acceptance of (b) is the essence of the Correspondence Principle, but how are we to determine (a)?

Consider, for example, the following alternative expressions for dynamical systems:

$$X_i(p_1, \ldots, p_n; \dot{p}_i) = 0 \qquad\qquad i = 1, \ldots, n \quad (1)$$

$$X_i(p_1, \ldots, p_n; \dot{p}_1, \ldots, \dot{p}_n) = 0 \qquad i = 1, \ldots, n \quad (2)$$

$$X_i(p_1, \ldots, p_n; \dot{p}_1, \ldots, \dot{p}_n; \ddot{p}_1, \ldots, \ddot{p}_n; \ldots) = 0 \quad i = 1, \ldots, n \quad (3)$$

To each of these systems there will correspond a different set of stability conditions. System (1) is a version of that used by Samuelson to prove that the Hicks conditions are neither necessary nor sufficient for stability, yet, as he himself noted, more complete generalizations such as (2) and (3) can be developed with different consequences for comparative statics. There is, therefore, an element of arbitrariness in the specification of dynamic systems in the absence of empirical information and there may on these grounds be a pragmatic justification for Hicks's method of developing 'stability conditions' that are 'timeless'. The Samuelson criterion is completely general and is an appropriate methodological approach, but for purposes of yielding practical results generality often implies emptiness.

The purpose of this paper, therefore, is to show that the Hicksian stability analysis is a useful contribution to the integration of statical and dynamical theory. First, I shall show that the perfect and imperfect stability conditions do correspond to the dynamic stability conditions of *some* dynamic processes irrespective of the pattern of signs of the price matrix. Second, I shall argue that, despite their usefulness in the form Hicks presented them, the perfect stability conditions are not completely general since they do not yield the information obtained by extending his method to the commodity 'adopted' as the standard commodity. Third, I shall show that generalized conditions can be obtained by interpreting his device of holding subsets of prices constant with respect to the standard commodity as an arbitrary method of forming various composite commodity groupings. Further I shall show that dynamic systems that fail to satisfy the generalized conditions will be unstable at *some* speeds of adjustment when a different commodity is adopted as the standard commodity in the dynamic system. And finally, I shall discuss the usefulness of the generalized Hicks conditions in devising dynamical rules for the *hyperstability* of 'policy systems'. [6] The illustrative examples are all taken from the theory of foreign exchange markets but the results, of course, apply to any generalized systems.

Our first task is to show that the Hicks conditions do, in a sense, correspond to the conditions of convergence of some dynamic systems. Let us take as an example a problem in devaluation theory. We can describe a closed static equilibrium system of $n+1$ currencies with prices (exchange rates) expressed in terms of currency 0, denoted by $p_1, \ldots, p_n$, as follows:

$$B_i = B_i(p_1, \ldots, p_n) = 0 \qquad i = 1, \ldots, n, \tag{4}$$

where B_i is the balance of payments of the ith country. In equilibrium each $B_i = 0$, while near the equilibrium we can write the system (4) as follows:

$$B_i = \sum_{j=1}^{n} b_{ij}(p_j - p_j^\circ) \qquad i = 1, \ldots, n \tag{5}$$

after expanding B_i in a Taylor series and omitting nonlinear terms.

Now let us suppose that the exchange rate of one country, say the rth country, appreciates in proportion to its balance of payments surplus according to the law

$$\dot{p}_r = k_r \sum_{j=1}^{n} b_{rj}(p_j - p_j^\circ), \tag{6}$$

while all other exchange rates adjust instantaneously to equilibrium. The solution of the differential system (6) is

$$p_r = p_r^\circ + A_r e^{k_r(\Delta/\Delta_{rr})t}, \tag{7}$$

where A_r is a constant that depends only on initial conditions,

$$\Delta \equiv \begin{vmatrix} b_{11} & b_{12} & \cdots & b_{1n} \\ b_{21} & b_{22} & \cdots & b_{2n} \\ \cdots & \cdots & \cdots & \cdots \\ b_{n1} & b_{n2} & & b_{nn} \end{vmatrix},$$

and Δ_{rr} is the co-factor (principal minor) of the element in its rth row and rth column.

For the dynamic process implied in equation (7) to be stable it is necessary and sufficient that $\Delta/\Delta_{rr} < 0$. But this condition is precisely (for the analogous problem in the Walrasian system) the Hicksian condition of imperfect stability for the rth currency; and when the method is applied to each currency (in succession, not simultaneously), we have the complete Hicksian conditions of imperfect stability, namely

$$\Delta/\Delta_{rr} < 0 \text{ for } r = 1, \ldots, n. \tag{8}$$

A similar analysis can help to show the usefulness of the Hicks conditions of perfect stability. Suppose that one exchange rate, say p_i, is held constant (relative to the numéraire). This amounts to dropping the ith row and column from Δ, so that if the original experiment were repeated, this time with the ith exchange rate constant, we would get, instead of equation (7),

$$p_r = p_r^\circ + A_r e^{k_r(\Delta_{ii}/\Delta_{ii,rr})t}, \tag{9}$$

and the stability condition $\Delta_{ii}/\Delta_{ii,rr} < 0$, which is one of the Hicksian conditions of perfect stability. Proceeding along these lines, holding one or another set of prices constant, we get the complete Hicks conditions of perfect stability.

But does this dynamic process have any economic plausibility ? Are we not, as Samuelson argued, allowing 'arbitrary modification of the dynamical equations of motion'. The answer is, in a sense, yes. But this can be the exact method needed in the theory of policy where our purpose is to *design* stable dynamic systems.

As an example, we might be interested in examining aspects of the stability of an exchange rate system such as that recently advocated by sixteen distinguished academic economists–a sliding parity system (with widened exchange rate margins) (Fellner, Machlup, Triffin *et al.*, 1966). Is it not precisely a set of conditions such as the Hicks conditions that would be involved ? We might ask, first, what would happen if, say, Britain (which we shall identify with country 1) adopted a sliding parity system while a subset of other countries $(2, \ldots, j)$ allowed their exchange rates to float, and the remaining countries, $k, \ldots, n$, kept their rates pegged to, say, the US dollar (the currency of country 0). Then if we suppose that balances of payments of countries whose rates float adjust instantaneously, while the pound adjusts slowly, the path of the pound over time would be

$$p_i = p_i^\circ + A e^{k_i(\Delta_{kk}, \ldots, nn/\Delta_{11}, kk, \ldots, nn)t} , \qquad (10)$$

for which knowledge of the Hicks conditions would be directly relevant. Thus the particular form of the dynamic system adopted–which countries are left out and which are left in–would depend on which of the Hicks conditions are satisfied. The Hicks method does, therefore, have a role to play in dynamic aspects of the theory of economic policy.

The Hicks *conditions*, however, are not exactly what we need for the theory of economic policy, because, as we shall see, they are incomplete even in terms of Hicks's own method. In the experiments Hicks conducts to derive his stability conditions he accords the numéraire–the standard commodity –a special role. In this section we shall consider the precise deficiencies in the statical information provided by the Hicks conditions.

This is best established by considering the comparative statics theorems implied by the Hicks conditions. Consider the equilibrium system

$$B_i(p_1, \ldots, p_n; \alpha) = 0 \qquad i = 1, \ldots, n , \qquad (11)$$

where, again, the B_i's are balances of payments, the p's are exchange rates and α is a parameter.

Differentiation of (11) with respect to α yields

$$\sum_{j=1}^{n} b_{ij}\frac{dp_j}{d\alpha} - \frac{\delta B_i}{\delta \alpha} \qquad i = 1,\ldots,n \tag{12}$$

and the solutions for the exchange rate changes are

$$\frac{dp_i}{d\alpha} = -\sum_{j=1}^{n} \frac{\delta B_j}{\delta \alpha} \frac{\Delta_{ji}}{\Delta} \qquad i = 1,\ldots,n. \tag{13}$$

Now consider an increase in demand for the currency of country i, such that $\delta B_i / \delta \alpha < 0$; while the excess demand for every other currency, at given exchange rates, is unchanged ($\delta B_j / \delta \alpha = 0$ for $i \neq j$). Then, instead of (13), we have simply

$$\frac{dp_i}{d\alpha} = -\frac{\delta B_i}{\delta \alpha} \frac{\Delta_{ii}}{\Delta}. \tag{14}$$

By the Hicks conditions of imperfect stability $\Delta_{ii}/\Delta < 0$ so $\delta B_i / \delta \alpha > 0$ implies $dp_i / d\alpha > 0$. Thus an increase in demand for the currency of the ith country raises the price of that currency after adjustment in all other exchange rates has been allowed for.

Similar implications follow from the conditions of perfect stability if we hold various subsets of other exchange rates constant relative to the numéraire. If, for example, the exchange rates of countries $k,\ldots,n$ are held constant, we get, instead of (14), the following equation,

$$\frac{dp_i}{d\alpha} = -\frac{\delta B_i}{\delta \alpha} \frac{\Delta_{ii,kk,\ldots,nn}}{\Delta_{kk,\ldots,nn}} > 0, \tag{15}$$

the inequality being an implication of one of the conditions of perfect stability.

How can an increase in demand occur in a closed system? Clearly only at the expense of other commodities (currencies) in the system. Cournot's Law (or Walras's Law in the context of the Walrasian system) ensures that

$$\sum_{i=0}^{n} \frac{\delta B_i}{\delta \alpha} \equiv 0, \tag{16}$$

where the summation, it should be emphasized, extends over *all* the commodities. The interpretation of (14) is therefore that an increase in demand for (say) pounds (the currency of country i) at the expense of dollars raises the dollar price of the pound. Now if other exchange rates are held constant relative to the dollar, the proposition holds, if the Hicksian perfect stability conditions are satisfied, when the shift of demand is interpreted as being from the dollar and all currencies whose exchange rates are kept fixed to the dollar. Note, however, that the Hicks conditions do not give us the sign of

$$\frac{dp_j}{d\alpha} = -\frac{\delta B_i}{\delta \alpha} \frac{\Delta_{ij}}{\Delta}, \tag{17}$$

so that we cannot specify, on the grounds of the Hicks conditions alone, whether a shift of demand from dollars to pounds raises or lowers the price of (say) the franc relative to the dollar.

But now we are in a position to see the narrow form of the mathematical implications of the Hicks conditions. Consider a shift of demand from the franc (currency j) to the pound (currency i). Then $\dfrac{\delta B_s}{\delta \alpha} = 0$ for $s \neq i, j$, while $\dfrac{\delta B_i}{\delta \alpha} = -\dfrac{\delta B_j}{\delta \alpha} > 0$ in view of (16); with no loss of generality we can make $\dfrac{\delta B_i}{\delta \alpha} = -\dfrac{\delta B_j}{\delta \alpha} = 1$. Substitution in (13) then gives the change in the dollar price of the pound and the franc

$$\frac{dp_i}{d\alpha} = -\frac{\Delta_{ii} - \Delta_{ji}}{\Delta} \tag{18}$$

$$\frac{dp_j}{d\alpha} = -\frac{\Delta_{ij} - \Delta_{ji}}{\Delta} \tag{19}$$

The Hicks conditions do not provide us with the sign of either (18) or (19), nor, by analogy to (17), should we expect them to. But, by analogy with (14) we should expect the difference

$$\frac{dp_i}{d\alpha} - \frac{dp_j}{d\alpha} = -\frac{\Delta_{ii} - \Delta_{ji} - \Delta_{ij} + \Delta_{ji}}{\Delta} \tag{20}$$

to be unambiguous in sign for any system in which units are chosen so that each $p_s = 1$, initially. When demand shifts from the franc to the pound we should not expect to be able to predict the sign of the change in the *dollar* price of the pound or franc, but we should be able to determine, on the basis of the Hicks conditions, the sign of the change in the *franc* price of the pound, the expression given in (20). But the Hicks conditions are of no help here, and this means that Hicks has not developed the mathematical implications of extending his method to the standard commodity.

The same information problem applies, *a fortiori*, when various subsets of prices are held constant. An implication of the Hicks conditions of perfect stability is that a shift of demand onto pounds raises the price of the pound even when various currencies remain pegged to the dollar; this amounts to treating the dollar and the other currencies pegged to it as a *composite* currency. By analogy the price of the pound should rise when demand shifts from a currency other than the dollar, say, the franc, while other currencies (e.g. the mark) are pegged to the *franc*.

Thus consider a shift of demand, at constant exchange rates, among three currencies i, j, and k, such that $\dfrac{\delta B_i}{\delta \alpha} + \dfrac{\delta B_j}{\delta \alpha} + \dfrac{\delta B_k}{\delta \alpha} \equiv 0$ and every other $\dfrac{\delta B_r}{\delta \alpha} = 0$.

Then, from (13), we have

$$\frac{dp_i}{d\alpha} = -\frac{\delta B_i}{\delta \alpha}\frac{\Delta_{ii}}{\Delta} - \frac{\delta B_j}{\delta \alpha}\frac{\Delta_{ji}}{\Delta} - \frac{\delta B_k}{\delta \alpha}\frac{\Delta_{ki}}{\Delta} \tag{21}$$

$$\frac{dp_j}{d\alpha} = -\frac{\delta B_i}{\delta \alpha}\frac{\Delta_{ij}}{\Delta} - \frac{\delta B_j}{\delta \alpha}\frac{\Delta_{jj}}{\Delta} - \frac{\delta B_k}{\delta \alpha}\frac{\Delta_{kj}}{\Delta} \tag{22}$$

$$\frac{dp_k}{d\alpha} = -\frac{\delta B_i}{\delta \alpha}\frac{\Delta_{ik}}{\Delta} - \frac{\delta B_j}{\delta \alpha}\frac{\Delta_{jk}}{\Delta} - \frac{\delta B_k}{\delta \alpha}\frac{\Delta_{kk}}{\Delta} . \tag{23}$$

Applying the restrictions that $\dfrac{dp_j}{d\alpha} = \dfrac{dp_k}{d\alpha} \equiv \dfrac{dp_{jk}}{d\alpha}$ and setting $\dfrac{\delta B_i}{\delta \alpha} = 1 = -\dfrac{\delta B_j}{\delta \alpha} - \dfrac{\delta B_k}{\delta \alpha}$, we can deduce the change in price of the pound relative to the mark and franc. The result is

$$\frac{dp_i}{d\alpha} - \frac{dp_{jk}}{d\alpha} = \frac{A}{\Delta(\Delta_{jj} - \Delta_{jk} - \Delta_{kj} + \Delta_{kk})} , \tag{24}$$

where A is the sum of the co-factors of the elements in the following matrix:

$$\begin{bmatrix} \Delta_{ii} & \Delta_{ij} & \Delta_{ik} \\ \Delta_{ji} & \Delta_{jj} & \Delta_{jk} \\ \Delta_{ki} & \Delta_{kj} & \Delta_{kk} \end{bmatrix}$$

The co-factor of, say, the element Δ_{jk} can be related to the second co-factors of Δ by Jacobi's ratio theorem,

$$- \begin{vmatrix} \Delta_{ii} & \Delta_{ij} \\ \Delta_{ki} & \Delta_{kj} \end{vmatrix} = -\Delta \cdot \Delta_{ii,kj},$$

so that A/Δ can be written entirely as the sum of second co-factors, and (24) can be rewritten as follows:

$$\frac{dp_i}{d\alpha} - \frac{dp_{jk}}{d\alpha} = - \frac{\left(\begin{matrix} \Delta_{jj,kk} - \Delta_{ji,kk} + \Delta_{ji,kj} \\ -\Delta_{ij,kk} + \Delta_{ii,kk} - \Delta_{ii,kj} \\ +\Delta_{ij,jk} - \Delta_{ii,jk} + \Delta_{ii,jj} \end{matrix} \right)}{\left(\begin{matrix} \Delta_{jj} - \Delta_{jk} \\ -\Delta_{kj} + \Delta_{kk} \end{matrix} \right)} > 0. \tag{25}$$

The inequality sign should hold if an increase in demand for one country's currency occurs at the expense of *any* other country, one other currency price remaining constant relative to that country. But the mathematical information is not given to us by the Hicks conditions. The reason is that the mathematical implications of the Hicks method have not been developed with respect to the currency adopted as numéraire.[7]

When we do extend Hicks's method to make it 'symmetrical' with respect to the numéraire (appreciating, say, the pound relative to, say, the *franc*, allowing various subsets of other currency markets to adjust) we get, of course, a set of conditions that specifies the signs of terms like those in equations (20) and (25). Along with the Hicks conditions, which can be written as

$$\frac{\Delta}{\Delta_{ii}} < 0; \frac{\Delta_{ii}}{\Delta_{ii,jj}} < 0; \frac{\Delta_{ii,jj}}{\Delta_{ii,jj,kk}} < 0; \ldots, \tag{26}$$

we get supplementary conditions of the form

$$\frac{\Delta}{\left(\begin{matrix} \Delta_{ii} - \Delta_{ij} \\ -\Delta_{ji} + \Delta_{jj} \end{matrix} \right)} < 0; \frac{\left(\begin{matrix} \Delta_{ii} - \Delta_{ij} \\ -\Delta_{ji} + \Delta_{jj} \end{matrix} \right)}{\left(\begin{matrix} \Delta_{jj,kk} - \Delta_{ji,kk} + \Delta_{ji,kj} \\ -\Delta_{ij,kk} + \Delta_{ii,kk} - \Delta_{ii,kj} \\ +\Delta_{ij,jk} - \Delta_{ii,jk} + \Delta_{ii,jj} \end{matrix} \right)} < 0, \text{etc.} \tag{27}$$

(The next ratio requires that the ratio of the denominator of the second ratio and the sum of sixteen third minors be negative; and so on for successive ratios. The last term in the conditions of (27) specifies that the sum of the $(n-1)$th minors (n^2 in number) be negative. But the $(n-1)$th minors are equivalent to the elements in the original determinant so the last condition simply requires that the sum of all the elements in the original determinant Δ be negative.)

This suggests an alternative – and simpler – way of developing the generalized conditions. Consider the augmented determinant

$$B \equiv \begin{vmatrix} b_{00} & b_{01} & \cdots & b_{0n} \\ b_{10} & b_{11} & \cdots & b_{1n} \\ \cdot & \cdot & \cdots & \cdot \\ b_{n0} & b_{n1} & \cdots & b_{nn} \end{vmatrix} \tag{28}$$

formed by bordering Δ with its column and row sums, with a change of sign, so that

$$\sum_{j=1}^{n} b_{ij} = -b_{i0}; \ \sum_{i=1}^{n} b_{ij} = -b_{0j}; \text{ and } b_{00} = \sum_{j=1}^{n} \sum_{i=1}^{n} b_{ij}. \tag{29}$$

Then the extended Hicks conditions can be stated simply as the requirement that principal minors of B arranged in successive order oscillate in sign, except for the (singular) determinant B itself.[8]

Because the elements in the augmented determinant B are interdependent the generalized conditions can be expressed entirely in terms of the 'normalized' determinant Δ. The supplemental conditions are

$$b_{00} < 0; \ \begin{vmatrix} b_{00} & b_{0i} \\ b_{i0} & b_{ii} \end{vmatrix} > 0; \ \begin{vmatrix} b_{00} & b_{0i} & b_{0j} \\ b_{i0} & b_{ii} & b_{ij} \\ b_{j0} & b_{ji} & b_{jj} \end{vmatrix} < 0, \text{ etc. }, \tag{30}$$

but in view of (29) these may be rewritten, in terms of elements excluding the 0th currency, as follows:

$$\sum_{i=1}^{n} \sum_{j=1}^{n} b_{ij} < 0; \ \begin{vmatrix} \sum_{\substack{s=1 \\ s \neq i}}^{n} \sum_{\substack{r=1 \\ r \neq i}}^{n} b_{rs} & \sum_{\substack{s=1 \\ s \neq i}}^{n} b_{si} \\ \sum_{\substack{s=1 \\ s \neq i}}^{n} b_{is} & b_{ii} \end{vmatrix} > 0, \text{ etc.} \tag{31}$$

with the last condition reducing to the basic determinant Δ itself. These forms are equivalent to (30) and imply the signs of the ratios in (27).

This representation has the intuitive appeal of starting with the matrix of *all* the currencies in the system.[9] Thus, instead of omitting the numéraire currency at the outset, we start with a non-normalized system of $n+1$ currencies, exchange rates being expressed in terms of an abstract unit of account (e.g. IMF par values) and apply the Hicks conditions allowing each currency the role of numéraire in turn.

The above conditions are more general than the Hicks conditions. Yet they still do not exhaust the information inherent in the Hicks methodology. The Hicks method of holding various subsets of prices constant with respect to one another can be regarded as a device for constructing 'composite commodities'; in the present context of currencies, I shall describe them as 'currency areas'. Now if we apply the Hicks method to a system based on arbitrary arrangements of countries in the currency areas, we get a further generalization of the results obtained by Hicks. When, for example, the mark is pegged to the dollar (the numéraire), the dollar and mark constitute a 'currency area'. But there is no reason to restrict the formation of currency areas in a uni-directional attachment to the dollar. A group of currencies could be 'attached' to the pound or the franc or any other currency, in principle. More importantly we can then allow entire currency areas to appreciate and require that the balance of payments of the areas worsen, various subsets of other currencies in the currency areas remaining unchanged.[10]

The remarkable fact is that the conditions resulting from making arbitrary currency alignments among the (non-dollar) countries and applying the Hicks method to the resulting matrix incorporate the conditions just developed as a special case. Thus consider the denominator of the first term in (27), $\begin{pmatrix} \Delta_{ii} - \Delta_{ij} \\ -\Delta_{ji} + \Delta_{jj} \end{pmatrix}$. This term is the result of combining the ith and jth currencies together to form a currency area of those two countries. With no loss of generality we can write $i = 1$ and $j = 2$. Then if the first and second rows and columns are replaced by their combined rows and columns, we have

$$\begin{vmatrix} \begin{matrix} b_{11}+b_{12} \\ + \\ +b_{21}+b_{22} \end{matrix} & \begin{matrix} b_{13}\ldots b_{1n} \\ + \ldots + \\ b_{23}\ldots b_{2n} \end{matrix} \\ \hline \begin{matrix} b_{31}+b_{32} \\ \cdot \cdot \cdot \cdot \cdot \\ b_{n1}+b_{n2} \end{matrix} & \begin{matrix} b_{33}\ldots b_{3n} \\ \cdot \cdot \cdot \cdot \cdot \\ b_{n3}\ldots b_{nn} \end{matrix} \end{vmatrix} \equiv \Delta_{11} - \Delta_{12} - \Delta_{21} + \Delta_{22},$$

as can be proved by straightforward expansion. Similarly, it can be shown that the denominator of the second term in (27) is the determinant formed by replacing the ith, jth and kth row and column of Δ by the amalgamated row and column.

When we now carry out Hicks's method for arbitrary arrangements of currency areas, extended over the whole range of currencies, we get a new set of conditions on the original $(n \times n)$ price matrix. These conditions can be expressed in a triangular arrangement of principal minors as follows:

$$b_{ii} < 0$$

$$\begin{vmatrix} b_{ii} b_{ij} \\ b_{ji} b_{jj} \end{vmatrix} > 0; \qquad \begin{vmatrix} b_{ii} + b_{ij} \\ + b_{ji} + b_{jj} \end{vmatrix} < 0$$

$$\begin{vmatrix} b_{ii} b_{ij} b_{ik} \\ b_{ji} b_{jj} b_{jk} \\ b_{ki} b_{kj} b_{kk} \end{vmatrix} < 0; \qquad \begin{vmatrix} b_{ii} + b_{ij} & b_{ik} \\ + b_{ji} + b_{jj} & b_{jk} \\ b_{ki} + b_{kj} & b_{kk} \end{vmatrix} > 0; \qquad \begin{vmatrix} b_{ii} + b_{ij} + b_{ik} \\ + b_{ji} + b_{jj} + b_{jk} \\ + b_{ki} + b_{kj} + b_{kk} \end{vmatrix} < 0$$

$$\tag{32}$$

$\cdots \cdots \cdots \cdots \cdots \cdots$ etc. $\cdots \cdots \cdots \cdots \cdots \cdots$

The conditions on the left side of the stability triangle are the conditions of perfect stability Hicks developed; they do not provide the information implicit in extending the analysis to the numéraire commodity. The conditions on the base of the triangle are those which result from extending the Hicksian method to the numéraire; they ignore the experiments resulting from allowing currency *areas* to appreciate. Finally, the conditions on the right side of the triangle are the conditions applicable when various sets of prices are raised in the same proportion, other prices remaining constant. More generally, the Hicks conditions on the left correspond to Hicksian adjustments when each currency (commodity) is treated in isolation; the adjacent conditions to their right are the Hicksian conditions when in the ith and jth goods move in the same proportion; and so on. The entire conditions are needed if the logic of Hicks's method is carried out to the bitter end.[11]

An important implication of the general conditions is that a system satisfying the Hicks conditions, but not the general conditions, will be stable or unstable depending on which currency is adopted as the key currency.[12] Consider, for example, a world of three currencies, dollars (currency 0), pounds (currency 1), and francs (currency 2) and suppose that the balances of payments of the three countries are related to exchange rates according to the equations:

$$B_0 = \cdot5p_0 + 1\cdot5p_1 - 2p_2$$
$$B_1 = -p_0 - 2p_1 + 3p_2 \tag{33}$$
$$B_2 = \cdot5p_0 + \cdot5p_1 - p_2 \, ,$$

where the exchange rates are defined in, and the B_i are expressed in, an abstract unit of account (I M F par value units). (Equilibrium exchange rates are unity or any multiple of unity since the system is homogeneous of degree 0.)

Let us consider a dynamic system in which the dollar is constant with respect to its par value so that the dollar becomes the effective numéraire. Let the par values of the pound and franc adjust in proportion to B_1 and B_2 respectively. We then have the following dynamic system:

$$\dot{p}_1 = k_1[-\bar{p}_0 - 2p_1 + 3p_2]$$
$$\dot{p}_2 = k_2[-\cdot5\bar{p}_0 + \cdot5p_1 - p_2] \, . \tag{34a}$$

In this system, the Hicks conditions of perfect stability, narrowly interpreted, are satisfied (since $b_{11} = -2 < 0$; $b_{22} = -1 < 0$ and

$$\begin{vmatrix} b_{11} & b_{12} \\ b_{21} & b_{22} \end{vmatrix} = \cdot5 > 0)$$ and the system is dynamically stable regardless of

the (positive and finite) values of k_1 and k_2.

Consider, however, a system in which the par value of the franc is fixed so that it becomes the 'key currency' instead of the dollar. The dynamic system then becomes

$$\dot{p}_0 = k_0[\cdot5p_0 + 1\cdot5p_1 - 2\bar{p}_2]$$
$$\dot{p}_1 = k_1[-p_0 - 2p_1 + \bar{p}_2] \tag{34b}$$

for which the Hicks conditions are not satisfied. It is dynamically stable or unstable according to whether $k_0 \gtrless 4k_1$.

This result could be predicted at once by applying the general conditions as given in the stability triangle (32). The sum of the coefficients in (34a) are positive so that the general conditions are not satisfied.

The general conditions are necessary conditions for a system to be stable regardless of the currency (commodity) chosen as key currency (standard commodity) and regardless of how quickly the various exchange rates adapt to disequilibrium. This proposition is perfectly general in the sense that it is valid in the n-currency case.[13]

I shall conclude this paper by showing how the Hicks conditions, extended as above, can be useful in devising dynamic mechanisms that are 'strongly stable'. The problem could be approached from the direction of the Correspondence Principle, which, in a narrow version of it, suggests that we apply to comparative statics the conditions that the characteristic equation of the systems have negative real parts. The justification for this narrow version lies in the observation that the systems we know are not characterized by instability. But there is no reason, in principle, why stronger conditions could not be applied. We could, following Hicks (and Samuelson) require that the system be stable no matter which subsets of market variables are held constant. Alternatively, we could use conditions that the roots be real or complex according to whether we observe cycles in the system under investigation.[14] If, for example, we observe an absence of cycles in the real world we know at once that the Hicks conditions are sufficient conditions for dynamic stability.

In the theory of policy (under incomplete information) the problem is often to choose among different dynamic systems, or different degrees of centralization of a given dynamic system; this is often expressed in terms of allocating, dynamically, instruments to targets (the problem of effective market classification), and we may want to construct '*strongly* stable' systems: first, because systems near the borderline of stability may become unstable if disturbed by outside shocks; second, because the cost of adjustment may be higher if the system, even though stable, oscillates in its approach to equilibrium; third, because slight errors in manipulating rates of changes in instrumental variables (interest rates, exchanges rates, etc.) may turn a weakly stable system into an unstable system; and finally, because the time involved in approaching equilibrium may be less under strongly stable systems and rapid adjustment may be preferred to slow adjustment.

We can consider, therefore, the problem of choosing a dynamic control mechanism with 'hyperstable' properties, in the sense that variables rise or fall whenever they are out of equilibrium; and show how the Hicks conditions can be of some help in constructing such a system when the precise location of an equilibrium is not known.

We take again as our example an international currency system. In a general hyperstable system it will be necessary to vary exchange rates taking into account the balances of payments of each country. The problem is to find out the weights each central bank should give their own balance of payments disequilibrium and that of the other countries.

Let B_i represent, as before, the balance of payments of the ith country, dependent upon the n exchange rates, according to the equation

$$B_i = \sum_{j=1}^{n} b_{ij}(p_j - p_j^\circ). \qquad i = 1, \ldots, n . \tag{35}$$

The problem is to find the values of the k_{ij}'s in

$$\frac{dp_i}{dt} = \sum_{j=1}^{n} k_{ij}B_j \qquad i = 1, \ldots, n \tag{36}$$

that will make the system hyperstable. (The 'speed' k_{ij} can be interpreted as the weight that country i has to give to the condition of the balance of payments of the jth country in adjusting its own exchange rate.)

It is readily shown that the system (36) is hyperstable if the k's are chosen so that

$$k_{ij} = \alpha_i \frac{\Delta_{ji}}{\Delta} \qquad i, j, = 1, \ldots, n , \tag{37}$$

where α_i is a negative real constant and the Δ_{ji}'s are, as before, the co-factors of Δ. The condition (37) means that the hyperstable speeds are weighted elements of the inverse of the price matrix.

To prove this proposition we need to prove that the dynamic system

$$\dot{p}_i = \alpha_i \sum_{j=1}^{n} \frac{\Delta_{ji}}{\Delta} B_j \qquad i = 1, \ldots, n \tag{38}$$

is hyperstable. Substituting for B_i from (35) gives us

$$\dot{p}_i = \alpha_i \sum_{j=1}^{n} \sum_{k=1}^{n} \frac{\Delta_{ji}}{\Delta} b_{jk}(p_k - p_k^\circ) \qquad i = 1, \ldots, n . \tag{39}$$

But, from the properties of any determinant, the typical term

$$\sum_{j=1}^{n} \frac{\Delta_{ji}}{\Delta} b_{jk}$$

has a value of unity for $k = i$ and a value of zero for $k \neq i$. The system (39) therefore reduces to

$$\dot{p}_i = \alpha_i(p_i - p_i^\circ) , \tag{40}$$

which is necessarily hyperstable for any $\alpha_i < 0$ since it has a solution

$$p_i = p_i^\circ + Ae^{\alpha_i t} .[15] \tag{41}$$

It is instructive to write out the hyperstable system (38) in detail in order to see clearly the implications of Hicksian perfect stability for dynamics:

$$\dot{p}_1 = \alpha_1 \frac{\Delta_{11}}{\Delta} B_1 + \alpha_1 \frac{\Delta_{21}}{\Delta} B_2 + \ldots + \alpha_1 \frac{\Delta_{n1}}{\Delta} B_n$$

$$\dot{p}_2 = \alpha_2 \frac{\Delta_{21}}{\Delta} B_1 + \alpha_2 \frac{\Delta_{22}}{\Delta} B_2 + \ldots + \alpha_2 \frac{\Delta_{n2}}{\Delta} B_n \tag{42}$$

$$\cdots \cdots \cdots \cdots \cdots \cdots \cdots \cdots$$

$$\dot{p}_n = \alpha_n \frac{\Delta_{n1}}{\Delta} B_1 + \alpha \frac{\Delta_{n2}}{\Delta} B_2 + \ldots + \alpha \frac{\Delta_{nn}}{\Delta} B_n .$$

We shall also find it convenient to consider a reduced system in which we choose the α_i, the *rate* at which each p_i is restored to equilibrium (with a negative sign), to be equal to the corresponding Hicksian conditions of imperfect stability as given in (9), that is, we equate

$$\alpha_i = \frac{\Delta}{\Delta_{ii}} < 0 \tag{43}$$

to get

$$\dot{p}_1 = B_1 + \frac{\Delta_{21}}{\Delta_{11}} B_2 + \ldots + \frac{\Delta_{n1}}{\Delta_{11}} B_n$$

$$\dot{p}_2 = \frac{\Delta_{12}}{\Delta_{22}} B_1 + B_2 + \ldots + \frac{\Delta_{n2}}{\Delta_{22}} B_n \tag{44}$$

$$\cdots \cdots \cdots \cdots \cdots \cdots \cdots \cdots$$

$$\dot{p}_n = \frac{\Delta_{1n}}{\Delta_{nn}} B_1 + \frac{\Delta_{2n}}{\Delta_{nn}} B_2 + \ldots + B_n .$$

Two observations can immediately be made about (44). First, if the elements of the inverse matrix all have the same sign hyperstability implies that positive weights be assigned to each balance of payments. Thus, 'Britain' should depreciate (appreciate) more rapidly the greater the deficits (surpluses) in the balance of payments of other countries, for any given deficit in her own balance (this implies corresponding changes in the US balance). But from Mosak's theorem the elements in the inverse will all have the same sign if the original currency matrix $[b_{ij}]$ is a gross substitute matrix provided $[b_{ij}]$ is Hicksian; and it will be Hicksian provided the dollar is also (reciprocally) a substitute for all other currencies.

The second point to notice about (44) is that 'Britain' should attach less weight to the balance of payments of other countries' currencies than to her own balance if currencies are all substitutes for one another; this follows because every ratio $\Delta_{ji}/\Delta_{ii} < 1$ for $j \neq i$.[16]

Leaving now the special case of gross substitutes, to return to the more general case represented by equations (42), we can find immediate implications of the Hicks conditions. First, if the Hicks conditions are satisfied 'normal' adjustments are implied in the sense that, *ceteris paribus* a deficit in a country's balance of payments suggests depreciation and a surplus appreciation; this follows because every $k_{ii} = \Delta_{ii}/\Delta > 0$ given the Hicks conditions of imperfect stability and $\alpha_i < 0$.

But more than this can be said. The following identities have to hold, from our definitions and Jacobi's ratio theorem,

$$\begin{vmatrix} k_{ii} & k_{ij} \\ k_{ji} & k_{jj} \end{vmatrix} = \alpha_i\alpha_j \begin{vmatrix} \Delta_{ii} & \Delta_{ij} \\ \Delta_{ji} & \Delta_{jj} \end{vmatrix} \equiv \alpha_i\alpha_j\Delta\Delta_{ii,jj} > 0 , \tag{45}$$

the inequality following at once from the Hicks conditions of perfect stability. Proceeding to the last term we have

$$\begin{vmatrix} k_{11} & \cdots & k_{1n} \\ \cdots & \cdots & \cdots \\ k_{n1} & \cdots & k_{nn} \end{vmatrix} = \alpha_1 \ldots \alpha_n \begin{vmatrix} \Delta_{11} & \cdots & \Delta_{1n} \\ \cdots & \cdots & \cdots \\ \Delta_{n1} & \cdots & \Delta_{nn} \end{vmatrix} \equiv d_i \ldots \alpha_n\Delta(-1)^n > 0 . \tag{46}$$

More generally, if the basic matrix $[b_{ij}]$ is Hicksian, the matrix of the speeds required for hyperstability must satisfy the conditions that every principal minor be positive, i.e.

$$k_{ii} > 0; \quad \begin{vmatrix} k_{ii} & k_{ij} \\ k_{ji} & k_{jj} \end{vmatrix} > 0; \text{ etc.} \tag{47}$$

Analogous conditions hold for the extended Hicks conditions if the system is to be hyperstable regardless of the currency used as the 'key currency'. In this sense the Hicks conditions alone are sufficient to establish in a weak sense the correctness of exchange rate policies directed at correcting 'own' balances of payments.

These developments conform to the conclusions of economic intuition; indeed, they may be interpreted as bringing the mathematical treatment of the subject closer to the level of common sense. They nevertheless suggest that the Hicksian stability analysis is not lacking in significance for the integration of dynamical and statical theory.[17]

ACKNOWLEDGMENT

The substance of this article was prepared while the author was a
Visiting Professor at McGill University in 1963–4, where he enjoyed
many helpful conversations on the subject with J. C. Weldon.

NOTES AND REFERENCES

[1] Strictly, the problem is not trivial even in the case of exchange of
two commodities; first, because of complications associated with the
possibility of time derivatives of various orders of price changes entering
the excess demand (X) functions, in a system such as $X(P, \dot{p}, \ddot{p}, \ldots) = 0$;
second, because of nonlinearities in the excess demand function; and third,
because market exchange of two commodities among many people may
involve adjustments of quantities toward budget constraints, giving rise
to the more complicated dynamics such as Marshall postulated in his
foreign trade analysis.

[2] Let $X_i = X_i(p_1, \ldots, p_n)$ be the excess demand functions for com-

modities $i = 1, \ldots, n$. By differentiation $dX_i = \sum_{j=1}^{n} b_{ij} dp_j$, where $b_{ij} \equiv \dfrac{\delta X_i}{\delta p_j}$.

Solving for the dp_i we get $dp_i = \sum_{j=1}^{n} \dfrac{\Delta_{ji}}{\Delta} dX_j$, where Δ is the determinant
of the system and Δ_{ji} its first co-factors. When all other prices adapt so

that every $dX_j = 0$ except dX_i, we have the solutions $dp_i = \dfrac{\Delta_{ii}}{\Delta} dX_i$; if

various prices $k, \ldots, n$, are held constant with respect to the numéraire

we get instead $dp_i = \dfrac{\Delta_{ii,kk, \ldots, nn}}{\Delta_{kk, \ldots, nn}} dX_i$. Imperfect stability requires that

$\dfrac{\Delta_{ii}}{\Delta} < 0$ for $i = 1, \ldots, n$, while perfect stability requires that

$\dfrac{\Delta_{ii,kk, \ldots, nn}}{\Delta_{kk, \ldots, nn}} < 0$ for any subset of commodities $k, \ldots, n$, excluding com-

modity i. The Hicksian perfect stability conditions are thus

$$\dfrac{\Delta}{\Delta_{ii}} < 0; \quad \dfrac{\Delta_{ii}}{\Delta_{ii,jj}} < 0; \quad \dfrac{\Delta_{ii,jj}}{\Delta_{ii,jj,kk}} < 0; \ldots b_{ii} < 0,$$

the first condition being the condition of imperfect stability.

[3] It is slightly ironic that Marshall in his 1879 manuscript on foreign
trade utilized the link between dynamics processes and stability, but not
explicitly the link between stability and comparative statics; whereas
Hicks utilized the link between stability and comparative statics but not
the link between dynamics and stability. Samuelson used both links in his
integration of dynamics and statics.

[4] Actually, Metzler's example (p. 285) that the Hicks conditions are not sufficient for stability to be independent of the speeds of adjustment contains a numerical error that destroys his demonstration (the second cubic of his footnote 12 should read $\lambda^3 + 4\lambda^2 + 3\cdot4\lambda + 13\cdot2 = 0$ instead of $\lambda^3 + 4\lambda^2 + 2\cdot6\lambda + 13\cdot2 = 0$ and in the first (correct) cubic the Routh conditions are satisfied). But a slight adjustment to his counter example can nevertheless demonstrate his point; if, for example, speeds are chosen so that, in his terminology, $k_1 = k_3 = 1$, giving the cubic $\lambda^3 + (2+k_2)\lambda^2 + (1+1\cdot2k_2)\lambda + 6\cdot6k_2 = 0$, the Routh conditions will not be satisfied for values of k_2 somewhat less than unity.

[5] In this connection Samuelson (1941) writes: '. . . In principle the Hicks procedure is clearly wrong, although in some empirical cases it may be useful to make the hypothesis that the equilibrium is stable even without the "equilibrating" action of some variable which may be arbitrarily held constant.' Samuelson provides an example in connection with the Keynesian system later in his paper.

[6] See, for example, Mundell (1962) and the references there to the 'principle of effective market classification'.

[7] This is perhaps apparent immediately since the Hicks conditions can be expressed in terms of the commodity chosen as numéraire, the excess demand for which is never allowed to go to zero. On this point (but without apparent recognition of its implications) see O. Lange (1944, p. 92).

[8] More compactly, we can state the conditions as requiring that every first minor of B be 'Hicksian'. Not all the conditions are independent, however, since $B_{00} \equiv B_{11} \equiv \ldots \equiv B_{nn}$ in view of the characteristics of B.

[9] One might think that Hicks really intended his conditions to extend over the entire range of excess demand coefficients (including the numéraire); this would be incorrect, since the last (augmented) determinant is singular. Alternatively, it might be thought that Hicks intended the conditions to apply no matter what commodity were taken as numéraire. The latter interpretation seems to be fortified by a footnote which states:
     . . . can be seen at once if we adopt the device of treating X (momentarily) as the standard commodity, and therefore regarding the increased demand for X as an increased supply of the old standard commodity M . . . (Hicks, 1939, p. 75).
If this device were adopted to derive the Hicks conditions it would indeed result in conditions equivalent to the above stability conditions. Yet this interpretation would conflict, not only with all subsequent interpretations of the Hicks conditions by other writers on stability, but also with Hicks's (1939, p. 315) own explicit statement in the Mathematical Appendix which specifies that the conditions must hold 'for the market in every $X_r (r = 1, 2, 3, \ldots, n-1)$', that is, the market

for the numéraire (the nth commodity) is omitted. In any case his discussion on pages 68–71 fails to make the point clear, while his third graph in Figure 16, which he asserts is stable, is actually totally stable only if the line along which there is zero excess demand for the standard commodity (not drawn in his figures) is inelastic with reference to the abscissa. The discussion is not completely clear, however, and I am therefore inclined to interpret Hicks as actually intending to give full coverage to the numéraire but not completing the mathematical implications of doing so.

[10] In Mundell (1961) I considered the problem of 'optimum' currency areas in terms of its attributes for stabilization policy, optimum exploitation of the functions of money, etc.; the present analysis suggests an additional criterion in terms of stability conditions.

[11] Stability conditions should, in principle, be 'invariants' in the sense that they are independent of the choice of units in which commodities are measured; this corresponds to Lange's (1944, p. 103) 'Principle of Invariance'. The above stability conditions are invariants only if, as is assumed in the case of the foreign exchange market analysis, the b_{ij}'s are all measured in equivalent currency units.

In the general case, however, where prices respond to excess demands denominated in physical quantity units, the units in which b_{ij} ($j = 1, \ldots, n$) is measured differs from the units in which b_{kj} ($j = 1, \ldots, n$) is measured. This means that invariant stability conditions require that each row of every stability determinant involving the sum of elements be multiplied by an arbitrary number reflecting units of measurement. Thus 'unit-invariant' stability in the general case involves the sign of terms like $\left(\begin{array}{c} k_i b_{ii} + k_i b_{ij} \\ + k_j b_{ji} + k_j b_{jj} \end{array} \right) < 0$. For arbitrary values of k_i and k_j extended over the entire range of the $(n+1) \times (n+1) B$ determinant, and given the homogeneity postulate, the general conditions then imply that all goods are gross substitutes.

[12] From a historical point of view, it is somewhat amusing that although the Hicks conditions are not symmetrical with respect to the commodity chosen as numéraire, neither are the (normalized) dynamic systems used to refute the validity of the Hicks conditions as true dynamic stability conditions.

[13] The proof in the general case follows by analogy to the proof of Metzler (1945, pp. 280–5) when his method is extended to include the augmented system.

[14] I applied this method to the problem of disentangling lags in expectational and cash balance adjustments in Mundell (1965a).

[15] More directly the matrix equation $\dot{p} = kB\alpha(p - p^\circ)$ reduces to $\dot{p} = \alpha(p - p^\circ)$ if $k = B^{-1}$.

The usefulness of this result lies not so much in providing a policy
maker with the rules of adjustment, since there is no problem if the basic
matrix is known, and the rule gives insufficient information if the basic
matrix is not known. The point is rather that pieces of information about
the inverse may be sufficient to distract policy makers from mistakes, and
that conditions like the Hicks conditions may be a sufficient guide to the
relative importance to be attached to particular instruments.

[16] I have discussed the implications of this condition in some detail
(Mundell, 1965b).

[17] Even the gap between true dynamic stability and Hicksian Stability
may be bridged by integrating Hicksian stability conditions with the
Samuelson 'Le Chatelier Principle' (Samuelson, 1960a) which can be
expressed entirely in terms of the Hicksian determinants. Hicksian
stability and dynamic stability mesh together under appropriate conditions
of gross substitutes, gross complements and symmetry, a common link
being sign-symmetry; and sign-symmetry of the inverse of the basic
Hicksian matrix is sufficient for at least one of the Le Chatelier conditions
to hold ($\Delta\Delta_{ii,jj} - \Delta_{ii}\Delta_{jj} < 0$ if Δ_{ij} and Δ_{ji} have the same sign).

A further implication of the Hicks conditions was called to my attention by Daniel McFadden who had proved, in a paper presented at the
1963 Econometrica Society meetings in Boston, Massachusetts, that if
the Hicks conditions of perfect stability are satisfied, a stable dynamic
system of the form $\dot{p} = KB(p - p^\circ)$ can always be found for a diagonal
K matrix with positive diagonal coefficients; the result also holds in the
global form. Prior to McFadden's result, and unknown to him, a local
version of the theorem had been published; see M. E. Fisher and A. T.
Fuller (1958).

In the context of the currency problem discussed above the theorem
means that, if the Hicks conditions are satisfied, it is always possible to
find a stable dynamic system in which exchange rates are adjusted to 'own'
balances of payments only.

19

Two Generalizations of the Elasticity of Substitution

Paul A. Samuelson

I. *One Good and Multiple Factors*

Review. In 1932 Hicks defined the useful concept called the elasticity of substitution, in the form

$$\sigma = \sigma_{12} = \frac{F_1 F_2}{F F_{12}} = \sigma_{21},\tag{1}$$

where $F(V_1, V_2)$ is a homogeneous first-degree neoclassical production function and where subscripts depict partial differentiation with respect to the indicated variable (such as $F_i = \partial F(V_1, V_2)/\partial V_i$, etc.). In 1933, Joan Robinson defined a related concept, designed to serve as a criterion of change in relative shares:

$$\sigma^{(R)} = -\frac{d(V_1/V_2)/(V_1/V_2)}{d(W_1/W_2)/(W_1/W_2)},\tag{2}$$

where W_i refers to the price of the V_i factor. And it was soon demonstrated that these are identical coefficients when applied to a two-variable neoclassical production function, whose partial derivatives provide the marginal-productivity determinants of factor prices.

When more than two inputs are involved, the problem of generalizing the Hicks σ coefficient becomes complex. Champernowne, Pigou, and others, in pursuit of the question of how the change in a factor price, W_i, affects the amount demanded of a different factor, V_j, have moved in the direction of defining a square matrix of partial-elasticities of substitution, of the type $[F_i F_j / F F_{ij}]$. Aside from being complex, this approach has led to little in the way of definite results and has moved away from the task of providing a criterion of change in relative factor shares.

New Approach. I have long found it convenient in lectures to generalize σ to more than two variables by moving in a different direction. Thus,

467

for a homogeneous first-degree production function $F(V_1, V_2, \ldots, V_n)$, $n \geqslant 2$, I define different σ's, of the form $(\sigma_1, \ldots, \sigma_n)$, with the property that each σ_i provides a criterion of change in the relative share of the ith factor as V_i increases with other V_j held constant–or, what is the same thing, as every V_j / V_i diminishes in the same proportion.

One natural way of approaching my concept is to rewrite the $n = 2$ Hicks coefficient, σ_{12}, in asymmetric notations:

$$\sigma_{12} = \frac{F_1 F_2}{F F_{12}} = -\frac{F_1 F_2}{F} \frac{V_2}{V_1 F_{11}} = -\frac{F_1}{V_1 F_{11}} \left(1 - \frac{F_1 V_1}{F} \right)$$

or, for $i = 1, 2$,

$$\sigma_i = -\left(\frac{F_i}{V_i F_{ii}} \right) \left(1 - \frac{F_i V_i}{F} \right) = \frac{\partial \log V_i}{\partial \log F_i} (1 - \alpha_i) = -E_{V_i F_i}(1 - \alpha_i), \quad (3)$$

where $(E_{V_i F_i})$ is the elasticity of the *ceteris paribus* marginal-product demand curve for the ith factor, α_i is the relative factor share of the ith factor, and $1 - \alpha_i$ is the relative share of the rest of the factors.

It is evident that this formula can hold for any one of three or more factors. Thus, I end up defining

$$\sigma_1 = -E_{V_1 F_1}(1 - \alpha_1)$$
$$\sigma_2 = -E_{V_2 F_2}(1 - \alpha_2)$$
$$\sigma_3 = -E_{V_3 F_3}(1 - \alpha_3) \qquad\qquad\qquad (4)$$
$$\cdot \cdot \cdot \cdot \cdot \cdot \cdot \cdot \cdot \cdot \cdot$$
$$\sigma_n = -E_{V_n F_n}(1 - \alpha_n).$$

Criterion of Relative Shares. I can now easily prove the theorem that σ_i does provide an indicator of relative shares.

Theorem 1: If $Q = F(V_1, \ldots, V_n) \equiv \lambda^{-1} F(\lambda V_1, \ldots, \lambda V_n)$

$$W_i = \partial F(V_1, \ldots, V_n) / \partial V_i \qquad (i = 1, \ldots, n),$$

$$\alpha_i = W_i V_i / Q = F_i V_i / F$$

then $\dfrac{\partial \alpha_i}{\partial V_i} \gtreqless 0$ depending on whether

$$\sigma_i = -\frac{F_i}{V_i F_{ii}} \left(1 - \frac{F_i V_i}{F} \right) = -E_{V_i F_i}(1 - \alpha_i) \gtreqless 1$$

To prove this, note that the algebraic sign of

$$\frac{\partial \log \alpha_i}{\partial \log V_i} = \frac{\partial \log F_i}{\partial \log V_i} + 1 - \frac{\partial \log F}{\partial \log V_i}$$

$$= \frac{1}{E_{V_iF_i}} + 1 - \alpha_i - \frac{1}{E_{V_iF_i}}[1 + E_{V_iF_i}(1-\alpha_i)] \tag{5}$$

is plus, zero, or minus depending on which of these signs the last bracket has, which directly proves the theorem.

Equality of Generalized Hicks and Robinson Coefficients. More specifically, let us rewrite Robinson's definition

$$\sigma^{(R)} = -\frac{d(V_1/V_2)/(V_1/V_2)}{d(W_1/W_2)/(W_1/W_2)}$$

$$= -\frac{\partial \log (V_1/V_2)/\partial V_1}{\partial \log (W_1/W_2)/\partial V_1}$$

$$= -\frac{1}{\dfrac{\partial \log \left(\dfrac{W_1 \, V_1}{W_2 \, V_2}\right)}{\partial \log V_1} - 1}$$

$$= \frac{1}{1 - \dfrac{\partial \log \left(\dfrac{\alpha_1}{1-\alpha_1}\right)}{\partial \log V_1}} . \tag{6}$$

I now generalize this to $n \geqslant 2$, in the form

Theorem 2.
$$\sigma_i^{(R)} = \frac{1}{1 - \dfrac{\partial \log \dfrac{\alpha_i}{1-\alpha_i}}{\partial \log V_i}}$$

$$= \frac{1}{1 - \dfrac{1}{1-\alpha_i}\dfrac{\partial \log \alpha_i}{\partial \log V_i}} = \frac{1}{1 - \dfrac{1}{1-\alpha_i}\left[\dfrac{1}{E_{V_iF_i}} + 1 - \alpha_i\right]}$$

$$= \frac{1}{1/\sigma_i} = \sigma_i .$$

This proves the identity of my *n*-dimensional generalization of the 1932 Hicks coefficient with my *n*-dimensional generalization of the 1933 Robinson coefficient.

Some Cases of Constant σ_i. This completes my first generalization. Some simple applications can now be indicated.

First, consider the n-dimensional Cobb-Douglas case. For

$$F(V_1, \ldots, V_n) = aV_1^{k_1}V_2^{k_2} \quad V_n^{k_n}, \quad \sum_1^n k_j = 1$$

$$\sigma_i = -\frac{F_i}{V_iF_{ii}}\left(1 - \frac{F_iV_i}{F}\right)$$

$$= -\frac{1}{k_i - 1}(1 - k_i) = 1 . \tag{7}$$

Hence, for the C-D case, the new coefficient is identically unity, as anyone would wish it to be.

Second, consider the obvious n-dimensional analogue of the Solow-Champernowne-Bergson so-called constant-elasticity-of-substitution function

$$Q = [a_1V_1^{(\sigma-1)/\sigma} + \ldots + a_nV_n^{(\sigma-1)/\sigma}]^{\sigma/(\sigma-1)} .$$

For this

$$\sigma_i = -\frac{F_i}{V_iF_{ii}}\left(1 - \frac{F_iV_i}{F}\right) \tag{8}$$

$$= -\frac{1}{\left(\dfrac{\sigma-1}{\sigma} - 1\right)(1 - \alpha_i)}(1 - \alpha_i) = \sigma \quad (i = 1, \ldots, n) .$$

Hence, this n-dimensional CES function does indeed have a constant σ_i that is the same for all factors.

This raises an interesting question. What n-dimensional $F(V_1, \ldots, V_n)$ has constant but unequal values for $(\sigma_1, \ldots, \sigma_n)$? For $n = 2$, we know there exists no such function since, by definition $\sigma_1 \equiv \sigma_2$ when $n = 2$. This alerts us to the fact that, for any $n > 2$, not all the $(\sigma_1, \ldots, \sigma_n)$ can be independently constant. Thus, if

$$\sigma_2 = \sigma_3 = \ldots = \sigma_n \equiv 1 ,$$

it is quite evident that we must be in the Cobb-Douglas case with σ_1 also unity. Likewise, if

$$\sigma_2 = \sigma_3 = \ldots = \sigma_n = \sigma \neq 1 ,$$

we must be in the generalized CES family with σ_1 also equal to σ.

Certainly the $(\sigma_1, \ldots, \sigma_n)$ must be connected by the relation

$$\alpha_1 + \ldots + \alpha_n = 1 = \sum_1^n \left(1 + \frac{\sigma_i}{E_{V_iF_i}}\right) = n + \sum_{i=1}^n \frac{\sigma_i}{E_{V_iF_i}} . \tag{9}$$

Suppose we try to impose constancy on $(n-1)$ of the σ's, say $(\sigma_2, \ldots, \sigma_n)$. Then we impose on the $(n-1)$ dimensional function

$$F(1, V_2/V_1, \ldots, V_n/V_1),$$

$(n-1)$ partial differential equations of the form

$$-\frac{\partial F(1,v_2,\ldots,v_n)/\partial v_i}{v_i \partial^2 F(1,v_2,\ldots,v_n)/\partial v_i^2}\left[1 - \frac{v_i\partial F(1,v_2,\ldots,v_n)/\partial v_i}{F(1,v_2,\ldots,v_n)}\right] \equiv \bar{\sigma}_i$$

$$(i = 2,\ldots,n). \qquad (10)$$

Whatever the most general solution, $F(1,v_2,\ldots,v_n)$, to these equations may be, it is too much to expect that, for arbitrary $\bar{\sigma}_2, \ldots, \bar{\sigma}_n$,

$$\sigma_1 = -\frac{\partial F(1,V_2/V_1,\ldots,V_n/V_1)/\partial V_1}{V_1\partial^2 F(1,V_2/V_1,\ldots,V_n/V_1)/\partial V_1^2}$$

$$\left[1 - \frac{V_1\partial F(1,V_2/V_1,\ldots,V_n/V_1)/\partial V_1}{F(1,V_2/V_1,\ldots,V_n/V_1)}\right] \qquad (11)$$

should turn out also to be a constant. I omit proof of this assertion.

Equivalent Approach via Leontief Physical-Composite Factor. The present σ_i involves the ith factor against all the rest. Thus, in computing σ_1, we change V_1, above, holding $(V_2, \ldots, V_n)$ constant. Holding any such inputs constant ought to be capable of being regarded as a case of holding some single *composite* physical factor bundle constant, and thus should be capable of being handled by the old $n = 2$ definition of 1932. In 1936, Leontief defined physical composite goods in connection with the economic theory of index numbers. Thus, consider the homogeneous function

$$Q = F(V_1, V_2, V_3, \ldots, V_n).$$

Subject the inputs to the new restrictions

$$V_1 = V_I$$
$$V_2 = \bar{V}_2 V_{II}$$
$$\ldots$$
$$V_n = \bar{V}_n V_{II}$$

to get
$$Q = F(V_I, \bar{V}_2 V_{II}, \ldots, \bar{V}_n V_{II})$$
$$= F(V_I, V_{II}; \bar{V}_2, \ldots, \bar{V}_n) \qquad (13)$$
$$= \Phi(V_I, V_{II}) \text{ for short.}$$

Now it is easy to verify that Φ has all the properties of a well-behaved concave homogeneous-first-degree neoclassical production function in 2 variables. We can apply the old 1932 definition, $\sigma_{I,II}$, to it. Obviously, we get the same coefficient as in my new definition of σ_1.

Theorem 3. If $\Phi(V_I,V_{II}) \equiv F(V_I,\overline{V}_2V_{II},\ldots,\overline{V}_nV_{II})$,

$$\sigma_{I,II} = \frac{\Phi_I\Phi_{II}}{\Phi\Phi_{I,II}} = -\frac{F_1}{V_1F_{11}}\left(1-\frac{F_1V_1}{F}\right) - \sigma_1$$

at any initial point $(V_I,V_{II}; V_1,\ldots,V_n) =$
$$(V_1,1; V_1,\overline{V}_2,\ldots,\overline{V}_n).$$

To prove this, merely note that $1-\alpha_1$ and $1-\alpha_I$ are the same thing, and so are the *ceteris paribus* marginal-productivity elasticities $E_{V_1F_1}$ and $E_{V_IF_I}$.

Alternative Approach via Hicks Price-composite Factor. One of Sir John's most interesting contributions to economic theory has been the use of price-composite commodities. These are in a certain sense dual to the Leontief-Ricardo physical doses of commodities, and also have well-behaved properties. This approach leads to a somewhat different set of E-of-S coefficients $(\sigma_1^*,\sigma_2^*,\ldots,\sigma_n^*)$, and to various intermediate coefficients.

Mechanically, we can abruptly define any one of the new set of co-efficients simply as follows:

$$\sigma_i^* = -\left(\frac{\partial \log V_i}{\partial \log W_i}\right)_{\substack{\text{certain other } V\text{'s constant}\\ \text{certain other } W\text{'s constant}}} (1-\alpha_i) \qquad (14)$$

The first term on the right represents a factor-demand elasticity. Which factor demand? That depends on what our *ceteris paribus* assumptions are. Thus, let $i = 1$ and suppose we decide to hold $V_2,\ldots,V_r$ constant and hold $W_{r+1},\ldots,W_n$ constant, thereby letting

$$(W_2,\ldots,W_r,V_{r+1},\ldots,V_n)$$

vary *mutatis mutandis* as W_1 and V_1 vary, varying as they will and must to maintain the optimizing marginal product-conditions

$$W_1 = \frac{\partial F(V_1,\ldots,V_n)}{\partial V_1}$$

$$W_2 = \frac{\partial F(V_1,\ldots,V_n)}{\partial V_2}$$

$$\cdots\cdots\cdots\cdots\cdots \qquad (15)$$

$$W_n = \frac{\partial F(V_1,\ldots,V_n)}{\partial V_n}.$$

Clearly, for $r = n$, we are holding *all* other physical inputs constant and we are back in my original (Leontief equivalent) case. This could be considered the extreme short-run case, where no other factors adjust.

At the other extreme is the hypothetical long-run in which a (small) industry can hire all other factors at constant factor prices. (This is hypothetical, because in many situations the ironical remark, 'You should live so long!' is indicated.) For this extreme and a homogeneous production function, *all* the elasticities end up infinite! Why? Because any last real factor price is completely determined–along a horizontal, infinitely-elastic demand curve–once *all* other real factor prices are stipulated, as the recent concept of the Factor-Price Frontier makes evident.

Between the extreme short run and the extreme long run, we can define a whole set of intermediate runs. And by the Le Chatelier principle, it is easy to show that

$$0 \leqslant \sigma_1 = [\sigma_1^*]_{r=n} \leqslant [\sigma_1^*]_{r=n-1} \leqslant \ldots \leqslant [\sigma_1^*]_{r=2} \leqslant [\sigma_1^*]_{r=1} = \infty. \qquad (16)$$

It is gratifying that all these various approaches end up in general agreement with Sir John's recent afterthoughts on his seminal *Theory of Wages* (Hicks, 1932).

II. *Intercommodity Substitution and Homothetic General Equilibrium*

The Multi-commodity Problem. From the beginning of his 1932 discussion, Sir John Hicks had clearly in mind that an increased scarcity of one factor would result in less of a rise in its price if people can shift away from consuming goods which use much of it in favor of consuming now-relatively-cheapened goods that use little of it. Since Machlup's 1935 discussion of this problem, it has tended to be eclipsed by more technical analysis of single commodity cases (like my Part I).

It is no joke to have to analyze the incidence of anything, a tax change or a factor-supply change, in a full general equilibrium model. What I propose to do here, very briefly, is to exhibit a beautifully simple special case of general equilibrium where intercommodity substitutions become transparently obvious.

Uniform, Homothetic Tastes. Heroically, assume with me that all people have the same tastes whether rich or poor, so that every dollar gets spent always in the same way. This is known to require uniform, homothetic indifference contours, which can be summarized by a cardinal utility function that is homogeneous of the first degree, and which will be concave in the well-behaved case. Thus

$$u = u[Q_1, Q_2, \ldots, Q_m] \equiv \lambda^{-1} u[\lambda Q_1, \lambda Q_2, \ldots, \lambda Q_m], \qquad (17)$$

where Q_j represents the total amount produced and consumed of the jth commodity. u has all the properties of a neoclassical production function and, as will be seen, plays the role of real social output (or real-dollar output), being able by virtue of the homotheticity axiom to solve rigorously the traditional index-number problem.

Each commodity Q_j is assumed to be produced by a concave, homogeneous-of-first-degree production function, that depends on the

$$[V_{1j}, V_{2j}, \ldots, V_{nj}] = [V_{ij}]$$

inputs devoted to its industry; and of course the total V_i of the ith factor is allocated among the m commodity industries: hence

$$Q_j = F^j(V_{1j}, \ldots, V_{nj}). \qquad (j = 1, 2, \ldots, m) \qquad (18)$$

$$V_i \geqslant V_{i1} + V_{i2} + \ldots + V_{im}, \qquad (i = 1, 2, \ldots, n) \qquad (19)$$

Competitive equilibrium is led, as if by an Invisible Hand, to solve the following maximum problem:

Subject to $V_i \geqslant V_{i1} + \ldots + V_{im}$

$$\max_{\{V_{ij}\}} u[F_1(V_{11}, \ldots, V_{n1}), \ldots, F_m(V_{1m}, \ldots, V_{nm})] = U(V_1, V_2, \ldots, V_n).$$

$$\qquad (20)$$

This last function, which depicts (maximized) real social output as being (optimally) manufactured out of available factor-input aggregates, is easily seen to have *all* the properties of a neoclassical physical production function. Thus, all of the single-good analysis of Part I's $F(V_1, \ldots, V_n)$ can be applied without qualification to $U(V_1, \ldots, V_n)$.

In particular, I can define total elasticity-of-substitution coefficients $(\bar{\sigma}_1, \ldots, \bar{\sigma}_n)$ that already take into account inter-commodity as well as intra-commodity substitutions, namely

$$\bar{\sigma}_i = -\left[\frac{U_i}{V_i U_{ii}}\right]\left[1 - \frac{V_i U_i}{U}\right] = -E_{V_i U_i}[1 - \alpha_i] \quad (i = 1, \ldots, n) \ (21)$$

where the subscript notation writes $\partial U / \partial V_i$ as U_i, etc.

Intuition tells us that these total $\bar{\sigma}$'s will tend to be (if anything) more elastic than the single-good technical E-of-S applied to a single industry production factor $F^j(\cdot)$. Thus, suppose there were no technical substitutions possible, so that every production function were of the fixed-coefficient form

$$Q_j = \text{Min}\left[\frac{V_{1j}}{a_{1j}}, \ldots, \frac{V_{nj}}{a_{nj}}\right]. \tag{22}$$

Then, provided the input-requirements vectors $[a_{1j}, \ldots, a_{nj}]$ were not all proportional (and thus of equal factor intensity), the fact that

$$u(Q_1, \ldots, Q_m)$$

permits some smooth inter-commodity substitution would permit $(\bar{\sigma}_1, \ldots, \bar{\sigma}_n)$ to be positive rather than zero. Of course, if all industry production functions were of the same factor intensities, with

$$F_1(x_1, \ldots, x_n) \equiv F_2(x_1, \ldots, x_n) \equiv \ldots \equiv F_m(x_1, \ldots, x_n), \tag{23}$$

changes in a factor total, like V_1, would have no effect on relative commodity prices and induce no inter-commodity substitutions. In such a singular case, my total $\bar{\sigma}_i$ would be identical with, and not greater than, the common intra-industry technical σ_i.

Intuitive Conclusions. If one works out the algebra of total $\bar{\sigma}_i$ of $U(V_1, \ldots, V_m)$ in terms of the technical σ's of the component

$$F^j(V_{1j}, \ldots, V_{nj})$$

functions and the consumer substitution properties of the $u(Q_1, \ldots, Q_m)$ function, then common sense rules will be verified:

Total elasticity of substitution is greater

(1) the greater is intra-industry technical substitutability in the $F^j(\cdot)$ functions;

(2) the greater is consumer substitutability in the $u(\cdot)$ function;

(3) the greater is the difference in factor intensities among industries.

To highlight the final factor-intensity point, consider the singular case where each industry uses a single input unique to itself, or

$$Q_j = F^j(V_{jj}) = \frac{V_j}{a_{jj}} = 1 \, . \, V_j \text{ by convention} \, .$$

Then only inter-commodity substitutions by consumer come into play, and all of the substitutability comes from the consumer side. In this limiting case

$$U(V_1, \ldots, V_m) \equiv u(V_1, \ldots, V_m) \tag{24}$$

and the total elasticity of substitution

$$\bar{\sigma}_i = -\frac{u_i}{V_i U_{ii}} \left[1 - \frac{V_i u_i}{u} \right] \tag{25}$$

becomes purely a consumption coefficient.

Equilibrium Conditions. All of the 1932 and 1963 Hicksian insights were confirmed by the analysis. For completeness, I write down the optimality conditions that enable us to define the $U(V_1, \ldots, V_m)$ function of (20). We solve the indicated Kuhn-Tucker problem in (concave) non-linear programming, by attaining the saddle-point conditions for

$$u\left[F^1(V_{11}, \ldots, V_{n1}), \ldots, F^m(V_{1m}, \ldots, V_{nm}) \right] + \sum_{i=1}^{n} w_i \left[V_i - \sum_{j=1}^{m} V_{ij} \right]. \tag{26}$$

Necessary and sufficient conditions for this are that the non-negative primal variable (V_{ij}) and dual variables (w_i) satisfy the inequalities

$$\frac{\partial u}{\partial Q_j} \frac{\partial F^j}{\partial V_{ij}} - w_i \leqslant 0, (i = 1, \ldots, n; j = 1, \ldots, m) \tag{27}$$

$$V_i - \sum_{j=1}^{m} V_{ij} \geqslant 0$$

$$\sum_{1}^{n} \left(V_i - \sum_{j=1}^{m} V_{ij} \right) w_j + \sum_{i=1}^{n} \sum_{j=1}^{m} \left(w_i - \frac{\partial u}{\partial Q_j} \frac{\partial F^j}{\partial V_{ij}} \right) V_{ij} = 0$$

$$w_i \geqslant 0, V_{ij} \geqslant 0.$$

In the regular, smooth case of classical interior maximization, this becomes equivalent to

$$\frac{\partial u}{\partial Q_j} \frac{\partial F^j}{\partial V_{ij}} - w_i = 0 \qquad (i = 1, \ldots, n; j = 1, \ldots, m) \tag{28}$$

$$V_i - \sum_{j=1}^{m} V_{ij} = 0$$

and $$\frac{\partial U}{\partial V_i} = w_i. \tag{29}$$

My uniform-homothetic case is manageable in general equilibrium form because all income effects are nicely balanced out. As soon as we permit different individuals to have different tastes and factor endowments, income effects enormously complicate the general equilibrium analysis. Thus, it is well known that the demand for a factor may be positively sloped when income effects are sufficiently badly-behaved. Indeed if the owners of a factor happen to have particularly strong tastes for commodities that require this factor in great intensity, we can easily encounter multiplicity of equilibria and instability: 'bootstrap operations' are then possible in which it pays much for owners of a factor to shift their demands a little toward goods requiring themselves. (This can provide an economic rationale for campaigns by Negroes or other minority groups to spend money 'among your own people'.) One must not ignore hard problems, or call them non-statical, just because they are hard.

I shall mention only one extreme case of unbalanced income effects. Suppose each factor spent all its money on a single good and that this happened in every case to be produced by that factor alone. Then the conditions of equilibrium would degenerate into $m = n$ entirely independent markets: that is, equilibrium would simply entail

$$Q_i = \frac{V_i}{a_{ii}} \qquad (i = 1, \ldots, n = m). \tag{30}$$

Relative prices and relative social shares are quite indeterminate. Although the intra-industry technical elasticity of substitution is in every case infinite, a total elasticity of substitution will be undefined.

I conclude with the observation that unrestricted general equilibrium is very complicated. And if you ask a very complicated question you must expect its answer to involve a very complicated analysis.

III. *Historical Postscript*

J.R. Hicks (1932, pp. 117–20, 241–7) presents the original definition of σ for the two-factor case, both as an indicator of relative shares and as a component of elasticity of derived factor demand. Joan Robinson (1933, pp. 256–62, 330) gives the definition of $\sigma^{(R)}$ for the two-factor case, and proves that a monopolist will have $\partial V_2 / \partial w_1 \gtreqless 0$ depending on whether product demand elasticity is greater or less than the elasticity of substitution. A.C. Pigou (1934) and D.G. Champernowne (1935) show how complicated becomes the incidence of a factor price change in an n-variable model of partial elasticities of substitution. See R.G.D. Allen (1938, pp. 341–5, 372–4, 504–5, 512–13, 520) for n-variable generalization in terms of partial elasticities of substitution $[\sigma_{ij}]$, along with reference to Hicks-Allen consumption measures. R.F. Kahn (1933) proves the equivalence of the two definitions in the case of 2-factor constant returns. J.R. Hicks (1963, p. 373) provides a compact proof.

The formulas for $(\sigma_1, \ldots, \sigma_n)$ of my lectures come close to Hicks's (1963, pp. 339–40, 378–81, 293–5) discussions. For $n = 2$, equation (8) of p. 379 is identical with my (3), and below (8) of p. 379 appears the equivalent to my (4), which is obviously derivable from 1932 formulas on pp. 244 and 246 when elasticities of product demand and of other factor supply are set respectively equal to infinity and zero. Applying his (8) definition to $\Phi(V_I, V_{II}) = F(V_I, V_{II} \overline{V}_2, \ldots, V_{II} \overline{V}_n)$, Hicks will arrive at the same as my (σ_i). To get $[\sigma_i^*]_r$ we apply (8) or my (3) to $\psi_r(V_I, V_{II})$ defined as

Subject to $w_{r+1} r_{+1} + V \ldots + w_n V_n \leqslant V_{II}$

$$\underset{V_{r+1}, \ldots, V_n}{\text{Max}} \quad F(V_I, V_{II} \overline{V}_2, \ldots, V_{II} \overline{V}_r, V_{r+1}, \ldots, V_n)$$

$$= \psi(V_I, V_{II}; \overline{V}_2, \ldots, \overline{V}_r; w_{r+1}, \ldots, w_n)$$

$$= \psi_r(V_I, V_{II}) .$$

The discussion of pp. 377–81 is couched in terms suggesting that

$$\Phi(V_I, V_{II}) \equiv F[V_1, V_{II}(V_2, \ldots, V_n)] ,$$

which would presuppose a special 'tree' property on F; but I doubt that such an implication is intended. For discussion of the Le Chatelier principle see P. A. Samuelson (1947, pp. 36, 38, 81, 168; 1966, chapters 42–4).

For intercommodity substitution of my Part II, see Hicks (1932, p. 120; 1963, pp. 297–9, 340–1, 381–4). F. Machlup (1935) has also emphasized this general equilibrium approach. Incidentally, my strong case of uniform-homothetic tastes (or of every dollar spent in the same way, anywhere) is known to be the only case where 'collective indifference curves' can *rigorously* generate observed market equilibria involving multiple individuals. (Samuelson, 1966, chapter 78). From the non-classical writings on the economic theory of index numbers, by Könus, Staehle, Frisch, Leontief, and others, it is known that unitary income elasticities are mandatory if there is to be a price index holding for all income levels.

Rather than burden the text with the algebra of computing my total $\bar{\sigma}_i$, I present here a brief summary that ought to be relatable to the 1963 algebra of pp. 381–4.

At a critical point where

$$\frac{\partial F(x_1, \ldots, x_n; \alpha)}{\partial x_i} = 0 , \tag{31}$$

we can evaluate the total change in F due to a parameter α, $F(\alpha)$, by the simplifying formulas (Samuelson, 1947, pp. 34–5).

$$F'(\alpha) = F_x \frac{dx}{d\alpha} + F_\alpha = 0 + F_\alpha \tag{32}$$

$$F''(\alpha) = \frac{d}{d\alpha}\left[F_x \frac{dx}{d\alpha} \right] + F_{\alpha\alpha} + F_{\alpha x}\frac{dx}{d\alpha} = 0 + F_{\alpha\alpha} - F_{\alpha x}F_{xx}^{-1}F_{x\alpha}, \tag{33}$$

where $\ [f_x, f_\alpha] = [\partial f/\partial x_i, \partial f/\partial\alpha]$

$$\begin{bmatrix} f_{xx} & f_{x\alpha} \\ f_{\alpha x} & f_{\alpha\alpha} \end{bmatrix} = \begin{bmatrix} \dfrac{\partial^2 f}{\partial x_i \partial x_j} & \dfrac{\partial^2 f}{\partial x_i \partial\alpha} \\ \dfrac{\partial^2 f}{\partial\alpha\partial x_j} & \dfrac{\partial^2 f}{\partial\alpha^2} \end{bmatrix}.$$

If f is identified with the Lagrangian saddlepoint expression of (26), we can calculate

$$[\partial^2 U/\partial V_i\partial V_j] = [\partial w_i/\partial V_j]$$

expression by the above kinds of formulas; this will involve square matrices of no less than $nm + n$ columns.

To reduce the problem to matrices of only $n + m$ columns I write the equilibrium conditions with the help of the minimum-unit-cost-of-production functions $A^j(w_1, \ldots, w_m)$, which are dual to the $F^j(V_{1j}\ldots, V_{nj})$ production functions, being concave and homogeneous of the first degree and known to have as partial derivatives

$$\frac{\partial A^j}{\partial w_i} = A_i^j = a_{ij}. \tag{34}$$

Equilibrium is defined by

$$V_i = \sum_{k=1}^{m} A_i^k(w_1, \ldots, w_n)Q_k \qquad (i = 1, \ldots, n) \tag{35}$$

$$0 = A^j(w_1, \ldots, w_n) - \partial u[Q_1, \ldots, Q_m]/\partial Q_j \qquad (j = 1, \ldots, m),$$

with

$$\begin{bmatrix} \dfrac{\partial w_i}{\partial V_j} \end{bmatrix} = \left[\begin{array}{c|c} \sum\limits_k A_{ij}^k Q_k & a_{ij} \\ \hline a_{ji} & -u_{ij} \end{array} \right]^{-1} \begin{bmatrix} I \\ 0 \end{bmatrix},$$

a negative semi-definite matrix by virtue of $[u_{ij}]$ and $[A_{ij}^k]$ all having that property.

For the special case where $m = n$, and $[a_{ij}]$ is a non-singular matrix of constants (the fixed-coefficient case), with an inverse $[a_{ij}]^{-1} = [a^{(ij)}]$, we can compute directly

$$\left[\frac{\partial^2 U}{\partial V_i \partial V_j}\right] = \left[\sum_{r=1}^{m} \sum_{s=1}^{m} \frac{\partial^2 u}{\partial Q_r \partial Q_s} u^{(ir)} u^{(js)}\right]. \tag{36}$$

This shows that total $\bar{\sigma}_i$ is finite and positive, even when every technical production function involves zero substitutability; it is the $[\partial^2 u / \partial Q_r \partial Q_s]$ inter-commodity substitution that produces the over-all elasticity of factor demand, in confirmation of economic intuition. (It will be noted that I have not found it useful to handle the homothetic case by separating out income and substitution effects. A direct approach seems more helpful.)

ACKNOWLEDGMENTS

I should like to thank my colleagues and former students Eytan Sheshinski and David Levhari for helpful criticisms of this paper and acknowledge financial aid from the National Science Foundation.

20

Short-run Adjustment of
Employment to Output

Robert M. Solow

It is no trick any more to derive linear decision rules from quadratic profit or loss functions. Nevertheless, this note is devoted to one more such exercise. It is justified, I hope, because the particular application is an important one, on which much empirical work has already been done. (For recent examples, and further references, see Ball and St Cyr (1966) and Brechling (1965)).

Casual observation suggests that changes in production by a firm, industry, or group of industries are typically followed by changes in employment only with a lag. This process of adjustment is one of the main sources of the observed pattern of short-run fluctuations in productivity. Econometric analysis confirms the existence of the lag. Almost all the econometric work on this subject proceeds by fitting the simple linear first-order adjustment process:

$$E_t - E_{t-1} = h(E_t^* - E_{t-1}).$$

Here E stands for employment, measured in men or manhours, and E^* stands for the 'target' level of employment, the level of employment which, if it had been achieved last period, would be left unchanged in this period. The parameter h is expected to be between zero and one; it is the fraction of the gap between the current target level of employment and the inherited level of employment from last period that will be eliminated in the current period.

The linear first-order adjustment process supplies a convenient regression model as soon as assumptions are made relating E^* to observable data, like output, other inputs, prices, time, or anything else. The model has given generally successful results when it has been applied to data from manufacturing industries in the US, the UK, and still other countries. Some puzzles remain, however.

The object of this note is to show how the linear first-order adjustment process (or rather its continuous-time analogue) can be deduced as the solution to a cost-minimizing problem. Some rather stiff assumptions are required. This suggests to me that it might pay to explore the empirical utility of more complicated adjustment models, in the hope that some of the other anomalies in current empirical work might be eliminated in the process.

I shall summarize the underlying cost model very briefly, because I have used it before (Solow, to appear) for a slightly different purpose. We are to imagine a typical firm planning its employment over a short horizon, of length T. The horizon is short enough so that capital and other factors are essentially constant. A firm that expects a particular output schedule can then translate it into a 'labor-requirements' schedule; the labor-requirement at each instant of time is designated E_t^*, and corresponds to the target-level of employment mentioned earlier. The firm's actual employment is E_t. It is not necessary that $E_t = E_t^*$ at any particular time. Employment can exceed labor requirements; the extra labor (sometimes described as 'hoarded') can be put to work doing maintenance or other housekeeping tasks not usually measured as part of output, or else work can simply be spread. Labor requirements can exceed employment; I shall interpret this to mean that overtime is being worked, if employment is measured in men, or that the intensity of work is increased beyond normal levels. In either case there will have to be premium pay or wage bonuses.

Instantaneous costs fall into three categories.

(1) wE represents ordinary wage costs, when the wage rate w is assumed to (or is expected to be) constant over the planning period;

(2) $v\dot{E}^2$ represents hiring-and-firing and other frictional costs associated with changes in the level of employment, assumed (for simplicity) to be symmetrical with respect to increases and decreases;

(3) $a(E^*-E)^2+b(E^*-E)$ is a component of costs which is zero when $E = E^*$, positive when $E^* > E$ (reflecting overtime premia, deterioration of quality, etc.), and negative when $E > E^*$ (reflecting the value of the housekeeping services performed by hoarded labor, whose wages have already been accounted for under (1)), at least when E is not too much bigger than E^*.

The planning period T is short enough so that discounting can be neglected. The firm plans its employment policy $E(t)$ to minimize cumulated costs throughout the planning period:

$$\int_0^T [wE + v\dot{E}^2 + a(E^* - E)^2 + b(E^* - E)]\,dt .$$

I now make the crucial assumption that the firm expects E^* to be *constant*. This need not mean that the firm can never change its estimate of E^*, but only that, whenever it plans, it plans for a constant output until the short horizon. If its expectation changes, it re-plans. One must suppose the planning period to be so short that productivity change can be neglected.

Under this assumption the integrand in the cost integral does not contain t explicitly. It is easy, therefore, to write down the first integral of the Euler equation. It is

$$wE + v\dot{E}^2 + a(E^* - E)^2 + b(E^* - E) - 2v\dot{E}^2 = C =$$

a constant of integration.

Therefore the optimal employment policy satisfies

$$\dot{E}^2 = \frac{1}{v}[wE + a(E^* - E)^2 + b(E^* - E) - C].$$

Now consider more closely the cost component $a(E^* - E)^2 + b(E^* - E)$. If one plots this as a function of E it equals zero at $E = E^*$ and has a slope at that point equal to $-b$. If one imagines that the overtime premium for the first overtime minute is very near zero, and goes higher as the extent of overtime increases, and that the housekeeping work waiting to be done in the first idle minute is worth very nearly the going wage to the firm, and is worth less at the margin as the amount of labor-hoarding rises, then it is natural to assume that $b = w$. Then

$$\dot{E}^2 = \frac{1}{v}[a(E^* - E)^2 + wE^* - C].$$

An optimal policy must clearly have the property that $\dot{E} = 0$ when $E = E^*$, because E^* is expected to be constant. This boundary condition fixes the constant of integration: $C = wE^*$. It then follows that

$$\dot{E} = \sqrt{\frac{a}{v}}(E^* - E).$$

This is the continuous-time version of the linear first-order adjustment process. The speed-of-adjustment parameter $h = \sqrt{(a/v)}$. Naturally enough, it is bigger the bigger is a (that is, the more costly it is to let E deviate substantially from E^*) and the smaller is v (that is, the less costly it is to make sudden changes in employment).

In the econometric literature, the custom is to make E^* a function of output, time (to allow for productivity increase), and perhaps a measure of capital stock. This procedure can perhaps be justified on the assumption that the horizon extends for one unit of time (usually a quarter of a year), so that E^* is re-set that frequently. Nevertheless, one is entitled to the feeling that a lot of weight is being placed on the assumption of constant expected labor-requirements during the planning period. If the 'correct' adjustment process is rather different, statistical results from the linear first-order process may be systematically biased.

If we allow E^* to be any function of time, the Euler equation for cost minimization is:

$$\ddot{E} = -\frac{a}{v}(E^*-E)+\frac{w-b}{2v}.$$

(If discounted costs are minimized, $-r\dot{E}$ is added to the right-hand side, where r is the discount rate.) The appropriately formulated adjustment process is second-order. Unfortunately it may be the case that the data simply will not support an analysis depending on second differences of employment with respect to time.

21

Time Preference, the Consumption Function, and Optimum Asset Holdings

H. Uzawa

I. *Introduction*

The problem of demand for money and other assets has been recently studied by Douglas (1966) and Sidrauski (1965) within the framework of a rational individual faced with the choice of a consumption schedule which is optimal with respect to the individual's time preference structure. In both papers, the intertemporal utility function upon which the consumer's choice is based is represented by a discounted integral of the stream of instantaneous utility levels, where future utilities are discounted by a rate which is kept constant independently of time profile of the utility stream associated with each consumption schedule. Thus, if a consumer is permitted to hold his assets either in the form of real cash balances or in the form of perpetuities yielding a constant rate of interest and if his instantaneous utility function is linear and homogeneous, he will either postpone his consumption until the very last moment or will consume as much as possible, according to whether the subject rate of discount is lower than the rate of interest. The only case in which the individual would desire to possess two types of assets simultaneously is one where his subject rate of discount is precisely equal to the rate of interest. Douglas has avoided this difficulty by having the level of bond holdings as one of the components for instantaneous utility level, while Sidrauski has introduced real capital as an alternative asset for which the rate of return varies with the amount held. In this paper, we shall instead start with an analysis of an individual's time preference structure, to derive a certain specific formulation regarding the rate by which he discounts future levels. We shall then proceed to examine the behavior of an individual consumer who decides the allocation of his income between consumption and savings and the choice of portfolio balances in such manner that the resulting consumption stream is most preferred in terms of his time preference structure. The analysis will be first carried out for the simple case in which the individual is permitted to hold his assets only in the form of bonds for which the expected rate of interest is constant, and then for a more general case in which he may hold his assets in the form of money and bonds and other types for which the rates of return may vary.

II. *Time Preference*

The analysis presented here is based upon a re-examination of the concept of time preference, which originates with Boehm-Bawerk (1959) and Fisher (1907), and for which an elaborated analysis has been recently done by Koopmans (1960). It is the rate by which future income (or utility) is discounted to the present, summarizing the preference structure of an individual economic unit regarding present and future consumption. To define the concept of time preference more precisely, let us first consider a special case where future consumption is concentrated at a certain time, say t. The preference structure of an individual unit then is described in terms of indifference curves, as typically depicted in Figure 1, where the horizontal axis represents the utility level u_0 resulting from present consumption, while the utility level of future consumption u_t is measured along the vertical axis. Each indifference curve is assumed to be convex toward the origin and to intersect with the horizontal axis (by a linear transition, if necessary).

Let u_0 and u_t be the levels of present and future utility, to be represented by a point A in Figure 1, and let U be the level of present utility at the point B at which the indifference curve through A intersects with the horizontal axis. Thus an increase in present utility from u_0 to U exactly compensates a decrease in future utility from u_t to 0. The ratio $u_t/(U-u_0)$, if we subtract one, represents the rate by which future utility is discounted to make it comparable with the present utility.

We may then define the rate of *time preference* $\Delta_{0,t}$:

$$\Delta_{0,t} = \frac{u_t}{U-u_0} - 1; \tag{1}$$

namely, $\quad U = u_0 + \dfrac{u_t}{1+\Delta_{0,t}},$ \hfill (2)

and the level U may be used to describe the preference structure of the individual in consideration. The rate of time preference $\Delta_{0,t}$ depends upon the utility levels of present and future consumption, and it is easily seen that an increase in the present utility along the indifference curve will result in a decrease in the rate of time preference; namely, the higher the level of real income today, the lower is the rate by which the individual discounts tomorrow's real income.

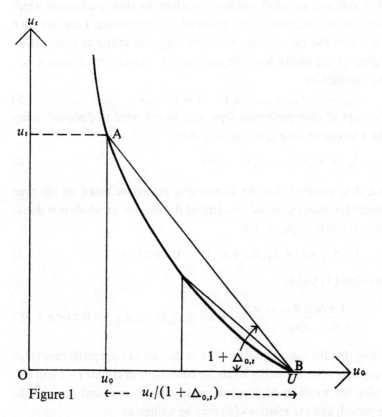

Figure 1

The concept of time preference is extended to the general case where future consumption is made at various time points, say $t = 1, \ldots, n$. Any utility stream is represented by a vector with $n+1$ components, $(u_0, u_1, \ldots, u_n)$, where u_0 is the utility level for present consumption and $u_1, \ldots, u_n$ refer to those for future consumption. Assuming that each indifference surface always intersects with the u_0-axis, it is possible to find n rates of time preference, $\Delta_{0,1}, \ldots, \Delta_{0,n}$, such that

$$U = u_0 + \frac{u_1}{1+\Delta_{0,1}} + \ldots + \frac{u_n}{1+\Delta_{0,n}} \tag{3}$$

represents the level of present utility which is indifferent with the given utility stream $(u_0, u_1, \ldots, u_n)$. The rate of time preference $\Delta_{0,t}$ now depends upon the entire time profile of the utility stream, to be indicated by the functional notation

$$\Delta_{0,t} = \Delta_{0,t}(u_0, \ldots, u_n) \qquad t = 1, \ldots, n. \tag{4}$$

In what follows, we shall confine ourselves to time preference which satisfies certain consistency and independency postulates. First, we shall postulate that the rate of time preference $\Delta_{0,t}$ for utility at time t is independent of the utility levels beyond time t; namely, the function $\Delta_{0,t}$ may be specified as

$$\Delta_{0,t} = \Delta_{0,t}(u_0, u_1, \ldots, u_t) \qquad t = 1, \ldots, n. \tag{5}$$

The concept of time preference then may be extended to discount utility at time t to one at time s, whenever $s < t$:

$$\Delta_{s,t} = \Delta_{s,t}(u_s, \ldots, u_t) \qquad s < t. \tag{6}$$

Second, it is assumed that the discounting procedure based on the time preference function (6) is independent of the manner in which it is done; in particular, it is required that

$$1 + \Delta_{0,t} = (1 + \Delta_{0,s})(1 + \Delta_{s,t}), \qquad 0 < s < t < n. \tag{7}$$

The relation (7) yields

$$\frac{1 + \Delta_{0,t}(u_0, \ldots, u_t)}{1 + \Delta_{0,t-1}(u_0, \ldots, u_{t-1})} = 1 + \Delta_{t-1,t}(u_{t-1}, u_t), \qquad 0 < t < n, \tag{8}$$

indicating that the logarithmic increase in the rate of time preference (plus one) depends upon the utility levels for consumption at time $t - 1$ and t.

Finally, the structure of time preference remains invariant through the entire period, and the relations (8) may be written as:

$$\frac{1 + \Delta_{0,t}(u_0, \ldots, u_t)}{1 + \Delta_{0,t-1}(u_0, \ldots, u_{t-1})} = 1 + \delta(u_{t-1}, u_t), \tag{9}$$

with a certain function δ.

If consumption is made continuously over an infinite time period, the structure of time preference is in general described in terms of the intertemporal utility functional:

$$U = \int_0^\infty u_t \, e^{-\Delta_t} \, dt, \tag{10}$$

where the rate of time preference Δ_t depends upon the time profile of a continuous utility stream $u_t (0 < t < \infty)$, and the relation (8) then may be transformed to the following:

$$\dot{\Delta}_t = \delta(u_t), \qquad (\Delta_0 = 0) \tag{11}$$

It will be assumed that $u(c)$ is a concave utility function satisfying

$$u(c) > 0, \qquad u'(c) > 0, \qquad u''(c) < 0, \qquad \text{for all } c > 0. \tag{12}$$

It is assumed that the function δ, to be referred to simply as the time preference function, satisfies the following conditions:

$$\delta(u) > 0, \qquad \delta'(u) > 0, \qquad \delta''(u) > 0, \qquad \text{for all } u > 0, \tag{13}$$

and $\quad \delta(u) - \delta'(u)u > 0. \tag{14}$

The condition (14) above indicates that between two stationary consumption streams the one with higher level of instantaneous utility is preferred. The second assumption in (13) requires that an increase in the consumption level at a certain future date will increase the rate of discount for all consumption made afterward, while the third assumption is required to derive a continuous consumption function, as in detail discussed below.

III. *Optimum Savings and Consumption Schedule*

The specific structure of time preference, as derived in the previous section, will now be used to examine the pattern of behavior for an individual consumer with regard to transitory, as well as permanent, adjustments of his holdings of cash and other assets. We shall begin with a simple case in which the individual consumer is allowed to hold his assets only in the form of interest-yielding bonds. It is simply assumed that bonds are quoted in terms of real output and yield interests, payable in output, at whatever rate will prevail in the market at the time of payments. At a certain moment of time 0, the consumer possesses a fixed sum of bonds, say b_0, and expects to receive wages w_t. The income stream he expects to receive then depends upon the amounts of accumulated savings, in the form of bond holdings, and he is primarily concerned with attaining the time path of consumption which is most preferred, in terms of his time preference structure, among all the feasible consumption paths consistent with his initial asset holdings and the state of expectations regarding future rates of interest and wage payments.

Let b_t be the amount of bonds the consumer plans to hold at each moment of time t. Then the level y_t of his income (in real terms) at time t is given by

$$y_t = r_t b_t + w_t,\tag{15}$$

which will be divided between consumption c_t and savings $\dot{b}_t$; namely,

$$y_t = c_t + \dot{b}_t,\tag{16}$$

with the initial bond holdings b_0.

The optimum paths of consumption and bond holdings thus are determined, among others, relative to the state of expectations regarding to real wages, real transfer payments, and real rate of interest, all of which in general vary through time. However, it will be assumed in the rest of the paper that the consumer expects real wages, real transfer payments, and real rate of interest to remain at certain constant, permanent, levels such that the resulting patterns of consumption and savings coincide with those which would have been derived under more general circumstances. Such a procedure in fact would be justified only after we have made a thorough examination of the general case, but it will be adopted here as a first approximation to enable us to get some insight into the complex structure of optimum resource allocation over time.

The analytical framework may now be summarized before we proceed to examine its structure in detail. We consider an individual consumer who possesses a fixed amount of assets to be held in the form of bonds. He expects the real rate of interest to be constant, r, and to receive wage payments fixed in real terms, w. His utility level u_t at each moment of time t is related to consumption c_t:

$$u_t = u(c_t),\tag{17}$$

and he is concerned with maximizing the total utility:

$$\int_0^\infty u_t\, e^{-\Delta_t}\, dt\tag{18}$$

subject to the constraints:

$$\dot{\Delta}_t = \delta(u_t), \quad \text{with } \Delta_0 = 0,\tag{19}$$

$$\dot{b}_t = y_t - c_t, \quad \text{with given } b_0,\tag{20}$$

where the real income y_t is given by

$$y_t = rb_t + w,\tag{21}$$

IV. *Solution of the Optimum Problem*

The first step in simplifying the optimum problem consists of a transformation of the time variable t into one in terms of which the rate of time preference becomes constant; namely,[1] if we take Δ as the independent variable instead of t in the maximand and (18), we get, in view of (19), that

$$\int_0^\infty u\, e^{-\Delta}\, dt = \int_0^\infty \frac{u}{\delta(u)}\, e^{-\Delta}\, d\Delta ,\qquad (22)$$

while the differential equation (19) is transformed to

$$b^\circ\left(=\frac{db}{d\Delta}\right)=\frac{y-c}{\delta(u)},\ \text{with a given}\ b(0)=b_0 ,\qquad (23)$$

where b° in general indicates $db/d\Delta$.

Since the real rate of interest r is constant through time, the differential equation (23) is reduced to one involving y instead of b; that is,

$$y^\circ\left(=\frac{dy}{d\Delta}\right)=\frac{r}{\delta(u)}(y-c),\qquad (24)$$

with the given initial condition $y(0) = rb_0 + w$.

The optimum problem now is converted to that of maximizing (22) subject to the differential equation (23) or (24). In the present form, it is possible to apply the mathematical techniques of the calculus of variations, as developed by, e.g. Ramsey (1928), Koopmans (1963).

By introducing the imputed price of investment $\lambda = \lambda(\Delta)$ for each level of accumulated rate of time preference, the imputed value of income H is defined by:

$$H = u(c)+\lambda(y-c) .\qquad (25)$$

The present value of the imputed income H, to be discounted at the prevailing rate of preference $\delta = \delta(u(c))$, is given by

$$\frac{H}{\delta(u)}\, e^{-\Delta} .\qquad (26)$$

The optimum consumption c is determined at the level at which the present value (27) of the imputed income is maximized; namely, by taking the first order condition, we get

$$u'(c)-\lambda-\frac{\delta'(u)u'(c)}{\delta(u)}H = 0 .\qquad (27)$$

The solution c to the first order condition (27) in fact is a maximum of (26), as is easily seen from the assumptions (12–14).

To explain the condition (27), let us rewrite it as

$$u' = \lambda + \frac{\delta' u'}{\delta} H \,, \tag{28}$$

the left-hand side of which is nothing but the marginal utility of consumption, while the right-hand side is the sum of the imputed value of investment λ and the marginal increase in the present value of the imputed income due to a marginal decrease in the rate of time preference.

The differential equation describing the dynamic path of the imputed price $\lambda = \lambda(\Delta)$ is obtained from the Euler-Lagrange condition; namely, we have

$$\frac{\lambda^{\circ}}{\lambda} = \frac{\delta(u) - r}{\delta(u)} \,, \tag{29}$$

which indicates that capital gains are always equal to the interest charges minus the competitive rent.

The optimum path of the asset accumulation is then characterized as one which, by a proper choice of imputed prices λ, constitutes a bounded solution to the system of differential equations (24) and (29), together with (27). The structure of the differential equations (24) and (29), however, is more easily analyzed by transforming them into those involving y and c. Let us denote

$$\phi(y,c,\lambda) = u'(c) - \frac{\delta(u(c))u'(c)}{\delta(u(c))} H \,, \tag{30}$$

which by a differentiation yields

$$\phi_y y^{\circ} + \phi_c c^{\circ} + \phi_\lambda \lambda^{\circ} = 0 \,, \tag{31}$$

along the path satisfying (27).

Substituting (24) and (29) into (31) and re-arranging, we get

$$c^{\circ} = \frac{r - \delta - \delta' u'(y - c)}{\delta \left(\dfrac{u'\delta''(u + u'(y - c))}{\delta - u\delta'} - \dfrac{u''}{u'} \right)} \,, \tag{32}$$

where $\delta' = \delta'(u)$, $u' = u'(c)$, etc.

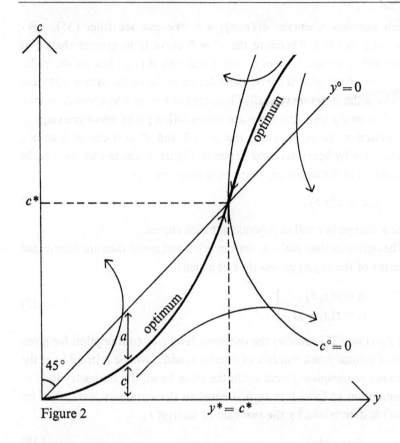

Figure 2

The rate of change in income level y is zero if and only if $c = y$; namely, the $y° = 0$ curve is described by the 45° line starting at the origin on the (c,y)-plane, as indicated in Figure 2. Real income y tends to increase below the $y° = 0$ curve, while it tends to decrease above the $y° = 0$ curve. On the other hand, the $c° = 0$ curve is characterized by:

$$r - \delta(u) - \delta'(u)u'(c)(y-c) = 0 , \tag{33}$$

or

$$y = c + \frac{1}{\delta'u'}(r-\delta) . \tag{34}$$

To see the shape of the $c° = 0$ curve, differentiate (34) with respect to c to get

$$\left(\frac{dy}{dc}\right)_{c°=0} = -\frac{r-\delta}{\delta'u'}\left(\frac{\delta''u'}{\delta'} + \frac{u''}{u'}\right) , \tag{35}$$

which vanishes whenever $\delta((u(c)) = r$. We can see from (35), $y \gtreqless c$ according to $r \gtreqless \delta$. Therefore the $c^\circ = 0$ curve is in general shaped as illustrated in Figure 2. Since $x^\circ > 0$ if and only if (c,y) lies on the right-hand side of the $c^\circ = 0$ curve, the solution paths to the system (24) and (29) have the structure typically illustrated in Figure 2 by arrowed curves. It is then easily seen that there are two solution paths which converge to the stationary point at which the $y^\circ = 0$ and $c^\circ = 0$ curves intersect, as indicated by heavy arrowed curves in Figure 2. Let the solution paths converging to the stationary point be denoted by

$$c = c(y,r), \tag{36}$$

since a change in r will in general shift such curves.

The optimum time paths of consumption and assets then are determined in terms of the $c(y,r)$ curves thus obtained:

$$\left.\begin{array}{l} c_t = c(y_t,r) \\ \dot{y}_t = r(y_t - c_t). \end{array}\right\} \tag{37}$$

The function (35) specifies the optimum level c of consumption for given level of income y and real rate of interest r, and it will be referred to as the *short-run consumption function*. On the other hand, the stationary level of consumption c^* (which in turn is equal to the stationary level y^* of income) is determined by the real rate of interest r:

$$c^* = c^*(r), \tag{38}$$

which will be referred to as the *long-run consumption function*.

v. *The Long-Run Consumption Function $c^*(r)$*

The long-run level of consumption c^* has been defined as that level of consumption which would have been eventually reached if the real rate of interest were to remain at a certain constant level r, throughout the whole period of adjustment. It is independent of the initial level of the asset holding or of initial income level, since it is determined at the level at which the rate of time preference is equal to the real rate of interest, that is,

$$\delta(u(c^*)) = r. \tag{39}$$

The long-run level c^* of real consumption thus is one for which the rate of time preference $\delta(u(c^*))$ is precisely equal to the market (real) rate of

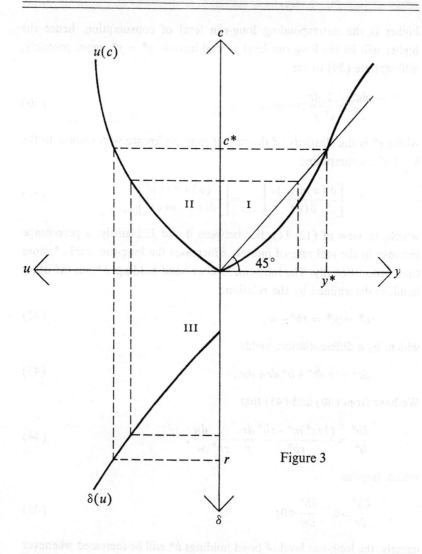

Figure 3

interest r. The determination of c^* is now typically described in Figure 3, where the first quadrant is simply copied from Figure 2. In the second quadrant, the horizontal axis represents the utility level u, while the vertical axis in the third quadrant measures the rate of time preference δ. The utility level for each consumption is specified by the $u(c)$-curve, while the $\delta(u)$-curve relates the rate of time preference δ with the utility level u. For a given real rate of interest r, the long-run level $c^*(r)$ of consumption is thus uniquely determined, and the higher the real rate of interest r, the higher is the corresponding long-run level of consumption, hence the higher will be the long-run level of real income $c^* = y^*$, more precisely, differentiate (39) to get

$$\frac{dc^*}{c^*} = \frac{1}{\varepsilon^*} \frac{dr}{r},$$
(40)

where ε^* is the elasticity of the rate of time preference with respect to the level of consumption:

$$\varepsilon^* = \left[\frac{\delta'(u)u'(c)c}{\delta(u)} \right]_{c=c^*} = \left[\frac{\delta'(u)u}{\delta(u)} \frac{u'(c)c}{u(c)} \right]_{c=c^*},$$
(41)

which, in view of (12–14), lies between 0 and 1. Namely, a percentage increase in the real rate of interest r increases the long-run level c^* more than proportionally. The long-run level of bond holdings b^*, on the other hand, is determined by the relation:

$$c^* = y^* = rb^* + w,$$
(42)

which, by a differentiation, yields

$$dc^* = r\, db^* + b^*\, dr + dw.$$
(43)

We have from (40) and (43) that

$$\frac{db^*}{b^*} = \frac{(1/\varepsilon^*)c^* - rb^*}{rb^*} \frac{dr}{r} - \frac{w}{rb^*} \frac{dw}{w},$$
(44)

which implies

$$\frac{\partial b^*}{\partial r} > 0, \quad \frac{\partial b^*}{\partial w} < 0;$$
(45)

namely, the long-run level of bond holdings b^* will be increased whenever there is an increase in the rate of interest r or a decrease either in real wages or transfer payments.

VI. *The Short-run Consumption Function* $c(y,r)$

In Section IV, we have shown that the optimum level of consumption c is uniquely determined for given income y and real rate of interest r. The structure of the short-run consumption $c(y,r)$ is illustrated in Figure 4, where part of Figure 2 has been reproduced. It is first seen that an increase

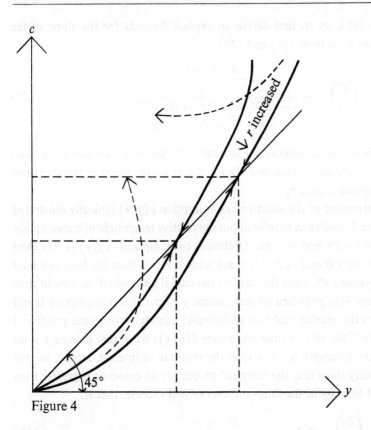

Figure 4

in income y is always associated with an increase in the optimum level of consumption, that is,

$$\partial c / \partial y > 0 . \tag{46}$$

Second, it can be shown that a decrease in the real rate of interest r shifts the optimum path uniformly to the left, thus resulting an increase in optimum consumption for a given level of income y, that is,

$$\partial c / \partial r < 0 . \tag{47}$$

Since an increase in r results in an upward movement (along the 45° line) of the long-run level of consumption, the proposition (47) will be proved if we can show that the slope of the optimum path is always increased whenever there is an increase in r; in other words, it suffices to show that

$$\frac{\partial}{\partial r}\left(\frac{dc}{dy}\right)_{\text{opt.}} > 0, \qquad y < y^* . \tag{48}$$

To see (48), let us first derive an explicit formula for the slope of the optimum path from (24) and (29):

$$\left(\frac{dc}{dy}\right)_{\text{opt.}} = \frac{1}{y-c} \frac{1-\dfrac{\delta+\delta'u'(y-c)}{r}}{\dfrac{u'\delta''(u+u'(y-c))}{\delta-u\delta'} - \dfrac{u''}{u'}}, \tag{49}$$

which is increased whenever r is increased. Similarly, we can show that, when $y > y^*$, an increase in r always decreases the slope of the short-run consumption schedule.

The structure of the short-run consumption $c(y, r)$ typically illustrated in Figure 4 enables us to infer about the relative magnitude of consumption compared with real income. Optimum consumption $c(y, r)$ is less than real income y if and only if the real income is less than the long-run level of real income y^*, while the latter is the case if and only if the rate of time preference $\delta(u(y))$ when all real income y is spent on consumption is still less than the market real rate of interest; namely, savings are positive if and only if the rate of time preference $\delta(u(y))$ when real income y is all spent on consumption is less than the real rate of interest. Hence, we can particularly show that the marginal propensity to consume is greater than or equal to unity at the long-run level of real income, that is,

$$\left(\frac{\partial c}{\partial y}\right)_{y=y^*} \geqslant 1. \tag{50}$$

VII. *Demand for Money and Other Assets*
The analysis presented above may be extended without much difficulty to a more general case in which each individual consumer is permitted to hold his assets either in the form of cash, from which he derives certain utility, or in the form of bonds, interest payments for which will be annually added to his income. At a certain moment of time, say 0, the consumer has a fixed amount, A_0, of assets, to be given in dollar terms, and expects to receive wages W_t for indefinite future all in money terms. The expected income stream will now depend upon the expected rates of interest as well as upon the way in which his asset holdings are divided between cash and bond. The consumer is again concerned with the time-path of consumption which is most preferred among all feasible time-paths of consumption.

Let M_t and B_t be respectively the amounts of cash balances and bond holdings the consumer plans to possess at each moment of time t. The total monetary value A_t of his asset holdings will then be

$$A_t = M_t + \pi_t B_t, \tag{51}$$

where π_t is the market price of bonds which the consumer expects to prevail at time t. On the other hand, the level of his nominal income Y_t at time t will be composed of interests and wages payments:

$$Y_t = i_t B_t + W_t, \tag{52}$$

where i_t is the coupon rate of interest; that is, the unit of bond is expected to yield interests in the amount i_t at time t.

The money income Y_t will be divided between consumption expenditure C_t, increases in cash balances $\dot{M}_t$, and in bond holdings $\dot{B}_t$:

$$Y_t = C_t + \dot{M}_t + i_t \dot{B}_t. \tag{53}$$

It is assumed that the level of utility depends upon the amount of real cash balances as well as upon real consumption (Patinkin, 1956; Archibald and Lipsey, 1958–9, pp. 1–23; Douglas, 1966; Sidrauski, 1965). If p_t is the general price level expected at time t, real consumption c_t and real cash balances m_t will be

$$c_t = C_t / p_t, \quad m_t = M_t / p_t,$$

and the utility level u_t will be given by

$$u_t = u(c_t, m_t).$$

The optimum plan then is the one which maximizes the total utility defined by (10) among all possible paths of consumption and real cash balances consistent with his initial value A_0 of assets and the state of his expectations regarding increases in the general price level and in the price of bond, as well as regarding the bond rate of interest. Let the expected money rate of interest and rate of increase in the general price level be denoted by

$$\rho_t = \frac{i_t}{\pi_t} + \frac{\dot{\pi}_t}{\pi_t}, \quad \psi_t = \frac{\dot{p}_t}{p_t}.$$

To simplify the formulation, we introduce the following real variables (which are in general denoted by small letters):

$a_t = A_t / p_t$: real value of the asset holdings,

$b_t = \pi_t B_t / p_t$: the market value of the bond holdings in real terms,

$m_t = M_t / p_t$: real cash balances,

$c_t = C_t/p_t$: real consumption,
$w_t = W_t/p_t$: the expected real wages,
$y_t = Y_t/p_t$: real income.
Then the relations (51–53) may be rewritten as:

$$a_t = m_t + b_t \,, \tag{54}$$

$$\begin{aligned}
c_t + \dot{m}_t + \dot{b}_t &= (\rho_t - \psi_t) b_t + w_t - {}_t m_t \psi \\
&= r_t b_t + w_t - \psi_t m_t \,,
\end{aligned} \tag{55}$$

where $r_t = \rho_t - \psi_t$ is the expected real rate of interest.

In view of (54), the equation (55) is reduced to

$$\dot{a}_t = (r_t a_t + w_t) - (\rho_t m_t + c_t) \,, \tag{56}$$

of which the first term on the right-hand side, $r_t a_t + w_t$, corresponds to the concept of real income, while the second term, $\rho_t m_t + c_t$, represents the virtual level of consumption, being the sum of the alternative cost of holding real cash balances at m_t and of real consumption c_t.

The optimum paths of consumption, real cash balances, and bond holdings thus are determined relative to the state of expectations regarding to real wages, real rate of interest, and money rate of interest which will be again assumed to be fixed at certain levels.

In summary, we consider an individual consumer who possesses a fixed amount ($a_0 = A_0/p_0$) in real terms to be held either in the form of real cash balances or in the form of bonds. He expects the real and money rates of interest to be constant, r and ρ, respectively, and to receive wage and transfer payments fixed in real terms, w and τ. His utility level at each moment of time t, u_t, is related to consumption c_t and real cash balances m_t:

$$u_t = u(c_t, m_t) \,, \tag{57}$$

and he is concerned with maximizing the total utility:

$$\int_0^\infty u_t e^{-\Delta t} \, dt \tag{58}$$

subject to the constraints:

$$\dot{\Delta}_t = \delta(u_t) \,, \quad \text{with } \Delta_0 = 0 \,, \tag{59}$$

$$\dot{a}_t = y_t - x_t \,, \quad \text{with given } a_0 \,, \tag{60}$$

$$a_t = m_t + b_t \,, \tag{61}$$

where real income y_t and the virtual level of consumption x_t are respectively defined by

$$y_t = r a_t + w \,, \tag{62}$$

$$x_t = c_t + \rho m_t \,. \tag{63}$$

It may be first noted that, along any optimum path, consumption c and real cash balances m are determined so as to maximize the level of utility $u(c,m)$ subject to the constraint that

$$c + \rho m = x . \tag{64}$$

Such a combination (c,m) of consumption and real cash balances is obtained at the point at which the marginal rate of substitution between them is equal to the money rate of interest ρ:

$$\frac{u_m}{u_c} = \rho , \tag{65}$$

so that c and m are uniquely determined by the level of virtual consumption x. In Figure 5, the horizontal axis represents real cash balances m, while the level of real consumption is measured along the vertical axis, and the optimum combination (c,m) of consumption and real cash balances moves along the income-consumption path, as the virtual level of consumption x is increased from zero to infinity; we may write:

$$c = c(x,\rho) , \qquad m = m(x,\rho) , \tag{66}$$

to indicate their dependency upon the money rate of interest ρ. The maximum level of utility will then be denoted by

$$u(c,m) = U(x,\rho) . \tag{67}$$

It will be assumed that both consumption and real cash balances are superior goods in the sense that an increase in the virtual level of consumption x will increase both optimum consumption and real cash balances:

$$\frac{\partial c}{\partial x} > 0 , \quad \frac{\partial m}{\partial x} > 0 . \tag{68}$$

The effects of an increase in the money rate of interest ρ is, on the other hand, to shift the income-consumption path uniformly upward; it will be assumed that

$$\frac{\partial c}{\partial \rho} > 0 , \quad \frac{\partial m}{\partial \rho} < 0 . \tag{69}$$

It is easily seen that the utility function $u(x) = U(x; \rho)$ satisfies the following conditions

$$u(x) > 0 , \qquad u'(x) > 0 , \qquad u''(x) < 0 , \qquad \text{for all } x > 0 . \tag{70}$$

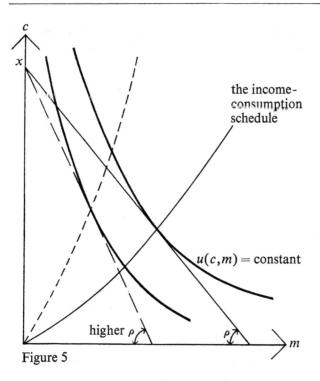

the income-
consumption
schedule

$u(c,m) = $ constant

higher ρ

ρ

m

Figure 5

In terms of the new utility function $u(x) = U(x,\rho)$, the optimum problem is reduced to one in which the total utility (58) is maximized subject to the constraints (59) and (60), where

$$u_t = U(x_t; \rho).\qquad(71)$$

The optimum path of the virtual level of consumption x_t and the real income y_t will then be obtained with the aid of the following differential equations:

$$\dot{y} = r(y-x),\qquad(72)$$

$$\dot{x} = \frac{r-\delta-\delta'u'(y-x)}{\dfrac{u'\delta''[u+u'(y-x)]}{\delta-\delta'u}-\dfrac{u''}{u'}},\qquad(73)$$

where $u' = u'(x) = \partial U/\partial x$ denotes the marginal utility of virtual consumption x, etc. The stable solution paths of the differential equations (72–3) determine the short-run consumption schedule; namely, let

$$x = x(y,r,\rho)\qquad(74)$$

represent the stable branches of the solution paths, as illustrated by the heavy arrowed curves in Figure 2, where real consumption c is now replaced by the virtual level of consumption x for the vertical axis.[2] Then the optimum path of asset accumulation is attained by adjusting the virtual level of consumption according to the schedule (74) and by determining the allocation of the virtual level of consumption x between real consumption c and real cash balances m in such a manner that the marginal rate of substitution between real consumption and real cash balances is equal to the money rate of interest ρ; namely,

$$c(y,r,\rho) = c(x,\rho)$$
$$m(y,r,\rho) = m(x,\rho),$$

where $x = x(y,r,\rho)$.

The effects of a change in the real rate of interest r upon the short-run consumption and demand for real cash balances are easily examined, since it does not involve a change in the shape of the utility function $u(x) = U(x; \rho)$. By applying the analysis presented for the simpler case, an increase in the real rate of interest r is shown to decrease the virtual level of short-run consumption x, thus resulting with decreases both in real consumption and real cash balances, that is,

$$\frac{\partial c}{\partial r} < 0, \quad \frac{\partial m}{\partial r} < 0. \tag{75}$$

On the other hand, an increase in real income y is easily shown to result in increases in both real consumption and real cash balances; that is,

$$\frac{\partial c}{\partial y} > 0, \quad \frac{\partial m}{\partial y} > 0. \tag{76}$$

The long-run virtual level of consumption x^* is determined at the level at which the rate of time preference is equated to the real rate of interest r:

$$\delta(u(x^*)) = r;$$

the long-run levels of real consumption c^* and real cash balances m^* are then determined by the real rate of interest r, together with the money rate of interest ρ upon which the shape of the utility function $u(x)$ depends; that is,

$$c^* = c^*(r,\rho), \qquad m^* = m^*(r,\rho).$$

The long-run levels c^* and m^* are more precisely characterized by the requirements

$$u_m - \rho u_c = 0 ,$$

$$\delta(u(c, m)) = r ,$$

which, by a differentiation, yield

$$\begin{pmatrix} u_{mc} - \rho u_{cc}, & -(\rho u_{cm} - u_{mm}) \\ 1 & \rho \end{pmatrix} \begin{pmatrix} dc^* \\ dm^* \end{pmatrix} = \begin{pmatrix} u_c & d\rho \\ (1/\delta' u_c) & dr \end{pmatrix} ;$$

hence,

$$\frac{\partial c^*}{\partial \rho} = \frac{\rho u_c}{\Delta^*} > 0, \quad \frac{\partial c^*}{\partial r} = \frac{\rho u_{cm} - u_{mm}}{\Delta^*} \frac{1}{\delta' u_c} > 0 ,$$

$$\frac{\partial m^*}{\partial \rho} = -\frac{u_c}{\Delta^*} < 0, \quad \frac{\partial m^*}{\partial r} = \frac{u_{cm} - \rho u_{cc}}{\Delta^*} \frac{1}{\delta' u_c} > 0 ,$$

where $\quad \Delta^* = -\rho^2 u_{cc} + \rho u_{cm} - u_{mm} > 0 .$

Thus an increase in the real rate of interest increases both the long-run levels of real consumption and real cash balances, while an increase in the money rate of interest results with an increase in the long-run level of real consumption and a decrease in the long-run real cash balances.

ACKNOWLEDGMENTS

This work was in part supported by the National Science Foundation. I am indebted to Harry Johnson, Michael Lav, John Scadding, and Miguel Sidrauski for their comments and criticisms.

NOTES AND REFERENCES

[1] The transformation introduced here is similar to what Allais (1966) has termed the psychological time.

[2] Such a curve will shift whenever there is a change either in the real rate of interest r or in the money rate of interest ρ, to be indicated by the functional notation (74).

22

The Demand for Money Expectations
and Short and Long Rates

Alan A. Walters

The expositions by Sir John Hicks (1935; 1946) of theories of money and interest rates are classics of economic theory. Much of what is now accepted as established theory was developed from those pages of lucid prose. Modern theorists spend much of their time extending and reinterpreting Hicksian notions. This is the purpose of this note on the demand for money and interest rates.

The two Hicksian ideas to be explored here are contained in *A Suggestion* and in *Value and Capital*. Among the many innovations in *A Suggestion* was the introduction of transaction cost or 'friction' as an explanation for the holding of money balances. In the usual economic model it was assumed that the process of acquiring and selling assets was costless. Hicks pointed out that if we could switch from paper or real assets to money without incurring costs there was no reason to hold money for *transactions* purposes. If therefore transactions balances were held it must be because there were costs of acquiring money by running down other assets. Later work by Baumol and Tobin showed how this transactions cost could be integrated formally into an inventory theory of transactions balances. The other main contribution of Hicks was to formulate the relationship between short term and long term interest rates. In *Value and Capital* he showed that the long term interest rate was a geometric function of the short term interest rates which were expected to rule in the future. This simple theory has been extended and developed. Hypotheses have been tested against data and the theory has not yet been convincingly discredited (Meiselman, 1962). In this note we shall deal with one of the problems of integrating the 'friction' explanation of liquidity preference for transactions balances with the short and the long term rates of interest.

Expectations – Short and Long Rate

The liquidity preference function, as it emerged in the *General Theory*, dichotomized desired real money balances. First there are transactions balances, which are a function of the level of income; this is the demand for money to spend. The second category is the demand for money as an asset. This desired asset holdings in the form of money was thought to be primarily a function of the rate of interest on paper securities. In Hicks's (1937) famous paper on Mr Keynes and the 'Classics' the dichotomy is formally stated as:

$L = L_1(Y) + L_2(r)$, where L_1 is the transaction demand for money and L_2 is the asset demand.

The rate of interest entering into the asset demand was clearly identified as the *long* term rate. Transactors will sell their long term paper assets and hold money if they believe that the ruling long rate of interest is unduly low. A future increase in the interest rate will enable them to purchase $2\frac{1}{2}$ per cent consols at a lower price than rules at present. To be a little more precise, the interest rate which enters into the asset demand for money must also be associated with *expectations* about future rates. It is the conjunction of today's price with expected future prices, and the associated degrees of belief with these expectations that determines the asset demand for money.[1]

Let us continue the fiction that the only forms of wealth are paper assets and money. Paper assets can be of two kinds, however, the short and the long term. Corresponding we have a short and a long interest rate. It is clear that the rates and the expected rates that enter into the asset demand for money are for *long* term securities.

Obviously there is no direct measure of the long term rate expected in future periods. But in *Value and Capital*, Hicks set out a theory which related expected short rates to existing long and short rates. If we make three important assumptions (a) that persons hold securities to maturity and (b) that there are single valued expectations and (c) there are no transactions costs, the rates of interest must satisfy the equation [2]

$$(1+R)^n = (1+r_1)(1+r_2^e)(1+r_3^e) \ldots (1+r_n^e),$$

where R is the 'long' term rate of interest, that is, the rate on a security
   which matures in n periods;

r_1 is the rate on one period loans in the first period;

r_i^e is the expected short run rate in the ith period.

Given the long rate R and the short rate r, one can calculate the geometric average of future expected discount factors $(1+r^e)$. A sort of average of expected short rates is implied by the existing long rate and short rates. But individual expected short rates (even granted we restrict the rates to strictly positive values) may assume any values.

This theory derives expected short rates from short and long rates. In the demand for money, however, as distinct from investigations of the term structure of interest rates, we are primarily concerned with getting measures of the expected long rate from evidence of the short and long rate. Since the essence of the asset demand for money is the shift between money and long term paper because of the chance of capital loss and gain, it is clearly not possible to employ this theory which *assumes* that the investor holds long term paper assets until they mature. Let us examine now a transactor who considers transfers *between* short and long term securities each period. Letting the period tend to be arbitrarily short (which is sensible in view of our assumption of zero transaction cost) we obtain

$$r_t = R_t - \left(\frac{1}{R_t} \cdot \frac{dR}{dt}\right)^e,$$

where $\left(\frac{1}{R_t} \cdot \frac{dR}{dt}\right)^e$ is the expected rate of change in the yield on consols. In discrete form this equation becomes

$$r_t = R_t - \left(\frac{R_{t+1}^e - R_t}{R_{t+1}^e}\right),$$

where R_{t+1}^e is the expected yield on consols in the next $(t+1)$th period (Hicks, 1946). The formulae simply reflect the fact that the money rate of return on short term paper must be the same as the rate of return on long. The latter consists of two parts: R_t, the yield per £, and the expected change in the capital value – the bracketed expectation on the right-hand side – which we denote by $\dot{R}_t^e$.

The singular advantage of this formulation is that it does give us method of measuring the expected long rate of interest. The expected rate of change of the long rate is simply the difference between the existing long and short rates. Before examining the consequences on the formulation of the demand for money one might enquire whether the two groups of transactors, those who always hold investments to maturity and those who continuously revise their short and long position, can live side by side in the same economy. This is of course an academic question (in the pejorative sense) since it is difficult to imagine that single expectations could be a useful analytical procedure for the market determination of interest rates. From the formal relationships, we obtain for large n,

$$(1+R_t)^n = (1+r_t)(1+r_{t+1}^e)(1+r_{t+2}^e)\ldots(1+r_{t+n-1}^e)$$

$$(1+R_t)^n = (1+R_t-\dot{R}_t^e)(1+r_{t+1}^e)\ldots\ldots(1+r_{t+n-1}^e).$$

This describes the relationship between expected short rates and expected change in the long rate as a function of the long rate (one can easily calculate it as a function of the short rate instead). If the long rate is expected to increase the expected short rate must also rise,[3] and if R_t^e is negative the expected short rates will, on the average, fall. The expected rates go up and down together.

At this level of abstraction (and it includes zero switching cost and no opportunities to buy real assets) we might enquire into the expectations effects of the equation:

$$R-r = \left(\frac{1}{R}\frac{dR}{dt}\right)^e$$

on liquidity preference. The value $(R-r)$ measures the difference in the rates of interest on irredeemable bonds and on short term bills or even money at call. The latter may be regarded as a very close substitute for money, whereas the former is the most illiquid asset (that is, with an unsure value at any date). Anyone who wished to keep liquid would keep most of his assets in bills or on call and short notice. The difference $(R-r)$ measures the income return on illiquidity, excluding expected capital gains. An empirical measure of this return has been used in studies of the demand for money.[4] The difference $R-r$ is taken as the empirical correlate of Keynes's '*the* rate of interest' in the liquidity preference function.

In most discussions of the demand for money the expected long rate of interest is entered as a separate variable. But it is clear that the equilibrium condition for the individual with single-valued expectations requires that the income rate of return on illiquidity be equal to the expected rate of change of the yield on consols. This means that, in equilibrium, the two measures are the same: the income rate of return on non-money assets is equal to the expected rate of change. In an equilibrium analysis therefore there is no need for the expectations term; it is already included.

A more difficult task is to interpret the expectations generated by this simple approach. Consider for simplicity that the government operates only in the bill market and not directly in the long market. Flooding the market with Treasury bills will drive the price down and r will rise. If we assume for a moment that the yield on consols is unchanged, this would mean that the representative individual would expect a *fall* in the yield on consols (that is, the price to rise). To put it more accurately–when r rises R will be unchanged only if there is expected to be a fall in the yield (a rise in the price) of consols.

This is, of course, not the typical pattern of movements in R and r. Usually when r increases R also increases but by not quite so much. Movements in short rates have a greater amplitude than these for long term bonds. With this pattern we get a similar, but not so extreme, result. If when r rises, R also goes up by a smaller amount, it must again be consistent with a revision of expectations *downwards* for R the yield on consols. This implies that when the rate of return on illiquidity $(R-r)$ goes down, the investor expects consol rates to go down.

With government operating at the short end of the market, and with the damped effect on consol yields, the expectations pattern is consistent with many verbal accounts of market behaviour. Tight money in this month will drive up the bill rate, but the yield on consols will not go up so much because it is expected to fall 'back to normal' in the following months. Expectations are counter to rate movements; they are regressive.

Consider now a government policy that *twists* the term structure. Suppose for example the government wishes to maintain lower long term rates, perhaps because of funding operations, and yet it wishes at the same time to raise short term rates, perhaps to counter excess demand. This is not an unusual state of affairs, because one of the aims of conventional debt management is to reduce the interest burden on the Exchequer. This particular twist of the term structure can be achieved, however, only if there exists a *downward* revision of expectations of the long rate. This is of course the *same* direction as the movement of the long rate itself. The expectation is revised *with* the movement not against it. To get long rates down the government must somehow persuade the market that in the future they may be expected to fall even more, so that capital appreciation of the bond will offset the low yield.

There is then a marked difference between the case where the long and money rates move together and where the term structure is twisted. In the former case consistent expectations of movements in R are regressive 'back to where we were before', whereas, in the latter case they must be reinforcing. Creating reinforcing expectations is one of the central problems of this debt-monetary policy.

It is clearly now sensible to remove the assumption that people can hold assets only in the form of money or short or long term securities. Suppose then they may also hold real assets and suppose that these assets are riskless. The attraction of holding a real asset consists of two elements, first the rate of return on £1 (current value) worth of real capital (say m), and secondly the change in the value of £1's worth of capital. If we write P for the level of prices of capital goods then over the period t to $t+dt$, £1's worth of capital will increase in value by an amount $\dfrac{1}{P}\dfrac{dP}{dt}$. So that the sum of the two elements of rate of return is

$$(m)^e + \left(\frac{1}{P}\frac{dP}{dt}\right)^e ,$$

where the superscript e refers to the expectation of the measure in brackets. Equilibrium in the asset market clearly requires

$$r = R - \left(\frac{1}{R}\frac{dR}{dt}\right)^e = m + \left(\frac{1}{P}\frac{dP}{dt}\right)^e .$$

[Note that it might be more sensible to retain a superscript on m since, typically, profits are not measured on real assets until long after they are earned.] From this equation we can, in principle, measure the expected change in prices. It is given by

$$\left(\frac{1}{P}\frac{dP}{dt}\right)^e = r - m ,$$

that is, the difference between the bill rate and rate of return on assets. If the price level is expected to rise the equilibrium bill rate will exceed the current money rate of return on real assets.[5]

Up to this point we have made the naïve assumptions that the individual's expectations are single valued, that he has no aversion to risk and that there are no transaction costs. If his expectations really were single valued then the exercise would be conducted on a razor's edge. A slight discrepancy between r and $R - [(R)^{-1}(dR/dt)]^e$ would send him either entirely into bonds or entirely into bills (the real asset option can be interpreted similarly); indeed if $r > R - [(R)^{-1}(dR/dt)]^e$ and we imagined that he could *issue* bonds, he would create and sell bonds and buy bills without limit!

One way to rationalize this formulation is simply to regard the single value as a certainty equivalent. This involves many difficulties which we cannot examine here. Alternatively the model may be extended by using a multivalue expectations hypothesis [6] with a utility function depending on not only the expected return but also on the variance of the return. This incorporates risk but not uncertainty into the model.[7] But it does provide the possibility of a choice between the non-risky and risky assets without the phenomena of complete 'plunging'.

A proper analysis of the effects of risk is beyond the scope of this paper, but we must indicate some of the consequences. The simplest way to integrate risk into the equations is to regard risk as abhorrent to the 'representative' transactor and write

$$R = R - \left(\frac{1}{R}\frac{dR}{dt}\right)^e - \rho_B = m + \left(\frac{1}{P}\frac{dP}{dt}\right)^e - \rho_A,$$

where ρ_B and ρ_A are normally positive and measure the 'risk premium' of bonds and real assets. The risk premium would depend on the degree of 'riskiness' which would depend on many factors. It is, for example, plausible to suppose that the estimated variance of future issues would change according to current history; a period of bond support policy (as before 1947) would, for example, generate an almost zero variance of future values of the yield.[8] The risk premium ρ_B is then near enough zero. This discussion suggests that it is difficult to isolate and measure factors which would be closely associated with the risk premium; here it seems that the econometric method must yield pride of place to the historical approach.

The last factor which influences transactions is, of course, the cost of making the transactions itself. If the expected gain of switching into long securities is less than the transaction cost incurred he will keep his portfolio short. With single expectations this introduces a discontinuity into behaviour—and it may be the cause of local stability. Fortunately we can regard transactions costs as being almost constant over time. The inclusion of transactions costs in the model is however not a simple matter in empirical terms. The inequality for switching from shorts to longs (ignoring the risk premium) is

$r < R - [R^{-1}(dR/dt)]^e$ — transaction cost per £1 unit,

whereas for switching from longs to short the inequality is reversed and the sign of unit transactions cost is changed. The direction of the change matters critically.

This discussion of both risk premiums and transactions costs suggests good reasons why $R - r$ must be interpreted very carefully as an indicator of the expected change in the consol yield. Nevertheless, it seems worth while examining the statistics to see if there is any regularity in this relationship. We cannot obtain any direct measure of the expected proportional change in the yield; we can only measure the actual proportional change. Thus we can compare $R_t - r_t$ with the realized $(R_{t+1} - R_t)/R_{t+1}$. The deviation between these two measures will then be due to

(a) the difference between the expected proportional change and the realized change;

(b) the risk premium;

(c) transaction costs;

(d) variations in the minimum feasible period for loans;

(e) differences in tax treatment of income and capital gains.

We have compared monthly averages of R_t (the yield on consols) and r_t (the yield on Treasury Bills) for each month from 1957 to 1964 (Figure 1). Figures are plotted only for years. The axes are $R_t - r_t$ and $(R_{t+1} - R_t)/R_{t+1}$.

The dominant impression of *all* years is one of randomness. There seems to be virtually no relationship at all between the realized proportional growth of consol yields and the difference between the long and the short rate. This is confirmed by a calculation of the correlation coefficient ($r = 0.10$); true the coefficient is positive but it is clearly too small to be significant. Another aspect of the statistics is that the variation of $R_t - r_t$ is much less r than the variation of the proportional changes in consol yield.

If we observe individual sub-periods we see that much more distinct patterns emerge. Quite strong positive relationships appear in years of low activity when the cycle is turning upwards 1957, 1960 and 1961; whereas essentially zero or even negative relationships appeared in the high activity

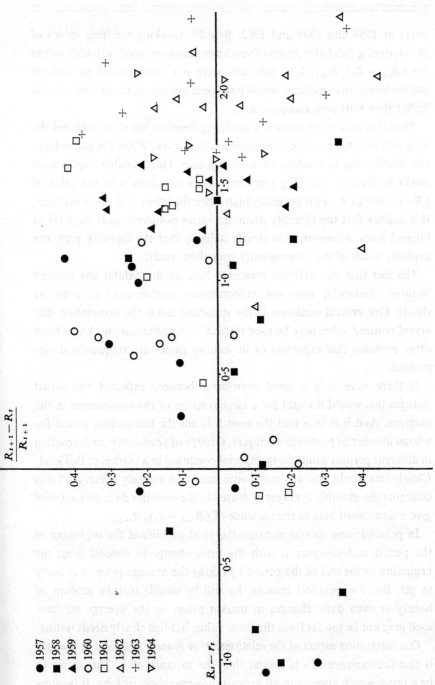

Figure 1

years of 1958 and 1959 and 1962. Broadly speaking the high values of $R_t - r_t$ during this latter group of years were not associated with high values for $(R_{t+1} - R_t)/R_{t+1}$. Low bill rates were not compensated by realized capital losses on consols; it would have been advantageous to hold consols rather than bills over this period.

Thus it is only when there is a small gap between the short rate and the long rate that the positive relationship is dominant. When the gap is large the relationship is random or even negative. One possible explanation might be that the 'liquidity premium' varies positively with the value of $(R-r)$. Since $(R-r)$ is generally high when the levels of R and r are high, this implies that the liquidity premium varies positively with the level of interest rates. However, it is clearly unlikely that the liquidity premium explains much of the heterogeneity over these years.

The fact that the statistics presented here do not exhibit any marked positive relationship does not, unfortunately, enable us to discredit the theory. One critical weakness in the statistical test is the assumption that actual realized value may be used instead of expectations; we know from other evidence that expectations in security prices are frequently disappointed.

If there were only a small correlation between expected and actual changes this would account for a large fraction of the randomness in the diagram. And it is true that the month is not the transaction period for a large number of portfolio managers. Groups of speculators each reacting in different periods would be the natural condition in a market of this kind. Clearly this would blur any systematic measured monthly effect. And it is clear that the monthly averages of R used in the statistics do in fact actually give a downward bias to the variance of $(R_{t+1} - R_t)/R_{t+1}$.

In principle one should measure the yield on bills at the beginning of the period and compare it with the price change in consols from the beginning to the end of the period by taking the average price he is likely to get. But for technical reasons, he will be unable to take account of hourly or even daily changes in market price. So the average we have used may not be too far from the 'best' value, but this clearly needs testing.

One interesting aspect of the relationship of R and r observed in practice is that the variance of r is greater than the variance of R. This seems to be a result which appears in all periods, however short or long. It is interesting to use this observed empirical relationship to see the implications for the expectation $(R^e_{t+1} - R_t)/R^e_{t+1}$ or, approximately, $[(dR/dt)R^{-1}]^e$, which we write as $\dot{R}^e$:

$$r = R - \dot{R}^e$$

$$\text{var}(r) = \text{var}(R) + \text{var}(\dot{R}^e) - 2\,\text{cov}(R, \dot{R}^e).$$

Thus if the variance of r exceeds the variance of R,

$$\text{var}(\dot{R}^e) - 2\,\text{cov}(R, \dot{R}^e) > 0,$$

which implies

$$\frac{\text{cov}(R, \dot{R}^e)}{\text{var}(\dot{R}^e)} < \tfrac{1}{2}.$$

This means that the regression of R (the level of consol rate) on the expected change of consol rate ($\dot{R}^e$) must be less than 0·5. This places an upper limit on reinforcing expectations, for $\text{var}(r) > \text{var}(R)$.

One special case of some interest is where the expected change is not correlated with the level of the rate. Then it follows that

$$\text{var}(r) = \text{var}(R) + \text{var}(\dot{R}^e).$$

The difference between the variance of r and the variance of R measures the variance of the expected change in rates.

Probably the most interesting cases are those when $\text{cov}(R, \dot{R}^e) < 0$, i.e. when the expectations are regressive. The high or the low rate is expected to return to 'normal'. This is clearly consistent with $\text{var}(r) > \text{var}(R)$. Suppose that $\text{var}(r) = \lambda\,\text{var}(R)$ then

$$(\lambda - 1)\,\text{var}(R) = \text{var}(\dot{R}^e) - 2\,\text{cov}(R, \dot{R}^e);$$

that is, correlation $(R, \dot{R}^e) = \tfrac{1}{2}\left[\dfrac{\sigma^2_{\dot{R}^e} - (\lambda - 1)\sigma^2_R}{\sigma_R \sigma_{\dot{R}^e}}\right]$, $\quad \lambda > 1$.

Clearly the sign of the correlation – positive indicating reinforcing, negative indicating regressive expectations – turns on the variances $\sigma^2_{\dot{R}^e}$ and σ^2_R as well as λ. The smaller the variance of expected changes *cet. par.*, the larger the correlation between R and $\dot{R}^e$; the correlation will be negative if

$$\sigma^2_R < (\lambda - 1)\sigma^2_r.$$

Returning to our model we can show that, for this period

$$(\lambda - 1)\,\text{var}(R) = \text{var}(\dot{R}^e) - 2\,\text{cov}(R, \dot{R}^e),$$

which in percentage units appears as

$$0\text{·}045 = \text{var}(\dot{R}^e) - 2\,\text{cov}(R, \dot{R}^e).$$

If the expectations are regressive with respect to the level of interest rates (that is, negative $\text{cov}(R, \dot{R}^e)$), then the covariance in percentage units must exceed -0.0225; this ensures a strictly positive var $(\dot{R}^e)$. We can also find a limit to the value of var $(\dot{R}^e)$, by finding the square of the correlation coefficient between R and $\dot{R}^e$ in terms of the variance $(\dot{R}^e)$ and the numerical values of λ and var (R) given above. The correlation is given by

$$\tfrac{1}{2}\left[\frac{\sigma_{\dot{R}^e}}{\sigma_R} - (\lambda-1)\frac{\sigma_R}{\sigma_{\dot{R}^e}}\right];$$

so, on inserting a value of $+1$ for the correlation and the measured values for λ and σ_R, we find that

$$\sigma_{\dot{R}^e}^2 = 0.00556 .$$

For a correlation of -1, we get

$$\sigma_{\dot{R}^e}^2 = 0.0013 ,$$

and, for a correlation of zero ,

$$\sigma_{\dot{R}^e}^2 = 0.00375 .$$

All these values are clearly very, very small compared with the value of var $(R_{t+1} - R_t)/R_{t+1}$ observed in practice, roughly

$$10^3 \text{ var } (\dot{R}^e) = \text{var } [(R_{t+1} - R_t)/R_{t+1}] .$$

Unfortunately one can draw only the most tentative inferences from this sort of data. But, for what they are worth, the suggestion emerges that transactors typically behave as if they expected the consol yield to move on the average by only a very small amount compared with the actual average movement which in fact occurs. It does not seem that 'transactions costs' are large enough to explain the smallness of the implied variance of expected changes. And it is difficult to measure the effects of 'liquidity premiums', but one may conjecture that they cannot explain the immense gulf between the implied variance of expected values and the realized variance.

The conclusion must be that it is extraordinarily difficult to test directly the theory of expectations outlined here. The fact that the negative results of direct testing, using realized values as a surrogate of expected outcomes, does not discredit the theory. It suggests that indirect testing may be more appropriate. One such test would be achieved by incorporating this expectations hypothesis directly into a study of the demand for money.

An empirical analysis of this kind is beyond the scope of the present paper. But the results do suggest that the expectations are regressive in character; high R's are associated with low $R-r$ and so imply low (or negative) $\dot{R}^e$. This is then entirely consistent with the 'normal level' hypothesis of Keynes and Hicks.

Note on Units. It must be observed that the rate of change is calculated as $(R_{t+1}-R_t)/R_t$ which means that it is in terms of proportional charges. Normally the rates of interest are measured in percentage terms so there is a factor of 100 involved on the R.H.S. of the equation. Secondly, since we have twice measured periods as one month, whereas yield is calculated as an *annual* rate, a factor of 12 must also be entered on the L.H.S. of the equation. Thus if we measure r and R in percentage terms and the time period is one month,

$$\frac{1}{12}(R_t-r_t) = \left(\frac{100}{R_t}\frac{dR}{dt}\right)^e.$$

In *annual* terms

$$\text{correlation } [R_t,(R_{t+1}-R_t)/R_{t+1}] = -0\cdot1578$$

$$\text{var}(R) = \left(\frac{144}{10,000}\right)0\cdot2958$$

$$\text{var}(r) = \left(\frac{144}{10,000}\right)0\cdot8306$$

$$\text{var}[(R_{t+1}-R_t)/R_{t+1}] = \left(\frac{1}{10,000}\right)3\cdot97$$

$$\lambda = 2\cdot8082 .$$

Short Rates and Transaction Balances

In this section we examine the question of the interest elasticity of demand for transactions balances. The point of departure is the inventory model of Baumol. He showed that the average quantity of money which people would wish to hold for transactions purposes was inversely related to 'the rate of interest' (with an elasticity of $-\frac{1}{2}$) and to the cost of acquiring cash. This 'square-root' theory was a consequence of assuming that expenditures are a constant unchanging stream. As Hicks pointed out the essential feature of expenditure (and also many forms of income) is that many items are random events. For example the break-down of a car is not usually an event which one can accurately predict. Thus it seems worthwhile examining the consequences of a stochastic expenditure function on the desired stock of money. When the expenditure is random it is natural, though not essential, to specify that when a man runs out of money he can borrow at some 'penalty' rate of interest (k).

Here we examine the value of the interest elasticity of demand for transactions balances where there is provision for borrowing to meet unforeseen expenditure. The model is appropriate for financial conditions where the issue is to maintain liquid assets in the form of money (bank deposits) or to invest them as deposits of a building society or other non-bank financial institution. The essential feature of deposits in the financial institution is that a period of notice must be given before the depositor can withdraw his deposit in the form of cash. In return for foregoing liquidity the depositor earns a rate of interest.

Consider a man who has two assets – cash in a drawing or current account and a credit balance in a deposit or in a non-bank financial institution. The former asset we shall call money. On his deposit account he earns interest of £r per period T. In order to draw money from his deposit account notice of a period T is required. If at any time his cash balance drops to zero he can borrow without limit, but he has to pay £k per £1 per period T for this facility. We suppose that $k > r > 0$. But each time he draws money from his deposit account he incurs a cost £a per occasion. There is apparently no cost per occasion of borrowing – but as we shall see below, this effect has in fact been included in the model.

The man's expenditure during the period 0 to T, T to $2T$, etc. is described by a probability density function $f(x)\,dx$, $0 \leqslant x \leqslant \infty$, where the T is a constant and the distribution is the same over time. Correspondingly, we define the distribution function:

$$F(m) = \int_m^\infty f(x)\,dx\,,$$

where m is soon to be defined as a quantity of money.

The truncated first moment is defined as

$$\phi(m) = \int_m^\infty xf(x)\,dx\,.$$

We assume that the man behaves as if he knows the parameters of the distribution function, that is, we rule out the problems of uncertainty. This is an important omission since rationale of the 'precautionary motive' in the *General Theory* was couched in terms of uncertainty.

Suppose that the man fixes two values of his money stock M and m, analogous to the S, s of inventory theory. The former (M) is the maximum possible value of his money stock and the latter (m) is the value at which he gives notice of withdrawing money. He will then receive $£(M-m)$ after a delay of T days. If, during these T days, he has spent nothing his money stock will rise to M, the maximum. Consequently his *actual balance* in the current account may be less than m by an amount equal to $(M-m)$ or $2(M-m)$ etc., which is the quantity of money for which notice has been given. Thus the actual balance of money at the time of ordering will be m, or $2m-M$, or $4m-3M$, etc. And these quantities may be negative, so that the man may be in debt when he gives notice of withdrawal.

The questions which arise from this formulation are

(1) What values of M and m would the man choose for a given density function ?

(2) What are the reactions to changes in r and k and in expected quantity of money as the interest rates change ?

We can represent the time series of a typical set of transactions by plotting the actual stock of money and the extent of the debt. When the stock of money drops below m at time t_0, notice of withdrawal is given and the money arrives at time t_0+T. But, in the meantime, the quantity of money both in the current account and for which notice of withdrawal has been given has fallen to less than m at time t_1. Thus more money is requested and is acquired at time t_1+T. We see that just after t_4 there are very substantial expenditures incurred which cause the man to use overdraft facilities. So great are the expenses that even the arrival of money at time t_4+T does not suffice to get him out of the overdraft state. He gives notice that he wants more money at t_5, and almost immediately afterwards he gives notice again of withdrawal, and so on (Figure 2).

Obviously the first steps of a least cost path will be determined to a large extent by the initial stock of money (the initial conditions). The economic interest in initial conditions is fairly small and most of our concern is with the structure of the system after it has settled down. We want to find the expected stock of money (m^*), the expected borrowing (b^*) and the expected number of times we transfer from the deposit to the current account. The expected costs of transactions in a period of length T are given by

$$E(K) = aE(\text{no. of transfers}) + k \cdot b^* + r \cdot m^* \, .$$

All costs are supposed to be linear. The cost of credit does not increase as the amount borrowed increases. The transfer expenses are related to the expected number of transfers; the amount transferred is the same on each occasion $(d = M - m)$.

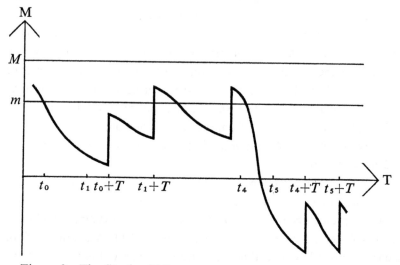

Figure 2   The Stock of Money

Now consider the problem of finding m^* and b^*. Suppose that we reckon the expected debt during the period as a half the sum of the expected debts immediately after receiving money at $t_i + T$, and just before receiving the new draft of money at time $t_{i+1} + T$.

In Figure 2 the debt at $t_4 + T$ is shown on the diagram together with the debt just before the new draft of money arrives at $t_5 + T$. The expected value of the debt at $t_4 + T$ clearly depends on the amount of money disbursed in the period from t_4 to $t_4 + T$, so that

$$E(\text{debt just after } t_4 + T) = \int_m^\infty (x - m) f(x) \, dx .$$

Notice that it does not matter if he receives transfers of money during this period; the transactor started at t_4 with a stock of money (including money on order) equal to m; that is, his *actual* stock of money *plus* money for which notice of withdrawal had been given amount to m. Similarly we can find the expected debt just before the money arrives in the current account at time $t_5 + T$:

$$E(\text{debt just before } t_5 + T) = \int_m^\infty (x - M) f(x)\, dx \, .$$

Thus the definition of the expected debt over the period $t_4 + T$ to $t_5 + T$ is

$$b^* = \tfrac{1}{2} \int_m^\infty (x - m) f(x)\, dx + \tfrac{1}{2} \int_M^\infty (x - M) f(x)\, dx$$

$$= \tfrac{1}{2} [\phi(m) - mF(m) + \phi(M) - MF(M)] \, .$$

The expected quantity of money m^* may be found in a similar way. And so

$$m^* = \tfrac{1}{2} \int_0^M (M - x) f(x)\, dx + \tfrac{1}{2} \int_0^m (m - x) f(x)\, dx$$

$$= \tfrac{1}{2} [M\{1 - F(M)\} - \{\bar{x} - \phi(M)\} + m\{1 - F(m)\} - \{\bar{x} - \phi(m)\}] \, .$$

The assumption that the expected quantity of money (and debt) is the arithmetic average of the stock (debt) at $t_3 + T$ and the stock (debt) at $t_4 + T$ is, of course, incorrect. In particular, when the man runs into debt in this period, this assumption *over*estimates both the stock of money and the amount of the debt. In Figure 3 we assume that AB, for simplicity, a straight line, indicates the stock of money A just after $t_3 + T$ and the debt at B just before $t_4 + T$. The formulae we have adopted would regard m (the mid point of AD) as the expected quantity of money and b (mid point of CB) as the expected borrowing. To find the true money stock we join the mid point (F) of AE to the mid point (G) of ED and find the point at which the line joining these mid points intersects the line mb, giving the true average money stock as n in the diagram.

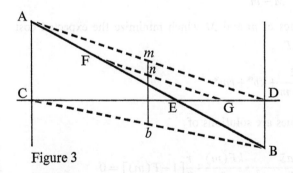

Figure 3

In addition to this overestimation of the quantity of money and of the amount of debt, we also overestimate the interest cost of both money and debt when the man runs into debt in the period. We should strictly charge an interest rate r (per £ per period T) on an amount F for only the fraction of CE/CD of the period $t_3 + T$ to $t_4 + T$. Instead we charge interest for the whole period. A similar effect appears on the debt side. One can, however, argue that the upward biases in the quantity and cost of money and debt are realistic and more closely approximate actual behaviour and costs when the man runs into debt. We can regard the extra cost as the cost of arranging for the loan or overdraft facility. Similarly, we might observe that the man on running into debt would tend to retain some currency. He would not run into debt before spending all his current account or currency.

But, of course, this argument should also be applied when the man is already in debt at the beginning of the period. The utility of cash in conducting quick and small transactions is considerably greater than that of a checking account. The implication is that we should amend our model to include stocks of two types: currency and current account deposits. This more complicated, but more realistic, 'two-bin' model has not been explored here.

The expected number of transfers from deposit account to cash is given by

$$
\begin{array}{l}
\text{Exp. no. of} \\
\text{transfers in} \\
\text{period } T
\end{array}
=
\frac{\text{Average expenditure in period } T}{\text{Amount transferred on each occasion}}
$$

$$
= \frac{\bar{x}}{M - m}.
$$

We now find the values of m and M which minimize the expected cost function for a period T:

$$
E(K) = \frac{a\bar{x}}{M - m} + kb^* + rm^*
$$

and the stationary values are solutions of

$$
\frac{\partial E(K)}{\partial m} = \frac{a\bar{x}}{(M-m)^2} - \frac{kF(m)}{2} + \frac{r}{2}[1 - F(m)] = 0
$$

$$
\frac{\partial E(K)}{\partial M} = \frac{-a\bar{x}}{(M-m)^2} - \frac{kF(M)}{2} + \frac{r}{2}[1 - F(M)] = 0.
$$

These reduce to

$$F(M)+F(m) = \frac{2r}{k+r}$$

and

$$(M-m)^2\{F(m)-F(M)\} = \frac{4a\bar{x}}{k+r}.$$

The solution of these equations is not an obvious task since they are not of any simple form. We here restrict the analysis to a particular distribution function–the rectangular case. This will enable us to sharpen the results.

If we suppose that the distribution of expenditure is uniform over the range $(0,2\bar{x})$, and, if $m < M < 2\bar{x}$, that is, $a < 8r^3\bar{x}/(k+r)^2$, we obtain

$$(M-m)^3 = \frac{8a\bar{x}^2}{k+r}$$

and

$$M+m = \frac{4k\bar{x}}{k+r}.$$

Thus

$$m = \frac{2k\bar{x}}{k+r} - \left(\frac{a\bar{x}}{k+r}\right)^{\frac{1}{3}}$$

and

$$M = \frac{2k\bar{x}}{k+r} + \left(\frac{a\bar{x}}{k+r}\right)^{\frac{1}{3}}.$$

When the cost of withdrawing cash (a) is below the critical bound the quantity of cash withdrawn on each occasion is $2\left(\dfrac{a\bar{x}}{k+r}\right)^{\frac{1}{3}}$.

If on the other hand $m < 2\bar{x} < M$, that is, if $a > 8r^3\bar{x}/(k+r)^2$, then we have the case where the cost of withdrawing cash is above the critical bound and the equations take the form

$$F(M) = 0$$

$$1 - \frac{m}{2x} = \frac{2r}{k+r}$$

$$(M-m)^2\left(1 - \frac{m}{2\bar{x}}\right) = \frac{4a\bar{x}}{k+r}.$$

The solutions are

$$m = 2\bar{x}\left(\frac{k-r}{k+r}\right)$$

$$M = 2\bar{x}\left(\frac{k-r}{k+r}\right) + \sqrt{2\frac{a\bar{x}}{r}}.$$

The amount of money ordered on each occasion is then $\sqrt{(2a\bar{x}/r)}$. The reader will quickly recognize that this is the same as the 'square-root' formula of Baumol model – but in this model it refers simply to the money ordered on each occasion and not to the *stock* of cash as in the Baumol model. The results are tabulated below.

Range	If a is	$M-m$	m
$m<M<2\bar{x}$	$<\dfrac{8r^3\bar{x}}{(k+r)^2}$	$2\left(\dfrac{a\bar{x}^2}{k+r}\right)^{\frac{1}{3}}$	$\dfrac{2k\bar{x}}{k+r}-\tfrac{1}{2}(M-m)$
$m<2\bar{x}<M$	$>\dfrac{8r^3\bar{x}}{(k+r)^2}$	$\sqrt{\dfrac{2a\bar{x}}{r}}$	$2\bar{x}\left(\dfrac{k-r}{k+r}\right)$

Some general conclusions are worth noting. The borrowing rates and lending rates enter into all M and m, as we should expect. A higher rate of interest will reduce the amount of money acquired on each occasion and increase the expected frequency of withdrawals. But only if a is below the critical bound will the penal rate (k) influence the quantity withdrawn $(M-m)$; if a is high *only* the lending rate (r) will have an influence. This is because M is then chosen so high relative to the upper bound of expenditure $(2\bar{x})$. The maximum he will spend in the interval t_i to t_i+T is $2\bar{x}$ and this is less than M but it exceeds m by $4\bar{x}r(k+r)^{-1}$; this then measures the maximum debt borrowed at penal rates.

The important issue is the reaction of changes in m^*, the expected stock of money, to changes in interest rates. In particular we first seek a value of dk/dr if such a value exists, which will result in a zero elasticity of demand for money with respect to the lending rate of interest (r). Thus we return to our general formulation with any frequency function $f(x)$.

Now $$\frac{dm^*}{dr}=\frac{\partial m^*}{\partial r}+\left(\frac{\partial m^*}{\partial k}\right)\left(\frac{dk}{dr}\right)=0\,,$$

if $$\frac{dk}{dr}=\frac{\partial m^*}{\partial r}\bigg/\frac{\partial m^*}{\partial k}\,.$$

We can rewrite $\dfrac{\partial m^*}{\partial r}$ as

$$\frac{\partial m^*}{\partial r} = \frac{\partial m^*}{\partial F(M)}\frac{\partial F(M)}{\partial r} + \frac{\partial F(m)}{\partial r}\frac{\partial F(m)}{\partial r}$$

and

$$\frac{\partial m^*}{\partial F(M)} = \frac{1}{2}\left[\frac{\partial M}{\partial F(M)} + \frac{\partial \phi(M)}{\partial F(M)} + \frac{\partial M . F(M)}{\partial F(M)}\right]$$

$$= \frac{1}{2}\left[-\frac{1}{f(M)} + M - M + \frac{F(M)}{f(M)}\right]$$

$$= \frac{1}{2f(M)}[F(M)-1].$$

Similarly

$$\frac{\partial m^*}{\partial F(m)} = \frac{1}{2f(m)}[F(m)-1]$$

and

$$\frac{\partial F(M)}{\partial r} = -f(M)\frac{\partial M}{\partial r}.$$

With similar results for the other three differential coefficients, it follows that

$$\frac{\partial M}{\partial r} = \frac{1}{2}[1-F(M)]\frac{\partial M}{\partial r} + \frac{1}{2}[1-F(m)]\frac{\partial m}{\partial r}$$

and

$$\frac{\partial m^*}{\partial k} = \frac{1}{2}[1-F(M)]\frac{\partial M}{\partial k} + \frac{1}{2}[1-F(m)]\frac{\partial m}{\partial k}.$$

Thus

$$\begin{bmatrix}\dfrac{\partial M}{\partial r}\\[2ex] \dfrac{\partial m}{\partial r}\end{bmatrix}$$

$$= \frac{2\Delta^{-1}}{(k+r)^2}\begin{bmatrix}-k(m-m)[2\{F(m)-F(M)\}+(M-m)f(m)]-2a\bar{x}f(m)\\[2ex] -k(M-m)[2\{F(m)-F(M)\}+(M-m)f(M)]+2a\bar{x}f(M)\end{bmatrix}$$

where $\Delta = 2(M-m)\{f(M)+f(m)\}\{F(m)-F(M)\}+$
$$+2(M-m)^2f(m)f(M).$$

Similarly,
$$
\begin{bmatrix} \dfrac{\partial M}{\partial k} \\[2mm] \dfrac{\partial m}{\partial k} \end{bmatrix}
$$

$$
= \frac{2\Delta^{-1}}{(k+r)^2}
\begin{bmatrix}
r(M-m)[2\{F(m)-F(M)\}+(M-m)f(m)]-2a\bar{x}f(m) \\[2mm]
r(M-m)[2\{F(m)-F(M)\}+(M-m)f(M)]+2a\bar{x}f(M)
\end{bmatrix}.
$$

Unfortunately this general formulation is unmanageable and we are driven again to examine the results for a specific frequency function $f(x)$. We now return once more to the assumption that $f(x)$ is rectangularly distributed over the range $(0,2\bar{x})$.

For the values of $\partial m^*/\partial r$ and $\partial m^*/\partial k$ we obtain

(A) for $a < 8r^3\bar{x}(k+r)^{-2}$ or $M < 2\bar{x}$

$$
\frac{\partial m^*}{\partial r} = \frac{-2k^2\bar{x}}{(k+r)^3} - \frac{1}{6\bar{x}}\frac{(a\bar{x}^2)^{\frac{3}{2}}}{(k+r)^{\frac{5}{2}}}
$$

$$
\frac{\partial m^*}{\partial k} = \frac{2k\bar{x}r}{(k+r)^3} - \frac{1}{6\bar{x}}\frac{(a\bar{x}^2)^{\frac{3}{2}}}{(k+r)^{\frac{5}{2}}}
$$

(i) As a becomes small the following result emerges

$$
\frac{dk}{dr} = \frac{\partial m^*/\partial r}{\partial m'^*/\partial k} \to \frac{k}{r} \text{ as } a \to 0.
$$

It can easily be shown that this result emerges for *all* admissible frequency functions. As $a \to 0$ the expected costs of holding cash and of borrowing become symmetrical; proportionate changes therefore leave the expected cash balance unchanged.

(ii) Now consider the other extreme as $a \to 8r^3\bar{x}(k+r)^{-2}$ from below. Then we have

$$
\frac{dk}{dr} \to \frac{k}{r} + \frac{r+k}{3k-r}.
$$

As a increases the borrowing rate must increase proportionately more than the lending rate in order to leave the demand for money unchanged.

For example if, at some point, $k = 2r$, the demand for money would be unchanged at the above value of a if

$$\left[\frac{dk}{dr}\right]_{k=2r} = 2 \cdot 6 \, .$$

(B) for $a > 8r^3\bar{x}(k+r)^{-2}$, that is $m < 2\bar{x} < M$, we have

$$\frac{\partial m^*}{\partial r} = -\frac{4k^2\bar{x}}{(k+r)^3} - \sqrt{\frac{a\bar{x}}{8r^3}}$$

$$\frac{\partial m^*}{\partial k} = \frac{4k\bar{x}r}{(k+r)^3} \, ,$$

so that the solution for dk/dr as a approaches $8r^3\bar{x}(k+r)^{-2}$ from above is

$$\frac{dk^*}{dr} = -\frac{\partial m^*/r}{\partial m^*/k} \rightarrow \frac{k}{r} + \frac{(k+r)^2}{4kr} \, .$$

Evaluating this result at $k = 2r$ we obtain

$$\frac{dk}{dr} \rightarrow 3 \cdot 125$$

as $a \rightarrow 8r^3\bar{x}(k+r)^{-2}$ from above.

The result suggests that as $a_+ \rightarrow 0$, proportional movements of the borrowing rate and lending rate will produce no effect on the expected amount of money demanded. The transactions balances will be independent of interest rate movements. Indeed if the borrowing rate changes proportionately more than the lending rate, decreases in rates will result in *smaller* transactions balances.

As $k \rightarrow r$ from above it is clear that the value dk/dr approaches a value of 2 for all admissible values of a (that is, including both $a > 8r^3\bar{x}(k+r)^{-3}$ and $a < 8r^3\bar{x}(k+r)^{-3}$). This implies that if the lending rate is only fractionally below the borrowing rate, absolute movements in the borrowing rate must be at least twice as large as those in the lending rate in order to give rise to null or perverse effects.

These simple results are a consequence of the special form of the distribution function. In this particular form there is only one parameter the mean $\bar{x}$ and this enormously simplifies the result. Experiments with more complicated distribution functions, the exponential and normal suitably truncated, suggest that the broad orders of magnitude of dk/dr are not wildly different from the rectangular distribution. But no neat analytical results are available, nor has any extensive numerical study been carried out.

On empirical grounds there is not much to be said. It is difficult to say what is the structure of lending and borrowing rates from casual empirical evidence. One finds that in periods of monetary stringency the borrowing rate rises much more steeply than the rate on deposit accounts. But even if it did not the phenomenon of credit rationing might well accompany a small rise in the borrowing rate. This would mean that the equivalent free market rate would be higher than the actual value of k. Credit rationing would then result in the creditors of good reputation holding smaller quantities of money than they would in a non-discriminating market. This is about as far as we can go without a full scale enquiry. However, the theory suggests the hypothesis that changes in 'the' rate of interest have only a small effect on his transaction balances. This brings us back almost to the Keynesian dependence on the speculative motive for the interest elasticity of the liquidity preference function. (One should also include Tobin's argument that risk aversion will give an interest elasticity.) Almost but not quite. The analysis has suggested that differences in the movements of borrowing and lending rates have some effect. This is a new hypothesis which is unfortunately extremely difficult to test.

Another fairly clear implication from this model is the role of the short term rate of interest – or the rate of interest on 'short notice' loans. In the analysis of the transactions demand for money the man puts his money into an account and can withdraw that nominal quantity of money after giving suitable notice. The rate of interest here is clearly the short term rate. Thus the transactions demand for cash depends on the short run rates of lending and borrowing. The long run rate (R) on irredeemable bonds affects only the speculative or idle balances. The liquidity function then appears as

$$L = L_1(r, k, Y) + L_2[(R-r), R, \text{wealth}],$$

where the difference $(R-r)$ is an indicator of expectations. The argument above suggests that the extended Keynesian form

$$L = L_1(Y) + L_2[(R-r), R, \text{wealth}]$$

is probably a good approximation in practice. This requires testing empirically.

ACKNOWLEDGMENTS

The ideas in this section were developed in 1961 and 1962. A first draft was written in December 1961 but this proved to be full of errors. This is an amended and expanded version of that original note. A. Charnes has pointed out to me ways of extending the theory and integrating it by using the functional form of the basic equation. His comments have been most valuable. I have also benefited considerably from R.C.O. Matthews, while Peter Fisk and Richard Barrett pointed out important errors. Responsibility for remaining errors lies with the author.

NOTES AND REFERENCES

[1] It is also clear that the asset demand for money is a function of the wealth of the individual. If a person is perfectly certain that the interest rate is going to fall substantially he will borrow up to the hilt to finance purchases of consols. If, on the other hand, he is perfectly certain it will rise (and if there are no other purchasable assets) he will sell all and hold only money. In principle he would also *issue* consols without limit and hold money instead; but this would no doubt strain the credulity of creditors.

[2] Note that this equation in principle regards the investor as being able to reinvest interest payments at the yield on consols *in the initial period*. This is however not possible. I am indebted to Adolf Buse for this point.

[3] This depends on R being less than unity.

[4] See for example Richard Selden (1956). Notice that Selden used the rate on savings deposits as a measure of r. This is clearly the most appropriate measure for household balances; but it moves conventionally in steps and has a much smaller amplitude than bill rate. For business balances it seems that the rate paid by financial institutions for short money is the right one to use.

[5] During a prolonged price rise the *accounting* return on assets will usually be much greater than the current return because of accounting conventions of valuing assets at cost rather than market price.

[6] These have been developed by Tobin and Groves and Bierwag.

[7] Risk exists when the parameters of the probability distribution are known; uncertainty when they are unknown.

[8] One of the difficulties with the model of Tobin and Groves and Bierwag is that the variance is exogenous and in particular *independent* of the expected value; the models do not generate variance adjustment processes.

Sir John Hicks

Biographical and Bibliographical Data

BIOGRAPHICAL

Born 8 April 1904 at Warwick. Educated at Greyfriars Preparatory
school, Leamington; at Clifton College; and at Balliol College, Oxford
(1922–6). First class, mathematical moderations, 1923; second class,
philosophy, politics and economics, 1925. Research work on labour
economics, under supervision of G. D. H. Cole, 1925–6. Assistant
lecturer, then lecturer London School of Economics 1926–35.

(On leave, to take temporary charge of teaching of economics in
University of the Witwatersrand, Johannesburg, South Africa, for one
term in 1928.)

Married, December 1935, Ursula Kathleen Webb (Somerville College,
Oxford, and L.S.E.), managing editor, *Review of Economic Studies*,
1933–61. (Ursula Hicks was lecturer in Public Finance, Oxford, 1948–63,
and a fellow of Linacre College, Oxford, 1963–6.)

Fellow of Gonville and Caius College, Cambridge, and University
Lecturer in Economics, 1935–8.

Stanley Jevons Professor of Political Economy, University of Manchester,
1938–46. (President, Manchester Statistical Society, 1943–5).

Official Fellow of Nuffield College, Oxford, 1946–52. (Lectured at
Chicago and other American universities, 1946; visiting lecturer, Delhi
School of Economics, 1950; member of Revenue Allocation Commission,
Nigeria, 1950.)

Drummond Professor of Political Economy, Oxford, 1952–65; pro-
fessorial fellow of All Souls College. (Member of Royal Commission
on Taxation of Income and Profits, 1951–4; appointed – with Ursula
Hicks – to enquire into Finance and Taxation in Jamaica, 1954; visiting
lecturer, Columbia University, New York, 1958; at di Tella Institute,
Buenos Aires, 1962; at Economic Research Institute, University of

Osaka, Japan, 1960; at Northwestern University and Purdue University,
USA, 1965.)
Research fellow of All Souls College, and emeritus professor, Oxford,
1965– . (Visiting fellow, Australian National University, Canberra, 1967.)
Fellow of the Econometric Society, 1937; Fellow of the British Academy,
1942; foreign member, Royal Swedish Academy, 1948; foreign member,
Academia dei Lincei, Italy, 1952; honorary member, American
Economic Association, 1950; honorary member, American Academy,
1958; honorary fellow of Nuffield College, 1958; president of Royal
Economic Society 1960–2; knighted 1964.
Honorary doctor, Technical University of Lisbon, 1956; honorary
D. Litt, University of Glasgow, 1965; honorary D. Litt. University of
Manchester, 1966.

BIBLIOGRAPHICAL

1928   Wage-fixing in the building industry. *Economica*
1930   Early history of industrial conciliation. *Economica*
       Edgeworth, Marshall and the indeterminateness of wages.
       Economic Journal
1931   Theory of uncertainty and profit. *Economica*
       Review of Amulree: *Industrial Arbitration. Economica.*
       Chapter on 'Quotas' in Beveridge *et al., Tariffs: The
       Case Examined*
1932   THEORY OF WAGES. London: Macmillan
       Marginal productivity and the principle of variation; followed by
       a reply to Henry Schultz. *Economica*
       Reviews of Goodfellow: *Economic History of South Africa.*
           Economic Journal
           Simiand: *Le salaire. Economic Journal*
           Mises and Spiethof (eds): *Probleme der Wertlehre.*
           Economic Journal
           Bresciani-Turroni: *Le vicende del Marco Tedesco. Economica*
1933   Review of Taussig: *Wages and Capital* (reprint). *Economica*
       Gleichgewicht und Konjunktur. *Zeitschrift für Nationalökonomie*
1934   A reconsideration of the theory of value (with R. G. D. Allen).
       Economica

A note on the elasticity of supply. *Review of Economic Studies*
Léon Walras. *Econometrica*
Reviews of Isles: *Wage Policy and the Price Level. Economic Journal*
　Myrdal: 'Monetary equilibrium'. In Hayek (ed) *Beiträge*
　zur Geldtheorie. Economica

1935　A suggestion for simplifying the theory of money (reprinted in
　CRITICAL ESSAYS). *Economica*
　The theory of monopoly (a survey). *Econometrica*
　Wages and interest: the dynamic problem (reprinted in
　THEORY OF WAGES, 2nd edition 1963). *Economic Journal*
　Reviews of Dupuit: *De l'utilité et de sa mesure* (Turin reprint).
　　Economica
　　von Stackelberg: *Marktform und Gleichgewicht. Economic*
　　Journal
　　Roos: *Dynamic Economics. Economic Journal*

1936　Mr Keynes's theory of employment. *Economic Journal*
　Distribution and economic progress; a revised version (reprinted
　in THEORY OF WAGES, 2nd edition 1963). *Review of Economic*
　Studies
　Review of Pigou: *Economics of Stationary States. Economic*
　Journal
　Economics and the social sciences. Contribution to a symposium
　on *The Social Sciences*. Institute of Sociology

1937　Mr Keynes and the 'Classics' (reprinted in CRITICAL STUDIES).
　Econometrica
　LA THÉORIE MATHÉMATIQUE DE LA VALEUR. Translated by
　G. Lutfalla. Paris: Hermann. This is effectively a first draft
　of the mathematical appendix to VALUE AND CAPITAL

1939　VALUE AND CAPITAL. Oxford: Clarendon Press
　Public finance in the national income (with Ursula Hicks).
　Review of Economic Studies
　Mr Hawtrey on bank rate; followed by a reply to Hawtrey.
　Manchester School of Economic and Social Studies
　Foundations of welfare economics. *Economic Journal*
　Reviews of Allen: *Mathematical Analysis for Economists.*
　　Economica
　　Pool: *Wage Policy and Industrial Fluctuation. Economica*

1940   Valuation of social income. *Economica*
1941   TAXATION OF WAR WEALTH (with Ursula Hicks and
         L. Rostas). Oxford: Clarendon Press
         Rehabilitation of consumer's surplus. *Review of Economic Studies*
         Education in economics (Manchester Statistical Society)
1942   THE SOCIAL FRAMEWORK: AN INTRODUCTION TO
         ECONOMICS. Oxford: Clarendon Press
         The monetary theory of D. H. Robertson. *Economica*
         Maintaining capital intact. *Economica*
         Consumer's surplus and index-numbers. *Review of
         Economic Studies*
         Review of Davis: *Theory of Econometrics. Economic Journal*
1943   STANDARDS OF LOCAL EXPENDITURE (with Ursula Hicks).
         Cambridge University Press (for the National Institute of
         Economic and Social Research)
         Review article on Rist: *History of Monetary Theory. Economic
         History Review*
1944   Four consumer's surpluses. *Review of Economic Studies*
         Inter-relations of shifts in demand. *Review of Economic Studies*
         VALUATION FOR RATING (with Ursula Hicks and C. E. V. Leser).
         Cambridge University Press (for the National Institute
         of Economic and Social Research)
1945   THE INCIDENCE OF LOCAL RATES IN GREAT BRITAIN (with
         Ursula Hicks). Cambridge University Press (for the National
         Institute of Economic and Social Research)
         Recent contributions to general equilibrium economics. *Economica*
         Théorie de Keynes après neuf ans. *Revue d'économie politique*
         Generalised theory of consumer's surplus. *Review of Economic
         Studies*
         Review of Pigou: *Lapses from Full Employment. Economic Journal*
         THE SOCIAL FRAMEWORK OF THE AMERICAN ECONOMY
         (adaptation by A. G. Hart). New York: Oxford University Press
1946   VALUE AND CAPITAL, 2nd edition. Oxford: Clarendon Press
1947   World recovery after war (reprinted in ESSAYS IN WORLD
         ECONOMICS). *Economic Journal*
         Full employment in a period of reconstruction. *Nationaløkonomisk
         Tidsskrift*

The empty economy. *Lloyds Bank Review*
1948 Valuation of social income (reply to Kuznetz). *Economica*
Review of Sewell Bray: *Precision and Design in Accounting.*
Economic Journal
1949 THE PROBLEM OF BUDGETARY REFORM. Oxford: Clarendon
Press
Devaluation and world trade (reprinted in ESSAYS IN WORLD
ECONOMICS). *Three Banks Review*
Les courbes d'indifférence collective. *Revue d'économic politique*
Mr Harrod's dynamic economics. *Economica*
1950 A CONTRIBUTION TO THE THEORY OF THE TRADE CYCLE.
Oxford: Clarendon Press
Mr Ichimura on related goods. *Review of Economic Studies*
Articles on Value, Demand, Interest, Wages, and Rent, in
Chambers's Encyclopaedia
1951 Report of Revenue Allocation Commission, Nigeria (part II
by J. R. H.)
Free trade and modern economics (reprinted in ESSAYS IN
WORLD ECONOMICS). Manchester Statistical Society
Review of Menger: *Principles* (Dingwall-Hoselitz translation).
Economic Journal
1952 SOCIAL FRAMEWORK, 2nd edition. Oxford: Clarendon Press
Review article on Scitovsky: *Welfare and Competition. American
Economic Review*
Contribution to a symposium on *Monetary Policy. Bulletin of
Oxford University Institute of Statistics*
1953 Inaugural Lecture: Long-term dollar problem (reprinted in
ESSAYS IN WORLD ECONOMICS). *Oxford Economic Papers*
1954 The process of imperfect competition. *Oxford Economic Papers*
Robbins on Robertson on Utility. *Economica*
Review of Myrdal: *Political Element* (translated by Streeten).
Economic Journal
1955 FINANCE AND TAXATION IN JAMAICA (with Ursula Hicks).
Jamaica Government
Economic Foundations of wage policy (reprinted in ESSAYS
IN WORLD ECONOMICS). *Economic Journal*
1956 A REVISION OF DEMAND THEORY. Oxford: Clarendon Press

Instability of wages (reprinted in ESSAYS IN WORLD
ECONOMICS). *Three Banks Review*
Methods of dynamic analysis. In *25 Essays in Honour of Erik
Lindahl*. Stockholm

1957   Review article on Patinkin: A rehabilitation of classical
economics? (reprinted in CRITICAL ESSAYS). *Economic Journal*
Development under population pressure (reprinted in ESSAYS
IN WORLD ECONOMICS). Central Bank, Ceylon

1958   Measurement of real income. *Oxford Economic Papers*
A 'value and capital' growth model. *Review of Economic Studies*
Future of the rate of interest (reprinted in CRITICAL ESSAYS).
Manchester Statistical Society
A world inflation (reprinted in ESSAYS IN WORLD ECONOMICS).
Irish Bank Review

1959   ESSAYS IN WORLD ECONOMICS, including, as well as papers
mentioned above: National economic development in the
international setting; Manifesto on welfarism; Unimproved
value rating (East Africa); A further note on import bias;
The factor-price equalisation theorem. Oxford: Clarendon
Press
Review of Leibenstein: *Economic Backwardness and Economic
Growth*. *Economic Journal*

1960   SOCIAL FRAMEWORK, 3rd edition. Oxford: Clarendon Press
Linear theory (reprinted in SURVEYS OF ECONOMIC THEORY,
vol. 3)

1961   Prices and the turnpike: the story of a mare's nest. *Review of
Economic Studies*
Pareto revealed. *Economica*
Marshall's Third Rule (reprinted in THEORY OF WAGES, 2nd
edition). *Oxford Economic Papers*

1962   Liquidity (reprinted in CRITICAL ESSAYS). *Economic Journal*
Evaluation of consumer's wants (reprinted in *Journal of Business*,
University of Chicago). Grenoble Colloquium of Centre
national de recherche scientifique
Reviews of Meade: *A Neo-classical Growth Model*. *Economic
Journal*
Sen: *Choice of Techniques*. *Economic Journal*

1963 International trade: the long view. Cairo: Central Bank of Egypt
THEORY OF WAGES, 2nd edition with reprints and commentary.
London: Macmillan
The reform of budget accounts (with Ursula Hicks). *Bulletin
of Oxford University Institute of Statistics*
Review of Friedman: Capitalism and Freedom. *Economica*

1965 CAPITAL AND GROWTH. Oxford: Clarendon Press
Dennis Robertson. British Academy, reprinted as memoir
prefixed to Robertson, *Essays in Money and Interest*. London:
Collins, 1966
Review of Lipsey: *Positive Economics*. *Economica*

1966 AFTER THE BOOM. Institute of Economic Affairs
Growth and anti-growth. *Oxford Economic Papers*

1967 CRITICAL ESSAYS IN MONETARY THEORY, including, as well as
papers mentioned above (some in much revised versions),
The two triads; Monetary theory and history; Thornton's
Paper Credit; A note on the *Treatise*; The Hayek story.
Oxford: Clarendon Press

1968 Saving, investment and taxation. *Three Banks Review*

List of Works Referred to

ALDCROFT, D. H. (1964) The entrepreneur and the British economy, 1870–1914 *Economic History Review* (2nd Ser.) 17, 113–34.

ALLAIS, M. (1966) A restatement of the quantity theory of money: the hereditary, relativistic and logistic formulation of the demand for money. *American Economic Review* 56.

ALLEN, R. G. D. (1938) *Mathematical analysis for economists.* London.
(1959) *Mathematical economics.* 2nd ed. London.

AMES, E. & ROSENBERG, N. (1963) Changing technological leadership and industrial growth. *Economic Journal* 73, 13–31.

ARCHIBALD, G. C. & LIPSEY, R. G. (1958) Monetary and value theory: a critique of Lange and Patinkin. *Review of Economic Studies* 26, 1–22.

ARROW, K. J. (1958) The measurement of price changes. The relationship of prices to economic stability and growth (compendium of papers submitted by panellists appearing before the Joint Economic Committee, 31 March 1958.)
(1962a) The economic implications of learning by doing. *Review of Economic Studies* 29, 155–73.
(1962b) Optimal capital adjustment. In K. J. Arrow, S. Karlin and H. Scarf (eds.) *Studies in applied probability and management science,* chapter 1. Stanford.
(1964) Optimal capital policy, the cost of capital, and myopic decision rules. *Annals of the Institute of Statistical Mathematics* 16, 21–30.

ARROW, K. J., BECKMANN, M. & KARLIN, S. (1958) Optimal expansion of the capacity of the firm. In K. J. Arrow, S. Karlin & H. Scarf (eds.) *Studies in the mathematical theory of inventory and production,* chapter 7. Stanford.

ARROW, K. J., BLOCK, H. & HURWICZ, L. (1959) On the stability of competitive equilibrium, 2. *Econometrica* 27, 82–109.

ARROW, K. J., CHENERY, H. B., MINHAS, B. & SOLOW, R. M. (1961) Capital-labor substitution and economic efficiency. *Review of Economics and Statistics* 43, 225–50.

ARROW, K. J. & ENTHOVEN, A. C. (1961) Quasi-concave programming. *Econometrica* 29, 779–800.

ARROW, K. J., HARRIS, T. E. & MARSCHAK, J. (1951) Optimal inventory policy. *Econometrica* 19, 250–72.

ARROW, K.J. & HURWICZ, L. (1958) On the stability of the competitive equilibrium, 1. *Econometrica* 26, 522–52.

ASHWORTH, W. (1966) The late Victorian economy. *Economica* (N.S.) 33, 17–33.

ATKINSON, T.R. (1956) *The pattern of financial asset ownership*. Princeton. (1964) Survey of financial characteristics of consumers. *Federal Reserve Bulletin.*

ATSUMI, H. (1965) Neoclassical growth and the efficient program of capital accumulation. *Review of Economic Studies* 32, 127–36.
(1966) Efficient capital accumulation in open models. (Doctoral dissertation, University of Rochester.)

BAGEHOT, W. (1962) *Lombard Street* . . . *With a new introd. by F. C. Genovese.* Homewood, Illinois.

BALASSA, B. (1965) Tariff protection in industrial countries: an evaluation. *Journal of Political Economy* 73, 573–94.

BALDWIN, R.E. (1960) The effect of tariffs on international and domestic prices. *Quarterly Journal of Economics* 74, 65–78.

BALL, R.J. & DRAKE, P.S. (1964) The relationship between aggregate consumption and wealth. *International Economic Review* 5, 63–81.

BALL, R.J. & ST.CYR, E.B.A. (1966) Short term employment functions in British manufacturing industry. *Review of Economic Studies* 33, 179–207.

BASMANN, R.L. (1963) Remarks concerning the application of exact finite sample distribution functions of GLC estimators in econometric statistical inference. *Journal of American Statistical Association* 58, 943–76.
(1965) The role of the economic historian in the testing of professed 'economic laws'. *Explorations in Entrepreneurial History* (2nd Ser.) 2, 159–86.

BELLMAN, R. (1957) *Dynamic programming*. Princeton.

BERILL, K. (1960) International trade and the rate of economic growth. *Economic History Review* (2nd Ser.) 12, 351–9.

BERNSTEIN, B. & TOUPIN, R.A. (1962) Some properties of the Hessian matrix of a strictly convex function. *Journal für die reine und angewandte Mathematik* 210, 65–72.

BHAGWATI, J. (1963) Some recent trends in the pure theory of international trade. In *International trade theory in a developing world* (International Economic Association) London.
(forthcoming) Gains from trade once again. *Economic Journal.*

BHAGWATI, J. & JOHNSON, H.G. (1961) A generalized theory of the effects of tariffs on the terms of trade. *Oxford Economic Papers* (N.S.) 13, 225–53.

BHAGWATI, J. & RAMASWAMI, V.K. (1963) Domestic distortions, tariffs, and the theory of optimum subsidy. *Journal of Political Economy* 71, 44–50.

BLAU, G. (1944) Some aspects of the theory of futures trading. *Review of Economic Studies* 12, 1–30.

BODKIN, R. G. (1966) *American Economic Review* 56.

BOEHM-BAWERK, E. VON (1959) *Positive theory of capital.* Tr. by G. D. Huncke. South Holland, Illinois.

BRECHLING, F. P. R. (1965) The relationship between output and employment in British manufacturing industries. *Review of Economic Studies* 32, 187–216.

BROWN, M. (1966) *On the theory and measurement of technological change.* Cambridge, England.

BROWN, M. & DE CANI, J. S. (1963) Technological change and the distribution of income. *International Economic Review* 4, 289–309.

BROWN, M. & POPKIN, J. (1962) A measure of technological change and returns to scale. *Review of Economics and Statistics* 44, 402–11.

BURNS, A. F. (1934) *Production trends in the United States since 1870.* New York.

CAIRNCROSS, A. K. (1953) *Home and foreign investment, 1870–1913.* Cambridge, England.

CARR, E. H. (1946) *The twenty years' crisis, 1919–1939.* 2nd ed. London.

CHAMPERNOWNE, D. G. (1935) A mathematical note on substitution. *Economic Journal* 45, 246–58.

(1964) Expectations and the links between the economic future and the present. In R. Lekachman (ed.) *Keynes's General Theory: reports of three decades,* 174–202. London.

CHASE, S. B., jr. (1963) *Asset prices in economic analysis.* Berkeley & Los Angeles.

CHENERY, H. B. (1960) Patterns of industrial growth. *American Economic Review* 50, 624–54.

(1961) Comparative advantage and development policy. *American Economic Review* 51, 18–51.

CHOW, G. (1960) Tests of equality between sets of coefficients in two linear regressions. *Econometrica* 28, 591–605.

CLAPHAM, J. H. (1944) *The Bank of England.* 2 vols. Cambridge, England.

CLOWER, R. W. (1963a) Classical monetary theory revisited. *Economica* (N.S.) 30, 165–70.

(1963b) Permanent income and transitory balances: Hahn's paradox. *Oxford Economic Papers* (N.S.) 15, 177–90.

COMMONS COMMITTEE ON BANK ACTS (1857) *Accounts and Papers.* London.

COOPER, C. A. & MASSELL, B. F. (1965) Towards a general theory of customs unions for developing countries. *Journal of Political Economy* 73, 461–76.

COPPOCK, D. J. (1956) The climacteric of the 1890s: a critical note. *Manchester School of Economic and Social Studies* 24, 1–31.

(1963) Mr Saville on the Great Depression: a reply. *Manchester School of Economics and Social Studies* 31, 171–84.

(1964) British industrial growth during the 'Great Depression', 1873–96: a pessimist's view. *Economic History Review* (2nd Ser.) 17, 389–96.

CORDEN, W. M. (1963) The tariff. In A. Hunter (ed.) *The economics of Australian industry.* Melbourne.

COURT, A. T. (1939) Hedonic price indexes with automotive examples. In *The dynamics of automobile demand*. New York.

DAVID, P. A. & DE KLUNDERT, T. VAN (1965) Biased efficiency growth and capital-labor substitution in the U. S., 1899–1960. *American Economic Review* 55, 357–94.

DELL, S. (1966) *A Latin American common market?* London.

DHRYMES, P. J. (1965) Some extensions and tests for the CES class of production functions. *Review of Economics and Statistics* 47, 357–66.

DIVISIA, F. (1928) *Economique rationnelle*. Paris.

DOBB, M. (1963) *Economic growth and underdeveloped countries*. London.

DORFMAN, R., SAMUELSON, P. A. & SOLOW, R. M. (1958) *Linear programming and economic analysis*. New York.

DOUGLAS, A. J. (1966) Studies in monetary dynamics. (Doctoral dissertation, Stanford University.)

DRESCH, F. W. (1938) Index numbers and general economic equilibrium. *Bulletin of the American Mathematical Society* 44, 134–40.

EINZIG, P. (1962) *The history of foreign exchange*. London.

EISNER, R., FRIEDMAN, M. & HOUTHAKKER, H. S. (1958) The permanent income hypothesis (comments and reply.) *American Economic Review* 48, 972–93.

FARRELL, M. J. (1959) The new theories of the consumption function. *Economic Journal* 69, 678–96.

FEAVEARYEAR, A. E. (1963) *The pound sterling*. 2nd ed. Oxford.

FELLNER, W. J. et al. (1966) *Maintaining and restoring balance in international payments*. Princeton.

FETTER, F. W. (1965) *Development of British monetary orthodoxy*. Cambridge, Mass.

FISHER, F. M. (1962) *A priori information and time series analysis: essays in economic theory and measurement*. Amsterdam.

(1965) Embodied technical change and the existence of an aggregate capital stock. *Review of Economic Studies* 32, 263–88.

FISHER, I. (1907) *The rate of interest*. New York.

(1930) *The theory of interest*. New York.

FISHER, M. E. & FULLER, A. T. (1958) On the stabilization of matrices and the convergence of linear iterative processes. *Proceedings of the Cambridge Philosophical Society* 54, 417–25.

FISHER, M. R. (1957) A reply to the critics. *Bulletin of Oxford University Institute of Statistics* 19, 179–99.

FLETCHER, T. W. (1961) The great depression of English agriculture, 1873–96. *Economic History Review* (2nd Ser.) 13, 417–32.

FORD, A. G. (1962) *The gold standard, 1880–1914*. Oxford.

(1964) Bank rate, the British balance of payments, and the burdens of adjustment, 1870–1914. *Oxford Economic Papers* (N.S.) 16, 24–39.

(1965) Overseas lending and internal fluctuations, 1870–1914. *Yorkshire Bulletin of Economic and Social Research* 17, 19–31.

FRANKEL, M. (1955) Obsolescence and technological change in a maturing economy. *American Economic Review* 45, 296–319.

(1956) [Obsolescence and technological change]:reply. *American Economic Review* 46, 652–6.

FRIEDMAN, M. (1957a) Savings and the balance sheet. *Bulletin of Oxford University Institute of Statistics* 19, 125–36.

(1957b) *A theory of the consumption function*. Princeton.

FRIEND, I. (1957) Some conditions for progress in the study of savings. *Bulletin of Oxford University Institute of Statistics* 19, 165–70.

FRIEND, I. & TAUBMAN, P. (1966) The aggregate propensity to save:some concepts and their application to international data. *Review of Economics and Statistics* 48, 113–23.

GALE, D. (1966) *On optimal development in a multi-sector economy*. (Mimeographed.)

GALE, D. & NIKAIDO, H. (1965) The Jacobian matrix and global univalence of mappings. *Mathematische Annalen* 159, 81–93.

GALENSON, W. & LEIBENSTEIN, H. (1955) Investment criteria, productivity, and economic development. *Quarterly Journal of Economics* 69, 343–70.

GANTMAKHER, F. R. (1959) *Applications of the theory of matrices*. New York.

GAYER, A. D., ROSTOW, W. W. & SCHWARTZ, A. J. (1953) *The growth and fluctuation of the British economy, 1790–1850*. 2 vols. Oxford.

GOLDBERGER, A. S. (1964) *Econometric theory*. New York.

GOLDSMITH, R. W. (1956) *A study of saving in the United States*. Princeton.

GORDON, D. F. (1956) Obsolescence and technological change:comment. *American Economic Review* 46, 646–52.

GORMAN, W. M. (1954) Klein aggregates and conventional index numbers. (In Report of the Innsbruck Conference of the Econometric Society.) *Econometrica* 22, 113–15.

(1965) Capital aggregation in vintage models. (Rome Conference of the Econometric Society, September 1965.)

GRILICHES, Z. (1961) Hedonic price indexes for automobiles: an econometric analysis of quality change. *The Price Statistics of the Federal Government* (National Bureau of Economic Research, General Series no. 73). New York.

(1963) The sources of measured productivity growth: United States agriculture, 1940–60. *Journal of Political Economy* 71, 331–46.

(1964) Research expenditures, education, and the aggregate agricultural production function. *American Economic Review* 54, 961–74.

HABAKKUK, H. J. (1962) *American and British technology in the nineteenth century*. Cambridge, England.

HAGEN, E. E. (1958) An economic justification of protectionism. *Quarterly Journal of Economics* 72, 496–514.

HANSON, N. R. (1958) *Patterns of discovery*. Cambridge, England.

HARROD, R. F. (1951) Notes on trade cycle theory. *Economic Journal* 61, 261–75.
(1964) Are monetary and fiscal policies enough? *Economic Journal* 74, 903–15.

HAWTREY, R. G. (1938) *A century of bank rate*. London.
(1940) Mr Kaldor on the forward market. *Review of Economic Studies* 7, 202–5.

HICKS, J. R. (1932) *The theory of wages*. London.
(1935) A suggestion for simplifying the theory of money. *Economica* (N.S.) 2, 1–19.
(1937) Mr Keynes and the 'Classics'. *Economica*.
(1939) *Value and capital*. Oxford.
(1946) *Value and capital*. 2nd ed. Oxford.
(1950) *A contribution to the theory of the trade cycle*. Oxford.
(1950–1) Free trade and modern economics. *Transactions of the Manchester Statistical Society* 118th Session, 1–25.
(1959) *Essays in world economics*. Oxford.
(1963) *Theory of wages*. 2nd ed. London.
(1965) *Capital and growth*. Oxford.

HOFFMANN, W. G. (1955) *British industry, 1700–1950*. Oxford.

HOFSTEN, E. A. G. VON (1952) *Price indexes and quality changes*. Stockholm.

HOMER, S. (1963) *History of interest rates*. New Brunswick, N.J.

HORWICH, G. (1966) *A framework for monetary policy*. (Krannert Quantitative Inst. Ser.) Homewood, Illinois

HOUTHAKKER, H. S. (1951–2) Compensated changes in quantities and qualities consumed. *Review of Economic Studies* 19, 155–64.
(1959) The scope and limits of futures trading. In A. Abramovitz *et al.*, *The allocation of economic resources*. Stanford.
(1961a) The present state of consumption theory. *Econometrica* 29, 704–40.
(1961b) Systematic and random elements in short-term price movements. *American Economic Review* 51, *Papers and Proceedings* 164–72.

HOUTHAKKER, H. S. & TAYLOR, L. D. (1966) *Consumer demand in the United States, 1929–1970*. Cambridge, Mass.

HUGHES, J. R. T. (1956) The commercial crisis of 1857. *Oxford Economic Papers* (N.S.) 8, 194–222.
(1960) *Fluctuations in trade, industry and finance*. Oxford.
(1966) Fact and theory in economic history. *Explorations in Entrepreneurial History* (2nd Ser.) 3, 75–100.

HUGHES, J. R. T. & ROSENBERG, N. (1963) The United States business cycle before 1860: some problems of interpretation. *Economic History Review* (2nd Ser.) 15, 476–93.

JENKS, L. H. (1938) *The migration of British capital to 1875*. London.

JOHANSEN, L. (1959) Substitution versus fixed production coefficients in the theory of economic growth: a synthesis. *Econometrica* 27, 157–76.

JOHNSON, H. G. (1964) Tariffs and economic development. *Journal of Development Studies* 1, 3–30.

(1965a) An economic theory of protectionism, the tariff bargaining, and the formation of customs unions. *Journal of Political Economy* 73, 256–83.

(1965b) Optimal trade intervention in the presence of domestic distortions. In *Trade, growth, and the balance of payments: essays in honor of Gottfried Haberler*. Chicago & Amsterdam.

(1966) Trade preferences and developing countries. *Lloyds Bank Review* 80, 1–18.

JORGENSON, D. W. (1965) Anticipations and investment behavior. In J. S. Duesenberry *et al.* (eds.) *Quarterly econometric model of the United States*. Chicago.

JORGENSON, D. W. & GRILICHES, Z. (1967) *The explanation of productivity change.* (Working Paper 105, Institute of Business and Economic Research) Berkeley.

KAHN, R. F. (1933) The elasticity of substitution and the relative share of a factor. *Review of Economic Studies* 1, 72–8.

KALDOR, N. (1939) Speculation and economic stability. *Review of Economic Studies* 7, 1–27.

KALDOR, N. & MIRRLEES, J. A. (1962) A new model of economic growth. *Review of Economic Studies* 29, 174–90.

KARLIN, S. (1959) *Mathematical methods and theory in games, programming and economics.* Reading, Mass. & London.

KEMP, M. C. (1960) The Mill-Bastable infant-industry dogma. *Journal of Political Economy* 68, 65–7.

(1964) *The pure theory of international trade.* Englewood Cliffs, N.J.

(1966a) Note on Marshallian conjecture. *Quarterly Journal of Economics* 80, 481–4.

(1966b) The gain from international trade and investment: a neo-Heckscher-Ohlin approach. *American Economic Review* 56, 788–809.

KENDALL, M. G. & STUART, A. (1961) *The advanced theory of statistics.* Vol. 2. New York.

KENDRICK, J. W. (1961) *Productivity trends in the United States.* Princeton.

KENNEDY, C. (1964) Induced bias in innovation and the theory of distribution. *Economic Journal* 74, 541–7.

KEYNES, J. M. (1923) Some aspects of commodity markets. *Manchester Guardian Commercial, Reconstruction in Europe.*

(1930) *A treatise on money.* London.

(1936) *The general theory of employment, interest and money.* London.

KINDLEBERGER, C. P. (1961) Foreign trade and economic growth: lessons from Britain and France, 1850 to 1913. *Economic History Review* (2nd Ser.) 14, 289–305.

KING, W. T. C. (1936) *History of the London discount market.* London.

KLEIN, L. R. (1946) Macroeconomics and the theory of rational behaviour, 1 and 2. *Econometrica* 14, 93–108.

(1958) The British propensity to save. *Journal of the Royal Statistical Society* 121, 60–96.

KLEIN, L. R. & KOSOBUD, R. F. (1961) Some econometrics of growth: great ratios of economics. *Quarterly Journal of Economics* 75, 173–98.

KLEIN, L. R. & LIVIATAN, N. (1957) The significance of income variability on savings behaviour. *Bulletin of Oxford University Institute of Statistics* 19, 151–60.

KOO, A. Y. C. (1953) Duty and non-duty imports and income distribution. *American Economic Review* 43, 51–75.

KOOPMANS, T. C. (1960) Stationary ordinary utility and impatience. *Econometrica* 28, 287–309.

(1963) On a concept of optimum economic growth. (Unpublished manuscript).

(1965) On the concept of optimal growth. In *Semaine d'Etude sur le Rôle de l'Analyse Econométrique dans la Formulation de Plans de Développement*, 1e partie. (Pontificiae Academiae Scientiarum Scripta Varia, 28, i.)

KURAHASHI, K. (1963) The optimum capacity of production facilities. (Paper presented at the International Meeting of the Institute of Management Sciences, Tokyo.)

KUZNETS, S. (1954) *Economic change*. London.

(1961) *Capital in the American economy: its formation and financing*. Princeton.

LANCASTER, K. J. (1966) A new approach to consumer theory. *Journal of Political Economy* 74, 132–57.

LANDSBERGER, M. (1966) Windfall income and consumption: comment. *American Economic Review* 56.

LANGE, O. (1944) *Price flexibility and full employment*. Bloomington.

LARSON, A. B. (1961) Estimation of hedging and speculative positions in futures markets. *Stanford University Food Research Institute Studies* 2, 203–12.

LAYTON, W. T. (1920) *An introduction to the study of prices*. London.

LEBERGOTT, S. (1957) Annual estimates of unemployment in the United States, 1900–1950. In Universities-National Bureau Committee for Economic Research, *The measurement and behavior of unemployment*, 213–41. Princeton.

LEONTIEF, W. W. (1947a) Introduction to a theory of the internal structure of functional relationships. *Econometrica* 15, 361–73.

(1947b) A note on the interrelation of subsets of independent variables of a continuous function with continuous first derivatives. *Bulletin of the American Mathematical Society* 53, 343–50.

(1951) *The structure of American economy, 1919–1939*. 2nd ed. New York & London.

LERNER,A.P. (1936) The symmetry between import and export taxes. *Economica* (N.S.) 3, 306–13.

LINDBECK,A. (1963) *A study in monetary analysis.* Stockholm.

LIPSEY,R. (1957) The theory of customs unions: trade diversion and welfare. *Economica* (N.S.) 24, 40–6.

— (1960) The theory of customs unions: a general survey. *Economic Journal* 70, 496–513.

LIVIATAN,N. (1965) On the long-run theory of consumption and real balances. *Oxford Economic Papers* (N.S.) 17, 205–18.

— (1966) A generalization of the composite good theorem for imperfect markets. *Review of Economic Studies* 33, 45–56.

— (forthcoming) Topics in price and capital theory.

LLOYD,C. (1964) The real-balance effect and the Slutsky equation. *Journal of Political Economy* 72, 295–9.

LYDALL,H.F. & LANSING,J.B. (1959) A comparison of the distribution of personal income and wealth in the United States and Great Britain. *American Economic Review* 49, 43–67.

MACARIO,S. (1964) Protectionism and industrialisation in Latin America. *Economic Bulletin for Latin America* 9, 61–101.

MACDONALD,R.A. (1912) The rate of interest since 1844. *Journal of the Royal Statistical Society* 75, 361–79.

MCFADDEN,D. (1966) Cost, revenue and profit functions: a cursory review. (Working Paper 86, Institute of Business and Economic Research) Berkeley.

MACHLUP,F. (1935) The commonsense of the elasticity of substitution. *Review of Economic Studies* 2, 202–13.

MCKENZIE,L.W. (1960) Matrices with dominant diagonals and economic theory. In *Stanford Symposium on Mathematical Methods in the Social Sciences.* Stanford.

— (1963) Turnpike theorems for a generalized Leontief model. *Econometrica* 31, 165–80.

— (1967) Maximal paths in the von Neumann model. In E. Malinvaud and M.O.L. Bacharach (eds.) *Activity analysis in the theory of growth and planning,* chapter 2. London.

MCKINNON,R.I. (1966) Intermediate products, differential tariffs: a generalisation of Lerner's symmetry theorem. *Quarterly Journal of Economics* 80, 584–615.

MAIZELS,A. (1963) *Industrial growth and world trade.* Cambridge, England.

MALINVAUD,E. (1953) Capital accumulation and efficient allocation of resources. *Econometrica* 21, 233–68.

— (1962) Efficient capital accumulation: a corrigendum. *Econometrica* 30, 570–3.

MALMGREN,H.B. (1961) Information, expectations, and the theory of the firm. *Quarterly Journal of Economics* 75, 399–421.

MALMQUIST, S. (1953) Index numbers and indifference surfaces. *Trabajos de Estadistica* 4, 209–42.

MANDELBROT, B. (1962) Paretian distributions and income maximization. *Quarterly Journal of Economics* 76, 57–85.

(1963) The variation of certain speculative prices. *Journal of Business* 36, 394–419.

MANSFIELD, E. (1961) Technical change and the rate of imitation. *Econometrica* 29, 741–66.

MARGLIN, S. A. (1963) *Approaches to dynamic investment planning.* Amsterdam.

MARKOWITZ, H. M. (1959) *Portfolio selection* (Cowles Foundation Mon. 16). New York.

MARSCHAK, J. (1949) Role of liquidity under complete and incomplete information. *American Economic Review* 39, *Papers and Proceedings,* 182–95.

MARSHALL, A. (1923) *Money, credit and commerce.* London.

(1926) *Memorandum on the fiscal policy of international trade.* (H. of C. No. 321, 1908). Repr. in A. Marshall, *Official Papers,* 369–420, London, 1926. Page references are to the *Official Papers.*

MASSÉ, P. (1946) *Les réserves et la régulation de l'avenir dans la vie économique.* 2 vols. Paris.

MATTHEWS, R. C. O. (1959) *The trade cycle.* Cambridge, England.

MAYER, T. (1963) The permanent income theory and occupational groups. *Review of Economics and Statistics* 45, 16–22.

MEADE, J. E. (1955) *The theory of customs unions.* Amsterdam.

(1961) *A neo-classical theory of economic growth.* London.

MEIER, G. M. (1963) *International trade and development.* New York.

MEISELMAN, D. (1962) *The term structure of interest rates.* Englewood Cliffs.

METZLER, L. A. (1945) Stability of multiple markets: the Hicks conditions. *Econometrica* 13, 277–92.

(1949a) Tariffs, the terms of trade, and the distribution of national income. *Journal of Political Economy* 57, 1–29.

(1949b) Tariffs, international demand, and domestic prices. *Journal of Political Economy* 57, 345–51.

MEYER, J. R. (1965) An input output approach to evaluating the influence of exports on British industrial production in the nineteenth century. *Explorations in Entrepreneurial History.*

MIRRLEES, J. A. (1965) Optimum accumulation under uncertainty. (Mimeographed).

MITCHELL, B. R. & DEANE, P. (1962) *Abstract of British historical statistics.* Cambridge, England.

MODIGLIANI, F. & BRUMBERG, R. E. (1954) Utility analysis and the consumption function: an interpretation of cross section data. In K. K. Kuruhara (ed.) *Post-Keynesian economics.* London.

MODIGLIANI, F. & COHEN, K. J. (1961) *The role of anticipations and plans in economic behavior and their use in economic analysis and forecasting.* Chicago.

MORGAN, E. V. (1943) *The theory and practice of central banking.* Cambridge, England.

MORISHIMA, M. (1958) A dynamic analysis of structural change in a Leontief model. *Economica* (N.S.) 25, 119–25.

— (1964) *Theory of growth: the von Neumann revolution.* (Institute for Mathematical Studies in the Social Sciences, Technical Report No. 130) Stanford.

MUNDELL, R. A. (1957) International trade and factor mobility. *American Economic Review* 47, 321–35.

— (1961) A theory of optimum currency areas. *American Economic Review* 51, 657–65.

— (1962) The appropriate use of monetary and fiscal policy for internal and external stability. *International Monetary Fund Staff Papers* 9, 70–7.

— (1965a) Growth, stability and inflationary finance. *Journal of Political Economy* 73, 97–109.

— (1965b) The homogeneity postulate and the laws of comparative statics in the Walrasian and Metzleric systems. *Econometrica* 33, 349–56.

MUSSON, A. E. (1959) The great depression in Britain, 1873–1896: a reappraisal. *Journal of Economic History* 19, 199–228.

— (1963) British industrial growth during the 'great depression', 1873–96: some comments. *Economic History Review* (2nd Ser.) 15, 529–33.

— (1964) British industrial growth 1873–96: a balanced view. *Economic History Review* (2nd Ser.) 17, 397–403.

MYINT, H. (1964) *The economics of the developing countries.* London.

MYRDAL, G. (1956) *An international economy.* New York & London.

NATAF, A. (1948) Sur la possibilité de la construction de certains macro-modèles. *Econometrica* 16, 232–44.

— (1965) Discussion of Fisher (1965) and Gorman (1965) at the Rome Conference of the Econometric Society, September 1965.

NATIONAL BUREAU OF ECONOMIC RESEARCH. (1961) *The price statistics of the Federal Government.* New York.

NERLOVE, M. (1958) *The dynamics of supply.* Baltimore.

NERLOVE, M. & ARROW, K. J. (1962) Optimal advertising policy under dynamic conditions. *Economica* (N.S.) 29, 129–42.

NEWMAN, P. K. (1959) Some notes on stability conditions. *Review of Economic Studies* 27, 1–9.

NEWMAN, P. K. & WOLFE, J. N. (1961) A model for the long-run theory of value. *Review of Economic Studies* 29, 51–61.

NURKSE, R. (1959) *Patterns of trade and development.* Stockholm.

PALGRAVE, R. H. I. (1903) *Bank rate and the money market.* London.

PATINKIN, D. (1956) *Money, interest and prices.* Evanston, Illinois.

PATTERSON,G. (1965) Would tariff preferences help economic development? *Lloyds Bank Review* 76, 18–30.

(1966) *Discrimination in international trade; the policy issues: 1945–1965.* Princeton.

PHELPS-BROWN,E.H. & HANDFIELD JONES,S.J. (1952) The climacteric of the 1890s: a study in the expanding economy. *Oxford Economic Papers* (N.S.) 4, 266–307.

PIGOU,A.C. (1934) The elasticity of substitution. *Economic Journal* 44, 232–41.

PLATT,J.R. (1964) Strong inference. *Science* 146, 347–53.

PONTRYAGIN,L.S. *et al.* (1962) *The mathematical theory of optimal processes.* Authorized translation from the Russian. New York.

POWER,J.H. (1963) Industrialisation in Pakistan: a case of frustrated take-off? *Pakistan Development Review* 3, 191–207.

PYATT,F.G. (1964) *Priority patterns and the demand for household durable goods.* Cambridge, England.

RADHU,G.M. (1965) The relation of indirect tax changes to price changes in Pakistan. *Pakistan Development Review* 5, 54–63.

RADNER,R. (1961) Paths of economic growth that are optimal with regard only to final states: a turnpike theorem. *Review of Economic Studies* 28, 98–104.

RAMSEY,F.P. (1928) A mathematical theory of savings. *Economic Journal* 38, 543–59.

RICARDO,D. (1824) *Plan for the establishment of a National Bank.* London.

RICHARDSON,H.W. (1965) Retardation in Britain's industrial growth, 1870–1913. *Scottish Journal of Political Economy* 12, 125–49.

RICHTER,M.K. Invariance axioms and economic indices. (Unpublished paper).

ROBBINS,L. (1954) *The economist in the twentieth century*, pp. 137–8. London.

ROBINSON,J. (1933) *The economics of imperfect competition.* London.

(1954) The production function and the theory of capital. *Review of Economic Studies* 21, 81–106.

(1956) *The accumulation of capital.* London.

ROLPH,E.R. (1954) *The theory of fiscal economics.* Berkeley & Los Angeles.

SAMUELSON,P.A. (1941) The stability of equilibrium: comparative statics and dynamics. *Econometrica* 9, 97–120.

(1942) The stability of equilibrium: linear and non-linear systems. *Econometrica* 10, 1–25.

(1944) The relation between Hicksian stability and true dynamic stability. *Econometrica* 12, 256–7.

(1947) *Foundations of economic analysis.* Cambridge, Mass.

(1950) Evaluation of real national income. *Oxford Economic Papers* (N.S.) 2, 1–29.

(1953–4) Prices of factors and goods in general equilibrium. *Review of Economic Studies* 21, 1–20.

(1960a) An extension of the Le Chatelier principle. *Econometrica* 28, 368–79.

(1960b) Structure of a minimum equilibrium system. In R. W. Pfouts (ed.) *Essays in economics and econometrics in honor of Harold Hotelling.* Chapel Hill.

(1961) The evaluation of social income: capital formation and wealth. In International Economic Association. *The theory of capital.* London.

(1965a) A theory of induced innovation along Kennedy-Weisäcker lines. *Review of Economics and Statistics* 47, 343–56.

(1965b) Proof that properly anticipated prices fluctuate randomly. *Industrial Management Review* 6, 41–9.

(1965c) Rational theory of warrant pricing. *Industrial Management Review* 6, 13–32.

(1966) *Collected scientific papers.* Ed. by J. E. Stiglitz. 2 vols. Cambridge, Mass.

SAMUELSON, P. A. & SOLOW, R. M. (1956) A complete capital model involving heterogeneous capital goods. *Quarterly Journal of Economics* 70, 537–62.

SAUL, S. B. (1960) *Studies in British overseas trade, 1870–1914.* Liverpool.

SAVILLE, J. (1961) Some retarding factors in the British economy before 1914. *Yorkshire Bulletin of Economic and Social Research* 13, 51–60.

SAYERS, R. S. (1957) *Central banking after Bagehot.* Oxford.

SCHLOTE, W. (1952) *British overseas trade from 1700 to the 1930s.* Oxford.

SCHUMPETER, J. A. (1954) *History of economic analysis.* New York.

SECRET COMMITTEE OF THE HOUSE OF LORDS. (1847–8) *Accounts and Papers.* London.

SECRET COMMITTEE ON THE CAUSES OF THE RECENT COMMERCIAL DISTRESS, etc. (1847–8) *Accounts and Papers.* London.

SELDEN, R. (1956) In M. Friedman (ed.) *Studies in the quantity theory of money.* Chicago.

SELECT COMMITTEE ON THE BANK ACTS AND THE RECENT COMMERCIAL DISTRESS. Report and evidence. (1857–8) *Accounts and Papers.* London.

SELECT COMMITTEE ON THE OPERATION OF THE BANK ACT. (1857) *Accounts and Papers.* London.

SHACKLE, G. S. (1952) *Expectation in economics.* 2nd ed. Cambridge, England.

SIDRAUSKI, M. (1965) Inflation, optimum consumption, and real cash balances (Paper presented at the New York meetings of the Econometric Society, 1965.)

SIMON, H. A. (1951) Effects of technological change in a linear model. In T. C. Koopmans (ed.) *Activity analysis of production and allocation,* 260–77. New York.

SOHMEN, E. (1958) The effect of devaluation on the price level. *Quarterly Journal of Economics* 72, 273–83.

SOLOW, R. M. (1960) Investment and technical progress. In *Stanford symposium on mathematical methods in the social sciences,* 89–104. Stanford.

(forthcoming) Distribution in the long and short run. (Proceedings of International Economic Association Conference on the Distribution of National Income.)

SPIRO, A. (1962) Wealth and the consumption function. *Journal of Political Economy* 70, 339–54.

STIGLER, G. J. (1963) *Capital and rates of return in manufacturing industries.* Princeton.

STONE, J. R. N. (1956) *Quantity and prices indexes in national accounts*, chapter 4. Paris.

STROTZ, R. H. (1955–6) Myopia and inconsistency in dynamic utility maximisation. *Review of Economic Studies* 23, 165–80.

SUITS, D. (1963) The determinants of consumer expenditure: a review of present knowledge. In *Impacts of monetary policy*. Englewood Cliffs.

THOMAS, B. (1954) *Migration and economic growth*. Cambridge, England.

TORRENS, R. (1857) *The principles and practical operation of Sir Robert Peel's Act of 1844 explained and defended.* 2nd ed. London.

UNITED NATIONS CONFERENCE ON TRADE AND DEVELOPMENT. (1964) *Towards a new trade policy for development: report by the Secretary-General.* New York.

UZAWA, H. (1961) Causal indeterminacy of the Leontief input-output system *Kikan Riron Keizaigaku* 12, 49–59.

(1964) Duality principles in the theory of cost and production. *International Economic Review* 5, 216–20.

VALAVANIS, S. (1955) A denial of Patinkin's contradiction. *Kyklos* 8, 351–68.

VINER, J. (1950) *The customs union issue*. London.

WALLIS, W. A. (1951) Tolerance intervals for linear regression. In *Proceedings of the Second Berkeley Symposium on Mathematical Statistics and Probability*, 43–51. Berkeley & Los Angeles.

WALTERS, A. A. (1963) Production and cost functions: an econometric survey. *Econometrica* 31, 1–66.

WEIZSACKER, C. C. VON (1965) Existence of optimal programs of accumulation for an infinite time horizon. *Review of Economic Studies*.

WHITAKER, J. K. (1966) Vintage capital models and econometric production functions. *Review of Economic Studies* 33, 1–18.

WICKSELL, K. (1958) The influence of the rate of interest on commodity prices. In *Selected papers on economic theory*. Cambridge, Mass.

(1965) *Interest and prices*. New York.

WINTER, S. G. jr. (1965) Some properties of the closed linear model of production. *International Economic Review* 6, 199–210.

WORKING, H. (1953) Hedging reconsidered. *Journal of Farm Economics* 35, 544–61.

For Product Safety Concerns and Information please contact our
EU representative GPSR@taylorandfrancis.com Taylor & Francis
Verlag GmbH, Kaufingerstraße 24, 80331 München, Germany